BASEBALLHQ.COM'S **2023**

MINOR LEAGUE BASEBALL ANALYST

PRESENTED BY BASEBALLHQ.COM | 18TH EDITION

BRENT HERSHEY, EDITOR | CHRIS BLESSING & JEREMY DELONEY, ASSOCIATE EDITORS

TRIUMPH
BOOKS

This book is available in quantity at special discounts for your group or organization. For further information, contact:

Triumph Books LLC
814 North Franklin Street
Chicago, Illinois 60610
(312) 337-0747
www.triumphbooks.com

Printed in U.S.A.
ISBN: 978-1-63727-187-2

Data provided by TheBaseballCube.com and Baseball Info Solutions

Cover design by Brent Hershey
Front cover photograph by Brent Skeen - USA TODAY Sports

MINOR LEAGUE BASEBALL ANALYST

Editor
Brent Hershey

Associate Editors
Chris Blessing
Jeremy Deloney

· · · · · ·

Tech/Data/Charts
Matt Cederholm
Neil FitzGerald
Ray Murphy

Graphic Design
Brent Hershey

**Player Commentaries
by MLB Organization**
Chris Blessing:
Arizona, Atlanta, Cincinnati,
Chicago (AL), Cleveland, Kansas City,
Los Angeles (AL), Miami, New York (AL),
New York (NL), Tampa Bay
Jeremy Deloney:
Boston, Milwuakee, Minnesota,
Pittsburgh, Oakland, Seattle,
San Diego, San Francisco, Toronto
Rob Gordon:
Chicago (NL), Colorado, Detroit,
Los Angeles (NL), St. Louis
Brent Hershey:
Baltimore, Philadelphia, Washington
Doug Otto:
Houston
Matthew St-Germain:
Texas

Articles
Chris Blessing
Jeremy Deloney
Rob Gordon
Brent Hershey
Doug Otto
Shelly Verougstraete

HQ100
Chris Blessing, Jeremy Deloney
Rob Gordon, Brent Hershey,
Doug Otto, Nick Richards,
Matthew St-Germain,
Shelly Verougstraete

Editing Support
Ryan Bloomfield
Brandon Kruse

TABLE OF CONTENTS

INTRODUCTION

Prospect Promotions in Year One: Observations

by Brent Hershey

While most of the baseball world (fantasy and otherwise) is rightfully focused on the on-the-field MLB rules changes in 2023 like the pitch clock, bigger bases, and banning the shift, we want to focus our gaze elsewhere. Let's take a minute to muse on a shift that affects prospects specifically: how the new Collective Bargaining Agreement (CBA) has altered prospect promotions to the big leagues.

When the new CBA was signed in March of 2022, there were a few new rules aimed at getting the best players on the field, quicker. As you're likely aware, under the previous agreement, during certain times of the year it was standard practice for MLB teams to hold off on promoting MLB-ready talent—in a way, NOT putting their best team on the field—to gain an extra year of team-controlled salary. Promoting a prospect to a team's active roster starts the player's arbitration and free agency clock, essentially two aspects of the "countdown" until a player would get to sell his services on the open market (a.k.a. "free agency").

MLB teams implemented this tactic in a couple ways, but the most notable scenario was a player who produced well enough to make the team's 26-man roster in spring training, but who the team sent down to Triple-A at the beginning of the season to work on "defense" or "pitch sequencing" (wink-wink) only to be miraculously cured of those ills once the team was sure the free agency and/or arbitration dates had safely passed, assuring the club of another year of cost-assured control at the end of the player's tenure with the club. From a purely business perspective—to keep costs down for the team while projecting a production level out of the young players that would far exceed their salary—it made sense. The rules didn't prohibit such roster shenanigans, and it was a good business decision.

But it was a very bad baseball one—players, agents, and informed fans couldn't help to feel somewhat cheated, in the sense this loophole allowed clubs to NOT place their best possible product on the field at various times.

So in the negotiations last Spring, the Player's Union made this issue one of their priorities, and in the final agreement, a new stipulation is in place by way of incentivizing MLB teams if these rookie players hit the ground running early in their MLB careers.

A player needs to have rookie eligibility, fewer than 60 days of service time at the beginning of his rookie year and is on two Top-100 rookie lists (from Baseball America, MLB.com, ESPN media outlets). If the club places him on their Opening Day roster, and at any point over the next three seasons the player wins Rookie of the Year or finishes in the Top 3 in the MVP or Cy Young Award voting, then the team gets an additional draft pick after the first round.

So, how did it play out in Year 1 of the new CBA, and what can that tell us about how prospect promotion will be handled going forward?

It's early and admittedly the sample size is small, but it seems like teams were paying attention to the incentives. We never can be 100% certain of how things would have played out under the old rules, but it's fair to say that Julio Rodríguez (#2 on 2022 HQ100) would have been a prime candidate for the "wink-wink" demotion. He was one of the game's top prospects who excelled and showed he was MLB-ready via his spring training performance, when he hit .412/.487/.794 in 34 AB. Under the old CBA, would that have been enough to make the club out of March, if the Mariners knew that keeping him down for approximately six weeks could benefit them with delaying his arbitration year?

The Mariners, though, didn't and Rodríguez was on the Opening Day roster. And, ahh, yeah … he delivered. After a bit of a slow start, Rodríguez caught fire in time to be selected to the All-Star Game and then finished with an amazing .284 BA, with 28 HR and 25 SB, eventually winning the American League Rookie of the Year hardware. It was a remarkable achievement for the 21-year-old on a personal level. And the Seattle ballclub got something out of it as well, with an extra draft pick after the 2023 first round, the number 29 overall pick.

But that was just one team, in one "perfect" scenario, both from the team and player perspective. Or was it?

Via a cursory look back at the 2022 HQ100 list, each of the Top 6 prospects from last year seemed on track to make their clubs on Opening Day. Bobby Witt, Jr. (1); Spencer Torkelson (4) and CJ Abrams (6) all did make the roster. Both Adley Rutschman (3) and Riley Greene (5) suffered spring training injuries that kept them out, but were well on their way had they stayed healthy. One could interpret that as clubs "taking their shot" in a new era.

Were there any other clues on how MLB clubs might handle this stipulation going forward? We might be able to get a sense by "working backwards," and noting how several of the Rookie of the Year placers were handled re: Opening Day assignments.

Rutschman finished second in the AL voting, even with his debut delayed until May 21 due to a triceps injury. Steven Kwan, who finished third, also made the Opening Day roster—sure, the Guardians needed outfielders, but was the team swayed by the award possibilities? Tough to say.

In the NL, the two biggest rookie surprises were on the Braves: Rookie of the Year winner Michael Harris was promoted from AA on May 28, and runner-up Spencer Strider, who did have a 2021 cameo, was on the Opening Day roster but didn't start his first game until Memorial Day. Even so, both far exceeded most "public" 2022 expectations. But because Rookie of the Year winner Harris was not active on Opening Day, the Braves will receive no additional draft pick compensation.

A secondary consideration in this new rule is whether teams are not only considering it on the "front end" of a season (whether to place a rookie on their Opening Day roster) but on the "back end" as well, as a means for preparing for the year following.

We couldn't help but notice the 2022 journey of Corbin Carroll and Gunnar Henderson. These were two players near the top of 2022 prospect lists, players not really ready by Opening Day, but ones who did excel in the high minors for most of the season. By mid-season, these two had risen to the top of several Top Prospect lists, and their performance seemed to have warranted consideration for their MLB activation sometime during the summer. And indeed, they were activated—Carroll on August 29; Henderson on August 31. Though it might not have been obvious at the time, it could be argued that teams were attempting to thread the needle between getting as many MLB ABs as possible for these two down the stretch; but not so many that they would lose their rookie (and thus Rookie of the Year) eligibility for 2023.

In the end, thread met needle: Carroll finished with 115 AB; Henderson with 116, both short of the 130 AB threshold necessary to maintain rookie status for 2023. And, assuming both stay the season on the Opening Day 2023 roster, the Diamondbacks and Orioles thus remain in line for a possible additional draft pick at some point if Carroll or Henderson were to win 2023 Rookie of the Year, or even better, place in the top 3 for their league's MVP sometime in the next three seasons. Extend the the 2023 list a bit further, and players like Josh Jung, Triston Casas and Ezequiel Tovar are also in similar spots—late-2022 callups who retained rookie status.

Again, it's only one year of data points, but if this pattern continues, it will have implications for those in one-year fantasy leagues with in-season pickups. So often in-season fantasy analysts, come July or so, warn that any given week's rookie callup is "your last chance" at an impact rookie via your league's Free Agent Budget (FAB). "Spend up," some say, "the cupboard is bare after this one." While there are plenty of other factors to consider as one makes FAB bids each week (team needs/context, in-season FAB management) the new CBA stipulations and how at least two big-league teams responded to it in 2022 call these analysts' conclusions into question.

While no, rostering a player for a three- or four-week stretch (as you would have for Carroll or Henderson) does not have the same percentage impact on your team's overall standings as adding a comparable player in June, there is also the argument to make that for those in close, tight races in September, finding the best players to provide that push to the finish are just valuable in their own right. And having the FAB resources to make competitive bids on players like Carroll or Henderson can be a big advantage for a team in the hunt for a championship.

It will be interesting to see if this scenario plays itself out again in 2023; where perceived top 2024 prospects who are deemed ready, get the call at just the right time to maximize both 2023 plate appearances/IP as well as their chances for a lucrative (on both the team and player front) return that would come with a Rookie of the Year or other post-season award placement. We'll be watching.

•

Long-time readers of the *Minor League Baseball Analyst* may have noticed something a bit new a few pages back. For the first time, we've included an official masthead so we can give all the contributors to the MLBA the recognition they deserve.

And it also makes it a bit easier to just who is putting together the player profiles. Via the list on the masthead, all player-based information in the boxes—including the skills grades, commentaries and player ratings—are the primary work of one analyst. Assignments are divided up by organization, so that our analysts get to know an MLB team's system from top to bottom.

That means, if you are reading a box commentary about a player in the Toronto system, that author is Jeremy Deloney. If it's a Marlin, those are Chris Blessing's words. Given our emphasis on seeing players in person—and the daunting task when the book covers 900+ players—we did share information and insights with each other, tapping the strength of our team. In addition, each writer filled in the gaps with various scouting and front-office contacts.

Though the player-box section is the meat of the book, there are many other great features and structure to help you prepare for your next minor-league game (or fantasy-league draft). Let's quickly run through the features and structure.

The Insights section provides some narrative details and tools you can use as you prepare for getting the most out of your farm system and the rookies that will emerge during the 2023 baseball season. All the essays are designed to help you assemble your teams, as well as give you some food for thought on the prospect landscape.

As usual, several of the essays address our unique player grading system and some perspectives on how we've used it in the past. Again this year, the first Insights essay is a "Primer" on the subject, where we explain in more detail the grading process, and give some real-life examples of what we mean when we give a player an "8C" grade, for instance.

Additional topics in this edition include a detailed essay why we so rarely assign a "10" rating to a pitcher; work on how plate discipline metrics can give us insight into expected walk and strikeout rates; how MLB's "taking over" of the minor leagues affect player evaluation; the reviews of the 2022 Arizona Fall League and the MLB First Year Player Draft; and previews of both prospects to know about from 2023 college baseball and the 2023prep ranks. If the past is any indication, no doubt many of these players mentioned in the essays will soon be fantasy cornerstones. For keeper leagues, the time to get on board is now.

Up next is the HQ100—our signature list of the top 100 fantasy baseball prospects for 2023. The HQ100 is a compilation of eight individual lists (MLBA authors Chris Blessing, Jeremy Deloney, Rob Gordon Brent Hershey, Doug Otto and Matthew St-Germain, as well as BaseballHQ.com prospect-savvy writers Nick Richards and Shelly Verougstraete). This list is ranked by overall fantasy value, in an attempt to balance raw skill level, level of polish/refinement, risk in terms of age/level, and overall potential impact value. And then Deloney suggests 10 more "Sleepers" just outside the HQ100, players who just missed in 2023 or who could make the jump to the list in 2024.

Though the player profiles make up the bulk of the book, don't miss the tools that follow: the Major League Equivalencies; the Organization Grades; the Top Prospects by organization, by position, and by specific skills; the Top 75 prospects for 2023 only; an archive of our Top 100 lists; the glossary and a list of minor league affiliates. Whew … there's a lot of information in these pages.

But for now—if you have a suggestion to share, email us at support@baseballhq.com. Otherwise, grab a shovel and dig in. A better fantasy farm system awaits.

Player Grade Primer

by Brent Hershey

What follows is a quick primer on our background and grading system that we hope gives you the proper context to consume the player grades you find in each player box, and referenced in some of the essays. Feel free to refer to this repeatedly as you work your way through this book. Our hope is that the context provides a clear sense of making the most out of our evaluations.

Background

Yes, these are prospect reports, and in one sense they are like the many other quality prospect lists and discussions you'll find in pre-season books and websites that aim to prepare you for the 2023 season. There is one specific characteristic, however, about the *Minor League Baseball Analyst* evaluations that we feel makes them stand out: They are compiled, evaluated and ranked *specifically with fantasy baseball in mind*. We know that you're not just looking for the best prospects; you want the best *fantasy* prospects. Our writers write and editors edit with the goal of how much a player will contribute to a fantasy baseball roster. Among a few of their considerations that may help you:

Position(s) matters. For instance, almost all fantasy leagues require a catcher. Given the lower bar offensively for that position, we attempt to adjust when we evaluate backstops. Finding a catcher who consistently contributes on offense can be a challenging endeavor. Given how much emphasis is put on a rookie catcher's defense, and learning to manage a big-league staff upon his promotion, it often takes time for the bat to "catch up." We attempt to account for that, because finding a reliable catcher who can contribute to your fantasy squad is a huge built-in advantage. And knowing who to stay away from can be just as valuable.

Speed matters. Given the recent MLB downturn in stolen bases and SB attempts overall, those players who are successfully able to compile stolen bases continue to increase in value. Of course, SB totals in the minors are not always the best proxy for MLB SB success—pitchers and catchers are better equipped at the majors, for one thing, and there's always the question of whether the player can either hit or get on base enough. And we haven't even broached the subject of having a manager who uses that weapon in today's launch-angle environment. All that's to say we take special care in evaluating speed-first players, because if they make it and can become reliable SB sources at the MLB level, they will have a unique skill set for impacting our fantasy baseball teams.

Defense matters. This point has long been touted on the opposite side: Defense doesn't matter when evaluating MLB prospects for fantasy utility; we only worry about the bat. But given the growing importance in the real-life game on position flexibility and players able to play multiple positions, it's past time to consider defensive flexibility as an important part of prospect evaluation. Prospects who are able to play MLB-quality defense at several positions are many times more likely to get opportunities to play (which equals more AB) than, say, a player who is merely adequate defensively at just one position. The MLB game's shift to carrying more pitchers on the active roster almost means that bench players especially *have* to be capable at several positions. And it's even better if some of a teams' starting eight position players can "double up" on positions. So while no, it doesn't matter how many errors in the field a certain top-hitting shortstop makes for fantasy baseball purposes, it may matter just how many positions a player can adequately man that will be the difference between a big-league roster spot and one at Triple-A.

A pitcher's "stuff" matters. With strikeouts in the game continuing to rise, and with some multi-inning relievers knocking on the 100-K door each year, pitchers who can get whiffs continue to garner attention. Now, it's obviously only one tool: As Alex Reyes or Brusdar Graterol shows, having some baseline of control, command, secondary pitches still matter—and a lack of such will eventually force a pitcher to the bullpen. But in general, we'll rate a high-K, wild pitcher higher than a Low-A change-up artist with a 2.00 ERA. Yes, a pitcher's stuff can improve, but showing the raw skills of pitch movement and getting swings-and-misses seems to project better to fantasy success than pitchers cruising on average velocity and overall arsenal but pinpoint control.

There are more elements to this complex process, of course, but those are just some examples of elements that this volume's writers take into account that may differ from other "baseball-only value" lists.

Lastly, with the above, it may seem curious that we still break up our writing assignments by MLB team—after all, beyond -only leagues, which MLB team a player is on has very little bearing as to a player's future value. The answer, for now … is that it's just the easiest way to produce this material. In our case—like other outlets—we have one analyst solely responsible for each individual organization (see specific assignments in the introductory essay). It helps with our workload of attempting to see with live looks as many of these players as we can throughout the season. And it helps because each of the evaluators fills in the gaps with information from contacts who have seen the players in person.

The Grade

Minor League Baseball Analyst and BaseballHQ.com's unique grading system was developed by Deric McKamey, a former prospect writer and current scout for the St. Louis Cardinals. The system debuted in the 2007 edition of this book, and we've been using it in subsequent MLBAs and on our site ever since. While the scale is listed on the introductory Batters and Pitchers pages, sometimes there's some confusion for both new and old readers on the specifics of the system. So we'll take some time here to explain how we best intend to use it along with some examples of current MLB players.

The system is a two-part scale: A number grade comes first, which represents a player's upside—at full MLB maturity, not at the present day. And then a letter grade follows, which attaches some probability that the player reaches that upside. Let's break these elements down even further.

Upside

Upside, of course, is what we're all chasing in this prospecting endeavor. We want to get the highest performing players onto our fantasy rosters, even if we have to wait a bit for the production to materialize. And that's exactly why we use this measure—we want to help identify which players have the highest upside, regardless of other factors.

As analysts, our goal is to be realistic as possible with this number grade. This is why not everyone is a 10—even though, in the purest technical sense, there's still the infinitesimal chance that you or I would be a Hall of Fame-caliber player. Each analyst brings their own perspective and experience to providing these number grades. It comes from years of scouting players, seeing comps, realizing who worked out, who improved, who didn't—and understanding to the best of their ability the "whys" behind those examples.

Let's run through the top five levels of number grades here with the "key"—but also with several corresponding established MLB players at their current level to help level-set our expectations. And of course, some of these players can still move up or down a tier as their careers develop. This is just a snapshot of who they are now:

Gr	Description	Current Example Player
10	Potential Hall of Famer	Mike Trout, Mookie Betts Jacob deGrom, Justin Verlander
9	Potential Elite Player	Trea Turner, Vlad Guerrero, Jr., Juan Soto Corbin Burnes, Aaron Nola, Edwin Diaz
8	Potential Solid Regular	Bryan Reynolds, Willie Adames, Andrew Benintendi Pablo Lopez, Joe Musgrove, Sonny Gray, David Bednar
7	Potential Average Regular	Carson Kelly, Michael A. Taylor, Kyle Farmer Marco Gonzales, Jose Quintana, Nick Pivetta
6	Potential Platoon Player	Cavan Biggio Joc Pederson, Dan Vogelbach Bailey Falter, Adrian Houser, Brad Keller

So as you consume these number grades, you may find the examples above helpful given some of their real-life production levels.

Probability/risk

The second part of the Grade is a letter, given in the A-E academic scale. The letter portion is best thought of as a proxy for risk: Essentially, it is the probability that the evaluator thinks the player will reach his upside grade. We break it down into percentages, like this:

A: 90% probability of reaching potential
B: 70% probability of reaching potential
C: 50% probability of reaching potential
D: 30% probability of reaching potential
E: 10% probability of reaching potential

It's best to remember that this is *not* how close a player is to the majors—though that is one small aspect of the letter grade—as in, proven production at higher levels of the minors usually increases a player's probability grade. For instance, a player who has performed well against AA competition has some aspect of a smaller risk than a Low-A teenager.

Other things that can affect a players' letter grade:

Quality makeup. Here are two examples of makeup that could affect a player's letter grade positively: A drivenness to put in the work to improve, and/or the ability to block out other distractions and keenly focus on his craft.

A sense of conquering foundational skills that can "set the table" for further overall improvement. Think of a Low-A pitcher with impeccable ability to throw strikes, or a Double-A hitter who can just put the bat on the ball. Even if there are other aspects of these players' skill sets that are deficient—say, the pitcher can't command his fastball and the hitter has not yet developed in-game power—sometimes the foundational skills are building blocks for skills that come later. Recognizing these different tools and knowing how to express them in the letter grade is one of the things we ask our evaluators to consider.

Note that a lower letter grade that indicates more risk may include:

Concerns about a player staying healthy. If he has trouble in the minors, how likely is that to continue as he climbs the ladder?

Lack of fundamental baseball skills. This is the flip side of the above. We see this in toolsy but undisciplined players, sometimes pure athletes who have come to baseball later in their youth and have to refine their hitting mechanics or strike zone judgment. A pitcher might throw hard and have a nasty offspeed swing and miss pitch, but can't find the plate.

Makeup that might hold a player back from improving. Of course, judging and grading makeup is one of the toughest calls. But that still goes into our thought process.

One essential takeaway: not all players with the same grade are created equal. That's why it's so important to not just look at the grade; the real work our crew does is in the written comments, where we break down a player's tools/skills and attempt to give a snapshot of the player's future. Related, don't obsess over the differences in the grade. Yes, for sure, an 8B and a 9C are very close and there is some merit to saying that every 8B could easily also be graded a 9C. But we ask our evaluators to make a call, and provide them space in the comments to give their understanding of this player's potential future. In the end, *you* make the call for *your* team. Some fantasy owners don't mind the risk, and just want to shoot for upside. It is likely those owners will have more 9Ds on their roster. Others may want more sure things, and are going to lean towards the 8As and 8Bs, or even 7As, who are meant to have lower risk in their profiles. It's just how this works.

Conclusion

We do all of this knowing that there will be instances when we will be wrong; and those when we'll be right—such as our early-career reports on Vlad Guerrero (9B) and our 2018 ceiling for Corbin Burnes (9E). Fantasy or not, both hits and misses are the nature of this business. But we hope you will find value in our work to help guide your decisions for your teams.

Search for the 10-Rated Pitcher

by Chris Blessing

The 10 potential rating is the most prized rating the authors of the *Minor League Baseball Analyst* (MLBA) can give to a prospect. A 10 rating means we believe a particular prospect has at least a 30% or greater probability of achieving a Hall of Fame type player outcome. Since my introduction to BaseballHQ.com and the MLBA eight offseasons ago, we've given out only ten of these Hall of Fame potential ratings. This year, I had the pleasure of contributing the lone 10 rating in our book, dishing out a 10D (30% probability to reach a Hall of Fame outcome) to Corbin Carroll (OF, ARI).

We've given five 10 ratings in the past six editions of the MLBA. The only year we didn't hand out a new 10 rating was 2021, when we reproduced our player boxes from the 2020 MLBA edition due to the lost minor league season because of COVID-19. Each 10 rating during this time span has been hitters, including Carroll this season.

We haven't thrown a 10 rating on a pitching prospect for a long time. It was 2017 to be exact. Lucas Giolito (10C) and Alex Reyes (10D) were our last two 10-rated pitching prospects, each achieving their ratings in consecutive seasons (2016 & 2017). Joining Giolito and Reyes in 2016 as a 10-rated pitcher was Kolby Allard (10D), which is the only 10 I've assigned to a pitcher. The thought of the Allard rating continues to haunt me as an evaluator, even though I'm probably the only one who still brings it up or cares. It's the biggest miss of my thirteen years playing prospect evaluator/scout in the public space.

Let's delve deeper into pitching projection, what a 10 rating looks like in real life and if we considered a 10 rating for any of the pitchers on this year's ranking. Before we get into the pitching side of pitching projection, I'll recap the process I use to determine a 10-rated prospect by delving into the process with Corbin Carroll.

The 10 rating process

I hand out a lot of 7 ratings (average regular). Using our evaluation scale, a 7 rating encompasses the ceiling of most prospects. 7A (90% probability) and 7B (70% probability) mean much more than a 7C (50%) or lower rating. 8 ratings (solid regular) are my second-most frequent potential rating assigned, followed by 6 ratings (platoon player) and 9 ratings (elite players). I've only assigned four 10 ratings in my MLBA history (Carroll, Wander Franco, Ronald Acuna Jr. and Allard).

Many factors contribute to a 10 rating for Corbin Carroll this year. Here is Carroll's player box.

> *Wiry athletic CF mashed his way through the upper minors to receive MLB callup. Shorter limbs aid compact swing with plus bat speed. Upright, slightly closed stance with slight load. Patient, all fields approach with natural loft off the bat. Average power in frame plays up due to swing mechanics and approach. Exceptional speed. 30/30 threat.*

I didn't do much statistical or data analysis of his big-league debut. Still, a .260/.330/.500 slash line was impressive. According to Baseball Savant, his sprint speed was in the 100th percentile. The data from the minor leagues really stood out, especially compared to his peers. Carroll's average exit velocity (EV) was near 90 mph, his 90th percentile EV was over 105 mph and he hit the ball nearly 50% of the time over 95 mph. A high percentage of his over 95 mph+ contact was lofted in the air. For a wiry, athletic body frame, it's quite impressive. Throw in his plus eye and his spray tendencies, Carroll overwhelmingly fit the 10 rating fantasy producer outcome potential. There was an injury caveat hanging over the Carroll profile. He tore his shoulder in 7th game of the 2021 season while following through after hitting a home run. He missed the rest of the season after surgery. It was an uncommon injury. I hedged a bit, grading Carroll a 10D (30% probability) instead of the 10C (50% probability) rating.

The Carroll shoulder injury and the hesitancy to grant a higher rating probability is relatable to our overall hesitancy to throw high ratings on prospect pitchers. No matter the pitcher, the risk of serious, career-altering injuries is ever-present. Look at what has become of Marlins prospect Sixto Sanchez, who debuted in 2020. He looked like a future ace, even pitching for the Marlins in the playoffs. However, he hasn't seen game action since due to shoulder issues, which included 2021 surgery to repair a tear the posterior capsule in his throwing shoulder and bursectomy surgery on the same shoulder last fall. Even so, I never considered Sanchez a 10-rated pitcher. He simply didn't bring enough swing-and-miss to the party to be a true, dominant, Hall of Fame caliber pitcher. To figure out who meets the criteria, we must identify what a 10-rated outcome looks like.

10 Rating pitching benchmarks

A Hall of Fame fantasy pitcher, year in and year out, provides stability and consistency across fantasy pitching rotations. Some hurlers will seep into the conversation for a year, maybe two, but most pitchers don't have staying power among the elite. There is always someone new on the verge of this conversation. However, it takes someone special to emerge from a one-year or two-year wonder to a dominant, Hall of Fame caliber hurler. Who knows, it could be Sandy Alcantara, the best pitcher in the National League last season and the only pitcher in baseball to throw 400 innings over the last two seasons.

There are four active pitchers who experienced stretches in their career considered to be Hall of Fame quality. During these stretches of brilliance, they piled up strikeouts, limited baserunners, avoided disastrous outings and did it with consistency over multiple seasons, and, in a few instances, for more than a decade. The active pitchers who have enjoyed these sorts of stretches in their careers and can clearly stake a claim to this category are Justin Verlander, Clayton Kershaw, Max Scherzer and Jacob deGrom. One could argue Gerrit Cole is in this exclusive company, too. 2023 could be the year he undoubtedly enters the 10-rating outcome category.

Prospect pedigree of 10-rated outcomes

With four identified 10-rated outcome examples, let's take a ride in the wayback machine to look at the prospect profiles of each pitcher.

Justin Verlander (MLBA graduation 2006)

Verlander predates the potential rating system created by former BHQ prospect guru and current MLB scout Deric McKamey. McKamey had Verlander's projected role as an #1 starter, rating his fastball as a +++++ pitch, his change-up as a +++ pitch and his curve as a ++ pitch. McKamey wrote the following commentary:

> *Led minor leagues with 1.29 ERA, getting dynamic movement to sinker and change-up. DET got him to stand taller and shorten his stride, allowing him to repeat delivery and improve command. Curveball could be tighter and needs to be more efficient. Shutdown in AUG due to a sore shoulder.*

The uncertainty related to the curveball likely would have curbed a 10 rating had the potential rating system been in place at that time. Having studied McKamey's work from the early days of the potential rating scale to better understand his system, this commentary, coupled by the pitch ratings, feels like a 9B rating (70% probability for an elite outcome).

The great thing about the Verlander profile is the foundational skills have been the catalyst for his dominance, like his feel for his powerful fastball and his overall command. He ditched his once-elite sinker he used masterfully in another era and continues to dominate today with a four-seam fastball. Verlander obviously tightened up his curve, added a slider and continued to work in a change-up, which became a fourth pitch during his stint in Houston.

Max Scherzer (MLBA graduation 2008)

By 2008, McKamey had developed the Potential Rating system, making a 10-rated prospect possible. Questions about Scherzer's stamina and his inability to change speeds contributed to a 9C prospect (50% probability for an elite outcome) for Scherzer. McKamey projected a #3 starter/setup reliever for Scherzer. His fastball and slider both rated out as ++++ pitches while his change-up rated out as a ++ pitch. Here is McKamey's commentary.

> *Blessed with arm strength and quick arm action, he generates plus velocity to fastball and movement to slider. Deceptive with low 3/4 slot and loves to challenge hitters inside. Struggles to change speeds and hasn't shown much stamina which may prompt move to relief.*

Scherzer was a later bloomer than Verlander, who won Rookie of the Year in his first full MLB season. It wasn't until Scherzer's fifth or sixth major league season before he started to peak, which corresponded with developing the ability to change speeds by introducing a curveball and improving the execution of his change-up. The tenacity and competitive spirit have always been a part of the profile. Scherzer just needed more time.

The most significant thing that sticks out about Scherzer has been a career willingness to change. In recent years, he's enhanced his repertoire by adding a cutter, which created another angle for hitters to deal with, guarding against the stuff from backing up due to any age-related regressions. Scherzer added the cutter in 2018, after two consecutive Cy Young Award-winning seasons.

Clayton Kershaw (MLBA graduation 2008)

Kershaw, like Scherzer, graduated during the 2008 season. I suspected Kershaw, given his prospect pedigree, was the only pitcher of the quintet to earn a 10 rating as a prospect. I was right. McKamey stuck a 10D rating (30% probability for a Hall of Fame outcome) on Kershaw with a projected role as a #1 starter. His fastball and change-up each earned ++++ ratings. His curveball earned a +++ rating. Here is McKamey's commentary.

> *Tall/projectable pitcher with overpowering fastball and good depth to curveball, being able to strikeout anyone. Repeats 3/4 delivery well giving him solid chang-eup and commands. Delivery lacks fluidity and tends to push baseball when tired. Dominated as one of league's youngest players.*

Kershaw was a different animal as a minor leaguer, compared to just about anyone over the last 20 years. The most difficult thing for me as a pitching evaluator is to project a curveball from a minor league mound to an MLB mound. Kershaw's curveball became elite. He added a slider, which also became elite. During his prime, he was operating with three elite pitches (FB, CB, SL) and sometimes flashing a fourth plus pitch (CU).

The fluidity of the delivery and his habit of pushing the baseball when he was tired stood out to me in the commentary, just because of the uniqueness of the delivery. I see others try to duplicate a Kershaw-esque delivery and tend to fall into the same pattern observed in Kershaw as a minor leaguer. MacKenzie Gore, once a top prospect, saw his stuff mostly fall apart as he struggled to maintain a similarly unique delivery. Who knows if Kershaw's delivery has contributed to his back issues. It's hard to speculate.

Jacob deGrom (MLBA graduation 2014)

deGrom is the most unique arm to become a Hall of Fame outcome in fantasy. While I wasn't a writer for BaseballHQ or MLBA in deGrom's prospect years, I was active at other sites like Bullpen Banter and RotoScouting. Like here, I had Mets coverage at both sites and was familiar with deGrom prior to his 2014 MLB debut and Rookie of the Year season. He was the definition of a 7C pitcher (50% probability of an average regular outcome). In fact, 7C was the potential rating assigned by former MLBA writer Chris Mallonee. deGrom was ranked 13th in the Mets organization, ranked behind several other active pitchers including Noah Syndergaard, Rafael Montero and Michael Fulmer. Here is Mallonee's commentary.

> *Didn't start pitching until his junior year of college and missed 2011 for Tommy John surgery, which is why he's an older prospect. Athletic frame with a plus fastball that he can dial up to 98 and a plus slider. His change-up is making progress and he will go to it on occasion but needs it to become a viable third pitch. Throws strikes and goes to breaking ball when he needs a swing and miss.*

deGrom was up to 98 with his two-seam fastball in 2013, mostly sitting in the low 90s and it was an extremely hittable pitch. deGrom couldn't put away hitters with his fastball, didn't get enough whiffs from his slider and his change-up flashed average. He had above-average command, repeated his delivery extremely well and oozed athleticism from a wiry frame. I questioned his durability at the time because he was rail-thin, though not as extreme as Triston McKenzie is today. Even now, deGrom doesn't have the same frame as most power pitchers.

As he has advanced in years, deGrom has turned a fringe-to-average two-seam fastball into an exceptional four-seam fastball. As his stuff has improved, so has his overall command. Some might chalk it up to being late to the mound and needing time to reach his potential. Others might say it is his work ethic. deGrom is an anomaly for me. He literally was on the same trajectory as Kyle Gibson and ended up in the same conversation as Justin Verlander, Max Scherzer and Clayton Kershaw.

Ace X-factor

What sets guys like Verlander and Scherzer apart from highly-rated pitching prospects who never develop to an elite-level competitor? One might say it's because guys like Verlander and Scherzer are wired differently as competitors compared to other pitchers. If it's true, how would we quantify it? Would we use a term like "makeup" to further project the sort of personalities or characteristics we could expect to take it to this Hall of Fame level as a competitor?

Getting into makeup in projection is messy for anyone in the public sphere. Sure, I'm well enough informed through contacts to know of some guys thought to have strong makeup and others with makeup concerns. As an evaluator in the public space, I stay as far away as I can from reporting on makeup. Mostly, it's relying on second- or third-hand information. I've seen some in the public space try to draw on a variety of assumptions. I don't want to work on assumptions.

However, we can see that the high-level guys who strive to constantly improve, blessed with health, will outperform those who are content with their abilities. There are several recent top pitching prospects who lost their competitive advantage for something within their control, like staying on a nutritional program or not getting to the next level in development because they were content with tools not honed for advanced competition. Essentially, without knowing makeup, it's nearly impossible to assign a 10 rating to a pitching prospect.

Projecting the next elite pitcher

If recent history has told us anything, projecting elite pitching has become increasingly difficult. I touched on our histories with both Lucas Giolito and Alex Reyes in the opening. Giolito has had short in-season spurts of greatness. However, after eight seasons of looks, it appears he'll go down as a solid mid-tier #1 starter. Reyes isn't starting anymore because of poor command. The future, at best, is as a mid-tier fantasy closer. There are other names too, like Michael Kopech, Forrest Whitley and MacKenzie Gore, all Top 10 overall fantasy prospects, but don't appear to be top pitchers in fantasy. Each guy above showed similar promise to Verlander, Scherzer and Kershaw in the minors. They simply couldn't get to the next level.

The three top pitchers in this year's HQ100 are Andrew Painter (RHP, PHI), Grayson Rodriguez (RHP, BAL) and Eury Perez (RHP, MIA). You can make a case for each guy becoming the next 10-rated pitching performer based on their toolshed profiles alone.

Painter has an exceptional fastball, two secondary offerings projecting to be ++++ pitches and a fourth pitch, a seldom used curveball, which projects as an average offering. Painter's poise on the mound and ability to command both his fastball and slider at an advanced also bode well in his development. Brent Hershey, who has MLBA Phillies coverage, has Painter's potential rating at 9B. I concur.

Rodriguez's calling card are four pitches rated as above-average-or-better pitches. He's also added a cutter as a fifth pitch to his repertoire, which also looks like an average-or-better pitch. Rodriguez missed half of last season with a lat strain. There is some concern with his long-term ability to throw his change-up frequently, given the screwball like movement of the pitch and the stress a pitch like that can put on an elbow. Like for Painter, Hershey had Orioles coverage and rated Rodriguez a 9B prospect. Again, I concur.

Perez is the only prospect boasting four potential ++++ pitches in his arsenal. He also has exceptional command of his pitches and shows the same sort of poise as Painter shows on the mound. He missed time this season due to a right shoulder strain. Since I have Marlins coverage, I rated Perez. I talked myself down from a 9B rating due to his shoulder injury. I rated him a 9C prospect.

10 Rating Pitching Conclusions

This article has created a good argument for the "prospect pitching is a crapshoot" crowd. To an extent, they are correct. However, these higher-reward guys, even on the verge of their MLB debuts, come with much more risk than the high-floor, mid-rotation starter profiles. I'm confident we've got at least two ace pitchers developing between Andrew Painter, Grayson Rodriguez, and Eury Perez. However, if a manager wants to roster any of these high-upside arms, they should mitigate their risks by also carrying pitching prospects with less exciting upsides but significantly higher floors, like a Logan Allen (LHP, CLE) profile or a Ryne Nelson (RHP, ARI) profile. Ky Bush (LHP, LAA) isn't a sexy roster add but he should eat innings and do so productively as an MLB arm. The only way to win the arms race in fantasy is to spread out risk across various profiles.

A 10-rating pitching outcome is out there. My money is on one of Painter, Rodriguez and Perez having 10-rating outcome. But they will have to prove it—and continue to improve—during their MLB careers.

!

Using Plate Discipline Metrics to Calculate Expected Walk and Strikeout Rates

by Doug Otto

A batter's ability to put the ball in play and/or get on base—arguably the most important prerequisite for success at the major league level—can make or break a hitter's career. For this reason, much of prospect evaluation comes down to accurately evaluating a batter's hit tool.

A batter's BB% and K% are standard ways to approximate hit tool and on-base skills, but more granular plate discipline metrics are often used to provide nuanced examinations of player profiles. Statistics such as contact% and swing% are some of the most popular plate discipline metrics used to describe a batter's particular approach and eye at the plate. These statistics may also be useful for predicting a batter's expected BB% and expected K%.

We can use data from the 2021 minor league season to "train" models on how to predict a batter's BB% and K% given their underlying plate discipline metrics, as demonstrated in Lucas Kelly's series of articles for FanGraphs.com[1] calculating expected BB% and K% for major league players.

Our methodology involved creating a correlation matrix across these metrics. Rather than calculate a table for every level of full-season minor league baseball, counting statistics for each individual player were aggregated across each level they played. Rate statistics to be used in the correlation matrix were then calculated for each player with at least 120 total PA for the entire 2021 minor league season. The final sample contained 1,678 batters.

For each of the variables identified to have strong correlations, we retained the variable that has the stronger correlation with either of the independent variables (i.e., BB% and K%). Based on the matrix, we kept zone% (i.e., the percentage of pitches seen that land in the zone), swing%, o-swing% (i.e., the percentage of pitches outside the zone that the batter swung at), contact%, o-contact%, and FpK% (i.e., the percentage of first pitches seen which are strikes). We also included the hitter's age as a control variable.

The next step was to run a regression model, one for each independent variable, to train the models on how to predict BB% and K% using the selected plate discipline metrics. Once the models were calculated, they were applied to the 2022 data to create predicted BB% and K% for each batter. Only batters with at least 120 total PA were included in the sample for analysis.

With these new expected BB% and K% statistics, let's take a look at some of the biggest estimated underperformers and overperformers for the 2022 season.

BB% Underperformers

Nick Yorke (2B, BOS)

Level	Total PA	BB%	xBB%	Difference
A+	373	8.8%	11.9%	-3.1%

Yorke, BaseballHQ's 59th overall prospect heading into 2022, had a disappointing follow-up to his blistering 2021 campaign, slashing .233/.303/.365 at High-A in 2022. Much of the 20-year-old's problems seemed to boil down to his cratered BA, likely fueled by a steep drop in LD% and a 28.8 h%. However, his plate discipline remained strong, as he showed a roughly average swing% and ct%. This is reflected in his xBB%, which thinks his below-average BB% should have been more average-to-above-average. Yorke is a decent buy-low in dynasty leagues with the caveat that his true talent level likely lies somewhere between his 2021 and 2022 performances.

Elly De La Cruz (SS, CIN)

Level	Total PA	BB%	xBB%	Difference
A+/AA	513	7.4%	10.4%	-3.0%

De La Cruz was one of the big breakout prospects of the 2022 season, climbing to Double-A as a 20-year-old on the strength of his raw power and speed. The SS has a higher ceiling than most other prospects, but his subpar plate discipline metrics present a decent risk that he may struggle to hit as he continues his climb to the majors. That being said, his plate discipline metrics suggest that he may be underperforming his true on-base potential as evidenced by his xBB%. Getting to a roughly average BB% would be a boon to De La Cruz's overall profile, and could help offset potential losses to his BA moving forward.

BB% Overperformers

Emmanuel Rodriguez (OF, MIN)

Level	Total PA	BB%	xBB%	Difference
A	198	28.3%	18.5%	9.8%

Rodriguez logged one of the more unique minor league seasons in recent memory, with walk and strikeout rates close to 30% while hitting .272 with 9 HR as a 19-year-old at Single-A. While the near-10% difference in his BB% and xBB% suggests he certainly overperformed given his plate discipline and contact profile, he still boasts the highest xBB% of any prospect at 18.5%. He's an intriguing prospect nonetheless given his advanced plate approach for his age, and is definitely worth watching to see if he can trim his K%.

Marcelo Mayer (SS, BOS)

Level	Total PA	BB%	xBB%	Difference
A	422	15.4%	10.5%	4.9%

Lauded as a toolsy, well-rounded player and one of the best in the 2021 draft, Mayer mostly looked the part, working his way through Single-A before ending the season in High-A. He hit for a decent average and kept strikeouts to a manageable level, while also showing an impactful combo of power and speed. The 19-year-old also showed patience at the plate as evidenced by his advanced walk rate. However, based on his underlying plate discipline data, xBB% sees him as closer to average than advanced. If this is a more accurate reflection of Mayer's plate discipline, he may end up as more of a "sum of his parts" prospect than a truly elite one.

K% Underperformers

Andy Pages (OF, LA)

Level	Total PA	K%	xK%	Difference
AA	578	24.7%	20.8%	3.9%

Pages has been one of the most prolific HR hitters in the minors over the last two seasons, tallying 26 in 132 games played in 2022. While he doesn't project as a plus hitter, he also isn't quite the hacker that might be suggested by his burgeoning track record of average-to-below-average strikeout rates and .236 average in 2022. His expected K% also points to some potential growth as hinted by his underlying plate discipline/contact skills. Pages could prove to be a very valuable power bat with solid hitting chops to boot.

Tyler Soderstrom (C, OAK)

Level	Total PA	K%	xK%	Difference
A+/AA/AAA	556	26.1%	22.7%	3.4%

Soderstrom struggled to begin the season, battling the cold Midwestern spring and suffering a thumb injury that cut into his playing time. He really turned it on in the second half, battling all the way from High-A to Triple-A all before his 21st birthday. While his aggressive approach sometimes led him astray, he managed to keep his K% to a respectable level. However, his xK% suggests there's more upside in his contact ability to limit strike-outs even further. It's possible his tepid start to the season could be obfuscating an even more impressive line here.

K% Overperformers

Joey Wiemer (OF, MIL)

Level	Total PA	K%	xK%	Difference
AA/AAA	550	26.7%	32.8%	-6.0%

Wiemer has endeared himself to many fantasy baseball fans thanks to his toolsy physicality and loud minor league offensive production. This production has come in spite of some worrying plate discipline and contact rates that call into question his projection as a major league hitter. He did seem to show some growth upon reaching Triple-A, where he cut his strikeouts and improved his OBP. However, his xK% is not buying it, as it expected Wiemer to have had a near-untenable K% rather than a so-so one. His ultra-aggressive approach and limited contact skills run the risk of being exposed in the majors without barring significant refinement.

Jordan Walker (3B, STL)

Level	Total PA	K%	xK%	Difference
AA/AAA	538	21.6%	26.1%	-4.5%

Walker, one of the top prospects in baseball thanks to his game-changing power and hitting ability as a 20-year-old, dominated Double-A while exhibiting good plate discipline. His xK% suggests he may have overperformed his true contact skills, however, pegging him as closer to average than below average. It's possible his positive run environment in Springfield helped mask some of his slight deficiencies making contact. Still, Walker's power and overall athleticism should still play if his contact skills settle in closer to average.

[1]*Kelly's analysis can be found at https://fantasy.fangraphs.com/linear-modeling-for-bb/*

MLB's Takeover of the Minor Leagues: Prospect Evaluation gets more Difficult

by Chris Blessing

During the 2020/2021 off-season, Major League Baseball launched a successful takeover attempt of the management aspect of the minor leagues. At first, the takeover was met with skepticism. MLB's track record supporting minor league talent was subpar at best. MLB looked like a villain with the lack of resources they provided teams. Thankfully, much of those behaviors have changed since Major League Baseball's takeover of the minor leagues. Still, there is work left to do. Here are some of the highlights from the rule changes MLB has implemented since taking over the minor leagues.

-      There was contraction. MLB contracted short-season, non-complex leagues. The Northwest League became High-A, the Pioneer League is now an independent partner league with MLB, the Appalachian League is now a collegiate summer league, and the New York-Penn League is now defunct with remnants spread across the South Atlantic League and the MLB Draft League. Over 40 teams across the country are no longer official affiliates of MLB teams.

Experimentation. MLB started to use the Minor Leagues as a place to experiment with potential rule changes. New MLB rules, such as pitch clocks, bigger bases and limits on defensive shifts, were tested the past two seasons. The automated strike zone, which will eventually make its debut in the big leagues—likely as a challenge system instead of a fully automated strike zone—has been experimented in the Low-A Florida State League for the past two seasons and has now pushed into Triple-A (Pacific Coast League and Charlotte in the International League).

Stadium standards. MLB baseball raised the minimum standards for minor league baseball facilities, often around clubhouse, indoor training/medical spaces, nutritional areas but also including some on-field stipulations. Minor League teams out of compliance have five years to fix any issues or risk losing their affiliation.

Housing. Teams are now required to provide furnished housing accommodation options for any player who wants accommodations. They must be reasonably close to the ballpark and must be a comfortable arrangement.

Travel. MLB has mandated changes to travel policies. They mandated 6-game series across full-season levels, allowing players to stay in one place for a week. They have reduced the distance between affiliates, creating smaller full-season leagues. If a team is traveling over 500 miles to its next location, for instance, they must travel via airplane and not bus, which could take up an teams' entire off-day.

These changes, including the experimental rule changes, have improved the quality of play in the minor leagues. There are still changes that need to be made. Organizations now have the option to pay their minor league players during spring training, extended spring training and Fall Instructional Leagues. However, this is not mandated. Player pay is perhaps the issue in need of improvement across the board. Strides have been made, but still, there are prospects who need to take on outside employment during the off-season to survive. Paying a living wage to players would be ideal so they can use working hours to hone their skills to improve their craft instead of working somewhere else.

Changes affecting evaluation and development

For the evaluator and the fantasy manager, these changes have made it much more difficult, to assess what is "real" about a prospect and what is fool's gold. Take the experimental automated strike zone—for the past two seasons, MLB chose to experiment with strike zone automation in the Florida State League (one of the three lowest-level full-season leagues).

In some respects, it's a good thing to have lower-level prospects utilize an automated zone. I had a minor league pitching coach tell me a decade ago the hardest lesson to teach a lower-level pitcher was the importance of throwing strikes. One thing an automated zone forces a pitcher to do is throw strikes. If he can't throw strikes, automation will expose him quicker than inexperienced human umpires and inexperienced hitters would.

But the change has made it difficult to truly value statistics from the Florida State League. Take Emmanuel Rodriguez (OF, MIN), for example. Rodriguez was a breakout performer in the first half for Fort Myers before a leg injury ended his season. The breakout was mostly built on improved BB% (15% in 2021 at complex ball vs. 30% in 2022) and batting eye (0.41 vs 1.10). Rodriguez slashed .272/.493/.552 with 9 HR and more walks than strikeouts (57 BB, 52 K in 47 games).

Here is some sourced data on Rodriguez: In 2022, he swung the bat less than 33% of the time, an ultra-low percentage. It was over 40% in 2021. His chase rate went from over 25% in 2021 to hover near 10% in 2022. Considering his "improved" BB% and Eye, the question is: Did Rodriguez make strides with his approach, or did he simply adjust to automation? Given how he maintained an in-zone whiff rate of over 25%—when other top prospects at the same level hover closer to 20%—it's likely the latter. If so, Rodriguez will face a significant fortune reversal once he gets to a level without strike zone automation.

New MLB rules present challenges with evaluation

Even some of the rules coming to MLB has been met with skepticism. Will bigger bases improve batting averages and stolen base tallies? Will shift restrictions improve offense overall? Will the pitch clock speed up the game and make for better gameplay?

From my experience on the minor league side…

The product will get a boost from the pitch clock. It likely won't have a tangible impact on statistical performance overall. However, gameplay will improve.

Shift restrictions will not have a huge impact on improving BA or run output. However, it should stop the decline of BA, which is presently at the lowest level since 1968 (.243 in 2022). Hitters will continue to sell out for loft and pitching is continually suited to rack up whiffs on hitters, pitching above swing paths. Until contact rates begin to neutralize, shift restrictions won't have a big impact on improving offensive skills.

Bigger bases have led to more stolen bases on the minor league level. The pitch clock and limits on throw-over rules have increased successful stolen base attempts since runners are able

to time pitchers extremely well. Some of the same standard evaluation practices exist as the competition level improves across the minors. At the upper levels, where pitchers hold runners on better and catchers' arms tend to be quicker and more accurate, stolen bases overall and stolen base percentages drop in comparison to the lower levels. However, the eye test suggests, the milliseconds gained by a well-timed jump and bigger bases, will increase stolen base numbers overall.

A player like Zac Veen (OF, COL) has shown an aptitude for timing his jump based on the pitch clock. Not everyone has the feel for baserunning as Veen has shown. He stole 55 bases in 64 attempts last season, adding 16 (in 18 attempts) more in the Arizona Fall League. Veen isn't a classic speedster, either. He produces average run times out of the box, home to first, and has shown above-average speed in the OF. But on the bases, statistically, he is a speed demon. It's likely causing the profile to be overvalued by analysts and fantasy managers. The upper minors will be a nice litmus test for a guy like Veen, who should play at the big-league level soon enough. If Veen can't steal bases at a high rate, what is he? His top hand dominant swing probably nets a high BA, 10-20 HR hitter (even at Coors) who might get managers 10-15 SB, which isn't likely more than a low solid regular outcome in most formats.

MLB, since banning the use of sticky substances on the mound, started using the Southern League and the Texas League (both Double-A leagues) to test pre-tacked baseballs. According to media reports, the experiment only lasted in the Southern League for two weeks for undisclosed reasons. Speaking to a few Southern League pitchers once this story broke in June of 2022, the consensus was the tack inadvertently caused gripping issues for several pitchers. The belief is that MLB will continue to run controlled experiments throughout the minor leagues, their partnered independent leagues and the Arizona Fall League until MLB finds the right pre-tack for pitchers to grip the baseball.

Other player development/evaluation challenges brought on by MiLB takeover

There are other factors, outside of the experimental rules, making it harder to evaluate prospects. The minor league playing field standards are more uniform than ever before. Still, there are places in need of major improvements. Either large renovations are planned for the existing ballparks or minor league organizations are in the process of building new stadiums to house their teams.

For instance, the Reds have a top 5 farm system. Currently, two of their affiliates fall way under the new standards MLB has set for facilities. The city of Daytona (FL) operates Low-A Daytona's Jackie Robinson Ballpark. They are attempting to budget over $30 million to get their stadium up to MLB standards. The Reds Double-A affiliate in Chattanooga will be getting a new stadium in 2025, replacing outdated AT&T Field. Both existing facilities were found to have numerous violations (supposedly in the triple digits) in a report by MLB baseball in 2020, when rumors of contraction first gained media attention. These inequalities between the facilities in the Reds organization, at a time of their rebuild, could be damning in their attempt at developing prospects.

Elly De La Cruz (SS, CIN) is the organization's best prospect. He finished 2022 at Double-A Chattanooga where his .305/.358/.553 slash was sick. However, his struggles with spin specifically warrant a return to Double-A to start 2023. Do the Reds push him to Triple-A Louisville, where the facilities are much better, or do they leave him in Double-A, where he has the best chance at working on spin recognition? This isn't a question the Braves or the Yankees—teams with top-flight affiliate facilities—need to ask. Of course, the Reds aren't the only ones with out of compliance facilities, but it affects them more because of the situation they are in with one of the best farm systems in baseball, in the middle of a rebuild.

Contraction, along with less rounds in the amateur draft, has accelerated timelines for players to reach the big leagues. Several 2021 draft picks from the prep ranks have already climbed to Double-A, including first round picks Jordan Lawlar (SS, ARI), Andrew Painter (RHP, PHI) and Colson Montgomery (SS, CHW). This was unheard of five years ago. Most prep guys spent their first full-seasons after their draft season at Low-A with a shot at High-A by late August. Now, prep guys are splitting the seasons almost equally between lower level, full-season affiliates. The players who adapt the quickest are being rewarded while there is concern for those who don't adapt or develop as quickly getting pushed along faster than would normally be warranted.

Conclusion

The MLB takeover of the minor leagues will continue to reap more pluses than minus over the next half decade or so for player development. It will eventually make evaluation standards easier. We will likely see some affiliate agreements terminate due to minor league organizations failing to gain support from local and state governments for improvements to bring their facilities up to MLB code. This will cause reshuffling across levels and leagues. Also, there is a chance at MLB expansion, which would add four affiliated minor league organizations per team added to MLB. It's believed, by 2027, there will be uniform facilities across the minor leagues.

Experimentation in the minor leagues with the goal of improving the MLB product will continue. Hopefully, it is not done at the cost of player development. With rule changes pushing to the big leagues this season and the automated strike zone experiments likely moving towards a challenge ball/strike system, the testing of pre-tack baseballs will become the most prominent experiment playing out in the minor leagues during the 2023 season. Most likely, there will be anomalies created by the pre-tack substance used in a particular controlled experiment across a league. We simply won't know until we observe it. Baseball HQ will continue to monitor for any changes to play or any changes to player development these experiments might cause.

2022 Arizona Fall League Recap

by Shelly Verougstraete

The Arizona Fall League has been considered a finishing school for prospects. All 30 MLB teams send players to get additional seasoning and the teams use this time to make 40-man roster decisions prior to the Rule 5 draft. In 2022, the league was filled with top-tier prospects like Jordan Walker (3B/OF, STL), Jordan Lawlar (SS, ARI), and Jackson Merrill (SS, SD). Pitching normally lags behind hitters, but this year's crop of pitchers might have been one of the worst in recent memory. That being said, there were some outstanding pitching performances that shocked even the deepest dynasty league players.

In the Minor League Baseball Analyst, we have typically covered the AFL with a "Risers and Fallers" article, but this year we decided it would be fun to give some love to prospects not on the HQ100—as some of the players could be fantasy waiver wire picks very soon.

Will Wagner (1B/3B, HOU), son of Billy Wagner, was one of the better offensive players in Arizona. Over 14 games for the Surprise Saguaros, he slashed .346/.433/.712 with three homers and one stolen base. Wagner was selected by the Houston Astros in the 18th round of the 2021 draft out of Liberty University and made it up to Double-A in his first full professional season. During 2022, he split time between High-A Ashville and Double-A Corpus Christi, slashing .261/.374/.394 with 10 homers and eight stolen bases. The 23-year-old's control of the strike zone and ability to get the barrel on the ball consistently are some of his bigger strengths. During the AFL, his power is what woke most scouts and evaluators up. His exit velocities were consistently high, reaching a max of 105 mph on a groundout. Wagner has all the makings of a late-round sleeper for Houston.

Colt Keith (3B, DET) has had an interesting professional career so far. He was drafted in the fifth (and final) round of the 2020 draft but didn't make his debut until the following year due to the minor league shutdown. 2021 was a fine year for Keith, as he slashed .286/.396/.393 with two homers and four stolen bases. Over the winter, the then 19-year-old worked on getting stronger and added around 20 pounds of muscle. Keith began the season in High-A and hit nine homers across 48 games before a shoulder injury in June ended his season. Luckily, the injury didn't require surgery and the 20-year-old was able to join the Salt River Rafters where he slashed .344/.463/.541 with three homers and three stolen bases. The Tigers system has been a disappointing one but Keith looks to be a piece in Detroit's future.

Tyler Hardman (3B, NYY) was a fifth-round senior sign of the New York Yankees in the 2021 draft out of the University of Oklahoma. In his first professional season, the 23-year-old hit .255/.320/.464 with 22 homers and 14 stolen bases across 111 games for High-A Hudson Valley and Double-A Somerset. He has always shown off above-average power and nothing changed this fall in Arizona. In 20 games for the Mesa Solar Sox, Hardman lived up to his name and smacked 6 long balls and was second in the league with 13 extra-base hits. Hardman is mostly viewed as an org-depth guy since New York's current roster is filled with 1B/DH types. However, he should begin the season back in Double-A and is just an injury away from smacking balls out of Yankee Stadium.

Zavier Warren (C, MIL) was a third-round draft pick out of Central Michigan University in the shrunken 2020 draft. During his time in college, Warren played all SS, 1B, 3B, SS, and C but was primarily SS by his senior year. After he was drafted, he played mostly third base but still caught 20 games. He didn't play catcher at all in 2022 and moved to the hot corner. During his time in the Valley of the Sun, he played first base as the Glendale Desert Dogs didn't have a better option there. The 23-year-old is a switch hitter and showed patience as he had the third highest K/BB ratio with a 22/16 mark. While he is not a heralded prospect, Warren showed enough to keep him in the conversation but is probably a year or two away as he is not on the 40-man roster at the moment.

No other prospect enjoyed themselves more in the Fall League than **Edouard Julien (OF, MIN)**. Julien was born in Quebec, Canada but went to school at Auburn University, where he was drafted in the 18th round. Julien is known for his hawk-like strike zone eye, and he rarely swings and misses outside the zone. After hitting .300/.441/.490 with 17 homers across 113 games for Double-A Wichita, he came to Glendale and said "Hold my beer." Over 21 games, the 23-year-old slashed .400/.563/.686 with five homers and six stolen bases. Julien has dabbled in the outfield but has played exclusively second base and DH in 2022 and is on the cusp of joining the Twins.

Connor Thomas (RHP, STL) was a fifth-round pick out of Georgia Tech and blossomed in Arizona in 2022. After putting up a 5.47 ERA, and 1.57 WHIP over 135 innings in Triple-A Memphis, he dropped a 1.75 ERA and 1.05 WHIP in six games for the Salt River Rafters. Thomas's fastball isn't much (it sits in the high 80s/low 90s) but he had enough finesse to fool even some of the better prospects. Can this work in the majors? Maybe, but he will fill the role of a back-end starter from a fantasy perspective.

Bryan Woo (RHP, SEA) was a sixth-round pick of the Mariners in the 2021 draft and had an excellent AFL. Over 10.2 innings, the 22-year-old stuck out 16 batters and posted a 0.84 ERA and matching 0.84 WHIP. His fastball sits in the mid-90s and has a high-80s change-up with a mid-80s slider that generates big time whiffs. He pounds the strike zone and has a repeatable delivery that should spell even more success as he moves up

the ranks. Woo's season also began in Arizona and started three games before the Mariners promoted him to Low-A Modesto. He finished the season in High-A Everett and had a 4.11 ERA, 1.31 WHIP, and 84/22 K/BB across all three levels. Woo still struggles with left-handed batters, but that is something the Mariners can help him overcome.

Christian Chamberlain (LHP, KC) was a dominating force in the Oregon State's 2020 rotation until the pandemic ended his season after four starts where he posted a miniscule 0.81 ERA. He was selected in the third round by Kansas City and was limited to 3.2 innings in 2021 after hamstring and shoulder injuries ended his season. Since returning, the 5'11" lefty has been used as a reliever. Chamberlain has an electric fastball that sits in the mid-90s and is hard for batters to square up due to his arm slot and above-average vertical movement. His curveball is a wipeout pitch that generates many swings and misses. The biggest obstacle in Chamberlain's way is lack of control but that is understandable due to the amount of time missed. The Royals' closer situation is locked in for the moment but Chamberlain has the stuff to be an excellent eighth-inning option for them in the near future.

It is hard to fathom a reliever having a hotter fall than **Evan Reifert (RHP, TAM)**. Across eight appearances, he struck out 25 of the 40 batters he faced while allowing just one hit. His standout pitch is his slider, which sits in the mid-80s with eye-popping spin rates. Reifert signed with the Brewers as an unsigned free agent in the pandemic-shortened 2020 draft and made his way to Tampa Bay in the Mike Brosseau trade. Control will be his biggest obstacle as he started the season in Double-A, but was sent back to High-A after posting seven walks in five games for Double-A Montgomery. His dominance in the Fall League should give Tampa Bay confidence whenever they call him up next year.

Emmet Sheehan (RHP, LA) was the Dodgers sixth-round pick out of Boston College in 2021. He started the season in High-A and was promoted to Double-A Tulsa to finish out the year. The biggest mark on Sheehan's resume is that he is inconsistent in throwing strikes which has led to some evaluators putting the reliever tag on him. Sheehan has a low-to mid-90s fastball with a low-80s slider and a plus change-up and showed flashes of brilliance—including a 10-strikeout game over Peoria—in the AFL.

2022 MLB First-Year Player Draft Recap
by Jeremy Deloney (AL) and Rob Gordon (NL)

AMERICAN LEAGUE

BALTIMORE ORIOLES

With five of the top 81 picks in the draft, the Orioles are ecstatic about their haul. With the first overall pick, they selected SS Jackson Holliday, a high-upside high schooler who they signed to a $8.19M bonus. He immediately becomes one of the top prospects in the system. Baltimore handed out five seven-figure bonuses, including a $1.325M bonus to SS Carter Young (17) from Vanderbilt and enjoyed the benefits of position players with their first four picks. They drafted OF Dylan Beavers (1s) and OF Jud Fabian (2s) from major colleges, and selected 3B Max Wagner (2) between them. While they didn't sign RHP Nolan McLean (3) from Oklahoma State, there are plenty of intriguing arms, including RHPs Trace Bright (5) and Preston Johnson (7).

Sleeper: LHP Jared Beck (13) has one of the more unique profiles of all draftees, standing 7'0". He doesn't throw particularly hard—88-92 mph—but he offers a deceptive, repeatable delivery.
Grade: A

BOSTON RED SOX

With three of the first 79 picks in the draft, the Red Sox took high school position players with each. SS Mikey Romero (1) and SS Cutter Coffey (2) give the system an injection of talented young infielders. They went well over slot to nab OF Roman Anthony (2s) with their third pick and he received the highest bonus of all Red Sox picks. They then went under slot from rounds 3 thru 8. As expected, college arms were in abundance in the top ten rounds, led by LHP Dalton Rogers (3), a short college reliever with a lower release point. All in all, the Red Sox draft left lots to be desired. There were no high-upside arms and most project as relievers. They also missed out on signing two promising young high school infielders in rounds 13 and 14.

Sleeper: C Brooks Brannon (9) is a big, physical high school backstop with plus raw power and an above-average arm but work to be done defensively.
Grade: D

CHICAGO WHITE SOX

Two trends stand out for Chicago's draft haul. For one, they much preferred college prospects, (19 of their 20 picks). The exception was first-rounder LHP Noah Schultz (1) from a high school in Illinois. He has a 6'9" frame with a deceptive delivery and can dominate with his fastball alone. The other trend was a strong slant towards pitching. Six of the first seven picks were pitchers. In rounds 2 and 3, the White Sox got big-time talent in college RHPs Peyton Pallette (2, Arkansas) and Jonathan Cannon (3, Georgia). Because of the big bonuses for Schultz, Pallette and Cannon, the White Sox went well under slot from rounds 8 thru 10. Their draft success will be almost entirely based on the top three picks.

Sleeper: INF/OF Brooks Baldwin (12) plays all over the diamond and saw time at five positions upon signing. He is a sound, disciplined hitter who uses his speed well and has good pull power.
Grade: B+

CLEVELAND GUARDIANS

The Guardians selected 21 players and signed them all, including four to seven-figure bonuses. Compared to other organizations, they preferred to spread their bonus pool and were able to sign a handful of high school players in later rounds, including RHP Jacob Zibin (10; $1.2M bonus) and LHP Jackson Humphries (8; $600k). OF Chase DeLauter (1) was the headliner and among the most toolsy prospects in the entire draft. There are some wrinkles to iron out, but the upside is impressive. The Guardians then decided on college arms, selecting RHP Justin Campbell (1s) and LHP Parker Messick (2) with their next two selections. OF Joe Lampe (3) is a legitimate CF with incredible speed and a patient approach that gets him on base consistently at a high clip.

Sleeper: RHP Dylan DeLucia (6) was outstanding in the College World Series for Mississippi and can start or relieve. He has a terrific fastball/slider combo that keeps hitters off-guard.
Grade: A-

DETROIT TIGERS

If you like college prospects, then the Tigers selections may be to your liking. Detroit selected all college players in their draft haul and signed them all except for their last pick in round 20. This was also a very top-heavy draft with 2B Jace Jung (1) and SS Peyton Graham (2) earning seven-figure bonuses. Both figure high in the Tigers future and both could advance rapidly through the minors. They added to their infield depth with four of their top five picks. RHP Troy Melton (4) from San Diego State was their only arm selected in the first 7 rounds. It was mostly pitchers after that, with 9 of their last 11 selections being collegiate hurlers. The Tigers mainly stayed on slot and spread out their bonus pool well after Jung and Graham. There are enough projects here that their draft could be a sneaky good one down the road.

Sleeper: SS Danny Serretti (6) wasn't as highly regarded as Jung or Graham, but is a steady switch-hitter with good tools across the board. He makes easy contact and can hit the ball hard. He reached Double-A in his first season.
Grade: B-

HOUSTON ASTROS

After selecting two college outfielders in the first two rounds, the Astros chose college arms with their next four. Pitching was the emphasis early with 7 pitchers selected with their top ten picks. From rounds 10 to 20, however, only 1 arm was drafted. Both OF Drew Gilbert (1) and OF Jacob Melton (2) received seven-figure bonuses and nobody else did, except OF Ryan Clifford (11) in later rounds. He was the first prep player chosen and has high-quality hitting skills. Gilbert and Melton give the Astros some intriguing prospects in the outfield. Both come from major Division 1 programs (Tennessee and Oregon State, respectively) and both provide ample tools with the bat and glove. The Astros are high on their pitching selections and believe RHP Andrew Taylor (2s) and RHP Nolan DeVos (5) could be significant sleepers.

Sleeper: 2B/SS Tim Borden (16) reached High-A upon signing and he does everything well. He showed vast improvement in his senior year at Louisville and even hit 6 HR in his pro debut covering 84 AB.
Grade: B+

KANSAS CITY ROYALS

This was mostly a conservative draft for the Royals as they focused on college players and spread out their bonus pool. The highlights, of course, were in the top two rounds with OF Gavin Cross (1) and 3B Cayden Wallace (2), two college hitters who could develop into everyday players in the future Royals lineup. After that, they opted for college pitchers with their next three picks. None of their top four pitchers selected made their pro debuts. They didn't choose a high school player until rounds 18 thru 20. They even signed two of those selections—OF Milo Rushford and SS Austin Charles (20). Overall, this was a solid draft, but lacked the reaches and high-upside prospects in the later rounds.

Sleeper: C Hayden Dunhurst (6) is a terrific defensive catcher with polished attributes and quality leadership traits. He gets on base consistently but will need to enhance his offensive arsenal.

Grade: B

LOS ANGELES ANGELS

The Angels weren't blessed with a wealthy bonus pool, but they maximized it with intriguing selections with their first three picks and a well-over-slot selection in round 11. SS Zach Neto (1) hit .320/.382/.492 with 4 HR and 4 SB in Double-A and the Angels believe he could reach the majors within a few years. He may come from a small school, but he has good upside. RHP Ben Joyce (3) is known for his premier fastball that regularly touches 100+ mph and he has an outstanding slider to boot. Whether he throws strikes is another story. RHP Jake Madden (4) is a power arm from the junior college ranks and he'll need time to develop, but the upside is huge. Prep RHP Caden Dana (11) was given the 2nd-highest bonus in the Angels draft, signing for $1.5M. The Angels did an excellent job of using their bonus pool creatively and believe they have a haul of both upside and polish.

Sleeper: RHP Victor Mederos (6) was one of three Angels selections from Oklahoma State and has the ingredients to become a mid-rotation starter. His performance hasn't matched his stuff yet, but professional coaching should help.

Grade: A-

MINNESOTA TWINS

Improving their infield prospects was a clear focal point and the Twins delivered in that regard, selecting shortstops with three of their top 5 picks, including #8 overall selection SS Brooks Lee (1) from Cal Poly. He immediately becomes one of the organization's best prospects due to his natural hitting ability. He could move quickly. The Twins chose from the college ranks for the first 13 rounds. Of their first 9 position players selected, all were either middle infielders or catchers. All three of their top picks received seven-figure bonuses, including LHP Connor Prielipp, who missed most of the college season due to Tommy John surgery, and SS Tanner Schobel, a fundamentally sound infielder from Virginia Tech. After going over slot for both Lee and Prielipp, the Twins went under slot for the rest of their top ten selections.

Sleeper: RHP Kyle Jones (7) was a senior sign out of Toledo and has arm action the Twins believe could add velocity. He has an excellent curveball that misses bats and could be a back-of-the-rotation guy.

Grade: B-

NEW YORK YANKEES

The Yankees picked towards the bottom of the first round and were pleased to select OF Spencer Jones (1), a tall, strong prospect from Vanderbilt. Overall, they chose nothing but players from the college or junior college ranks. Diving further, pitchers were chosen with 11 of their first 14 picks. The Yankees pretty much stayed on schedule with their selections, signing their top five picks for the exact slot value. RHP Chase Hampton (6) signed for more than slot and provides the organization with an arm that could be used as a starter or reliever. Other than Jones, the only other seven-figure bonus was given out to RHP Drew Thorpe (2), a relatively polished arm from Cal Poly. The depth of the system was enhanced with all 20 draft selections inked to deals.

Sleeper: RHP Matt Keating (9) owns a short, strong frame and could move quickly as a two-pitch reliever. He doesn't have premium velocity, but his curveball is a weapon and it misses bats.

Grade: C

OAKLAND ATHLETICS

The Athletics had a very interesting draft and wanted to find prospects with high ceilings. C Daniel Susac (1) had a strong pedigree from Arizona and he fits the bill of a near-ready big league backstop. OF Henry Bolte (2), however, is more of a long-term project out of the high school ranks, but he has as much upside as any high school bat. If he lives up to the billing, he could be a 25 HR/25 SB player in the majors. Then, Oakland selected two more position players with their next two picks, both from the college ranks. OFs Clark Elliott (2s) and Colby Thomas (3) could develop into solid players with more seasoning. 8 of the top 11 selections by the Athletics were position players. RHPs Jacob Watters (4) and Jack Perkins (5) were the lone arms. Unfortunately, they weren't able to come to terms with their selections from rounds 10 and 11.

Sleeper: 3B Brennan Milone (6) showed good hitting skills at Oregon and used those to hit .310 in Low-A upon signing. He offers above average power potential and should hit for BA as he cleans up his swing.

Grade: B-

SEATTLE MARINERS

Their first four picks all received at least $1 million signing bonuses with three coming from the high school ranks. SS Cole Young (1), RHP Walter Ford (2s) and RHP Ashton Izzi (4) all were inked from high school and give Seattle the type of upside they crave. Because of the large bonuses—which included 3B Tyler Locklear (2) from Virginia Commonwealth—the Mariners went under slot in rounds 5 thru 8. The headliner of all the picks may be Ford. He was young for the class and has extreme athleticism and power stuff. He will need time to develop and the Mariners will certainly give him that time. Izzi is all about projection and he should continue to add ticks to his fastball, though he needs work on his breaking balls. The addition of Locklear complements the draft haul well as he can inject significant power into the future lineup.

Sleeper: RHP Tyler Gough (9) is another intriguing prep arm who pitches above his age. He has several offerings and has excellent command and pitchability. The Mariners believe they can clean up his delivery.

Grade: A-

TAMPA BAY RAYS

Position players were in demand by the Rays. After prep 1B Xavier Isaac (1), they opted for three college players. OF Brock Jones (2) from Stanford fits the Rays model with premium athleticism and the potential to post a high OBP. The Rays also stockpiled college picks, though they are high on both Isaac and RHP Gary Gill Hill (6). In particular, Hill is very young with tons of projection and existing arm speed. College arms were selected in rounds 9 through 15. Tampa Bay is more than satisfied with mature, polished performers such as SS Chandler Simpson (2s) and OF Ryan Cermak (2s). Simpson brings a contact-oriented approach to the game and is extremely fast. Cermak hits the ball hard and projects well defensively as a true CF. This may not be a huge upside draft but is solid overall.

Sleeper: 1B Blake Robertson (7) is a big, lefty slugger from Oklahoma who can put a charge into the ball. He draws tons of walks and can shorten his stroke to make acceptable contact.
Grade: B

TEXAS RANGERS

The Rangers did not have a pick in rounds 2 or 3 so they loaded up on pitching with their first two selections. RHP Kumar Rocker (1) was the third overall pick and Texas believes they can work with him on his delivery and get him to the majors in short order. The best long-term pitcher in the draft could be RHP Brock Porter (4) who received an astounding $3.7M to keep him away from college. The next highest bonus was given to OF Tommy Specht (6) who only received $450k from the prep ranks. As this was a top-heavy draft that monopolized the bonus pool, Texas was not able to sign five of their selections despite signing Rocker for $2.5M under slot. Outside of the top two, very few of the selections will appear on any top prospect list for the foreseeable future.

Sleeper: RHP Luiz Ramirez (7) pitched well for Long Beach State and has solid command with average stuff. His stock dropped a bit due to a shoulder injury, but he will likely stick as a starter.
Grade: D

TORONTO BLUE JAYS

The Blue Jays enjoyed a diversified draft with five picks in the top 98 and a solid mix between high schoolers and college prospects. They are highest on two prep starters, LHP Brandon Barriera (1) and SS Tucker Toman (2s) who both immediately become two of their top prospects. Both were signed to seven-figure bonuses. They also chose two college middle infielders from major programs, selecting SS Josh Kasevich (2) from Oregon and 2B Cade Doughty (2s) from LSU. Because of going over slot to get the prep stars, the Blue Jays had to go under slot from rounds 3 thru 10. Thus, this is a top-heavy draft. OF Alan Roden (3) was a sound selection from Creighton and makes extreme contact but needs to add a bit more pop to his game. While a number of pitchers were drafted, none of them are considered among the Blue Jays better prospects.

Sleeper: LHP Mason Fluharty (5) from Liberty offers good size and is a career reliever. He throws consistent strikes and has a slider that could evolve into a plus offering at the major league level.
Grade: B-

NATIONAL LEAGUE

ARIZONA DIAMONDBACKS

The Diamondbacks had a hefty $15.1 million to spend on the draft and leveraged that into an impressive haul. With the 2nd overall pick, the Snakes drafted prep OF Druw Jones, the son of former major leaguer Andruw Jones. Jones is a legit 5-tool talent and has some of the best speed in the draft. With their second pick, the club rolled the dice on Mississippi State RHP Landon Sims (CB-A). Sims had Tommy John surgery in March, but when healthy has a plus FB/SL mix that will work either as a starter or in relief. With their next pick the club landed Texas 3B and Golden Spikes winner Ivan Melendez (2), who led D-1 with 32 HR. The Diamondbacks have used the draft and trades to build one of the deepest and most dynamic farm systems in baseball.

Sleeper: UNC Charlotte LHP Spencer Giesting (11) has lean, projectable frame and a high spin fastball, but struggles with control and command, posting a 4.46 ERA during his two years at UNC, but with a 12.5 K/9.
Grade: A

ATLANTA BRAVES

Despite having to wait until the 20th pick, the Braves ended up with four picks before the end of round 2, helping to restock a much-depleted farm system. With the 20th pick, the Braves landed RHP Owen Murphy, a dominant high schooler who overwhelmed hitters with a low-90s fastball and a solid 4-pitch mix. They also added high school RHPs J.R. Ritchie (CB-A) and Cole Phillips (2) before drafting Auburn RHP Blake Burkholder (2C) and Missouri State catcher Drake Baldwin (3). Murphy had the best pro debut, striking out 17 in just 12 IP. Overall, this was a solid if not spectacular haul, but the system remains one of the weakest in the NL.

Sleeper: Ignacio Alvarez (5) has an advanced understanding of the strike zone and rarely expands. He has a compact stroke and raw power, but his stroke is geared more towards line drives.
Grade: B

CHICAGO CUBS

The Cubs surprised many when they popped Cade Horton (RHP) with the 7th pick in the draft. Few denied the upside or the dominance Horton showed in the Big 12 conference tournament and College World Series run, but he had Tommy John surgery in early 2021 and needs to improve his command and develop a solid third pitch to reach his considerable upside. The Cubs went the high school route with their next three picks, with LHP Jackson Ferris (2), SS Christopher Paciolla (3), and RHP Nazier Mule (4). Mule has an electric 100 mph heater and has huge upside, but the success of this draft class hinges on the Cubs ability to help Horton hone his elite fastball/slider combination and add a viable third offering. If they can, Horton has the stuff to be a staff ace.

Sleeper: High school RHP Luis Rujano (13) is a big athletic kid who can get his fastball in the 94-96 range with good sink and backs it up with a potentially above-average slider. If he can develop a quality change-up, he has the size and velocity to make it to the majors.
Grade: C

CINCINNATI REDS

The Reds front office had to be thrilled that Cam Collier was still available when they picked at #18. Collier, the son of former major leaguer Lou Collier, fared well as a 17-year-old in his one year at Chipola College where he hit .333/.419/.537 with 8 HR. Right now he's more hit over power, but that should change as he matures. The club then picked up high school 3B Sal Stewart (1C), Mississippi State C Logan Tanner (2), and Oregon State OF Justin Boyd (CB-B) before adding their first arm with Florida State LHP Bryce Hubbart (3). Tanner has a double-plus arm behind the plate and has improved defensively; Stewart already has plus raw power, and Hubbart posted a solid career at FSU (3.71 ERA; 12 K/9). If Collier reaches his considerable upside, this will be a great draft for the Reds.

Sleeper: Monmouth LHP Rob Hensey (9) doesn't blow hitters away, but he pounds the strike zone with an above-average three-pitch mix. As a senior he had a K:BB figure of 102:13 in 81.1 IP.
Grade: A

COLORADO ROCKIES

The Rockies had the 5th-largest draft pool and selected a diverse pool of college players. The Rockies added two high-upside arms with Gonzaga RHP Gabriel Hughes (10th overall) and Miami LHP Carson Palmquist (3). Hughes features an easy mid-90s fastball and a potentially plus slider, and Palmquist has an excellent FB/SL mix that's tough on LHB. In between, the Rockies drafted Florida OF Sterlin Thompson (1C) and Tennessee OF Jordan Beck (CB-A). The Rockies went above-slot to sign their only prep player RHP Jackson Cox who has a good low-90s heater and advanced feel for a breaking ball. All-in-all this was a solid haul for what had been a fairly thin system.

Sleeper: Mississippi State OF Brad Cumbest (9) was one of the more consistent hitters in the SEC, slashing .302/.347/.584 with 15 HR. At 6'6", 235 he's one of the biggest position players in the draft and has huge raw power.
Grade: A-

LOS ANGELES DODGERS

The Dodgers had their 1st-round pick moved back 10 spots as a luxury tax penalty, but were still able to land Louisville catcher Dalton Rushing, one of the better college bats in the draft. All Rushing did was slash .404/.522/.740 in 104 AB between Rookie Ball and Low-A. The club also added Central Florida SS Alex Freeland (3), who also had a nice pro debut. Outside of Rushing, none of the Dodgers picks are solid bets to become MLB regulars. The Dodgers were limited by their MLB-low $4.2 million draft pool, which severely hampered their ability to add top-end talent.

Sleeper: TCU/Dallas Baptist RHP Jacob Meador (12) struggled with consistency and command throughout his collegiate career, but has a solid three-pitch mix highlighted by a 91-94 mph fastball and a potentially plus 12-to-6 curveball. The Dodgers have a tremendous track record with these kinds of players, making him a player worth watching.
Grade: C-

MIAMI MARLINS

The Marlins farm system has been depleted by graduations and injuries so the 2022 draft was a crucial opportunity to restock the system. They landed five Top 200 prospects, highlighted by LSU 3B Jacob Berry (6th overall). The switch-hitting Berry had the best combination of power and hit in the college class and posted a career line of .360/.450/.655 between Alabama and LSU, but he'll need to work hard to stick at 3B. The Marlins also landed two high school RHP in Jacob Miller (2) and Karson Milbrandt (3), before going college-heavy throughout the rest of the draft. Miller already sits in the low-90s, topping out at 95 and could add more as he matures. Milbrandt has a plus low-to-mid-90s fastball that has plus spin and life up in the zone. Berry has a high floor and should be on the fast track to the majors.

Sleeper: Louisville RHP Jared Poland (6), a former two-way player, focused exclusively on pitching in 2022 and went 5-5 with a 3.46 ERA and 32 BB/103 K in 83.1 IP. His fastball sits at 91-93 with north/south action from a high arm slot.
Grade: B+

MILWAUKEE BREWERS

The Brewers had to wait until the end of round one to make their first selection, Coastal Carolina SS Eric Brown Jr. and they signed him to an under-slot $2.05M. They used the savings to go over slot to land Canadian RHP Jacob Misiorowski (2) and Arkansas 2B Robert Moore (3). The club took just two pitchers in the first five rounds, landing Cal Poly RHP Will Rudy (5) in addition to Misiorowski and also signed four JuCo players. Overall this group lacks star power, though Moore (the son of former Royals' GM Dayton Moore) is a heady player who gets the most of his skills, but had a down year in 2022. If he can regain his form at the plate, this draft class will look a whole lot better than it does now.

Sleeper: High school 3B Luke Adams (12) has above-average raw power and the Brewers liked him enough to give him $282,500 as a late round pick. He has a lot of work to do, but he fared well in his pro debut, hitting .375/.512/.562 in 11 games.
Grade: D

NEW YORK METS

Not being able to sign RHP Kumar Rocker in 2021 might have been a blessing in disguise as they had picks #11 and #14 in 2022. The club used them to land Georgia Tech catcher Kevin Parada and high school SS Jett Williams. Despite being graded as the best backstop in the class, Parada fell and the Mets inked him to an over-slot $5.02 million deal. Parada slashed .361/.453/.709 with 26 HR as a draft-eligible sophomore and has consistently shown a knack for hitting and hitting for power. Williams has plus speed and should be able to stick at SS or CF, but at 5'8" power isn't likely to be a huge part of his game. The Mets also added Tennessee RHP Blake Tidwell and high school SS Nick Morabito in the second round. Tidwell started the year as the Volunteers Friday Night starter, but a shoulder injury limited him to just 39 IP.

Sleeper: RHP Paul Gervase (12) moved into the closer role at LSU in 2022 and was effective all year. At 6'10" 230 lbs his low-90s fastball gets on hitters faster than they anticipate though he doesn't have much else in his arsenal that plays up.
Grade: A

PHILADELPHIA PHILLIES

The Phillies went into the draft without a second-round pick, due to signing Nick Castellanos. With their first pick the Phillies landed high school OF Justin Crawford (#17 overall), son of former MLB All-Star Carl Crawford. Not surprisingly, Crawford has plus speed and was one of the better athletes in the draft class. The Phillies went college heavy the rest of the way, with 17 of their 20 picks coming from the collegiate ranks. That group was highlighted by Florida Atlantic OF Gabriel Rincones Jr (3), Miami RHP Alex McFarlane (4), and South Florida RHP Orion Kerkering (5). Rincones hit .346/.451/.658 and has a quick LH stroke and a knack for finding the barrel and McFarlane has a fastball that's been clocked up to 99 mph.

Sleeper: High school OF Emaarion Boyd (11) is a plus-plus runner with some feel for hitting. His contact-oriented approach isn't likely to lead to much power, but he could turn into a solid 4th OF.

Grade: B

PITTSBURGH PIRATES

The Pirates came into the 2022 draft with one of the better farm systems in baseball, but outside of first-rounder Termarr Johnson (#4 overall), this group is light on high-upside players. Despite being just 5'7", Johnson might have been the best pure hitter in the draft. The Pirates went with college pitchers with their next three picks, including Campbell RHP Thomas Harrington (CB-A), Florida LHP Hunter Barco (2), and Notre Dame 3B/RHP Jack Brannigan (3). Barco made just 9 starts before succumbing to Tommy John surgery, but has one of the better sliders in the draft. Two-way player Brannigan has a double-plus arm and can touch 100 mph on the mound with a potentially plus slider but terrible control. He also has plus speed and is a good defender at 3B. He played exclusively in the field in his pro debut, but hit just .211 and is likely to get a look on the mound next spring.

Sleeper: Oklahoma OF Tanner Tredaway (10) slashed .370/.414/.549 as a senior. He is a plus runner with good bat-to-ball skills, but is not going to hit for much power.

Grade: A-

SAN DIEGO PADRES

The Padres had a healthy $10 million to spend on the 2022 draft and invested those resources wisely, acquiring four Top 100 pre-draft prospects. With their top two picks, the Padres went with prep hurlers RHP Dylan Lesko (#15 overall) and LHP Robby Snelling (CB-A). Lesko already features a 92-95 mph heater and maybe the best change-up in the draft class, while Snelling has a low-90s fastball and a plus curve. Both have mid-rotation upside. The club continued to add pitching depth, selecting Iowa RHP Adam Mazur (2) and Duke RHP Henry Williams (3) before finally taking a position player with high school backstop Lamar King Jr. (4). While the Padres didn't land any elite prospects, Lesko and Snelling both have the potential to have long professional careers and provide the club with much-needed rotational depth.

Sleeper: Jakob Marsee (6) was one of the leaders of the Central Michigan squad that made an impressive postseason run. As a college junior, Marsee had more walks than strikeouts and had a solid pro debut, hitting .240/.422/.410 with 30 BB/20K in 67 AB.

Grade: A-

SAN FRANCISCO GIANTS

The Giants picked last in Round One and selected lightly-regarded LHP/1B Reggie Crawford, who missed the 2022 season recovering from Tommy John surgery. They used the savings to land East Carolina LHP Carson Whisenhut (2) who slid in the draft after being suspended for a failed drug test. Whisenhut was considered one of the top collegiate arms at the beginning of the season and did not look rusty in a limited pro debut: 0.00 ERA with 1 BB/14 K in 7.2 IP. The club went pitching heavy throughout; their first six picks were starting pitchers. Whisenhut could be a huge win for the Giants, but the rest of the draft class lacks star power.

Sleeper: Oregon State OF Wade Meckler (8) is just 5'10", 180 lbs but has plus speed and a mature approach at the plate. Meckler raked in his pro debut, hitting .367/.500/.544 in 79 AB between rookie ball and Low-A.

Grade: B

ST. LOUIS CARDINALS

The Cardinals went college-heavy and focused on pitching, taking college starters with 7 of their first 10 picks. With the 22nd overall pick the Redbirds landed Oregon State ace LHP Cooper Hjerpe, who fits the Cardinals model to a T. He doesn't blow hitters away but attacks the zone with a solid three-pitch mix from a deceptive, low 3/4s arm slot. They also added San Diego LHP Brycen Mautz (2) and Texas LHP Pete Hansen (3), before adding their first position player in Oklahoma backstop Jimmy Crooks III (4). Hansen and Mautz have yet to make their pro debuts, but Crooks hit well, slashing .296/.396/.468 at Low-A Palm Beach. The club then went over-slot to land UCLA RHP Max Rajcic (6) and all five players landed in the Cardinals Top 30 prospects heading into 2023.

Sleeper: California RHP Joseph King (9) doesn't blow hitters away but has a good idea of how to pitch and his overhand arm slot, low-90s fastball, and above-average change-up keep hitters off-balance.

Grade: B+

WASHINGTON NATIONALS

The Nationals added both a potential All-Star caliber player with high school OF Elijah Green (#5 overall) and some much-needed depth with college players including Oklahoma RHP Jake Bennett (2), Tennessee OF Trey Lipscomb (3), Baylor OF Jared McKenzie (5), and TCU RHP Riley Cornelio (7). Green was in the conversation to go 1/1 in the draft and the Nats were thrilled he slid to them at #5. While there are some concerns about swing-and-miss tendencies, Green is an elite athlete and has the potential to be a 30/30 hitter if he can find a way to make enough contact. McKenzie also had an impressive debut, hitting .400 in 79 AB at Low-A. There are concerns that Lipscomb's monster season at Tennessee owed as much to a hitter-friendly home park as his innate talent, but he did slash .355/.428/.717 for the Volunteers and had a solid pro debut. Beyond Green, the Nats added several players who have a chance to have lengthy big league careers.

Sleeper: Georgia Tech RHP Marquis Grissom Jr. (13), while raw on the mound, he possesses a low-to-mid-90s fastball that tops out at 96 mph. Grissom struggled with command but is very athletic and had a solid, if limited, pro debut.

Grade: A-

High School Players to Watch in 2023

by Chris Blessing

Here is our annual list of draft-eligible high school seniors who project as top MLB fantasy prospects heading into their prep season, beginning in mid-February in some states and extending into June in northern states. With the 2023 draft once again scheduled for All-Star weekend in July, there is sure to be changes in rankings between now and then. Last year's 12th-ranked prep draft prospect pre-season, Jackson Holliday (SS, BAL), ended up being the 1st overall pick after a dynamic spring. This ranking is merely a guideline for those managers who can roster anyone within the universe or those dynasty managers looking for a preview of their first-year player drafts in the summer and/or next offseason.

High school draft prospects have the most leverage among all prospects, meaning some of the best prep prospects on this list may decide to go to school if they believe they can improve their bonus earning potential by sticking with their college commitment. It's been a nice gamble for some prospects, including Jack Leiter (RHP, TEX), a potential 1st-rounder in the 2019 draft, and Matt McClain (SS, CIN), a 1st-rounder in the 2018 draft who decided not to sign with the Diamondbacks. However, sometimes it's not the right choice, like what took place with Mike Vasil (RHP, NYM), who was a potential 1st-round pick in 2018 and chose to go to the University of Virginia. He was drafted in the 8th round of the 2021 draft, costing himself millions of dollars.

Eight prep position players and four prep pitchers were drafted in the first round of last year's draft. Additionally, three prep pitchers and one prep position player earned first-round money signing outside the first round. This year's prep class isn't as deep or top-heavy as the past two seasons. Right now, only OF Walker Jenkins and OF Max Clark project as Top 10 picks. Last year, four of the top five overall picks were prep position players. Even though this year's class is lighter, it doesn't mean scouts won't be crisscrossing the United States, Canada, and Puerto Rico in search of premium high school talent.

1. Walker Jenkins, OF – *South Brunswick HS (NC), L/R 6-3, 210*
Jenkins, committed to the University of North Carolina, boasts potentially plus hit and power tools. Against advanced competition during the summer showcase circuit, the left-handed slugger showed a feel for hard contact to all fields and potential to hit 30+ HR at projection. Projects best as power-hitting RF long-term with enough athleticism to keep profile alive in CF.

2. Maxwell Clark, OF – *Franklin Community HS (IN), L/L 6-1, 190*
Clark is a super athletic left-handed hitting OF prospect who has the best combination of hit and speed in this prep class. Committed to Vanderbilt, Clark utilizes a patient approach with a willingness to hit liners to all fields. He possesses plus-plus speed and will likely stick in CF long-term. He will need to get more aggressive on pitches middle-in to play up his power potential.

3. Kevin McGonigle, SS – *Monsignor Bonnor HS (PA), L/R 5-11, 185*
Committed to Auburn University, McGonigle possesses one of the best hit tools in this prep class. At the Area Code Games in San Diego in 2022, he hit an impressive HR out to CF, creating buzz for his power potential. A SS, McGonigle has terrific hands, instincts and footwork, ala Dansby Swanson, despite possessing below-average speed.

4. Thomas White, LHP – *Phillips Academy (MA), L/L 6-5, 210*
White is the best pitching prospect in this year's prep draft class. Committed to Vanderbilt, White creates smooth, easy velocity, sitting in the low-to-mid 90s with his 4-seam fastball with explosive movement, especially commanded up in the zone. He has a feel for spin, throwing mostly a curveball, and has a feel for a late-tumbling change-up.

5. Arjun Nimmala, SS – *Strawberry Crest HS (FL), R/R 6-1, 170*
Nimmala is a quick-twitch athletic SS who impressed scouts throughout various circuits during the early summer. A Florida State commit, Nimmala has one of the quickest swings in the draft class. He displays raw plus power during batting practice, which hasn't translated into games yet, mostly due to a flatter swing trajectory. There's room to add more power to the frame too.

6. Aidan Miller, SS - *JW Mitchell HS (FL), R/R 6-2, 205*
Committed to the University of Arkansas, Miller abused international competition playing for Team USA last summer. It's a power-over-hit profile, and not the cleanest setup. However, Miller produces plus bat speed with raw power already showing up in games. There's plus power in frame and swing. A SS now, he's better equipped to handle 3B as a pro with a double-plus arm.

7. Noble Meyer, RHP – *Jesuit HS (OR), R/R 6-5, 200*
Meyer is a projectable RHP with a wiry frame, a deceptive low 3/4s-to-sidearm slot and an ever-improving fastball. Committed to the University of Oregon, Meyer utilizes his size well within his delivery, playing up his fastball, which sat mid-90s during the showcase circuit. His slider also projects as a plus pitch, operating as Meyer's out pitch. He has solid command of his arsenal.

8. Blake Mitchell, C – *Sinton HS (TX), L/R 6-1, 200*
Mitchell, committed to Louisiana State University, is the best catching prospect in this prep class. He's a two-way player with potential as a pro prospect on the mound. At the plate, it's a power-over-hit profile, with raw plus pop that plays to all fields. During the showcase circuit, Mitchell struggled getting barrel to velocity. However, he took advantage of launching mistake pitches.

9. Dillon Head, OF – *Homewood Flossmoor HS (IL), L/L 6-0, 180*
Head is one of the best athletes of this year's prep class. Committed to Clemson, Head employs a slasher approach and does well with peppering the middle of the field with line drive and ground ball contact. It's hit tool over power tool, mostly taking advantage of Head's exceptional run tool. Contacts believe power will eventually come to the profile with pro coaching help.

10. Roch Cholowsky, SS – *Hamilton HS (AZ), R/R 6-2, 185*
Cholowsky, committed to the UCLA, has a tremendous feel for getting on base. A linear swing plane provides a contact approach presently. Cholowsky utilizes the middle of the diamond well. He relies heavily on plus hand/eye coordination, which helps temper an aggressive approach. There's above-average power in frame, doesn't show up in game. Cholowsky sticks at SS.

11. Charlee Soto, RHP – *Reborn Christian Academy (FL), S/R 6-5, 197*
Soto is one of the biggest risers in this year's draft. Committed to the University of Central Florida, Soto will be 17 years old on draft day. He operates from a high 3/4s slot with repeatable mechanics and an improving 4-seam fastball. During the summer circuit, his fastball has sat in the mid-90s. Soto has an advanced feel for selling a fading change-up with occasional tumble.

12. Bryce Eldridge, RHP – *James Madison HS (VA), L/R 6-7, 222*
Committed to the University of Alabama, Eldridge has some of the best projectable size in this year's prep class. It's a long, lanky body frame with room to grow. Eldridge sits in the low-to-mid 90s with his 4-seam fastball with a chance for more velocity as he gets stronger. He has a feel for spin with his curveball currently outperforming his slider. He also throws a change-up.

More to Watch

Antonio Anderson, SS, North Atlanta HS (GA) – Switch-hitting, likely 3B prospect has solid hit/power foundation. Committed to Georgia Tech.

Braden Holcomb, SS, Foundation Academy (FL) – Power-over-hit prospect with strong, athletic frame. Committed to Vanderbilt.

Cameron Johnson, LHP, IMG Academy (FL) – Size plus deceptive slot plays up explosive fastball. Committed to Louisiana State University.

Colin Houck, SS, Parkview HS (GA) – Two-sport star is now committed full-time to baseball after turning down Power 5 offers to play QB. Committed to Mississippi State University.

Eric Bitonti, SS, Aquinas HS (CA) – Potential double-plus power bat fits best as long-term 3B. Committed to the University of Oregon.

Liam Peterson, RHP, Calvary Christian Academy (FL) – Added velocity to 4-seam FB over summer at the cost of his control. Committed to the University of Florida.

Roman Martin, SS, Servite HS (CA) – Athletic, hit-tool-over-power prospect has projectable body and could get to above-average power. Committed to UCLA.

Travis Sykora, RHP, Round Rock HS (TX) – Athletic mature hurler with terrific feel for spin is older for the class. Committed to the University of Texas.

College Players to Watch in 2023

by Chris Lee

After a 2022 MLB Draft that was weaker on high-end college players (and particularly pitchers) than in most years, 2023 promises better things. The Southeastern Conference—year in and year out, college baseball's best league—dominates our list of fantasy prospects this season with its top four (and seven of its Top 10) players. With most SEC games available through ESPN's streaming network, Friday, Saturday and Sunday nights could mean appointment TV for owners looking to get a step ahead in dynasty leagues.

Here's a head start on who to watch for the 2023 season and its upcoming draft.

1. Dylan Crews, OF—*LSU, R/R, 6-0, 203*
Crews has a combination of high upside, solid skills and a lengthy, stable track record. He has hit .356/.458/.691 with 40 home runs for his career, won co-national Freshman of the Year honors and followed that with a co-Southeastern Conference Player of the Year campaign. He draws high marks with both his hit tool and his power; the one small knock on him as a hitter is contact ability, but an 17% career K% is better than most college power bats. He's not a bad runner—he's played some center at LSU and swiped 17 bags—and profiles as a guy who can hit in the middle of an MLB order for a long time.

2. Enrique Bradfield Jr., OF—*Vanderbilt, L/L, 6-1, 160*
The Commodore center fielder has started and produced since the day he stepped on campus. His 80-grade speed has made him such a base-stealing nightmare (he wasn't caught in 46 attempts last season) that teams, lacking any conventional means to stop him, took to throwing repeatedly to first (he drew 17 pickoff throws in two trips to first in one SEC tournament game). Bradfield upped his home run output from one to eight with a flat swing that generates loft while his K% remained the same from his 14% freshman season. He'll have value in both average and on-base leagues, and phenomenal defense in center (think Lorenzo Cain) adds to his real-baseball value.

3. Wyatt Langford, OF—*Florida, R/R, 6-1, 225*
No collegiate hitter had his stock rise faster last season than Langford, who had four at-bats as a freshman and then had a .355/.447/.719, 26-HR sophomore year, with solid BB% (12%) and K% (15%) totals. Langford followed that with a nice summer (.333/.407/.381) for Team USA. Langford is regarded as a five-tool talent, with power considered the best of those tools, and even a little speed (7 SB, 3 triples). Langford also has an outstanding work ethic; he transitioned to left field last season and will man center in 2023, replacing the departed Jud Fabian.

4. Chase Dollander, RHP—*Tennessee, R/R, 6-3, 192*
The reigning SEC pitcher of the year has just about everything you want, from pitch mix (high-90s fastball, high-80s slider, curve, change-up) to command (8.3 Cmd) to dominance (35%

K%). One of Dollander's best attributes is an ability to place pitches exactly on the black. The biggest question is the lack of a lengthy track record. Dollander threw 79 innings last year thanks to a bone bruise courtesy of a line drive, and just 49 innings as a freshman at Georgia Southern, and he was just ordinary (8 ER over 16 1/3 innings, though 18 Ks) over his last three starts of 2022. Still, Dollander is an elite arm and if he remains healthy and duplicates last year's production over a full season, there won't be much to pick apart.

5. Brayden Taylor, 3B—TCU, L/R, 6-1, 175

Taylor has been remarkably consistent, hitting .319/.450/.574 for his TCU career while stealing successfully on 25 of 26 attempts. Taylor's walks eclipsed his strikeouts for the second straight year (20% vs. 15% in 2022) and he's got a reputation for hitting to all fields and not chasing out of the zone. He played DH on Team USA last year, but saw time at second, third and short for the Horned Frogs and figures to start his pro career at third.

6. Jacob Gonzalez, SS—*Ole Miss, L/R, 6-2, 200*

Gonzalez has been unafraid of the spotlight , splitting Freshman of the Year honors with Crews in 2021 and then leading the Rebels to a national title. In two seasons, he's hit .315/.424/.560 with 18 HR and his best attribute has been an elite Eye (1.30) and ability to control the strike zone (11 K%). He won't run but projects as a decent left-side-of-the-infield power source who might be able to help in average and on-base percentage.

7. Matt Shaw, SS—*Maryland, R/R, 5-11, 185*

Shaw hit .291/.381/.604 at Maryland, then, strengthened his draft stock by winning Cape Cod League MVP. Shaw gets high marks for hitting (and showing power) to all fields and for respectable K (16%) and walk (12%) rates. Versatility may be his calling card— Shaw has played several positions and could perhaps do the same professionally, and figures to help a bit in most statistical categories, too.

8. Paul Skenes, RHP/C/1B—*LSU, R/R, 6-6, 235*

College baseball's best two-way player will get a change of scenery. Skenes, who spent his first two years at Air Force, was the only Division I player to reach double digits in both home runs (11) and saves (10) as a freshman. In 2022 he moved to the rotation and this time hit double figures in wins (10) and homers (13). Skenes is expected to play both ways at LSU, and will likely be drafted as a pitching prospect thanks to a fastball that tops out near 100, a mid-80s slider and a change-up. Skenes is good enough that he could be drafted in the top five rounds as a hitter alone, but a 22% K rate at a much lower level of pitching than he'll see this year dampens his stock there.

9. Hurston Waldrep, RHP—*Florida, R/R, 6-2, 205*

Waldrep will see if the dominance he exhibited in Conference USA (37% K%) translates to the SEC, where he'll join one of the country's best programs at developing pitching prospects. Blessed with a mid-to-high-90s fastball, a hard slider that grades as a plus pitch and a change-up, Waldrep has some work to do on control

(he had a respectable 9% BB%, but hit six men and threw 13 wild pitches). This will be his second season as a collegiate starter after throwing 16 1/3 relief innings as a freshman.

10. Jacob Wilson, SS—*Grand Canyon, R/R, 6-3, 175*

The son of former MLB shortstop Jack Wilson, Jacob Wilson is a throwback. He complied an incredible 2.6% K rate as a sophomore in 246 at-bats, smacking five more home runs (12) than he had strikeouts. That came against Western Athletic Conference competition, but Grand Canyon played against one of the country's best non-conference schedules. Wilson followed that up with a .364/.462/.455 line over 11 at-bats (one K) with Team USA. He's a hit-over-power guy and he probably won't contribute much in steals (he's got just one in his collegiate career) but there's value in a high-average middle infielder who could score a lot of runs.

More to watch:

Maui Ahuna, SS—*Tennessee*

Jake Gelof, 3B—*Virginia*

Travis Honeyman, OF—*Boston College*

Rhett Lowder, RHP—*Wake Forest*

Yohandy Morales, 3B—*Miami*

Will Sanders, RHP—*South Carolina*

Brandon Sproat, RHP—*Florida*

Kyle Teel, C—*Virginia*

Juaron Watts-Brown, RHP—*Oklahoma State*

1	Corbin Carroll	OF	ARI		51	Brandon Pfaadt	RHP	ARI
2	Gunnar Henderson	SS	BAL		52	Sal Frelick	OF	MIL
3	Jordan Lawlar	SS	ARI		53	Oswald Peraza	SS	NYY
4	Jackson Chourio	OF	MIL		54	Endy Rodriguez	C	PIT
5	Jordan Walker	OF	STL		55	Edwn Arroyo	SS	CIN
6	Anthony Volpe	SS	NYY		56	Max Meyer	RHP	MIA
7	Grayson Rodriguez	RHP	BAL		57	Henry Davis	C	PIT
8	Elly De La Cruz	SS	CIN		58	Harry Ford	C	SEA
9	Eury Perez	RHP	MIA		59	Brennen Davis	OF	CHC
10	Andrew Painter	RHP	PHI		60	Cam Collier	3B	CIN
11	James Wood	OF	WAS		61	Emmanuel Rodriguez	OF	MIN
12	Ezequiel Tovar	SS	COL		62	Mick Abel	RHP	PHI
13	Francisco Alvarez	C	NYM		63	Logan O'Hoppe	C	LAA
14	Jackson Holliday	SS	BAL		64	Brayan Rocchio	SS	CLE
15	Druw Jones	OF	ARI		65	Tink Hence	RHP	STL
16	Marcelo Mayer	SS	BOS		66	Cade Cavalli	RHP	WAS
17	Ricky Tiedemann	LHP	TOR		67	Connor Norby	2B	BAL
18	Miguel Vargas	3B	LA		68	Zach Neto	SS	LAA
19	Josh Jung	3B	TEX		69	George Valera	OF	CLE
20	Daniel Espino	RHP	CLE		70	Coby Mayo	3B	BAL
21	Triston Casas	1B	BOS		71	DL Hall	LHP	BAL
22	Kyle Harrison	LHP	SF		72	Jackson Jobe	RHP	DET
23	Royce Lewis	SS	MIN		73	Brady House	SS	WAS
24	Evan Carter	OF	TEX		74	Will Brennan	OF	CLE
25	Robert Hassell III	OF	WAS		75	Esteury Ruiz	OF	OAK
26	Noelvi Marte	SS	CIN		76	Jace Jung	2B	DET
27	Gavin Williams	RHP	CLE		77	Matt Mervis	1B	CHC
28	Colton Cowser	OF	BAL		78	Tanner Bibee	RHP	CLE
29	Marco Luciano	SS	SF		79	Gavin Cross	OF	KC
30	Jasson Dominguez	OF	NYY		80	Kevin Alcantara	OF	CHC
31	Brett Baty	3B	NYM		81	Garrett Mitchell	OF	MIL
32	Curtis Mead	3B	TAM		82	Jordan Westburg	SS	BAL
33	Termarr Johnson	2B	PIT		83	Yainer Diaz	C	HOU
34	Kyle Manzardo	1B	TAM		84	Quinn Priester	RHP	PIT
35	Pete Crow-Armstrong	OF	CHC		85	Andy Pages	OF	LA
36	Tyler Soderstrom	C	OAK		86	Spencer Jones	OF	NYY
37	Bobby Miller	RHP	LA		87	Michael Busch	2B	LA
38	Hunter Brown	RHP	HOU		88	Oscar Colas	OF	CHW
39	Diego Cartaya	C	LA		89	Chase DeLauter	OF	CLE
40	Taj Bradley	RHP	TAM		90	Jack Leiter	RHP	TEX
41	Elijah Green	OF	WAS		91	Emerson Hancock	RHP	SEA
42	Colson Montgomery	SS	CHW		92	Dustin Harris	OF	TEX
43	Masyn Winn	SS	STL		93	Colt Keith	3B	DET
44	Bo Naylor	C	CLE		94	Junior Caminero	3B	TAM
45	Brooks Lee	SS	MIN		95	Jacob Berry	3B	MIA
46	Jackson Merrill	SS	SD		96	Ceddanne Rafaela	OF	BOS
47	Zac Veen	OF	COL		97	Ryan Pepiot	RHP	LA
48	Adael Amador	SS	COL		98	Owen White	RHP	TEX
49	Kevin Parada	C	NYM		99	Jose Acuña	SS	TEX
50	Gavin Stone	RHP	LA		100	Wilmer Flores	RHP	DET

Sleepers Outside the HQ100

by Jeremy Deloney

Most who follow minor league baseball already know the vast majority of top prospects. A cursory review of the HQ100 will likely result in debate over who should be ranked higher or lower. Such is life when putting together a cumulative list of votes from several minor league experts.

One of the more enjoyable aspects of assessing minor league prospects is identifying those players who have a credible shot at jumping into the HQ100 at some point—whether by midseason or the following season. These are players who should be on your radar for the future. It could be argued that some of these "sleepers" should currently be in the HQ100 as evidenced by their placements on individual Top 100 lists. Others may have the requisite skills to warrant a move in the near future. We highlight several of these players below.

AMERICAN LEAGUE

Drafted in the 5th round in the 2021 draft out of junior college, 21-year-old **Mason Auer (OF, TAM)** has already exceeded expectations with his athleticism and natural talent. He split the 2022 campaign between Low-A and High-A and batted .290/.372/.487 with 21 doubles, 15 HR and 48 SB. The right-handed hitter was consistent and steady all season long and excelled with his double-plus speed and elite arm strength. With bat speed and a clean swing, he should grow into at least average power. His ultimate success may be dependent on whether he can continue to improve his hit tool. He uses all fields in his approach and makes consistent, hard contact. If Auer realizes his full potential, he could produce 30 HR and 30 SB at the big league level.

The Guardians are blessed with incredible depth at the middle infield spots and 20-year-old **Angel Martinez (INF, CLE)** is certainly included in that impressive mix. The switch-hitter played most of the 2022 season in High-A before getting a promotion to Double-A in late August. Despite being young for each level, he batted .278/.378/.471 with 23 doubles, 13 HR and 12 SB. He improved across the board from 2021 and started to show more pop, particularly from the left side, while maintaining his high baseball intellect and ability to put bat to ball. Martinez also excels with the glove and has seen action at all of 2B, SS and 3B. He has the quickness and arm to be proficient at any of those spots. The Guardians feel very confident in his abilities and they placed him on the 40-man roster in the offseason.

After being named the Pac-12 Player of the Year, **Jacob Melton (OF, HOU)** was selected in the 2nd round of the 2022 draft by the Astros. The 22-year-old quickly acclimated himself to pro ball and hit .324/.424/.577 with 4 HR in 71 AB in Low-A. He is a premium athlete with plentiful tools and even has some projection remaining. There have been questions about the development of his hit tool as he combines an aggressive approach with a swing that features moving parts. The rest of his tools are quite striking. The left-handed hitter is a true CF with enough of an arm that could profile best in RF. He exhibits plus raw power to all fields. The Astros believe he can improve his swing mechanics with

professional repetition while maintaining his power. Additionally, he could either hit at the top or middle of the lineup.

Lazaro Montes (OF, SEA) has yet to make his stateside debut, but the Mariners are rightfully intrigued with his athleticism and power projection. The left-handed hitter will play the entire 2023 season at age 18 and will likely be headed to Low-A to begin the year. He feasted on pitching in the Dominican Summer League, batting .284/.422/.585 with 10 HR and 3 SB in 176 AB. He was signed to a whopping $2.5M bonus out of Cuba in January 2022 and already has a mature frame (6'3", 210 lbs) that should continue to get stronger with more professional development. Because of his youth, there is a lot of polish needed to his overall game. Regardless, the upside is extremely high. Montes projects as a slugging RF who hits 30+ HR and gets on base at a high clip.

The Royals were looking for quality hitters in the 2022 draft and they found one with **Cayden Wallace (3B, KC)**, who they selected in the 2nd round out of the University of Arkansas. He hit .294/.369/.468 with 2 HR and 8 SB in his pro debut (109 AB in Low-A). They foresee a power-hitting corner infielder who could advance quickly through the minors. The 21-year-old has well-above-average bat speed and natural strength which, combined with a compact stroke, give him outstanding power potential from the right side. He has a mature approach at the plate and isn't shy about working counts to get on base. While he can be pull-happy and can improve with pitch recognition, he has both a high ceiling and floor. Defensively, he has as strong an arm as any infielder in the system.

NATIONAL LEAGUE

The Giants have a number of quality position player prospects and **Aeverson Arteaga (SS, SF)** may be the most underrated of the lot. The 19-year-old was terrific in Low-A in 2022 when he hit .270/.345/.431 with an organizational-high 35 doubles, 14 HR and 11 SB in 508 AB. There may be a lot of swing-and-miss in his offensive package right now (his 155 Ks were third-highest in the organization), but he should continue to get better with refinement to his approach and swing. The right-handed hitter has excellent bat speed and makes plenty of loud contact with high exit velocity. Arteaga should grow into 20+ HR power. He is an outstanding defender with quick, soft hands and well-above-average range. He is a prospect that should stay at SS long-term, though the Giants may opt to play him at other positions for versatility.

Oftentimes, a lefty college draftee is stereotyped as a soft-tossing pitchability prospect with limited upside. The Cardinals selected **Cooper Hjerpe (LHP, STL)** in the first round (22nd overall pick) in 2022 and believe he will evolve into something more than that. He has yet to throw a professional pitch, but will likely begin his career at Low-A in 2023. The 21-year-old relies on many attributes from that stereotype: deception, sequencing and a deep repertoire. The difference is that Hjerpe could add a few more ticks to his 90-93 mph fastball. It plays up due to his extension and his low 3/4 slot. With two breaking balls and a change-up that features heavy, late action, he could become a mid-rotation starter. This is a pitcher who also could advance quickly upon dominating the lower minors.

Cade Horton (RHP, CHC) underwent Tommy John surgery in February 2021 and didn't return to the mound at the University of Oklahoma until late March 2022. He struggled initially, but was downright dominant during the College World Series. As a result, the Cubs drafted him with the 7th overall pick, much higher than forecasted prior to the 2022 season. The 21-year-old has a plus, lively fastball that sits in the mid-90s and reaches 98 mph with arm-side run. He complements the heater with a nasty slider and slow curveball. He has the velocity and movement to pitch up in the zone and also has cutting action on his slider. Some may point to his lack of track record, but the Cubs are focused on his present pitch mix and upside potential.

With the 20th overall pick the 2022 draft, the Braves chose **Owen Murphy (RHP, ATL)** from an Illinois high school. Atlanta has experienced much success in the past with prep hurlers and believe the 19-year-old could be an ideal candidate to front a potential future rotation. He doesn't have great size, but he features advanced skills for his age and has an athletic delivery that could lead to more velocity down the road. He has a plus fastball already in the low-90s and it plays up due to its ride and carry up in the strike zone. Murphy also exhibits a plus slider with cutting action and a slower curveball to give hitters different looks and shapes. Because he throws with good command and control, it wouldn't be a surprise to see him have easy success in the lower minors in 2023.

In one of the biggest trades in years, the Nationals sent OF Juan Soto to the Padres and received an impressive lot of prospects, including **Jarlin Susana (RHP, WAS),** who may be the least known of the bunch. The tall and strong righty was signed in January 2022 for a $1.7M bonus by San Diego from the Dominican Republic. He stands 6'6" 235 lbs and has premium velocity in the upper 90s. He can pop 103 mph on the gun at times. Because of his youth (he'll play 2023 at just 19 years old) and inexperience, there is plenty of development time ahead. Susana needs to improve his command, but the overall repertoire is more than sufficient to project future stardom. He will be in Low-A for 2023 and will work on his developing change-up to match his elite fastball and slider.

POSITIONS: Up to four positions are listed for each batter and represent those for which he appeared in at least 15 games in 2021. Positions are shown with their numeric designation (2=CA, 3=1B, 7=LF, 0=DH, etc.)

BATS: Shows which side of the plate he bats from—right (R), left (L) or switch-hitter (S).

AGE: Player's age, as of April 1, 2023.

DRAFTED: The year, round, and school that the player performed at as an amateur if drafted, or where the player was signed from, if a free agent.

EXP MLB DEBUT: The year a player is expected to debut in the major leagues.

H/W: The player's height and weight.

FUT: The role that the batter is expected to have for the majority of his major league career, not necessarily his greatest upside.

SKILLS: Each skill a player possesses is graded and designated with a "+", indicating the quality of the skills, taking into context the batter's age and level played. An average skill will receive three "+" marks.

- **PWR:** Measures the player's ability to drive the ball and hit for power.
- **BAVG:** Measures the player's ability to hit for batting average and judge the strike zone.
- **SPD:** Measures the player's raw speed and base-running ability. When we've measured run times (point of bat-to-ball contact to foot hitting first base), we've included these next to the SPD box.
- **DEF:** Measures the player's overall defense, which includes arm strength, arm accuracy, range, agility, hands, and defensive instincts.

PLAYER STAT LINES: Player statistics for the last five teams that he played for (if applicable), including college and the major leagues.

TEAM DESIGNATIONS: Each team that the player performed for during a given year is included.

LEVEL DESIGNATIONS: The level for each team a player performed is included. "AAA" means Triple-A, "AA" means Double-A, "A+" means high Class-A, "A" means full-season low Class-A, and "Rk" means rookie level. Prior to 2020, an "A-" referred to short-season Class-A, a level between rookie level and full-season low-A. Starting in 2021, that level no longer exists.

SABERMETRIC CATEGORIES: Descriptions of all the sabermetric categories appear in the glossary.

CAPSULE COMMENTARIES: For each player, a brief analysis of their skills/statistics, and their future potential is provided.

ELIGIBILITY: Eligibility for inclusion is the standard for which Major League Baseball adheres to; less than 130 major league at-bats and less than 45 days on the 26-man MLB roster.

POTENTIAL RATINGS: The Potential Ratings are a two-part system in which a player is assigned a number rating based on his upside potential (1-10) and a letter rating based on the probability of reaching that potential (A-E).

Potential

10:	Hall of Famer	5:	MLB reserve
9:	Elite player	4:	Top minor leaguer
8:	Solid regular	3:	Average minor leaguer
7:	Average regular	2:	Minor league reserve
6:	Platoon player	1:	Minor league roster filler

Probability Rating

A: 90% probability of reaching potential
B: 70% probability of reaching potential
C: 50% probability of reaching potential
D: 30% probability of reaching potential
E: 10% probability of reaching potential

SKILLS: Scouts usually grade a player's skills on the 20-80 scale, and while most of the grades are subjective, there are grades that can be given to represent a certain hitting statistic or running speed. These are indicated on this chart:

Scout Grade	HR	BA	Speed (L)	Speed (R)
80	39+	.320+	3.9	4.0
70	32-38	.300-.319	4.0	4.1
60	25-31	.286-.299	4.1	4.2
50 (avg)	17-24	.270-.285	4.2	4.3
40	11-16	.250-.269	4.3	4.4
30	6-10	.220-.249	4.4	4.5
20	0-5	.219-	4.5	4.6

CATCHER POP TIMES: Catchers are timed (in seconds) from the moment the pitch reaches the catcher's mitt until the time that the middle infielder receives the baseball at second base. This number assists both teams in assessing whether a base-runner should steal second base or not.

1.85	+
1.95	MLB average
2.05	–

Abreu,Wilyer — 789 — Boston

EXP MLB DEBUT: 2023 | H/W: 6-0 217 | FUT: Starting OF | 7D

Bats L | Age 23 | 2017 FA (VZ)

Year	Lev	Team	AB	R	H	HR	RBI	Avg	OB	Slg	OPS	bb%	ct%	Eye	SB	CS	x/h%	Iso	RC/G
2019	A-	Tri City	70	8	16	1	7	229	280	329	609	7	77	0.31	2	3	31	100	2.91
2019	A	Quad Cities	122	13	33	1	6	270	346	385	731	10	76	0.48	4	5	30	115	4.76
2021	A+	Asheville	287	52	77	16	50	268	354	495	849	12	66	0.38	10	11	42	226	6.56
2022	AA	Corpus Christi	329	81	82	15	54	249	393	459	852	19	67	0.72	23	1	48	210	6.85
2022	AA	Portland	128	25	31	4	19	242	409	375	784	22	65	0.80	8	2	29	133	6.00

Pwr +++ | BAvg ++ | Spd +++ | Def +++

Acquired from HOU in August, finished 2nd in minors in BB while establishing highs in HR and SB. Too much swing and miss hinders BA potential and lacks ideal swing mechanics. Sells out for power and too many flyballs mutes speed. Spike in pop due to more loft in stroke. Has become more patient at plate. Decent athlete who plays all OF spots.

Acosta,Maximo — 46 — Texas

EXP MLB DEBUT: 2026 | H/W: 6-1 187 | FUT: Reserve 2B | 6B

Bats R | Age 20 | 2019 FA (VZ)

Year	Lev	Team	AB	R	H	HR	RBI	Avg	OB	Slg	OPS	bb%	ct%	Eye	SB	CS	x/h%	Iso	RC/G
2021	Rk	ACL Rangers	61	11	15	1	5	246	281	393	675	5	75	0.20	7	2	33	148	3.73
2022	A	Down East	404	62	106	4	35	262	329	361	690	9	78	0.46	44	17	29	99	4.13

Pwr + | BAvg ++ | Spd +++ | Def ++

Big '19 IFA signing lost '20 to pandemic and most of '21 to thoracic outlet surgery, so '22 really was first taste. Pretty average across the board, projection for above-average hit and speed, but body and Knoblauch swing says no power's coming and he struggles against LHP. Body may slow so he's likely a 2B, and one without power. Utility future.

Acosta,Victor — 46 — Cincinnati

EXP MLB DEBUT: 2026 | H/W: 5-11 170 | FUT: Starting SS | 7E

Bats B | Age 18 | 2021 FA (DR)

Year	Lev	Team	AB	R	H	HR	RBI	Avg	OB	Slg	OPS	bb%	ct%	Eye	SB	CS	x/h%	Iso	RC/G
2021	Rk	DSL Padres	186	45	53	5	31	285	406	484	890	17	76	0.84	26	7	42	199	7.19
2022	Rk	ACL Padres	111	17	27	2	11	243	339	360	699	13	73	0.53	5	7	26	117	4.37
2022	Rk	ACL Reds	28	5	6	0	1	214	333	357	690	15	75	0.71	0	0	67	143	4.58

Pwr ++ | BAvg +++ | Spd +++ | Def +++

Athletic SS prospect, acquired in mid-season deal, was SD's 2020-2021 top international signing. Athletic, wiry frame with room to grow. Hitchy load delays bat getting to hit position, preventing above-average bat speed from getting barrel out in front of the plate, and depressing hard contact. Above-average speed with solid range, should stick at SS.

Acuna,Jose — 46 — Texas

EXP MLB DEBUT: 2024 | H/W: 5-10 181 | FUT: Starting SS | 8D

Bats R | Age 21 | 2018 FA (VZ)

Year	Lev	Team	AB	R	H	HR	RBI	Avg	OB	Slg	OPS	bb%	ct%	Eye	SB	CS	x/h%	Iso	RC/G
2021	A	Down East	413	77	110	12	74	266	344	404	749	11	73	0.45	44	11	27	138	4.88
2022	A+	Hickory	205	45	65	8	29	317	414	483	897	14	71	0.57	28	6	28	166	7.17
2022	AA	Frisco	152	21	34	3	18	224	302	349	650	10	76	0.47	12	3	32	125	3.60

Pwr ++ | BAvg ++ | Spd ++++ | Def +++

Lil' bro ascended to AA and held own whilst continuing to show prime time tools. Smaller-in-stature, he dominated at A+ Hickory across the board, though stumbled a bit in AA at age 20. Plus speed continued to burn bright but the juice peeled back at Frisco. Despite hit concerns and AA h%-related BA crater, maintained solid plate discipline.

Adams,Jordyn — 789 — Los Angeles (A)

EXP MLB DEBUT: 2024 | H/W: 6-2 181 | FUT: Starting CF | 7E

Bats R | Age 23 | 2018 (1) HS (NC)

Year	Lev	Team	AB	R	H	HR	RBI	Avg	OB	Slg	OPS	bb%	ct%	Eye	SB	CS	x/h%	Iso	RC/G
2019	A	Burlington	372	52	93	7	31	250	339	358	696	12	75	0.53	12	5	26	108	4.27
2019	A+	Inland Empire	35	7	8	1	1	229	325	400	725	13	60	0.36	0	1	38	171	5.16
2021	A+	Tri-City	277	37	60	5	27	217	289	310	599	9	58	0.24	18	4	23	94	3.03
2022	A+	Tri-City	219	31	50	0	22	228	296	306	602	9	75	0.39	18	3	28	78	3.00
2022	AA	Rocket City	209	33	52	4	20	249	317	359	676	9	67	0.30	15	0	25	110	3.98

Pwr ++ | BAvg ++ | Spd +++++ | Def ++++

Quick-twitch, athletic OF prospect continues to struggle with bat. Former 2-sport athlete with D1 scholarship offers in football. Long, lean physique with powerful lower half. Continues to tinker with swing mechanics. The swing is rough, especially in the load and swing path. Plus power in frame, plays below average in games. Exceptional runner.

Aguilar,Starlin — 5 — Seattle

EXP MLB DEBUT: 2026 | H/W: 5-11 170 | FUT: Starting 3B | 8E

Bats L | Age 19 | 2021 FA (DR)

Year	Lev	Team	AB	R	H	HR	RBI	Avg	OB	Slg	OPS	bb%	ct%	Eye	SB	CS	x/h%	Iso	RC/G
2021	Rk	DSL Mariners	183	38	45	2	21	246	349	361	710	14	78	0.71	0	2	36	115	4.63
2022	Rk	ACL Mariners	175	13	51	0	20	291	322	337	660	4	76	0.19	0	1	14	46	3.46

Pwr + | BAvg +++ | Spd ++ | Def ++

Young, strong INF with high upside due to projection and current tools. Power hasn't yet arrived as he makes soft contact. Plate approach can be advanced and has chance to hit for high BA. Uses whole field and has plus hand-eye coordination. Doesn't walk much. Foot speed is below average and limited range is questionable for 3B.

Alcantara,Kevin — 89 — Chicago (N)

EXP MLB DEBUT: 2025 | H/W: 6-6 188 | FUT: Starting OF | 8D

Bats R | Age 20 | 2018 FA (DR)

Year	Lev	Team	AB	R	H	HR	RBI	Avg	OB	Slg	OPS	bb%	ct%	Eye	SB	CS	x/h%	Iso	RC/G
2019	Rk	GCL Yankees	123	19	32	1	13	260	278	358	636	2	78	0.11	3	3	25	98	3.09
2021	Rk	FCL Yankees	27	5	10	1	3	370	452	519	970	13	70	0.50	2	0	20	148	8.16
2021	Rk	ACL Cubs	92	27	31	4	21	337	419	609	1028	12	70	0.46	3	0	39	272	9.18
2022	A	Myrtle Beach	428	76	117	15	85	273	356	451	807	11	71	0.45	14	3	34	178	5.79

Pwr ++++ | BAvg +++ | Spd +++ | Def +++

Impressive full-season debut, showing both speed and power. Aggressive approach does result in plenty of swing-and-miss, but also draws plenty of walks. Still growing into his enormous frame, but showed improved understanding of his swing and the strike zone. Will be hard-pressed to stick in CF; has enough arm for RF.

Alexander,Blaze — 6 — Arizona

EXP MLB DEBUT: 2023 | H/W: 6-0 160 | FUT: Starting SS | 7C

Bats R | Age 23 | 2018 (11) HS (FL)

Year	Lev	Team	AB	R	H	HR	RBI	Avg	OB	Slg	OPS	bb%	ct%	Eye	SB	CS	x/h%	Iso	RC/G
2019	A	Kane County	343	56	90	7	47	262	343	382	725	11	74	0.47	14	4	26	120	4.62
2021	A+	Hillsboro	339	60	74	10	38	218	308	372	680	11	63	0.35	17	4	39	153	4.20
2022	Rk	ACL DBacks	8	1	2	1	1	250	333	625	958	11	75	0.50	0	0	50	375	7.15
2022	AA	Amarillo	317	48	97	17	54	306	371	539	911	9	71	0.36	10	6	38	233	7.08
2022	AAA	Reno	27	8	7	2	4	259	355	519	873	13	70	0.50	0	0	43	259	6.56

Pwr +++ | BAvg ++ | Spd +++ | Def +++

Strong, athletic SS prospect improved contact rate to post career best line. Lean, muscular build with plus raw power. Upright stance with hitch in load. Plus bat speed on a linear swing plane. Aggressive approach, struggles with chasing better spin. Above-average power if swing trajectory improves. Solid defender with strong arm.

Allen,Jay — 8 — Cincinnati

EXP MLB DEBUT: 2025 | H/W: 6-2 190 | FUT: Starting CF | 7C

Bats R | Age 20 | 2021 (1) HS (FL)

Year	Lev	Team	AB	R	H	HR	RBI	Avg	OB	Slg	OPS	bb%	ct%	Eye	SB	CS	x/h%	Iso	RC/G
2021	Rk	ACL Reds	61	20	20	3	11	328	406	557	963	12	80	0.67	14	1	35	230	7.55
2022	A	Daytona	241	48	54	3	21	224	335	332	666	14	70	0.55	31	6	33	108	4.03
2022	A+	Dayton	74	13	17	0	8	230	269	297	567	5	74	0.21	12	4	18	68	2.34

Pwr ++ | BAvg +++ | Spd +++ | Def +++

Toolsy, athletic RHH OF struggled with consistent hard contact in full season debut. Former 2-sport HS athlete. Upright, open stance. Bat wrap causes delay loading hands. Struggles to get barrel out in front of the plate. Frame capable of adding muscle, likely above-average raw power. Above-average runner who handles CF.

Almonte,Ariel — 9 — Cincinnati

EXP MLB DEBUT: 2026 | H/W: 6-1 170 | FUT: Starting OF | 8E

Bats L | Age 19 | 2021 FA (DR)

Year	Lev	Team	AB	R	H	HR	RBI	Avg	OB	Slg	OPS	bb%	ct%	Eye	SB	CS	x/h%	Iso	RC/G
2021	Rk	DSL Reds	162	35	45	5	33	278	378	438	816	14	68	0.50	15	6	33	160	6.17
2022	Rk	ACL Reds	140	28	40	6	24	286	379	493	872	13	65	0.43	1	0	43	207	7.11

Pwr ++++ | BAvg +++ | Spd ++ | Def +++

Powerful COF prospect continued domination of rookie league competition. Long-levered frame with room to build muscle. Chase rate and whiff rate increased compared to '21, which tempered hit tool projection. Raw plus power in frame and in uppercut swing. Power plays in game from CF to RF. Below-average runner. Plus arm carry RF projection.

Alvarez,Francisco — 2 — New York (N)

EXP MLB DEBUT: 2022 | H/W: 5-11 233 | FUT: Starting C | 9C

Bats R | Age 21 | 2018 FA (VZ)

Year	Lev	Team	AB	R	H	HR	RBI	Avg	OB	Slg	OPS	bb%	ct%	Eye	SB	CS	x/h%	Iso	RC/G
2021	A	St. Lucie	48	12	20	2	12	417	556	646	1201	24	85	2.14	2	2	35	229	11.30
2021	A+	Brooklyn	279	55	69	22	58	247	342	538	879	13	71	0.49	6	3	52	290	6.63
2022	AA	Binghamton	253	43	70	18	47	277	367	553	920	12	72	0.51	0	0	49	277	7.20
2022	AAA	Syracuse	158	31	37	9	31	234	370	443	813	18	67	0.65	0	0	41	209	6.07
2022	MLB	New York (N)	12	3	2	1	1	167	286	500	786	14	67	0.50	0	0	100	333	5.49

Pwr ++++ | BAvg ++++ | Spd + | Def +++

Stocky, strong C prospect made MLB debut after minor league power burst. XXL frame at physical projection. Short arms aid compact stroke. Open stance with minimal trigger. Struggled with spin in minors, contributing to high whiff and chase rate. Plus power plays to all fields. Impacts the ball at high EV. Slow runner. Improved receiving skills.

Alvarez, Ignacio — 5 — Atlanta

EXP MLB DEBUT: 2024　H/W: 6-0　190　FUT: Reserve IF　6C

Bats R　Age 19
2022 (5) Riverside CC

Pwr +
BAvg +++
Spd +++
Def +++

Year	Lev	Team	AB	R	H	HR	RBI	Avg	OB	Slg	OPS	bb%	ct%	Eye	SB	CS	x/h%	Iso	RC/G
2022	Rk	FCL Braves	43	11	12	1	5	279	380	419	799	14	86	1.17	4	0	25	140	5.76
2022	A	Augusta	51	14	15	0	6	294	486	373	858	27	82	2.11	4	1	20	78	7.39

2022 5th round pick taken out of CA junior college ranks hit well in pro debut. Slight open stance with solid trigger. Shorter levers allow for compact swing. It's a linear swing with not much power potential. Physically maxed out. All-fields approach was advanced for level. It will likely play until upper levels. A solid defender at SS/3B.

Amador, Adael — 46 — Colorado

EXP MLB DEBUT: 2025　H/W: 6-0　160　FUT: Starting 2B　9D

Bats B　Age 19
2019 FA (DR)

Pwr ++
BAvg ++++
Spd +++
Def +++

Year	Lev	Team	AB	R	H	HR	RBI	Avg	OB	Slg	OPS	bb%	ct%	Eye	SB	CS	x/h%	Iso	RC/G
2021	Rk	ACL Rockies	164	41	49	4	24	299	398	445	843	14	82	0.93	10	7	31	146	6.29
2022	A	Fresno	449	100	131	15	57	292	407	445	852	16	85	1.30	26	12	30	154	6.46

Switch-hitting SS has an advanced feel for hitting and controls the strike zone as well as any player in the minors. Uses leg kick to start swing and identifies spin early with a quick bat and compact stroke. Rockets balls into gaps with average to a tick above raw power. Runs well, but arm and instincts could push him over to 2B down the line.

Amaya, Jacob — 6 — Miami

EXP MLB DEBUT: 2023　H/W: 6-0　180　FUT: Reserve SS　6A

Bats R　Age 24
2017 (11) HS (CA)

Pwr ++
BAvg ++
Spd ++
Def ++++

Year	Lev	Team	AB	R	H	HR	RBI	Avg	OB	Slg	OPS	bb%	ct%	Eye	SB	CS	x/h%	Iso	RC/G
2019	A	Great Lakes	386	68	101	6	58	262	380	394	774	16	78	0.89	4	4	35	132	5.58
2019	A+	Rancho Cuca	80	14	20	1	13	250	310	375	685	8	81	0.47	1	3	50	125	4.06
2021	AA	Tulsa	417	60	90	12	41	216	303	343	646	11	75	0.50	5	0	31	127	3.49
2022	AA	Tulsa	182	39	48	9	26	264	374	500	874	15	84	1.10	3	1	46	236	6.61
2022	AAA	Oklahoma City	294	46	76	8	45	259	364	381	745	14	72	0.59	3	1	25	122	5.02

One of the best defenders in the system. Good first step quickness results in plus range with some hands and enough arm to stick at short. High motor player who earns praise for how he plays. Improved physicality led to career high in HR and increases odds of carving out a starting role. If he can hit, the glove will keep him in the majors. Traded to Miami in M. Rojas deal.

Amaya, Miguel — 2 — Chicago (N)

EXP MLB DEBUT: 2023　H/W: 6-2　230　FUT: Starting C　7C

Bats R　Age 24
2015 FA (PN)

Pwr ++
BAvg ++
Spd +
Def +++

Year	Lev	Team	AB	R	H	HR	RBI	Avg	OB	Slg	OPS	bb%	ct%	Eye	SB	CS	x/h%	Iso	RC/G
2018	A	South Bend	414	54	106	12	52	256	336	403	740	11	78	0.55	1	0	33	147	4.75
2019	A+	Myrtle Beach	341	50	80	11	57	235	339	402	741	14	80	0.78	2	0	44	167	4.93
2021	AA	Tennessee	79	11	17	1	13	215	380	304	684	21	72	0.95	2	0	29	89	4.49
2022	Rk	ACL Cubs	37	4	8	2	4	216	341	378	719	16	65	0.54	0	0	25	162	4.59
2022	AA	Tennessee	97	15	27	4	19	278	369	485	854	13	71	0.50	0	0	41	206	6.50

Missed most of 2021 and the start of 2022 recovering from Tommy John surgery and was then shut down with a broken foot. When healthy is an above-average to plus defender. Blocks and receives well with a strong, accurate arm. At the plate uses a contact-oriented approach, but power is going to be average or a tick below.

Angeles, Euribiel — 46 — Oakland

EXP MLB DEBUT: 2024　H/W: 5-11　175　FUT: Starting 2B　7C

Bats R　Age 20
2018 FA (DR)

Pwr +
BAvg +++
Spd +++
Def +++

Year	Lev	Team	AB	R	H	HR	RBI	Avg	OB	Slg	OPS	bb%	ct%	Eye	SB	CS	x/h%	Iso	RC/G
2021	A	Lake Elsinore	362	65	124	3	56	343	396	461	857	8	83	0.52	18	6	25	119	6.16
2021	A+	Fort Wayne	72	12	19	1	8	264	338	361	699	10	78	0.50	1	1	26	97	4.24
2022	A+	Lansing	363	29	101	2	32	278	311	353	663	4	84	0.29	8	6	22	74	3.59

Acquired from SD in April 2022. Contact-oriented hitter who goes gap-to-gap with quick hands and bat. Produces doubles and has speed to log XBH. Rarely draws walks with aggressive approach due to ease of bat-to-ball. Versatile defender with hands and feet to play both MIF spots. Lack of arm strength isn't ideal for SS.

Anthony, Roman — 8 — Boston

EXP MLB DEBUT: 2026　H/W: 6-3　200　FUT: Starting OF　8E

Bats L　Age 18
2022 (2) HS (FL)

Pwr +++
BAvg ++
Spd +++
Def ++

Year	Lev	Team	AB	R	H	HR	RBI	Avg	OB	Slg	OPS	bb%	ct%	Eye	SB	CS	x/h%	Iso	RC/G
2022	Rk	FCL Red Sox	35	5	15	0	7	429	487	486	973	10	89	1.00	1	0	13	57	7.59
2022	A	Salem	37	2	7	0	5	189	286	243	529	12	89	1.25	0	0	29	54	2.70

Long-term project with scintillating potential to be well-rounded player. Has natural strength and offers enticing power potential from left side. Strong and athletic frame should result in both power and speed production. Lacks contact ability, but needs more at bats and more consistent swing mechanics. Plays CF and likely to end up in corner.

Antuna, Yasel — 7 — Washington

EXP MLB DEBUT: 2024　H/W: 6-0　199　FUT: Reserve OF　7D

Bats B　Age 23
2016 FA (DR)

Pwr +++
BAvg ++
Spd ++
Def +

Year	Lev	Team	AB	R	H	HR	RBI	Avg	OB	Slg	OPS	bb%	ct%	Eye	SB	CS	x/h%	Iso	RC/G
2018	A	Hagerstown	323	44	71	6	27	220	290	331	621	9	76	0.41	8	7	31	111	3.15
2019	Rk	GCL Nationals	6	1	1	0	0	167	375	167	542	25	83	2.00	0	0	0	0	3.11
2021	A+	Wilmington	405	55	92	12	65	227	306	385	691	10	75	0.46	4	4	42	158	4.10
2022	A+	Wilmington	332	66	78	10	44	235	371	370	742	18	73	0.82	26	6	31	136	5.08
2022	AA	Harrisburg	91	9	13	1	4	143	278	220	498	16	64	0.52	1	2	38	77	1.40

Once a sought-after international sign, bat has not developed as hoped. Switch-hitter but much better from the LH side; lacks strength to drive the ball from either side. Average runner; nabbed 27 SB across two levels. Was a double-digit guy prior to rules tweak. Was taken off 40-man roster this winter and looks career UT player at best.

Antunez, Wuilfredo — 8 — Cleveland

EXP MLB DEBUT: 2026　H/W: 6-0　150　FUT: Starting OF　7E

Bats L　Age 20
2019 FA (VZ)

Pwr +++
BAvg +++
Spd ++++
Def ++++

Year	Lev	Team	AB	R	H	HR	RBI	Avg	OB	Slg	OPS	bb%	ct%	Eye	SB	CS	x/h%	Iso	RC/G
2022	Rk	ACL Indians	78	21	23	4	13	295	433	538	971	20	78	1.12	11	4	39	244	8.18
2022	A	Lynchburg	6	0	2	0	0	333	600	500	1100	40	67	2.00	0	0	50	167	12.14

Wiry, toolsy CF prospect debuted mid-season at complex, earning August callup to Low-A. Athletic frame with lots of room to grow. Upright stance with minimal load. Swing has lift to it and flashed power during ACL. There's average power with potential for more. Fast runner with good defensive coverage skills. Could stick in CF.

Ardoin, Silas — 2 — Baltimore

EXP MLB DEBUT: 2026　H/W: 6-0　215　FUT: Starting C　7D

Bats R　Age 22
2022 (4) Texas

Pwr ++
BAvg ++
Spd +
Def ++++

Year	Lev	Team	AB	R	H	HR	RBI	Avg	OB	Slg	OPS	bb%	ct%	Eye	SB	CS	x/h%	Iso	RC/G
2022	NCAA	Texas	240	48	65	12	50	271	373	513	885	14	81	0.85	1	0	51	242	6.72
2022	Rk	FCL Orioles B	8	1	0	0	1	0	529	0	529	53	75	4.50	0	0		0	2.59
2022	A	Delmarva	44	5	10	0	8	227	346	250	596	15	59	0.44	0	0	10	23	3.11

Defense-first backstop with MLB bloodlines (Danny is his father). Superlative with the glove - blocks, frames, receives well above average. Question is will he hit enough. Has shown good eye and walk rates in college, but quality of contact needs to improve. Has fringe-average power and some natural strength that showed up in 2022 college season.

Arias, Gabriel — 456 — Cleveland

EXP MLB DEBUT: 2022　H/W: 6-1　217　FUT: Starting SS　7B

Bats R　Age 23
2016 FA (VZ)

Pwr +++
BAvg ++
Spd ++++
Def ++++

Year	Lev	Team	AB	R	H	HR	RBI	Avg	OB	Slg	OPS	bb%	ct%	Eye	SB	CS	x/h%	Iso	RC/G
2019	A+	Lake Elsinore	477	62	144	17	75	302	337	470	806	5	73	0.20	8	4	29	168	5.36
2021	AAA	Columbus	436	64	124	13	55	284	343	454	797	8	75	0.35	5	1	36	170	5.44
2022	Rk	ACL Indians	13	2	3	0	0	231	375	308	683	19	46	0.43	1	0	33	77	5.92
2022	AAA	Columbus	288	46	69	13	36	240	300	406	707	8	73	0.32	5	1	32	167	4.08
2022	MLB	Cleveland	47	9	9	1	5	191	309	319	628	15	66	0.50	1	0	33	128	3.43

Athletic SS prospect made MLB debut after struggling with contact in Triple-A. Power-over-hit prospect. Upright, closed stance with bat wrap and leg lift. Linear swing plane conducive to line drive contact. Frame and max EV indicate more power present than swing trajectory currently allows. Aggressive approach overall. Strong arm and rangy SS.

Arias, Roderick — 6 — New York (A)

EXP MLB DEBUT: 2027　H/W: 6-2　178　FUT: Starting SS　8E

Bats B　Age 18
2022 FA (DR)

Pwr +++
BAvg ++
Spd ++++
Def ++++

Year	Lev	Team	AB	R	H	HR	RBI	Avg	OB	Slg	OPS	bb%	ct%	Eye	SB	CS	x/h%	Iso	RC/G
2022	Rk	DSL Yankees 2	108	25	21	3	11	194	360	370	731	21	57	0.61	10	2	52	176	5.52

Wiry and athletic switch-hitting SS struggled with in zone contact during professional debut in the Dominican. Better profile as LHH. Struggled mightily in limited RH chances. Plus power in frame, didn't play due to rough, top heavy swing. Plus run tool aids SB potential. Skilled defender with plus range and solid arm at SS.

Arroyo,Edwin — 6 — Cincinnati
EXP MLB DEBUT: 2025 | H/W: 6-0 175 | FUT: Starting SS | 8C

Bats B Age 19 — 2021 (2) HS (PR) — Pwr ++++ — BAvg +++ — Spd +++ — Def ++++

Year	Lev	Team	AB	R	H	HR	RBI	Avg	OB	Slg	OPS	bb%	ct%	Eye	SB	CS	x/h%	Iso	RC/G
2021	Rk	ACL Mariners	71	16	15	2	10	211	309	324	633	12	63	0.38	4	1	27	113	3.38
2022	Rk	ACL Reds	6	1	0	0	1	0	250	0	250	25	67	1.00	2	0		0	
2022	A	Daytona	97	16	22	1	16	227	292	381	674	8	68	0.29	4	2	45	155	4.08
2022	A	Modesto	364	76	115	13	67	316	376	514	890	9	75	0.39	21	4	34	198	6.67

Athletic, switch-hitting SS prospect had breakout first half before mid-season trade from SEA. Power-over-hit prospect. Wide open stance with little load and moderate leg lift from both sides of the plate. Uppercut-oriented swing creates lots of loft. Plus power potential at maturity. Above-average runner; 27 for 33 in SB attempts. Plus SS.

Arroyo,Michael — 56 — Seattle
EXP MLB DEBUT: 2027 | H/W: 5-10 160 | FUT: Starting 3B | 8D

Bats R Age 18 — 2022 FA (CB) — Pwr ++ — BAvg +++ — Spd ++ — Def ++

Year	Lev	Team	AB	R	H	HR	RBI	Avg	OB	Slg	OPS	bb%	ct%	Eye	SB	CS	x/h%	Iso	RC/G
2022	Rk	DSL Mariners	153	46	48	4	22	314	417	484	900	15	78	0.82	4	4	33	170	7.13

High-profile signing who spent all 2022 in DSL. Shows evidence of all five tools with power potentially a longer-term play. Compact swing generates line drive contact at present and has advanced knowledge of strike zone. Rarely fans with quality hand-eye coordination. Runs well and has the range and arm to play either SS or 3B.

Arteaga,Aeverson — 6 — San Francisco
EXP MLB DEBUT: 2025 | H/W: 6-1 170 | FUT: Starting SS | 8C

Bats R Age 20 — 2019 FA (VZ) — Pwr +++ — BAvg +++ — Spd ++++ — Def ++++

Year	Lev	Team	AB	R	H	HR	RBI	Avg	OB	Slg	OPS	bb%	ct%	Eye	SB	CS	x/h%	Iso	RC/G
2021	Rk	ACL Giants O	197	42	58	9	43	294	368	503	871	10	65	0.33	8	0	38	208	6.97
2021	A	San Jose	3	0	0	0	0	0	0	0	0	0	67	0.00	0	0		0	
2022	A	San Jose	503	87	136	14	84	270	335	431	767	9	69	0.32	11	6	38	161	5.22

Athletic, smooth SS with excellent tools across board with potential for more. Needs to address swing and miss and aggressive approach, but has high upside. Swings very fast bat and makes loud contact with high exit velocity. Led org in doubles with potential 20+ HR upside. Fast, quick actions at SS with plus range and arm strength.

Auer,Mason — 89 — Tampa Bay
EXP MLB DEBUT: 2024 | H/W: 6-1 210 | FUT: Starting OF | 9D

Bats R Age 22 — 2021 (5) San Jacinto JC — Pwr +++ — BAvg +++ — Spd ++++ — Def ++++

Year	Lev	Team	AB	R	H	HR	RBI	Avg	OB	Slg	OPS	bb%	ct%	Eye	SB	CS	x/h%	Iso	RC/G
2020	NCAA	Missouri St	9	0	1	0	0	111	273	111	384	18	78	1.00	0	1	0	0	0.44
2021	NJCAA	San Jacinto	204	60	76	11	56	373	526	627	1153	24	78	1.47	34	3	34	255	10.94
2021	Rk	FCL Rays	34	7	9	0	3	265	375	324	699	15	79	0.86	10	1	22	59	4.59
2022	A	Charleston	232	46	68	4	31	293	376	478	855	12	79	0.65	24	3	38	185	6.45
2022	A+	Bowling Green	226	38	65	11	31	288	356	496	852	10	73	0.39	24	4	34	208	6.19

Athletic, strong RHH OFer emerged as solid all-around prospect in 2022. Hit for average and power in lower levels. Upright stance with direct load. All-fields approach with solid discipline. Got to hard contact nearly 40% of the time. Above-average power potential. Plus speed powered 48 SB season. Double-plus arm, fits RF.

Azuaje,Alexeis — 4 — Philadelphia
EXP MLB DEBUT: 2026 | H/W: 5-10 155 | FUT: Starting 2B | 7C

Bats R Age 20 — 2018 FA (VZ) — Pwr ++ — BAvg +++ — Spd +++ — Def ++

Year	Lev	Team	AB	R	H	HR	RBI	Avg	OB	Slg	OPS	bb%	ct%	Eye	SB	CS	x/h%	Iso	RC/G
2021	Rk	FCL Phillies	45	17	18	5	16	400	449	867	1316	8	89	0.80	4	0	61	467	10.97
2022	Rk	FCL Phillies	17	1	3	0	1	176	176	235	412	0	71	0.00	1	1	33	59	
2022	A	Clearwater	137	23	39	1	8	285	315	380	694	4	69	0.14	15	4	26	95	4.07

Intriguing player with some good bat-on-ball skills that come from a line drive swing. Can get over-aggressive and chase, thinking he can reach everything, so current strikeout totals are high/walks are low. Smaller-framed, but with some added strength, hit tool could get to average power. Passable defense at 2B but limited there.

Bae,Ji-hwan — 468 — Pittsburgh
EXP MLB DEBUT: 2022 | H/W: 6-1 185 | FUT: Starting 2B | 7C

Bats L Age 23 — 2018 FA (KR) — Pwr ++ — BAvg +++ — Spd ++++ — Def +++

Year	Lev	Team	AB	R	H	HR	RBI	Avg	OB	Slg	OPS	bb%	ct%	Eye	SB	CS	x/h%	Iso	RC/G
2021	Rk	FCL Pirates Black	4	2	2	0	1	500	500	500	1000	0	100		0	0	0	0	6.83
2021	Rk	FCL Pirates Gold	3	1	1	1	1	333	333	###	1667	0	100		0	0	100	1000	12.52
2021	AA	Altoona	320	63	89	7	31	278	355	413	767	11	74	0.46	20	8	27	134	5.19
2022	AAA	Indianapolis	419	81	121	8	53	289	362	430	791	10	81	0.60	30	8	31	141	5.46
2022	MLB	Pittsburgh	33	5	11	0	6	333	371	424	796	6	82	0.33	3	0	27	91	5.30

Made MLB debut after finishing 2nd in org in SB and continuing to show defensive versatility and easy contact skills. Exhibits incredible speed to steal bags. Adding to power thanks to loftier swing and strength, but not really his game. Puts bat to ball and can drive to gaps. Lacks range and quickness, but makes fundamental plays.

Baez,Joshua — 89 — St. Louis
EXP MLB DEBUT: 2025 | H/W: 6-4 220 | FUT: Starting OF | 8E

Bats R Age 19 — 2021 (2) HS (MA) — Pwr ++++ — BAvg ++ — Spd ++ — Def +++

Year	Lev	Team	AB	R	H	HR	RBI	Avg	OB	Slg	OPS	bb%	ct%	Eye	SB	CS	x/h%	Iso	RC/G
2021	Rk	FCL Cardinals	76	18	12	2	8	158	289	303	592	16	63	0.50	5	0	50	145	2.86
2022	Rk	FCL Cardinals	38	4	9	1	5	237	326	395	720	12	63	0.36	6	1	44	158	4.89
2022	A	Palm Beach	63	11	18	3	16	286	392	540	932	15	52	0.37	4	3	50	254	9.78

Wrist injury limited him to 32 G and he's had just 177 pro AB. He has an aggressive, all-or-nothing approach with above-average bat speed and plus raw power. Not surprisingly, that comes at the price of plenty of swing-and-miss and he owns a career 35% K rate. Runs a tick above average and enough arm to handle RF.

Bailey,Patrick — 2 — San Francisco
EXP MLB DEBUT: 2024 | H/W: 6-1 210 | FUT: Starting C | 7C

Bats B Age 23 — 2020 (1) North Carolina St — Pwr +++ — BAvg ++ — Spd + — Def ++++

Year	Lev	Team	AB	R	H	HR	RBI	Avg	OB	Slg	OPS	bb%	ct%	Eye	SB	CS	x/h%	Iso	RC/G
2020	NCAA	NC St	54	20	16	6	20	296	465	685	1150	24	67	0.94	1	0	56	389	11.24
2021	Rk	ACL Giants B	5	3	2	0	0	400	571	400	971	29	80	2.00	0	0	0	0	8.99
2021	A	San Jose	177	45	57	7	24	322	415	531	946	14	73	0.60	1	1	40	209	7.76
2021	A+	Eugene	135	13	25	2	15	185	281	296	577	12	68	0.42	6	0	44	111	2.63
2022	A+	Eugene	267	49	60	12	51	225	345	419	764	16	73	0.68	1	1	45	195	5.25

Fundamentally-sound C who returned to High-A and had solid season. Better from left side and generates more pop. Works counts to get on base and uses whole field. Too much swing and miss while trying to swing for fences. Very good backstop with quick, accurate arm. Best receiver and blocker in org.

Balcazar,Leonardo — 46 — Cincinnati
EXP MLB DEBUT: 2026 | H/W: 5-10 167 | FUT: Starting SS | 8E

Bats R Age 18 — 2021 FA (VZ) — Pwr ++++ — BAvg +++ — Spd ++++ — Def +++

Year	Lev	Team	AB	R	H	HR	RBI	Avg	OB	Slg	OPS	bb%	ct%	Eye	SB	CS	x/h%	Iso	RC/G
2021	Rk	DSL Reds	112	26	29	6	15	259	336	536	872	10	74	0.45	8	4	52	277	6.53
2022	Rk	ACL Reds	143	25	46	4	26	322	398	476	873	11	71	0.43	13	1	26	154	6.77

Shorter-statured RHH SS with power potential enjoyed great US debut. Lean, athletic frame with room to grow. Quick twitch athlete. Slightly open, upright stance with minimal load and slight toe tap. Compact swing with plus bat speed. Power has played in games to all fields. Potential for 25+ HR at projection. Plus runner, 13 for 14 in SB attempts.

Ball,Bryce — 3 — Chicago (N)
EXP MLB DEBUT: 2024 | H/W: 6-6 240 | FUT: Reserve 1B | 6C

Bats L Age 24 — 2019 (24) Dallas Baptist — Pwr +++ — BAvg + — Spd ++ — Def ++

Year	Lev	Team	AB	R	H	HR	RBI	Avg	OB	Slg	OPS	bb%	ct%	Eye	SB	CS	x/h%	Iso	RC/G
2019	Rk	Danville	145	37	47	13	38	324	413	676	1089	13	79	0.73	0	0	53	352	9.09
2019	A	Rome	86	14	29	4	14	337	367	547	913	4	77	0.20	0	0	34	209	6.57
2021	A+	Rome	170	24	35	6	31	206	357	394	751	19	65	0.68	0	0	54	188	5.42
2021	A+	South Bend	184	24	38	7	21	207	348	380	729	18	66	0.65	0	0	45	174	4.95
2022	AA	Tennessee	486	77	129	11	76	265	357	405	762	12	75	0.57	1	4	34	140	5.20

Huge framed LHH has plus raw power. Average bat speed and a pull-heavy approach limit in-game power, though he does draw plenty of walks and understands the strike zone. Can be beat by velo and quality breaking balls. Fringe defender at 1B with below-average speed and will need to hit for more power to carve out a big league role.

Ballesteros,Moises — 23 — Chicago (N)
EXP MLB DEBUT: 2025 | H/W: 5-10 195 | FUT: Starting C | 7D

Bats L Age 19 — 2021 FA (VZ) — Pwr ++ — BAvg +++ — Spd + — Def ++

Year	Lev	Team	AB	R	H	HR	RBI	Avg	OB	Slg	OPS	bb%	ct%	Eye	SB	CS	x/h%	Iso	RC/G
2021	Rk	DSL Cubs Red	154	22	41	3	25	266	389	390	779	17	84	1.29	6	1	32	123	5.68
2022	Rk	ACL Cubs	97	12	26	7	18	268	355	536	891	12	80	0.68	0	0	46	268	6.50
2022	A	Myrtle Beach	109	17	27	3	15	248	354	394	749	14	74	0.64	0	1	37	147	5.07

Signed for $1.2 million, he had a solid state-side debut. Smooth LH stroke with feel for barrel and good pitch recognition. Contact-heavy approach as he shoots line drives into gaps, but has current limited over-the-fence power. Receives the ball well with strong arm, but lacks agility and needs to improve blocking skills.

Barber,Colin | 89 | Houston

EXP MLB DEBUT: 2024 | H/W: 6-0 200 | FUT: Reserve OF | 6B

Bats L Age 22	Year	Lev	Team	AB	R	H	HR	RBI	Avg	OB	Slg	OPS	bb%	ct%	Eye	SB	CS	x/h%	Iso	RC/G
2019 (4) HS (CA)	2019	Rk	GCL Astros	99	19	26	2	6	263	381	394	775	16	71	0.66	2	1	31	131	5.63
Pwr ++	2021	A+	Asheville	42	10	9	3	7	214	353	452	805	18	48	0.41	1	1	44	238	7.61
BAvg +++	2022	Rk	FCL Astros	3	0	0	0	0	0	0	0	0	0	100		0	0		0	
Spd ++	2022	Rk	FCL Astros O	7	0	2	0	0	286	286	286	571	0	86	0.00	0	0	0	0	2.18
Def +++	2022	A+	Asheville	218	35	65	7	33	298	383	450	833	12	74	0.53	7	4	28	151	6.08

OF prospect with strong hit tool has struggled to stay on field over past couple of seasons. Strong bodied with frame close to maxed out. Slightly crouched stance at plate with level swing and leg kick. Has good eye and patience at plate and tends to lay off pitches outside the zone. Inefficient base-stealer with minimal power. Projects as 4th OF.

Barger,Addison | 56 | Toronto

EXP MLB DEBUT: 2023 | H/W: 6-0 175 | FUT: Starting 3B | 7C

Bats L Age 23	Year	Lev	Team	AB	R	H	HR	RBI	Avg	OB	Slg	OPS	bb%	ct%	Eye	SB	CS	x/h%	Iso	RC/G
2018 (6) HS (FL)	2021	A	Dunedin	325	53	81	18	80	249	324	492	816	10	62	0.29	7	0	51	243	6.28
Pwr +++	2021	A+	Vancouver	19	1	3	0	2	158	158	211	368	0	68	0.00	0	0	33	53	
BAvg +++	2022	A+	Vancouver	260	46	78	14	53	300	361	558	919	9	71	0.33	7	2	47	258	7.22
Spd ++	2022	AA	New Hampshire	176	26	55	9	29	313	376	528	905	9	72	0.36	2	2	36	216	6.94
Def +++	2022	AAA	Buffalo	31	8	11	3	9	355	444	677	1122	14	84	1.00	0	1	36	323	9.26

Aggressive INF who led org in OPS while posting career highs in HR and SB. Added strength and power and has skill set to emerge. Was very good on 3 levels and split time between SS and 3B with the latter the more likely long-term. Added greater loft to swing and saw exit velo rise. Needs to make more contact to sustain BA.

Barrios,Johan | 56 | Milwaukee

EXP MLB DEBUT: 2027 | H/W: 6-3 180 | FUT: Starting 3B | 8E

Bats R Age 18	Year	Lev	Team	AB	R	H	HR	RBI	Avg	OB	Slg	OPS	bb%	ct%	Eye	SB	CS	x/h%	Iso	RC/G
2022 FA (VZ)																				
Pwr ++																				
BAvg +++																				
Spd +++																				
Def +++	2022	Rk	DSL Brewers 2	120	22	35	0	13	292	351	350	701	8	74	0.35	3	4	14	58	4.26

Lean, athletic INF who was big international signee. Tall frame has plenty of room to add muscle and strength. Offers major power potential from right side and has quick bat to put ball in play. Projection is unmatched in org. Very raw skills, though has natural SS actions. May move to 3B down line with plus arm strength.

Barrosa,Jorge | 8 | Arizona

EXP MLB DEBUT: 2023 | H/W: 5-9 165 | FUT: Starting CF | 7B

Bats B Age 22	Year	Lev	Team	AB	R	H	HR	RBI	Avg	OB	Slg	OPS	bb%	ct%	Eye	SB	CS	x/h%	Iso	RC/G
2017 FA (VZ)	2019	A-	Hillsboro	223	25	56	1	26	251	316	336	652	9	86	0.66	8	4	27	85	3.78
Pwr ++	2021	A	Visalia	147	30	49	3	16	333	364	449	813	5	79	0.23	9	4	22	116	5.31
BAvg +++	2021	A+	Hillsboro	242	41	62	4	21	256	318	405	723	8	80	0.46	20	7	40	149	4.54
Spd ++++	2022	A+	Hillsboro	40	5	12	1	6	300	333	450	783	5	88	0.40	4	1	33	150	4.99
Def ++++	2022	AA	Amarillo	434	85	120	12	51	276	371	438	809	13	82	0.81	22	11	37	161	5.78

Speedy, defensively skilled switch-hitting CF prospect posted terrific offensive season. Smaller stature with short limbs. Cleaned up swing mechanics from both sides to get to harder contact. Added uppercut trajectory to LH swing, adding new dimension to slasher profile. Utilizes entire field offensively. Dynamic defender, will stick in CF.

Basabe,Osleivis | 456 | Tampa Bay

EXP MLB DEBUT: 2024 | H/W: 6-1 188 | FUT: Starting MIF | 8D

Bats R Age 22	Year	Lev	Team	AB	R	H	HR	RBI	Avg	OB	Slg	OPS	bb%	ct%	Eye	SB	CS	x/h%	Iso	RC/G
2017 FA (VZ)	2019	A-	Spokane	10	0	3	0	1	300	300	300	600	0	90	0.00	0	0	0	0	2.63
Pwr ++	2021	A	Charleston	278	51	79	2	35	284	345	385	730	9	86	0.67	18	4	23	101	4.69
BAvg ++++	2021	A+	Bowling Green	16	2	4	1	1	250	333	438	771	11	63	0.33	0	0	25	188	5.34
Spd ++++	2022	A+	Bowling Green	216	41	68	4	22	315	362	463	825	7	84	0.47	7	5	32	148	5.65
Def +++	2022	AA	Montgomery	228	39	76	0	25	333	397	461	857	10	89	0.96	14	0	34	127	6.34

Contact-oriented MIF prospect hit for over .300 in High-A and Double-A. Athletic frame, near physical projection. Open, upright swing with direct load to hit position. Plus hand-eye coordination carries hit tool. Will expand zone. Slasher approach. Hits off top hand, producing topspin liners. Plus runner. Fits best defensively at 2B.

Basallo,Samuel | 2 | Baltimore

EXP MLB DEBUT: 2027 | H/W: 6-3 180 | FUT: Starting C | 8E

Bats L Age 18	Year	Lev	Team	AB	R	H	HR	RBI	Avg	OB	Slg	OPS	bb%	ct%	Eye	SB	CS	x/h%	Iso	RC/G
2021 FA (DR)																				
Pwr ++++																				
BAvg +++																				
Spd ++	2021	Rk	DSL Orioles	134	18	32	5	19	239	333	410	744	12	76	0.59	1	0	41	172	4.85
Def ++	2022	Rk	FCL Orioles B	158	22	44	6	32	278	341	424	765	9	77	0.41	1	0	25	146	4.88

Bat-first catcher who led the Florida complex league in HR. Logs superior exit velocity numbers that legitimize his current power and point to more in his future. With a large frame as a teenager, he'll need to monitor the length of his swing. His size also affect whether he can stay at CA despite a strong arm. A move to 1B could be in his future.

Bastidas,Abel | 6 | Detroit

EXP MLB DEBUT: 2025 | H/W: 6-2 165 | FUT: Starting SS | 7B

Bats B Age 19	Year	Lev	Team	AB	R	H	HR	RBI	Avg	OB	Slg	OPS	bb%	ct%	Eye	SB	CS	x/h%	Iso	RC/G
2021 FA (VZ)																				
Pwr ++																				
BAvg +++																				
Spd +++	2021	Rk	DSL Tigers	181	24	34	2	27	188	319	276	596	16	75	0.76	12	5	26	88	3.12
Def ++++	2022	Rk	FCL Tigers East	154	18	40	3	26	260	360	409	769	13	79	0.73	4	6	38	149	5.36

Switch-hitter has plus bat speed and an advanced understanding of the strike zone, but needs to answer questions about long-term power development. Should grow into more power as he fills out his lean frame, but needs to use his lower half more effectively. Plus to double-plus defender with silky smooth actions at short with plus range and arm.

Baty,Brett | 57 | New York (N)

EXP MLB DEBUT: 2022 | H/W: 6-3 210 | FUT: Starting OF | 8B

Bats L Age 23	Year	Lev	Team	AB	R	H	HR	RBI	Avg	OB	Slg	OPS	bb%	ct%	Eye	SB	CS	x/h%	Iso	RC/G
2019 (1) HS (TX)	2021	A+	Brooklyn	181	27	56	7	34	309	390	514	904	12	71	0.45	4	3	39	204	7.21
Pwr +++	2021	AA	Binghamton	151	16	41	5	22	272	364	424	788	13	70	0.49	2	0	32	152	5.58
BAvg ++++	2022	AA	Binghamton	340	73	106	19	59	312	394	544	938	12	71	0.47	2	3	39	232	7.55
Spd +++	2022	AAA	Syracuse	22	3	8	0	1	364	440	364	804	12	73	0.50	0	1	0	0	5.78
Def +++	2022	MLB	New York (N)	38	4	7	2	5	184	225	342	567	5	79	0.25	0	0	29	158	2.10

Longer-levered 3B prospect does well to stay compact with swing, contributing to plus hit tool. Strong frame with some room to grow. Already impacts the ball like a plus power hitter. Linear swing creates more topspin than loft, contributing to lower HR totals. Patient approach, works liners to all fields. Fringe 3B defensively. Might be LF.

Beavers,Dylan | 9 | Baltimore

EXP MLB DEBUT: 2025 | H/W: 6-4 206 | FUT: Starting OF | 8D

Bats R Age 21	Year	Lev	Team	AB	R	H	HR	RBI	Avg	OB	Slg	OPS	bb%	ct%	Eye	SB	CS	x/h%	Iso	RC/G
2022 (1) California																				
Pwr +++	2022	NCAA	California	213	62	62	17	50	291	428	634	1062	19	75	0.94	7	4	58	343	9.39
BAvg +++	2022	Rk	FCL Orioles B	9	1	1	0	0	111	273	222	495	18	78	1.00	0	0	100	111	2.06
4.21 Spd +++	2022	A	Delmarva	64	13	23	0	13	359	461	531	992	16	83	1.09	6	1	39	172	8.49
Def ++	2022	A+	Aberdeen	14	0	4	0	2	286	375	286	661	13	64	0.40	0	0	0	0	3.92

Lanky OF whose long levers and bat speed create his average power. Uppercut swing, but doesn't engage lower half which creates timing issues. Very advanced approach; doesn't chase and history of double-digit walk rates. Solid run tool plays up due to hustle, aggressiveness and field energy. Likely a corner OF profile; will need to hit.

Beck,Jordan | 7 | Colorado

EXP MLB DEBUT: 2025 | H/W: 6-3 225 | FUT: Starting OF | 8D

Bats R Age 21	Year	Lev	Team	AB	R	H	HR	RBI	Avg	OB	Slg	OPS	bb%	ct%	Eye	SB	CS	x/h%	Iso	RC/G
2022 (1) Tennessee																				
Pwr +++																				
BAvg ++	2022	NCAA	Tennessee	252	70	75	18	61	298	388	595	983	13	75	0.60	6	4	48	298	7.95
Spd +++	2022	Rk	ACL Rockies	49	9	15	1	10	306	404	469	873	14	78	0.73	0	0	40	163	6.78
Def +++	2022	A	Fresno	39	11	11	2	9	282	462	487	949	25	77	1.44	0	0	36	205	8.14

Mashed his way into 1st round consideration. Strong, athletic frame with a quick bat and in-game power. Good understanding of the strike zone and an ability to barrel the ball, but aggressive approach and trouble with breaking balls creates swing-and-miss, though fared well in pro debut. Runs well with a strong arm and profiles as an above-avg RF.

Beltre,Manuel | 46 | Toronto

EXP MLB DEBUT: 2026 | H/W: 5-9 155 | FUT: Starting 2B | 7D

Bats R Age 18	Year	Lev	Team	AB	R	H	HR	RBI	Avg	OB	Slg	OPS	bb%	ct%	Eye	SB	CS	x/h%	Iso	RC/G
2021 FA (DR)																				
Pwr ++																				
BAvg ++	2021	Rk	DSL Blue Jays	182	39	41	2	29	225	371	346	717	19	82	1.27	10	4	37	121	5.04
Spd +++	2022	Rk	FCL Blue Jays	171	25	40	1	23	234	321	310	631	11	76	0.54	9	4	25	76	3.46
Def +++	2022	A	Dunedin	21	3	8	1	3	381	409	571	981	5	86	0.33	0	0	25	190	7.07

Small-framed INF who was high-profile signing in 2021 and showed potential in first year in U.S. Brings advanced approach to plate and controls bat to make easy contact, though fairly weak. Needs to add muscle to lean frame to realize power potential. Has chance to add value with bat and glove at peak. Very fast with quick actions.

Bergolla,William — 6 — Philadelphia

EXP MLB DEBUT: 2027 | H/W: 5-11 165 | FUT: Starting SS | 8E

Bats L Age 18 — 2022 FA (VZ)

Pwr ++ | BAvg +++ | Spd ++ | Def ++++

Year	Lev	Team	AB	R	H	HR	RBI	Avg	OB	Slg	OPS	bb%	ct%	Eye	SB	CS	x/h%	Iso	RC/G
2022	Rk	DSL Phillies White	71	18	27	0	14	380	463	423	886	13	96	3.67	2	3	11	42	6.93

A priority sign from the 2022 international class showed great SS instincts and fundamentals in his shortened DSL season. Advanced eye at the plate, discerns balls from strikes, and is currently a gap hitter with a simple level stroke from the left side. Strength/power gains will be key to his future offensive development; time is on his side.

Bernabel,Warming — 5 — Colorado

EXP MLB DEBUT: 2024 | H/W: 6-0 180 | FUT: Starting 3B | 8D

Bats R Age 20 — 2018 FA (DR)

Pwr +++ | BAvg +++ | Spd +++ | Def ++

Year	Lev	Team	AB	R	H	HR	RBI	Avg	OB	Slg	OPS	bb%	ct%	Eye	SB	CS	x/h%	Iso	RC/G
2021	Rk	ACL Rockies	74	18	32	6	31	432	468	743	1212	6	84	0.42	5	1	34	311	9.88
2021	A	Fresno	83	9	17	1	7	205	267	313	580	8	83	0.50	4	1	41	108	2.79
2022	A	Fresno	262	52	83	10	54	317	385	504	889	10	85	0.74	21	6	35	187	6.50
2022	A+	Spokane	105	18	32	4	17	305	318	486	803	2	84	0.12	2	2	34	181	4.95

Pure hitter with an advanced ability to find the barrel with minimal swing-and-miss. Can be overly aggressive at the plate, which cuts into his power output, but makes plenty of contact (14% K rate). Power is mostly to the pull side and he isn't going to be a true masher. Was drafted as a SS, but moved to 3B where he is a fringe-average defender.

Bernal,Leonardo — 2 — St. Louis

EXP MLB DEBUT: 2026 | H/W: 6-0 200 | FUT: Starting C | 7D

Bats B Age 19 — 2021 FA (PN)

Pwr ++ | BAvg +++ | Spd + | Def +++

Year	Lev	Team	AB	R	H	HR	RBI	Avg	OB	Slg	OPS	bb%	ct%	Eye	SB	CS	x/h%	Iso	RC/G
2021	Rk	DSL Cardinals Blue	158	23	33	5	29	209	286	373	659	10	82	0.61	3	1	45	165	3.74
2022	A	Palm Beach	156	22	40	7	29	256	310	455	765	7	79	0.38	1	1	40	199	4.81

Was one of the youngest players in the FSL and held his own in 45 G. Switch-hitter is physically mature and shows potential on both sides of the ball. Good understanding of strike zone and ability to put the bat on the ball. Should develop at least average power and he moves up. Continues to make gains on defense and should stick at the position.

Berry,Jacob — 5 — Miami

EXP MLB DEBUT: 2024 | H/W: 6-0 212 | FUT: Starting OF | 7B

Bats B Age 21 — 2022 (1) LSU

Pwr ++++ | BAvg ++ | Spd ++ | Def ++

Year	Lev	Team	AB	R	H	HR	RBI	Avg	OB	Slg	OPS	bb%	ct%	Eye	SB	CS	x/h%	Iso	RC/G
2022	NCAA	LSU	208	47	77	15	48	370	443	630	1072	11	89	1.23	0	0	31	260	8.49
2022	Rk	FCL Marlins	16	1	2	0	2	125	176	125	301	6	63	0.17	0	0	0	0	-1.89
2022	A	Jupiter	125	19	33	3	24	264	333	392	725	9	82	0.57	1	1	30	128	4.53

2022 1st round pick enjoyed solid debut in Low-A. Physical maxed-out physique. Slightly open, upright LHH with a hitchy load. Unorthodox swing with length and above-average bat speed, doesn't get to hard contact enough. Linear swing trajectory depresses raw plus power potential. Below average runner, struggles with hands and throws as 3B.

Binelas,Alex — 35 — Boston

EXP MLB DEBUT: 2024 | H/W: 6-3 225 | FUT: Starting 3B | 7E

Bats L Age 22 — 2021 (3) Louisville

Pwr +++ | BAvg + | Spd ++ | Def ++

Year	Lev	Team	AB	R	H	HR	RBI	Avg	OB	Slg	OPS	bb%	ct%	Eye	SB	CS	x/h%	Iso	RC/G
2021	NCAA	Louisville	195	43	50	19	63	256	329	621	949	10	74	0.41	4	1	62	364	7.27
2021	Rk	ACL Brewers Gold	21	4	6	0	2	286	423	286	709	19	71	0.83	1	1	0	0	4.81
2021	A	Carolina	118	29	37	9	27	314	377	636	1013	9	72	0.36	0	0	54	322	8.35
2022	A+	Greenville	216	41	53	14	43	245	358	495	854	15	68	0.55	8	0	47	250	6.54
2022	AA	Portland	211	30	35	11	35	166	254	379	633	11	63	0.32	0	0	63	213	3.29

Tall, powerful INF who finished 3rd in org in HR despite sub-par BA and lackluster hit tool. Has ton of swing and miss and limited pitch recognition skills. Swing can get very long, though quick and smooth. Willing to draw walks and hits ball hard when contact made. Not a strong defender at either 1B or 3B.

Bishop,Hunter — 89 — San Francisco

EXP MLB DEBUT: 2024 | H/W: 6-5 210 | FUT: Starting OF | 8E

Bats L Age 24 — 2019 (1) Arizona St

Pwr +++ | BAvg ++ | Spd ++++ | Def +++

Year	Lev	Team	AB	R	H	HR	RBI	Avg	OB	Slg	OPS	bb%	ct%	Eye	SB	CS	x/h%	Iso	RC/G
2021	Rk	ACL Giants B	25	5	4	0	3	160	300	200	500	17	60	0.50	1	1	25	40	1.48
2021	A	San Jose	8	1	0	0	0	0	111	0	111	11	13	0.14	0	0		0	-10.10
2021	A+	Eugene	12	1	2	0	1	167	286	250	536	14	67	0.50	0	0	50	83	2.16
2022	Rk	ACL Giants B	2	0	0	0	0	0	0	0	0	0	100		0	0		0	-2.66
2022	A+	Eugene	315	51	74	13	44	235	303	406	710	9	63	0.26	20	2	35	171	4.51

Athletic OF who has as exciting tools, but can't stay on field due to various maladies. Not much time after July due to oblique. Owns outstanding bat speed with strength and natural loft in lefty stroke. Hits for power to all fields, but can be pull-conscious. Swings and misses too often. Can play CF, but likely corner OF with plus speed.

Black,Tyler — 48 — Milwaukee

EXP MLB DEBUT: 2024 | H/W: 6-2 190 | FUT: Starting 2B | 7B

Bats L Age 22 — 2021 (1) Wright St

Pwr ++ | BAvg ++++ | Spd +++ | Def ++

Year	Lev	Team	AB	R	H	HR	RBI	Avg	OB	Slg	OPS	bb%	ct%	Eye	SB	CS	x/h%	Iso	RC/G
2020	NCAA	Wright St	46	6	11	1	5	239	340	370	709	13	80	0.78	0	2	27	130	4.55
2021	NCAA	Wright St	183	64	70	13	59	383	491	683	1174	18	86	1.56	11	1	40	301	10.27
2021	Rk	ACL Brewers Blue	6	4	3	1	2	500	750	###	1750	50	67	3.00	2	0	33	500	22.16
2021	A	Carolina	81	11	18	0	6	222	376	272	648	20	64	0.69	3	2	22	49	4.00
2022	A+	Wisconsin	231	45	65	4	35	281	399	424	823	16	81	1.02	13	6	32	143	6.22

Patient, contact-oriented INF with natural hitting skills. Makes consistent hard contact with simple, short stroke and works counts to get on base. Uses all fields with good bat speed and could add to power arsenal with added loft and leverage. Runs fairly well and has some CF experience, but fits best at 2B due to fringy range and arm.

Blakely,Werner — 5 — Los Angeles (A)

EXP MLB DEBUT: 2025 | H/W: 6-3 185 | FUT: Starting OF | 7D

Bats L Age 21 — 2020 (4) HS (MI)

Pwr +++ | BAvg +++ | Spd ++++ | Def ++

Year	Lev	Team	AB	R	H	HR	RBI	Avg	OB	Slg	OPS	bb%	ct%	Eye	SB	CS	x/h%	Iso	RC/G
2021	Rk	ACL Angels	148	22	27	3	19	182	331	284	615	18	53	0.48	15	2	33	101	3.56
2022	A	Inland Empire	183	36	54	5	40	295	434	470	904	20	62	0.64	24	2	37	175	8.25

Tall, athletic IF prospect tinkered with swing to post good returns in full season debut. Upright, open setup with a bat wrap at the load. It's plus bat speed once the bat gets moving. Advanced approach for age. Works counts and works the opposite field gap well. Swing is much more linear than debut. Plus runner, best suited for OF.

Bleis,Miguel — 8 — Boston

EXP MLB DEBUT: 2026 | H/W: 6-3 170 | FUT: Starting CF | 8D

Bats R Age 19 — 2021 FA (DR)

Pwr +++ | BAvg +++ | Spd ++++ | Def +++

Year	Lev	Team	AB	R	H	HR	RBI	Avg	OB	Slg	OPS	bb%	ct%	Eye	SB	CS	x/h%	Iso	RC/G
2021	Rk	DSL Red Sox Red	119	17	30	4	17	252	321	420	741	9	79	0.48	7	4	37	168	4.67
2022	Rk	FCL Red Sox	153	28	46	5	27	301	344	542	886	6	71	0.22	18	3	50	242	6.83

Tall, athletic CF who was 4th in FCL in OPS and will look to make statement in full season ball. Very exciting upside due to presence of all five tools. Makes consistent, hard contact and has mostly pull side power now. Bat speed and projected strength gains could lead to all-fields pop down road. Runs very well now and could stick in CF.

Bliss,Ryan — 46 — Arizona

EXP MLB DEBUT: 2024 | H/W: 5-9 165 | FUT: Reserve IF | 6C

Bats R Age 23 — 2021 (2) Auburn

Pwr ++ | BAvg ++ | Spd ++++ | Def +++

Year	Lev	Team	AB	R	H	HR	RBI	Avg	OB	Slg	OPS	bb%	ct%	Eye	SB	CS	x/h%	Iso	RC/G
2020	NCAA	Auburn	77	21	29	2	17	377	415	597	1012	6	94	1.00	5	2	38	221	7.69
2021	NCAA	Auburn	211	50	77	15	45	365	427	654	1081	10	86	0.77	6	5	39	289	8.60
2021	Rk	ACL DBacks	7	1	3	0	1	429	429	571	1000	0	71	0.00	2	0	33	143	8.04
2021	A	Visalia	158	22	41	6	23	259	316	443	759	8	75	0.33	11	4	39	184	4.85
2022	A+	Hillsboro	426	68	91	10	37	214	286	343	628	9	72	0.36	31	12	35	129	3.22

Athletic, short-statured MIF struggled mightily in High-A. Upright, slight open stance with moderate leg lift, hesitates getting bat going. Aggressive, opposite field approach. Longer swing length than in college. Not getting to contact out in front of plate. Above-average bat speed present, may recover. Fits best at 2b but serviceable at SS.

Bolte,Henry — 89 — Oakland

EXP MLB DEBUT: 2026 | H/W: 6-3 195 | FUT: Starting CF | 8D

Bats R Age 19 — 2022 (2) HS (CA)

Pwr +++ | BAvg ++ | Spd ++++ | Def +++

Year	Lev	Team	AB	R	H	HR	RBI	Avg	OB	Slg	OPS	bb%	ct%	Eye	SB	CS	x/h%	Iso	RC/G
2022	Rk	ACL Athletics	33	5	7	0	2	212	316	212	528	13	42	0.26	0	1	0	0	2.80

High-upside slugger with plentiful tools. Very raw with stick as he chases out of zone and owns long swing. Power potential is double-plus and has bat speed to produce hard contact. Has exceptional speed for SB and CF defense. Has frame to add even more strength, but could slow down. Only has average arm and could move to corner.

Bonaci,Brainer | 46 | Boston | EXP MLB DEBUT: 2025 | H/W: 5-10 164 | FUT: Utility player | 7D

Bats B Age 20	Year	Lev	Team	AB	R	H	HR	RBI	Avg	OB	Slg	OPS	bb%	ct%	Eye	SB	CS	x/h%	Iso	RC/G
2018 FA (VZ)																				
Pwr +																				
BAvg +++	2021	Rk	FCL Red Sox	139	27	35	2	17	252	350	403	753	13	73	0.57	12	0	46	151	5.23
Spd +++	2021	A	Salem	49	5	11	0	8	224	269	327	596	6	84	0.38	0	0	36	102	2.98
Def +++	2022	A	Salem	397	86	104	6	50	262	397	385	783	18	78	1.00	28	6	30	123	5.80

Disciplined infielder who finished 2nd in CAR in both OBP and walks. Brings keen instincts to both sides of game and has good feel for contact. Needs to get stronger and will never be power guy, but has bat path for doubles to gaps. Solid middle INF with plus arm strength and enough range to play either spot. Likely utility guy with good skills.

Bowen,Jase | 489 | Pittsburgh | EXP MLB DEBUT: 2024 | H/W: 6-0 190 | FUT: Utility player | 6B

Bats R Age 22	Year	Lev	Team	AB	R	H	HR	RBI	Avg	OB	Slg	OPS	bb%	ct%	Eye	SB	CS	x/h%	Iso	RC/G
2019 (11) HS (OH)																				
Pwr +++	2019	Rk	GCL Pirates	130	15	29	0	7	223	299	315	614	10	73	0.40	5	2	28	92	3.22
BAvg ++	2021	A	Bradenton	354	51	78	14	60	220	285	384	669	8	69	0.29	16	1	36	164	3.69
Spd +++	2022	A	Bradenton	367	60	102	14	66	278	346	450	795	9	70	0.35	20	2	32	172	5.53
Def ++	2022	A+	Greensboro	102	11	18	3	8	176	215	324	538	5	66	0.14	5	0	44	147	1.78

Versatile prospect who returned to Low-A and showed improvement with BA and SLG. Finished 3rd in FSL in SLG. K rate continues to climb, but has added more offensive punch while hitting to all fields. BA in question as he can be beaten with velocity and breaking balls. Runs well. Plays all over diamond, including CF.

Bowman,Cooper | 46 | Oakland | EXP MLB DEBUT: 2025 | H/W: 6-0 205 | FUT: Starting 2B | 7D

Bats R Age 23	Year	Lev	Team	AB	R	H	HR	RBI	Avg	OB	Slg	OPS	bb%	ct%	Eye	SB	CS	x/h%	Iso	RC/G
2021 (4) Louisville	2021	NCAA	Louisville	191	42	56	8	22	293	369	455	825	11	83	0.72	20	4	27	162	5.72
Pwr ++	2021	Rk	FCL Yankees	9	3	4	1	1	444	444	889	1333	0	56	0.00	2	0	50	444	15.50
BAvg ++	2021	A	Tampa	93	17	22	3	22	237	317	441	758	11	72	0.42	11	1	55	204	5.13
Spd ++++	2022	A+	Hudson Valley	299	54	65	8	35	217	339	355	693	16	68	0.57	35	6	37	137	4.39
Def ++	2022	A+	Lansing	115	12	24	3	12	209	266	304	570	7	67	0.24	12	0	21	96	2.23

Outstanding athlete who was acquired from NYY at deadline. Exhibits plus speed and adept at stealing bases. Brings disciplined approach to plate and waits for pitches to drive. Can fall behind in count and be subject to weak contact. Not much power in swing, though could add loft. Mostly plays 2B with limited arm and range.

Boyd,Emaarion | 79 | Philadelphia | EXP MLB DEBUT: 2027 | H/W: 6-1 177 | FUT: Starting CF | 7D

Bats R Age 19	Year	Lev	Team	AB	R	H	HR	RBI	Avg	OB	Slg	OPS	bb%	ct%	Eye	SB	CS	x/h%	Iso	RC/G
2022 (11) HS (MS)																				
Pwr ++																				
BAvg ++																				
Spd +++++	2022	Rk	FCL Phillies	29	6	10	0	2	345	441	379	820	15	83	1.00	7	2	10	34	6.11
Def ++++	2022	A	Clearwater	7	1	3	0	0	429	429	429	857	0	100		1	0	0	0	5.47

Top-of-the-scale speedster. When combined with this natural athleticism, is a no-doubt centerfielder and stolen base threat. Question is whether there is enough batted ball quality to carve out a full-time role. A bit of physical projection left, but peppering balls into the gaps should be his focus. Unlikely to be a power threat.

Boyd,Justin | 8 | Cincinnati | EXP MLB DEBUT: 2025 | H/W: 6-0 201 | FUT: Starting OF | 7D

Bats R Age 22	Year	Lev	Team	AB	R	H	HR	RBI	Avg	OB	Slg	OPS	bb%	ct%	Eye	SB	CS	x/h%	Iso	RC/G
2022 (2) Oregon St																				
Pwr ++																				
BAvg +++	2022	NCAA	Oregon State	241	72	90	9	53	373	485	577	1061	18	76	0.90	24	7	30	203	9.48
Spd ++++	2022	Rk	ACL Reds	3	2	2	0	0	667	667	###	1667	0	100		1	0	50	333	13.79
Def +++	2022	A	Daytona	71	11	13	0	4	183	266	239	505	10	59	0.28	5	0	31	56	1.56

Athletic, RHH OF prospect reworked body and improved overall ability to slash .373/.490/.577 for Oregon State. Struggled in pro debut. Upright, closed stance with slight load to get hands to hit position. It's a linear swing plane with a gap-to-gap approach. Below average power potential. Struggled getting to hard contact in pro debut. Plus runner.

Bradley,Tucker | 79 | Kansas City | EXP MLB DEBUT: 2023 | H/W: 6-0 206 | FUT: Reserve OF | 6C

Bats L Age 24	Year	Lev	Team	AB	R	H	HR	RBI	Avg	OB	Slg	OPS	bb%	ct%	Eye	SB	CS	x/h%	Iso	RC/G
2020 FA (Georgia)																				
Pwr ++	2020	NCAA	Georgia	61	17	24	6	23	393	513	738	1251	20	95	5.00	8	1	38	344	10.94
BAvg +++	2021	A	Columbia	23	2	8	0	3	348	444	391	836	15	87	1.33	3	1	13	43	6.34
Spd +++	2021	A+	Quad Cities	307	53	86	6	42	280	367	430	797	12	75	0.55	9	1	34	150	5.70
Def +++	2022	AA	NW Arkansas	396	73	116	12	53	293	379	455	834	12	79	0.65	19	6	32	162	6.04

Hit-over-power COF posted solid season at Double-A. Solid frame at physical projection. Upright, open stance allowing hands to glide to hit position. It's a line drive oriented swing and doesn't generate great angles off the bat, depressing carry. Power is likely below-average at maturity. Average speed and an average defender. Lacks carry tool.

Breaux,Josh | 2 | New York (A) | EXP MLB DEBUT: 2023 | H/W: 6-1 220 | FUT: Starting C | 6D

Bats R Age 25	Year	Lev	Team	AB	R	H	HR	RBI	Avg	OB	Slg	OPS	bb%	ct%	Eye	SB	CS	x/h%	Iso	RC/G
2018 (2) McLennan CC	2019	A	Charleston (Sc)	199	28	54	13	49	271	322	518	840	7	70	0.25	0	0	43	246	5.90
Pwr +++	2021	A+	Hudson Valley	250	34	63	17	46	252	313	504	817	8	71	0.30	0	0	46	252	5.59
BAvg +	2021	AA	Somerset	100	14	24	6	17	240	269	500	769	4	74	0.15	1	0	58	260	4.75
Spd +	2022	AA	Somerset	211	24	43	13	29	204	270	436	706	8	70	0.30	1	0	53	232	4.09
Def +++	2022	AAA	Scranton/WB	159	20	38	6	21	239	292	403	695	7	69	0.24	1	0	32	164	4.01

Power-first RHH C prospect continues to struggle with hit tool. Strong catcher's frame with plus power potential in BP. Upright, closed stance. Drops hands triggering to hit position. Super aggressive approach with high swing-and-miss issues. Has improved work behind the plate and can stick as reserve if hit tool allows.

Brennan,Will | 789 | Cleveland | EXP MLB DEBUT: 2022 | H/W: 6-0 200 | FUT: Starting OF | 8A

Bats L Age 25	Year	Lev	Team	AB	R	H	HR	RBI	Avg	OB	Slg	OPS	bb%	ct%	Eye	SB	CS	x/h%	Iso	RC/G
2019 (8) Kansas St	2021	A+	Lake County	238	42	69	4	30	290	357	441	799	10	82	0.58	13	4	39	151	5.54
Pwr +++	2021	AA	Akron	150	28	42	2	20	280	357	360	717	11	81	0.62	2	2	19	80	4.51
BAvg ++++	2022	AA	Akron	135	16	42	4	39	311	388	504	892	11	88	1.06	5	2	40	193	6.70
Spd +++	2022	AAA	Columbus	393	53	124	9	68	316	369	471	839	8	87	0.62	15	1	32	155	5.85
Def +++	2022	MLB	Cleveland	42	6	15	1	8	357	386	500	886	5	90	0.50	2	1	20	143	6.12

Hitterish LHH OF made late MLB debut after breakout season. Short, athletic build; utilizes closed, upright swing with smooth load. Solid approach with plus contact skills and will work all fields but best at RCF gap. Power mostly pull-oriented. Should hit 20-25 HR regularly with hit tool leading way. Solid defender. Offense will carry COF role.

Brito,Juan | 4 | Cleveland | EXP MLB DEBUT: 2025 | H/W: 5-11 162 | FUT: Starting MIF | 7D

Bats B Age 21	Year	Lev	Team	AB	R	H	HR	RBI	Avg	OB	Slg	OPS	bb%	ct%	Eye	SB	CS	x/h%	Iso	RC/G
2018 FA (DR)																				
Pwr +++																				
BAvg +++																				
Spd +++	2021	Rk	ACL Rockies	88	20	26	3	11	295	398	432	830	15	76	0.71	5	4	23	136	6.08
Def +++	2022	A	Fresno	402	91	115	11	72	286	402	470	872	16	82	1.10	17	9	40	184	6.80

Switch-hitting, offensive minded MIF was acquired in Nolan Jones trade with COL this off-season. Discerning eye with good plate skills, especially from the LH side. Open, upright stance from both sides of the plate. More of a contact approach from RH side. Power to the average pull side as LHH, much less as RHH. Defensively solid at 2B.

Brown, Jr.,Eric | 6 | Milwaukee | EXP MLB DEBUT: 2025 | H/W: 5-10 190 | FUT: Starting SS | 7C

Bats R Age 22	Year	Lev	Team	AB	R	H	HR	RBI	Avg	OB	Slg	OPS	bb%	ct%	Eye	SB	CS	x/h%	Iso	RC/G
2022 (1) Coastal Carolina																				
Pwr ++																				
BAvg +++	2022	NCAA	Coastal Carolina	206	60	68	7	40	330	437	544	980	16	86	1.39	12	5	41	214	8.05
Spd +++	2022	Rk	ACL Brewers Gold	13	7	4	0	1	308	471	538	1009	24	69	1.00	4	0	75	231	9.86
Def +++	2022	A	Carolina	84	16	22	3	7	262	347	440	788	12	80	0.65	15	2	36	179	5.40

Exciting, aggressive INF who does everything relatively well. Profiles as bat-first with average power and ideal barrel control. Willing to draw walks due to keen understanding of strike zone. Runs bases hard and fast and has potential to have 15+ HR with 20+ SB. Swing path geared more toward line drives. Strong arm works at SS.

Brown,Dasan | 8 | Toronto | EXP MLB DEBUT: 2024 | H/W: 6-0 185 | FUT: Starting OF | 8D

Bats R Age 21	Year	Lev	Team	AB	R	H	HR	RBI	Avg	OB	Slg	OPS	bb%	ct%	Eye	SB	CS	x/h%	Iso	RC/G
2019 (3) HS (ON)																				
Pwr ++	2021	A	Dunedin	198	33	42	4	16	212	284	323	608	9	63	0.27	22	6	31	111	3.02
BAvg ++	2022	Rk	FCL Blue Jays	16	5	3	0	1	188	278	250	528	11	56	0.29	2	1	33	63	2.04
Spd +++++	2022	A	Dunedin	140	35	39	4	12	279	357	450	807	11	68	0.38	11	6	36	171	5.96
Def ++++	2022	A+	Vancouver	151	25	45	2	11	298	358	411	768	8	67	0.28	11	3	29	113	5.38

Best athlete in org with double plus speed. Had solid season after poor 21 and finished strong. Set high in HR, though more of a groundball guy. Lot of swing and miss in profile and struggles with pitch recognition. Starting to get on base more consistently to use speed. Has frame to add weight. Plus defender in CF with average arm.

Brown,Vaun — 79 — San Francisco

EXP MLB DEBUT: 2024 | H/W: 6-1 215 | FUT: Starting OF | 7B

Bats R | Age 24 | 2021 (10) Florida Southern

Pwr +++ | BAvg +++ | Spd ++++ | Def +++

Year	Lev	Team	AB	R	H	HR	RBI	Avg	OB	Slg	OPS	bb%	ct%	Eye	SB	CS	x/h%	Iso	RC/G
2021	NCAA	Florida Southern	111	40	43	13	31	387	447	793	1240	10	77	0.46	9	2	44	405	10.82
2021	Rk	ACL Giants O	79	24	28	2	14	354	407	620	1027	8	63	0.24	8	1	46	266	9.84
2022	A	San Jose	228	50	79	14	41	346	411	636	1047	10	71	0.37	23	3	42	289	9.07
2022	A+	Eugene	157	50	55	9	34	350	430	611	1042	12	67	0.42	21	3	38	261	9.46
2022	AA	Richmond	2	0	0	0	0	0	0	0	0	0	100		0	0		0	-2.66

Breakout prospect was great at two levels and led all minors in BA and OPS while leading org in SB. Has muscular build, but still has plus speed to go along with power. Has holes in swing and will swing and miss frequently. Doubts about BA potential are legit as he can overswing. Dominates LHP. Good corner OF with average arm.

Buelvas,Brayan — 89 — Oakland

EXP MLB DEBUT: 2025 | H/W: 5-11 155 | FUT: Starting OF | 8E

Bats R | Age 20 | 2018 FA (CB)

Pwr ++ | BAvg ++ | Spd +++ | Def +++

Year	Lev	Team	AB	R	H	HR	RBI	Avg	OB	Slg	OPS	bb%	ct%	Eye	SB	CS	x/h%	Iso	RC/G
2021	A	Stockton	347	54	76	16	50	219	294	412	706	10	73	0.39	17	7	41	193	4.20
2022	Rk	ACL Athletics	23	4	6	1	4	261	370	522	892	15	74	0.67	4	0	50	261	7.10
2022	A+	Lansing	236	28	46	7	26	195	249	352	601	7	76	0.30	7	4	48	157	2.76

Instinctual OF who missed time midyear with hamstring issue. Hasn't developed much offense despite previous accolades. Struggles with long swing and inability to read spin. Mostly goes to gaps with flat swing path. Has some power in tank, but not consistent production. Runs very well and can play CF with enough range and arm.

Bunnell,Cade — 346 — Atlanta

EXP MLB DEBUT: 2024 | H/W: 6-0 190 | FUT: Reserve IF | 6C

Bats L | Age 25 | 2019 (40) Indiana

Pwr +++ | BAvg ++ | Spd +++ | Def +++

Year	Lev	Team	AB	R	H	HR	RBI	Avg	OB	Slg	OPS	bb%	ct%	Eye	SB	CS	x/h%	Iso	RC/G
2019	NCAA	Indiana	46	7	9	1	3	196	275	283	557	10	61	0.28	0	1	22	87	2.19
2019	Rk	GCL Braves	64	17	9	1	4	141	382	203	585	28	58	0.93	0	0	22	63	2.76
2021	A	Augusta	393	78	85	17	50	216	364	433	796	19	56	0.53	13	2	55	216	6.68
2022	A+	Rome	222	36	41	7	24	185	349	315	664	20	51	0.52	3	0	34	131	4.53
2022	AA	Mississippi	146	24	44	8	32	301	424	568	992	18	60	0.53	0	1	48	267	9.66

Versatile IF prospect had a Jekyll and Hyde like season, split between High-A and Double-A. Struggled to buy contact in High-A, excelled in Double-A. Slightly closed, upright stance. Power over hit profile with solid eye and lots of swing-and-miss. LHH is a hacker with plus raw above-average power to all fields. Playable at multiple positions.

Burleson,Alec — 7 — St. Louis

EXP MLB DEBUT: 2022 | H/W: 6-2 212 | FUT: Starting OF | 8D

Bats L | Age 24 | 2020 (2) East Carolina

Pwr ++++ | BAvg +++ | Spd + | Def ++

Year	Lev	Team	AB	R	H	HR	RBI	Avg	OB	Slg	OPS	bb%	ct%	Eye	SB	CS	x/h%	Iso	RC/G
2021	A+	Peoria	42	8	12	4	10	286	375	595	970	13	64	0.40	1	0	42	310	8.28
2021	AA	Springfield	260	34	75	14	44	288	337	488	825	7	77	0.32	2	0	32	200	5.49
2021	AAA	Memphis	154	19	36	4	22	234	310	357	667	10	82	0.63	0	1	31	123	3.84
2022	AAA	Memphis	432	68	143	20	87	331	373	532	906	6	84	0.43	4	0	32	201	6.40
2022	MLB	St. Louis	48	4	9	1	3	188	264	271	535	9	81	0.56	1	0	22	83	2.14

Led all AAA hitters with .331 average en route to his MLB debut. Aggressive approach at the plate is mitigated by extreme contact skills with minimal swing-and-miss. Spread out, no-stride setup helps keep the bat in the zone with a flat bat path. Above-average power and should continue to make strides as he gains experience. Fringe defender.

Busch,Michael — 4 — Los Angeles (N)

EXP MLB DEBUT: 2023 | H/W: 6-1 210 | FUT: Starting 2B | 8D

Bats L | Age 25 | 2019 (1) North Carolina

Pwr ++++ | BAvg +++ | Spd + | Def +

Year	Lev	Team	AB	R	H	HR	RBI	Avg	OB	Slg	OPS	bb%	ct%	Eye	SB	CS	x/h%	Iso	RC/G
2019	Rk	AZL Dodgers La	13	1	1	0	0	77	143	77	220	7	85	0.50	0	0	0	0	-1.47
2019	A	Great Lakes	11	4	2	0	2	182	471	182	652	35	73	2.00	0	0	0	0	4.48
2021	AA	Tulsa	409	84	109	20	67	267	374	484	858	15	68	0.54	2	3	44	218	6.70
2022	AA	Tulsa	108	31	33	11	29	306	432	667	1098	18	67	0.67	1	0	52	361	10.28
2022	AAA	Oklahoma City	444	87	118	21	79	266	340	480	820	10	70	0.38	3	2	45	214	5.88

Uses a slightly open stance with quick LH stroke and good barrel awareness to hunt for pitches he can drive. Does have some swing-and-miss that will prevent him from being a .300 hitter, but understands the strike zone and is willing to take his walk. Has worked hard to improve defensively but for now is a player without a clear defensive position.

Butler,Lawrence — 39 — Oakland

EXP MLB DEBUT: 2025 | H/W: 6-3 210 | FUT: Starting 1B | 8D

Bats L | Age 22 | 2018 (6) HS (GA)

Pwr ++++ | BAvg +++ | Spd +++ | Def ++

Year	Lev	Team	AB	R	H	HR	RBI	Avg	OB	Slg	OPS	bb%	ct%	Eye	SB	CS	x/h%	Iso	RC/G
2019	A-	Vermont	192	20	34	4	22	177	275	286	562	12	53	0.29	1	0	32	109	2.61
2021	A	Stockton	335	62	88	17	67	263	367	499	865	14	61	0.42	26	4	47	236	7.33
2021	A+	Lansing	50	14	17	2	8	340	389	540	929	7	70	0.27	3	1	35	200	7.36
2022	Rk	ACL Athletics	9	0	1	0	0	111	111	111	222	0	56	0.00	0	0	0	0	-3.48
2022	A+	Lansing	293	52	79	11	41	270	357	468	825	12	64	0.38	13	5	42	198	6.44

Versatile prospect who missed most of 2nd half with arm injury. Got off to slow start before showcasing patient, power approach. Uses entire field and is better hitter than some suggest. Will always swing and miss, particularly with breaking balls. Can be too passive at times. Runs very well for size. Plays both 1B and outfield corners.

Caissie,Owen — 79 — Chicago (N)

EXP MLB DEBUT: 2024 | H/W: 6-4 190 | FUT: Starting OF | 7D

Bats L | Age 20 | 2020 (2) HS (ON)

Pwr +++ | BAvg ++ | Spd ++ | Def +++

Year	Lev	Team	AB	R	H	HR	RBI	Avg	OB	Slg	OPS	bb%	ct%	Eye	SB	CS	x/h%	Iso	RC/G
2021	Rk	ACL Cubs	109	20	38	6	20	349	474	596	1070	19	64	0.67	1	2	37	248	10.52
2021	A	Myrtle Beach	73	15	17	1	9	233	371	329	700	18	62	0.57	0	0	29	96	4.79
2022	A+	South Bend	378	57	96	11	58	254	341	402	743	12	67	0.40	11	6	34	148	5.02

Slightly open, upright stance with hands high pre-load. Has a moderately quick bat and plenty of raw power to all fields, but also lots of swing-and-miss within the zone. Ball jumps off his bat when he makes contact, but needs to do so more frequently. Average runner with enough arm strength to play either corner slot.

Callihan,Tyler — 45 — Cincinnati

EXP MLB DEBUT: 2024 | H/W: 6-1 205 | FUT: Reserve 3B | 6C

Bats L | Age 22 | 2019 (3) HS (FL)

Pwr ++ | BAvg +++ | Spd ++ | Def ++

Year	Lev	Team	AB	R	H	HR	RBI	Avg	OB	Slg	OPS	bb%	ct%	Eye	SB	CS	x/h%	Iso	RC/G
2019	Rk	Billings	20	3	8	1	7	400	429	650	1079	5	80	0.25	2	0	25	250	8.54
2019	Rk	Greeneville	204	27	51	5	26	250	282	422	703	4	77	0.20	9	3	39	172	4.03
2021	A	Daytona	87	14	26	2	10	299	358	437	795	8	85	0.62	5	1	31	138	5.35
2022	A	Daytona	117	18	33	3	13	282	339	419	757	8	84	0.53	9	1	30	137	4.84
2022	A+	Dayton	211	27	49	4	20	232	289	384	673	7	71	0.28	6	2	41	152	3.87

Was eased back into field after 2021 Tommy John surgery recovery. Spent season up/down between A-Ball affiliates. Hit over power prospect lacked explosion through zone with bat, contributing to dip in hard contact consistency. Short, compact swing with slight uppercut trajectory. Below average game power. Defensively challenged at 2B and 3B.

Caminero,Junior — 46 — Tampa Bay

EXP MLB DEBUT: 2025 | H/W: 5-11 157 | FUT: Starting 3B | 9D

Bats R | Age 19 | 2019 FA (DR)

Pwr ++++ | BAvg +++ | Spd +++ | Def +++

Year	Lev	Team	AB	R	H	HR	RBI	Avg	OB	Slg	OPS	bb%	ct%	Eye	SB	CS	x/h%	Iso	RC/G
2021	Rk	DSL Indians Red	146	26	43	9	33	295	380	534	914	12	81	0.71	2	0	40	240	6.85
2022	Rk	FCL Rays	132	18	43	5	31	326	395	492	887	10	84	0.71	7	1	26	167	6.47
2022	A	Charleston	107	19	32	6	20	299	348	505	852	7	79	0.36	5	0	28	206	5.79

Power hitting lower minors prospect went on power barrage in US debut. Bigger than listed height and weight. Slightly open, upright stance. Busy setup with lots of motion will need to cut down to maintain hit tool. Advanced contact skills at level. Double-plus raw power in swing and frame. Could be 30+ HR masher. Challenged defensively at SS.

Campos,Roberto — 89 — Detroit

EXP MLB DEBUT: 2025 | H/W: 6-2 200 | FUT: Starting OF | 8E

Bats R | Age 19 | 2019 FA (CU)

Pwr ++++ | BAvg ++ | Spd ++ | Def +++

Year	Lev	Team	AB	R	H	HR	RBI	Avg	OB	Slg	OPS	bb%	ct%	Eye	SB	CS	x/h%	Iso	RC/G
2021	Rk	FCL Tigers West	136	20	31	8	19	228	314	441	755	11	70	0.41	3	0	42	213	4.89
2022	A	Lakeland	403	52	104	5	50	258	325	385	710	9	76	0.41	7	3	35	127	4.40

Tooled-up prospect is already physically mature with some of the best raw power in the system, but aggressive approach and uppercut swing prevents him from getting to it in game action. Still primarily a CF, he lacks range and quickness to stick and a shift to RF seems inevitable. Still only 19, but will need to show more soon.

Canario,Alexander — 89 — Chicago (N)

EXP MLB DEBUT: 2023 | H/W: 6-1 165 | FUT: Starting OF | 8D

Bats R | Age 22 | 2016 FA (DR)

Pwr ++++ | BAvg ++ | Spd +++ | Def +++

Year	Lev	Team	AB	R	H	HR	RBI	Avg	OB	Slg	OPS	bb%	ct%	Eye	SB	CS	x/h%	Iso	RC/G
2021	A	San Jose	238	43	56	9	29	235	328	433	761	12	67	0.42	15	3	46	197	5.32
2021	A+	South Bend	170	19	38	9	28	224	267	429	696	6	73	0.22	6	5	42	206	3.83
2022	A+	South Bend	89	17	25	7	22	281	354	584	938	10	61	0.29	3	0	52	303	8.25
2022	AA	Tennessee	310	51	77	24	61	248	327	552	878	10	71	0.40	17	3	57	303	6.56
2022	AAA	Iowa	65	16	15	6	14	231	359	538	897	17	68	0.62	3	0	53	308	7.07

Plus bat speed and raw strength; makes loud contact when barrels the ball, and had a breakout 2022 where led MiLB with 37 HR. Can drift into the zone and his big load makes him beatable by high heat and soft stuff away. Above-average speed; swiped a career-best 23 bags. Major winter league injury (ankle, shoulder) will delay his 2023 season.

Canzone,Dominic — 379 — Arizona
EXP MLB DEBUT: 2023 | H/W: 6-1 190 | FUT: Starting OF | 7D

Bats L Age 25	Year	Lev	Team	AB	R	H	HR	RBI	Avg	OB	Slg	OPS	bb%	ct%	Eye	SB	CS	x/h%	Iso	RC/G
2019 (8) Ohio State	2021	A+	Hillsboro	171	22	45	7	25	263	330	468	798	9	75	0.40	18	3	40	205	5.44
Pwr +++	2021	AA	Amarillo	130	25	46	7	27	354	421	592	1013	10	78	0.54	1	1	35	238	8.14
BAvg +++	2022	Rk	ACL DBacks	8	2	2	0	1	250	333	500	833	11	63	0.33	0	0	50	250	7.24
Spd ++	2022	AA	Amarillo	55	18	22	6	20	400	476	855	1331	13	89	1.33	1	0	59	455	11.49
Def ++	2022	AAA	Reno	331	61	94	16	68	284	340	489	829	8	78	0.38	14	2	37	205	5.66

Strong 1B/OF prospect started tapping into raw power potential in 2022. Maxed out physically. Upright, open stance. Drops hands in load. Solid bat control with above-average bat speed. Aggressive approach, will expand. Handles upper velocity well, especially up in zone. Works all fields. Power to pull side and CF. Below average runner.

Cappe,Yiddi — 56 — Miami
EXP MLB DEBUT: 2025 | H/W: 6-3 175 | FUT: Starting 3B | 9E

Bats R Age 20	Year	Lev	Team	AB	R	H	HR	RBI	Avg	OB	Slg	OPS	bb%	ct%	Eye	SB	CS	x/h%	Iso	RC/G
2021 FA (CU)																				
Pwr ++++																				
BAvg +++	2021	Rk	DSL Marlins	189	31	51	2	27	270	337	402	739	9	81	0.54	9	8	39	132	4.81
Spd +++	2022	Rk	FCL Marlins	118	23	36	6	25	305	354	517	871	7	84	0.47	6	4	36	212	6.04
Def +++	2022	A	Jupiter	158	18	44	3	15	278	305	380	685	4	86	0.27	7	1	20	101	3.75

Quick twitch, athletic SS prospect dominated the complex with power game. Wiry frame with room to grow. Upright open stance with slight trigger. Plus-plus bat speed combined with plus hand/eye coordination. Struggles expanding zone. Raw plus power in swing, should get there if calms approach. Above-average runner, likely grows off SS.

Carreras,Julio — 6 — Colorado
EXP MLB DEBUT: 2024 | H/W: 6-2 190 | FUT: Starting SS | 7D

Bats R Age 23	Year	Lev	Team	AB	R	H	HR	RBI	Avg	OB	Slg	OPS	bb%	ct%	Eye	SB	CS	x/h%	Iso	RC/G
2018 FA (DR)																				
Pwr +++	2019	Rk	Grand Junction	262	51	77	5	38	294	355	466	821	9	76	0.40	14	8	35	172	5.86
BAvg ++	2021	A	Fresno	362	61	92	7	44	254	301	392	693	6	72	0.24	15	4	34	138	4.04
Spd +++	2022	A+	Spokane	402	59	116	11	59	289	339	473	812	7	74	0.29	17	5	43	184	5.67
Def ++++	2022	AA	Hartford	60	11	14	0	13	233	292	350	642	8	65	0.24	2	0	43	117	3.70

Lean, athletic player is an above-average to plus defender with good range, a quick release and enough arm to stick at short or handle 3B. Employs a high leg kick and an aggressive approach as chases power to the pull side. Approach does lead to plenty of swing-and-miss and he rarely walks, but did stroke 42 doubles and 11 home runs in 2022.

Carroll,Corbin — 8 — Arizona
EXP MLB DEBUT: 2022 | H/W: 5-10 165 | FUT: Starting CF | 10D

Bats L Age 22	Year	Lev	Team	AB	R	H	HR	RBI	Avg	OB	Slg	OPS	bb%	ct%	Eye	SB	CS	x/h%	Iso	RC/G
2019 (1) HS (WA)	2021	A+	Hillsboro	23	9	10	2	5	435	552	913	1465	21	70	0.86	3	1	50	478	15.99
Pwr ++++	2022	Rk	ACL DBacks Reds	6	2	3	1	1	500	625	###	1625	25	50	0.67	0	0	33	500	23.69
BAvg ++++	2022	AA	Amarillo	227	62	71	16	39	313	418	643	1061	15	70	0.60	20	3	49	330	9.58
Spd +++++	2022	AAA	Reno	129	25	37	7	22	287	399	535	934	16	72	0.67	11	2	49	248	7.66
Def ++++	2022	MLB	Arizona	104	13	27	4	14	260	313	500	813	7	70	0.26	2	1	56	240	5.81

Wiry athletic CF mashed his way through the upper minors to receive MLB callup. Shorter limbs aid compact swing with plus bat speed. Upright, slightly closed stance with slight load. Patient, all fields approach with natural loft off the bat. Average power in frame plays up due to swing mechanics and approach. Exceptional speed. 30/30 threat.

Cartaya,Diego — 2 — Los Angeles (N)
EXP MLB DEBUT: 2024 | H/W: 6-3 219 | FUT: Starting C | 9C

Bats R Age 21	Year	Lev	Team	AB	R	H	HR	RBI	Avg	OB	Slg	OPS	bb%	ct%	Eye	SB	CS	x/h%	Iso	RC/G
2018 FA (VZ)																				
Pwr ++++	2019	Rk	AZL Dodgers Mota	135	25	40	3	13	296	349	437	786	8	77	0.35	1	0	33	141	5.23
BAvg +++	2021	A	Rancho Cuca	114	31	34	10	31	298	394	614	1008	14	68	0.49	0	0	47	316	8.71
Spd +	2022	A	Rancho Cuca	131	31	34	9	31	260	370	550	920	15	66	0.52	0	0	56	290	7.67
Def ++++	2022	A+	Great Lakes	231	43	58	13	41	251	362	476	838	15	68	0.53	1	0	45	225	6.38

Has a good understanding of the strike zone and advanced approach at the plate, laying off balls and hunting FB. Does have some swing-and-miss, but he draws plenty of walks. Best tool is his above-average power. Moves well behind the plate with good hands, but he isn't consistent blocking balls with avg pop times, but does have a plus arm.

Carter,Evan — 8 — Texas
EXP MLB DEBUT: 2023 | H/W: 6-4 190 | FUT: Starting CF | 9C

Bats L Age 20	Year	Lev	Team	AB	R	H	HR	RBI	Avg	OB	Slg	OPS	bb%	ct%	Eye	SB	CS	x/h%	Iso	RC/G
2020 (2) HS (TN)																				
Pwr +++																				
BAvg ++++	2021	A	Down East	106	22	25	2	12	236	421	387	808	24	74	1.21	12	4	44	151	6.42
Spd ++++	2022	A+	Hickory	376	78	108	11	66	287	384	476	860	14	80	0.79	26	12	36	189	6.50
Def +++	2022	AA	Frisco	21	8	9	1	7	429	538	714	1253	19	71	0.83	2	1	44	286	12.66

He continued to show one of the most polished toolsets in the game through two levels in 2022. Long arms belie exceptional plate coverage and zone awareness, as most guys this tall struggle with swing holes. Lanky, frame portends more power to come. Plus speed works both in OF and on bases. At least average defensively in CF.

Casas,Triston — 3 — Boston
EXP MLB DEBUT: 2022 | H/W: 6-4 252 | FUT: Starting 1B | 8A

Bats L Age 23	Year	Lev	Team	AB	R	H	HR	RBI	Avg	OB	Slg	OPS	bb%	ct%	Eye	SB	CS	x/h%	Iso	RC/G
2018 (1) HS (FL)	2021	AA	Portland	275	57	78	13	52	284	392	484	876	15	77	0.78	6	3	35	200	6.67
Pwr ++++	2021	AAA	Worcester	33	6	8	1	7	242	390	485	875	20	76	1.00	1	0	63	242	7.13
BAvg +++	2022	Rk	FCL Red Sox	14	3	6	1	3	429	529	857	1387	18	86	1.50	0	0	67	429	13.02
Spd +	2022	AAA	Worcester	264	45	72	11	38	273	381	481	862	15	74	0.68	0	0	44	208	6.61
Def +++	2022	MLB	Boston	76	11	15	5	12	197	358	408	766	20	70	0.83	1	0	40	211	5.25

Huge-framed slugger who reached BOS thanks to mature approach and mammoth power. Could evolve into 35+ HR monster with middle of order skills. Uses entire field and solid understanding of strike zone enhances offensive package. Hasn't been great in BA department yet due to struggles with LHP. Sound defender with soft hands and strong arm.

Cavaco,Keoni — 5 — Minnesota
EXP MLB DEBUT: 2025 | H/W: 6-2 195 | FUT: Starting 3B | 7E

Bats R Age 21	Year	Lev	Team	AB	R	H	HR	RBI	Avg	OB	Slg	OPS	bb%	ct%	Eye	SB	CS	x/h%	Iso	RC/G
2019 (1) HS (CA)																				
Pwr ++	2019	Rk	GCL Twins	87	9	15	1	6	172	209	253	462	4	60	0.11	1	1	33	80	0.68
BAvg ++	2021	Rk	FCL Twins	9	2	2	0	2	222	300	333	633	10	67	0.33	1	0	50	111	3.59
Spd +++	2021	A	Fort Myers	236	27	55	2	24	233	287	301	588	7	62	0.20	5	2	18	68	2.71
Def +++	2022	A	Fort Myers	368	34	85	11	59	231	274	397	671	6	63	0.16	7	4	40	166	3.95

Repeated Low-A and set easy high in HR, but still poor year overall. Finished with 6th lowest OPS in FSL and continues to struggle with plate approach. Raw tools are very impressive, highlighted by plus power. Rarely draws walks and swing mechanics still crude. Hits LHP well. Solid defensive 3B with strong arm.

Cedeno,Nerwilian — 4 — San Diego
EXP MLB DEBUT: 2026 | H/W: 5-11 175 | FUT: Utility player | 7D

Bats B Age 21	Year	Lev	Team	AB	R	H	HR	RBI	Avg	OB	Slg	OPS	bb%	ct%	Eye	SB	CS	x/h%	Iso	RC/G
2018 FA (VZ)																				
Pwr ++																				
BAvg ++																				
Spd +++	2021	Rk	ACL Padres	54	8	13	2	7	241	349	537	886	14	63	0.45	2	0	85	296	7.78
Def +++	2022	A	Lake Elsinore	270	60	69	6	54	256	356	400	756	13	71	0.53	18	8	33	144	5.24

Short, lean INF who had solid campaign in Low-A. Has played 1B and SS previously, but now mostly at 2B. Has average defensive skills with enough range, quickness and arm to be adept. Has added strength to frame and starting to make harder contact. Focuses on line drives to gaps with occasional pull power. Exhibits average speed.

Cerda,Allan — 89 — Cincinnati
EXP MLB DEBUT: 2023 | H/W: 6-3 170 | FUT: Reserve OF | 6C

Bats R Age 23	Year	Lev	Team	AB	R	H	HR	RBI	Avg	OB	Slg	OPS	bb%	ct%	Eye	SB	CS	x/h%	Iso	RC/G
2017 FA (NY)	2019	Rk	Greeneville	132	22	29	9	27	220	322	470	792	13	58	0.36	2	2	52	250	6.17
Pwr ++++	2021	A	Daytona	227	42	55	14	42	242	333	524	858	12	63	0.36	1	7	58	282	6.97
BAvg +	2021	A+	Dayton	77	15	21	3	13	273	356	519	876	11	74	0.50	1	1	57	247	6.74
Spd +++	2022	A+	Dayton	201	38	44	13	31	219	354	488	841	17	55	0.46	3	3	61	269	7.49
Def +++	2022	AA	Chattanooga	207	36	41	11	25	198	333	401	734	17	63	0.55	4	1	49	203	5.00

Power-first OF prospect continued struggles with hit tool across two levels in '23. Discerning eye prevents OBP from bottoming out. Uppercut trajectory guides power tool. Hit 24 HR between 2 levels. Contact issues plus fly ball rates killing BABIP cause of low BA. Above-average runner with plus arm. Defensively fits best in RF.

Cermak,Ryan — 89 — Tampa Bay
EXP MLB DEBUT: 2025 | H/W: 6-1 205 | FUT: Starting CF | 8E

Bats R Age 21	Year	Lev	Team	AB	R	H	HR	RBI	Avg	OB	Slg	OPS	bb%	ct%	Eye	SB	CS	x/h%	Iso	RC/G
2022 (2) Illinois St																				
Pwr +++																				
BAvg +++																				
Spd ++++	2022	NCAA	Illinois St	194	45	66	19	43	340	429	696	1124	13	77	0.68	8	1	47	356	9.60
Def ++++	2022	Rk	FCL Rays	22	5	6	2	5	273	304	636	941	4	59	0.11	3	0	50	364	8.34

Speedy collegiate OF was drafted in 2022 during Competitive Balance Round B. Athletic frame with room to add additional lean muscle. Upright stance with noisy trigger to hit position. Above-average bat speed with uppercut trajectory. Impacted ball better in 2022. Raw plus power plays as average now, could get to more. Speedy runner. Sticks in CF.

Cerny, Logan — 8 — Houston

EXP MLB DEBUT: 2025 | H/W: 6-1 185 | FUT: Utility player | 6C

Bats R Age 23
2021 (10) Troy
Pwr ++
BAvg +++
Spd +++
Def +++

Year	Lev	Team	AB	R	H	HR	RBI	Avg	OB	Slg	OPS	bb%	ct%	Eye	SB	CS	x/h%	Iso	RC/G
2020	NCAA	Troy	31	8	6	2	7	194	359	419	778	21	45	0.47	0	1	50	226	7.43
2021	NCAA	Troy	193	49	64	15	47	332	414	694	1108	12	66	0.41	12	3	56	363	10.55
2021	Rk	FCL Phillies	20	6	5	0	2	250	423	400	823	23	60	0.75	6	1	40	150	7.36
2021	A	Clearwater	15	1	2	0	0	133	235	133	369	12	73	0.50	0	1	0	0	-0.23
2022	A	Fayetteville	316	59	80	15	54	253	350	472	821	13	65	0.43	35	7	44	218	6.28

OF prospect showed power/speed production at Single-A. Selective at plate but subpar contact skills drive up Ks, drag down BA. Upward swing plane results in pulled fly balls. Plus raw speed supports stolen base success, future in CF. Toolsy, but hit tool lags behind.

Cespedes, Yoelqui — 89 — Chicago (A)

EXP MLB DEBUT: 2023 | H/W: 5-9 205 | FUT: Starting OF | 7D

Bats R Age 25
2021 FA (CU)
Pwr +++
BAvg ++
Spd +++
Def +++

Year	Lev	Team	AB	R	H	HR	RBI	Avg	OB	Slg	OPS	bb%	ct%	Eye	SB	CS	x/h%	Iso	RC/G
2021	A+	Salem	176	34	49	7	20	278	328	494	822	7	68	0.23	10	2	49	216	5.97
2021	AA	Birmingham	94	14	28	1	7	298	320	404	724	3	71	0.11	8	4	21	106	4.33
2022	AA	Birmingham	458	65	118	17	59	258	302	437	739	6	66	0.19	33	12	40	179	4.75

Powerful, athletic OF struggled with swing decisions and whiffs in 2022. Shorter statured, he applies open stance with slight load. Struggles with aggression and heavy pull approach. Raw plus power doesn't play due to holes in hit tool. Piles up strikeouts during low points. Above-average runner handles CF well. 20/20 upside.

Charles, Austin — 6 — Kansas City

EXP MLB DEBUT: 2026 | H/W: 6-6 215 | FUT: Starting OF | 7E

Bats R Age 19
2022 (20) HS (CA)
Pwr +++
BAvg +++
Spd +++
Def +++

Year	Lev	Team	AB	R	H	HR	RBI	Avg	OB	Slg	OPS	bb%	ct%	Eye	SB	CS	x/h%	Iso	RC/G
2022	Rk	ACL Royals Blue	11	1	3	0	0	273	273	273	545	0	64	0.00	0	0	0	0	1.70

Tall, athletic raw MIF with huge frame; has tremendous room to add bulk. Open, upright stance with uppercut oriented swing plane. Long levers struggle covering the zone causing present whiff risk. It's plus raw power if physique and swing develops. Size likely forces move off dirt where athleticism will play in COF.

Cho, Won-Bin — 7 — St. Louis

EXP MLB DEBUT: 2026 | H/W: 6-3 200 | FUT: Starting OF | 7D

Bats L Age 19
2022 FA (KR)
Pwr +++
BAvg ++
Spd +++
Def +++

Year	Lev	Team	AB	R	H	HR	RBI	Avg	OB	Slg	OPS	bb%	ct%	Eye	SB	CS	x/h%	Iso	RC/G
2022	Rk	FCL Cardinals	76	10	16	1	3	211	375	316	691	21	64	0.74	6	4	31	105	4.64

Korean OF opted to sign out of HS instead of starting his career in the KBO. Has good size and athleticism, but is raw in some aspects of the game. Plus bat speed and above-average raw power from a tall, projectable frame. Mixed results in pro debut, but did show solid plate discipline. Runs well and with an above-average arm and RF seems like his future home.

Chourio, Jackson — 8 — Milwaukee

EXP MLB DEBUT: 2024 | H/W: 6-1 165 | FUT: Starting CF | 9C

Bats R Age 19
2021 FA (VZ)
Pwr ++++
BAvg +++
Spd ++++
Def +++

Year	Lev	Team	AB	R	H	HR	RBI	Avg	OB	Slg	OPS	bb%	ct%	Eye	SB	CS	x/h%	Iso	RC/G
2021	Rk	DSL Brewers 2	159	31	47	5	25	296	385	447	831	13	82	0.82	8	3	28	151	5.99
2022	A	Carolina	250	51	81	12	47	324	372	600	972	7	70	0.25	10	2	49	276	8.06
2022	A+	Wisconsin	127	24	32	8	24	252	312	488	800	8	76	0.35	4	1	44	236	5.24
2022	AA	Biloxi	23	0	2	0	4	87	160	130	290	8	52	0.18	2	1	50	43	-2.33

Elite prospect who reached AA at age 18 in first year in US. Has explosive athleticism that appears in swing mechanics, CF defense and on base. Plays game with aggression and has elite bat speed and major power potential. Whips bat thru zone and makes easy contact. Can expand zone at times. Only fringy arm strength is question mark.

Chourio, Jaison — 8 — Cleveland

EXP MLB DEBUT: 2027 | H/W: 6-1 162 | FUT: Starting CF | 7E

Bats B Age 17
2022 FA (VZ)
Pwr +++
BAvg +++
Spd +++
Def +++

Year	Lev	Team	AB	R	H	HR	RBI	Avg	OB	Slg	OPS	bb%	ct%	Eye	SB	CS	x/h%	Iso	RC/G
2022	Rk	DSL Indians 2	132	32	37	1	28	280	448	402	849	23	83	1.82	14	4	30	121	7.03

Switch-hitting brother of Brewers prospect Jackson made professional debut in DSL. Wiry frame with room to grow. Crouching, open stance with easy load, gets to hit position quickly. Swing plane is flat and struggled getting to consistent hard contact. Discerning eye with solid plate skills overall. Above-average defender with chance for CF.

Clarke, Denzel — 8 — Oakland

EXP MLB DEBUT: 2024 | H/W: 6-5 220 | FUT: Starting CF | 8D

Bats R Age 22
2021 (4) Cal St Northridge
Pwr +++
BAvg ++
Spd ++++
Def +++

Year	Lev	Team	AB	R	H	HR	RBI	Avg	OB	Slg	OPS	bb%	ct%	Eye	SB	CS	x/h%	Iso	RC/G
2020	NCAA	CSUN	40	12	16	3	9	400	467	775	1242	11	63	0.33	5	2	50	375	13.16
2021	NCAA	CSUN	142	30	46	8	25	324	429	570	999	15	72	0.65	15	2	41	246	8.58
2021	Rk	ACL Athletics	19	2	6	1	1	316	409	579	988	14	68	0.50	1	2	50	263	8.64
2022	A	Stockton	156	37	46	7	26	295	402	545	947	15	64	0.50	14	2	50	250	8.51
2022	A+	Lansing	187	30	39	8	21	209	312	406	718	13	58	0.35	16	1	49	198	5.08

Elite athlete with as much speed as any in org. Very rough around edges and needs major polish. Plate approach needs work and swing can get out of whack. Natural tools are outstanding. Puts significant charge into ball and has plus power potential. Can go to opposite field with quick stroke. Should stick in CF with quality routes.

Clase, Jonatan — 8 — Seattle

EXP MLB DEBUT: 2024 | H/W: 5-8 150 | FUT: Starting CF | 7D

Bats B Age 20
2018 FA (DR)
Pwr ++
BAvg +++
Spd ++++
Def +++

Year	Lev	Team	AB	R	H	HR	RBI	Avg	OB	Slg	OPS	bb%	ct%	Eye	SB	CS	x/h%	Iso	RC/G
2021	Rk	ACL Mariners	49	12	12	2	10	245	327	388	715	11	69	0.40	16	0	25	143	4.37
2022	A	Modesto	423	91	113	13	49	267	365	463	828	13	69	0.49	55	10	41	196	6.36

Emerging, athletic OF who led CAL and org in SB in breakout campaign. Best attributes are speed and strike zone awareness. Gets on base at high clip and leverages double-plus speed. Has limited size in diminutive frame and generates fringy power. Has sufficient range to stick in CF with average arm. Needs to add strength.

Clifford, Ryan — 7 — Houston

EXP MLB DEBUT: 2026 | H/W: 6-3 200 | FUT: Starting OF | 7D

Bats L Age 19
2022 (11) HS (NC)
Pwr +++
BAvg +++
Spd +
Def ++

Year	Lev	Team	AB	R	H	HR	RBI	Avg	OB	Slg	OPS	bb%	ct%	Eye	SB	CS	x/h%	Iso	RC/G
2022	Rk	FCL Astros O	36	8	8	1	5	222	417	389	806	25	56	0.75	2	0	50	167	7.06
2022	A	Fayetteville	41	5	11	1	5	268	412	390	802	20	63	0.67	0	0	27	122	6.37

OF prospect signed away from Vanderbilt commit. Exhibits impressive contact ability and smooth left-handed swing to project for above average hit tool and showed mature patience at plate in small-sample pro debut. Moderate bat speed and present physical maturity limit power projection.

Coffey, Cutter — 45 — Boston

EXP MLB DEBUT: 2026 | H/W: 6-2 190 | FUT: Starting 3B | 8E

Bats R Age 18
2022 (2) HS (CA)
Pwr ++
BAvg ++
Spd ++
Def +++

Year	Lev	Team	AB	R	H	HR	RBI	Avg	OB	Slg	OPS	bb%	ct%	Eye	SB	CS	x/h%	Iso	RC/G
2022	Rk	FCL Red Sox	32	7	4	0	0	125	282	156	438	18	66	0.64	1	0	25	31	0.59

Promising, athletic INF with good tools and potential to be above average in several categories. Versatile defender with premium arm strength, though may not have enough range for SS. Not particularly fast, but is good baserunner. Swings a quick bat and has good strength at present. Struggles with long swing and contact.

Colas, Oscar — 89 — Chicago (A)

EXP MLB DEBUT: 2023 | H/W: 6-1 209 | FUT: Starting OF | 8C

Bats L Age 24
2022 FA (CU)
Pwr ++++
BAvg +++
Spd +++
Def +++

Year	Lev	Team	AB	R	H	HR	RBI	Avg	OB	Slg	OPS	bb%	ct%	Eye	SB	CS	x/h%	Iso	RC/G
2022	A+	Winston-Salem	244	37	76	7	42	311	368	475	844	8	78	0.41	1	1	30	164	5.98
2022	AA	Birmingham	206	39	63	14	33	306	350	563	913	6	74	0.26	1	2	38	257	6.70
2022	AAA	Charlotte	31	5	12	2	4	387	424	645	1069	6	61	0.17	1	1	33	258	10.20

Power-hitting, former Cuban pro player made MiLB debut after 3 years out of baseball. Open stance with an easy load and quick, linear swing that gets to hard contact, especially middle-in. Struggled with spin as competition improved and aggressive approach was exposed. Needs a swing tweak to get to raw plus power. Profiles best in RF.

Collier,Cam

5 | Cincinnati | EXP MLB DEBUT: 2025 | H/W: 6-2 210 | FUT: Starting 3B | 9E

Bats L Age 18
2022 (1) Chipola JC
Pwr ++++
BAvg ++++
Spd +++
Def +++

Year	Lev	Team	AB	R	H	HR	RBI	Avg	OB	Slg	OPS	bb%	ct%	Eye	SB	CS	x/h%	Iso	RC/G
2022	NJCAA	Chipola	177	35	59	8	47	333	416	537	953	12	81	0.76	5	0	34	203	7.44
2022	Rk	ACL Reds	27	7	10	2	4	370	500	630	1130	21	78	1.17	0	2	30	259	10.19

Sweet-swinging teenage 3B prospect bet on self by enrolling in junior college 2 years early to get drafted in '22 1st round. It's an open, upright stance with a short, compact uppercut swing. He cleaned up his load during '22 season. Advanced approach for age, will work up the middle and to pull side for power. Plus power at projection.

Colmenarez,Carlos

46 | Tampa Bay | EXP MLB DEBUT: 2026 | H/W: 5-10 170 | FUT: Starting SS | 7E

Bats L Age 19
2021 FA (VZ)
Pwr ++
BAvg +++
Spd ++++
Def +++

Year	Lev	Team	AB	R	H	HR	RBI	Avg	OB	Slg	OPS	bb%	ct%	Eye	SB	CS	x/h%	Iso	RC/G
2021	Rk	DSL Rays	97	7	24	0	12	247	305	289	593	8	69	0.27	7	6	13	41	2.74
2022	Rk	FCL Rays	126	36	32	1	19	254	343	381	724	12	67	0.41	13	2	34	127	4.92

Former top international free agent signing has solid but unspectacular US debut. Athletic frame with some room to grow. Slight open stance with busy load and big leg kick. Linear swing plane with nothing really standing out offensive game. Below-average power potential. Slick defender at SS. Plus runner with SB potential carrying fantasy profile.

Conine,Griffin

79 | Miami | EXP MLB DEBUT: 2024 | H/W: 6-1 210 | FUT: Reserve OF | 6C

Bats L Age 25
2018 (2) Duke
Pwr ++++
BAvg +
Spd ++
Def +++

Year	Lev	Team	AB	R	H	HR	RBI	Avg	OB	Slg	OPS	bb%	ct%	Eye	SB	CS	x/h%	Iso	RC/G
2018	A-	Vancouver	206	24	49	7	30	238	302	427	729	8	69	0.30	5	0	47	189	4.65
2019	A	Lansing	304	59	86	22	64	283	363	576	938	11	59	0.30	2	0	50	293	8.57
2021	A+	Beloit	235	45	58	23	59	247	370	587	957	16	56	0.45	3	0	55	340	9.13
2021	AA	Pensacola	159	18	28	13	25	176	234	447	680	7	48	0.15	0	1	61	270	5.01
2022	AA	Pensacola	414	55	89	24	74	215	334	435	769	15	56	0.40	1	1	46	220	6.01

Power-hitting LHH, son of former Marlins All-star Jeff, continues to struggle with limited contact tool. Powerful frame is at physical projection. Open, upright stance features bat wrap that compromises swing reactions. Above-average bat speed with uppercut swing trajectory. Plus power in swing and frame. 30% in zone whiff rate haunts profile.

Conley,Cal

6 | Atlanta | EXP MLB DEBUT: 2024 | H/W: 5-10 185 | FUT: Utility player | 6B

Bats B Age 23
2021 (4) Texas Tech
Pwr ++
BAvg +++
Spd +++
Def ++++

Year	Lev	Team	AB	R	H	HR	RBI	Avg	OB	Slg	OPS	bb%	ct%	Eye	SB	CS	x/h%	Iso	RC/G
2020	NCAA	Texas Tech	70	15	26	3	24	371	436	643	1079	10	84	0.73	5	0	46	271	8.87
2021	NCAA	Texas Tech	225	46	74	15	55	329	386	587	973	9	83	0.55	7	1	38	258	7.29
2021	A	Augusta	140	21	30	2	9	214	286	307	593	9	76	0.42	8	3	27	93	2.80
2022	A	Augusta	309	62	76	10	40	246	302	414	717	7	81	0.42	23	7	34	168	4.30
2022	A+	Rome	177	32	46	6	25	260	332	429	761	10	72	0.38	13	1	37	169	5.05

Switch-hitting, versatile MIF performed solidly across lower level affiliates. Shorter statured; close to physical projection. Slight open stance with short trigger. Compact swing. All fields approach from LH side. Up-the-middle approach from RH side. Below-average power projection. Power plays only to pull field. Defensively skilled SS.

Consuegra,Stanley

89 | New York (N) | EXP MLB DEBUT: 2024 | H/W: 6-2 167 | FUT: Starting OF | 7E

Bats R Age 22
2017 FA (DR)
Pwr +++
BAvg ++
Spd +++
Def ++++

Year	Lev	Team	AB	R	H	HR	RBI	Avg	OB	Slg	OPS	bb%	ct%	Eye	SB	CS	x/h%	Iso	RC/G
2018	Rk	DSL Mets 2	52	9	10	2	13	192	311	365	677	15	90	1.80	5	0	40	173	4.42
2018	Rk	GCL Mets	189	23	41	2	26	217	282	344	625	8	78	0.41	4	4	41	127	3.31
2021	Rk	FCL Mets	74	10	20	2	10	270	308	500	808	5	72	0.19	3	3	60	230	5.68
2022	A	St. Lucie	255	38	64	8	32	251	320	431	752	9	70	0.34	8	8	41	180	5.00
2022	A+	Brooklyn	226	33	54	5	27	239	295	381	676	7	73	0.29	4	2	37	142	3.83

Physically strong OF prospect has struggled with whiffs despite putting together solid lower minors campaign. Athletic frame with still room to grow into raw plus power profile. Hitchy load creates issues reacting to pitches. Plus bat speed, will extend early, sometimes going out and around the baseball. Sells out for pull power. Versatile OF.

Corona,Kenedy

789 | Houston | EXP MLB DEBUT: 2025 | H/W: 5-11 185 | FUT: Reserve OF | 6C

Bats R Age 23
2019 FA (VZ)
Pwr ++
BAvg ++
Spd ++
Def +++

Year	Lev	Team	AB	R	H	HR	RBI	Avg	OB	Slg	OPS	bb%	ct%	Eye	SB	CS	x/h%	Iso	RC/G
2019	Rk	GCL Mets	151	35	47	5	21	311	381	483	864	10	83	0.68	11	2	32	172	6.25
2019	A-	Brooklyn	3	1	0	0	1	0	500	0	500	50	33	1.50	0	0	###	0	-2.18
2021	A	Fayetteville	201	30	49	2	22	244	293	343	636	7	74	0.26	19	7	31	100	3.29
2022	A	Fayetteville	165	32	43	9	30	261	344	491	835	11	74	0.49	8	2	44	230	5.98
2022	A+	Asheville	245	56	71	10	37	290	363	498	861	10	74	0.44	20	6	39	208	6.37

OF prospect had productive season across Single-A and High-A. Close to maxed-out frame, generates power from muscular lower-half in lieu of limited bat speed. Good runner in OF but inefficient on base paths. Level swing-plane results in high GB%. Decent contact skills, does good job fighting off outside pitches. Profiles as "sum-of-his-parts" OF.

Cowser,Colton

8 | Baltimore | EXP MLB DEBUT: 2023 | H/W: 6-3 195 | FUT: Starting CF | 8B

Bats L Age 23
2021 (1) Sam Houston St
Pwr +++
BAvg +++
4.23 Spd ++++
Def +++

Year	Lev	Team	AB	R	H	HR	RBI	Avg	OB	Slg	OPS	bb%	ct%	Eye	SB	CS	x/h%	Iso	RC/G
2021	Rk	FCL Orioles Orange	22	8	11	1	8	500	560	773	1333	12	82	0.75	3	2	36	273	12.20
2021	A	Delmarva	98	22	34	1	26	347	467	429	895	18	81	1.16	4	2	18	82	7.27
2022	A+	Aberdeen	229	42	59	4	22	258	380	410	790	16	66	0.57	16	1	42	153	6.11
2022	AA	Bowie	176	49	60	10	33	341	453	568	1021	17	68	0.63	2	2	33	227	9.25
2022	AAA	Norfolk Tides	105	23	23	5	11	219	305	429	734	11	64	0.34	0	0	52	210	4.90

In first full pro season, shot up through three levels to the cusp of MLB. Has a solid, balanced swing and makes hard contact. Advanced approach, though can be too passive at times and strikes out more than one would expect, especially via whiffs in the zone. Better than advertised in CF; not a burner, but could stay there. Has the bat for a corner.

Cox,Brenner

7 | Washington | EXP MLB DEBUT: 2027 | H/W: 6-3 195 | FUT: Starting CF | 8E

Bats L Age 18
2022 (4) HS (TX)
Pwr ++
BAvg +++
Spd ++++
Def +++

Year	Lev	Team	AB	R	H	HR	RBI	Avg	OB	Slg	OPS	bb%	ct%	Eye	SB	CS	x/h%	Iso	RC/G
2022	Rk	FCL Nationals	35	4	10	1	5	286	375	400	775	13	60	0.36	2	0	20	114	5.88

Two-sport athlete signed away from a University of Texas committment. Owns a classic lefty swing with tools aplenty, including projectable power, a feel to hit, speed and range to stay in CF, and RF arm strength if he needed to move. Held his own in 10 complex-level games; could repeat that level in 2023 as he needs reps. On the rise.

Crawford,Justin

8 | Philadelphia | EXP MLB DEBUT: 2026 | H/W: 6-3 175 | FUT: Starting CF | 8D

Bats L Age 19
2022 (1) HS (NV)
Pwr ++
BAvg ++
Spd ++++
Def ++++

Year	Lev	Team	AB	R	H	HR	RBI	Avg	OB	Slg	OPS	bb%	ct%	Eye	SB	CS	x/h%	Iso	RC/G
2022	Rk	FCL Phillies	37	6	11	0	5	297	381	351	732	12	84	0.83	8	3	9	54	4.89
2022	A	Clearwater	21	2	3	0	0	143	217	143	360	9	57	0.22	2	1	0	0	-1.08

Classic prep athlete befitting of Carl Crawford's son. Projectable frame, tons of speed, good routes and overall plus glove in center field. Quality of hit tool less certain; ground-ball heavy and lots of whiffs in teeny Low-A sample. Could add strength for a bit more pop, though unlikely to exceed average power. Needs more polish/reps.

Crooks,Jimmy

2 | St. Louis | EXP MLB DEBUT: 2025 | H/W: 6-1 210 | FUT: Starting C | 7E

Bats L Age 21
2022 (4) Oklahoma
Pwr +++
BAvg ++
Spd ++
Def ++

Year	Lev	Team	AB	R	H	HR	RBI	Avg	OB	Slg	OPS	bb%	ct%	Eye	SB	CS	x/h%	Iso	RC/G
2022	NCAA	Oklahoma	249	49	76	9	51	305	408	506	914	15	77	0.75	10	4	41	201	7.27
2022	A	Palm Beach	79	12	21	3	7	266	363	468	831	13	72	0.55	0	0	38	203	6.19

4th rounder had a solid pro debut at Low-A. Strong, stocky frame and has worked hard to improve behind the dish. Blocks and receives the ball well, but is not particularly agile while arm is just a tick above-average. Lack of elite bad speed means he hunts for balls he can crush to the pull-side and can be beat by high heat and breaking balls away.

Cross,Gavin

8 | Kansas City | EXP MLB DEBUT: 2024 | H/W: 6-3 210 | FUT: Starting OF | 9D

Bats L Age 22
2022 (1) Virginia Tech
Pwr ++++
BAvg +++
Spd +++
Def +++

Year	Lev	Team	AB	R	H	HR	RBI	Avg	OB	Slg	OPS	bb%	ct%	Eye	SB	CS	x/h%	Iso	RC/G
2022	NCAA	Virginia Tech	244	70	80	17	50	328	401	660	1061	11	83	0.73	12	0	49	332	8.61
2022	Rk	ACL Royals Blue	10	4	5	1	3	500	583	###	1583	17	80	1.00	0	0	60	500	15.76
2022	A	Columbia	99	20	29	7	22	293	421	596	1017	18	69	0.71	4	2	48	303	9.12

Athletic, power hitting OF prospect made pro debut after '22 1st round selection. Upright, stiff open stance with minimal load; gets into swing seamlessly. Solid hit tool foundation should limit BA crash due to power sell out. Plus raw power plays due to steep launch angle and strength in frame. Above-average runner with 10-15 SB potential.

Crouch,Josh

2 | **Detroit** | EXP MLB DEBUT: 2024 | H/W: 6-0 200 | FUT: Starting C | **7D**

Bats R Age 24
2021 (11) Central Florida

- Pwr + +
- BAvg + +
- Spd + +
- Def + + +

Year	Lev	Team	AB	R	H	HR	RBI	Avg	OB	Slg	OPS	bb%	ct%	Eye	SB	CS	x/h%	Iso	RC/G
2021	NCAA	Central Florida	209	45	65	15	36	311	419	574	994	16	80	0.95	0	1	38	263	8.03
2021	A	Lakeland	87	12	20	2	16	230	272	333	605	5	64	0.16	0	0	20	103	2.78
2022	A	Lakeland	36	7	12	0	5	333	415	417	831	12	72	0.50	0	0	25	83	6.34
2022	A+	West Michigan	335	43	97	10	61	290	362	445	807	10	83	0.68	1	0	33	155	5.56
2022	AA	Erie	24	1	4	1	4	167	167	292	458	0	75	0.00	0	0	25	125	0.44

Breakout performance in full-season debut. Worked hard to improve on both sides of the ball. Body is lean and strong and improved blocking and receiving make him an above-average defender. Removed leg kick to shorten stroke and made more contact. All-fields approach should allow him to hit for average and power. Gets the most out of average tools.

Crow-Armstrong,Pete

8 | **Chicago (N)** | EXP MLB DEBUT: 2024 | H/W: 6-0 184 | FUT: Starting CF | **8B**

Bats L Age 20
2020 (1) HS (CA)

- Pwr + + +
- BAvg + + + +
- Spd + + + +
- Def + + + +

Year	Lev	Team	AB	R	H	HR	RBI	Avg	OB	Slg	OPS	bb%	ct%	Eye	SB	CS	x/h%	Iso	RC/G
2021	A	St. Lucie	24	6	10	0	4	417	548	500	1048	23	75	1.17	2	3	20	83	9.90
2022	A	Myrtle Beach	158	39	56	7	27	354	433	557	990	12	79	0.67	13	4	27	203	7.98
2022	A+	South Bend	265	50	76	9	34	287	323	498	821	5	74	0.20	19	7	41	211	5.65

Breakout campaign in full-season debut after coming over in Baez deal. Smooth LH stroke and simple approach enable him to stay on time against velo and handle off-speed offerings, but struggled with contact once moved up to A+. Plus speed and defense along with ability to get on base, make him an ideal top-of-the-order bat. Potential Gold Glove D.

Cruz,Armando

6 | **Washington** | EXP MLB DEBUT: 2026 | H/W: 5-10 160 | FUT: Starting SS | **7D**

Bats R Age 19
2021 FA (DR)

- Pwr +
- BAvg + +
- Spd + +
- Def + + + + +

Year	Lev	Team	AB	R	H	HR	RBI	Avg	OB	Slg	OPS	bb%	ct%	Eye	SB	CS	x/h%	Iso	RC/G
2021	Rk	DSL Nationals	177	22	41	1	17	232	295	305	600	8	85	0.59	11	4	24	73	3.11
2022	Rk	FCL Nationals	207	41	57	2	20	275	312	362	674	5	81	0.28	6	5	21	87	3.70
2022	A	Fredericksburg	15	3	4	0	2	267	353	333	686	12	87	1.00	0	0	25	67	4.41

Does everything in the field; makes both the flashy plays and the routine look easy from SS. His bat, however, is the big question. He makes ample contact with quick hands, but right now does not have the strength to do damage. Still a teenager, lots of time to improve, but needs physicality to make his mark.

Cruz,Trei

56 | **Detroit** | EXP MLB DEBUT: 2024 | H/W: 6-2 204 | FUT: Reserve IF | **6C**

Bats B Age 24
2020 (3) Rice

- Pwr + +
- BAvg + +
- Spd + + +
- Def + + +

Year	Lev	Team	AB	R	H	HR	RBI	Avg	OB	Slg	OPS	bb%	ct%	Eye	SB	CS	x/h%	Iso	RC/G
2021	Rk	FCL Tigers East	4	0	1	0	0	250	250	500	750	0	75	0.00	0	0	100	250	4.87
2021	A	Lakeland	111	23	18	2	9	162	354	288	642	23	72	1.06	11	2	50	126	3.91
2021	A+	West Michigan	82	10	13	0	6	159	337	244	580	21	57	0.63	1	1	46	85	2.99
2022	A+	West Michigan	386	63	90	8	52	233	359	365	725	16	71	0.68	15	4	34	132	4.89
2022	AA	Erie	25	3	5	0	0	200	333	200	533	17	72	0.71	1	0	0	0	2.17

Toolsy switch-hitter has yet to click. Patient approach with good strike zone awareness and improved contact, but lacks bat speed to tap into above-average raw power. Average runner/range with a solid arm split time between SS and 3B, but lacks the power necessary for 3B and could end up in UT role.

Cueva,Danyer

6 | **Texas** | EXP MLB DEBUT: 2027 | H/W: 6-1 160 | FUT: Reserve OF | **6C**

Bats L Age 18
2021 FA (VZ)

- Pwr + +
- BAvg +
- Spd + +
- Def +

Year	Lev	Team	AB	R	H	HR	RBI	Avg	OB	Slg	OPS	bb%	ct%	Eye	SB	CS	x/h%	Iso	RC/G
2021	Rk	DSL Rangers	202	48	57	1	25	282	353	381	734	10	76	0.46	9	4	26	99	4.78
2022	Rk	ACL Rangers	176	39	58	5	31	330	366	483	849	5	77	0.25	3	2	28	153	5.85
2022	A	Down East	18	0	2	0	0	111	111	111	222	0	72	0.00	0	0	0	0	-2.62

Big '21 International signing looks maxed out; unlikely to profile beyond the keystone. Limited power anchors the profile from projecting a starting future. 30% SwK was frightening, especially with a 26.7% FB, and really fell off as season waned. Not enough arm for RF so even a 4th OF role is questionable right now.

Davidson,Logan

56 | **Oakland** | EXP MLB DEBUT: 2024 | H/W: 6-3 185 | FUT: Starting 3B | **7D**

Bats B Age 25
2019 (1) Clemson

- Pwr + + +
- BAvg + +
- Spd + + +
- Def + + +

Year	Lev	Team	AB	R	H	HR	RBI	Avg	OB	Slg	OPS	bb%	ct%	Eye	SB	CS	x/h%	Iso	RC/G
2019	A-	Vermont	205	42	49	4	12	239	339	332	671	13	73	0.56	5	0	22	93	3.94
2021	AA	Midland	448	53	95	7	48	212	308	313	620	12	65	0.40	4	3	32	100	3.27
2022	AA	Midland	424	72	107	14	56	252	335	406	741	11	68	0.40	4	1	34	153	4.89

Tall INF who repeated AA and improved across board. Spent most of time at SS where he exhibits quality glovework with quick hands and average arm. Stock has declined due to inability to make consistent contact. Has upped HR output and maintains above average power potential. Swing tends to get long, but also draws walks.

Davis,Brennen

78 | **Chicago (N)** | EXP MLB DEBUT: 2023 | H/W: 6-4 210 | FUT: Starting CF | **8C**

Bats R Age 23
2018 (2) HS (AZ)

- Pwr + + +
- BAvg + + +
- Spd + + +
- Def + + +

Year	Lev	Team	AB	R	H	HR	RBI	Avg	OB	Slg	OPS	bb%	ct%	Eye	SB	CS	x/h%	Iso	RC/G
2021	AA	Tennessee	266	50	67	13	36	252	341	474	815	12	64	0.37	6	4	49	222	6.24
2021	AAA	Iowa	56	10	15	4	12	268	388	536	924	16	73	0.73	0	0	47	268	7.36
2022	Rk	ACL Cubs	14	2	2	1	2	143	250	357	607	13	64	0.40	0	0	50	214	2.65
2022	A+	South Bend	23	0	3	0	2	130	130	130	261	0	65	0.00	0	0	0	0	-2.47
2022	AAA	Iowa	141	16	27	4	13	191	305	319	624	14	63	0.44	0	1	37	128	3.31

Sidelined for much of the season with back injury. When active, struggled to make consistent contact and concerns about hit tool remain. Other tools are all above-average and he does draw walks. Can be beat by breaking balls down and away and swing can get long. May not be able to hit for both power and average. Plus speed and defense.

Davis,Henry

2 | **Pittsburgh** | EXP MLB DEBUT: 2023 | H/W: 6-2 210 | FUT: Starting C | **8B**

Bats R Age 23
2021 (1) Louisville

- Pwr + + + +
- BAvg + + +
- Spd + +
- Def + +

Year	Lev	Team	AB	R	H	HR	RBI	Avg	OB	Slg	OPS	bb%	ct%	Eye	SB	CS	x/h%	Iso	RC/G
2021	A+	Greensboro	19	6	5	2	3	263	391	684	1076	17	58	0.50	1	0	60	421	11.07
2022	Rk	FCL Pirates Black	3	0	0	0	0	0	0	0	0	0	67	0.00	0	0		0	-6.12
2022	A	Bradenton	11	2	4	1	2	364	417	727	1144	8	82	0.50	1	0	50	364	9.34
2022	A+	Greensboro	82	18	28	5	22	341	400	585	985	9	78	0.44	5	1	32	244	7.65
2022	AA	Altoona	116	19	24	4	18	207	281	379	661	9	74	0.40	3	1	50	172	3.64

Strong backstop who missed valuable time due to wrist. Combines plate patience and huge power to be potent weapon with bat. Has chance to hit for both BA and power and has ability to read spin and make hard contact. Uses entire field in simple approach, though can get pull happy. Continuing to improve with receiving. Owns plus arm.

De Andrade,Danny

6 | **Minnesota** | EXP MLB DEBUT: 2026 | H/W: 5-11 173 | FUT: Starting SS | **7D**

Bats R Age 18
2021 FA (VZ)

- Pwr +
- BAvg + +
- Spd + + +
- Def + + +

Year	Lev	Team	AB	R	H	HR	RBI	Avg	OB	Slg	OPS	bb%	ct%	Eye	SB	CS	x/h%	Iso	RC/G
2021	Rk	DSL Twins	178	16	47	0	16	264	321	348	670	8	85	0.56	6	2	30	84	3.96
2022	Rk	FCL Twins	178	27	43	4	23	242	315	371	686	10	81	0.56	4	2	33	129	4.06

Instinctual, defensive SS with chance to be offensive contributor. Aggressive approach at plate; lacks strength for HR power, though projectable frame could lead to above average pop. Has bat speed, barrel control, average foot speed. Good SS with enough range/arm strength. Has seen time at 3B.

De Jesus,Alex

56 | **Toronto** | EXP MLB DEBUT: 2025 | H/W: 6-2 170 | FUT: Starting 3B | **7C**

Bats R Age 21
2018 FA (DR)

- Pwr + + +
- BAvg + + +
- Spd +
- Def + +

Year	Lev	Team	AB	R	H	HR	RBI	Avg	OB	Slg	OPS	bb%	ct%	Eye	SB	CS	x/h%	Iso	RC/G
2021	A	Rancho Cuca	351	67	94	12	73	268	388	447	835	16	64	0.54	1	0	40	179	6.80
2022	Rk	FCL Blue Jays	6	2	3	1	3	500	571	###	1738	14	100		0	0	67	667	15.27
2022	A	Rancho Cuca	143	34	37	7	22	259	394	483	877	18	65	0.64	2	0	46	224	7.32
2022	A+	Great Lakes	195	27	55	4	26	282	372	421	793	13	67	0.43	0	1	31	138	5.90
2022	A+	Vancouver	90	10	19	2	13	211	304	333	637	12	60	0.33	0	0	37	122	3.65

Acquired from LA at deadline and intrigued with offensive outputs. Draws walks with sound approach, though has too many Ks for profile. Drives balls to gaps and has strength and bat speed to project to more HR power. Can use opposite field. Likely to be 3B as he lacks SS range. Has well below average speed.

De La Cruz,Carlos

379 | **Philadelphia** | EXP MLB DEBUT: 2024 | H/W: 6-8 210 | FUT: Starting OF | **8D**

Bats R Age 23
2017 FA (NY)

- Pwr + + + +
- BAvg + +
- 4.45 Spd + + +
- Def + + +

Year	Lev	Team	AB	R	H	HR	RBI	Avg	OB	Slg	OPS	bb%	ct%	Eye	SB	CS	x/h%	Iso	RC/G
2021	Rk	FCL Phillies	20	3	4	0	1	200	429	200	629	29	60	1.00	3	0	0	0	3.75
2021	A	Clearwater	122	10	18	2	11	148	230	238	467	10	54	0.23	2	0	39	90	0.85
2021	A+	Jersey Shore	62	10	15	3	14	242	299	452	750	7	63	0.22	0	0	47	210	5.11
2022	A+	Jersey Shore	214	29	57	10	24	266	326	463	789	8	65	0.25	5	2	37	196	5.59
2022	AA	Reading	151	21	42	7	23	278	314	510	824	5	70	0.18	1	0	48	232	5.77

Raw athlete with NBA frame made big strides becoming a baseball player. Made better contact which enabled all-fields power when was able to extend arms; eye-opening exit velos resulted. Long levers mean he'll always have swing holes, and he'll chase, but can punish mistakes in the zone. Above-average runner; covers ground; likely COR OF future.

De La Cruz,Elly

56 | Cincinnati | EXP MLB DEBUT: 2024 | H/W: 6-5 200 | FUT: Starting SS | 9C

Bats B Age 21
2018 FA (DR)

Tools	Year	Lev	Team	AB	R	H	HR	RBI	Avg	OB	Slg	OPS	bb%	ct%	Eye	SB	CS	x/h%	Iso	RC/G
Pwr ++++	2021	Rk	ACL Reds	50	13	20	3	13	400	444	780	1224	7	70	0.27	2	0	55	380	11.70
BAvg +++	2021	A	Daytona	197	22	53	5	29	269	304	477	782	5	67	0.15	8	5	45	208	5.50
Spd ++++	2022	A+	Dayton	281	53	85	20	52	302	357	609	966	8	67	0.26	28	4	47	306	8.09
Def +++	2022	AA	Chattanooga	190	34	58	8	34	305	359	553	912	8	66	0.25	19	2	48	247	7.50

Wiry, athletic switch-hitting SS continued to rake across multiple levels despite limited spin recognition skills. Slightly open, upright stance from both sides. Smoother load and more consistent swing plane from LH side. Exceptional power potential in swing. Utilizes opposite field gap to pull side for HR power. Near double-plus runner.

De La Cruz,Jose

79 | Detroit | EXP MLB DEBUT: 2025 | H/W: 6-1 216 | FUT: Starting OF | 8E

Bats R Age 21
2018 FA (DR)

Tools	Year	Lev	Team	AB	R	H	HR	RBI	Avg	OB	Slg	OPS	bb%	ct%	Eye	SB	CS	x/h%	Iso	RC/G
Pwr +++	2021	Rk	FCL Tigers East	159	20	43	4	15	270	341	415	756	10	64	0.29	7	7	33	145	5.36
BAvg +	2021	A	Lakeland	142	15	18	1	10	127	184	183	367	7	48	0.14	6	1	28	56	-0.84
Spd ++++	2022	Rk	FCL Tigers East	21	5	5	1	3	238	273	476	749	5	48	0.09	1	0	60	238	7.00
Def +++	2022	A	Lakeland	307	31	62	10	42	202	271	339	610	9	57	0.22	3	3	34	137	3.18

After impressive DSL debut in 2019, has not been able to duplicate at higher levels. Overly aggressive approach has led to extreme contact issues. Struggles to identify spin and lay off balls out of the zone. Plus bat speed and ball jumps off bat when he does make contact. Plus speed/arm.

de la Rosa,Jeremy

8 | Washington | EXP MLB DEBUT: 2025 | H/W: 6-0 199 | FUT: Starting CF | 8D

Bats L Age 21
2018 FA (DR)

Tools	Year	Lev	Team	AB	R	H	HR	RBI	Avg	OB	Slg	OPS	bb%	ct%	Eye	SB	CS	x/h%	Iso	RC/G
Pwr +++	2019	Rk	GCL Nationals	82	14	19	2	10	232	330	366	696	13	65	0.41	3	2	26	134	4.44
BAvg +++	2021	A	Fredericksburg	326	34	68	5	22	209	275	316	591	8	63	0.25	7	8	31	107	2.80
Spd ++++	2022	A	Fredericksburg	279	56	88	10	57	315	394	505	899	11	72	0.46	26	5	35	190	7.07
Def +++	2022	A+	Wilmington	118	10	23	1	10	195	269	271	540	9	69	0.32	13	2	26	76	2.01

Big strides in 2022, though late-season promotion to High-A, along with hamate surgery, somewhat quieted his second half. Improved contact rate and posted double-digit HR for the first time while playing good CF defense. Also runs well, notching 39 SB over two levels. No flashy tools, but headed towards solid-regular outcome.

De Los Santos,Deyvison

35 | Arizona | EXP MLB DEBUT: 2024 | H/W: 6-1 185 | FUT: Starting 1B | 8D

Bats R Age 19
2019 FA (DR)

Tools	Year	Lev	Team	AB	R	H	HR	RBI	Avg	OB	Slg	OPS	bb%	ct%	Eye	SB	CS	x/h%	Iso	RC/G
	2021	Rk	ACL DBacks	82	19	27	5	17	329	421	610	1031	14	71	0.54	1	1	41	280	9.03
Pwr ++++	2021	A	Visalia	145	26	40	3	20	276	335	421	756	8	70	0.30	2	0	38	145	5.04
BAvg +++	2022	A	Visalia	316	43	104	12	67	329	373	513	885	7	73	0.26	4	1	31	184	6.51
Spd ++	2022	A+	Hillsboro	158	24	44	9	33	278	309	506	815	4	66	0.13	1	0	41	228	5.74
Def ++	2022	AA	Amarillo	39	5	9	1	6	231	318	359	677	11	77	0.56	0	0	33	128	3.97

XXL frame RHH CIF powered way through lower level competition. Body already maxed out. Upright, slight closed stance with long-winded load. Opposite field approach with power playing mostly to RCF. Aggressive at the plate, chases with solid hand/eye coordination. Power is double-plus raw; 30+ HR if can get to pull power. 1B only defensively.

De Paula,Josue

8 | Los Angeles (N) | EXP MLB DEBUT: 2026 | H/W: 6-3 185 | FUT: Starting CF | 8E

Bats L Age 17
2022 FA (NY)

Tools	Year	Lev	Team	AB	R	H	HR	RBI	Avg	OB	Slg	OPS	bb%	ct%	Eye	SB	CS	x/h%	Iso	RC/G
Pwr +++																				
BAvg +++																				
Spd ++																				
Def ++	2022	Rk	DSL Dodgers Ba	186	42	65	5	30	349	445	522	966	15	83	1.03	16	6	31	172	7.85

Breakout campaign in the DSL; he is the nephew of NBA great Stephon Marbury rising up prospect charts. Already possessing above-average power and a quick LH stroke and ability to make consistent, hard contact. Should continue to add muscle to his lean, projectable frame. Relies on a slightly open stance to drive balls, mostly to the pull side.

DeLauter,Chase

8 | Cleveland | EXP MLB DEBUT: 2025 | H/W: 6-4 235 | FUT: Starting CF | 9E

Bats L Age 21
2022 (1) James Madison

Tools	Year	Lev	Team	AB	R	H	HR	RBI	Avg	OB	Slg	OPS	bb%	ct%	Eye	SB	CS	x/h%	Iso	RC/G
Pwr ++++																				
BAvg +++																				
Spd ++++																				
Def ++++																				

Burly, athletic OF with pristine eye and power for days missed most of 2022 college season with a broken foot. Looks like SEC linebacker with speed to match. Upright stance; long stride and quick load. Uppercut swing trajectory with good plate coverage. 30+ HR at projection with underlying hit skills. Plus-plus speed in CF; a 30/30 threat.

DeLoach,Zach

79 | Seattle | EXP MLB DEBUT: 2023 | H/W: 6-1 205 | FUT: Starting OF | 7B

Bats L Age 24
2020 (2) Texas A&M

Tools	Year	Lev	Team	AB	R	H	HR	RBI	Avg	OB	Slg	OPS	bb%	ct%	Eye	SB	CS	x/h%	Iso	RC/G
Pwr +++	2020	NCAA	Texas A&M	57	25	24	6	17	421	535	789	1325	20	95	4.67	6	0	38	368	11.73
BAvg +++	2021	A+	Everett	249	56	78	9	37	313	391	530	922	11	75	0.51	6	3	44	217	7.30
Spd +++	2021	AA	Arkansas	185	28	42	5	22	227	329	384	712	13	69	0.48	1	2	40	157	4.61
Def +++	2022	AA	Arkansas	418	79	108	14	73	258	366	409	775	15	72	0.60	4	1	30	151	5.43

Athletic, speedy OF who plays above tools, though underlying skills are solid. Adept hitter who reads spin and makes ample contact. Works deep into counts and barrels balls to all fields. Should see BA continue to rise with more consistent stroke. Struggles with LHP and hits ton of groundballs. Solid corner OF, but mostly due to instincts.

DeLuca,Jonny

7 | Los Angeles (N) | EXP MLB DEBUT: 2024 | H/W: 6-0 200 | FUT: Starting OF | 7E

Bats R Age 24
2019 (25) Oregon

Tools	Year	Lev	Team	AB	R	H	HR	RBI	Avg	OB	Slg	OPS	bb%	ct%	Eye	SB	CS	x/h%	Iso	RC/G
Pwr +++	2021	A	Rancho Cuca	223	48	64	15	43	287	374	592	966	12	78	0.65	13	2	55	305	7.63
BAvg ++	2021	A+	Great Lakes	164	27	38	7	21	232	296	421	717	8	79	0.43	7	0	39	189	4.28
Spd +++	2022	A+	Great Lakes	277	51	68	18	51	245	334	516	851	12	80	0.66	12	2	54	271	6.07
Def +++	2022	AA	Tulsa	104	22	31	7	20	298	348	606	954	7	84	0.47	5	0	48	308	7.04

Short, but athletic OF continues to make steady progress towards the majors and the Dodgers added him to 40-man roster. Intriguing mix of speed and power. Mature approach at the plate and is willing to draw walks and rarely swings and misses in the zone. Posted a career-high .541 SLG% and could carve out a 4th OF role. Solid defender in CF.

Diaz,Jordan

35 | Oakland | EXP MLB DEBUT: 2022 | H/W: 5-10 175 | FUT: Starting 1B | 7C

Bats R Age 22
2016 FA (CB)

Tools	Year	Lev	Team	AB	R	H	HR	RBI	Avg	OB	Slg	OPS	bb%	ct%	Eye	SB	CS	x/h%	Iso	RC/G
	2019	A-	Vermont	277	31	73	9	47	264	308	430	738	6	83	0.39	2	2	37	166	4.49
Pwr +++	2021	A+	Lansing	333	46	96	13	56	288	338	483	821	7	83	0.43	2	3	40	195	5.52
BAvg +++	2022	AA	Midland	379	48	121	15	58	319	357	507	863	5	84	0.36	0	0	34	187	5.89
Spd +	2022	AAA	Las Vegas	112	19	39	4	25	348	381	545	926	5	87	0.40	0	0	33	196	6.60
Def ++	2022	MLB	Oakland	49	3	13	0	1	265	294	327	621	4	86	0.29	0	0	23	61	3.13

Natural hitter who reached OAK despite slow start. Posted highest BA in org by using entire field and making easy, hard contact. Set career highs in HR and doubles and controls bat well. Transitioned from gap guy to HR prospect with added loft. Doesn't see many pitches and had 2nd lowest BB% in TL. Lacks foot speed and defense.

Diaz,Wilman

46 | Los Angeles (N) | EXP MLB DEBUT: 2026 | H/W: 6-2 182 | FUT: Utility player | 7E

Bats R Age 19
2021 FA (VZ)

Tools	Year	Lev	Team	AB	R	H	HR	RBI	Avg	OB	Slg	OPS	bb%	ct%	Eye	SB	CS	x/h%	Iso	RC/G
Pwr +																				
BAvg ++																				
Spd +++	2021	Rk	DSL Dodgers Sh	85	13	20	1	9	235	309	353	661	10	69	0.35	8	4	35	118	3.82
Def +++	2022	Rk	ACL Dodgers	197	26	33	2	15	168	215	223	439	6	59	0.15	3	2	21	56	0.27

Venezuelan infielder signed for $2.7 million in 2021, but has yet to find much success as a pro. Quick RH stroke and plus bat speed, but struggles to find the barrel and aggressive approach results in too much swing-and-miss. Plus speed and defense give him a chance if he can make adjustments at the plate, but they need to come soon.

Diaz,Yainer

23 | Houston | EXP MLB DEBUT: 2022 | H/W: 6-0 195 | FUT: Starting C | 8C

Bats R Age 24
2016 FA (DR)

Tools	Year	Lev	Team	AB	R	H	HR	RBI	Avg	OB	Slg	OPS	bb%	ct%	Eye	SB	CS	x/h%	Iso	RC/G
	2021	A	Fayetteville	48	3	11	1	7	229	229	333	563	0	92	0.00	1	0	27	104	2.34
Pwr ++++	2021	A+	Asheville	96	28	38	11	33	396	442	781	1224	8	82	0.47	2	0	39	385	10.05
BAvg +++	2022	AA	Corpus Christi	244	37	77	9	48	316	370	504	874	8	84	0.53	1	0	32	189	6.21
Spd +	2022	AAA	Sugar Land	201	38	59	16	48	294	336	587	924	6	81	0.33	1	0	44	294	6.54
Def +++	2022	MLB	Houston	8	0	1	0	1	125	222	250	472	11	75	0.50	0	0	100	125	1.45

Prototypical stocky catcher built upon '21 success by maintaining high batting average and continuing power growth. Chance for plus hit/power combo at peak. Tends to chase pitches outside the zone but gets away with it thanks to refined contact skills. Excellent LD% and impact power buoy BA/OBP. Projects to stick at C in majors.

Dingler,Dillon

2 | **Detroit** | EXP MLB DEBUT: 2023 | H/W: 6-3 210 | FUT: Starting C | **7D**

Bats R Age 24	Year	Lev	Team	AB	R	H	HR	RBI	Avg	OB	Slg	OPS	bb%	ct%	Eye	SB	CS	x/h%	Iso	RC/G
2020 (2) Ohio St	2020	NCAA	Ohio St	50	12	17	5	14	340	389	760	1149	7	86	0.57	1	2	59	420	9.17
Pwr ++	2021	A	Lakeland	12	1	4	0	2	333	333	417	750	0	75	0.00	0	0	25	83	4.45
BAvg ++	2021	A+	West Michigan	122	25	35	8	24	287	356	549	905	10	70	0.36	0	0	43	262	6.96
Spd ++	2021	AA	Erie	188	24	38	4	20	202	239	314	552	5	67	0.15	1	0	26	112	1.97
Def ++++	2022	AA	Erie	387	56	92	14	58	238	317	419	736	10	63	0.31	1	0	42	181	5.04

Looked to be on the fast-track to the majors, but propensity to swing-and-miss has stalled development. Lack of plus bat speed and length of swing raise concerns about hit tool. Remains agile and athletic behind the plate with a plus arm and improved blocking and receiving skills make it likely he will stick behind the dish.

Dirden,Justin

789 | **Houston** | EXP MLB DEBUT: 2023 | H/W: 6-3 209 | FUT: Reserve OF | **7D**

Bats L Age 25	Year	Lev	Team	AB	R	H	HR	RBI	Avg	OB	Slg	OPS	bb%	ct%	Eye	SB	CS	x/h%	Iso	RC/G
2020 FA (SE Missouri St)	2020	NCAA	SE Missouri St	70	20	29	9	26	414	474	900	1374	10	84	0.73	9	0	48	486	11.96
Pwr +++	2021	A	Fayetteville	202	46	54	11	41	267	388	535	923	17	63	0.54	8	1	54	267	8.14
BAvg ++	2021	A+	Asheville	83	13	24	4	17	289	379	542	921	13	69	0.46	2	3	42	253	7.61
Spd +++	2022	AA	Corpus Christi	349	64	113	20	73	324	395	616	1011	11	73	0.44	7	2	50	292	8.47
Def +++	2022	AAA	Sugar Land	128	18	31	4	28	242	297	398	696	7	69	0.25	5	1	39	156	4.10

Older OF prospect with above-average power and solid hit tool. Struggled a bit upon promotion to Triple-A. Drop in FB% stymied HR production, though ct% rate stayed consistent. Wide stance at plate with uppercut swing and aggressive approach. Decent base stealer who can play all 3 OF spots.

Dominguez,Jasson

8 | **New York (A)** | EXP MLB DEBUT: 2024 | H/W: 5-10 190 | FUT: Starting CF | **9D**

Bats B Age 20	Year	Lev	Team	AB	R	H	HR	RBI	Avg	OB	Slg	OPS	bb%	ct%	Eye	SB	CS	x/h%	Iso	RC/G
2019 FA (DR)	2021	Rk	FCL Yankees	20	5	4	0	1	200	385	200	585	23	70	1.00	2	0	0	0	3.07
Pwr ++++	2021	A	Tampa	186	26	48	5	18	258	333	398	731	10	64	0.31	7	3	31	140	4.93
BAvg +++	2022	A	Tampa	275	54	73	9	36	265	371	440	811	14	68	0.52	19	6	38	175	6.12
Spd ++++	2022	A+	Hudson Valley	157	33	48	6	22	306	394	510	904	13	78	0.68	17	1	33	204	6.98
Def +++	2022	AA	Somerset	19	5	2	1	1	105	227	368	596	14	74	0.60	1	0	100	263	2.86

Switch-hitting athletic CF prospect recovered from slow start to post impressing returns across 3 levels. Short, stocky muscular frame at physical projection. Open, upright stance from both sides of plate with occasional bat wrap. Plus-plus bat speed aids Up-the-middle approach. Raw plus-plus power in frame. Plus runner in space.

Doncon,Rayne

46 | **Los Angeles (N)** | EXP MLB DEBUT: 2025 | H/W: 6-2 176 | FUT: Starting SS | **8D**

Bats R Age 19	Year	Lev	Team	AB	R	H	HR	RBI	Avg	OB	Slg	OPS	bb%	ct%	Eye	SB	CS	x/h%	Iso	RC/G
2021 FA (DR)																				
Pwr +++																				
BAvg +++	2021	Rk	DSL Dodgers Ba	99	20	28	3	15	283	383	455	837	14	72	0.57	7	1	32	172	6.36
Spd +++	2022	Rk	ACL Dodgers	199	28	51	9	38	256	308	482	791	7	81	0.39	6	2	51	226	5.17
Def +++	2022	A	Rancho Cuca	40	6	10	3	8	250	302	475	777	7	88	0.60	0	0	30	225	4.78

Quick RHB with feel for the barrel and easy pull-side power and above-average speed. Makes consistent contact, but needs to be more selective in order to reach his full offensive potential. Decent range, but will need to work hard to stick at SS and could grow out of the position, though does have the power needed to handle 3B.

Doughty,Cade

45 | **Toronto** | EXP MLB DEBUT: 2024 | H/W: 6-1 195 | FUT: Starting 2B | **8D**

Bats R Age 22	Year	Lev	Team	AB	R	H	HR	RBI	Avg	OB	Slg	OPS	bb%	ct%	Eye	SB	CS	x/h%	Iso	RC/G
2022 (2) LSU																				
Pwr +++																				
BAvg +++																				
Spd +++	2022	NCAA	LSU	238	56	71	15	57	298	375	567	942	11	79	0.59	4	1	48	269	7.20
Def +++	2022	A	Dunedin	103	21	28	6	24	272	336	495	831	9	72	0.34	3	2	39	223	5.83

Fundamentally-sound MIF who has prevalence of all tools, though none stand out. Does everything well, including natural hitting ability with average bat speed and strength. Added loft to swing and could get to above average power in time. Has trouble with spin, though can make appropriate adjustments. Average defender with OK range.

Downs,Jeter

6 | **Washington** | EXP MLB DEBUT: 2022 | H/W: 5-11 195 | FUT: Starting SS | **7E**

Bats R Age 24	Year	Lev	Team	AB	R	H	HR	RBI	Avg	OB	Slg	OPS	bb%	ct%	Eye	SB	CS	x/h%	Iso	RC/G
2017 (1) HS (FL)	2019	A+	Rancho Cuca	412	78	111	19	75	269	354	507	861	12	76	0.56	23	8	50	238	6.39
Pwr +++	2019	AA	Tulsa	48	14	16	5	11	333	407	688	1095	11	79	0.60	1	0	44	354	8.91
BAvg +	2021	AAA	Worcester	357	39	68	14	39	190	268	333	602	10	63	0.29	18	3	34	143	2.77
Spd +++	2022	AAA	Worcester	284	56	56	16	33	197	292	412	704	12	65	0.38	18	4	50	215	4.31
Def +++	2022	MLB	Boston	39	4	6	1	4	154	175	256	431	3	46	0.05	0	0	33	103	0.56

Regressing prospect who repeated AAA and hit under .200 again. Made MLB debut despite horrific contact and high K rate. Fooled by breaking balls and has been far too aggressive. Still has bat speed and ability to use entire field. Has exhibited good power and owns enough speed to be 20/20 player, but may be a dream.

Doyle,Brenton

89 | **Colorado** | EXP MLB DEBUT: 2023 | H/W: 6-3 200 | FUT: Reserve OF | **7E**

Bats R Age 24	Year	Lev	Team	AB	R	H	HR	RBI	Avg	OB	Slg	OPS	bb%	ct%	Eye	SB	CS	x/h%	Iso	RC/G
2019 (4) Shepherd	2019	NCAA	Shepherd Univ	186	79	73	13	47	392	504	758	1262	18	88	1.91	19	5	49	366	11.41
Pwr ++++	2019	Rk	Grand Junction	180	42	69	8	33	383	474	611	1085	15	74	0.66	17	3	32	228	9.71
BAvg +	2021	A+	Spokane	390	70	109	16	47	279	331	454	785	7	66	0.22	21	6	31	174	5.46
Spd +++	2022	AA	Hartford	471	74	116	23	68	246	281	450	731	5	66	0.15	23	3	41	204	4.52
Def +++	2022	AAA	Albuquerque	36	8	14	3	9	389	463	778	1241	12	64	0.38	0	0	43	389	12.89

Impressive raw tools give him a chance to be a solid 4th OF. Strong, powerful frame with good bat speed results in above-power and stroked a career best 26 HR. But poor pitch recognition, especially on breaking balls out of the zone, leads to plenty of swing-and-miss and without an adjustment he's unlikely to hit for both power and average.

Dunham,Elijah

79 | **New York (A)** | EXP MLB DEBUT: 2023 | H/W: 6-0 213 | FUT: Starting OF | **7C**

Bats L Age 24	Year	Lev	Team	AB	R	H	HR	RBI	Avg	OB	Slg	OPS	bb%	ct%	Eye	SB	CS	x/h%	Iso	RC/G
2019 (40) Indiana																				
Pwr +++	2020	NCAA	Indiana	59	12	23	1	11	390	486	559	1045	16	86	1.38	1	0	35	169	8.90
BAvg +++	2021	A	Tampa	98	32	27	4	25	276	423	500	923	20	77	1.09	11	4	44	224	7.68
Spd +++	2021	A+	Hudson Valley	241	40	62	9	32	257	319	448	768	8	74	0.35	17	1	45	191	5.03
Def +++	2022	AA	Somerset	415	67	103	17	63	248	342	448	790	12	75	0.57	37	7	45	200	5.49

Tweener LHH OF struggled getting to loft in 2022 season at Double-A. Athletic build, close to projection. Crouched, open stance with slight trigger. Slasher approach with patience. Top hand heavy swing, generates tons of topspin contact, depressing above-average raw power profile. Versatile defender. Arm likely plays as regular in LF.

Dunhurst,Hayden

2 | **Kansas City** | EXP MLB DEBUT: 2025 | H/W: 5-11 220 | FUT: Starting C | **7E**

Bats L Age 22	Year	Lev	Team	AB	R	H	HR	RBI	Avg	OB	Slg	OPS	bb%	ct%	Eye	SB	CS	x/h%	Iso	RC/G
2022 (6) Mississippi																				
Pwr ++																				
BAvg ++																				
Spd ++	2022	NCAA	Mississippi	169	30	39	6	30	231	366	385	750	18	59	0.52	0	0	36	154	5.61
Def ++++	2022	Rk	ACL Royals Blue	7	2	3	0	1	429	600	714	1314	30	71	1.50	0	0	67	286	14.76

Glove first C struggled offensively during draft season. Solid athletic frame with good actions behind the plate and a strong arm. Defense will carry profile. Discerning eye at the plate, carried solid OBP. Upright stance with uppercut power stroke. Struggles getting to consistent hard contact, tanking BA and HR potential. Limited wood bat history.

Edwards,Xavier

456 | **Miami** | EXP MLB DEBUT: 2023 | H/W: 5-10 175 | FUT: Reserve IF | **6C**

Bats B Age 23	Year	Lev	Team	AB	R	H	HR	RBI	Avg	OB	Slg	OPS	bb%	ct%	Eye	SB	CS	x/h%	Iso	RC/G
2018 (1) HS (FL)	2018	A-	Tri-City	86	21	27	0	5	314	433	360	793	17	83	1.20	10	0	15	47	5.95
Pwr +	2019	A	Fort Wayne	307	44	103	1	30	336	395	414	808	9	89	0.86	20	9	17	78	5.64
BAvg +++	2019	A+	Lake Elsinore	196	32	59	0	13	301	348	367	715	7	90	0.74	14	2	15	66	4.48
Spd ++++	2021	AA	Montgomery	291	40	88	0	27	302	379	368	747	11	86	0.86	19	11	18	65	5.05
Def +++	2022	AAA	Durham	349	48	86	5	33	246	329	350	679	11	79	0.57	7	4	29	103	4.05

Switch-hitting slasher MIF, struggled with impacting the ball in terrible Triple-A season. Acquired from TAM in off-season. Short-statured, athletic frame. RH profile has better chance at sticking in big leagues than LH profile. Hard-hit rate is in poor range, mostly due to being overmatched as LHH. Plus runner. Doesn't have range to stick at SS.

Elliott,Clark

79 | **Oakland** | EXP MLB DEBUT: 2025 | H/W: 6-0 183 | FUT: Starting OF | **7D**

Bats L Age 22	Year	Lev	Team	AB	R	H	HR	RBI	Avg	OB	Slg	OPS	bb%	ct%	Eye	SB	CS	x/h%	Iso	RC/G
2022 (2) Michigan																				
Pwr ++																				
BAvg +++																				
Spd +++	2022	NCAA	Michigan	243	73	82	16	69	337	449	630	1078	17	77	0.88	19	4	44	292	9.43
Def +++	2022	Rk	ACL Athletics	1	1	0	0	0	0	500	0	500	50	100		0	0		0	4.75

Athletic OF with profile to be solid contributor with bat and glove. Mature hitting approach accentuates solid hit tool and has power potential, but needs more loft. Has bat speed to catch up to good FB. Draws walks and uses speed well. Plays all OF positions with excellent range, though likely heading to corner.

Encarnacion-Strand,Chr | 5 | Cincinnati | EXP MLB DEBUT: 2023 | H/W: 6-0 224 | FUT: Starting 1B | 8D

Bats R Age 23	Year	Lev	Team	AB	R	H	HR	RBI	Avg	OB	Slg	OPS	bb%	ct%	Eye	SB	CS	x/h%	Iso	RC/G
2021 (4) Oklahoma State	2021	NCAA	Oklahoma St	227	47	82	15	66	361	413	661	1074	8	78	0.40	4	2	43	300	8.78
Pwr + + +	2021	A	Fort Myers	87	17	34	4	18	391	424	598	1022	5	70	0.19	2	0	24	207	8.48
BAvg + + +	2022	A+	Cedar Rapids	294	52	87	20	68	296	361	599	960	9	71	0.35	7	1	53	303	7.73
Spd + +	2022	AA	Chattanooga	136	13	42	7	29	309	338	522	860	4	72	0.16	0	0	33	213	6.03
Def +	2022	AA	Wichita	54	11	18	5	17	333	379	685	1064	7	74	0.29	1	1	44	352	8.67

With a super-aggressive approach, he dominated two levels in '22; came over in Mahle trade. Upright, open stance. Always ready to swing. Plus hand/eye coordination prevents outrageous K-rates. Uppercut swing, gets to hard contact, especially in FB counts. 25+ HR power if hit tool allows. Defensively challenged. Likely DH only.

Escotto,Maikol | 46 | Pittsburgh | EXP MLB DEBUT: 2025 | H/W: 6-0 180 | FUT: Starting 2B | 7D

Bats R Age 20	Year	Lev	Team	AB	R	H	HR	RBI	Avg	OB	Slg	OPS	bb%	ct%	Eye	SB	CS	x/h%	Iso	RC/G
2018 FA (DR)																				
Pwr + + +	2021	A	Bradenton	320	61	75	7	38	234	345	347	692	14	64	0.47	22	5	28	113	4.44
BAvg + +	2022	Rk	FCL Pirates Black	10	3	3	0	0	300	417	300	717	17	60	0.50	3	0	0	0	5.15
Spd + + +	2022	A	Bradenton	87	11	22	2	13	253	323	391	714	9	75	0.41	3	6	36	138	4.40
Def + + +	2022	A+	Greensboro	146	17	24	6	19	164	213	342	555	6	60	0.16	5	3	50	178	2.10

Strong, athletic INF with impressive skills. Performance hasn't lived up to expectations, but hope is not lost. Frame could add strength and has potential to hit for BA and power. Uses simple stroke, but can swing under pitches. Has good footwork and clean, quick hands to make routine plays. Likely 2B full time.

Espinoza,Lizandro | 46 | St. Louis | EXP MLB DEBUT: 2025 | H/W: 5-7 158 | FUT: Utility player | 6C

Bats R Age 20	Year	Lev	Team	AB	R	H	HR	RBI	Avg	OB	Slg	OPS	bb%	ct%	Eye	SB	CS	x/h%	Iso	RC/G
2019 FA (VZ)																				
Pwr +																				
BAvg + + +	2021	Rk	DSL Cardinals Red	117	27	34	0	8	291	381	385	765	13	82	0.81	10	6	26	94	5.38
Spd + +	2022	Rk	FCL Cardinals	104	17	25	1	15	240	319	394	713	10	72	0.41	4	1	40	154	4.63
Def + +	2022	A	Palm Beach	69	10	11	1	3	159	194	246	441	4	58	0.10	1	0	27	87	0.33

Short utility player struggled to do much damage in state-side debut and was over-matched when moved up to Low-A. Still young, but there isn't much power so the BA/contact will need to carry him. Fortunately he has a quick stroke and mature understanding of the strike zone. Runs a tick above average and isn't likely to stick at SS as he moves up.

Fabian,Jud | 8 | Baltimore | EXP MLB DEBUT: 2024 | H/W: 6-1 195 | FUT: Starting CF | 8D

Bats R Age 22	Year	Lev	Team	AB	R	H	HR	RBI	Avg	OB	Slg	OPS	bb%	ct%	Eye	SB	CS	x/h%	Iso	RC/G
2022 (2) Florida																				
Pwr + + + +	2022	NCAA	Florida	234	63	56	24	55	239	399	598	997	21	71	0.90	9	4	63	359	8.52
BAvg + + +	2022	Rk	FCL Orioles B	10	2	5	0	3	500	688	600	1288	38	60	1.50	1	0	20	100	16.46
4.51 Spd + + +	2022	A	Delmarva	44	16	17	3	9	386	481	841	1322	15	80	0.89	0	0	71	455	12.57
Def + + + + +	2022	A+	Aberdeen	24	1	4	0	4	167	310	208	519	17	67	0.63	0	2	25	42	1.89

Projects to have plus power from solid build and broad shoulders; hits the ball hard when he makes contact. Hit tool inconsistent; will wait on and drive outer-half strikes, but also swing through hittable fastballs. Enough here for a 20-HR bat. Superlative defense in CF despite only average footspeed; jumps and routes outstanding.

Feliciano,Mario | 2 | Detroit | EXP MLB DEBUT: 2021 | H/W: 6-1 200 | FUT: Starting C | 7D

Bats R Age 24	Year	Lev	Team	AB	R	H	HR	RBI	Avg	OB	Slg	OPS	bb%	ct%	Eye	SB	CS	x/h%	Iso	RC/G
2016 (2) HS (PR)	2021	Rk	ACL Brewers Gold	25	7	9	0	4	360	385	560	945	4	76	0.17	0	0	44	200	7.41
Pwr + +	2021	AAA	Nashville	105	12	22	3	19	210	239	314	553	4	75	0.15	1	0	23	105	1.90
BAvg + + +	2021	MLB	Milwaukee	0	1	0	0	0					100			0	0			
Spd + +	2022	AAA	Nashville	285	31	78	6	38	274	317	386	703	6	82	0.35	2	2	26	112	4.05
Def + + +	2022	MLB	Milwaukee	4	0	1	0	0	250	400	250	650	20	75	1.00	0	0	0	0	4.03

Athletic, agile catcher who has appeared in majors last two years. Power has not developed as much as hoped. Exhibits BP power and can put charge into ball, but hasn't translated to games. Has nice swing and hits LHP. Offensive skill ahead of defense. Has strong arm, but hasn't been effective at stopping basestealers.

Feliz,George | 8 | Seattle | EXP MLB DEBUT: 2026 | H/W: 5-11 160 | FUT: Starting CF | 8E

Bats R Age 20	Year	Lev	Team	AB	R	H	HR	RBI	Avg	OB	Slg	OPS	bb%	ct%	Eye	SB	CS	x/h%	Iso	RC/G
2019 FA (DR)																				
Pwr +																				
BAvg + +																				
Spd + + +	2021	Rk	DSL Mariners	173	32	48	5	25	277	356	451	807	11	73	0.46	8	1	33	173	5.75
Def + + +	2022	Rk	ACL Mariners	150	18	29	2	16	193	275	307	582	10	64	0.31	12	3	34	113	2.70

Athletic OF who needs to fill out lean frame. All about projection and has chance to make impact with both bat and glove. Hits lot of groundballs now, but working on swing to make harder contact. Better selectivity would help. Good speed and owns baserunning instincts. Plays quality CF and will focus on routes and jumps.

Fernandez,Yanquiel | 9 | Colorado | EXP MLB DEBUT: 2025 | H/W: 6-2 198 | FUT: Starting OF | 7D

Bats L Age 20	Year	Lev	Team	AB	R	H	HR	RBI	Avg	OB	Slg	OPS	bb%	ct%	Eye	SB	CS	x/h%	Iso	RC/G
2019 FA (CU)																				
Pwr + + +																				
BAvg + +																				
Spd + +	2021	Rk	DSL Rockies	177	29	59	6	34	333	407	531	938	11	85	0.85	0	0	39	198	7.21
Def +	2022	A	Fresno	475	76	135	21	109	284	339	507	846	8	76	0.34	5	1	44	223	5.97

Strong, physically mature hitter out of Cuba has above-average to plus power. Lots of motion pre-swing, but gets to the ball on time and can crush velo with high exit rates. Overly aggressive at the plate, leading to swing-and-miss and tends to expand the zone. Average speed with a strong arm, but is a fringe defender in RF.

Fernandez,Yeiner | 24 | Los Angeles (N) | EXP MLB DEBUT: 2025 | H/W: 5-9 170 | FUT: Starting C | 7D

Bats R Age 20	Year	Lev	Team	AB	R	H	HR	RBI	Avg	OB	Slg	OPS	bb%	ct%	Eye	SB	CS	x/h%	Iso	RC/G
2019 FA (VZ)																				
Pwr + +																				
BAvg + + +	2021	Rk	ACL Dodgers	141	24	45	2	15	319	364	454	818	7	81	0.37	1	3	31	135	5.59
Spd +	2021	A	Rancho Cuca	31	4	16	1	10	516	545	645	1191	6	90	0.67	0	0	13	129	9.43
Def + +	2022	A	Rancho Cuca	363	76	106	10	68	292	372	430	801	11	85	0.84	3	2	26	138	5.57

Diminutive, but athletic backstop has an advanced feel for hitting and owns a .312 career BA. Plus ability to control the strike zone and walks almost as often as he Ks. Fringe power could prevent him from carving out a full-time role in the majors, but the hit tool will carry and plays 2B as well. Raw behind the plate, but shows good instincts.

Figuero,Gleider | 5 | Texas | EXP MLB DEBUT: 2026 | H/W: 6-0 165 | FUT: Reserve 1B | 7E

Bats L Age 18	Year	Lev	Team	AB	R	H	HR	RBI	Avg	OB	Slg	OPS	bb%	ct%	Eye	SB	CS	x/h%	Iso	RC/G
2021 FA (DR)																				
Pwr + + +																				
BAvg + +	2021	Rk	DSL Rangers	156	23	36	2	28	231	348	359	707	15	80	0.90	3	2	33	128	4.70
Spd +	2022	Rk	ACL Rangers	125	29	35	9	31	280	357	616	973	11	74	0.45	7	1	54	336	7.86
Def +	2022	A	Down East	24	0	5	0	1	208	269	208	478	8	67	0.25	0	0	0	0	0.95

Plus-first-named CI made good state-side transition with tools support. Compact player has upper-body projection on athletic, CA-ish build and cannon arm. Surface stats while ok hiding more as there's power and all-fields approach. Ignore SB numbers; not part of future. Only 74 AB but big LHP struggles and 22% SwK.

Fletcher,Dominic | 789 | Arizona | EXP MLB DEBUT: 2023 | H/W: 5-9 185 | FUT: Starting CF | 7C

Bats L Age 25	Year	Lev	Team	AB	R	H	HR	RBI	Avg	OB	Slg	OPS	bb%	ct%	Eye	SB	CS	x/h%	Iso	RC/G
2019 (2) Arkansas																				
Pwr + + +	2019	A	Kane County	214	33	68	5	28	318	381	463	844	9	77	0.44	1	1	29	145	6.09
BAvg + + +	2021	AA	Amarillo	402	60	106	15	56	264	307	445	752	6	73	0.23	3	3	36	182	4.71
Spd + + +	2022	AA	Amarillo	127	28	44	7	34	346	407	591	998	9	80	0.52	4	2	34	244	7.80
Def + + + +	2022	AAA	Reno	396	70	119	5	38	301	368	452	820	10	78	0.48	5	6	35	152	5.88

Improved contact rate and hard contact rate to post stellar offensive numbers. Upright, slight open stance with quick trigger, utilizes shorter limbs to advantage. Plus hand/eye coordination but chases out of zone. All-fields approach with average overall power, especially to pull gap. Defensive ability carries in CF.

Florial,Estevan | 8 | New York (A) | EXP MLB DEBUT: 2020 | H/W: 6-1 195 | FUT: Starting CF | 7C

Bats L Age 25	Year	Lev	Team	AB	R	H	HR	RBI	Avg	OB	Slg	OPS	bb%	ct%	Eye	SB	CS	x/h%	Iso	RC/G
2015 FA (DR)	2021	AA	Somerset	35	5	8	4	6	229	308	629	936	10	74	0.44	0	1	75	400	6.99
Pwr + + +	2021	AAA	Scranton/WB	312	65	68	13	41	218	311	404	715	12	64	0.38	13	7	46	186	4.63
BAvg + +	2021	MLB	New York	20	3	6	1	2	300	440	550	990	20	70	0.83	1	0	50	250	8.85
Spd + + +	2022	AAA	Scranton/WB	403	66	114	15	46	283	368	481	849	12	65	0.39	39	10	42	199	6.74
Def + + + +	2022	MLB	New York (A)	31	4	3	0	1	97	176	97	273	9	58	0.23	2	0	0	0	-2.54

Wiry, athletic LHH OF prospect suffering from prospect fatigue showed improved hit tool in Triple-A. Open, upright stance with direct trigger and leg lift. Plus-plus bat speed still present. Struggles with bat path and in zone swing and miss. Has calmed approach but still struggles with breakers immensely. Plus defensive CF skills carry profile.

Ford,Harry

2 | **Seattle** | EXP MLB DEBUT: 2025 | H/W: 5-10 200 | FUT: Starting C | **8B**

Bats R Age 20	Year	Lev	Team	AB	R	H	HR	RBI	Avg	OB	Slg	OPS	bb%	ct%	Eye	SB	CS	x/h%	Iso	RC/G
2021 (1) HS (GA)																				
Pwr +++																				
BAvg +++																				
Spd ++++	2021	Rk	ACL Mariners	55	12	16	3	10	291	391	582	972	14	75	0.64	3	0	63	291	8.08
Def +++	2022	A	Modesto	390	89	107	11	65	274	408	438	846	18	71	0.77	23	5	36	164	6.74

Patient, athletic backstop who may be fastest catcher in baseball. Has very bright future predicated on offense and improving receiving. Has bat speed and strength to project to above average power and draws tons of walks with discerning eye. Drives ball to all fields with excellent barrel control. Strong arm is highlight.

Foscue,Justin

4 | **Texas** | EXP MLB DEBUT: 2023 | H/W: 6-0 205 | FUT: Starting 2B | **7B**

Bats R Age 24	Year	Lev	Team	AB	R	H	HR	RBI	Avg	OB	Slg	OPS	bb%	ct%	Eye	SB	CS	x/h%	Iso	RC/G
2020 (1) Mississippi St	2020	NCAA	Mississippi St	53	10	16	2	16	302	456	491	946	22	94	5.00	1	0	38	189	8.07
Pwr +++	2021	Rk	ACL Rangers	11	4	3	1	3	273	333	636	970	8	64	0.25	1	0	67	364	8.36
BAvg +++	2021	A+	Hickory	125	34	37	14	35	296	376	736	1112	11	69	0.41	1	1	70	440	9.99
Spd +	2021	AA	Frisco	93	14	23	2	13	247	307	387	694	8	69	0.28	0	1	39	140	4.17
Def +	2022	AA	Frisco	400	60	115	15	81	288	360	483	842	10	84	0.68	3	4	41	195	5.98

Fully mature, compact MI whose bat needs to carry him; so far it has. Spent 2022 at AA with more FB than GB and a 7% SwK hinting at upside. Lots of pull. Lack of speed, arm, and range says he's a 2B with no SB, but one with slightly above-average BA and power outcomes. Destroys LHP, holds own against RHP, and clutch with men on base.

Fox,Jake

48 | **Cleveland** | EXP MLB DEBUT: 2025 | H/W: 6-0 185 | FUT: Utility player | **7D**

Bats L Age 20	Year	Lev	Team	AB	R	H	HR	RBI	Avg	OB	Slg	OPS	bb%	ct%	Eye	SB	CS	x/h%	Iso	RC/G
2021 (3) HS (FL)																				
Pwr +++																				
BAvg +++																				
Spd ++++	2021	Rk	ACL Indians	42	10	17	0	6	405	479	429	908	13	79	0.67	7	0	6	24	7.09
Def +++	2022	A	Lynchburg	380	74	94	5	44	247	370	374	744	16	76	0.82	21	3	36	126	5.20

Athletic, LHH MIF prospect struggled getting to hard contact with lofted swing trajectory. Open, upright stance with small bat wrap. Swing geared towards lofted contact extends too early, causing length in swing. Solid eye with plus contact skills. Should hit for BA and get on-base. A fast runner, there's a chance for 20 SB.

Fraizer,Matt

789 | **Pittsburgh** | EXP MLB DEBUT: 2024 | H/W: 6-3 220 | FUT: Starting OF | **7D**

Bats L Age 25	Year	Lev	Team	AB	R	H	HR	RBI	Avg	OB	Slg	OPS	bb%	ct%	Eye	SB	CS	x/h%	Iso	RC/G
2019 (3) Arizona																				
Pwr ++																				
BAvg ++	2021	A+	Greensboro	303	64	95	20	50	314	399	578	976	12	76	0.58	14	6	39	264	7.83
Spd ++++	2021	AA	Altoona	132	20	38	3	18	288	352	492	844	9	74	0.38	1	2	47	205	6.26
Def ++	2022	AA	Altoona	439	56	96	6	44	219	276	333	609	7	74	0.31	18	1	32	114	2.96

Large, fast OF who suffered thru miserable campaign. Couldn't solve LHP as erratic swing mechanics hindered BA. Has significant loft in lefty swing that leads to lazy flyballs. Has the strength to hit for plus power, but tough to get to. Owns plus speed, but doesn't get on base enough to use it. Best in LF as arm strength a tad short.

Franklin,Christian

78 | **Chicago (N)** | EXP MLB DEBUT: 2024 | H/W: 5-11 195 | FUT: Starting OF | **7E**

Bats R Age 23	Year	Lev	Team	AB	R	H	HR	RBI	Avg	OB	Slg	OPS	bb%	ct%	Eye	SB	CS	x/h%	Iso	RC/G
2021 (4) Arkansas																				
Pwr +++	2020	NCAA	Arkansas	63	21	24	3	11	381	466	619	1085	14	78	0.71	3	1	33	238	9.38
BAvg +	2021	NCAA	Arkansas	215	55	59	13	54	274	398	544	942	17	64	0.56	11	3	51	270	8.36
Spd +++	2021	Rk	ACL Cubs	11	4	5	0	3	455	571	455	1026	21	82	1.50	3	0	0	0	9.17
Def +++	2021	A	Myrtle Beach	65	13	13	1	5	200	366	292	658	21	65	0.74	1	4	31	92	4.06

An intriguing set of tools, but has seen limited action since turning pro and missed all of 2022 following knee surgery. When healthy has above-average speed and raw power, but struggles against breaking balls and velocity up in the zone. Remains to be seen if he can stay healthy and hit for average. Above-average defender.

Franklin,Jesse

79 | **Atlanta** | EXP MLB DEBUT: 2024 | H/W: 6-1 215 | FUT: Starting OF | **7C**

Bats L Age 24	Year	Lev	Team	AB	R	H	HR	RBI	Avg	OB	Slg	OPS	bb%	ct%	Eye	SB	CS	x/h%	Iso	RC/G
2020 (3) Michigan																				
Pwr +++																				
BAvg +++																				
Spd +++	2021	A+	Rome	360	55	88	24	61	244	310	522	832	9	68	0.30	19	4	57	278	6.02
Def ++	2022	AA	Mississippi	55	6	13	2	9	236	311	400	711	10	67	0.33	2	0	31	164	4.43

Strong, powerful OF prospect lost most of the '22 season after Tommy John surgery. Played in only 15 games. Upright, open stance with slight bat wrap during trigger. Improved approach in small sample, chasing less and getting to harder contact. Raw plus power. It's probably above-average power at maturity. LHH, struggles in same-handed matchups.

Frelick,Sal

78 | **Milwaukee** | EXP MLB DEBUT: 2023 | H/W: 5-10 180 | FUT: Starting CF | **8C**

Bats L Age 22	Year	Lev	Team	AB	R	H	HR	RBI	Avg	OB	Slg	OPS	bb%	ct%	Eye	SB	CS	x/h%	Iso	RC/G
2021 (1) Boston College	2021	A	Carolina	71	17	31	1	12	437	500	592	1092	11	86	0.90	6	2	26	155	9.12
Pwr ++	2021	A+	Wisconsin	60	7	10	1	5	167	286	267	552	14	78	0.77	3	0	30	100	2.54
BAvg ++++	2022	A+	Wisconsin	79	12	23	2	9	291	391	456	847	14	82	0.93	6	3	35	165	6.35
Spd ++++	2022	AA	Biloxi	224	40	71	5	25	317	373	464	837	8	85	0.61	9	2	28	147	5.85
Def +++	2022	AAA	Nashville	189	38	69	4	25	365	423	508	931	9	92	1.19	9	3	25	143	6.99

Short, premier athlete who reached AAA in first full season as pro. Finished 4th in minors in BA. One of most difficult hitters to fan due to quick bat and exceptional hand-eye coordination. Focuses on getting on base at top of lineup. Not much pop in game, but could have average HR output. Brings elite speed to basepaths and CF.

Galiz,Jesus

2 | **Los Angeles (N)** | EXP MLB DEBUT: 2025 | H/W: 6-0 183 | FUT: Starting C | **7D**

Bats R Age 19	Year	Lev	Team	AB	R	H	HR	RBI	Avg	OB	Slg	OPS	bb%	ct%	Eye	SB	CS	x/h%	Iso	RC/G
2021 FA (VZ)																				
Pwr ++																				
BAvg +++																				
Spd +	2021	Rk	DSL Dodgers Ba	101	14	22	0	12	218	269	287	556	6	83	0.41	2	0	27	69	2.47
Def ++	2022	Rk	ACL Dodgers	85	15	20	4	13	235	323	471	794	11	71	0.44	0	0	60	235	5.60

Athletic backstop held his own as 18-yr-old in Rookie Ball. Agile behind the plate with a quick release and strong arm. At the plate, uses a small leg kick to start swing with above bat speed. Has a good understanding of the strike zone, but is contact-over-power for now, but shows potential for more as he matures and gets stronger.

Garcia,Eduardo

6 | **Milwaukee** | EXP MLB DEBUT: 2025 | H/W: 6-2 160 | FUT: Starting SS | **8E**

Bats R Age 20	Year	Lev	Team	AB	R	H	HR	RBI	Avg	OB	Slg	OPS	bb%	ct%	Eye	SB	CS	x/h%	Iso	RC/G
2018 FA (VZ)	2021	Rk	ACL Brewers Blue	13	3	5	1	3	385	429	769	1198	7	85	0.50	0	1	60	385	9.91
Pwr ++	2021	Rk	ACL Brewers Gold	122	24	29	3	24	238	290	443	733	7	67	0.23	2	2	55	205	4.86
BAvg ++	2021	A	Carolina	33	8	11	0	7	333	436	455	890	15	61	0.46	1	0	36	121	8.25
Spd ++	2022	A	Carolina	347	43	91	10	48	262	301	403	704	5	65	0.16	14	2	29	141	4.28
Def ++++	2022	A+	Wisconsin	105	11	26	5	17	248	248	419	667	0	62	0.00	1	0	31	171	3.55

Outstanding defender with fundamental skills, quickness and plus arm strength. Will stick at SS due to range and soft, quick hands. Hitting is another story. Finished 2nd in org in Ks and alarmingly draws few walks. Has some bat potential with strong swing and power projection. Exhibits good bat skills, but needs better approach.

Garcia,Maikel

6 | **Kansas City** | EXP MLB DEBUT: 2022 | H/W: 6-0 145 | FUT: Utility player | **7C**

Bats R Age 23	Year	Lev	Team	AB	R	H	HR	RBI	Avg	OB	Slg	OPS	bb%	ct%	Eye	SB	CS	x/h%	Iso	RC/G
2016 FA (VZ)	2021	A	Columbia	195	40	59	1	26	303	416	415	832	16	83	1.15	24	3	29	113	6.41
Pwr ++	2021	A+	Quad Cities	217	38	61	3	24	281	353	396	749	10	82	0.60	11	3	25	115	4.92
BAvg +++	2022	AA	NW Arkansas	323	63	94	4	33	291	371	409	780	11	81	0.68	27	3	31	118	5.39
Spd ++++	2022	AAA	Omaha	164	41	45	7	28	274	343	463	806	9	74	0.40	12	5	38	189	5.53
Def +++	2022	MLB	Kansas City	22	1	7	0	2	318	348	364	711	4	77	0.20	0	0	14	45	4.11

Wiry, athletic SS prospect turned successful minor league season into MLB debut. Frame hasn't put on much strength during pro career so likely close to physical projection. Hit-over-power prospect. Steady approach at plate. Works primarily up-the-middle and to RCF gap. Patient, will get on base. Plus runner, should steal bases and sticks at SS.

Garcia,Yhoswar

8 | **Philadelphia** | EXP MLB DEBUT: 2026 | H/W: 6-0 150 | FUT: Starting CF | **8E**

Bats R Age 21	Year	Lev	Team	AB	R	H	HR	RBI	Avg	OB	Slg	OPS	bb%	ct%	Eye	SB	CS	x/h%	Iso	RC/G
2020 FA (VZ)																				
Pwr ++																				
BAvg +++	2021	A	Clearwater	70	7	16	0	8	229	289	271	561	8	67	0.26	11	2	13	43	2.29
Spd ++++	2022	Rk	FCL Phillies	6	0	2	0	1	333	429	333	762	14	83	1.00	3	1	0	0	5.32
Def ++++	2022	A	Clearwater	126	26	26	1	16	206	286	310	595	10	72	0.40	29	6	31	103	2.90

Suffered severe ankle sprain in mid-May that kept him out for most the season. Mostly singles hitter presently, but can fly: 32 SB in 37 games. Unlikely to produce much extra-base power and still makes some questionable swing decisions. Second year in a row that leg injuries cut short his season; needs to stay on the field. Top-flight CF defender.

Garcia,Yunior

39 | **Los Angeles (N)** | EXP MLB DEBUT: 2025 | H/W: 6-0 198 | FUT: Starting 1B | **7E**

Bats R Age 21
2017 FA (DR)

- Pwr + + +
- BAvg + + +
- Spd +
- Def +

Year	Lev	Team	AB	R	H	HR	RBI	Avg	OB	Slg	OPS	bb%	ct%	Eye	SB	CS	x/h%	Iso	RC/G
2019	Rk	AZL Dodgers La	72	8	17	3	22	236	247	403	649	1	64	0.04	0	1	35	167	3.28
2021	Rk	ACL Dodgers	110	20	33	4	16	300	358	473	831	8	74	0.34	2	0	30	173	5.87
2022	A	Rancho Cuca	334	58	102	13	74	305	368	512	880	9	78	0.44	2	0	41	207	6.47
2022	A+	Great Lakes	33	2	5	0	1	152	152	152	303	0	64	0.00	0	0	0	0	-1.92

Breakout season at Low-A posting a .900 OPS earning a late-season promotion to High-A. Plus bat speed and impressive raw power started showing up in game action after injuries limited his pro debut. Slightly open RH stance and drives balls with authority to all fields. Below-average defender is limited to LF, 1B, or DH.

Gelof,Zack

45 | **Oakland** | EXP MLB DEBUT: 2023 | H/W: 6-3 205 | FUT: Starting 3B | **7B**

Bats R Age 23
2021 (2) Virginia

- Pwr + + +
- BAvg + + +
- Spd + + +
- Def + + +

Year	Lev	Team	AB	R	H	HR	RBI	Avg	OB	Slg	OPS	bb%	ct%	Eye	SB	CS	x/h%	Iso	RC/G
2021	Rk	ACL Athletics	2	1	2	0	2	1000	###	###	2000	0	100		2	0	0	0	16.32
2021	A	Stockton	124	26	37	7	22	298	392	548	940	13	71	0.53	11	2	43	250	7.68
2021	AAA	Las Vegas	12	3	7	0	6	583	615	667	1282	8	83	0.50	0	0	14	83	11.17
2022	AA	Midland	354	54	96	13	61	271	357	438	794	12	69	0.43	9	2	32	167	5.67
2022	AAA	Las Vegas	35	7	9	5	5	257	316	714	1030	8	69	0.27	1	0	67	457	8.37

Instinctual INF who is advancing rapidly. Missed all of June and July and struggled upon return. Uses disciplined approach to find pitches to drive. Added patience and strike zone recognition to solid hitting skills. Power continues to evolve. Athletic, agile frame allows him to run well and exhibit quality defense at both 2B and 3B.

Genao,Angel

46 | **Cleveland** | EXP MLB DEBUT: 2026 | H/W: 5-9 150 | FUT: Starting SS | **7D**

Bats B Age 18
2021 FA (DR)

- Pwr + + +
- BAvg + + +
- Spd + + +
- Def + + + +

Year	Lev	Team	AB	R	H	HR	RBI	Avg	OB	Slg	OPS	bb%	ct%	Eye	SB	CS	x/h%	Iso	RC/G
2021	Rk	DSL Indians Blue	151	36	40	1	14	265	416	364	780	21	81	1.34	16	0	23	99	5.95
2022	Rk	ACL Indians	149	22	48	2	18	322	388	416	804	10	73	0.40	6	3	19	94	5.67
2022	A	Lynchburg	28	3	5	0	3	179	281	214	496	13	82	0.80	0	1	20	36	1.96

Defensively skilled SS had successful US debut in the ACL. Wiry frame with room to grow. Switch hitter has similar stances and loads from each side of the plate and fairly clean swing mechanics. Contact-oriented overall. Struggled recognizing better spin led to some chase issues. Great reactions with plus range and arm at SS.

Gentry,Tyler

79 | **Kansas City** | EXP MLB DEBUT: 2023 | H/W: 6-2 210 | FUT: Starting OF | **8D**

Bats R Age 24
2020 (3) Alabama

- Pwr + + +
- BAvg + + +
- Spd + + +
- Def + + +

Year	Lev	Team	AB	R	H	HR	RBI	Avg	OB	Slg	OPS	bb%	ct%	Eye	SB	CS	x/h%	Iso	RC/G
2020	NCAA	Alabama	56	19	24	4	21	429	515	750	1265	15	82	1.00	2	2	42	321	11.43
2021	A+	Quad Cities	147	29	38	6	28	259	381	449	830	16	63	0.53	4	0	42	190	6.71
2022	A+	Quad Cities	128	22	43	5	23	336	426	516	941	14	70	0.51	2	2	28	180	7.87
2022	AA	NW Arkansas	274	57	88	16	63	321	408	555	962	13	76	0.61	8	4	36	234	7.68

A breakout performer in 2022, he reworked swing mechanics to get hands quicker to the hit position, improving reaction time and getting to consistent swing path. Cut down whiff risk. Utilizes entire field with patient approach. Average pull power started to play. Still, might not be enough over-the-fence power to stick as COF.

Gilbert,Drew

8 | **Houston** | EXP MLB DEBUT: 2024 | H/W: 5-9 185 | FUT: Starting CF | **8D**

Bats L Age 22
2022 (1) Tennessee

- Pwr + +
- BAvg + + + +
- Spd + +
- Def + + +

Year	Lev	Team	AB	R	H	HR	RBI	Avg	OB	Slg	OPS	bb%	ct%	Eye	SB	CS	x/h%	Iso	RC/G

Impressive college season with Tennessee resulted in 1st-round selection. Displays a patient approach with excellent contact skills and solid power, though it's mostly gap power at present. Has a crouched, open stance at the plate and controls the zone with a clean, level bat path. Short-statured with muscular frame and minimal room for projection.

Gomez,Antonio

2 | **New York (A)** | EXP MLB DEBUT: 2025 | H/W: 6-2 210 | FUT: Starting C | **7E**

Bats R Age 21
2018 FA (VZ)

- Pwr + + +
- BAvg + +
- Spd + +
- Def + + +

Year	Lev	Team	AB	R	H	HR	RBI	Avg	OB	Slg	OPS	bb%	ct%	Eye	SB	CS	x/h%	Iso	RC/G
2019	Rk	GCL Yankees	47	9	12	1	7	255	300	404	704	6	85	0.43	0	0	42	149	4.18
2021	Rk	FCL Yankees	95	18	29	2	16	305	405	474	879	14	67	0.52	4	0	38	168	7.30
2021	A	Tampa	61	10	12	2	7	197	310	328	638	14	70	0.56	1	0	33	131	3.43
2022	A	Tampa	325	36	82	8	48	252	325	369	694	10	69	0.35	1	3	24	117	4.16

Grip and rip, physically strong RHH C prospect struggled to carry BP power into games. Aggressive approach, struggles with spin recognition, accounting for most of whiffs. Raw plus power plays average due to limits on hit tool and flatter, linear swing trajectory. Produces mostly topspin contact. Improving defensive profile behind the dish.

Gomez,Moises

79 | **St. Louis** | EXP MLB DEBUT: 2023 | H/W: 5-11 200 | FUT: Reserve OF | **7E**

Bats R Age 24
2015 FA (VZ)

- Pwr + + + +
- BAvg +
- Spd + +
- Def +

Year	Lev	Team	AB	R	H	HR	RBI	Avg	OB	Slg	OPS	bb%	ct%	Eye	SB	CS	x/h%	Iso	RC/G
2018	A	Bowling Green	471	67	132	19	82	280	329	503	832	7	71	0.25	4	3	45	223	5.97
2019	A+	Charlotte	428	55	94	16	66	220	298	402	700	10	62	0.29	3	3	47	182	4.52
2021	AA	Montgomery	269	34	46	8	23	171	247	309	555	9	57	0.23	5	3	46	138	2.26
2022	AA	Springfield	224	53	72	23	54	321	394	705	1100	11	60	0.30	7	3	56	384	10.97
2022	AAA	Memphis	218	36	58	16	40	266	342	541	883	10	61	0.30	3	0	45	275	7.27

Picked up as a FA and had a monster season between Double and Triple-A, mashing a career high and minor league best 39 HR. Extremely aggressive approach with an all or nothing swing generates easy plus power but also lots of swing-and-miss (35% K rate) and ridiculous .402 BABIP says .292 BA is unattainable. Still you gotta love the power.

Gonzales,Nick

4 | **Pittsburgh** | EXP MLB DEBUT: 2023 | H/W: 5-10 195 | FUT: Starting 2B | **8B**

Bats R Age 23
2020 (1) New Mexico St

- Pwr + + +
- BAvg + + + +
- Spd + + +
- Def + + +

Year	Lev	Team	AB	R	H	HR	RBI	Avg	OB	Slg	OPS	bb%	ct%	Eye	SB	CS	x/h%	Iso	RC/G
2020	NCAA	New Mexico St	58	28	26	12	36	448	595	###	1750	27	83	2.10	4	1	62	707	17.60
2021	A+	Greensboro	324	53	98	18	54	302	379	565	944	11	69	0.40	7	2	46	262	7.80
2022	Rk	FCL Pirates Black	7	1	3	0	3	429	429	857	1286	0	86	0.00	1	0	67	429	11.04
2022	A	Bradenton	3	0	0	0	1	0	250	0	250	25	33	0.50	0	0		0	-5.88
2022	AA	Altoona	259	47	68	7	33	263	368	429	796	14	65	0.48	5	3	41	166	6.06

Natural hitter who missed time with foot and heel injuries. Makes exceptional contact with strike zone knowledge and elite hand-eye coordination. Smashes line drives to gaps and can turn on velocity for HR. Can try to do too much with stick and overswing. Runs well, though not a burner and is solid defender at 2B.

Gonzalez,Gabriel

79 | **Seattle** | EXP MLB DEBUT: 2025 | H/W: 5-10 165 | FUT: Starting OF | **9E**

Bats R Age 19
2021 FA (VZ)

- Pwr + + +
- BAvg + + +
- Spd + + +
- Def + + +

Year	Lev	Team	AB	R	H	HR	RBI	Avg	OB	Slg	OPS	bb%	ct%	Eye	SB	CS	x/h%	Iso	RC/G
2021	Rk	DSL Mariners	188	39	54	7	36	287	359	521	880	10	81	0.60	9	3	48	234	6.52
2022	Rk	ACL Mariners	126	20	45	5	17	357	396	548	943	6	83	0.38	5	3	31	190	6.87
2022	A	Modesto	126	31	36	2	17	286	353	389	741	9	83	0.62	4	1	22	103	4.77

Physical, raw corner OF who hit well at two levels. Received large bonus upon signing due to intriguing tools. Still has room for growth and development. Makes loud contact with mature approach and level swing path. Power projects to plus status as he continues to add muscle. Runs well now, though likely to slow down as he ages.

Gonzalez,Martin

46 | **Seattle** | EXP MLB DEBUT: 2027 | H/W: 5-10 165 | FUT: Starting SS | **8E**

Bats R Age 18
2022 FA (DR)

- Pwr + +
- BAvg + +
- Spd + + +
- Def + + +

Year	Lev	Team	AB	R	H	HR	RBI	Avg	OB	Slg	OPS	bb%	ct%	Eye	SB	CS	x/h%	Iso	RC/G
2022	Rk	DSL Mariners	172	28	40	3	24	233	353	326	679	16	50	0.37	2	4	25	93	5.15

Short, quick INF who has significant development time ahead. High upside due to projectable frame and solid defensive attributes. Has advanced approach, but also struck out in half of AB in DSL. Could hit for BA down line along with average power. More of a groundball guy today. Speed and defense are best present abilities.

Goodman,Hunter

23 | **Colorado** | EXP MLB DEBUT: 2024 | H/W: 6-1 210 | FUT: Starting C | **8E**

Bats R Age 23
2021 (4) Memphis

- Pwr + + + +
- BAvg + +
- Spd +
- Def + +

Year	Lev	Team	AB	R	H	HR	RBI	Avg	OB	Slg	OPS	bb%	ct%	Eye	SB	CS	x/h%	Iso	RC/G
2021	NCAA	Memphis	202	40	62	21	51	307	397	678	1075	13	74	0.57	9	0	52	371	9.09
2021	Rk	ACL Rockies	60	16	18	2	12	300	391	517	908	13	77	0.64	1	0	50	217	7.16
2022	A	Fresno	282	53	82	22	68	291	351	592	943	8	72	0.33	4	2	49	301	7.27
2022	A+	Spokane	197	39	62	12	34	315	351	589	940	5	69	0.18	1	0	47	274	7.41
2022	AA	Hartford	44	5	10	2	4	227	277	364	640	6	73	0.25	1	0	20	136	3.05

Offensive minded backstop has the best raw power in the system and mashed across 3 stops. Good understanding of the strike zone and hunts balls he can rocket to pull side. Ultra aggressive approach means there will be plenty of swing-and-miss and few walks, but when he connects the ball flies. Fringe defender will have to work hard to stick at C.

Gorski, Matt — 8 — Pittsburgh

EXP MLB DEBUT: 2023 **H/W:** 6-4 198 **FUT:** Starting OF **8E**

Bats R Age 25
2019 (2) Indiana

Pwr	++++
BAvg	++
Spd	+++
Def	+++

Year	Lev	Team	AB	R	H	HR	RBI	Avg	OB	Slg	OPS	bb%	ct%	Eye	SB	CS	x/h%	Iso	RC/G
2021	A+	Greensboro	358	62	80	17	56	223	291	416	707	9	65	0.27	18	1	44	193	4.34
2022	A	Bradenton	17	1	3	1	1	176	222	353	575	6	65	0.17	1	0	33	176	2.09
2022	A+	Greensboro	126	34	37	17	37	294	378	754	1132	12	69	0.44	9	1	59	460	10.07
2022	AA	Altoona	141	27	39	6	28	277	346	489	836	10	67	0.32	10	2	41	213	6.33
2022	AAA	Indianapolis	2	0	1	0	0	500	500	500	1000	0	50	0.00	1	0	0	0	11.13

Sleeper prospect who was promoted to AA mid-year. Posted 20/20 season despite missing time with strained quad. Set highs in both HR and SB and showed more polished hit tool. Ks are an issue, though made more consistent contact than previous year. Also increased walk rate. True CF with range and enough arm.

Graham, Peyton — 6 — Detroit

EXP MLB DEBUT: 2025 **H/W:** 6-3 185 **FUT:** Starting SS **8D**

Bats R Age 22
2022 (2) Oklahoma

Pwr	+++
BAvg	+++
Spd	++++
Def	+++

Year	Lev	Team	AB	R	H	HR	RBI	Avg	OB	Slg	OPS	bb%	ct%	Eye	SB	CS	x/h%	Iso	RC/G
2022	NCAA	Oklahoma	278	75	93	20	71	335	395	640	1036	9	75	0.41	34	2	44	306	8.47
2022	A	Lakeland	100	19	27	1	13	270	336	370	706	9	71	0.34	7	1	26	100	4.39

Slid out of 1st rd due to concerns about top-end power; draws comps to Yelich due to frame and projectability. Good feel for barrel; quick hands and bat speed should enable him to hit, but high leg kick and aggressive approach prevent him from getting into lower half. Good range and enough arm to stick at SS.

Gray, Joe — 89 — Milwaukee

EXP MLB DEBUT: 2024 **H/W:** 6-1 214 **FUT:** Starting CF **7E**

Bats R Age 23
2018 (2) HS (MS)

Pwr	+++
BAvg	+
Spd	++++
Def	+++

Year	Lev	Team	AB	R	H	HR	RBI	Avg	OB	Slg	OPS	bb%	ct%	Eye	SB	CS	x/h%	Iso	RC/G
2018	Rk	AZL Brewers	77	14	14	2	9	182	337	325	662	19	68	0.72	6	0	50	143	4.00
2019	Rk	Rocky Mountain	110	19	18	3	9	164	252	300	552	11	67	0.36	3	2	44	136	2.13
2021	A	Carolina	190	40	55	12	53	289	395	632	1026	15	68	0.54	12	0	62	342	9.32
2021	A+	Wisconsin	215	32	47	8	37	219	285	381	667	9	67	0.29	11	3	36	163	3.70
2022	A+	Wisconsin	462	58	89	15	54	193	273	353	626	10	62	0.29	17	2	45	160	3.32

Athletic, strong OF who had horrendous year after breakout in 2021. Can't seem to solve High-A pitching. Can be free swinger by chasing balls out of zone and often too passive for own good. Has plus speed and above average raw power. Range and arm strength are also positive. Just can't make enough contact to be asset.

Green, Elijah — 8 — Washington

EXP MLB DEBUT: 2026 **H/W:** 6-3 225 **FUT:** Starting CF **9E**

Bats R Age 19
2022 (1) HS (FL)

Pwr	++++
BAvg	++
Spd	+++
Def	++++

Year	Lev	Team	AB	R	H	HR	RBI	Avg	OB	Slg	OPS	bb%	ct%	Eye	SB	CS	x/h%	Iso	RC/G
2022	Rk	FCL Nationals	43	9	13	2	9	302	388	535	923	12	51	0.29	1	0	46	233	9.79

His top-of-the-scale power and speed skills in an athletic package stood out in the 2022 class. Son of NFL TE Eric Green, his tools are explosive and more fully developed than most prepsters. He's a sure-fire center fielder with a strong arm. Only blemish right now is an alarming swing-and-miss tendency, which will require future attention.

Greene, Isaiah — 789 — Cleveland

EXP MLB DEBUT: 2025 **H/W:** 6-1 180 **FUT:** Starting CF **7E**

Bats L Age 21
2020 (2) HS (CA)

Pwr	+++
BAvg	++
Spd	++++
Def	+++

Year	Lev	Team	AB	R	H	HR	RBI	Avg	OB	Slg	OPS	bb%	ct%	Eye	SB	CS	x/h%	Iso	RC/G
2021	Rk	ACL Indians	152	31	44	1	16	289	422	368	791	19	72	0.83	5	4	23	79	6.01
2022	A	Lynchburg	371	65	84	4	43	226	387	340	726	21	69	0.85	39	4	31	113	5.17

Long, lanky LHH OF prospect struggled with hard contact in full-season debut. Athletic frame with room to grow. Best tool is plus foot speed. Upright, slightly open stance with bat wrap. Substandard bat speed, needs to do better job incorporating lower half. There's above-average power potential in eventual frame. Solid defender in CF.

Groshans, Jordan — 56 — Miami

EXP MLB DEBUT: 2022 **H/W:** 6-3 200 **FUT:** Starting 3B **7C**

Bats R Age 23
2018 (1) HS (TX)

Pwr	++
BAvg	+++
Spd	+++
Def	++

Year	Lev	Team	AB	R	H	HR	RBI	Avg	OB	Slg	OPS	bb%	ct%	Eye	SB	CS	x/h%	Iso	RC/G
2021	AA	New Hampshire	278	46	81	7	40	291	369	450	818	11	78	0.56	0	0	37	158	5.83
2022	A	Dunedin	19	2	4	0	0	211	250	263	513	5	74	0.20	0	0	25	53	1.59
2022	AAA	Buffalo	240	30	60	1	24	250	345	296	641	13	81	0.76	2	0	15	46	3.71
2022	AAA	Jacksonville	113	14	34	2	10	301	402	416	817	14	83	1.00	1	0	26	115	6.00
2022	MLB	Miami	61	9	16	1	2	262	308	311	619	6	79	0.31	0	0	6	49	2.92

Former HQ100 prospect, traded mid-season from TOR, made MLB debut. Tall frame with shorter arms drives contact skill. Slight open, upright stance with minimal trigger. Top hand heavy swing, depresses loft, crashing power potential. Patient, all-fields approach. Will let balls travel deep in zone and knock them the other way. Lacks SS range.

Guilarte, Daniel — 6 — Milwaukee

EXP MLB DEBUT: 2026 **H/W:** 6-0 160 **FUT:** Starting SS **8E**

Bats R Age 19
2021 FA (VZ)

Pwr	+
BAvg	+++
Spd	++++
Def	+++

Year	Lev	Team	AB	R	H	HR	RBI	Avg	OB	Slg	OPS	bb%	ct%	Eye	SB	CS	x/h%	Iso	RC/G
2022	Rk	ACL Brewers Blue	124	17	38	0	20	306	399	371	770	13	75	0.61	8	3	21	65	5.45

Lean, wiry INF who was high profile international signee. Had splendid campaign in ACL by showcasing advanced skills for age. Level swing path produces hard contact and has bat speed and strike zone knowledge. Power could be forthcoming with additional strength. Hits too many groundballs. Should stay at SS with plus speed and arm.

Gutierrez, Abrahan — 2 — Pittsburgh

EXP MLB DEBUT: 2024 **H/W:** 6-0 214 **FUT:** Starting C **7E**

Bats R Age 23
2016 FA (VZ)

Pwr	++
BAvg	+++
Spd	++
Def	+++

Year	Lev	Team	AB	R	H	HR	RBI	Avg	OB	Slg	OPS	bb%	ct%	Eye	SB	CS	x/h%	Iso	RC/G
2018	Rk	GCL Phillies West	162	24	51	1	30	315	355	407	762	6	90	0.63	2	2	24	93	4.92
2019	A	Lakewood	289	23	71	4	27	246	312	318	631	9	79	0.45	3	1	18	73	3.28
2021	A	Bradenton	68	16	20	0	4	294	429	471	899	19	81	1.23	0	0	50	176	7.56
2021	A	Clearwater	177	30	51	5	32	288	411	429	841	17	82	1.19	0	0	29	141	6.40
2022	A+	Greensboro	377	51	97	12	56	257	347	411	758	12	70	0.46	4	2	35	154	5.15

Improving catcher who performed at High-A after 2 years in Low-A. Showed more polish with both bat and glove. Posted easy career high in HR while being more selective and chasing less. Still doesn't make consistent, hard contact due to length in swing. Improved receiving behind plate with fringy arm strength.

Gutierrez, Anthony — 8 — Texas

EXP MLB DEBUT: 2026 **H/W:** 6-3 180 **FUT:** Starting OF **8D**

Bats R Age 18
2022 FA (VZ)

Pwr	++
BAvg	+++
Spd	+++
Def	++

Year	Lev	Team	AB	R	H	HR	RBI	Avg	OB	Slg	OPS	bb%	ct%	Eye	SB	CS	x/h%	Iso	RC/G
2022	Rk	ACL Rangers	81	13	21	1	8	259	286	407	693	4	80	0.19	6	3	38	148	3.94
2022	Rk	DSL Rangers 2	91	22	32	3	16	352	404	538	943	8	80	0.44	5	3	34	187	7.14

Young DSL debutee makes it stateside same season and holds own. Great frame to dream on a five-tool future and the current production to back that up. Across the profile there's nascent building blocks but the normal teenager aggressiveness. Speed and instincts give 4th OF floor but probably more a RF long term with the SB likely dwindling.

Guzman, Denzer — 6 — Los Angeles (A)

EXP MLB DEBUT: 2025 **H/W:** 6-1 180 **FUT:** Starting 3B **8D**

Bats R Age 19
2021 FA (DR)

Pwr	++++
BAvg	+++
Spd	++
Def	+++

Year	Lev	Team	AB	R	H	HR	RBI	Avg	OB	Slg	OPS	bb%	ct%	Eye	SB	CS	x/h%	Iso	RC/G
2021	Rk	DSL Angels	141	21	30	3	27	213	311	362	672	12	83	0.83	11	7	47	149	4.13
2022	Rk	ACL Angels	192	38	55	3	33	286	338	422	760	7	77	0.34	3	1	31	135	4.93
2022	A	Inland Empire	17	2	3	0	2	176	391	176	568	26	41	0.60	1	0	0	0	3.23

Athletic, strong SS prospect showcased offensive upside in US debut. Projectable frame with power to come. Upright stance with a solid load. Gets to plus bat speed in uppercut swing. Solid approach and feel for barrel. Markers for plus power in frame and swing. 25+ HR potential. Lacks range at SS. Fits best at 3B long term. Below-average runner.

Hall, Anthony — 9 — New York (A)

EXP MLB DEBUT: 2025 **H/W:** 6-2 200 **FUT:** Starting OF **7D**

Bats L Age 22
2022 (4) Oregon

Pwr	+++
BAvg	+++
Spd	+++
Def	+++

Year	Lev	Team	AB	R	H	HR	RBI	Avg	OB	Slg	OPS	bb%	ct%	Eye	SB	CS	x/h%	Iso	RC/G
2022	NCAA	Oregon	225	53	75	14	56	333	398	640	1038	10	81	0.56	4	2	48	307	8.34
2022	Rk	FCL Yankees	1	0	0	0	0	0	0	0	0	0	100		0	0		0	-2.66

Athletic LHH OF prospect suffered wrist injury in first pro AB. Open, upright stance with small bat wrap at the hitting position. All-field approach, will let ball travel deep in zone and go the other way. Average power potential, mostly to the pull side. Apt at splitting gaps with liners. Above-average runner.

Halpin,Petey — 8 — Cleveland
EXP MLB DEBUT: 2024 | H/W: 6-0 185 | FUT: Starting CF | **7C**

Bats L Age 20
2020 (3) HS (CA)
- Pwr + +
- BAvg + + +
- Spd + + + +
- Def + + +

Year	Lev	Team	AB	R	H	HR	RBI	Avg	OB	Slg	OPS	bb%	ct%	Eye	SB	CS	x/h%	Iso	RC/G
2021	A	Lynchburg	221	34	65	1	18	294	355	425	781	9	77	0.42	11	9	32	131	5.38
2022	A+	Lake County	382	68	100	6	36	262	340	385	724	11	76	0.49	16	7	31	123	4.63

Athletic, hitterish LHH struggled out of the gate before slashing .303/.392/.465 over last 65 games. Open, upright stance with moderate leg lift & slight bat wrap in load. Linear swing plane conducive to topspin contact. Athletic frame with some room to grow. Below average raw power. Plus runner; 16 SB. Above-average in CF.

Hamilton,David — 46 — Boston
EXP MLB DEBUT: 2023 | H/W: 5-10 175 | FUT: Utility player | **6B**

Bats L Age 25
2019 (8) Texas
- Pwr + +
- BAvg + +
- Spd + + + +
- Def + + +

Year	Lev	Team	AB	R	H	HR	RBI	Avg	OB	Slg	OPS	bb%	ct%	Eye	SB	CS	x/h%	Iso	RC/G
2021	A+	Wisconsin	270	50	71	5	31	263	348	422	770	11	79	0.60	41	6	37	159	5.30
2021	AA	Biloxi	133	16	33	3	12	248	324	414	738	10	76	0.47	11	3	36	165	4.80
2022	AA	Portland	463	81	116	12	42	251	331	402	733	11	74	0.47	70	8	32	151	4.72

Short, quick INF who was 3rd in minors in SB in first full pro season. Split time between 2B and SS and has strong fundamentals to player either well. Arm best at 2B. Focuses on easy contact, but not much oomph in swing. Has been solid against LHP and uses keen eye to get on base. Fits utility profile.

Hardman,Tyler — 5 — New York (A)
EXP MLB DEBUT: 2024 | H/W: 6-3 204 | FUT: Starting 3B | **7D**

Bats R Age 24
2021 (5) Oklahoma
- Pwr + + +
- BAvg + +
- Spd + +
- Def + + + +

Year	Lev	Team	AB	R	H	HR	RBI	Avg	OB	Slg	OPS	bb%	ct%	Eye	SB	CS	x/h%	Iso	RC/G
2021	NCAA	Oklahoma	216	49	87	12	49	403	484	676	1160	14	74	0.61	3	2	38	273	10.61
2021	Rk	FCL Yankees	6	2	2	0	2	333	429	667	1095	14	100		0	0	100	333	9.58
2021	A	Tampa	101	18	24	4	17	238	300	406	706	8	55	0.20	4	1	38	168	4.98
2022	A+	Hudson Valley	397	53	104	22	79	262	330	479	808	9	66	0.29	14	4	38	217	5.82
2022	AA	Somerset	15	0	1	0	2	67	67	67	133	0	60	0.00	0	0	0	0	-4.70

Strong-bodied RHH 3B prospect slugged 28 HR across two minor league levels and the Arizona Fall League. Wide open, upright stance with a slight hitch in load, which was improved from 2021. Power-oriented swing, maximizing pull potential with approach. Present in-zone swing-and-miss depresses profile. Quick reactions at 3B with strong arm.

Harris,Brett — 5 — Oakland
EXP MLB DEBUT: 2024 | H/W: 6-3 208 | FUT: Starting 3B | **7C**

Bats R Age 24
2021 (7) Gonzaga
- Pwr + +
- BAvg + + +
- Spd + + +
- Def + + +

Year	Lev	Team	AB	R	H	HR	RBI	Avg	OB	Slg	OPS	bb%	ct%	Eye	SB	CS	x/h%	Iso	RC/G
2021	NCAA	Gonzaga	197	52	70	6	43	355	433	543	976	12	87	1.08	7	5	34	188	7.72
2021	Rk	ACL Athletics	3	2	2	0	3	667	800	667	1467	40	100		0	0	0	0	15.92
2021	A+	Lansing	81	14	18	3	11	222	292	370	663	9	75	0.40	3	1	33	148	3.58
2022	A+	Lansing	102	22	31	7	18	304	413	578	992	16	79	0.90	0	0	45	275	8.07
2022	AA	Midland	315	51	90	10	45	286	350	441	791	9	80	0.50	11	5	30	156	5.28

Breakout prospect who continues to fly under radar. Consistently good all season and finished 3rd in org in BA. Reads spin well and has the swing and quick hands to make easy contact. Hits for fringe-average power and that development will dictate future. Doesn't own any plus tool, but does most things well. Solid defender at 3B.

Harris,Dustin — 7 — Texas
EXP MLB DEBUT: 2023 | H/W: 6-2 185 | FUT: Starting 1B | **8D**

Bats L Age 23
2019 (11) St. Petersburg Col
- Pwr + + + +
- BAvg + +
- Spd + +
- Def +

Year	Lev	Team	AB	R	H	HR	RBI	Avg	OB	Slg	OPS	bb%	ct%	Eye	SB	CS	x/h%	Iso	RC/G
2019	Rk	AZL A's Green	125	23	41	1	16	328	396	448	844	10	84	0.70	9	4	29	120	6.14
2019	A-	Vermont	84	10	27	0	10	321	400	345	745	12	77	0.58	0	3	7	24	4.94
2021	A	Down East	259	54	78	10	53	301	382	483	865	12	81	0.71	20	1	31	181	6.33
2021	A+	Hickory	145	32	54	10	32	372	424	648	1072	8	83	0.52	5	1	37	276	8.47
2022	AA	Frisco	331	58	85	17	66	257	340	471	812	11	78	0.57	19	5	41	215	5.61

2022 production feels down compared to 2021, but h% drop hid solid metrics including plate discipline development. 40% FB and 10% SwK indicates growth potential in his BA and the unicorn wheels continue to produce against superior C. Moved almost entirely to LF; still ironing out kinks. Can struggle against RHP.

Haskin,Hudson — 789 — Baltimore
EXP MLB DEBUT: 2024 | H/W: 6-2 200 | FUT: Starting CF | **7B**

Bats R Age 23
2020 (2) Tulane
- Pwr + + +
- BAvg + + +
- 4.28 Spd + + + +
- Def + + +

Year	Lev	Team	AB	R	H	HR	RBI	Avg	OB	Slg	OPS	bb%	ct%	Eye	SB	CS	x/h%	Iso	RC/G
2020	NCAA	Tulane	66	18	22	1	14	333	450	500	950	18	85	1.40	1	0	36	167	7.92
2021	A	Delmarva	217	44	60	5	33	276	343	415	758	9	72	0.37	17	5	32	138	5.02
2021	A+	Aberdeen	91	15	25	0	9	275	347	385	731	10	80	0.56	5	2	32	110	4.81
2022	AA	Bowie	387	58	102	15	56	264	337	455	792	10	74	0.43	5	3	40	191	5.43

Versatile and athletic, can hold down CF defensively but bat is challenged in a corner, even though his launch angle improved in 2022 and got to some more power. Has a good eye at the plate, makes good in-AB adjustments and willing to run when we gets on. Hustling, spark plug profile even if tools fall a bit short of top-of-the-order type.

Hassell III,Robert — 8 — Washington
EXP MLB DEBUT: 2023 | H/W: 6-2 195 | FUT: Starting CF | **9C**

Bats L Age 21
2020 (1) HS (TN)
- Pwr + + +
- BAvg + + + +
- Spd + + +
- Def + + +

Year	Lev	Team	AB	R	H	HR	RBI	Avg	OB	Slg	OPS	bb%	ct%	Eye	SB	CS	x/h%	Iso	RC/G
2021	A	Lake Elsinore	365	77	118	7	65	323	415	482	897	14	80	0.77	31	6	35	159	7.02
2021	A+	Fort Wayne	78	10	16	4	11	205	287	410	698	10	68	0.36	3	0	44	205	4.14
2022	A+	Fort Wayne	304	49	91	10	55	299	377	467	844	11	78	0.58	20	3	33	168	6.11
2022	A+	Wilmington	38	9	8	0	3	211	318	237	555	14	68	0.50	3	0	13	26	2.36
2022	AA	Harrisburg	108	9	24	1	12	222	306	296	602	11	68	0.37	1	0	25	74	2.95

Part of the Soto haul, the lanky CFer did struggle to make contact more than anticipated after the move East. But he has good ball/strike recognition and has been lauded for his hit tool. Uses speed on the bases and in the field. Jury is still out on his power ceiling; his frame and athleticism hints at more, but right now hits a ton of grounders.

Head,Hudson — 89 — Pittsburgh
EXP MLB DEBUT: 2024 | H/W: 6-1 180 | FUT: Starting OF | **7D**

Bats L Age 21
2019 (3) HS (TX)
- Pwr + +
- BAvg + +
- Spd + + +
- Def + + +

Year	Lev	Team	AB	R	H	HR	RBI	Avg	OB	Slg	OPS	bb%	ct%	Eye	SB	CS	x/h%	Iso	RC/G
2019	Rk	AZL Padres	120	19	34	1	12	283	363	417	780	11	76	0.52	3	3	32	133	5.49
2021	A	Bradenton	348	67	74	15	50	213	341	394	735	16	61	0.50	3	1	43	181	5.19
2022	A+	Greensboro	359	60	84	10	40	234	323	387	710	12	61	0.33	13	8	37	153	4.82

Toolsy, athletic OF who is still waiting to pop. Highly thought of due to natural skill and talent, but struggles to put it all together. Swings and misses far too often and can be beaten by FB up in zone. Will work counts and exhibit above average power at times. Just not consistent enough with stick. Solid defender who runs well.

Helman,Michael — 458 — Minnesota
EXP MLB DEBUT: 2023 | H/W: 6-1 195 | FUT: Utility player | **6B**

Bats R Age 26
2018 (11) Texas A&M
- Pwr + +
- BAvg + +
- Spd + + +
- Def + +

Year	Lev	Team	AB	R	H	HR	RBI	Avg	OB	Slg	OPS	bb%	ct%	Eye	SB	CS	x/h%	Iso	RC/G
2018	A	Cedar Rapids	107	20	38	2	15	355	389	486	875	5	87	0.43	4	5	24	131	6.07
2019	A+	Fort Myers	284	26	56	3	25	197	243	282	524	6	86	0.43	3	3	30	85	2.10
2021	A+	Cedar Rapids	398	71	98	19	57	246	332	462	794	11	78	0.59	21	5	45	216	5.42
2022	AA	Wichita	144	34	40	6	20	278	370	472	842	13	78	0.66	10	0	35	194	6.14
2022	AAA	St. Paul	368	67	92	14	40	250	324	416	739	10	78	0.50	30	5	35	166	4.64

Versatile prospect who fits utility profile. Spent most of year in AAA and set highs in both HR and SB. Has become more consistent power threat with more loft in stroke. Attacking pitches early in count and driving to all fields. Can play any position on diamond with easy arm strength. Smart ballplayer with high IQ. No plus tool.

Henderson,Gunnar — 5 — Baltimore
EXP MLB DEBUT: 2022 | H/W: 6-2 210 | FUT: Starting 3B | **9B**

Bats L Age 21
2019 (2) HS (AL)
- Pwr + + + +
- BAvg + + +
- Spd + + + +
- Def + + +

Year	Lev	Team	AB	R	H	HR	RBI	Avg	OB	Slg	OPS	bb%	ct%	Eye	SB	CS	x/h%	Iso	RC/G
2021	A+	Aberdeen	243	34	56	9	35	230	339	432	771	14	64	0.46	11	1	50	202	5.67
2021	AA	Bowie	15	4	3	0	0	200	294	267	561	12	33	0.20	0	0	33	67	5.83
2022	AA	Bowie	157	41	49	8	35	312	455	573	1028	21	76	1.08	12	2	45	261	9.12
2022	AAA	Norfolk Tides	250	60	72	11	41	288	382	504	886	13	69	0.49	10	1	39	216	7.09
2022	MLB	Baltimore	116	12	30	4	18	259	348	440	788	12	71	0.47	1	1	40	181	5.58

Yet another step forward with power/speed combo that got him to the majors in 2022. Hit ball extremely hard in both minors and majors that point to significant future HR numbers. Will always have some swing and miss that will mute the BA a bit, but all-fields pop and SB ability like from an infielder is golden. An All-Star trajectory.

Hendrick,Austin — 89 — Cincinnati
EXP MLB DEBUT: 2025 | H/W: 6-0 195 | FUT: Starting OF | **7E**

Bats L Age 21
2020 (1) HS (PA)
- Pwr + + + +
- BAvg +
- Spd + + +
- Def + + +

Year	Lev	Team	AB	R	H	HR	RBI	Avg	OB	Slg	OPS	bb%	ct%	Eye	SB	CS	x/h%	Iso	RC/G
2021	A	Daytona	209	30	44	7	29	211	365	388	753	20	52	0.51	4	2	52	177	6.32
2022	A	Daytona	127	19	26	7	21	205	284	402	685	10	54	0.24	2	0	42	197	4.58
2022	A+	Dayton	261	39	58	14	48	222	300	448	748	10	59	0.27	14	5	53	226	5.39

Powerful, athletic former 1st rd pick continues struggles with contact. Upright, closed stance with a hitchy load. It's an extreme uppercut swing trajectory with plus bat speed. Terrible approach with over 40% whiff rate and high chase rate in lower levels. Raw double-plus power. Gets to solid hard contact when not whiffing. Above-average runner.

Hernaiz,Darell

456 | Baltimore | EXP MLB DEBUT: 2025 | H/W: 6-1 190 | FUT: Starting 2B | 8D

Bats R Age 21 — 2019 (5) HS (TX)

Pwr +++ / BAvg +++ / Spd +++ (4.20) / Def ++++

Year	Lev	Team	AB	R	H	HR	RBI	Avg	OB	Slg	OPS	bb%	ct%	Eye	SB	CS	x/h%	Iso	RC/G
2021	A	Delmarva	372	62	103	6	52	277	328	358	685	7	81	0.40	22	6	17	81	3.88
2022	A	Delmarva	127	25	36	6	25	283	326	512	838	6	83	0.36	9	0	42	228	5.64
2022	A+	Aberdeen	226	41	69	5	29	305	367	456	823	9	81	0.51	22	3	30	150	5.74
2022	AA	Bowie	53	6	6	1	8	113	190	189	378	9	70	0.31	1	1	33	75	-0.41

Athletic, quick-twitch IFer with surprisingly robust hit and power projection who played at three levels in 2022. Has very good contact rates and exit velocity numbers justify the burgeoning pop - likely never plus, but more than expected from his smaller build. Likely settles in as bat-first 2B or valuable play-everywhere UT. Current speed for SB.

Hernandez,Cristian

6 | Chicago (N) | EXP MLB DEBUT: 2025 | H/W: 6-2 175 | FUT: Starting SS | 8D

Bats R Age 19 — 2021 FA (DR)

Pwr +++ / BAvg +++ / Spd ++++ / Def ++++

Year	Lev	Team	AB	R	H	HR	RBI	Avg	OB	Slg	OPS	bb%	ct%	Eye	SB	CS	x/h%	Iso	RC/G
2021	Rk	DSL Cubs Blue	158	38	45	5	22	285	399	424	823	16	75	0.77	21	3	24	139	6.10
2022	Rk	ACL Cubs	157	21	41	3	21	261	318	357	674	8	66	0.25	6	3	20	96	3.87

An uber talented teenager has the highest upside of any player in the system. Plus bat speed and projectable raw power. Plus speed and arm should allow him to stick at SS. If he can control the strike zone and keep his stroke short, he has the tools to be an All-Star SS.

Hernandez,Diego

89 | Kansas City | EXP MLB DEBUT: 2023 | H/W: 6-0 150 | FUT: Starting OF | 7D

Bats L Age 22 — 2017 FA (DR)

Pwr ++ / BAvg ++ / Spd ++++ / Def ++++

Year	Lev	Team	AB	R	H	HR	RBI	Avg	OB	Slg	OPS	bb%	ct%	Eye	SB	CS	x/h%	Iso	RC/G
2021	Rk	ACL Royals Blue	3	0	0	0	0	0	0	0	0	0	67	0.00	0	0		0	-6.12
2021	Rk	ACL Royals Gold	12	1	1	0	1	83	214	83	298	14	67	0.50	1	1	0	0	-1.63
2021	A	Columbia	266	47	73	1	19	274	352	335	687	11	75	0.48	34	10	16	60	4.16
2022	A+	Quad Cities	330	55	92	7	29	279	333	418	752	8	78	0.38	27	8	30	139	4.79
2022	AA	NW Arkansas	124	23	37	2	11	298	360	379	739	9	77	0.43	13	4	16	81	4.65

Athletic, speedy OF prospect posted strong returns with bat, split between High-A and Double-A. Calling card is double-plus run tool. Stole 40 bases in 115 games last year and played plus defense in CF. High BA slash approach with low average EV. Struggles with zone and spin recognition. Chased at significant rate. Below-average pull power.

Hernandez,Heriberto

79 | Tampa Bay | EXP MLB DEBUT: 2024 | H/W: 6-1 195 | FUT: Starting OF | 7C

Bats R Age 23 — 2017 FA (DR)

Pwr ++++ / BAvg ++ / Spd ++ / Def ++

Year	Lev	Team	AB	R	H	HR	RBI	Avg	OB	Slg	OPS	bb%	ct%	Eye	SB	CS	x/h%	Iso	RC/G
2019	Rk	AZL Rangers	192	42	66	11	48	344	425	646	1070	12	70	0.47	3	3	48	302	9.64
2019	A-	Spokane	8	4	3	0	1	375	500	375	875	20	63	0.67	3	0	0	0	7.80
2021	A	Charleston	254	57	64	12	44	252	373	453	826	16	65	0.54	7	4	42	201	6.45
2022	A+	Bowling Green	419	70	107	24	89	255	358	499	857	14	63	0.43	6	2	50	243	6.94

Three True Outcomer is former C prospect; best season in Rays organization. Strong, powerful frame. Patient approach, works counts and takes walks. Capable of 30+ HR at projection. Struggled early to get to consistent hard contact, got to it late in year. Swing-and-miss in profile with near 30% in zone whiff rate. Challenged defensively. Slow.

Hernandez,Maikol

6 | Baltimore | EXP MLB DEBUT: 2027 | H/W: 6-3 175 | FUT: Starting SS | 7D

Bats R Age 19 — 2021 FA (VZ)

Pwr ++ / BAvg ++ / Spd +++ / Def ++++

Year	Lev	Team	AB	R	H	HR	RBI	Avg	OB	Slg	OPS	bb%	ct%	Eye	SB	CS	x/h%	Iso	RC/G
2021	Rk	DSL Orioles	130	20	30	0	15	231	333	308	641	13	75	0.61	4	3	30	77	3.72
2022	Rk	FCL Orioles B	148	20	23	0	10	155	251	203	454	11	60	0.32	7	2	30	47	0.69

Athletic infielder has height and lean frame to put on some bulk and strength. Current clean swing mechanics, but yet to show average hit or power, though has good strike zone awareness. Plays a rangy shortstop with quality arm; should be a plus defender there if his size doesn't move him off the position. Long-term project.

Herrera,Ivan

2 | St. Louis | EXP MLB DEBUT: 2022 | H/W: 5-11 220 | FUT: Starting C | 7C

Bats R Age 22 — 2016 FA (PN)

Pwr ++ / BAvg ++ / Spd ++ / Def +++

Year	Lev	Team	AB	R	H	HR	RBI	Avg	OB	Slg	OPS	bb%	ct%	Eye	SB	CS	x/h%	Iso	RC/G
2019	A+	Palm Beach	58	7	16	1	5	276	333	328	661	8	72	0.31	0	0	6	52	3.52
2021	AA	Springfield	363	50	84	17	63	231	340	408	748	14	74	0.63	2	3	36	176	4.91
2021	AAA	Memphis	4	0	0	0	0	0	0	0	0	0	100		0	0		0	-2.66
2022	AAA	Memphis	235	41	63	6	34	268	370	396	766	14	78	0.73	5	1	27	128	5.26
2022	MLB	St. Louis	18	0	2	0	1	111	200	111	311	10	56	0.25	0	0	0	0	-2.00

Athletic backstop continues to make gains defensively. He receives and blocks the ball well with a strong, accurate arm. Bounced back offensively and made MLB debut. Quick RH stroke with average raw power, but doesn't get to it regularly in game action and seems to have opted for a contact-over-power approach at the plate.

Hickey,Nathan

2 | Boston | EXP MLB DEBUT: 2024 | H/W: 6-0 210 | FUT: Starting C | 7D

Bats L Age 23 — 2021 (5) Florida

Pwr ++++ / BAvg ++ / Spd + / Def +

Year	Lev	Team	AB	R	H	HR	RBI	Avg	OB	Slg	OPS	bb%	ct%	Eye	SB	CS	x/h%	Iso	RC/G
2021	NCAA	Florida	221	40	70	9	50	317	426	525	951	16	82	1.08	1	1	37	208	7.68
2021	Rk	FCL Red Sox	20	4	5	0	1	250	423	350	773	23	60	0.75	0	0	40	100	6.41
2021	A	Salem	8	1	1	0	1	125	364	125	489	27	75	1.50	0	0	0	0	1.95
2022	A	Salem	140	31	38	7	39	271	430	507	937	22	72	1.00	0	1	50	236	8.01
2022	A+	Greenville	115	19	29	9	23	252	381	539	920	17	66	0.62	0	0	52	287	7.67

Consistent, strong backstop who achieved in first full season. Has room to grow defensively as receiving and blocking are both sub-par. Owns strong, though inaccurate arm with slower transfer. Will have time to develop. Brings disciplined approach to plate with good power to pull side. Bat speed leads to hard contact. Potential to grow into BA.

Hicklen,Brewer

7 | Kansas City | EXP MLB DEBUT: 2022 | H/W: 6-2 208 | FUT: Reserve OF | 6C

Bats R Age 27 — 2017 (7) Ala-Birmingham

Pwr +++ / BAvg ++ / Spd ++++ / Def +++

Year	Lev	Team	AB	R	H	HR	RBI	Avg	OB	Slg	OPS	bb%	ct%	Eye	SB	CS	x/h%	Iso	RC/G
2018	A+	Wilmington	71	11	15	1	3	211	253	310	563	5	63	0.15	6	0	33	99	2.26
2019	A+	Wilmington	419	70	110	14	51	263	348	427	775	12	67	0.39	39	14	31	165	5.51
2021	AA	NW Arkansas	362	70	88	16	57	243	338	434	772	13	64	0.39	40	4	39	191	5.57
2022	AAA	Omaha	480	85	119	28	85	248	329	502	831	11	58	0.29	35	2	52	254	6.93
2022	MLB	Kansas City	4	1	0	0	0	0	0	0	0	0	0	0.00	0	0		0	

Former collegiate 2-sport athlete made MLB debut despite high Triple-A strikeout rate. Struck out 202 times in 480 AB with over 30% in zone whiff rate. Slightly open stance with minimal trigger and pull-dominant approach. Closes off plate and struggles with spin out of the zone. Plus raw power in frame. Average power potential in bigs. Plus runner.

Hill,Darius

9 | Chicago (N) | EXP MLB DEBUT: 2023 | H/W: 6-1 190 | FUT: Reserve OF | 6C

Bats L Age 25 — 2019 (20) West Virginia

Pwr + / BAvg +++ / Spd ++ / Def ++

Year	Lev	Team	AB	R	H	HR	RBI	Avg	OB	Slg	OPS	bb%	ct%	Eye	SB	CS	x/h%	Iso	RC/G
2019	A	South Bend	85	10	19	1	3	224	283	306	588	8	91	0.88	1	1	26	82	3.11
2021	A	Myrtle Beach	32	2	12	0	5	375	375	469	844	0	78	0.00	1	0	25	94	5.55
2021	AA	Tennessee	249	40	69	5	31	277	336	357	693	8	81	0.47	2	2	14	80	4.01
2022	AA	Tennessee	185	34	57	6	18	308	354	486	840	7	87	0.54	3	2	35	178	5.74
2022	AAA	Iowa	343	48	109	3	35	318	357	434	792	6	85	0.40	4	2	28	117	5.22

Has a mature, patient approach at the plate and is a contact-over-power prospect. Quick LH stroke is and geared toward gap-to-gap and line drives. Doesn't draw a ton of walks, but also rarely swings and misses (13% K rate) and did stroke a career-high 9 HR. Average to a tick above speed and will likely occupy a 4th OF role in the bigs.

Hinds,Rece

79 | Cincinnati | EXP MLB DEBUT: 2024 | H/W: 6-4 215 | FUT: Starting OF | 7C

Bats R Age 22 — 2019 (2) HS (FL)

Pwr +++ / BAvg ++ / Spd +++ / Def +++

Year	Lev	Team	AB	R	H	HR	RBI	Avg	OB	Slg	OPS	bb%	ct%	Eye	SB	CS	x/h%	Iso	RC/G
2021	Rk	ACL Reds	34	6	10	2	5	294	368	676	1045	11	62	0.31	1	1	70	382	10.29
2021	A	Daytona	167	33	42	10	27	251	306	515	821	7	69	0.25	6	2	52	263	5.81
2022	Rk	ACL Reds	16	2	1	0	0	63	167	63	229	11	63	0.33	2	2	0	0	-3.01
2022	A+	Dayton	247	33	58	10	26	235	300	425	725	9	57	0.21	13	5	40	190	5.25
2022	AA	Chattanooga	29	3	9	2	4	310	310	655	966	0	59	0.00	0	1	56	345	8.90

Power RHH OF prospect had second straight season shortened by injury. This time it was fractured hamate bone. Upright, open stance. Cleaned up load to get to hit position quicker. Super aggressive in-zone; over 40% whiff rate. Plus-plus bat speed with uppercut swing trajectory. Plus power in frame and swing. Power and strong arm carries in RF.

Hiraldo,Miguel

4 | Toronto | EXP MLB DEBUT: 2025 | H/W: 5-11 197 | FUT: Starting 2B | 8E

Bats R Age 22 — 2017 FA (DR)

Pwr +++ / BAvg ++ / Spd ++++ / Def ++

Year	Lev	Team	AB	R	H	HR	RBI	Avg	OB	Slg	OPS	bb%	ct%	Eye	SB	CS	x/h%	Iso	RC/G
2018	Rk	DSL Blue Jays	214	41	67	2	33	313	380	453	833	10	86	0.77	15	6	34	140	6.01
2019	Rk	Bluefield	237	43	71	7	37	300	339	481	820	6	85	0.39	11	3	39	181	5.47
2019	A	Lansing	4	0	1	0	0	250	250	750	1000	0	100		0	0	100	500	7.78
2021	A	Dunedin	390	66	97	7	52	249	336	390	725	12	72	0.46	29	5	38	141	4.75
2022	A+	Vancouver	398	47	92	11	55	231	280	382	662	6	68	0.21	28	5	37	151	3.62

Athletic, strong INF who has seen stock fall based upon poor plate approach and below average defense. Remains a bat-first prospect with good power potential. Set high in HR with short, quick stroke and above average bat speed. Has difficulty with breaking balls and can be too pull happy. Has hands and arm to improve as 2B.

Holland,Will — 68 — Minnesota
EXP MLB DEBUT: 2024 | H/W: 5-10 181 | FUT: Utility player | **6C**

Bats R Age 24	Year	Lev	Team	AB	R	H	HR	RBI	Avg	OB	Slg	OPS	bb%	ct%	Eye	SB	CS	x/h%	Iso	RC/G
2019 (5) Auburn																				
Pwr ++	2019	Rk	Elizabethton	125	22	24	7	16	192	273	376	649	10	65	0.32	8	1	38	184	3.38
BAvg ++	2021	A	Fort Myers	252	40	54	10	27	214	305	401	706	12	61	0.33	19	5	48	187	4.68
Spd ++++	2022	A+	Cedar Rapids	276	45	62	6	35	225	321	362	683	12	64	0.40	21	4	35	138	4.27
Def +++	2022	AA	Wichita	98	21	23	3	14	235	348	378	725	15	60	0.44	11	2	26	143	5.11

Athletic prospect with as much speed as any in org. Set career best in SB and got on base more consistently due to more discerning eye and pitch recognition. Still strikes out far too much for someone with limited punch. Swing path is erratic and doesn't hit for BA. Can play both SS and CF with impressive range.

Holliday,Jackson — 6 — Baltimore
EXP MLB DEBUT: 2025 | H/W: 6-1 175 | FUT: Starting SS | **9D**

Bats L Age 19	Year	Lev	Team	AB	R	H	HR	RBI	Avg	OB	Slg	OPS	bb%	ct%	Eye	SB	CS	x/h%	Iso	RC/G
2022 (1) HS (OK)																				
Pwr +++																				
BAvg ++++																				
4.14 Spd ++++	2022	Rk	FCL Orioles B	22	6	9	1	3	409	594	591	1185	31	91	5.00	3	0	22	182	11.46
Def +++	2022	A	Delmarva	42	8	10	0	6	238	439	333	772	26	76	1.50	1	1	40	95	6.12

Top overall pick has exemplary combination of polish and projection. Frame has room to add strength and bulk to a foundation of simple, linear swing path with hands that explode and beget good carry. Knows the strike zone; low whiff rates, impressive exit velos. Premium athlete; game looks easy. Hands/range/arm to stay at SS. Sky-high upside.

Hopkins,TJ — 79 — Cincinnati
EXP MLB DEBUT: 2023 | H/W: 6-0 195 | FUT: Reserve OF | **6C**

Bats R Age 26	Year	Lev	Team	AB	R	H	HR	RBI	Avg	OB	Slg	OPS	bb%	ct%	Eye	SB	CS	x/h%	Iso	RC/G
2019 (9) So Carolina	2019	NCAA	South Carolina	214	49	61	11	42	285	365	519	884	11	77	0.55	18	4	41	234	6.58
Pwr ++	2019	Rk	Billings	202	40	54	5	30	267	330	426	756	9	74	0.37	12	2	35	158	4.95
BAvg ++	2021	AA	Chattanooga	257	42	69	5	33	268	336	436	771	9	72	0.37	3	0	38	167	5.30
Spd +++	2022	AA	Chattanooga	373	57	97	17	66	260	332	464	796	10	69	0.34	6	5	41	204	5.59
Def +++	2022	AAA	Louisville	94	11	24	4	14	255	314	436	750	8	69	0.28	2	0	38	181	4.82

Solid COF prospect pushed onward to Triple-A in 2022. Near physical projection. Open, upright stance with slight trigger at load. Average bat speed, struggles with bigger velocity, especially up. Has swing-and-miss in profile. Maximizes power potential with solid lofted ball profile to pull field. Average runner.

Horwitz,Spencer — 3 — Toronto
EXP MLB DEBUT: 2023 | H/W: 6-0 190 | FUT: Starting 1B | **7C**

Bats L Age 25	Year	Lev	Team	AB	R	H	HR	RBI	Avg	OB	Slg	OPS	bb%	ct%	Eye	SB	CS	x/h%	Iso	RC/G
2019 (24) Radford	2019	A-	Tri-City	42	6	8	1	3	190	209	286	495	2	86	0.17	0	0	25	95	1.47
Pwr ++	2021	A+	Vancouver	389	65	113	10	62	290	399	445	843	15	83	1.06	4	5	35	154	6.36
BAvg +++	2021	AA	New Hampshire	16	3	6	2	4	375	375	875	1250	0	88	0.00	0	0	67	500	9.60
Spd +	2022	AA	New Hampshire	232	46	69	10	39	297	407	517	925	16	77	0.80	3	1	43	220	7.43
Def ++	2022	AAA	Buffalo	171	31	42	2	12	246	358	363	721	15	76	0.73	4	1	38	117	4.83

Patient 1B who led org in BB and finished 2nd in doubles. Reached AAA and has chance to get to TOR. Makes easy contact with simple swing, enhanced by strong batting eye. Uses entire field and only struggles against LHP, limiting BA. Poor defender and doesn't run well. May have to add power.

House,Brady — 6 — Washington
EXP MLB DEBUT: 2026 | H/W: 6-4 215 | FUT: Starting 3B | **9D**

Bats R Age 19	Year	Lev	Team	AB	R	H	HR	RBI	Avg	OB	Slg	OPS	bb%	ct%	Eye	SB	CS	x/h%	Iso	RC/G
2021 (1) HS (GA)																				
Pwr ++++																				
BAvg +++																				
Spd ++	2021	Rk	FCL Nationals	59	14	19	4	12	322	394	576	970	11	78	0.54	0	0	37	254	7.52
Def +++	2022	A	Fredericksburg	176	24	49	3	31	278	324	375	699	6	66	0.20	1	0	22	97	4.21

Big power from a mature frame, though only got two months into first full season before back issues shut him down. Some have never been sold on his hit tool, and he did have trouble making consistent contact in 2022. Right now plays an OK shortstop, though consensus is growing that he'll be better suited at 3B as he makes his way to the majors.

Howard,Ed — 6 — Chicago (N)
EXP MLB DEBUT: 2024 | H/W: 6-2 185 | FUT: Reserve SS | **7E**

Bats R Age 21	Year	Lev	Team	AB	R	H	HR	RBI	Avg	OB	Slg	OPS	bb%	ct%	Eye	SB	CS	x/h%	Iso	RC/G
2020 (1) HS (IL)																				
Pwr +																				
BAvg ++																				
Spd +++	2021	A	Myrtle Beach	302	33	68	4	31	225	269	315	583	6	68	0.18	7	2	24	89	2.49
Def ++++	2022	A+	South Bend	82	8	20	1	11	244	319	317	636	10	77	0.47	3	0	15	73	3.39

16th pick in 2020 came into the league with questions about his hit tool that have largely been confirmed and he now owns a career .602 OPS. Struggles with breaking ball and pitch recognition. Plus athlete is one of the best defensive SS in the minors with good range and a strong, accurate arm. Runs well, but not a SB threat. The clock is ticking.

Howell,Korry — 8 — San Diego
EXP MLB DEBUT: 2023 | H/W: 6-3 180 | FUT: Utility player | **6B**

Bats R Age 24	Year	Lev	Team	AB	R	H	HR	RBI	Avg	OB	Slg	OPS	bb%	ct%	Eye	SB	CS	x/h%	Iso	RC/G
2018 (12) Kirkwood CC	2018	Rk	AZL Brewers	103	15	32	0	6	311	393	350	743	12	77	0.58	12	4	13	39	4.96
Pwr ++	2019	A	Wisconsin	293	35	69	2	22	235	321	317	639	11	68	0.39	19	8	25	82	3.55
BAvg ++	2021	A+	Wisconsin	258	65	64	12	36	248	336	465	801	12	66	0.39	20	3	44	217	5.88
Spd ++++	2021	AA	Biloxi	98	18	23	4	15	235	318	429	747	11	55	0.27	4	3	43	194	5.82
Def +++	2022	AA	San Antonio	146	37	37	6	20	253	363	486	849	15	64	0.48	12	1	49	233	6.91

Versatile prospect was acquired from MIL in April and ended season in June due to wrist. Terrific athlete who has plus speed and is quality defender, but doesn't hit much yet. Gets on base consistently with keen eye and possesses at least average raw power. Struggles with spin and swings over pitches. Needs to make more contact.

Infante,Sammy — 5 — Washington
EXP MLB DEBUT: 2025 | H/W: 6-1 185 | FUT: Starting 3B | **7D**

Bats R Age 21	Year	Lev	Team	AB	R	H	HR	RBI	Avg	OB	Slg	OPS	bb%	ct%	Eye	SB	CS	x/h%	Iso	RC/G
2020 (2) HS (FL)																				
Pwr +++																				
BAvg ++																				
Spd +++	2021	Rk	FCL Nationals	121	19	26	3	15	215	312	364	675	12	64	0.40	3	4	38	149	4.14
Def +++	2022	A	Fredericksburg	367	59	77	17	56	210	287	406	693	10	65	0.31	15	4	48	196	4.17

Power-over-hit cornerman with athletic swing and raw pop, but too often sells out and the result is a sky-high whiff rate and rough BA numbers. Does sport a double-digit walk rate, but tweaking his swing for more contact is paramount to future success, especially as a third baseman. Was not young for his draft class, but still time.

Isola,Alex — 23 — Minnesota
EXP MLB DEBUT: 2024 | H/W: 6-1 215 | FUT: Reserve C | **7E**

Bats R Age 24	Year	Lev	Team	AB	R	H	HR	RBI	Avg	OB	Slg	OPS	bb%	ct%	Eye	SB	CS	x/h%	Iso	RC/G
2019 (29) Texas Christian	2019	Rk	Elizabethton	25	7	10	1	8	400	400	600	1000	0	60	0.00	1	0	30	200	9.13
Pwr +++	2019	A	Cedar Rapids	56	7	15	2	9	268	328	429	756	8	84	0.56	0	0	33	161	4.80
BAvg ++	2021	A+	Cedar Rapids	362	47	88	17	52	243	340	425	765	13	75	0.60	1	0	36	182	5.08
Spd +	2022	Rk	FCL Twins	6	2	1	1	3	167	444	667	1111	33	67	1.50	0	0	100	500	10.20
Def ++	2022	AA	Wichita	210	33	60	10	40	286	380	471	852	13	79	0.71	0	1	32	186	6.21

Bat-first backstop with intriguing size and strength. Missed lot of time mid-season due to injury, but returned with aplomb. Worked on swing and became more fluid and strong. Consistently puts charge into ball while maintaining good walk rate. Speed and defense are below par. Can play 1B and will need to stay healthy and hit.

Issac,Xavier — 3 — Tampa Bay
EXP MLB DEBUT: 2026 | H/W: 6-4 240 | FUT: Starting 1B | **8E**

Bats L Age 19	Year	Lev	Team	AB	R	H	HR	RBI	Avg	OB	Slg	OPS	bb%	ct%	Eye	SB	CS	x/h%	Iso	RC/G
2022 (1) HS (NC)																				
Pwr ++++																				
BAvg +++																				
Spd +																				
Def ++	2022	Rk	FCL Rays	19	4	4	0	5	211	286	368	654	10	84	0.67	0	0	75	158	3.99

XXL frame, 1B-only power prospect was surprised 1st round pick in 2022 draft. Strong, stocky frame will need attention. Upright, slight open stance with direct trigger to hit position. Plus bat speed with present feel for barrel. Exceptional raw power, will likely play in game. Foundational hit tool willing to go with pitch to opposite field.

Jackson,Jeremiah — 46 — Los Angeles (A)
EXP MLB DEBUT: 2024 | H/W: 6-0 165 | FUT: Starting 2B | **7E**

Bats R Age 23	Year	Lev	Team	AB	R	H	HR	RBI	Avg	OB	Slg	OPS	bb%	ct%	Eye	SB	CS	x/h%	Iso	RC/G
2018 (2) HS (AL)	2018	Rk	AZL Angels	82	13	26	5	14	317	371	598	968	8	70	0.28	6	1	42	280	7.93
Pwr +++	2019	Rk	Orem	256	47	68	23	60	266	329	605	934	9	63	0.25	5	1	57	340	7.88
BAvg ++	2021	Rk	ACL Angels	21	5	8	2	4	381	409	714	1123	5	67	0.14	2	0	38	333	10.01
Spd +++	2021	A	Inland Empire	167	29	44	8	46	263	356	527	883	13	61	0.37	11	3	57	263	7.67
Def +++	2022	AA	Rocket City	307	44	66	14	44	215	301	404	705	11	75	0.49	7	4	45	189	4.22

Toolsy, athletic 2B struggles with lack of feel for hit tool. Quick-twitch athlete. Potential for plus body strength. Closed, upright stance with bat wrap. Plus bat speed with uppercut trajectory swing. Doesn't consistently combine loft and hard contact due to struggles chasing out of the zone. Above-average runner. Plus defender at 2B.

ensen,Carter | 2 | Kansas City | EXP MLB DEBUT: 2025 | H/W: 6-1 210 | FUT: Starting C | 8E

Bats L Age 19
2021 (3) HS (MO)
Pwr ++++
BAvg +++
Spd ++
Def +++

Year	Lev	Team	AB	R	H	HR	RBI	Avg	OB	Slg	OPS	bb%	ct%	Eye	SB	CS	x/h%	Iso	RC/G
2021	Rk	ACL Royals Blue	2	1	1	0	0	500	500	###	1500	0	50	0.00	0	0	100	500	22.52
2021	Rk	ACL Royals Gold	55	8	15	1	7	273	385	382	766	15	65	0.53	4	0	20	109	5.63
2022	A	Columbia	393	66	89	11	50	226	361	382	743	17	74	0.81	8	6	42	155	5.13

Offensively drivenn CA struggled with average in Low-A despite advanced approach. Upright, open stance. Swing is geared towards lift with plus power potential carrying profile. Gets to hard contact often. Discerning eye, will take walks. Fly ball tendencies lead to low BABIP, depressing BA potential. Improved defensively as season wore on.

imenez,Gilberto | 89 | Boston | EXP MLB DEBUT: 2024 | H/W: 5-11 212 | FUT: Starting OF | 8E

Bats R Age 22
2017 FA (DR)
Pwr ++
BAvg ++
Spd ++++
Def +++

Year	Lev	Team	AB	R	H	HR	RBI	Avg	OB	Slg	OPS	bb%	ct%	Eye	SB	CS	x/h%	Iso	RC/G
2019	A-	Lowell	234	35	84	3	19	359	393	470	863	5	84	0.34	14	6	20	111	5.96
2021	A	Salem	373	64	114	3	56	306	339	405	744	5	77	0.22	13	8	22	99	4.59
2022	A+	Greenville	380	49	102	5	34	268	302	366	667	5	74	0.18	20	9	25	97	3.56

Excellent athlete whose development has stalled. Continues to flail at pitches out of zone and approach far too aggressive to be worthwhile. Rarely draws walks and power hasn't developed as anticipated. BA has been OK, but likely to fall at upper levels. Has prevalence of all tools and has incredible speed. Good defender with strong arm.

imenez,Leo | 6 | Toronto | EXP MLB DEBUT: 2024 | H/W: 5-11 215 | FUT: Starting 2B | 7D

Bats R Age 21
2017 FA (PN)
Pwr ++
BAvg ++
Spd +++
Def +++

Year	Lev	Team	AB	R	H	HR	RBI	Avg	OB	Slg	OPS	bb%	ct%	Eye	SB	CS	x/h%	Iso	RC/G
2019	Rk	Bluefield	215	34	64	0	22	298	360	377	737	9	80	0.50	2	1	23	79	4.77
2019	A	Lansing	6	0	1	0	0	167	167	167	333	0	67	0.00	0	0	0	0	-1.38
2021	Rk	FCL Blue Jays	13	6	5	0	2	385	500	538	1038	19	92	3.00	1	0	40	154	9.12
2021	A	Dunedin	168	35	53	1	19	315	475	381	856	23	79	1.46	4	1	17	65	7.07
2022	A+	Vancouver	244	45	56	6	40	230	306	385	692	10	76	0.47	7	3	41	156	4.14

Steady, athletic INF who has improved with bat by adding strength and driving balls with greater exit velocity. BA dropped as he learned new swing mechanics. Rarely chases out of zone and also puts bat to ball consistently. Quick defender who makes all routine plays at SS. Owns average arm with soft hands.

ohnson,Ivan | 4 | Cincinnati | EXP MLB DEBUT: 2023 | H/W: 6-0 190 | FUT: Starting 2B | 7D

Bats B Age 24
2019 (4) Chipola JC
Pwr +++
BAvg ++
Spd +++
Def +++

Year	Lev	Team	AB	R	H	HR	RBI	Avg	OB	Slg	OPS	bb%	ct%	Eye	SB	CS	x/h%	Iso	RC/G
2019	NCAA	Chipola Col	189	54	72	9	49	381	475	587	1063	15	80	0.92	14	6	28	206	9.03
2019	Rk	Greeneville	188	27	48	6	22	255	320	415	735	9	76	0.39	11	4	35	160	4.60
2021	A	Daytona	186	27	49	6	23	263	357	457	814	13	67	0.44	8	5	45	194	6.17
2021	A+	Dayton	98	17	26	4	18	265	357	439	796	13	60	0.36	3	2	35	173	6.19
2022	AA	Chattanooga	180	32	47	4	25	261	311	428	739	7	63	0.20	4	1	40	167	5.09

Oft-injured MIF prospect struggled to stay on the field dealing with wrist and shoulder injuries. Switch-hitter with better hit tool from RH side but better power potential from LH side. Struggled recouping bat speed after injury. It's above-average raw power, likely plays as average but only if bat speed returns. Solid defender at 2B.

ohnson,Termarr | 46 | Pittsburgh | EXP MLB DEBUT: 2025 | H/W: 5-7 175 | FUT: Starting 2B | 8B

Bats L Age 18
2022 (1) HS (GA)
Pwr +++
BAvg ++++
Spd +++
Def ++

Year	Lev	Team	AB	R	H	HR	RBI	Avg	OB	Slg	OPS	bb%	ct%	Eye	SB	CS	x/h%	Iso	RC/G
2022	Rk	FCL Pirates Black	23	0	3	0	0	130	310	217	528	21	65	0.75	2	0	67	87	2.11
2022	A	Bradenton	40	7	11	1	6	275	420	450	870	20	68	0.77	4	1	45	175	7.33

Advanced hitter with hand-eye coordination, pitch recognition and strong stroke. Quick hand and wrist action can put charge into balls and has potential for plus power to all fields. Simply needs pro AB. Knows balls and strikes and willing to wait. Likely limited to 2B due to lack of range, but is fundamentally sound. Face of franchise potential.

ohnston,Troy | 3 | Miami | EXP MLB DEBUT: 2023 | H/W: 6-0 205 | FUT: Starting 1B | 7C

Bats L Age 25
2019 (17) Gonzaga
Pwr +++
BAvg +++
Spd ++
Def ++

Year	Lev	Team	AB	R	H	HR	RBI	Avg	OB	Slg	OPS	bb%	ct%	Eye	SB	CS	x/h%	Iso	RC/G
2021	A	Jupiter	83	12	29	1	13	349	426	446	871	12	86	0.92	0	0	21	96	6.50
2021	A+	Beloit	357	54	103	14	72	289	386	473	860	14	75	0.63	6	1	36	185	6.51
2022	AA	Pensacola	329	42	96	10	49	292	355	450	804	9	78	0.45	3	0	32	158	5.48
2022	AAA	Jacksonville	97	9	15	4	8	155	287	330	617	16	75	0.75	1	0	60	175	3.23

Tweener profile 1B/COF prospect continues march to eventual big league debut. Upright, open stance with minimal load. Quick hands and solid base propel above-average bat speed. Gap approach, hasn't cashed in on pull over-the-fence power. Will need pull power feature to carry starting roll. Below-average defender in OF, wroks best at 1B.

ones,Brock | 78 | Tampa Bay | EXP MLB DEBUT: 2025 | H/W: 6-0 197 | FUT: Starting CF | 8E

Bats L Age 22
2022 (2) Stanford
Pwr ++++
BAvg ++
Spd ++++
Def +++

Year	Lev	Team	AB	R	H	HR	RBI	Avg	OB	Slg	OPS	bb%	ct%	Eye	SB	CS	x/h%	Iso	RC/G
2022	Rk	FCL Rays	19	4	4	0	2	211	375	211	586	21	68	0.83	2	2	0	0	2.99
2022	A	Charleston	49	15	14	4	12	286	426	653	1079	20	57	0.57	9	3	64	367	11.53

Former 2-sport player in college was selected in 2nd round of 2022 draft. Compact, muscular frame. Plus athlete. Open stance with stiff trigger. Handles middle-in pitches well and doesn't chase out of the zone. Up-the-middle to pull approach. Raw plus power plays to CF and gaps. Could hit 25+ HR if developed. Plus runner with skills for CF.

ones,Druw | 8 | Arizona | EXP MLB DEBUT: 2025 | H/W: 6-4 180 | FUT: Starting CF | 9C

Bats R Age 19
2022 (1) HS (GA)
Pwr ++++
BAvg ++++
Spd ++++
Def ++++

Year	Lev	Team	AB	R	H	HR	RBI	Avg	OB	Slg	OPS	bb%	ct%	Eye	SB	CS	x/h%	Iso	RC/G

Quick twitch, athlete CF prospect, taken 2nd overall in draft, is son of former MLB All-Star Andruw Jones. Long and lean with room to grow physically. Missed pro debut due to shoulder injury. Plus tools across the board. Plus bat speed with a linear swing plane. Raw plus power in frame. Will play as swing matures. 30/30 potential performer.

ones,Greg | 6 | Tampa Bay | EXP MLB DEBUT: 2024 | H/W: 6-2 175 | FUT: Starting SS | 7C

Bats B Age 25
2019 (1) UNC Wilmington
Pwr +++
BAvg ++
Spd ++++
Def +++

Year	Lev	Team	AB	R	H	HR	RBI	Avg	OB	Slg	OPS	bb%	ct%	Eye	SB	CS	x/h%	Iso	RC/G
2019	NCAA	UNC Wilmington	223	70	76	5	36	341	471	543	1014	20	80	1.25	42	10	34	202	8.93
2019	A-	Hudson Valley	191	39	64	1	24	335	404	461	864	10	71	0.39	19	8	28	126	6.79
2021	A+	Bowling Green	220	48	64	13	38	291	373	527	901	12	66	0.39	27	2	36	236	7.31
2021	AA	Montgomery	54	8	10	1	2	185	241	296	538	7	61	0.19	7	0	30	111	1.92
2022	AA	Montgomery	319	54	76	8	40	238	298	392	690	8	60	0.21	37	5	39	154	4.49

Speedy, switch-hitting SS prospect continues to struggle with swing and miss. Wiry, athletic frame with plus raw strength. Upright stance from both sides of plate. Struggles with swing decisions and cutting off the plate, especially from the LH side. Hit tool is average from RH side. So is overall power potential. Plus runner, swipes bases.

ones,Spencer | 89 | New York (A) | EXP MLB DEBUT: 2025 | H/W: 6-7 225 | FUT: Starting OF | 9E

Bats L Age 21
2022 (1) Vanderbilt
Pwr ++++
BAvg +++
Spd +++
Def +++

Year	Lev	Team	AB	R	H	HR	RBI	Avg	OB	Slg	OPS	bb%	ct%	Eye	SB	CS	x/h%	Iso	RC/G
2022	NCAA	Vanderbilt	230	62	85	12	60	370	447	643	1090	12	72	0.50	14	1	42	274	9.75
2022	Rk	FCL Yankees	10	3	5	1	4	500	545	900	1445	9	80	0.50	2	0	40	400	13.22
2022	A	Tampa	83	18	27	3	8	325	398	494	892	11	78	0.56	10	0	30	169	6.67

Tall, powerful athletic LHH OF prospect was selected by NYY in first round. Open, upright stance with smooth trigger, gets hands quickly to hit position. Up-the-middle approach with average patience. Does well to get to contact despite longer levers, supplementing hit tool. Raw plus-plus power. Plays to CF mostly in games. Above-average runner.

ordan,Blaze | 35 | Boston | EXP MLB DEBUT: 2025 | H/W: 6-2 220 | FUT: Starting 1B | 8C

Bats R Age 20
2020 (3) HS (MS)
Pwr ++++
BAvg +++
Spd +
Def ++

Year	Lev	Team	AB	R	H	HR	RBI	Avg	OB	Slg	OPS	bb%	ct%	Eye	SB	CS	x/h%	Iso	RC/G
2021	Rk	FCL Red Sox	69	12	25	4	19	362	413	667	1080	8	81	0.46	1	0	48	304	8.77
2021	A	Salem	36	7	9	2	7	250	289	444	734	5	78	0.25	0	0	33	194	4.22
2022	A	Salem	370	48	106	8	57	286	351	446	797	9	82	0.55	4	1	38	159	5.46
2022	A+	Greenville	93	12	28	4	11	301	375	441	816	11	71	0.41	1	0	18	140	5.73

Powerful INF who finished 3rd in CAR in BA and 2nd in walks. Possesses good hitting skills for power profile. Works counts and makes good contact despite natural loft. Using all fields more consistently. Destroys LHP and should be platoon option at worst. Lacks foot speed and agility at 3B and likely to move to 1B full time.

Jorge,Carlos — 4 — Cincinnati

EXP MLB DEBUT: 2026 | H/W: 5-10 160 | FUT: Starting 2B | 8E

Bats L Age 19 | 2021 FA (DR)
Pwr +++ | BAvg +++ | Spd ++++ | Def +++

Year	Lev	Team	AB	R	H	HR	RBI	Avg	OB	Slg	OPS	bb%	ct%	Eye	SB	CS	x/h%	Iso	RC/G
2021	Rk	DSL Reds	159	38	55	3	33	346	432	579	1010	13	80	0.75	27	5	38	233	8.55
2022	Rk	ACL Reds	119	32	31	7	21	261	389	529	918	17	66	0.61	27	4	52	269	7.87

Short-statured LHH 2B prospect impressed with strength and ability to run. Frame has room to add bulk. Upright, open stance with leg lift and smooth load. Short, compact swing with uppercut trajectory. Easy hit mechanics overall. Solid eye, will work the opposite way. Packs a punch; also 27 for 31 in SB.

Jorge,Dyan — 6 — Colorado

EXP MLB DEBUT: 2025 | H/W: 6-3 170 | FUT: Starting SS | 7D

Bats R Age 20 | 2022 FA (CU)
Pwr ++ | BAvg +++ | Spd ++++ | Def +++

Year	Lev	Team	AB	R	H	HR	RBI	Avg	OB	Slg	OPS	bb%	ct%	Eye	SB	CS	x/h%	Iso	RC/G
2022	Rk	DSL Rockies	15	2	5	0	5	333	375	467	842	6	73	0.25	0	0	40	133	6.20
2022	Rk	DSL Colorado	191	35	61	4	20	319	393	450	843	11	84	0.74	13	10	26	131	6.07

Cuban SS signed late but landed a hefty $2.8 million bonus. Plus runner with good range, soft hands, and enough arm to stick at short. Mature approach at the plate and is able to find the barrel regularly without being overly aggressive. Power development will be key and he could surpass expectations with double-digit SB and HR.

Julien,Edouard — 4 — Minnesota

EXP MLB DEBUT: 2023 | H/W: 6-2 195 | FUT: Starting 2B | 7C

Bats L Age 23 | 2019 (18) Auburn
Pwr +++ | BAvg +++ | Spd ++ | Def ++

Year	Lev	Team	AB	R	H	HR	RBI	Avg	OB	Slg	OPS	bb%	ct%	Eye	SB	CS	x/h%	Iso	RC/G
2021	A	Fort Myers	147	41	44	3	24	299	477	456	933	25	63	0.93	21	2	36	156	8.84
2021	A+	Cedar Rapids	247	52	61	15	48	247	394	494	888	20	64	0.67	13	3	51	247	7.53
2022	AA	Wichita	400	77	120	17	67	300	438	490	928	20	69	0.78	19	7	33	190	7.97

Ultra-patient 2B who led TL in OBP while finishing 6th in minors in walks. Rarely chases pitches and has exquisite knowledge on what pitches he can hit hard. Has upped production with more bat speed and strength. Still swings and misses, particularly against velocity. Struggles with LHP. Not much value on defense.

Jung,Jace — 4 — Detroit

EXP MLB DEBUT: 2025 | H/W: 6-0 205 | FUT: Starting 2B | 9D

Bats L Age 22 | 2022 (1) Texas Tech
Pwr ++++ | BAvg ++++ | Spd ++ | Def ++

Year	Lev	Team	AB	R	H	HR	RBI	Avg	OB	Slg	OPS	bb%	ct%	Eye	SB	CS	x/h%	Iso	RC/G
2022	NCAA	Texas Tech	224	68	75	14	57	335	473	612	1085	21	81	1.40	5	0	44	277	9.60
2022	A+	West Michigan	108	16	25	1	13	231	376	333	709	19	74	0.89	1	0	32	102	4.83

Younger brother of Josh Jung has an advanced approach at the plate and rarely chases out of the zone. Unorthodox setup raises questions about how hit tool will translate in pro ball, but quick lefty stroke results in consistent contact and above-average power. Below-average defender with limited speed raises questions about future position.

Jung,Josh — 5 — Texas

EXP MLB DEBUT: 2022 | H/W: 6-2 214 | FUT: Starting 3B | 9D

Bats R Age 25 | 2019 (1) Texas Tech
Pwr ++++ | BAvg +++ | Spd + | Def +++

Year	Lev	Team	AB	R	H	HR	RBI	Avg	OB	Slg	OPS	bb%	ct%	Eye	SB	CS	x/h%	Iso	RC/G
2021	AA	Frisco	169	25	52	10	40	308	357	544	902	7	75	0.31	2	2	37	237	6.58
2021	AAA	Round Rock	135	29	47	9	21	348	425	652	1077	12	75	0.53	0	0	49	304	9.25
2022	Rk	ACL Rangers	25	4	6	3	5	240	321	600	921	11	80	0.60	0	0	50	360	6.53
2022	AAA	Round Rock	99	15	27	6	24	273	301	525	826	4	70	0.13	1	0	48	253	5.66
2022	MLB	Texas	98	9	20	5	14	204	235	418	654	4	60	0.10	2	0	50	214	3.63

Much ballyhooed prospect debuted with massive power and whiff rates, though 13.2 SwK not awful. Watched lots of strikes, difficulty with SL and SI. Still projects as All-Star caliber player but hit tool questions now more pronounced. Cannon arm and suitable hot corner range locks in starting gig for extended MLB burn, but speed well below average.

Kasevich,Josh — 56 — Toronto

EXP MLB DEBUT: 2024 | H/W: 6-0 200 | FUT: Starting 3B | 7C

Bats R Age 22 | 2022 (2) Oregon
Pwr ++ | BAvg +++ | Spd +++ | Def +++

Year	Lev	Team	AB	R	H	HR	RBI	Avg	OB	Slg	OPS	bb%	ct%	Eye	SB	CS	x/h%	Iso	RC/G
2022	NCAA	Oregon	245	53	76	7	44	310	372	445	817	9	93	1.50	6	0	24	135	5.69
2022	A	Dunedin	107	18	28	0	7	262	331	336	667	9	92	1.22	0	2	29	75	4.20

Consistent INF who plays a simple game. Has tremendous plate discipline and gets on base at high clip. Also puts bat to ball consistently with level swing path. Makes hard contact to all fields, though may need to pull ball more for HR. Hits lot of groundballs. Not the fleetest of foot, but is smart baserunner. Strong arm likely to land at 3B.

Kath,Wes — 5 — Chicago (A)

EXP MLB DEBUT: 2025 | H/W: 6-3 200 | FUT: Starting 3B | 8E

Bats L Age 20 | 2021 (2) HS (AZ)
Pwr +++ | BAvg ++ | Spd ++ | Def +++

Year	Lev	Team	AB	R	H	HR	RBI	Avg	OB	Slg	OPS	bb%	ct%	Eye	SB	CS	x/h%	Iso	RC/G
2021	Rk	ACL White Sox	104	15	22	3	15	212	268	337	604	7	60	0.19	1	0	23	125	2.96
2022	A	Kannapolis	383	56	91	13	42	238	341	397	738	14	61	0.41	2	0	37	159	5.22
2022	AA	Birmingham	47	1	8	0	3	170	235	191	427	8	51	0.17	0	0	13	21	0.22

Infielder struggled with whiffs in full season debut. It's an open, upright stance with a bat wrap into a sweet, compact swing with not a lot of flexibility. Swing cuts off the outer half playing for pull power and can get beat by gas up. Above-average power potential should play with more contact. Strong arm, sticks at 3B.

Kavadas,Niko — 3 — Boston

EXP MLB DEBUT: 2024 | H/W: 6-1 235 | FUT: Starting 1B | 8E

Bats L Age 24 | 2021 (11) Notre Dame
Pwr ++++ | BAvg ++ | Spd + | Def +

Year	Lev	Team	AB	R	H	HR	RBI	Avg	OB	Slg	OPS	bb%	ct%	Eye	SB	CS	x/h%	Iso	RC/G
2021	Rk	FCL Red Sox	22	4	5	1	2	227	414	455	868	24	73	1.17	0	0	60	227	7.10
2021	A	Salem	21	6	6	1	4	286	483	524	1007	28	67	1.14	0	0	50	238	9.62
2022	A	Salem	192	35	55	14	48	286	443	609	1052	22	64	0.77	1	1	60	323	10.28
2022	A+	Greenville	120	27	37	10	28	308	454	592	1046	21	65	0.76	0	0	38	283	9.82
2022	AA	Portland	81	9	18	2	10	222	351	333	684	16	51	0.40	0	0	28	111	5.12

Hulking slugger who fits typical mashing profile. Finished 2nd in org in both HR and K while also leading in walks. Can differentiate between balls and strikes and brings double-plus power to the plate. Has been tough getting to power at times due to lofty, vicious stroke. Power-only 1B with poor speed and agility.

Keegan,Dominic — 23 — Tampa Bay

EXP MLB DEBUT: 2025 | H/W: 6-0 210 | FUT: Starting C | 7C

Bats R Age 22 | 2022 (4) Vanderbilt
Pwr +++ | BAvg +++ | Spd ++ | Def ++

Year	Lev	Team	AB	R	H	HR	RBI	Avg	OB	Slg	OPS	bb%	ct%	Eye	SB	CS	x/h%	Iso	RC/G
2022	NCAA	Vanderbilt	229	47	85	14	67	371	463	646	1109	15	78	0.76	2	0	39	275	9.68
2022	Rk	FCL Rays	17	2	7	0	5	412	500	647	1147	15	76	0.75	1	0	57	235	10.84
2022	A	Charleston	23	4	6	2	6	261	320	522	842	8	74	0.33	0	0	33	261	5.64

Hit-first prospect, drafted as catcher, made pro debut after 4th round selection. Catcher frame with strong base. Open, upright stance with direct load to hit position. Up-the-middle approach, works count. Most XBH in college went to CF and the gaps. Above-average power potential. Needs to find pull power to play. Has work to do to stick at C.

Keirsey,DaShawn — 8 — Minnesota

EXP MLB DEBUT: 2024 | H/W: 6-2 195 | FUT: Reserve OF | 6C

Bats L Age 25 | 2018 (4) Utah
Pwr ++ | BAvg ++ | Spd ++++ | Def ++++

Year	Lev	Team	AB	R	H	HR	RBI	Avg	OB	Slg	OPS	bb%	ct%	Eye	SB	CS	x/h%	Iso	RC/G
2019	Rk	Elizabethton	23	4	5	0	3	217	379	217	597	21	65	0.75	1	0	0	0	3.12
2019	A	Cedar Rapids	124	9	17	0	11	137	246	161	408	13	68	0.45	2	1	12	24	0.12
2021	Rk	FCL Twins	11	4	4	0	0	364	364	364	727	0	91	0.00	1	0	0	0	3.99
2021	A+	Cedar Rapids	141	17	28	7	24	199	289	433	722	11	65	0.36	10	3	54	234	4.72
2022	AA	Wichita	425	61	115	7	48	271	322	395	717	7	75	0.30	42	7	31	125	4.36

Athletic, fast OF who had best pro season to date. Led TL in SB and started to drive ball more consistently. Doubles production dramatically increased as result. Doesn't reach seats often, but more a byproduct of contact-approach than lack of strength. Needs to get on base more. Strong arm in CF with plus range.

Keith,Colt — 45 — Detroit

EXP MLB DEBUT: 2024 | H/W: 6-3 211 | FUT: Starting 3B | 8D

Bats L Age 21 | 2020 (5) HS (MS)
Pwr +++ | BAvg +++ | Spd ++ | Def ++

Year	Lev	Team	AB	R	H	HR	RBI	Avg	OB	Slg	OPS	bb%	ct%	Eye	SB	CS	x/h%	Iso	RC/G
2021	Rk	FCL Tigers East	7	2	5	0	4	714	800	857	1657	30	100		0	0	20	143	16.97
2021	Rk	FCL Tigers West	2	0	1	0	1	500	500	###	2000	0	100		0	0	100	1000	18.22
2021	A	Lakeland	147	32	47	1	21	320	435	422	857	17	73	0.77	4	1	21	102	6.87
2021	A+	West Michigan	68	7	11	1	6	162	250	250	500	11	60	0.30	0	0	27	88	1.35
2022	A+	West Michigan	193	38	58	9	31	301	372	544	916	10	78	0.52	4	0	45	244	6.98

Breakout campaign derailed by shoulder injury but was back in action in AFL. Tall frame with broad shoulders and added strength give him tools to hit for power. Quick bat, ability to lay off pitches out of the zone, and bat-to-ball skills result in plus hit tool. Moves well for size with avg speed and a plus arm and should stick at 3B.

Kessinger,Grae | 6 | Houston | EXP MLB DEBUT: 2024 | H/W: 6-2 204 | FUT: Reserve IF | 6B

Bats R Age 25	Year	Lev	Team	AB	R	H	HR	RBI	Avg	OB	Slg	OPS	bb%	ct%	Eye	SB	CS	x/h%	Iso	RC/G
2019 (2) Mississippi	2019	NCAA	Mississippi	270	67	89	7	50	330	418	474	892	13	87	1.17	16	3	28	144	6.80
Pwr +++	2019	A-	Tri City	41	5	11	0	3	268	318	366	684	7	90	0.75	1	1	36	98	4.21
BAvg ++	2019	A	Quad Cities	170	25	38	2	17	224	327	294	621	13	81	0.81	8	2	21	71	3.46
Spd ++	2021	AA	Corpus Christi	297	46	62	9	26	209	275	330	605	8	73	0.33	12	5	29	121	2.77
Def +++	2022	AA	Corpus Christi	421	72	89	16	58	211	322	366	688	14	73	0.61	23	10	35	154	4.13

Older SS built on Double-A reprise with more speed, power. Pull-heavy swing geared toward loft helps make most of power. Upright stance in box with quiet load and leg kick. Struggles to stay on time resulting in lots of pop-ups, low BA. Inefficient base stealer, needs to pick better spots. Quality fielder with soft hands and good instincts.

King, Jr.,Lamar | 2 | San Diego | EXP MLB DEBUT: 2026 | H/W: 6-3 215 | FUT: Starting C | 8E

Bats R Age 19	Year	Lev	Team	AB	R	H	HR	RBI	Avg	OB	Slg	OPS	bb%	ct%	Eye	SB	CS	x/h%	Iso	RC/G
2022 (4) HS (MD)																				
Pwr +++																				
BAvg +																				
Spd +																				
Def +++	2022	Rk	ACL Padres	9	1	1	0	1	111	200	111	311	10	78	0.50	0	0	0	0	-0.77

High upside backstop who has years of development ahead. Very crude hit tool with stiff, unusual swing mechanics. BA potential in question as a result. Could grow into plus to double-plus power if potential realized. Has natural strength and loft to give ball ride. Has good agility for size with strong, accurate arm.

Kinney,Cooper | 45 | Tampa Bay | EXP MLB DEBUT: 2026 | H/W: 6-3 200 | FUT: Starting 2B | 7E

Bats L Age 20	Year	Lev	Team	AB	R	H	HR	RBI	Avg	OB	Slg	OPS	bb%	ct%	Eye	SB	CS	x/h%	Iso	RC/G
2021 (1) HS (TN)																				
Pwr +++																				
BAvg +++																				
Spd +++																				
Def ++	2021	Rk	FCL Rays	35	9	10	0	5	286	444	371	816	22	74	1.11	2	0	20	86	6.58

Tall, powerful OF prospect missed entire season after shoulder surgery in the spring. LHH with plus underlying hit tool. Patient approach, will work long counts. Short, compact swing with all-fields approach. Struggles getting to lift now but has above-average power in frame and bat speed. Average runner. Likely relegated to 2B as pro.

Kjerstad,Heston | 9 | Baltimore | EXP MLB DEBUT: 2024 | H/W: 6-3 205 | FUT: Starting OF | 8D

Bats L Age 24	Year	Lev	Team	AB	R	H	HR	RBI	Avg	OB	Slg	OPS	bb%	ct%	Eye	SB	CS	x/h%	Iso	RC/G
2020 (1) Arkansas																				
Pwr ++++																				
BAvg +++																				
4.44 Spd ++	2022	A	Delmarva	80	17	37	2	17	463	538	650	1188	14	79	0.76	0	0	30	188	10.82
Def +++	2022	A+	Aberdeen	163	28	38	3	20	233	302	362	664	9	71	0.34	1	0	34	129	3.75

Big bat from 2020 draft got in first game action in two years due to injury. Some rust remained, but big power metrics returned and he mashed his way to the AFL MVP in 2022. All-fields pop with persistent whiffs currently; making better swing decisions a growing edge. Long and lean body with a right-field arm; it's a 25+ homer bat at maturity.

Koss,Christian | 456 | Boston | EXP MLB DEBUT: 2023 | H/W: 6-1 182 | FUT: Starting 2B | 7D

Bats R Age 25	Year	Lev	Team	AB	R	H	HR	RBI	Avg	OB	Slg	OPS	bb%	ct%	Eye	SB	CS	x/h%	Iso	RC/G
2019 (12) UC Irvine																				
Pwr ++																				
BAvg +++																				
Spd +++	2021	A+	Greenville	428	65	116	15	55	271	320	451	771	7	77	0.31	10	4	34	180	4.95
Def +++	2022	AA	Portland	488	69	127	17	84	260	296	430	727	5	72	0.18	16	5	35	170	4.34

Steady, all-fields hitter who set highs in HR and SB. Advancing one level per year and uses compact stroke to put charge into ball. Ton of Ks despite lack of plus power and can sell out. Sits on FB and may need to adjust approach to hit for higher BA. Heady INF with good speed and range. Strong arm suitable for any infield spot.

Kreidler,Ryan | 456 | Detroit | EXP MLB DEBUT: 2022 | H/W: 6-4 208 | FUT: Utility player | 7D

Bats R Age 25	Year	Lev	Team	AB	R	H	HR	RBI	Avg	OB	Slg	OPS	bb%	ct%	Eye	SB	CS	x/h%	Iso	RC/G
2019 (4) UCLA	2021	AA	Erie	347	67	89	15	36	256	319	429	749	8	66	0.27	10	4	34	173	4.94
Pwr ++	2021	AAA	Toledo	135	28	41	7	22	304	409	519	927	15	71	0.62	5	2	37	215	7.57
BAvg ++	2022	A+	West Michigan	13	3	3	0	4	231	412	385	796	24	77	1.33	2	0	67	154	6.40
Spd +++	2022	AAA	Toledo	202	29	43	8	22	213	332	411	743	15	64	0.50	15	1	51	198	5.20
Def +++	2022	MLB	Detroit	73	8	13	1	6	178	241	233	473	8	70	0.27	0	1	15	55	0.92

Tall, surprisingly athletic player generates above-average power, mostly to the pull side. Lack of explosive bat speed and length to swing results in too much swing-and-miss, though he does draw his fair share of walks. Smart, instinctive defender with first-step quickness, but seems destined to a UT role in the majors.

Labrada,Victor | 8 | Seattle | EXP MLB DEBUT: 2024 | H/W: 5-9 165 | FUT: Starting CF | 7D

Bats L Age 23	Year	Lev	Team	AB	R	H	HR	RBI	Avg	OB	Slg	OPS	bb%	ct%	Eye	SB	CS	x/h%	Iso	RC/G
2021 FA (CU)																				
Pwr ++	2021	A	Modesto	201	44	59	1	28	294	396	418	814	14	70	0.57	22	9	34	124	6.29
BAvg +++	2021	A+	Everett	203	35	50	6	27	246	311	399	710	9	69	0.30	10	6	32	153	4.36
Spd ++++	2022	A	Modesto	50	13	20	2	13	400	492	620	1112	15	84	1.13	3	1	35	220	9.60
Def +++	2022	A+	Everett	401	66	93	10	31	232	316	374	690	11	67	0.37	27	8	33	142	4.24

Undersized OF who suffered thru slow start, but quickly recovered to have strong season. At least 30 SB the last two years and set new high in HR. More of a slap approach and leverages elite speed at top of order. Plays game aggressively, including with approach. Can chase at times. May move to corner OF due to crude reads and routes.

Lampe,Joe | 78 | Cleveland | EXP MLB DEBUT: 2025 | H/W: 6-1 185 | FUT: Starting OF | 7D

Bats L Age 22	Year	Lev	Team	AB	R	H	HR	RBI	Avg	OB	Slg	OPS	bb%	ct%	Eye	SB	CS	x/h%	Iso	RC/G
2022 (3) Arizona State																				
Pwr ++																				
BAvg +++																				
Spd ++++	2022	NCAA	Arizona St	256	60	87	12	41	340	392	590	982	8	88	0.73	17	3	43	250	7.42
Def +++	2022	A	Lynchburg	10	0	1	0	1	100	182	100	282	9	40	0.17	0	0	0	0	-2.80

Athletic, contact-oriented LHH was 3rd rd pick in '22. Athletic frame close to physical projection. Upright stance with a bat wrap during the load. It's a flat linear swing with line drive and ground ball tendencies. Utilizes entire field approach and is selective. Below average raw power. Plus runner with good defensive instincts in CF.

Lara,Luis | 8 | Milwaukee | EXP MLB DEBUT: 2027 | H/W: 5-9 155 | FUT: Starting CF | 8D

Bats B Age 18	Year	Lev	Team	AB	R	H	HR	RBI	Avg	OB	Slg	OPS	bb%	ct%	Eye	SB	CS	x/h%	Iso	RC/G
2022 FA (VZ)																				
Pwr ++																				
BAvg +++																				
Spd ++++																				
Def +++	2022	Rk	DSL Brewers 1	200	39	52	2	21	260	330	385	715	10	86	0.75	7	7	33	125	4.60

Explosive athlete who has yet to appear in US. Uses short, quick stroke to put bat to ball and uses whole field. Diminutive frame needs muscle in order to get to average power potential. Exhibits clean, quick stroke from both sides of plate. Patrols CF with solid range and well above average speed. Could become leadoff hitter in time.

LaVastida,Bryan | 2 | Cleveland | EXP MLB DEBUT: 2022 | H/W: 6-0 200 | FUT: Reserve C | 6C

Bats R Age 24	Year	Lev	Team	AB	R	H	HR	RBI	Avg	OB	Slg	OPS	bb%	ct%	Eye	SB	CS	x/h%	Iso	RC/G
2018 (15) Hillsborough CC	2021	AA	Akron	103	16	30	3	17	291	365	466	831	10	73	0.43	2	3	37	175	6.09
Pwr ++	2021	AAA	Columbus	19	2	3	1	3	158	238	316	554	10	47	0.20	0	0	33	158	2.57
BAvg ++	2022	AA	Akron	174	22	34	5	14	195	247	328	575	6	74	0.27	5	1	32	132	2.35
Spd ++	2022	AAA	Columbus	147	24	33	4	16	224	301	374	675	10	76	0.46	2	1	36	150	3.88
Def +++	2022	MLB	Cleveland	12	0	1	0	0	83	267	83	350	20	67	0.75	0	0	0	0	-0.79

Stocky RHH C prospect struggled across 3 levels, including a 6 game MLB sample. Upright, slightly open stance with a bit of a hitch in the load. It's a linear swing with an opposite field approach. Power is limited because of how swing is oriented. Think 10-15 HR. Solid defender with a strong throwing arm. Has shot to stick as backup catcher.

Lavigne,Grant | 3 | Colorado | EXP MLB DEBUT: 2024 | H/W: 6-4 220 | FUT: Reserve 1B | 6B

Bats L Age 23	Year	Lev	Team	AB	R	H	HR	RBI	Avg	OB	Slg	OPS	bb%	ct%	Eye	SB	CS	x/h%	Iso	RC/G
2018 (1) HS (NH)	2019	A	Asheville	440	52	104	7	64	236	339	327	666	13	71	0.53	8	9	25	91	3.92
Pwr ++	2021	A	Fresno	260	49	73	7	40	281	375	442	817	13	72	0.53	7	2	33	162	6.04
BAvg +++	2021	A+	Spokane	111	17	25	2	18	225	353	342	696	17	65	0.56	2	1	32	117	4.58
Spd 0	2022	A+	Spokane	241	41	76	5	38	315	404	469	873	13	72	0.53	2	3	32	154	6.89
Def +	2022	AA	Hartford	208	29	51	5	24	245	346	370	716	13	68	0.48	0	0	27	125	4.66

1st round pick has been slow to develop and has yet to effectively tap into his raw power. Patient contact-oriented approach at the plate allows the hit tool to play up and is willing to draw walks, but at the price of power and he hit a career best 10 HR in '22. Strong showing in the AFL wasn't enough to get him on the 40-man roster.

Lawlar,Jordan — 6 — Arizona

EXP MLB DEBUT: 2024 | H/W: 6-2 190 | FUT: Starting SS | 9C

Bats R | Age 20 | 2021 (1) HS (TX)

Pwr ++++ | BAvg ++++ | Spd ++++ | Def +++

Year	Lev	Team	AB	R	H	HR	RBI	Avg	OB	Slg	OPS	bb%	ct%	Eye	SB	CS	x/h%	Iso	RC/G
2021	Rk	ACL DBacks	5	0	2	0	1	400	500	600	1100	17	80	1.00	1	0	50	200	10.07
2022	Rk	ACL DBacks	19	5	7	0	2	368	478	526	1005	17	68	0.67	0	0	29	158	9.49
2022	A	Visalia	174	44	61	9	32	351	438	603	1041	13	72	0.56	24	4	36	253	9.09
2022	A+	Hillsboro	111	31	32	3	17	288	378	477	855	13	70	0.48	13	1	41	189	6.68
2022	AA	Amarillo	85	18	18	4	11	212	295	353	648	11	67	0.36	2	1	22	141	3.34

Athletic SS prospect dominated the lower minors in his first full pro season. Lean, athletic frame with room to grow. Upright stance with easy load to hit position. Up-the-middle, patient approach. Uppercut swing trajectory with plus bat speed. Plus power raw, has yet to show up in games. Could be 30+ HR at projection. Fast runner.

Lee,Brooks — 6 — Minnesota

EXP MLB DEBUT: 2024 | H/W: 6-0 205 | FUT: Starting 3B | 8A

Bats B | Age 21 | 2022 (1) Cal Poly

Pwr +++ | BAvg ++++ | Spd ++ | Def +++

Year	Lev	Team	AB	R	H	HR	RBI	Avg	OB	Slg	OPS	bb%	ct%	Eye	SB	CS	x/h%	Iso	RC/G
2022	NCAA	Cal Poly	235	56	84	15	55	357	463	664	1126	16	88	1.64	3	1	49	306	9.64
2022	Rk	FCL Twins	17	2	6	0	3	353	353	471	824	0	100		0	0	33	118	5.38
2022	A+	Cedar Rapids	97	14	28	4	12	289	389	454	843	14	81	0.89	0	2	29	165	6.16
2022	AA	Wichita	8	1	3	0	0	375	375	375	750	0	75	0.00	0	0	0	0	4.24

Natural hitter with instincts, ability to make contact and hit for power. Swing conducive for hard contact from both sides. Should hit for very high BA with elite bat-to-ball ability. Exhibits at least average power and possible plus. Not much speed, but runs bases well. Played pro debut at SS, but may be best at 3B or 2B in future.

Lee,Hao Yu — 46 — Philadelphia

EXP MLB DEBUT: 2025 | H/W: 5-10 190 | FUT: Starting 2B | 8D

Bats R | Age 20 | 2021 FA (TW)

Pwr +++ | BAvg ++++ | Spd ++ | Def +++

Year	Lev	Team	AB	R	H	HR	RBI	Avg	OB	Slg	OPS	bb%	ct%	Eye	SB	CS	x/h%	Iso	RC/G
2021	Rk	FCL Phillies	22	9	8	1	5	364	440	773	1213	12	77	0.60	0	0	63	409	11.27
2022	Rk	FCL Phillies	6	4	3	1	1	500	625	###	1792	25	83	2.00	1	0	67	667	18.29
2022	A	Clearwater	258	37	73	7	50	283	371	415	785	12	78	0.63	10	7	26	132	5.42
2022	A+	Jersey Shore	35	5	9	1	2	257	350	486	836	13	74	0.56	3	0	56	229	6.30

One of the best pure hitters in the system, his barrel consistently found the ball in his first full pro season at age 19. Doesn't possess plus speed or power, but combines a simple setup and swing with great ball/strike awareness to make his mark. He's played around the infield but 2B seems to be his sweet spot. Pleasant developmental surprise.

Lee,Khalil — 789 — New York (N)

EXP MLB DEBUT: 2021 | H/W: 5-10 170 | FUT: Starting OF | 7D

Bats L | Age 24 | 2016 (3) HS (VA)

Pwr +++ | BAvg ++ | Spd +++ | Def +++

Year	Lev	Team	AB	R	H	HR	RBI	Avg	OB	Slg	OPS	bb%	ct%	Eye	SB	CS	x/h%	Iso	RC/G
2021	AAA	Syracuse	292	67	80	14	37	274	416	500	916	20	61	0.62	8	10	45	226	8.37
2021	MLB	New York	18	2	1	0	1	56	56	111	167	0	28	0.00	0	0	100	56	-4.08
2022	A	St. Lucie	29	5	7	0	2	241	313	414	726	9	62	0.27	1	3	57	172	5.34
2022	AAA	Syracuse	355	48	75	10	37	211	303	366	670	12	61	0.34	14	3	47	155	4.15
2022	MLB	New York (N)	2	1	1	1	3	500	500	###	2500	0	100		0	0	100	1500	20.12

Shorter-statured, athletic OF prospect has a knack for hard contact and whiffs. Body is at physical projection with average run tool remaining. Upright stance with quick trigger. At least plus bat speed with 93 MPH average EV. Lots of topspin off bat, depressing loft. Doesn't see spin at all. Versatile defender. Heady baserunner.

Lee,Korey — 2 — Houston

EXP MLB DEBUT: 2022 | H/W: 6-2 210 | FUT: Starting C | 8E

Bats R | Age 24 | 2019 (1) California

Pwr +++ | BAvg ++ | Spd ++ | Def ++++

Year	Lev	Team	AB	R	H	HR	RBI	Avg	OB	Slg	OPS	bb%	ct%	Eye	SB	CS	x/h%	Iso	RC/G
2021	A+	Asheville	109	24	36	3	14	330	397	459	855	10	78	0.50	1	0	22	128	6.17
2021	AA	Corpus Christi	185	25	47	8	27	254	317	443	760	8	81	0.49	3	1	38	189	4.82
2021	AAA	Sugar Land	35	2	8	0	4	229	270	343	613	5	74	0.22	0	0	50	114	3.06
2022	AAA	Sugar Land	404	74	96	25	76	238	300	483	783	8	69	0.28	12	1	49	245	5.25
2022	MLB	Houston	25	1	4	0	4	160	192	240	432	4	64	0.11	0	0	50	80	0.34

Former first round draft pick made MLB debut in '22. Generates power by catching pitches out front with quiet, level swing and aggressive pull-heavy approach. Mostly average contact profile and tends to chase pitches outside, but nothing egregious. Good defense with strong arm.

Leon,Pedro — 489 — Houston

EXP MLB DEBUT: 2023 | H/W: 5-10 170 | FUT: Starting OF | 8E

Bats R | Age 24 | 2021 FA (CU)

Pwr +++ | BAvg ++ | Spd ++++ | Def +++

Year	Lev	Team	AB	R	H	HR	RBI	Avg	OB	Slg	OPS	bb%	ct%	Eye	SB	CS	x/h%	Iso	RC/G
2021	Rk	FCL Astros	9	0	2	0	1	222	222	222	444	0	78	0.00	1	0	0	0	0.46
2021	AA	Corpus Christi	185	29	46	9	33	249	338	443	781	12	64	0.37	13	8	37	195	5.64
2021	AAA	Sugar Land	61	11	8	0	2	131	293	164	457	19	62	0.61	4	2	25	33	0.79
2022	AAA	Sugar Land	413	71	94	17	63	228	341	431	772	15	65	0.49	38	18	50	203	5.61

Athletic, short-statured OF/2B prospect shows solid power/speed ability but has struggled to hit for decent average in 2 seasons in affiliated pro ball. Upright stance at the plate with slight hitch in swing. Patient plate approach rescues OBP, as contact skills are subpar and lead to plenty of strikeouts. Significant pull-side power.

Leonard,Eddys — 6 — Los Angeles (N)

EXP MLB DEBUT: 2023 | H/W: 5-11 195 | FUT: Utility player | 7D

Bats R | Age 22 | 2017 FA (DR)

Pwr +++ | BAvg +++ | Spd +++ | Def +++

Year	Lev	Team	AB	R	H	HR	RBI	Avg	OB	Slg	OPS	bb%	ct%	Eye	SB	CS	x/h%	Iso	RC/G
2019	Rk	AZL Dodgers La	168	27	47	3	20	280	379	423	802	14	71	0.56	2	4	30	143	5.95
2019	A	Great Lakes	4	1	1	0	0	250	250	250	500	0	25	0.00	0	0	0	0	8.54
2021	A	Rancho Cuca	261	59	77	14	57	295	376	544	920	12	72	0.46	6	2	45	249	7.31
2021	A+	Great Lakes	164	30	49	8	24	299	365	530	895	9	74	0.40	3	1	41	232	6.75
2022	A+	Great Lakes	496	80	131	15	61	264	325	435	761	8	76	0.38	4	4	39	171	4.94

Took a step back after breakout in 2021, but has average to above tools across the board. Plus bat speed and barrel awareness give him a chance to hit at the major league level. Not a true burner but runs well with enough range and arm to play SS, 3B, and 2B. Surprising pop from his smaller frame and profiles as a super UT type.

Lewis,Ian — 45 — Miami

EXP MLB DEBUT: 2025 | H/W: 5-10 177 | FUT: Starting 2B | 7E

Bats B | Age 20 | 2019 FA (BM)

Pwr +++ | BAvg ++ | Spd ++++ | Def +++

Year	Lev	Team	AB	R	H	HR	RBI	Avg	OB	Slg	OPS	bb%	ct%	Eye	SB	CS	x/h%	Iso	RC/G
2021	Rk	FCL Marlins	149	24	45	3	27	302	350	497	847	7	84	0.46	9	4	40	195	5.98
2022	A	Jupiter	185	21	49	2	21	265	343	368	711	11	76	0.49	16	1	24	103	4.47

Short-statured, wiry switch-hitting MIF enjoyed solid full-season debut in Low-A. Slight open, upright swing with short trigger. Super aggressive approach, makes poor swing decisions. Slasher now; could open up to more of a power approach as launch angle improves. Above-average raw power present. Plus runner. Profile fits best at 2B.

Lewis,Royce — 68 — Minnesota

EXP MLB DEBUT: 2022 | H/W: 6-2 200 | FUT: Starting SS | 8B

Bats R | Age 23 | 2017 (1) HS (CA)

Pwr +++ | BAvg +++ | Spd ++++ | Def +++

Year	Lev	Team	AB	R	H	HR	RBI	Avg	OB	Slg	OPS	bb%	ct%	Eye	SB	CS	x/h%	Iso	RC/G
2019	A+	Fort Myers	383	55	91	10	35	238	288	376	664	7	77	0.30	16	8	33	138	3.57
2019	AA	Pensacola	134	18	31	2	14	231	290	358	648	8	75	0.33	6	2	39	127	3.50
2021	--	*Did Not Play*																	
2022	AAA	St. Paul	131	30	41	5	14	313	396	534	930	12	76	0.56	12	2	44	221	7.41
2022	MLB	Minnesota	40	5	12	2	5	300	317	550	867	2	88	0.20	0	0	50	250	5.73

Exceptional athlete who can't stay healthy. Produced in MIN before knee surgery ended year. Power starting to emerge as he has polished swing mechanics and added leverage. Bat speed and raw power border on elite and has smarts to identify hittable pitches. Future position in question, but not for lack of talent. Speed is best tool.

Lile,Daylen — 7 — Washington

EXP MLB DEBUT: 2027 | H/W: 6-0 195 | FUT: Starting OF | 7D

Bats L | Age 20 | 2021 (2) HS (KY)

Pwr +++ | BAvg ++ | Spd ++ | Def ++

Year	Lev	Team	AB	R	H	HR	RBI	Avg	OB	Slg	OPS	bb%	ct%	Eye	SB	CS	x/h%	Iso	RC/G
2021	Rk	FCL Nationals	64	16	14	0	10	219	367	250	617	19	69	0.75	2	1	14	31	3.47

Power-over-hit prepster whose 2022 erased by Tommy John surgery. Needs reps against pro pitching as questions abound regarding his hit tool despite aesthetically pleasing swing. Likely limited to left field due to shaky glove and sub-par arm. Timeline pushed back some due to surgery; likely to be a shake-the-rust-off year in 2023.

Lipcius,Andre — 45 — Detroit

EXP MLB DEBUT: 2023 | H/W: 6-1 190 | FUT: Reserve 3B | 6C

Bats R | Age 24 | 2019 (3) Tennessee

Pwr ++ | BAvg ++ | Spd ++ | Def +++

Year	Lev	Team	AB	R	H	HR	RBI	Avg	OB	Slg	OPS	bb%	ct%	Eye	SB	CS	x/h%	Iso	RC/G
2019	A	West Michigan	253	32	69	2	29	273	343	360	703	10	77	0.47	3	2	26	87	4.31
2021	A+	West Michigan	83	14	23	3	13	277	368	482	850	13	81	0.75	3	1	39	205	6.27
2021	AA	Erie	341	51	80	9	46	235	313	378	691	10	76	0.48	4	1	36	144	4.12
2022	AA	Erie	303	52	80	9	39	264	387	426	813	17	82	1.09	12	1	38	162	6.03
2022	AAA	Toledo	159	18	48	3	24	302	397	453	850	14	79	0.76	1	3	35	151	6.42

Continues to make steady progress, but power has not developed as anticipated, likely pushing him to a bench role. Plus understanding of the strike zone resulted in career best .391 OBP, but tentativeness and lack of bat speed make it unlikely to hit for enough power. Solid defender at 3B/2B.

Lipscomb,Trey

5 | **Washington** | EXP MLB DEBUT: 2025 | H/W: 6-1 200 | FUT: Starting 3B | **7C**

Bats R Age 22 — 2022 (3) Tennessee

Pwr ++ · BAvg +++ · Spd +++ · Def +++

Year	Lev	Team	AB	R	H	HR	RBI	Avg	OB	Slg	OPS	bb%	ct%	Eye	SB	CS	x/h%	Iso	RC/G
2022	NCAA	Tennessee	251	68	89	22	84	355	415	717	1132	9	85	0.70	4	1	49	363	9.16
2022	A	Fredericksburg	97	15	29	1	13	299	327	392	718	4	80	0.21	12	1	21	93	4.17

Lean and athletic, fit right into full-season ball after career at Tennessee. Upright stance, torso turn, whips bat through the zone. More of a gap-to-gap doubles approach with good contact; not much present raw power. Heady defender, good arm, average runner who steals bases on instinct. Tools not loud, but could contribute in multiple ways.

Locklear,Tyler

5 | **Seattle** | EXP MLB DEBUT: 2024 | H/W: 6-3 210 | FUT: Starting 3B | **7D**

Bats R Age 22 — 2022 (2) VCU

Pwr +++ · BAvg ++ · Spd ++ · Def ++

Year	Lev	Team	AB	R	H	HR	RBI	Avg	OB	Slg	OPS	bb%	ct%	Eye	SB	CS	x/h%	Iso	RC/G
2022	NCAA	VCU	224	77	90	20	78	402	506	799	1305	17	89	1.88	6	2	52	397	11.66
2022	Rk	ACL Mariners	6	0	2	0	2	333	429	500	929	14	83	1.00	0	0	50	167	7.60
2022	A	Modesto	117	19	33	7	29	282	323	504	827	6	75	0.24	0	0	36	222	5.48

Large-framed 3B with lot of raw thunder in bat. Knows the strike zone and will draw walks to get on base. Swing mechanics are a bit rough and needs revision to hit for BA as pro. Has incredible natural strength with average bat speed from right side. Secondary attributes are a bit short. Not much speed and limited agility at 3B.

Lockridge,Brandon

78 | **New York (A)** | EXP MLB DEBUT: 2023 | H/W: 6-1 185 | FUT: Starting OF | **6C**

Bats R Age 26 — 2018 (5) Troy

Pwr ++ · BAvg ++ · Spd ++++ · Def +++

Year	Lev	Team	AB	R	H	HR	RBI	Avg	OB	Slg	OPS	bb%	ct%	Eye	SB	CS	x/h%	Iso	RC/G
2018	A-	Staten Island	51	6	11	1	6	216	322	373	695	14	71	0.53	0	2	45	157	4.41
2019	A	Charleston (Sc)	498	69	125	12	56	251	313	410	723	8	72	0.32	22	8	40	159	4.53
2021	A+	Hudson Valley	125	18	32	3	22	256	306	408	714	7	78	0.33	5	1	34	152	4.27
2021	AA	Somerset	174	33	57	10	24	328	374	557	932	7	67	0.22	13	1	35	230	7.51
2022	AA	Somerset	418	67	96	14	49	230	291	378	669	8	70	0.29	18	4	34	148	3.68

Athletic OF with plus-plus run tool continues to struggle with aggressive approach. Athletic frame, at physical projection. Open, upright stance with bat wrap. Top hand heavy swing that depresses loft opportunities and limits power output. Present swing-and-miss, aggressive approach limit BA potential. Weak arm limits CF play.

Loftin,Nick

58 | **Kansas City** | EXP MLB DEBUT: 2023 | H/W: 6-1 180 | FUT: Utility player | **7B**

Bats R Age 24 — 2020 (1) Baylor

Pwr +++ · BAvg +++ · Spd +++ · Def +++

Year	Lev	Team	AB	R	H	HR	RBI	Avg	OB	Slg	OPS	bb%	ct%	Eye	SB	CS	x/h%	Iso	RC/G
2020	NCAA	Baylor	57	7	17	2	15	298	344	544	888	7	81	0.36	0	0	47	246	6.46
2021	A+	Quad Cities	356	67	103	10	57	289	364	463	828	11	83	0.70	11	2	36	174	5.89
2022	AA	NW Arkansas	363	78	98	12	47	270	350	421	772	11	84	0.79	24	4	31	152	5.17
2022	AAA	Omaha	153	26	33	5	19	216	264	359	623	6	73	0.24	5	2	36	144	2.96

Contact-oriented UT type struggled against advanced competition after Triple-A callup. Athletic frame near projection. Average to above-average tools across the board. Traded launch angle for consistent EV rate resulting in drop of BA and increase in HR power. Mostly average power to pull side. Above-average runner; think 15-20 SB.

Loperfido,Joey

34 | **Houston** | EXP MLB DEBUT: 2025 | H/W: 6-4 195 | FUT: Utility player | **6C**

Bats L Age 24 — 2021 (7) Duke

Pwr ++ · BAvg +++ · Spd +++ · Def +++

Year	Lev	Team	AB	R	H	HR	RBI	Avg	OB	Slg	OPS	bb%	ct%	Eye	SB	CS	x/h%	Iso	RC/G
2020	NCAA	Duke	53	12	14	0	6	264	400	358	758	18	77	1.00	5	1	21	94	5.59
2021	NCAA	Duke	193	51	70	7	27	363	431	591	1021	11	75	0.48	11	3	39	228	8.59
2021	A	Fayetteville	69	10	8	2	6	116	208	261	469	10	55	0.26	1	0	75	145	0.81
2022	A	Fayetteville	296	51	90	9	45	304	387	473	860	12	74	0.53	30	9	32	169	6.48
2022	A+	Asheville	96	19	34	3	24	354	431	552	983	12	74	0.52	2	2	35	198	8.22

Left-handed batter fared well against low-minors pitchers. Slightly crouched stance in box with level swing geared for line drives. Shows some aggressive tendencies at the plate, makes good contact. Steps up in box on every pitch. Runs well but is inefficient on base paths. Versatile defender who can play all over field.

Lopez,Dariel

45 | **Pittsburgh** | EXP MLB DEBUT: 2024 | H/W: 6-1 183 | FUT: Starting 3B | **7C**

Bats R Age 21 — 2018 FA (DR)

Pwr +++ · BAvg +++ · Spd + · Def ++

Year	Lev	Team	AB	R	H	HR	RBI	Avg	OB	Slg	OPS	bb%	ct%	Eye	SB	CS	x/h%	Iso	RC/G
2021	A	Bradenton	361	52	93	10	64	258	333	393	727	10	71	0.40	1	2	30	136	4.60
2022	A+	Greensboro	391	58	112	19	58	286	323	476	799	5	73	0.20	6	4	31	189	5.20

Under the radar INF who set highs in both HR and SB despite slow start. Advancing one level per year, but will need to tame aggressive approach. Hits for BA and is sound situational hitter. Goes to opposite fields and has strength and whippy bat to produce punch. Not a good defender and likely to be 3B full time. Not much speed in game.

Lopez,Otto

478 | **Toronto** | EXP MLB DEBUT: 2021 | H/W: 5-10 185 | FUT: Utility player | **6A**

Bats R Age 24 — 2016 FA (DR)

Pwr ++ · BAvg ++++ · Spd ++++ · Def +++

Year	Lev	Team	AB	R	H	HR	RBI	Avg	OB	Slg	OPS	bb%	ct%	Eye	SB	CS	x/h%	Iso	RC/G
2021	AAA	Buffalo	173	36	50	2	25	289	339	405	743	7	85	0.50	15	1	26	116	4.72
2021	MLB	Toronto	1	0	0	0	0	0	0	0	0	0	0	0.00	0	0		0	
2022	A	Dunedin	20	0	1	0	2	50	136	50	186	9	80	0.50	0	0	0	0	-2.20
2022	AAA	Buffalo	340	53	101	3	34	297	373	415	787	11	82	0.67	14	5	28	118	5.49
2022	MLB	Toronto	9	0	6	0	3	667	700	667	1367	10	89	1.00	0	1	0	0	11.90

Versatile prospect who has stints in majors. Good athlete who makes incredibly consistent contact while using speed effectively. Walk rate has climbed with better approach and will steal bases. Uses all fields, but not much pop in swing or strength. Plays all over field with average arm and quickness. Ideal utility player.

Luciano,Marco

6 | **San Francisco** | EXP MLB DEBUT: 2024 | H/W: 6-2 178 | FUT: Starting SS | **9C**

Bats R Age 21 — 2018 FA (DR)

Pwr ++++ · BAvg +++ · Spd ++ · Def ++

Year	Lev	Team	AB	R	H	HR	RBI	Avg	OB	Slg	OPS	bb%	ct%	Eye	SB	CS	x/h%	Iso	RC/G
2019	A-	Salem-Keizer	33	6	7	0	4	212	316	333	649	13	82	0.83	1	0	57	121	4.01
2021	A	San Jose	266	52	74	18	57	278	368	556	925	13	74	0.56	5	5	47	278	7.20
2021	A+	Eugene	129	16	28	1	14	217	273	295	568	7	58	0.19	1	0	21	78	2.56
2022	Rk	ACL Giants B	22	6	7	1	6	318	423	545	969	15	68	0.57	0	0	43	227	8.46
2022	A+	Eugene	205	27	54	10	30	263	335	459	793	10	75	0.43	0	0	37	195	5.31

Electric prospect who had limited time after early June, but showed improvement across board in all facets of game. Can be highlight reel with bat due to elite bat speed and incredible raw power. BA should continue to climb with swing adjustments as he can chase. Speed and defense are fringy and could move to 3B.

Lugo,Matthew

56 | **Boston** | EXP MLB DEBUT: 2024 | H/W: 6-1 187 | FUT: Starting 3B | **7B**

Bats R Age 21 — 2019 (2) HS (PR)

Pwr +++ · BAvg +++ · Spd +++ · Def +++

Year	Lev	Team	AB	R	H	HR	RBI	Avg	OB	Slg	OPS	bb%	ct%	Eye	SB	CS	x/h%	Iso	RC/G
2019	Rk	GCL Red Sox	136	19	35	1	12	257	331	331	662	10	74	0.42	3	0	20	74	3.77
2019	A-	Lowell	8	0	2	0	1	250	250	250	500	0	75	0.00	0	0	0	0	1.07
2021	A	Salem	418	61	113	4	50	270	331	364	695	8	78	0.40	15	4	25	93	4.14
2022	A+	Greenville	466	76	134	18	78	288	337	500	837	7	79	0.35	20	7	40	212	5.80
2022	AA	Portland	12	1	1	0	1	83	83	167	250	0	67	0.00	0	0	100	83	-2.32

Rapidly improving INF who is growing into body while maintaining fluidity and agility in field. Huge jump in power and hits doubles and HR with quick, direct stroke. Reads spin well and can go to opposite field. Runs well, though may slow down. Could stand to be more patient at plate. Good defender with average range and arm. Could move to 3B.

Machado,Estiven

46 | **Toronto** | EXP MLB DEBUT: 2025 | H/W: 5-10 170 | FUT: Starting 2B | **8E**

Bats B Age 20 — 2019 FA (VZ)

Pwr + · BAvg ++ · Spd +++ · Def +++

Year	Lev	Team	AB	R	H	HR	RBI	Avg	OB	Slg	OPS	bb%	ct%	Eye	SB	CS	x/h%	Iso	RC/G
2021	Rk	FCL Blue Jays	1	0	1	0	0	1000	###	###	2000	0	100		0	0	0	0	16.32
2022	A	Dunedin	339	45	89	1	32	263	337	345	682	10	71	0.39	6	3	26	83	4.13

Very athletic INF who sees action at both 2B and SS. Has excellent quickness and ideal footwork to be asset with glove. Arm works anywhere. Not much power production at present and buries ball into ground, but has above average power potential. Room to add lot of strength and has solid bat speed. Uses whole field.

Mack,Joe

2 | **Miami** | EXP MLB DEBUT: 2025 | H/W: 6-1 210 | FUT: Starting C | **8E**

Bats L Age 20 — 2021 (1) HS (NY)

Pwr ++++ · BAvg +++ · Spd ++ · Def +++

Year	Lev	Team	AB	R	H	HR	RBI	Avg	OB	Slg	OPS	bb%	ct%	Eye	SB	CS	x/h%	Iso	RC/G
2021	Rk	FCL Marlins	53	9	7	1	2	132	370	208	577	27	58	0.91	0	1	29	75	2.60
2022	Rk	FCL Marlins	27	2	8	2	3	296	387	519	906	13	74	0.57	0	0	25	222	6.81
2022	A	Jupiter	121	18	28	3	12	231	380	355	735	19	67	0.73	0	0	29	124	5.16

Hard-hitting LHH C prospect struggled with health in full season debut. Missed time with hamstring injury. Open, upright stance. Hands go direct to trigger. Linear swing with in zone swing and miss. Needs to cut down on swing length. Creates good angles to opposite field off bat. Power over hit profile. Strong defender. Will stick at catcher.

Made,Kevin

6 | **Chicago (N)** | EXP MLB DEBUT: 2024 | H/W: 5-10 160 | FUT: Starting SS | **7D**

Bats R Age 20 — 2019 FA (DR)

- Pwr +++
- BAvg ++
- Spd +++
- Def +++

Year	Lev	Team	AB	R	H	HR	RBI	Avg	OB	Slg	OPS	bb%	ct%	Eye	SB	CS	x/h%	Iso	RC/G
2021	A	Myrtle Beach	235	19	64	1	20	272	290	366	656	2	76	0.11	2	0	27	94	3.38
2022	A	Myrtle Beach	222	41	59	9	30	266	345	450	796	11	78	0.55	0	1	39	185	5.43
2022	A+	South Bend	130	14	21	1	14	162	268	246	515	13	76	0.61	3	0	38	85	1.97

Dominican SS signed for $1.5 million in 2019 and has been slow to develop. Overly aggressive approach at the plate is mitigated by quick hands and ability to make contact, but has limited his ability to consistently make hard contact. Above-average to plus defender with good range and a strong arm. Can play 3B and 2B as well.

Malloy,Justyn-Henry

57 | **Detroit** | EXP MLB DEBUT: 2023 | H/W: 6-2 212 | FUT: Starting OF | **7C**

Bats R Age 23 — 2021 (6) Georgia Tech

- Pwr +++
- BAvg +++
- Spd ++
- Def ++

Year	Lev	Team	AB	R	H	HR	RBI	Avg	OB	Slg	OPS	bb%	ct%	Eye	SB	CS	x/h%	Iso	RC/G
2021	NCAA	Georgia Tech	208	53	64	11	43	308	433	558	991	18	81	1.15	4	1	45	250	8.28
2021	A	Augusta	122	23	33	5	21	270	390	434	825	16	75	0.80	4	2	30	164	6.09
2022	A+	Rome	263	51	80	10	44	304	410	479	889	15	72	0.64	3	0	33	175	7.05
2022	AA	Mississippi	190	35	51	6	31	268	403	421	824	18	68	0.72	0	0	33	153	6.43
2022	AAA	Gwinnett	25	5	7	1	6	280	438	440	878	22	80	1.40	2	0	29	160	7.04

Strong-bodied '21 6th round pick performed across 3 levels in huge '22 season. Developed and near physical projection. Open stance with simple trigger to hit position, maximizing plus bat speed. Line drive approach, mostly pull oriented. Improved flyball angles as season wore on. Discerning eye with less than 20% chase rate. Poor defender at 3B.

Mangum,Jake

789 | **Miami** | EXP MLB DEBUT: 2023 | H/W: 6-1 179 | FUT: Reserve OF | **6C**

Bats B Age 27 — 2019 (4) Mississippi St

- Pwr +
- BAvg +++
- Spd +++
- Def +++

Year	Lev	Team	AB	R	H	HR	RBI	Avg	OB	Slg	OPS	bb%	ct%	Eye	SB	CS	x/h%	Iso	RC/G
2021	A+	Brooklyn	34	7	7	2	6	206	270	412	682	8	56	0.20	0	1	43	206	4.35
2021	AA	Binghamton	303	56	89	7	41	294	329	459	788	5	81	0.28	14	6	36	165	5.10
2022	Rk	FCL Mets	7	1	3	0	1	429	600	714	1314	30	100		0	0	33	286	13.17
2022	AA	Binghamton	143	20	39	2	13	273	329	399	728	8	76	0.35	7	2	26	126	4.55
2022	AAA	Syracuse	138	22	46	2	21	333	366	471	837	5	83	0.30	7	1	30	138	5.67

Versitile, contact-oriented switch-hitting OF prospect was acquired during the off-season from NYM. Upright, slight open stance from both sides of the plate. Hacker, will expand the zone but has plus hand-eye to limit whiffs. Slasher approach, will shoot gaps. Limited over-the-fence power. Solid runner, can play all 3 OF positions.

Manzardo,Kyle

3 | **Tampa Bay** | EXP MLB DEBUT: 2023 | H/W: 6-1 205 | FUT: Starting 1B | **8A**

Bats L Age 22 — 2021 (2) Washington St

- Pwr ++++
- BAvg ++++
- Spd +
- Def +++

Year	Lev	Team	AB	R	H	HR	RBI	Avg	OB	Slg	OPS	bb%	ct%	Eye	SB	CS	x/h%	Iso	RC/G
2020	NCAA	Washington St	62	21	27	3	14	435	485	694	1179	9	81	0.50	0	1	37	258	10.08
2021	NCAA	Washington St	197	43	72	11	60	365	437	640	1077	11	85	0.86	1	0	43	274	8.78
2021	Rk	FCL Rays	43	10	15	2	8	349	404	605	1009	9	86	0.67	0	0	47	256	7.82
2022	A+	Bowling Green	225	53	74	17	55	329	441	636	1076	17	80	0.98	0	0	46	307	9.20
2022	AA	Montgomery	99	18	32	5	26	323	407	576	983	12	81	0.74	1	1	47	253	7.86

Former 2nd round pick, sporting one of the best hit tools in minors, emerged as power prospect. Slightly open, semi upright LH stance with direct trigger to hit position. Plus-plus bat control with knack for hard contact. Change in swing trajectory unlocked power potential. Power plays to CF and pull side. Think 30+ HR at projection. Solid defender.

Marlowe,Cade

8 | **Seattle** | EXP MLB DEBUT: 2023 | H/W: 6-1 210 | FUT: Reserve OF | **6A**

Bats L Age 25 — 2019 (20) West Georgia

- Pwr +++
- BAvg +++
- Spd +++
- Def +++

Year	Lev	Team	AB	R	H	HR	RBI	Avg	OB	Slg	OPS	bb%	ct%	Eye	SB	CS	x/h%	Iso	RC/G
2021	A	Modesto	133	35	40	6	29	301	408	556	964	15	70	0.60	11	2	43	256	8.32
2021	A+	Everett	286	52	74	20	77	259	342	566	908	11	68	0.40	12	7	58	308	7.26
2021	AAA	Tacoma	3	0	2	0	1	667	750	###	1750	25	67	1.00	1	0	50	333	22.26
2022	AA	Arkansas	447	75	130	20	86	291	369	483	852	11	70	0.41	36	10	32	192	6.37
2022	AAA	Tacoma	52	8	13	3	16	250	339	519	858	12	56	0.30	6	0	54	269	7.73

Athletic, strong OF who plays well above tools. Set career high in SB while continuing to get on base at high clip. Has hit at least 23 HR each of last 2 seasons despite struggles with contact and LHP. Too much swing and miss in game, but has speed to beat out grounders. Very good CF with solid-average speed and instincts.

Marte,Noelvi

56 | **Cincinnati** | EXP MLB DEBUT: 2024 | H/W: 6-1 181 | FUT: Starting 3B | **8C**

Bats R Age 21 — 2018 FA (DR)

- Pwr ++++
- BAvg +++
- Spd ++++
- Def +++

Year	Lev	Team	AB	R	H	HR	RBI	Avg	OB	Slg	OPS	bb%	ct%	Eye	SB	CS	x/h%	Iso	RC/G
2021	A	Modesto	413	87	112	17	69	271	361	462	823	12	74	0.55	23	7	38	191	5.93
2021	A+	Everett	31	4	9	0	2	290	333	419	753	6	65	0.18	1	0	44	129	5.37
2022	A+	Dayton	106	12	31	4	13	292	390	443	834	14	78	0.74	10	3	26	151	6.05
2022	A+	Everett	342	62	94	15	55	275	354	462	816	11	75	0.50	13	6	36	187	5.71

Strong, athletic prospect, acquired in mid-season trade with SEA, spent fall working on defensive conversion to 3B. Has bulked up with room to grow, but former plus speed has been the cost. Open stance with some effort to get hands to hit position. Power-over-hit prospect with solid contact skills. Plus power plays from CF to pull side.

Martin,Austin

6 | **Minnesota** | EXP MLB DEBUT: 2023 | H/W: 6-0 185 | FUT: Starting SS | **7C**

Bats R Age 24 — 2020 (1) Vanderbilt

- Pwr +
- BAvg +++
- Spd +++
- Def +++

Year	Lev	Team	AB	R	H	HR	RBI	Avg	OB	Slg	OPS	bb%	ct%	Eye	SB	CS	x/h%	Iso	RC/G
2020	NCAA	Vanderbilt	53	15	20	3	11	377	476	660	1137	16	96	5.00	3	1	45	283	9.65
2021	AA	New Hampshire	196	43	55	2	16	281	395	383	778	16	73	0.70	9	3	25	102	5.67
2021	AA	Wichita	134	24	34	3	19	254	363	381	744	15	78	0.77	5	1	32	127	5.03
2022	Rk	FCL Twins	8	1	2	0	3	250	400	375	775	20	88	2.00	1	1	50	125	6.05
2022	AA	Wichita	336	59	81	2	32	241	334	315	650	12	84	0.87	34	5	22	74	3.90

Contact-hitting prospect who repeated AA, but finished lower in BA, OBP and SLG. One of toughest in minors to K and makes easy contact with pure hitting ability. Bat speed and plate discipline stand out, but where is the power? Hit very few HR and doubles with minimal exit velocity. SB jumped tremendously and hope is he lands on CF or SS.

Martin,Casey

6 | **Philadelphia** | EXP MLB DEBUT: 2024 | H/W: 5-11 175 | FUT: Reserve IF | **6A**

Bats R Age 24 — 2020 (3) Arkansas

- Pwr ++
- BAvg ++
- Spd ++++
- Def +++

Year	Lev	Team	AB	R	H	HR	RBI	Avg	OB	Slg	OPS	bb%	ct%	Eye	SB	CS	x/h%	Iso	RC/G
2020	NCAA	Arkansas	59	7	16	2	10	271	377	458	834	14	63	0.45	6	0	44	186	6.80
2021	A	Clearwater	264	33	59	6	35	223	298	356	654	10	74	0.41	15	3	39	133	3.60
2021	A+	Jersey Shore	110	15	15	1	7	136	228	200	428	11	53	0.25	2	4	33	64	0.15
2022	A+	Jersey Shore	398	42	72	5	33	181	224	281	505	5	75	0.22	17	2	39	101	1.49

Slight infielder whose power/speed combination in college raised expectations, but has yet to deliver in pro ball. SB ability best current asset; made better contact with aggressive approach in 2022 but results came up far short. Needs more strength to pepper the gaps. Can handle SS, but likely headed to a bench-UT future.

Martin,Mason

3 | **Pittsburgh** | EXP MLB DEBUT: 2023 | H/W: 6-0 220 | FUT: Starting 1B | **7E**

Bats L Age 23 — 2017 (17) HS (WA)

- Pwr ++++
- BAvg +
- Spd ++
- Def ++

Year	Lev	Team	AB	R	H	HR	RBI	Avg	OB	Slg	OPS	bb%	ct%	Eye	SB	CS	x/h%	Iso	RC/G
2019	A	Greensboro	301	58	79	23	83	262	360	575	935	13	66	0.45	8	2	57	312	7.85
2019	A+	Bradenton	176	32	42	12	46	239	323	528	852	11	63	0.34	0	1	62	290	6.75
2021	AA	Altoona	414	62	100	22	75	242	305	481	786	8	61	0.24	0	2	53	239	5.85
2021	AAA	Indianapolis	25	4	6	3	6	240	269	600	869	4	60	0.10	0	1	50	360	6.66
2022	AAA	Indianapolis	481	62	101	19	74	210	287	410	697	10	60	0.27	12	3	52	200	4.58

Powerful 1B who is all-or-nothing hitter. Raw power is as impressive as any in org, but inability to put bat to ball mutes offensive impact. Led org in Ks and has fanned at least 149 times each full season as pro. Recognizing pitches better, but just can't hit them. Has very limited foot speed and is below average 1B.

Martinez,Angel

46 | **Cleveland** | EXP MLB DEBUT: 2024 | H/W: 6-0 165 | FUT: Starting SS | **7B**

Bats B Age 21 — 2018 FA (DR)

- Pwr +++
- BAvg +++
- Spd +++
- Def +++

Year	Lev	Team	AB	R	H	HR	RBI	Avg	OB	Slg	OPS	bb%	ct%	Eye	SB	CS	x/h%	Iso	RC/G
2021	A	Lynchburg	377	62	91	7	46	241	319	382	701	10	77	0.49	13	6	36	141	4.31
2022	A+	Lake County	281	46	81	10	27	288	377	477	854	12	79	0.69	10	6	37	189	6.30
2022	AA	Akron	82	10	20	3	17	244	340	451	792	13	78	0.67	2	1	50	207	5.55

Heady, switch-hitting MIF with MLB bloodlines put together solid season between two aggressive assignments. Power driven hit tool from LH side, getting to lofted contact more, especially to the pull side gap. From RH side, swing is much more linear, depressing loft. Plus feel for zone and situations. Defensively, arm plays at SS/3B.

Martinez,Gabriel

79 | **Toronto** | EXP MLB DEBUT: 2025 | H/W: 6-0 170 | FUT: Starting OF | **8D**

Bats R Age 20 — 2018 FA (VZ)

- Pwr +++
- BAvg +++
- Spd ++
- Def ++

Year	Lev	Team	AB	R	H	HR	RBI	Avg	OB	Slg	OPS	bb%	ct%	Eye	SB	CS	x/h%	Iso	RC/G
2021	Rk	FCL Blue Jays	100	16	33	0	14	330	446	410	856	17	82	1.17	7	2	24	80	6.79
2021	A	Dunedin	12	1	4	0	1	333	385	417	801	8	67	0.25	0	1	25	83	5.93
2022	Rk	FCL Blue Jays	10	1	1	0	0	100	182	200	382	9	80	0.50	1	0	100	100	0.41
2022	A	Dunedin	240	46	69	11	46	288	347	483	831	8	81	0.49	3	1	36	196	5.67
2022	A+	Vancouver	102	11	33	3	13	324	378	490	869	8	83	0.53	0	0	33	167	6.19

Much improved prospect who was very good at two levels. Power was up across board with big spike in HR while continuing to hit doubles. Makes consistent contact and has good hit tool. Can be aggressive within strike zone due to contact. Some projectable power in frame, though not much speed. Corner OF with strong arm.

Martinez,Orelvis — 56 — Toronto

EXP MLB DEBUT: 2023 | H/W: 6-1 200 | FUT: Starting 3B | 9C

Bats R | Age 21 | 2018 FA (DR)

Pwr + + + + + | BAvg + + | Spd + + | Def + +

Year	Lev	Team	AB	R	H	HR	RBI	Avg	OB	Slg	OPS	bb%	ct%	Eye	SB	CS	x/h%	Iso	RC/G
2019	Rk	GCL Blue Jays	142	20	39	7	32	275	340	549	889	9	80	0.48	2	0	51	275	6.56
2021	A	Dunedin	283	49	79	19	68	279	354	572	927	10	70	0.39	4	1	54	293	7.39
2021	A+	Vancouver	112	17	24	9	19	214	279	491	770	8	75	0.36	0	1	54	277	4.77
2022	AA	New Hampshire	433	57	88	30	76	203	271	446	716	8	68	0.29	6	3	51	242	4.24

Young INF who led org in HR, though 3rd in Ks. Owns elite bat speed and hard, aggressive swing that produces double-plus power. Starting to pull ball more and has chance for 40+ HR. Hits lots of flyballs, but also strikes out in abundance. Limited range and speed, but has good hands. Has star potential based entirely on bat.

Martinez,Orlando — 79 — Los Angeles (A)

EXP MLB DEBUT: 2023 | H/W: 6-0 185 | FUT: Reserve OF | 6B

Bats L | Age 25 | 2017 FA (CU)

Pwr + + + | BAvg + + | Spd + + + | Def + + +

Year	Lev	Team	AB	R	H	HR	RBI	Avg	OB	Slg	OPS	bb%	ct%	Eye	SB	CS	x/h%	Iso	RC/G
2019	A+	Inland Empire	380	55	100	12	49	263	327	434	761	9	79	0.46	5	4	37	171	4.93
2021	AA	Rocket City	400	58	103	16	54	258	309	445	754	7	70	0.25	5	3	40	188	4.85
2022	Rk	ACL Angels	11	4	5	0	2	455	500	727	1227	8	64	0.25	0	0	60	273	13.24
2022	AA	Rocket City	141	25	43	4	33	305	384	454	838	11	77	0.55	6	4	28	149	6.08
2022	AAA	Salt Lake	244	27	61	5	34	250	304	393	698	7	76	0.32	3	3	34	143	4.11

Jack-of-many trades OF struggled transitioning swing gains to game action in 2022. Upright, open stance with a big load. Plus bat speed powers uppercut swing. Solid, gap-to-gap approach with average power to all fields. Struggles with spin, especially diving out of zone. Low BA potential. Average runner with position flexibility.

Martorella,Nathan — 3 — San Diego

EXP MLB DEBUT: 2025 | H/W: 6-1 224 | FUT: Starting 1B | 7D

Bats L | Age 22 | 2022 (5) California

Pwr + + | BAvg + + + | Spd + | Def + +

Year	Lev	Team	AB	R	H	HR	RBI	Avg	OB	Slg	OPS	bb%	ct%	Eye	SB	CS	x/h%	Iso	RC/G
2022	NCAA	California	228	47	76	11	46	333	420	553	972	13	87	1.17	1	0	36	219	7.63
2022	Rk	ACL Padres	31	4	12	1	10	387	457	613	1070	11	81	0.67	0	0	42	226	9.02
2022	A	Lake Elsinore	59	10	17	2	11	288	408	458	866	17	75	0.80	0	0	35	169	6.78

Strong 1B who had excellent first pro experience upon signing. Manages strike zone well and makes easy contact for his profile. Dead FB hitter who relies more on strength than bat speed and can struggle with spin. Gets on base at high clip, but has very limited speed. Not a strong defender, though not a liability with glove.

Mastrobuoni,Miles — 49 — Chicago (N)

EXP MLB DEBUT: 2022 | H/W: 5-11 185 | FUT: Utility player | 7C

Bats L | Age 27 | 2016 (14) Nevada

Pwr + + | BAvg + + + | Spd + + + | Def + +

Year	Lev	Team	AB	R	H	HR	RBI	Avg	OB	Slg	OPS	bb%	ct%	Eye	SB	CS	x/h%	Iso	RC/G
2019	AAA	Durham	11	0	1	0	0	91	167	91	258	8	64	0.25	0	0	0	0	-2.49
2021	AA	Montgomery	221	34	66	5	31	299	375	448	823	11	81	0.63	6	3	32	149	5.87
2021	AAA	Durham	161	25	47	0	14	292	384	391	775	13	70	0.50	2	4	28	99	5.67
2022	AAA	Durham	507	92	152	16	64	300	377	469	847	11	81	0.66	23	3	34	170	6.12
2022	MLB	Tampa Bay	16	1	3	0	0	188	235	188	423	6	63	0.17	1	0	0	0	0.01

Contact-oriented LHH enjoyed career best slash line in AAA, earning MLB callup. Shorter-statured frame, at physical projection. Spray approach with power strictly to pull side. Rarely chases, not a alot of whiffs. Below-average raw power, hit 16 HR benefiting from AAA ball. Versatile, plays several positions. Has average speed.

Matos,Luis — 8 — San Francisco

EXP MLB DEBUT: 2024 | H/W: 5-11 160 | FUT: Starting CF | 8D

Bats R | Age 21 | 2018 FA (VZ)

Pwr + + | BAvg + + + | Spd + + + | Def + + +

Year	Lev	Team	AB	R	H	HR	RBI	Avg	OB	Slg	OPS	bb%	ct%	Eye	SB	CS	x/h%	Iso	RC/G
2021	A	San Jose	451	84	141	15	86	313	353	494	847	6	86	0.46	21	5	36	182	5.77
2022	Rk	ACL Giants B	7	3	3	1	4	429	500	###	1500	13	86	1.00	0	0	67	571	13.53
2022	A+	Eugene	369	55	78	11	43	211	265	344	609	7	82	0.42	11	3	33	133	2.95

Athletic, strong OF who had miserable year and saw BA and SLG fall dramatically. Missed time due to strained quad. Still high on upside as he has ability to make loud, hard contact and ability to control strike zone. Hits flyballs, but can be easy out when he flails at breaking balls. Has speed, arm and range to be solid CF.

Mauricio,Ronny — 6 — New York (N)

EXP MLB DEBUT: 2023 | H/W: 6-3 166 | FUT: Starting 3B | 8D

Bats B | Age 22 | 2017 FA (DR)

Pwr + + + + | BAvg + + | Spd + + | Def + + + +

Year	Lev	Team	AB	R	H	HR	RBI	Avg	OB	Slg	OPS	bb%	ct%	Eye	SB	CS	x/h%	Iso	RC/G
2018	Rk	GCL Mets	197	26	55	3	31	279	314	421	735	5	84	0.32	1	6	35	142	4.49
2019	A	Columbia	470	62	126	4	37	268	302	357	660	5	79	0.23	6	10	23	89	3.50
2021	A+	Brooklyn	392	55	95	19	63	242	286	449	735	6	74	0.24	9	7	40	207	4.39
2021	AA	Binghamton	31	3	10	1	1	323	364	452	815	6	65	0.18	2	0	20	129	5.94
2022	AA	Binghamton	509	71	132	26	89	259	293	472	764	5	75	0.19	20	11	41	212	4.67

Tall, powerful 3B prospect has grown into wiry frame with still more power to come. Switch hitter with open stance and slight bat wrap from LH side, smoother trigger from RH side. Plus-plus bat speed from LH side. Hits in parts from RH side. Terrible patience, will chase FB up and breakers down and away at high frequency. Potentially plus 3B.

Mayer,Marcelo — 6 — Boston

EXP MLB DEBUT: 2024 | H/W: 6-3 188 | FUT: Starting SS | 9B

Bats L | Age 20 | 2021 (1) HS (CA)

Pwr + + + | BAvg + + + + | Spd + + | Def + + + +

Year	Lev	Team	AB	R	H	HR	RBI	Avg	OB	Slg	OPS	bb%	ct%	Eye	SB	CS	x/h%	Iso	RC/G
2021	Rk	FCL Red Sox	91	25	25	3	17	275	377	440	817	14	70	0.56	7	1	32	165	6.08
2022	A	Salem	252	46	72	9	40	286	406	504	910	17	69	0.65	16	0	50	218	7.68
2022	A+	Greenville	98	15	26	4	13	265	374	449	823	15	70	0.59	1	0	35	184	6.14

Elite prospect with significant tools and instincts. May not exhibit plus speed, but does everything well. Reached A+ in first full season and highlights advanced approach at plate with pitch recognition. Plus power should come as he adds more strength. Uses entire field and makes adjustments. Solid defender with quick hands and strong arm.

Mayo,Coby — 5 — Baltimore

EXP MLB DEBUT: 2024 | H/W: 6-5 215 | FUT: Starting 1B | 9D

Bats R | Age 21 | 2020 (4) HS (FL)

Pwr + + + + | BAvg + + | Spd + + | Def + + +

Year	Lev	Team	AB	R	H	HR	RBI	Avg	OB	Slg	OPS	bb%	ct%	Eye	SB	CS	x/h%	Iso	RC/G
2021	Rk	FCL Orioles B	71	17	23	3	13	324	415	535	950	13	82	0.85	6	0	39	211	7.51
2021	A	Delmarva	106	27	33	5	26	311	402	547	949	13	75	0.62	5	0	42	236	7.65
2022	Rk	FCL Orioles B	5	1	0	0	0	0	167	0	167	17	60	0.50	0	0		0	-4.34
2022	A+	Aberdeen	255	50	64	14	49	251	323	494	817	10	76	0.44	5	1	50	243	5.64
2022	AA	Bowie	128	21	32	5	20	250	314	398	713	9	61	0.24	0	0	28	148	4.63

Has the look of a classic, HR-slugging cornerman with bat speed and ability to manipulate the barrel to maximize it. Strikeout rate jumped at AA, but injury kept him from a full season. Strength to hit HRs into the wind as well as fight off good pitches. Passable at 3B now; likely 1B or OF in his future where bat is likely to be enough to carry.

McCann,Kyle — 23 — Oakland

EXP MLB DEBUT: 2024 | H/W: 6-2 217 | FUT: Starting C | 7D

Bats L | Age 25 | 2019 (4) Georgia Tech

Pwr + + + | BAvg + + | Spd + | Def + +

Year	Lev	Team	AB	R	H	HR	RBI	Avg	OB	Slg	OPS	bb%	ct%	Eye	SB	CS	x/h%	Iso	RC/G
2019	Rk	AZL A's Gold	20	10	8	2	7	400	520	###	1520	20	70	0.83	0	0	75	600	16.71
2019	A-	Vermont	198	23	38	7	25	192	283	343	626	11	59	0.31	0	0	39	152	3.38
2021	AA	Midland	320	40	53	8	39	166	272	275	547	13	57	0.34	1	0	36	109	2.15
2022	AA	Midland	370	61	88	20	65	238	333	449	782	13	61	0.37	2	0	43	211	5.80
2022	AAA	Las Vegas	24	4	4	1	1	167	259	375	634	11	63	0.33	0	0	75	208	3.44

Returned to AA for 2022 and was much better after atrocious 2021 campaign. Dramatically increased HR while becoming more selective with better pitch recognition. BA ability still muted as he can expand zone, particularly with breaking balls. Had 4th most Ks in TL. Has improved defensively, but still a ways to go. Owns strong arm.

McCray,Grant — 8 — San Francisco

EXP MLB DEBUT: 2024 | H/W: 6-2 190 | FUT: Starting OF | 8D

Bats L | Age 22 | 2019 (3) HS (FL)

Pwr + + + | BAvg + + + | Spd + + + + | Def + + +

Year	Lev	Team	AB	R	H	HR	RBI	Avg	OB	Slg	OPS	bb%	ct%	Eye	SB	CS	x/h%	Iso	RC/G
2019	Rk	AZL Giants	185	43	50	1	11	270	372	335	707	14	71	0.56	17	13	16	65	4.61
2021	Rk	ACL Giants O	55	16	17	1	6	309	406	455	861	14	64	0.45	3	1	29	145	7.25
2021	A	San Jose	80	8	20	2	12	250	302	400	702	7	63	0.20	4	1	30	150	4.50
2022	A	San Jose	436	92	127	21	69	291	374	525	900	12	66	0.39	35	10	40	234	7.40
2022	A+	Eugene	52	12	14	2	10	269	377	423	800	15	58	0.41	8	0	29	154	6.52

Athletic OF who easily set career high in HR and SB with dramatic jumps in both. Had breakout season with realization of power and speed. Produces pop thru above average bat speed and strength. Led org in walks, but also 2nd in Ks. Concern about hit tool due to swing and miss and struggles with spin.

McDonough,Tyler — 478 — Boston

EXP MLB DEBUT: 2024 | H/W: 5-10 180 | FUT: Utility player | 6C

Bats B | Age 24 | 2021 (3) NC State

Pwr + + | BAvg + + | Spd + + + | Def + + +

Year	Lev	Team	AB	R	H	HR	RBI	Avg	OB	Slg	OPS	bb%	ct%	Eye	SB	CS	x/h%	Iso	RC/G
2020	NCAA	NC St	65	17	23	3	16	354	468	554	1022	18	85	1.40	7	0	30	200	8.58
2021	NCAA	NC St	233	58	79	15	45	339	421	631	1052	12	79	0.69	13	4	47	292	8.71
2021	Rk	FCL Red Sox	13	2	4	0	1	308	308	538	846	0	69	0.00	0	0	75	231	6.38
2021	A	Salem	108	23	32	3	14	296	392	491	883	14	78	0.71	3	1	34	194	6.85
2022	A+	Greenville	457	60	105	9	48	230	303	357	660	10	65	0.30	21	5	34	127	3.83

Versatile, switch-hitting INF who faded down stretch. Led org in Ks despite lack of offensive punch. Works counts and can hit velocity. Hope is he can grow into average power where lack of contact would be acceptable. Steals bases with average speed and polished instincts. Sufficient defender who can play any position.

McIntosh,Paul | 2 | Miami | EXP MLB DEBUT: 2024 | H/W: 6-1 220 | FUT: Starting C | 7D

Bats R Age 25	Year	Lev	Team	AB	R	H	HR	RBI	Avg	OB	Slg	OPS	bb%	ct%	Eye	SB	CS	x/h%	Iso	RC/G
2022 NDFA West Virginia	2020	NCAA	West Virginia	58	10	12	3	14	207	246	414	660	5	86	0.38	0	2	50	207	3.47
Pwr +++	2021	NCAA	West Virginia	156	25	40	8	26	256	333	474	808	10	85	0.78	2	6	43	218	5.50
BAvg +++	2021	Rk	FCL Marlins	1	0	0	0	0	0	0	0	0	0	100		0	0		0	-2.66
Spd ++	2021	A	Jupiter	75	14	19	6	20	253	378	627	1004	17	73	0.75	0	0	74	373	8.57
Def ++	2022	AA	Pensacola	318	66	82	13	51	258	367	465	833	15	76	0.73	10	5	48	208	6.17

Former undrafted collegiate free agent excelled with the bat in first full-season as pro. Upright, slight open stance with no trigger and moderate leg lift. Above-average bat speed with slight uppercut swing trajectory. Raw power in frame. Patient approach at the plate. Extreme pull tendencies. Could hit 20+ HR. Challenged defensively at C.

McLain,Matt | 46 | Cincinnati | EXP MLB DEBUT: 2023 | H/W: 5-11 180 | FUT: Starting 2B | 8D

Bats R Age 23	Year	Lev	Team	AB	R	H	HR	RBI	Avg	OB	Slg	OPS	bb%	ct%	Eye	SB	CS	x/h%	Iso	RC/G
2021 (1) UCLA	2020	NCAA	UCLA	58	15	23	3	19	397	435	621	1056	6	78	0.31	1	0	30	224	8.45
Pwr +++	2021	NCAA	UCLA	183	47	61	9	36	333	438	579	1017	16	81	1.00	9	1	41	246	8.48
BAvg +++	2021	Rk	ACL Reds	7	2	3	0	0	429	429	1000	1429	0	100		0	0	100	571	11.98
Spd +++	2021	A+	Dayton	99	15	27	3	19	273	379	424	804	15	76	0.71	10	2	33	152	5.80
Def +++	2022	AA	Chattanooga	371	67	86	17	58	232	354	453	807	16	66	0.55	27	3	50	221	6.13

Sold out for loft and struggled with BA, whiffs throughout '22. Shorter-statured, he is at physical projection. Average-to-above-average tools across the board. Upright, open stance with uppercut swing. Swing lost ability to get to FB up. Discerning eye with patient approach. 20-25 HR power at projection. Above-average runner.

Mead,Curtis | 45 | Tampa Bay | EXP MLB DEBUT: 2023 | H/W: 6-2 171 | FUT: Utility player | 9B

Bats R Age 22	Year	Lev	Team	AB	R	H	HR	RBI	Avg	OB	Slg	OPS	bb%	ct%	Eye	SB	CS	x/h%	Iso	RC/G
2017 FA (AU)	2021	A	Charleston	191	36	68	7	35	356	403	586	989	7	84	0.50	9	2	43	230	7.59
Pwr ++++	2021	A+	Bowling Green	206	38	58	7	32	282	342	466	808	8	82	0.50	2	2	40	184	5.49
BAvg ++++	2021	AAA	Durham	14	3	6	1	2	429	429	786	1214	0	79	0.00	0	0	50	357	9.95
Spd ++	2022	AA	Montgomery	210	35	64	10	36	305	379	548	926	11	79	0.56	6	2	48	243	7.11
Def ++	2022	AAA	Durham	72	8	20	3	14	278	373	486	860	13	76	0.65	1	0	45	208	6.45

Strong, hitterish IF prospect put up big numbers in injury shortened season. Upright stance with little to no trigger. Has supreme body control at the plate with natural opposite field gap swing. Patient approach, makes good decisions, gets to hard contact. Raw power beginning to blossom while incorporating the pull field. Doesn't have a position.

Meadows,Parker | 8 | Detroit | EXP MLB DEBUT: 2023 | H/W: 6-5 205 | FUT: Reserve OF | 7D

Bats L Age 23	Year	Lev	Team	AB	R	H	HR	RBI	Avg	OB	Slg	OPS	bb%	ct%	Eye	SB	CS	x/h%	Iso	RC/G
2018 (2) HS (GA)	2019	A	West Michigan	443	52	98	7	40	221	296	312	607	10	74	0.42	14	8	24	90	2.97
Pwr ++	2021	A	Lakeland	11	2	3	0	1	273	273	364	636	0	73	0.00	0	0	33	91	3.05
BAvg +++	2021	A+	West Michigan	355	50	74	8	44	208	283	330	613	9	72	0.37	9	8	34	121	3.01
Spd +++	2022	A+	West Michigan	61	16	14	4	7	230	277	525	802	6	70	0.22	0	0	64	295	5.43
Def ++++	2022	AA	Erie	425	64	117	16	51	275	354	466	820	11	79	0.58	17	2	37	191	5.78

Younger brother of Tigers OF Austin, he had best season as a pro, slugging a career best .473 with 20 HR. Showed a more aggressive, pull-heavy approach without sacrificing plate discipline and posted an 11% BB rate at Double-A. Always considered a plus defender with above-average speed, now has a chance to carve out an MLB role.

Mears,Joshua | 89 | San Diego | EXP MLB DEBUT: 2024 | H/W: 6-3 230 | FUT: Starting OF | 8D

Bats R Age 22	Year	Lev	Team	AB	R	H	HR	RBI	Avg	OB	Slg	OPS	bb%	ct%	Eye	SB	CS	x/h%	Iso	RC/G
2019 (2) HS (WA)	2019	Rk	AZL Padres	166	30	42	7	24	253	344	440	784	12	64	0.39	9	1	33	187	5.71
Pwr ++++	2021	A	Lake Elsinore	242	45	59	17	48	244	342	529	871	13	53	0.32	10	5	53	285	8.25
BAvg +	2022	Rk	ACL Padres	56	10	15	3	10	268	359	571	931	13	54	0.31	2	0	67	304	9.56
Spd +++	2022	A+	Fort Wayne	184	29	41	14	34	223	285	511	796	8	51	0.18	1	1	61	288	7.02
Def +++	2022	AA	San Antonio	83	9	14	5	15	169	258	373	632	11	46	0.22	1	0	50	205	4.39

Hulking slugger who led org in Ks after miserable start to season. Hitting for BA may not be in cards due to ton of swing and miss. Makes very hard, loud contact and has light tower power to all fields. Very easy bat speed with lot of loft. Has good speed and can play CF, though RF more likely. Could have breakout with consistent contact.

Mejia,Jonathan | 6 | St. Louis | EXP MLB DEBUT: 2028 | H/W: 6-0 185 | FUT: Starting SS | 8E

Bats B Age 17	Year	Lev	Team	AB	R	H	HR	RBI	Avg	OB	Slg	OPS	bb%	ct%	Eye	SB	CS	x/h%	Iso	RC/G
2022 FA (DR)																				
Pwr +++																				
BAvg +++																				
Spd +++																				
Def +++	2022	Rk	DSL Cardinals Blue	165	33	44	5	34	267	389	479	868	17	71	0.69	3	2	50	212	7.01

Signed out of DR for $2M as one of the top international prospects in the '22 class. Showed why with an impressive pro debut in the DSL. Shows an advanced understanding of strike zone to go along with a quick bat and feel for the barrel. Quick first step and strong arm that should enable him to stick at SS.

Melendez,Ivan | 35 | Arizona | EXP MLB DEBUT: 2025 | H/W: 6-3 225 | FUT: Starting 1B | 7C

Bats R Age 23	Year	Lev	Team	AB	R	H	HR	RBI	Avg	OB	Slg	OPS	bb%	ct%	Eye	SB	CS	x/h%	Iso	RC/G
2022 (2) Texas																				
Pwr ++++	2022	NCAA	Texas	248	75	96	32	94	387	493	863	1356	17	79	1.02	1	0	54	476	12.61
BAvg ++	2022	Rk	ACL DBacks	1	1	0	0	0	0	667	0	667	67	100		0	0		0	7.21
Spd +	2022	Rk	ACL Dbacks	9	1	2	0	0	222	300	222	522	10	44	0.20	0	0	0	0	2.54
Def ++	2022	A	Visalia	87	11	18	3	8	207	289	368	656	10	77	0.50	0	0	39	161	3.62

Strong-bodied, power-first 1B prospect slugged his way to 2nd round of 2022 draft. Body is near projection. Upright stance with slight hitch in load. Gap-to-gap power approach. Uppercut trajectory enhances raw power; think 30+ HR at projection. Aggressive approach. Chases better spin. Defensively limited to 1B but power carries.

Melton,Jacob | 8 | Houston | EXP MLB DEBUT: 2024 | H/W: 6-3 208 | FUT: Starting OF | 8D

Bats L Age 22	Year	Lev	Team	AB	R	H	HR	RBI	Avg	OB	Slg	OPS	bb%	ct%	Eye	SB	CS	x/h%	Iso	RC/G
2022 (2) Oregon St																				
Pwr +++																				
BAvg +++	2022	NCAA	Oregon State	261	66	94	17	83	360	418	670	1089	9	80	0.51	21	1	46	310	8.93
Spd ++++	2022	Rk	FCL Astros	17	0	0	0	0	0	0	0	0	0	65	0.00	1	0		0	-6.32
Def +++	2022	A	Fayetteville	71	11	23	4	13	324	415	577	992	13	72	0.55	4	2	43	254	8.39

Earned PAC-12 Player of the Year award following excellent junior season. Shows 5-tool production with some projection remaining in athletic frame. Wide open stance in box with good feel for barrel despite noisy setup and slight hitch in swing. Plus speed in field and on base paths.

Mendez,Hendry | 9 | Milwaukee | EXP MLB DEBUT: 2026 | H/W: 6-2 175 | FUT: Starting OF | 7D

Bats L Age 19	Year	Lev	Team	AB	R	H	HR	RBI	Avg	OB	Slg	OPS	bb%	ct%	Eye	SB	CS	x/h%	Iso	RC/G
2021 FA (DR)																				
Pwr ++																				
BAvg ++	2021	Rk	ACL Brewers Blue	63	6	21	0	10	333	425	460	885	14	84	1.00	3	1	29	127	6.96
Spd +++	2021	Rk	DSL Brewers 1	54	10	16	1	9	296	377	481	859	11	96	3.50	0	0	44	185	6.54
Def ++	2022	A	Carolina	377	47	92	5	39	244	351	318	669	14	81	0.89	7	8	18	74	4.11

Projectable OF who has very impressive tools other than speed. Has advanced ability to read pitches and excellent bat speed from left side. Has patience to find pitch to drive, but K rate too high. Should get to at least average power and maybe more, but swing needs adjustments. Has enough arm for RF and will need to polish baserunning.

Mercedes,Yasser | 8 | Minnesota | EXP MLB DEBUT: 2027 | H/W: 6-2 175 | FUT: Starting CF | 8E

Bats R Age 18	Year	Lev	Team	AB	R	H	HR	RBI	Avg	OB	Slg	OPS	bb%	ct%	Eye	SB	CS	x/h%	Iso	RC/G
2022 FA (PR)																				
Pwr +++																				
BAvg +++																				
Spd +++																				
Def ++	2022	Rk	DSL Twins	155	34	55	4	20	355	422	555	977	10	77	0.51	30	5	36	200	7.93

Big bonus OF who enjoyed dazzling pro debut in DSL. Has athletic and projectable lean physique. If potential realized, could hit for both BA and power. Reads spin well for age, but can chase at times. Natural power in righty swing and has shown ability to make swing adjustments. CF play is crude and likely to end up in corner.

Merrill,Jackson | 6 | San Diego | EXP MLB DEBUT: 2025 | H/W: 6-3 195 | FUT: Starting SS | 8B

Bats L Age 19	Year	Lev	Team	AB	R	H	HR	RBI	Avg	OB	Slg	OPS	bb%	ct%	Eye	SB	CS	x/h%	Iso	RC/G
2021 (1) HS (MD)																				
Pwr +++																				
BAvg +++	2021	Rk	ACL Padres	107	19	30	0	10	280	342	383	725	9	75	0.37	5	1	30	103	4.67
Spd +++	2022	Rk	ACL Padres	30	5	13	1	6	433	452	700	1152	3	93	0.50	3	0	38	267	8.92
Def +++	2022	A	Lake Elsinore	197	33	64	5	34	325	384	482	866	9	79	0.45	8	5	28	157	6.30

Top prospect who missed time due to wrist, but played in AFL. Owns outstanding tools across board. Knows how to hit and has added strength and weight for more pop and durability. Can hit LHP with strong eye and nice bat speed. Should hit for both BA and power in time. Likely to stick at SS with soft, quick hands and strong arm.

Mervis,Matt | 3 | Chicago (N) | EXP MLB DEBUT: 2023 | H/W: 6-4 225 | FUT: Starting 1B | 8D

Bats L Age 24	Year	Lev	Team	AB	R	H	HR	RBI	Avg	OB	Slg	OPS	bb%	ct%	Eye	SB	CS	x/h%	Iso	RC/G
2020 NDFA Duke	2021	A	Myrtle Beach	245	38	50	9	42	204	306	367	673	13	73	0.55	6	0	42	163	3.91
Pwr ++++	2021	AAA	Iowa	14	2	4	0	2	286	333	357	690	7	71	0.25	0	0	25	71	4.09
BAvg +++	2022	A+	South Bend	100	17	35	7	29	350	381	650	1031	5	74	0.19	0	0	46	300	8.22
Spd +	2022	AA	Tennessee	203	34	61	14	51	300	363	596	959	9	77	0.43	2	0	51	296	7.37
Def ++	2022	AAA	Iowa	209	41	62	15	39	297	372	593	965	11	83	0.71	0	0	50	297	7.35

Tall frame with quick LH stroke that generates easy all-fields power. Upright stance w/ leg kick for timing and advanced understanding of the strike zone fueled monster season and continued to rake in AFL. Attacks heaters and mistakes in the zone. Well below average runner with a plus arm limits him to 1B or DH. But bat can do serious damage.

Mesa Jr.,Victor | 78 | Miami | EXP MLB DEBUT: 2024 | H/W: 6-0 195 | FUT: Starting OF | 7D

Bats L Age 21	Year	Lev	Team	AB	R	H	HR	RBI	Avg	OB	Slg	OPS	bb%	ct%	Eye	SB	CS	x/h%	Iso	RC/G
2018 FA (CU)																				
Pwr +++																				
BAvg ++																				
Spd +++	2021	A	Jupiter	428	66	114	5	71	266	319	402	721	7	76	0.32	12	5	32	136	4.47
Def +++	2022	A+	Beloit	460	53	112	5	50	243	322	346	667	10	78	0.53	10	4	30	102	3.90

Strong, LHH OF prospect couldn't get to consistent hard contact during High-A stint. Upright, open stance with long trigger, struggles getting bat started. Plus bat speed with slight uppercut swing trajectory, doesn't get to hard, lofted contact. Raw above-average power in frame, Could be average at maturity. Versatile defender. Best in LF.

Meza,Luis | 2 | Toronto | EXP MLB DEBUT: 2027 | H/W: 5-10 150 | FUT: Starting C | 8E

Bats R Age 18	Year	Lev	Team	AB	R	H	HR	RBI	Avg	OB	Slg	OPS	bb%	ct%	Eye	SB	CS	x/h%	Iso	RC/G
2022 FA (VZ)																				
Pwr ++																				
BAvg ++																				
Spd ++																				
Def +++	2022	Rk	DSL Blue Jays	96	6	22	0	8	229	267	292	559	5	80	0.26	2	0	23	63	2.33

High-profile international signee with bright future if tools continue to develop. Solid backstop for age. Exhibits agility and natural leadership qualities. Needs to refine both receiving and blocking. Has mature approach and pitch recognition skills. Makes easy contact and exhibits gap power now. Power development is key.

Mezquita,Brandol | 789 | Atlanta | EXP MLB DEBUT: 2025 | H/W: 6-0 170 | FUT: Reserve OF | 6C

Bats R Age 21	Year	Lev	Team	AB	R	H	HR	RBI	Avg	OB	Slg	OPS	bb%	ct%	Eye	SB	CS	x/h%	Iso	RC/G
2017 FA (DR)																				
Pwr ++	2019	Rk	GCL Braves	118	14	29	1	12	246	341	280	620	13	66	0.43	6	2	7	34	3.23
BAvg ++	2021	Rk	FCL Braves	146	18	45	3	25	308	388	452	840	12	66	0.38	15	4	29	144	6.64
Spd +++	2022	A	Augusta	331	57	93	3	46	281	360	375	735	11	69	0.41	14	5	23	94	4.92
Def +++	2022	A+	Rome	57	2	11	0	5	193	270	228	498	10	60	0.26	0	1	9	35	1.37

Athletic RHH OF prospect put up solid numbers in Low-A despite high K rate. Average frame with room to grow. Upright, slight open stance with little trigger. Linear swing, sometimes in parts. Struggles with strike zone awareness, especially with spin. Power-over-hit profile. Average raw power. Solid in CF defensively now but likely a corner OF long term.

Mieses,Luis | 79 | Chicago (A) | EXP MLB DEBUT: 2023 | H/W: 6-3 180 | FUT: Starting OF | 6C

Bats L Age 22	Year	Lev	Team	AB	R	H	HR	RBI	Avg	OB	Slg	OPS	bb%	ct%	Eye	SB	CS	x/h%	Iso	RC/G
2016 FA (DR)	2019	Rk	Great Falls	220	24	53	4	28	241	264	359	623	3	79	0.15	0	1	34	118	2.93
Pwr +++	2021	A	Kannapolis	203	31	62	6	41	305	347	463	810	6	84	0.39	0	0	31	158	5.34
BAvg +++	2021	A+	Salem	220	30	52	9	33	236	273	464	736	5	78	0.23	0	1	58	227	4.43
Spd ++	2022	A+	Winston-Salem	420	54	118	12	72	281	320	448	767	5	83	0.33	0	0	39	167	4.83
Def +++	2022	AA	Birmingham	97	12	29	3	16	299	327	443	770	4	79	0.20	1	0	28	144	4.71

Long, lanky hit-over-power prospect enjoyed best season as pro. Open, upright stance with a short bat wrap in load; it's a linear swing with some length. Struggles getting to hard contact consistently. Utilizes entire field in approach; has raw plus power that plays a hair under average. A slow runner, limited to COF.

Millas,Drew | 2 | Washington | EXP MLB DEBUT: 2024 | H/W: 6-2 202 | FUT: Reserve C | 7D

Bats B Age 25	Year	Lev	Team	AB	R	H	HR	RBI	Avg	OB	Slg	OPS	bb%	ct%	Eye	SB	CS	x/h%	Iso	RC/G
2019 (7) Missouri St	2021	A+	Lansing	220	34	56	3	28	255	372	359	731	16	82	1.05	10	2	29	105	5.02
Pwr ++	2021	A+	Wilmington	102	15	29	0	20	284	365	324	689	11	86	0.93	5	1	14	39	4.36
BAvg ++	2022	A	Fredericksburg	61	15	15	2	10	246	387	377	764	19	79	1.08	6	2	27	131	5.41
Spd +++	2022	A+	Wilmington	76	13	18	1	10	237	408	434	842	22	74	1.10	1	0	61	197	6.95
Def ++++	2022	AA	Harrisburg	152	12	32	3	16	211	281	296	577	9	65	0.28	1	1	22	86	2.45

Defense-first backstop with good arm and blocking/receiving skills that point to MLB backup floor. Unfortunately offense doesn't raise profile much. Shows great patience - excellent OBPs throughout his career - but payout-upon-contact is most often light. Better wheels than an average catcher; might not hit enough to use 'em.

Miller,Noah | 6 | Minnesota | EXP MLB DEBUT: 2025 | H/W: 6-1 190 | FUT: Starting SS | 7C

Bats B Age 20	Year	Lev	Team	AB	R	H	HR	RBI	Avg	OB	Slg	OPS	bb%	ct%	Eye	SB	CS	x/h%	Iso	RC/G
2021 (1) HS (WI)																				
Pwr +																				
BAvg ++																				
Spd +++	2021	Rk	FCL Twins	84	11	20	2	14	238	312	369	681	10	69	0.35	1	1	30	131	4.00
Def +++	2022	A	Fort Myers	383	62	81	2	24	211	342	279	621	17	71	0.69	23	7	22	68	3.47

Quick, instinctual SS who struggled with stick in first full pro season. Draws ton of walks with discerning eye at plate, but hasn't made hard contact. Too many Ks for profile. Should continue to add weight and expectation is for additional pop in time. Has swing path to hit for BA. Excellent SS with ample range and strong arm.

Misner,Kameron | 89 | Tampa Bay | EXP MLB DEBUT: 2024 | H/W: 6-4 218 | FUT: Starting OF | 7D

Bats L Age 25	Year	Lev	Team	AB	R	H	HR	RBI	Avg	OB	Slg	OPS	bb%	ct%	Eye	SB	CS	x/h%	Iso	RC/G
2019 (1) Missouri	2019	Rk	GCL Marlins	29	2	7	0	4	241	421	310	731	24	76	1.29	3	0	29	69	5.42
Pwr ++++	2019	A	Clinton	134	25	37	2	20	276	374	373	747	14	74	0.60	8	0	24	97	5.07
BAvg ++	2021	A+	Beloit	340	58	83	11	56	244	341	424	765	13	65	0.42	24	2	43	179	5.50
Spd +++	2021	AA	Pensacola	55	12	17	1	3	309	387	491	878	11	69	0.41	2	2	47	182	7.09
Def ++++	2022	AA	Montgomery	415	80	104	16	62	251	379	431	811	17	63	0.55	32	7	40	181	6.42

Power-first OF prospect struggled with in-zone swing-and-miss despite putting up productive line. Tall, athletic frame with plus raw strength; power plays mostly to pull side. Patient approach, works counts. Struggles with bat wrap in load and longer swing length. Above-average runner.

Mitchell,Garrett | 8 | Milwaukee | EXP MLB DEBUT: 2022 | H/W: 6-3 215 | FUT: Starting CF | 8B

Bats L Age 24	Year	Lev	Team	AB	R	H	HR	RBI	Avg	OB	Slg	OPS	bb%	ct%	Eye	SB	CS	x/h%	Iso	RC/G
2020 (1) UCLA	2021	AA	Biloxi	129	16	24	3	10	186	286	264	549	12	68	0.44	5	1	17	78	2.07
Pwr +++	2022	Rk	ACL Brewers Blue	12	5	1	0	0	83	313	167	479	25	67	1.00	1	0	100	83	1.38
BAvg ++++	2022	AA	Biloxi	166	29	46	4	25	277	341	428	768	9	69	0.31	7	1	33	151	5.28
Spd ++++	2022	AAA	Nashville	73	15	25	1	9	342	422	466	887	12	75	0.56	9	0	28	123	6.92
Def ++++	2022	MLB	Milwaukee	61	9	19	2	9	311	373	459	832	9	54	0.21	8	0	26	148	7.48

Plus athlete with double-plus speed and ability to be standout in CF. Could challenge for starting job in MIL in 2023. Made big league debut and was impressive. Consistent offensive producer who can hit LHP. Exhibits plate patience to get on base at high clip. Power hasn't yet appeared, but strength and bat speed are prevalent.

Montes,Lazaro | 9 | Seattle | EXP MLB DEBUT: 2027 | H/W: 6-3 210 | FUT: Starting OF | 8D

Bats L Age 18	Year	Lev	Team	AB	R	H	HR	RBI	Avg	OB	Slg	OPS	bb%	ct%	Eye	SB	CS	x/h%	Iso	RC/G
2022 FA (CU)																				
Pwr ++++																				
BAvg +++																				
Spd ++																				
Def ++	2022	Rk	DSL Mariners	176	34	50	10	41	284	403	585	988	17	58	0.47	3	1	56	301	9.91

Big-time bonus baby who finished 7th in DSL in OPS in first pro season. Owns significant upside, but needs time to polish natural talent. Leverages advanced eye at plate to identify pitches to destroy. Could grow into double-plus power and hit in middle of lineup. Has leverage and loft, but struggles to make consistent contact.

Montesino,Daniel | 37 | San Diego | EXP MLB DEBUT: 2027 | H/W: 6-0 180 | FUT: Starting 1B | 8E

Bats L Age 19	Year	Lev	Team	AB	R	H	HR	RBI	Avg	OB	Slg	OPS	bb%	ct%	Eye	SB	CS	x/h%	Iso	RC/G
2021 FA (VZ)																				
Pwr +++																				
BAvg +++																				
Spd ++																				
Def +	2021	Rk	DSL Padres	190	37	60	4	48	316	442	489	932	18	72	0.81	8	4	35	174	8.01

Missed season after Tommy John surgery, yet has promising future. High-profile international signing with lot of power potential and clean swing mechanics. Has disciplined eye at plate, but tendency to swing too hard. Has trouble with breaking balls. Not a particularly good defender and may end up at 1B where arm strength isn't mandatory.

Montgomery,Benny — 8 — Colorado — EXP MLB DEBUT: 2025 — H/W: 6-4 200 — FUT: Starting CF — 9D

Bats R Age 20 · 2021 (1) HS (PA) · Pwr +++ · BAvg ++ · Spd ++++ · Def ++++

Year	Lev	Team	AB	R	H	HR	RBI	Avg	OB	Sig	OPS	bb%	ct%	Eye	SB	CS	x/h%	Iso	RC/G
2021	Rk	ACL Rockies	47	7	16	0	6	340	404	383	787	10	81	0.56	5	1	6	43	5.37
2022	Rk	ACL Rockies	22	3	6	0	2	273	273	409	682	0	73	0.00	0	0	33	136	3.76
2022	A	Fresno	233	48	73	6	42	313	370	502	872	8	70	0.30	9	1	40	189	6.77

Athletic OF was limited to just 62G due to injury, but when healthy continued to put up impressive numbers. Plus runner has worked hard to simplify his setup and keep the barrel in the zone. Needs to be more selective to maximize his above-average raw power. Plus defender with good range and a strong arm and has the potential to be a 20/20 guy.

Montgomery,Colson — 6 — Chicago (A) — EXP MLB DEBUT: 2024 — H/W: 6-4 205 — FUT: Starting SS — 8C

Bats L Age 21 · 2021 (1) HS (IN) · Pwr +++ · BAvg +++ · Spd +++ · Def +++

Year	Lev	Team	AB	R	H	HR	RBI	Avg	OB	Sig	OPS	bb%	ct%	Eye	SB	CS	x/h%	Iso	RC/G
2021	Rk	ACL White Sox	94	16	27	0	7	287	374	362	736	12	77	0.59	0	1	26	74	4.93
2022	A	Kannapolis	170	31	55	4	26	324	413	476	890	13	75	0.62	0	1	31	153	6.97
2022	A+	Winston-Salem	132	22	34	5	14	258	380	417	796	16	80	1.00	1	0	29	159	5.72
2022	AA	Birmingham	48	5	7	2	7	146	180	292	472	4	69	0.13	0	0	43	146	0.67

Athletic with across-the-board above-average skills. Upright, slight open stance with simple load and a flat-angled swing, maximizing contact over EV. Lots of feel in approach. Will allow ball to travel and not afraid to swing inside-out. Raw above-average power; swing change needed to get to it. Solid runner and SS.

Moore,Robert — 46 — Milwaukee — EXP MLB DEBUT: 2025 — H/W: 5-9 170 — FUT: Starting 2B — 7C

Bats B Age 21 · 2022 (2) Arkansas · Pwr ++ · BAvg +++ · Spd ++ · Def +++

Year	Lev	Team	AB	R	H	HR	RBI	Avg	OB	Sig	OPS	bb%	ct%	Eye	SB	CS	x/h%	Iso	RC/G
2022	NCAA	Arkansas	241	48	56	8	44	232	346	427	774	15	81	0.91	5	2	52	195	5.44
2022	Rk	ACL Brewers Blue	11	1	1	0	1	91	167	182	348	8	91	1.00	0	0	100	91	0.67
2022	Rk	ACL Brewers Gold	4	2	1	0	1	250	400	250	650	20	75	1.00	1	0	0	0	4.03
2022	A	Carolina	110	14	29	3	14	264	341	418	760	11	75	0.46	6	2	38	155	5.06

Fundamentally-sound INF who plays above tools. Focus is on pitch selection, consistent contact and using entire field in simple approach. Gets on base and uses fringy speed and shrewd instincts to steal bases. Power not part of equation. Doesn't chase pitches and not afraid to hit with two strikes. Sound defensive player.

Morabito,Nick — 8 — New York (N) — EXP MLB DEBUT: 2026 — H/W: 5-11 185 — FUT: Starting OF — 7E

Bats R Age 19 · 2022 (2) HS (DC) · Pwr +++ · BAvg +++ · Spd ++++ · Def ++

Year	Lev	Team	AB	R	H	HR	RBI	Avg	OB	Sig	OPS	bb%	ct%	Eye	SB	CS	x/h%	Iso	RC/G
2022	Rk	FCL Mets	22	1	2	0	2	91	167	136	303	8	36	0.14	1	0	50	45	-1.86

2022 HS CF prospect had limited pro debut in Florida Complex League. Stockier athletic frame with plus run tool. Slightly closed stance with quick trigger. Linear swing with above-average bat speed. Opposite field approach. Raw average power. Improved pull power last spring. Converted IF. Weak arm.

Morissette,Cody — 4 — Miami — EXP MLB DEBUT: 2024 — H/W: 6-0 175 — FUT: Starting 2B — 7D

Bats L Age 23 · 2021 (2) Boston Col · Pwr +++ · BAvg ++ · Spd +++ · Def +++

Year	Lev	Team	AB	R	H	HR	RBI	Avg	OB	Sig	OPS	bb%	ct%	Eye	SB	CS	x/h%	Iso	RC/G
2020	NCAA	Boston Col	58	14	26	2	11	448	522	655	1178	13	90	1.50	3	2	31	207	10.08
2021	NCAA	Boston Col	165	29	53	6	33	321	398	497	895	11	80	0.64	8	1	30	176	6.71
2021	A	Jupiter	137	22	28	1	10	204	306	299	605	13	72	0.53	0	2	36	95	3.13
2022	Rk	FCL Marlins	6	1	2	0	1	333	333	500	833	0	83	0.00	0	0	50	167	5.48
2022	A+	Beloit	336	48	78	13	51	232	301	399	700	9	73	0.37	4	1	38	167	4.09

Shorter-statured, athletic SS prospect struggled getting to hard contact in High-A. LHH with open, upright stance. Bit of a hitchy load slowing swing reactions. Uppercut swing trajectory with extreme pull approach. Could get to average power by maturity. Above-average range due to plus reactions in the field. Average runner.

Morris,Tanner — 45 — Toronto — EXP MLB DEBUT: 2023 — H/W: 6-2 190 — FUT: Utility player — 6B

Bats L Age 24 · 2019 (5) Virginia · Pwr + · BAvg +++ · Spd + · Def ++

Year	Lev	Team	AB	R	H	HR	RBI	Avg	OB	Sig	OPS	bb%	ct%	Eye	SB	CS	x/h%	Iso	RC/G
2019	NCAA	Virginia	223	56	77	5	38	345	447	507	954	16	83	1.08	3	1	34	161	7.78
2019	A-	Tri-City	240	37	59	2	28	246	374	346	720	17	77	0.88	4	2	32	100	4.92
2021	A+	Vancouver	397	55	113	7	57	285	376	401	776	13	77	0.64	4	1	26	116	5.39
2022	AA	New Hampshire	154	35	48	5	11	312	424	468	891	16	81	1.00	1	3	27	156	6.98
2022	AAA	Buffalo	98	8	17	0	7	173	341	173	515	20	74	1.00	0	2	0	0	2.12

Natural-hitting INF who hit over .300 at AA, but under .200 in AAA. Limited time after June due to wrist injury. Posts very high BB rate and makes very easy contact with short, controllable stroke. Hits hard line drives to gaps, but has well below average HR power. Swing path not conducive to flyballs. Below average speed and quickness.

Morrobel,Yeison — 789 — Texas — EXP MLB DEBUT: 2026 — H/W: 6-2 170 — FUT: Starting OF — 7D

Bats L Age 19 · 2021 FA (DR) · Pwr + · BAvg +++ · Spd + · Def ++

Year	Lev	Team	AB	R	H	HR	RBI	Avg	OB	Sig	OPS	bb%	ct%	Eye	SB	CS	x/h%	Iso	RC/G
2021	Rk	DSL Rangers	185	33	50	1	30	270	372	411	783	14	86	1.20	8	4	36	141	5.74
2022	Rk	ACL Rangers	152	31	50	3	21	329	396	487	883	10	78	0.50	5	5	34	158	6.67
2022	A	Down East	26	3	6	0	3	231	310	269	580	10	77	0.50	2	1	17	38	2.74

Near $2M bonus quick-twitcher slimmed down and dropped a 144 wRC+ in stateside debut. Advanced bat adjustment ability portends future plus hit tool, but obviously raw now. Plate discipline played up but little juice as body waits on projection; probably not ever a banger nor burner. No splits but patience erodes against LHP.

Muncy,Max — 6 — Oakland — EXP MLB DEBUT: 2025 — H/W: 6-1 180 — FUT: Starting SS — 8D

Bats R Age 20 · 2021 (1) HS (CA) · Pwr +++ · BAvg ++ · Spd +++ · Def +++

Year	Lev	Team	AB	R	H	HR	RBI	Avg	OB	Sig	OPS	bb%	ct%	Eye	SB	CS	x/h%	Iso	RC/G
2021	Rk	ACL Athletics	31	3	4	0	4	129	206	129	335	9	61	0.25	1	0	0	0	-1.38
2022	A	Stockton	304	50	70	16	51	230	341	447	788	14	64	0.47	6	5	47	217	5.79
2022	A+	Lansing	168	19	38	3	19	226	301	375	676	10	64	0.30	13	1	45	149	4.17

Gifted INF who was promoted to High-A in July. Had most Ks in org, but 2nd most walks. Has natural tools across board with athleticism, speed and excellent defense. High K rate is a concern, but should get better as he becomes less aggressive. Body has room for more muscle and should add to above average power.

Muzziotti,Simon — 8 — Philadelphia — EXP MLB DEBUT: 2022 — H/W: 6-1 175 — FUT: Starting CF — 7C

Bats L Age 24 · 2015 FA (VZ) · Pwr ++ · BAvg +++ · Spd ++++ · Def ++++

Year	Lev	Team	AB	R	H	HR	RBI	Avg	OB	Sig	OPS	bb%	ct%	Eye	SB	CS	x/h%	Iso	RC/G
2022	Rk	FCL Phillies	2	0	0	0	0	0	0	0	0	0	100		0	0		0	-2.66
2022	A	Clearwater	8	0	0	0	0	0	111	0	111	11	50	0.25	0	0		0	-6.20
2022	AA	Reading	143	23	37	5	20	259	346	455	800	12	78	0.61	7	3	38	196	5.61
2022	AAA	Lehigh Valley	16	2	5	0	0	313	389	313	701	11	81	0.67	1	0	0	0	4.34
2022	MLB	Philadelphia	7	0	1	0	0	143	143	143	286	0	71	0.00	0	0	0	0	-1.83

Parlayed some strength gains into better batted-ball quality in 2022, but two leg injuries kept his AB total low in a season in which he badly needed reps. There is some newfound power/speed appeal, and his plus defensive chops in CF give him a reserve OF floor. At his age, an injury-free season is almost a must for his prospect status.

Naylor,Bo — 2 — Cleveland — EXP MLB DEBUT: 2022 — H/W: 6-0 205 — FUT: Starting C — 9D

Bats L Age 23 · 2018 (1) HS (ON) · Pwr ++++ · BAvg +++ · Spd +++ · Def ++++

Year	Lev	Team	AB	R	H	HR	RBI	Avg	OB	Sig	OPS	bb%	ct%	Eye	SB	CS	x/h%	Iso	RC/G
2019	A	Lake County	399	60	97	11	65	243	317	421	738	10	74	0.41	7	5	40	178	4.77
2021	AA	Akron	313	41	59	10	44	188	274	332	607	11	64	0.33	10	0	41	144	2.93
2022	AA	Akron	170	29	46	6	21	271	423	471	894	21	73	0.98	11	3	43	200	7.43
2022	AAA	Columbus	245	44	63	15	47	257	355	514	869	13	69	0.49	9	1	49	257	6.69
2022	MLB	Cleveland	8	0	0	0	0	0	0	0	0	0	38	0.00	0	0		0	-9.15

LHH C with MLB bloodlines had fantastic comeback season, putting offensive skillset together with power and on-base clip of more than 40%. Earned late season MLB debut. Open stance with a small bat wrap on load. Has advanced approach with a discerning eye and power to all fields (25+ HR at maturity). Makes great swing decisions. Plus framer at C.

Neto,Zach — 6 — Los Angeles (A) — EXP MLB DEBUT: 2024 — H/W: 6-0 185 — FUT: Starting SS — 8C

Bats R Age 22 · 2022 (1) Campbell · Pwr +++ · BAvg +++ · Spd +++ · Def +++

Year	Lev	Team	AB	R	H	HR	RBI	Avg	OB	Sig	OPS	bb%	ct%	Eye	SB	CS	x/h%	Iso	RC/G
2022	NCAA	Campbell	199	65	81	15	50	407	504	769	1273	16	90	2.05	19	1	49	362	11.24
2022	A+	Tri-City	25	2	5	1	4	200	310	400	710	14	84	1.00	1	0	40	200	4.59
2022	AA	Rocket City	122	22	39	4	23	320	362	492	853	6	76	0.28	4	2	33	172	5.99

Athletic, across-the-board talented SS made it to Double-A in pro debut. Unorthodox setup and path to contact. Solid all-fields approach. Gets to hard contact often, generating plus angles off the bat, including to the gaps. Above-average raw power. Could get to 25+ HR at projection. Plus arm with range at SS.

Noel,Jhonkensy
359 | Cleveland | EXP MLB DEBUT: 2024 | H/W: 6-3 250 | FUT: Starting OF | 8D

Bats R Age 21	Year	Lev	Team	AB	R	H	HR	RBI	Avg	OB	Slg	OPS	bb%	ct%	Eye	SB	CS	x/h%	Iso	RC/G
2017 FA (DR)	2021	A	Lynchburg	150	36	59	11	40	393	420	693	1114	4	82	0.26	2	1	37	300	8.72
Pwr +++++	2021	A+	Lake County	100	13	28	8	25	280	339	550	889	8	69	0.29	3	1	39	270	6.62
BAvg ++	2022	A+	Lake County	228	35	50	19	42	219	276	509	785	7	65	0.23	1	0	56	289	5.30
Spd ++	2022	AA	Akron	240	43	58	13	42	242	326	488	813	11	74	0.48	2	0	53	246	5.72
Def ++	2022	AAA	Columbus	17	2	3	0	0	176	222	235	458	6	59	0.14	0	0	33	59	0.72

XXL RHH 1B/OF prospect hit 32 HR across 3 levels but struck out 150 times. Open, crouched stance with hands back to minimize load. Plus-plus bat speed with some feel for hit. Struggles with spin recognition and over-aggressiveness. Exceptional raw power. If approach tones down, perennial threat for 40+ HR season. Solid athlete for size.

Nolasco,Rodolfo
9 | Pittsburgh | EXP MLB DEBUT: 2025 | H/W: 6-1 175 | FUT: Starting OF | 7D

Bats R Age 21	Year	Lev	Team	AB	R	H	HR	RBI	Avg	OB	Slg	OPS	bb%	ct%	Eye	SB	CS	x/h%	Iso	RC/G
2018 FA (DR)																				
Pwr +++																				
BAvg ++																				
Spd ++	2021	Rk	FCL Pirates Gold	134	27	38	8	32	284	400	552	952	16	68	0.60	0	0	47	269	8.18
Def +++	2022	A	Bradenton	280	40	67	11	48	239	328	425	753	12	61	0.34	7	4	42	186	5.44

Intriguing OF who missed most of last 2 months in first full year in minors. Adding strength to lean frame and has very fast bat that can give ball a ride. Dead fastball hitter with improving barrel control. Could grow into massive power producer, but swing mechanics need to be tweaked. Currently too much swing and miss.

Norby,Connor
4 | Baltimore | EXP MLB DEBUT: 2023 | H/W: 5-10 187 | FUT: Starting 2B | 8C

Bats R Age 22	Year	Lev	Team	AB	R	H	HR	RBI	Avg	OB	Slg	OPS	bb%	ct%	Eye	SB	CS	x/h%	Iso	RC/G
2021 (2) East Carolina	2021	Rk	FCL Orioles Orange	22	3	4	0	2	182	217	273	490	4	68	0.14	1	0	50	91	1.26
Pwr +++	2021	A	Delmarva	99	17	28	3	17	283	408	434	843	18	72	0.75	5	3	29	152	6.57
BAvg ++++	2022	A+	Aberdeen	186	27	44	8	20	237	304	425	729	9	73	0.36	6	3	39	188	4.48
Spd +++	2022	AA	Bowie	252	58	75	17	46	298	381	571	953	12	77	0.58	10	2	44	274	7.45
Def ++	2022	AAA	Norfolk Tides	39	7	14	4	7	359	405	718	1123	7	87	0.60	0	1	43	359	8.68

In first full pro season, just kept hitting and rose from A+ to AAA level. Quiet setup; short swing that can catch up to velo; patience but also some swing and miss. Biggest surprise was 29 HR, if that actualizes in MLB he's a special player. Even if not, he's a bat-first 2B option with moderate power and opportunistic speed, and he's close.

Nunez,Malcom
3 | Pittsburgh | EXP MLB DEBUT: 2024 | H/W: 5-11 205 | FUT: Starting 1B | 7D

Bats R Age 22	Year	Lev	Team	AB	R	H	HR	RBI	Avg	OB	Slg	OPS	bb%	ct%	Eye	SB	CS	x/h%	Iso	RC/G
2018 FA (CU)	2021	A+	Peoria	137	18	39	3	20	285	338	453	790	7	80	0.41	5	2	38	168	5.30
Pwr +++	2021	AA	Springfield	202	28	52	6	19	257	327	371	699	9	78	0.48	2	1	21	114	4.09
BAvg +++	2022	AA	Altoona	105	20	30	5	21	286	385	476	861	14	74	0.63	1	0	33	190	6.47
Spd +	2022	AA	Springfield	298	51	76	17	66	255	358	463	821	14	76	0.68	4	2	37	208	5.82
Def ++	2022	AAA	Indianapolis	13	1	3	1	1	231	412	462	873	24	62	0.80	0	0	33	231	7.27

Stocky, strong 1B who was acquired from STL at deadline. Overcame slow start, but got hot mid-year. Bat only prospect who set easy career high in HR while having some BA potential. Bat speed is very quick and makes acceptable contact. Could hit more flyballs for additional HR. Does not run well and lacks range.

Nunez,Nasim
6 | Miami | EXP MLB DEBUT: 2024 | H/W: 5-9 158 | FUT: Reserve SS | 6B

Bats B Age 22	Year	Lev	Team	AB	R	H	HR	RBI	Avg	OB	Slg	OPS	bb%	ct%	Eye	SB	CS	x/h%	Iso	RC/G
2019 (2) HS (GA)																				
Pwr +																				
BAvg +++	2021	A	Jupiter	189	33	46	0	10	243	362	265	626	16	76	0.76	33	10	7	21	3.55
Spd ++++	2022	A+	Beloit	300	53	74	2	27	247	391	323	714	19	66	0.69	49	11	22	77	4.99
Def ++++	2022	AA	Pensacola	142	22	37	0	14	261	367	303	670	14	75	0.67	21	5	16	42	4.12

Dynamic defensive SS with plus athleticism had best offensive season as pro. Shorter statured with wiry frame; upright closed stance. Slasher approach. Swing length is long in the tooth for type of hitter. Increased launch angle has contributed to some gap XBH power; though HR unlikely. Plus runner and among rangiest SS in minor leagues.

O'Hoppe,Logan
2 | Los Angeles (A) | EXP MLB DEBUT: 2022 | H/W: 6-2 185 | FUT: Starting C | 8C

Bats R Age 23	Year	Lev	Team	AB	R	H	HR	RBI	Avg	OB	Slg	OPS	bb%	ct%	Eye	SB	CS	x/h%	Iso	RC/G
2018 (23) HS (NY)	2021	AA	Reading	54	6	16	3	7	296	309	481	791	2	83	0.11	0	0	25	185	4.65
Pwr +++	2021	AAA	Lehigh Valley	21	2	4	1	3	190	261	381	642	9	81	0.50	0	0	50	190	3.35
BAvg +++	2022	AA	Reading	262	48	72	15	45	275	373	496	869	14	80	0.79	6	2	38	221	6.39
Spd ++	2022	AA	Rocket City	98	24	30	11	33	306	465	673	1138	23	78	1.32	1	2	47	367	10.18
Def +++	2022	MLB	LA Angels	14	1	4	0	2	286	375	286	661	13	79	0.67	0	0	0	0	3.87

Strong backstop continued making offensive gains in 2022. Acquired from PHI in mid-season deal. Closed stance. Utilizes strength well in contact-oriented swing. Patient approach, will work pull side and the gaps. Plus raw power in frame, mostly pull-oriented. 25+ HR possible with power approach. Solid athlete with plus agility behind dish.

O'Rae,Dylan
46 | Milwaukee | EXP MLB DEBUT: 2027 | H/W: 5-9 160 | FUT: Starting 2B | 7D

Bats L Age 19	Year	Lev	Team	AB	R	H	HR	RBI	Avg	OB	Slg	OPS	bb%	ct%	Eye	SB	CS	x/h%	Iso	RC/G
2022 (3) HS (ON)																				
Pwr +																				
BAvg +++																				
Spd ++++																				
Def ++	2022	Rk	ACL Brewers Gold	26	6	8	0	3	308	438	308	745	19	73	0.86	4	1	0	0	5.31

Slight-framed INF who will need lot of development time. Excellent quickness and double-plus speed highlight present tools, but needs to add significant strength to frame. Doesn't have strong arm either. Knows the strike zone and puts bat to ball in simple approach. XBH more a result of speed than gap power.

Ornelas,Jonathan
56 | Texas | EXP MLB DEBUT: 2024 | H/W: 6-0 196 | FUT: Utility player | 6B

Bats R Age 22	Year	Lev	Team	AB	R	H	HR	RBI	Avg	OB	Slg	OPS	bb%	ct%	Eye	SB	CS	x/h%	Iso	RC/G
2018 (3) HS (AZ)																				
Pwr +	2018	Rk	AZL Rangers	172	34	52	3	28	302	391	459	850	13	76	0.61	15	5	33	157	6.45
BAvg ++	2019	A	Hickory	413	61	106	6	38	257	325	373	698	9	75	0.41	13	4	31	116	4.22
Spd ++	2021	A+	Hickory	376	71	98	8	38	261	300	394	693	5	77	0.24	9	5	31	133	3.92
Def ++	2022	AA	Frisco	525	84	157	14	64	299	354	425	779	8	77	0.37	14	6	23	126	5.09

Stat-line scouting hides Texas League outcome inflation but he certainly performed beyond expectations and set himself up as a potential utility piece. Athletic frame and defensive versatility will get him reps, but focusing on contact over power most likely path to playing time as it is primarily a GB profile. Good against RHP, owns LHP.

Ornelas,Tirso
7 | San Diego | EXP MLB DEBUT: 2023 | H/W: 6-3 200 | FUT: Starting OF | 7C

Bats L Age 23	Year	Lev	Team	AB	R	H	HR	RBI	Avg	OB	Slg	OPS	bb%	ct%	Eye	SB	CS	x/h%	Iso	RC/G
2017 FA (MX)	2019	Rk	AZL Padres	88	6	18	0	11	205	278	227	506	9	75	0.41	4	0	11	23	1.64
Pwr ++	2019	A+	Lake Elsinore	332	41	73	1	30	220	311	292	603	12	73	0.48	3	1	23	72	3.08
BAvg +++	2021	A+	Fort Wayne	383	57	95	7	55	248	338	389	727	12	74	0.53	3	1	41	141	4.75
Spd ++	2022	AA	San Antonio	441	62	127	7	51	288	351	408	759	9	81	0.51	7	2	29	120	4.97
Def ++	2022	AAA	El Paso	14	2	3	0	2	214	267	286	552	7	86	0.50	0	0	33	71	2.54

Contact-oriented hitter who puts bat to ball and uses line drive stroke to use entire field. Not much power in his game (career high 8 HR) and lacks frontline bat speed. Hits LHP with aplomb and has hand-eye coordination to flick ball around. Solid baserunner with keen instincts. Possesses average arm strength and limited to LF.

Ortiz,Jhailyn
9 | Philadelphia | EXP MLB DEBUT: 2023 | H/W: 6-3 215 | FUT: Reserve OF | 7D

Bats R Age 24	Year	Lev	Team	AB	R	H	HR	RBI	Avg	OB	Slg	OPS	bb%	ct%	Eye	SB	CS	x/h%	Iso	RC/G
2015 FA (DR)	2018	A	Lakewood	405	51	91	13	47	225	286	375	662	8	63	0.24	2	2	36	151	3.76
Pwr ++++	2019	A+	Clearwater	430	57	86	19	65	200	262	381	643	8	65	0.24	2	3	43	181	3.34
BAvg ++	2021	A+	Jersey Shore	263	52	69	19	48	262	336	521	857	10	67	0.34	4	1	43	259	6.38
Spd ++	2021	AA	Reading	77	7	16	4	6	208	291	377	667	10	65	0.33	0	0	31	169	3.68
Def ++	2022	AA	Reading	448	67	106	17	61	237	303	415	719	9	63	0.26	9	2	42	179	4.69

Surprised with almost double-digit steals last year, but was signed for the power way back when, and that ship has almost sailed. Decent exit velo/barrel figures, plays an OK corner OF, but swings through many hittable fastballs and chases down-and-away breakers. Contact% is and poor - this is who he is. Reserve outfielder profile.

Ortiz,Joey
46 | Baltimore | EXP MLB DEBUT: 2023 | H/W: 5-11 175 | FUT: Starting SS | 8C

Bats R Age 24	Year	Lev	Team	AB	R	H	HR	RBI	Avg	OB	Slg	OPS	bb%	ct%	Eye	SB	CS	x/h%	Iso	RC/G
2019 (4) New Mexico St	2019	A-	Aberdeen	195	23	47	1	17	241	342	267	609	13	81	0.81	2	1	6	26	3.30
Pwr +++	2021	A+	Aberdeen	76	14	22	0	8	289	372	434	806	12	76	0.56	3	0	41	145	5.96
BAvg +++	2021	AA	Bowie	60	11	14	4	9	233	303	467	770	9	77	0.43	1	0	43	233	4.85
4.11 Spd ++	2022	AA	Bowie	435	69	117	15	71	269	332	455	787	9	81	0.51	2	1	40	186	5.24
Def ++++	2022	AAA	Norfolk Tides	104	22	36	4	14	346	398	567	966	8	84	0.53	6	1	36	221	7.34

Short-statured infielder with patience, contact, and now developing power. Lifted the ball more as season went on and finished on a hot streak. It's not massive pop, but add to above-average contact ability, some patience, and a no-doubt SS glove, and he becomes a very interesting player. Dash of speed; can also handle 2B/3B if necessary. Riser.

Osorio,Javier

46 | Detroit | EXP MLB DEBUT: 2027 | H/W: 6-0 165 | FUT: Starting SS | 7D

Bats R Age 18
2022 FA (VZ)
Pwr +++
BAvg +++
Spd +++
Def +++

Year	Lev	Team	AB	R	H	HR	RBI	Avg	OB	Slg	OPS	bb%	ct%	Eye	SB	CS	x/h%	Iso	RC/G
2022	Rk	DSL Tigers	154	17	27	1	12	175	253	227	480	9	56	0.24	15	3	22	52	1.08

Made his pro debut in the DSL where he struggled at the plate. Strong frame and plus bat speed should result in at least average to above power once he figures things out. Moves well at short with good range, soft hands, and a plus arm and should be able to stick as he moves up. Lots of upside, but lots of work to do.

Osuna,Alejandro

78 | Texas | EXP MLB DEBUT: 2025 | H/W: 6-0 185 | FUT: Reserve OF | 6B

Bats L Age 20
2020 FA (MX)
Pwr +
BAvg ++
Spd ++
Def ++

Year	Lev	Team	AB	R	H	HR	RBI	Avg	OB	Slg	OPS	bb%	ct%	Eye	SB	CS	x/h%	Iso	RC/G
2021	A	Down East	201	36	45	6	36	224	336	383	719	14	63	0.46	17	5	44	159	4.90
2022	A	Down East	273	54	84	8	44	308	388	451	839	12	81	0.71	32	15	26	143	6.03
2022	A+	Hickory	78	14	22	1	10	282	333	346	679	7	78	0.35	2	3	14	64	3.79

Big year; parlayed a contact-oriented approach into a successful repeat of A ball. 9.5% SwK across two levels also promising, and showed above-average SB outcomes even if the speed will likely play below this higher. Lack of power and a LF-fit probably means reserve OF but he'll get a chance to show 2022 wasn't a fluke.

Outman,James

789 | Los Angeles (N) | EXP MLB DEBUT: 2022 | H/W: 6-3 215 | FUT: Starting OF | 8D

Bats L Age 25
2018 (7) Sacramento St
Pwr +++
BAvg +++
Spd +++
Def +++

Year	Lev	Team	AB	R	H	HR	RBI	Avg	OB	Slg	OPS	bb%	ct%	Eye	SB	CS	x/h%	Iso	RC/G
2021	A+	Great Lakes	248	50	62	9	30	250	365	472	837	15	65	0.51	21	2	47	222	6.77
2021	AA	Tulsa	166	40	48	9	24	289	359	518	877	10	69	0.35	2	2	40	229	6.69
2022	AA	Tulsa	261	59	77	16	45	295	385	552	936	13	66	0.43	7	3	44	257	7.91
2022	AAA	Oklahoma City	212	42	62	15	61	292	385	627	1013	13	70	0.51	6	1	56	335	8.76
2022	MLB	Los Angeles	13	6	6	1	3	462	533	846	1379	13	46	0.29	0	0	50	385	20.93

Despite plus physicality and raw power, an overly aggressive approach led to too much swing-and-miss. Worked hard to retool stroke and become more selective. That approach paid off, earning him a brief stint in the majors. Has toned down his leg kick and now hunts for balls he can punish. Above-average speed and power; has tools to be a 20/20 guy.

Ovalles,Alexander

37 | Tampa Bay | EXP MLB DEBUT: 2024 | H/W: 6-0 184 | FUT: Reserve OF | 6C

Bats L Age 22
2017 FA (DR)
Pwr ++
BAvg +++
Spd +++
Def ++

Year	Lev	Team	AB	R	H	HR	RBI	Avg	OB	Slg	OPS	bb%	ct%	Eye	SB	CS	x/h%	Iso	RC/G
2019	A-	Spokane	91	13	17	2	15	187	253	319	571	8	74	0.33	3	1	47	132	2.43
2021	A	Charleston	315	45	78	8	46	248	338	378	716	12	78	0.63	5	4	29	130	4.52
2022	A+	Bowling Green	315	63	86	14	62	273	360	483	843	12	76	0.57	9	5	41	210	6.14
2022	AA	Montgomery	36	4	5	0	1	139	244	167	411	12	69	0.45	1	0	20	28	0.23
2022	AAA	Durham	6	0	1	0	2	167	286	167	452	14	67	0.50	0	0	0	0	0.74

Stocky OF/1B prospect had productive 2022 season. Athletic, near physical projection. Open stance with bat wrap. Has feel for zone, works counts. Struggles getting to barrel contact. Linear swing trajectory depresses loft. Top hand heavy hitter with lots of groundball contact in profile. Below-average power. Above-average runner.

Pacheco,Izaac

56 | Detroit | EXP MLB DEBUT: 2025 | H/W: 6-4 225 | FUT: Starting 3B | 8E

Bats L Age 20
2021 (2) HS (TX)
Pwr ++++
BAvg ++
Spd ++
Def ++

Year	Lev	Team	AB	R	H	HR	RBI	Avg	OB	Slg	OPS	bb%	ct%	Eye	SB	CS	x/h%	Iso	RC/G
2021	Rk	FCL Tigers West	106	16	24	1	7	226	339	330	669	15	59	0.42	1	0	29	104	4.38
2022	A	Lakeland	330	54	88	8	39	267	342	415	758	10	76	0.48	12	4	35	148	5.02
2022	A+	West Michigan	60	9	11	3	13	183	290	367	657	13	72	0.53	0	1	45	183	3.57

Solid production at Low-A, but struggled when promoted. Above-average to plus power if he can make enough contact. Quick LH bat, simple approach, and hands work well, but struggles to identify breaking balls and will chase out of the zone. Below average runner with a strong arm and was moved from SS to 3B where he should be able to stick.

Paciolla,Christopher

456 | Chicago (N) | EXP MLB DEBUT: 2026 | H/W: 6-2 185 | FUT: Starting 3B | 7D

Bats R Age 19
2022 (3) HS (CA)
Pwr +++
BAvg ++
Spd ++
Def ++

Year	Lev	Team	AB	R	H	HR	RBI	Avg	OB	Slg	OPS	bb%	ct%	Eye	SB	CS	x/h%	Iso	RC/G
2022	Rk	ACL Cubs	21	2	3	1	3	143	217	286	503	9	67	0.29	1	0	33	143	1.13

Athletic SS signed an over-slot deal for $900,000 and got into just 7 games in pro debut. Short, compact RH stroke with good bat to ball skills and the size and tools to hit for average and power, but poor pitch recognition and can be beat by breaking balls down and away. Tall, projectable frame and could add power as he matures. Lacks speed.

Pages,Andy

9 | Los Angeles (N) | EXP MLB DEBUT: 2023 | H/W: 6-1 212 | FUT: Starting OF | 8D

Bats R Age 22
2018 FA (CU)
Pwr ++++
BAvg ++
Spd ++
Def +++

Year	Lev	Team	AB	R	H	HR	RBI	Avg	OB	Slg	OPS	bb%	ct%	Eye	SB	CS	x/h%	Iso	RC/G
2018	Rk	AZL Dodgers	26	5	5	1	3	192	344	346	690	19	85	1.50	1	1	40	154	4.56
2018	Rk	DSL Dodgers	140	34	33	9	33	236	344	486	829	14	78	0.74	9	6	52	250	5.91
2019	Rk	Ogden	235	57	70	19	55	298	368	651	1019	10	66	0.33	7	6	61	353	8.98
2021	A+	Great Lakes	438	96	116	31	88	265	375	539	914	15	70	0.58	6	3	49	274	7.32
2022	AA	Tulsa	487	69	115	26	80	236	322	468	791	11	71	0.44	6	3	50	232	5.46

Surprisingly athletic player has some of the best power in the system and works hard to get balls into the air. When he does, they travel with good exit velo and backspin, but there is too much swing-and-miss to hit for power and average. Was moved from 3B to RF where he shows enough range and arm strength to be a tick above-average on defense.

Palma,Miguel

2 | Houston | EXP MLB DEBUT: 2025 | H/W: 5-10 170 | FUT: Starting C | 7C

Bats R Age 21
2018 FA (VZ)
Pwr +++
BAvg +++
Spd +
Def ++

Year	Lev	Team	AB	R	H	HR	RBI	Avg	OB	Slg	OPS	bb%	ct%	Eye	SB	CS	x/h%	Iso	RC/G
2021	Rk	FCL Astros	46	11	9	3	9	196	413	435	847	27	76	1.55	0	1	56	239	6.66
2021	A	Fayetteville	39	8	12	0	8	308	426	410	836	17	67	0.62	2	0	33	103	6.91
2022	A	Fayetteville	205	28	46	6	29	224	312	366	678	11	80	0.65	0	0	37	141	4.00
2022	A+	Asheville	104	15	34	7	29	327	369	587	956	6	79	0.32	0	0	35	260	7.05

20-year-old catcher pushed to High-A and succeeded despite drop off in underlying plate discipline and contact; likely aided by hitter-friendly venue. Short, stocky build. Upright stance with toe tap in swing and pull-heavy approach. Good receiver but struggles to control run game. Could move to 1B but will need to continue to make most of his tools.

Palmegiani,Damiano

35 | Toronto | EXP MLB DEBUT: 2024 | H/W: 6-1 195 | FUT: Starting 1B | 7D

Bats R Age 23
2021 (14) Southern NV
Pwr +++
BAvg ++
Spd ++
Def ++

Year	Lev	Team	AB	R	H	HR	RBI	Avg	OB	Slg	OPS	bb%	ct%	Eye	SB	CS	x/h%	Iso	RC/G
2021	NCAA	Southern Nevada	203	80	79	26	81	389	481	867	1348	15	81	0.95	14	4	53	478	12.21
2021	Rk	FCL Blue Jays	39	11	13	2	9	333	435	538	973	15	77	0.78	1	0	31	205	7.95
2022	A	Dunedin	195	30	50	11	37	256	335	508	843	11	76	0.49	2	0	52	251	6.02
2022	A+	Vancouver	228	44	51	13	46	224	317	443	760	12	74	0.52	3	0	47	219	4.94

Powerful INF with patient approach and acceptable contact rate. Power-over-hit tool at present, though has patient approach. Has long swing and can sell out for power, but shortens stroke with two strikes. Bat speed is impressive. Secondary skills are sub-par. Not a baseclogger, but not fast either. Below average defender at both 1B and 3B.

Parada,Kevin

2 | New York (N) | EXP MLB DEBUT: 2024 | H/W: 6-1 197 | FUT: Starting C | 9E

Bats R Age 21
2022 (1) Georgia Tech
Pwr ++++
BAvg ++++
Spd ++
Def ++

Year	Lev	Team	AB	R	H	HR	RBI	Avg	OB	Slg	OPS	bb%	ct%	Eye	SB	CS	x/h%	Iso	RC/G
2022	NCAA	Georgia Tech	258	79	93	26	88	360	427	709	1136	10	88	0.94	11	1	40	349	9.07
2022	Rk	FCL Mets	11	1	3	0	3	273	385	455	839	15	91	2.00	0	0	67	182	6.65
2022	A	St. Lucie	29	5	8	1	5	276	462	414	875	26	59	0.83	0	1	25	138	8.01

Strong-bodied C prospect, taken in 1st round of 2022 draft, had small but productive debut in Low-A. Frame has little projection left. Unusual stance. Solid all-fields approach with good plate discipline. Plus bat speed with varying trajectory. Plus power to all fields. Think 30+ HR at projection. Work-in-progress behind the plate.

Paris,Kyren

46 | Los Angeles (A) | EXP MLB DEBUT: 2024 | H/W: 6-0 180 | FUT: Reserve IF | 6C

Bats R Age 21
2019 (2) HS (CA)
Pwr ++
BAvg ++
Spd ++++
Def +++

Year	Lev	Team	AB	R	H	HR	RBI	Avg	OB	Slg	OPS	bb%	ct%	Eye	SB	CS	x/h%	Iso	RC/G
2021	A	Inland Empire	106	29	29	2	18	274	421	491	912	20	61	0.66	16	4	45	217	8.60
2021	A+	Tri-City	52	6	12	1	6	231	259	365	625	4	62	0.10	4	0	33	135	3.27
2022	Rk	ACL Angels	7	1	1	1	2	143	333	571	905	22	57	0.67	0	0	100	429	7.57
2022	A+	Tri-City	328	58	75	8	32	229	329	387	716	13	64	0.42	28	4	41	159	4.83
2022	AA	Rocket City	39	11	14	3	8	359	490	641	1131	20	64	0.71	5	0	36	282	11.36

Athletic RHH slasher struggled with contact rate, mostly in High-A. Speed over hit or power profile. Has good eye at plate. Often overmatched with velocity and spin. Near 35% whiff rate. Upright, slight open swing with a moderate load. Doesn't get to power in swing, best shooting line drives. Plus runner; 33 for 37 in SB attempts.

Patino,Wilderd

89 | **Arizona** | EXP MLB DEBUT: 2025 | H/W: 6-1 175 | FUT: Starting OF | **8E**

Bats R Age 21	Year	Lev	Team	AB	R	H	HR	RBI	Avg	OB	Slg	OPS	bb%	ct%	Eye	SB	CS	x/h%	Iso	RC/G
2017 FA (VZ)	2019	Rk	AZL Diamondbacks	106	18	37	1	21	349	410	472	882	9	70	0.34	13	3	22	123	6.99
Pwr +++	2021	Rk	ACL DBacks	28	2	7	0	1	250	250	357	607	0	68	0.00	0	2	29	107	2.79
BAvg +++	2021	A	Visalia	119	18	25	2	8	210	242	294	536	4	59	0.10	6	3	20	84	1.85
Spd +++	2022	A	Visalia	293	54	85	8	42	290	342	440	782	7	71	0.27	54	7	31	150	5.27
Def ++++	2022	A+	Hillsboro	73	14	21	1	11	288	325	397	722	5	66	0.16	13	2	29	110	4.60

Toolsy, oft-injured RHH posted solid rebound season. With a strong, athletic frame, he has struggled with leg injuries throughout career. Upright stance with hands direct to hitting position. Aggressive approach. Power-over-hit profile long term. Potential for 25+ HR in frame and swing. Plus runner; 67 for 76 in SB attempts. Long term RF.

Paulino,Eddinson

456 | **Boston** | EXP MLB DEBUT: 2025 | H/W: 5-10 155 | FUT: Starting 2B | **7C**

Bats L Age 20	Year	Lev	Team	AB	R	H	HR	RBI	Avg	OB	Slg	OPS	bb%	ct%	Eye	SB	CS	x/h%	Iso	RC/G
2018 FA (DR)																				
Pwr ++																				
BAvg +++																				
Spd +++	2021	Rk	FCL Red Sox	113	25	38	0	13	336	414	549	963	12	81	0.71	5	2	53	212	7.96
Def ++	2022	A	Salem	463	96	123	13	66	266	355	469	824	12	77	0.61	27	5	47	203	6.02

Breakout prospect who started slow, but ended well. Led CAR in doubles while producing HR despite none prior to season. Makes good contact with simple swing and uses hand-eye coordination to advantage. Hits for BA with line drive stroke and quick hands. Runs well and has enough arm and quickness for 2B and 3B.

Peguero,Liover

6 | **Pittsburgh** | EXP MLB DEBUT: 2022 | H/W: 6-2 200 | FUT: Starting SS | **8C**

Bats R Age 22	Year	Lev	Team	AB	R	H	HR	RBI	Avg	OB	Slg	OPS	bb%	ct%	Eye	SB	CS	x/h%	Iso	RC/G
2017 FA (DR)	2019	Rk	Missoula	143	34	52	5	27	364	413	559	972	8	76	0.35	8	1	29	196	7.65
Pwr +++	2019	A-	Hillsboro	84	13	22	0	11	262	326	357	683	9	80	0.47	3	1	27	95	4.12
BAvg +++	2021	A+	Greensboro	374	67	101	14	45	270	329	444	773	8	72	0.31	28	6	35	174	5.11
Spd ++++	2022	AA	Altoona	483	65	125	10	58	259	301	387	688	6	77	0.26	28	6	30	128	3.86
Def ++++	2022	MLB	Pittsburgh	3	0	1	0	0	333	500	333	833	25	33	0.50	0	0	0	0	13.10

Exciting INF who tailed off as season ended, but has tools aplenty. Has no obvious shortcoming and could be offensive-oriented SS. Has both power and speed in total package, but pop still emerging. Swings a very fast bat and is becoming more proficient with pitch recognition. Outstanding defender with plus range and strong arm.

Peraza,Oswald

46 | **New York (A)** | EXP MLB DEBUT: 2022 | H/W: 6-0 200 | FUT: Starting SS | **8C**

Bats R Age 22	Year	Lev	Team	AB	R	H	HR	RBI	Avg	OB	Slg	OPS	bb%	ct%	Eye	SB	CS	x/h%	Iso	RC/G
2016 FA (VZ)	2021	A+	Hudson Valley	111	20	34	5	16	306	374	532	906	10	78	0.50	16	1	44	225	6.79
Pwr +++	2021	AA	Somerset	326	51	96	12	40	294	341	466	807	7	75	0.28	20	8	31	172	5.41
BAvg +++	2021	AAA	Scranton/WB	28	5	8	1	2	286	333	393	726	7	82	0.40	2	1	13	107	4.23
Spd +++	2022	AAA	Scranton/WB	386	57	100	19	50	259	319	448	767	8	74	0.34	33	5	35	189	4.89
Def ++++	2022	MLB	New York (A)	49	8	15	1	2	306	382	429	810	11	82	0.67	2	0	27	122	5.69

Solid, athletic SS prospect with plus glove made MLB debut during pennant race. Slightly open, mostly upright stance. Aggressive approach with 30% minor league chase rate. Off-speed especially might be challenging. Pull oriented approach with good angles to LF and LCF on lofted contact. 20-25 HR power present. Above-average runner with SB feel.

Pereira,Everson

89 | **New York (A)** | EXP MLB DEBUT: 2023 | H/W: 6-0 191 | FUT: Starting OF | **8C**

Bats R Age 21	Year	Lev	Team	AB	R	H	HR	RBI	Avg	OB	Slg	OPS	bb%	ct%	Eye	SB	CS	x/h%	Iso	RC/G
2017 FA (VZ)	2021	Rk	FCL Yankees	8	3	3	1	3	375	545	###	1545	27	75	1.50	0	0	100	625	16.50
Pwr ++++	2021	A	Tampa	72	17	26	5	22	361	439	667	1106	12	71	0.48	4	1	42	306	9.96
BAvg +++	2021	A+	Hudson Valley	108	27	28	14	32	259	350	676	1026	12	65	0.39	5	2	61	417	8.89
Spd ++++	2022	A+	Hudson Valley	288	55	79	9	43	274	351	455	806	11	70	0.39	19	5	35	181	5.83
Def +++	2022	AA	Somerset	113	21	32	5	13	283	336	504	840	7	67	0.24	2	2	38	221	6.27

Oft-injured toolsy OF prospect finally eclipsed 100 games in his 5th season as a pro. Strong frame with still room to grow. Open, upright stance with bat wrap. Works counts but struggles with present swing-and-miss issues. Plus-plus raw power is fueled by frame and plus bat speed. Needs to add loft to get to 30+ HR potential. Plus runner.

Perez, Jr.,Robert

3 | **Seattle** | EXP MLB DEBUT: 2024 | H/W: 6-1 170 | FUT: Starting 1B | **7E**

Bats R Age 22	Year	Lev	Team	AB	R	H	HR	RBI	Avg	OB	Slg	OPS	bb%	ct%	Eye	SB	CS	x/h%	Iso	RC/G
2016 FA (VZ)	2019	A-	Everett	206	31	48	7	36	233	310	379	689	10	67	0.34	1	1	33	146	4.09
Pwr +++	2019	AAA	Tacoma	64	9	16	3	8	250	294	469	763	6	63	0.17	0	0	44	219	5.33
BAvg ++	2021	A	Modesto	401	62	113	15	77	282	338	456	794	8	72	0.30	0	0	34	175	5.40
Spd +	2022	A	Modesto	345	78	93	20	87	270	359	501	860	12	69	0.44	5	0	42	232	6.55
Def +	2022	A+	Everett	120	22	41	7	27	342	448	583	1031	16	72	0.68	1	1	34	242	9.05

Aggressive 1B who led SEA MiLBers in HR by improving approach and taking advantage of natural strength with loft-based swing. Set easy career high in HR while finishing 2nd in minors in RBI. Bat-only prospect with limited foot speed and below average defense. Can be pitched to with breaking balls. Can also be pull-conscious.

Perez,Hedbert

78 | **Milwaukee** | EXP MLB DEBUT: 2025 | H/W: 5-10 160 | FUT: Starting OF | **8E**

Bats L Age 20	Year	Lev	Team	AB	R	H	HR	RBI	Avg	OB	Slg	OPS	bb%	ct%	Eye	SB	CS	x/h%	Iso	RC/G
2019 FA (VZ)																				
Pwr ++++																				
BAvg +	2021	Rk	ACL Brewers Gold	120	19	40	6	21	333	375	575	950	6	72	0.24	2	0	43	242	7.46
Spd +++	2021	A	Carolina	65	5	11	1	7	169	182	246	428	2	62	0.04	0	0	27	77	0.03
Def ++	2022	A	Carolina	407	53	88	15	57	216	270	393	663	7	68	0.23	9	6	45	177	3.63

Short, strong OF who suffered thru poor year despite finishing 6th in CAR in HR. Added strength and exhibits requisite bat speed to hit mammoth HR. Trouble is getting to contact. Rarely draws walks and can be overly pull conscious. Free-swinging ways need to be tamed and has trouble with spin. Exhibits average speed, but limited to corner OF.

Perez,Junior

89 | **Oakland** | EXP MLB DEBUT: 2025 | H/W: 6-1 165 | FUT: Starting OF | **8E**

Bats R Age 21	Year	Lev	Team	AB	R	H	HR	RBI	Avg	OB	Slg	OPS	bb%	ct%	Eye	SB	CS	x/h%	Iso	RC/G
2017 FA (DR)																				
Pwr +++																				
BAvg ++	2019	Rk	AZL Padres 2	209	44	56	11	39	268	343	512	855	10	72	0.41	11	2	48	244	6.34
Spd +++	2021	A	Stockton	329	54	68	8	34	207	313	359	672	13	56	0.35	24	7	43	152	4.53
Def ++	2022	A	Stockton	398	74	99	15	62	249	361	425	786	15	63	0.47	32	7	38	176	5.94

Improving prospect who repeated Low-A and showed improvement. Increased HR, BB and SB and showed more loft in righty stroke. Produced consistently more loud contact, but still posts high K rate. Struggles with velocity. Has good power-speed combo. Lacks ideal hit tool and defense leaves lots to be desired.

Perez,Milkar

5 | **Seattle** | EXP MLB DEBUT: 2025 | H/W: 5-11 200 | FUT: Starting 3B | **7D**

Bats R Age 21	Year	Lev	Team	AB	R	H	HR	RBI	Avg	OB	Slg	OPS	bb%	ct%	Eye	SB	CS	x/h%	Iso	RC/G
2018 FA (NI)																				
Pwr ++																				
BAvg ++	2021	Rk	ACL Mariners	145	33	45	0	23	310	457	379	836	21	74	1.03	1	1	22	69	6.81
Spd +++	2021	A	Modesto	27	6	8	0	0	296	387	370	757	13	85	1.00	0	1	25	74	5.31
Def +++	2022	A	Modesto	179	17	26	0	17	145	323	168	491	21	67	0.80	1	0	15	22	1.49

Short, big-bodied 3B who suffered thru miserable season and hit under .200 in each month but one. Had difficulty making hard contact and became far too passive at plate. Can go to opposite field too often. Hope is for more aggression as well as loft in stroke. Has plenty of strength, but needs to use it. Cannon arm is best defensive attribute.

Perez,Rickardo

2 | **Philadelphia** | EXP MLB DEBUT: 2027 | H/W: 5-10 172 | FUT: Starting C | **7C**

Bats L Age 19	Year	Lev	Team	AB	R	H	HR	RBI	Avg	OB	Slg	OPS	bb%	ct%	Eye	SB	CS	x/h%	Iso	RC/G
2021 FA (VZ)																				
Pwr ++																				
BAvg +++																				
Spd +	2021	Rk	DSL Phillies Red	121	15	31	0	9	256	371	281	652	15	88	1.47	3	1	10	25	4.20
Def ++	2022	Rk	FCL Phillies	83	5	29	1	14	349	400	398	798	8	84	0.54	0	1	7	48	5.27

First stateside exposure had ups and downs. Makes very good contact from the left side; a balanced swing with bat speed; ingredients for a solid hit tool. But needs strength as the power is currently short; he would be overwhelmed with high-minors hard stuff currently. Thick body that will require attention; fringe-average defender. Long-termer.

Pinango,Yohendrick

7 | **Chicago (N)** | EXP MLB DEBUT: 2024 | H/W: 5-11 170 | FUT: Reserve OF | **6B**

Bats L Age 20	Year	Lev	Team	AB	R	H	HR	RBI	Avg	OB	Slg	OPS	bb%	ct%	Eye	SB	CS	x/h%	Iso	RC/G
2018 FA (VZ)																				
Pwr ++																				
BAvg +++	2021	A	Myrtle Beach	324	50	88	4	27	272	322	370	692	7	82	0.42	8	2	25	99	4.04
Spd ++	2021	A+	South Bend	97	9	28	1	9	289	337	381	718	7	88	0.58	0	0	21	93	4.42
Def ++	2022	A+	South Bend	464	65	116	13	63	250	296	394	690	6	81	0.34	14	1	34	144	3.89

Short, athletic OF has a quick bat and above-average bat to ball skills, giving him a chance to hit for average as he moves up. Busy hands and pre-pitch load creates length to swing and line-drive, all-fields approach limits long-term power upside. Average speed and OF defense, puts more pressure on the bat and power development.

Pineda, Israel — 2 — Washington

Bats R Age 23
2016 FA (VZ)

EXP MLB DEBUT: 2022 H/W: 5-11 188 FUT: Starting C **7C**

		Year	Lev	Team	AB	R	H	HR	RBI	Avg	OB	Slg	OPS	bb%	ct%	Eye	SB	CS	x/h%	Iso	RC/G
Pwr	+++	2021	A+	Wilmington	293	35	61	14	48	208	254	389	643	6	72	0.22	0	0	41	181	3.14
BAvg	++	2022	A+	Wilmington	246	31	65	8	45	264	325	443	768	8	72	0.31	2	2	40	179	5.11
Spd	+	2022	AA	Harrisburg	93	15	26	7	21	280	343	538	881	9	81	0.50	1	0	38	258	6.15
Def	++	2022	AAA	Rochester	21	3	2	1	5	95	269	286	555	19	67	0.71	0	0	100	190	2.15
		2022	MLB	Washington	13	1	1	0	0	77	143	77	220	7	46	0.14	0	0	0	0	-4.03

Pull-side power is the draw here; hits the ball hard and at the best angles for damage. 2022 was a career-best power year. Made MLB debut due to Ruiz's injury, but has not displayed adequate contact rates at upper levels. Has an OK arm, but other aspects of defense need work. Still needs development time in upper minors.

Pineda, Pedro — 8 — Oakland

Bats R Age 19
2021 FA (DR)

EXP MLB DEBUT: 2026 H/W: 6-1 170 FUT: Starting OF **8E**

		Year	Lev	Team	AB	R	H	HR	RBI	Avg	OB	Slg	OPS	bb%	ct%	Eye	SB	CS	x/h%	Iso	RC/G
Pwr	++	2021	Rk	ACL Athletics	62	15	16	1	8	258	387	403	790	17	55	0.46	3	3	31	145	6.94
BAvg	++	2021	Rk	DSL Athletics	35	4	7	0	1	200	300	286	586	13	63	0.38	3	2	29	86	2.93
Spd	++++	2022	Rk	ACL Athletics	3	0	0	0	0	0	0	0	0	0	0	0.00	0	0		0	
Def	+++	2022	A	Stockton	144	22	27	4	13	188	273	333	607	11	47	0.22	5	1	37	146	4.12

Toolsy OF with significant upside, but season cut short due to injury. Has a lot of power projection, but also crude hitting instincts with poor barrel control and pitch recognition. K rate was unacceptable and needs to tone down stroke. Body has room to add mass and should lead to consistent pop. Runs well and has strong arm.

Pinto, Adrian — 46 — Toronto

Bats R Age 20
2019 FA (VZ)

EXP MLB DEBUT: 2025 H/W: 5-6 156 FUT: Starting 2B **7C**

		Year	Lev	Team	AB	R	H	HR	RBI	Avg	OB	Slg	OPS	bb%	ct%	Eye	SB	CS	x/h%	Iso	RC/G
Pwr	+																				
BAvg	++																				
Spd	++++	2021	Rk	DSL Colorado	175	64	63	3	27	360	474	543	1017	18	90	2.11	41	8	35	183	8.71
Def	+++	2022	A	Dunedin	157	36	38	2	10	242	343	363	706	13	80	0.75	18	7	29	121	4.57

Sleeper INF who was acquired from COL before season. Has very small, compact frame with quick stroke and advanced ability to make contact. Can read spin and has strong understanding of strike zone. Has enough bat speed and strength, but HR not his game. Has plus speed. Likely targeted for 2B where his quick hands would suffice.

Placencia, Adrian — 46 — Los Angeles (A)

Bats B Age 19
2019 FA (DR)

EXP MLB DEBUT: 2025 H/W: 5-11 155 FUT: Utility player **7E**

		Year	Lev	Team	AB	R	H	HR	RBI	Avg	OB	Slg	OPS	bb%	ct%	Eye	SB	CS	x/h%	Iso	RC/G
Pwr	+++																				
BAvg	+++																				
Spd	++	2021	Rk	ACL Angels	143	29	25	5	19	175	310	343	653	16	66	0.57	4	2	44	168	3.76
Def	+++	2022	A	Inland Empire	382	83	97	13	64	254	378	427	804	17	63	0.54	21	8	39	173	6.33

Short-statured, strong switch-hitting MIF made strides with contact quality in 2022. Swing matured by utilizing lower half leverage better within an uppercut swing. Near 40% whiff rate. Struggles with velocity up and spin down. Above-average power potential in frame and swing. Think 25+ HR if hit tool plays. Fringe speed. Fits best at 2B.

Plummer, Nick — 789 — New York (N)

Bats L Age 26
2015 (1) HS (MI)

EXP MLB DEBUT: 2022 H/W: 5-10 200 FUT: Reserve OF **6C**

		Year	Lev	Team	AB	R	H	HR	RBI	Avg	OB	Slg	OPS	bb%	ct%	Eye	SB	CS	x/h%	Iso	RC/G
		2019	A+	Palm Beach	289	35	51	5	29	176	292	294	586	14	59	0.39	3	3	43	118	2.89
Pwr	+++	2021	AA	Springfield	311	52	88	13	46	283	387	489	876	15	65	0.49	9	8	39	206	7.22
BAvg	++	2021	AAA	Memphis	75	19	20	2	8	267	421	440	861	21	76	1.11	4	1	35	173	6.96
Spd	+++	2022	AAA	Syracuse	235	29	56	7	41	238	312	379	690	10	66	0.31	8	4	34	140	4.17
Def	+++	2022	MLB	New York (N)	29	4	4	2	6	138	167	379	546	3	59	0.08	0	0	75	241	1.80

Short-statured, strong OF prospect struggled during 1st year in NYM organization, including MLB stint. At physical projection currently. Crouch stance with no trigger. Uppercut swing but hits with heavy top hand causing topspin that depresses power projection. Patient approach with lots of whiffs in zone. Versatile defender with average speed.

Polanco, Shalin — 8 — Pittsburgh

Bats L Age 19
2021 FA (DR)

EXP MLB DEBUT: 2027 H/W: 5-11 168 FUT: Starting CF **7E**

		Year	Lev	Team	AB	R	H	HR	RBI	Avg	OB	Slg	OPS	bb%	ct%	Eye	SB	CS	x/h%	Iso	RC/G
Pwr	++																				
BAvg	++																				
Spd	+++	2021	Rk	DSL Pirates Black	157	16	32	3	22	204	286	338	623	10	72	0.41	6	2	38	134	3.24
Def	+++	2022	Rk	FCL Pirates Black	132	24	33	3	17	250	313	371	684	8	70	0.30	7	4	30	121	3.97

Lean, projectable OF who spent first year in US and showed good overall skills and tools. Added strength, but needs much more to realize power projection. Best present tool is speed and he can steal bases and track down balls in CF. Has clean, quick stroke, though has tendency to chase pitches out of zone.

Polcovich, Kaden — 4 — Seattle

Bats B Age 24
2020 (3) Oklahoma St

EXP MLB DEBUT: 2023 H/W: 5-8 180 FUT: Utility player **6C**

		Year	Lev	Team	AB	R	H	HR	RBI	Avg	OB	Slg	OPS	bb%	ct%	Eye	SB	CS	x/h%	Iso	RC/G
Pwr	++	2020	NCAA	Oklahoma St	64	20	22	2	21	344	494	578	1072	23	84	1.90	8	1	41	234	9.72
BAvg	++	2021	A+	Everett	214	55	58	10	47	271	402	505	907	18	70	0.73	16	3	45	234	7.53
Spd	+++	2021	AA	Arkansas	128	13	17	2	14	133	229	211	440	11	68	0.39	4	1	35	78	0.50
Def	+++	2022	AA	Arkansas	451	70	109	12	60	242	329	386	715	12	74	0.50	18	2	34	144	4.50

Athletic, versatile INF with quality secondary skills. Not much pop or natural hitting skills in toolbox. Swing can get long, particularly from right side and has trouble with spin. Focuses on seeing pitches and driving balls to gaps. Can play any position on diamond, though was mostly 2B in 22. Owns average arm and speed.

Pollard, Chandler — 456 — Texas

Bats R Age 18
2022 (5) HS (GA)

EXP MLB DEBUT: 2027 H/W: 6-2 173 FUT: Starting SS **8E**

		Year	Lev	Team	AB	R	H	HR	RBI	Avg	OB	Slg	OPS	bb%	ct%	Eye	SB	CS	x/h%	Iso	RC/G
Pwr	++																				
BAvg	++																				
Spd	+++++																				
Def	+++	2022	Rk	ACL Rangers	5	0	0	0	0	0	167	0	167	17	60	0.50	0	1		0	-4.34

Standout from 2022 class with best mix of tools. Tons of projection across body, with present bat speed and swing-adjustment ability. Non-predictive 8-game debut, but the tool grades are all at least average, with present plus-plus speed. Extreme range but average arm. Shortened up stroke and took to pro instruction well.

Pomares, Jairo — 7 — San Francisco

Bats L Age 22
2018 FA (CU)

EXP MLB DEBUT: 2024 H/W: 6-1 185 FUT: Starting OF **8D**

		Year	Lev	Team	AB	R	H	HR	RBI	Avg	OB	Slg	OPS	bb%	ct%	Eye	SB	CS	x/h%	Iso	RC/G
		2019	A-	Salem-Keizer	58	7	12	0	4	207	220	259	479	2	71	0.06	0	0	25	52	0.94
Pwr	+++	2021	A	San Jose	199	45	74	14	44	372	416	693	1109	7	73	0.28	0	0	49	322	9.54
BAvg	++++	2021	A+	Eugene	103	13	27	6	15	262	269	505	774	1	68	0.03	1	0	44	243	4.89
Spd	++	2022	Rk	ACL Giants O	15	5	8	3	7	533	563	###	1896	6	87	0.50	0	0	75	800	17.32
Def	++	2022	A+	Eugene	338	49	86	14	59	254	326	438	764	10	62	0.28	0	0	40	183	5.44

Career .304 hitter with natural and instinctual batting ability. Mostly average bat speed, but can hit velocity and breaking balls regardless of location. Produces loud contact and starting to pull ball more for power. Has average arm strength, but relegated to LF as he lacks routes and reads. Focus should be on batting eye and OF work.

Pouaka-Grego, Nikau — 6 — Philadelphia

Bats L Age 18
2022 FA (NZ)

EXP MLB DEBUT: 2027 H/W: 5-10 175 FUT: Starting 2B **8E**

		Year	Lev	Team	AB	R	H	HR	RBI	Avg	OB	Slg	OPS	bb%	ct%	Eye	SB	CS	x/h%	Iso	RC/G
Pwr	+++																				
BAvg	++																				
Spd	++																				
Def	++	2022	Rk	FCL Phillies	103	20	31	3	16	301	395	466	861	13	84	1.00	2	2	32	165	6.45

New Zealand teenager signed in Jan of 2022 and popped right into FSL complex ball. Made great contact with more punch than expected and showed command of the strike zone. A bit undersized but some room to grow. May have to move off SS but 2B could be the fit. Age/plate skills make him watchable.

Price, Collin — 2 — Houston

Bats R Age 23
2022 (6) Mercer

EXP MLB DEBUT: 2025 H/W: 6-6 205 FUT: Reserve C **7D**

		Year	Lev	Team	AB	R	H	HR	RBI	Avg	OB	Slg	OPS	bb%	ct%	Eye	SB	CS	x/h%	Iso	RC/G
Pwr	+++																				
BAvg	++																				
Spd	+	2022	NCAA	Mercer	203	53	64	18	58	315	455	626	1081	20	83	1.53	3	1	41	310	9.25
Def	+++	2022	A	Fayetteville	62	7	18	2	10	290	362	468	830	10	73	0.41	0	0	39	177	6.03

Senior sign catcher out of college. Improved stock due to jump in plate discipline and power. Continued to hit during short pro debut, showing patient approach and good ct%. Good defender, though DH, corner OF spot may be option as long as power translates to pro ball.

Prieto,Cesar | 45 | Baltimore | EXP MLB DEBUT: 2023 | H/W: 5-9 175 | FUT: Reserve IF | 7C

Bats L Age 23	Year	Lev	Team	AB	R	H	HR	RBI	Avg	OB	Slg	OPS	bb%	ct%	Eye	SB	CS	x/h%	Iso	RC/G
2022 FA (CU)																				
Pwr +++																				
BAvg +++																				
Spd ++	2022	A+	Aberdeen	97	13	33	7	20	340	373	619	991	5	84	0.31	3	1	39	278	7.23
Def ++	2022	AA	Bowie	368	44	94	4	37	255	285	348	632	4	84	0.26	2	5	28	92	3.19

Signed from Cuba in Jan 2022 and moved swiftly from High-A to Double-A in 2022. Fast bat from the left side produced solid power numbers with above-average contact. Able to turn around inside velocity and drive outer-half off speed pitches the other way. Smallish build best suited for 2B but can also play 3B. Bat-first IF UT.

Puason,Robert | 46 | Oakland | EXP MLB DEBUT: 2026 | H/W: 6-3 165 | FUT: Starting SS | 8E

Bats R Age 20	Year	Lev	Team	AB	R	H	HR	RBI	Avg	OB	Slg	OPS	bb%	ct%	Eye	SB	CS	x/h%	Iso	RC/G
2019 FA (DR)																				
Pwr +	2019	--	Did Not Play																	
BAvg ++	2021	A	Stockton	302	43	65	3	27	215	273	291	564	7	54	0.17	3	1	25	76	2.69
Spd ++++	2022	Rk	ACL Athletics	127	22	33	1	9	260	319	362	681	8	65	0.25	6	1	27	102	4.16
Def ++++	2022	A	Stockton	200	25	37	2	18	185	235	255	490	6	62	0.17	5	4	27	70	1.13

Regressing prospect who can't put it all together. Raw tools as impressive as any in org, but swing is out of whack and has insufficient approach to get on base or find good pitches to smash. Demoted from Low-A to Rookie ball in June. Struggles to make contact and rarely lofts ball. Has exceptional SS ability with range and arm.

Quero,Edgar | 2 | Los Angeles (A) | EXP MLB DEBUT: 2025 | H/W: 5-11 170 | FUT: Starting C | 8D

Bats B Age 20	Year	Lev	Team	AB	R	H	HR	RBI	Avg	OB	Slg	OPS	bb%	ct%	Eye	SB	CS	x/h%	Iso	RC/G
2021 FA (CU)																				
Pwr ++++																				
BAvg +++	2021	Rk	ACL Angels	87	21	22	4	24	253	409	506	915	21	68	0.82	1	1	59	253	7.90
Spd ++	2021	A	Inland Empire	34	2	7	1	6	206	308	353	661	13	53	0.31	1	0	43	147	4.48
Def +++	2022	A	Inland Empire	413	86	129	17	75	312	416	530	946	15	78	0.80	12	5	42	218	7.66

Offensively-skilled backstop took multiple steps forward in development during big 2022 campaign. Switch-hitter with power from both sides; light-tower variety from LH side. Game plans AB well, willing to work the other way when needed and work counts. Power to all fields, especially from LH side. 30+ HR potential. Solid defender.

Quero,Jeferson | 2 | Milwaukee | EXP MLB DEBUT: 2025 | H/W: 5-10 165 | FUT: Starting C | 8D

Bats R Age 20	Year	Lev	Team	AB	R	H	HR	RBI	Avg	OB	Slg	OPS	bb%	ct%	Eye	SB	CS	x/h%	Iso	RC/G
2019 FA (VZ)																				
Pwr +++																				
BAvg +++	2021	Rk	ACL Brewers Blue	68	15	21	2	8	309	413	500	913	15	85	1.20	4	3	38	191	7.20
Spd +	2022	A	Carolina	284	44	79	6	43	278	343	412	755	9	79	0.46	10	2	32	134	4.90
Def +++	2022	A+	Wisconsin	83	10	26	4	14	313	329	530	860	2	82	0.13	0	0	35	217	5.64

Athletic, agile backstop who got better as season wore on. Mature defensive skills and could become well above average. Receives pitches well with soft hands and exhibits plus arm strength with accuracy. Produced with bat despite average bat speed and power potential. Keeps bat in zone to make good contact.

Quintana,Roismar | 9 | Washington | EXP MLB DEBUT: 2026 | H/W: 6-1 175 | FUT: Starting OF | 8D

Bats R Age 20	Year	Lev	Team	AB	R	H	HR	RBI	Avg	OB	Slg	OPS	bb%	ct%	Eye	SB	CS	x/h%	Iso	RC/G
2020 FA (VZ)																				
Pwr ++++																				
BAvg +++																				
Spd ++	2021	Rk	FCL Nationals	13	3	4	1	5	308	526	692	1219	32	62	1.20	0	0	75	385	13.68
Def ++	2022	Rk	FCL Nationals	180	41	52	5	28	289	323	439	762	5	74	0.20	3	1	31	150	4.77

Repeated complex ball with good results in limited sample. Strong and well-proportioned, with all-fields power from the right side. Made decent contact in 2022, could be more selective at the plate as he moves up. Average runner is unlikely to be a base-stealer as frame fills out. Solid defender in RF; bat will need to prove he stays there.

Quintero,Geraldo | 56 | Atlanta | EXP MLB DEBUT: 2025 | H/W: 5-8 155 | FUT: Reserve IF | 6C

Bats B Age 21	Year	Lev	Team	AB	R	H	HR	RBI	Avg	OB	Slg	OPS	bb%	ct%	Eye	SB	CS	x/h%	Iso	RC/G
2019 FA (VZ)																				
Pwr ++																				
BAvg ++	2021	Rk	FCL Braves	121	23	25	0	6	207	304	273	577	12	79	0.65	12	5	20	66	2.89
Spd ++++	2022	A	Augusta	362	61	95	6	47	262	349	423	771	12	81	0.70	26	8	39	160	5.35
Def ++	2022	A+	Rome	80	12	19	2	12	238	322	363	685	11	73	0.45	8	3	32	125	4.05

Tiny switch-hitting MIF prospect made it up to High-A in 2022. Small athletic frame with some room for bulk. Open stance with a bat wrap triggering to the hit position. Linear swing plane. Struggles getting to hard contact. Much more fluid swing from LH side. Hits in parts as RH hitter. Contact and speed carry profile.

Rada,Nelson | 8 | Los Angeles (A) | EXP MLB DEBUT: 2026 | H/W: 5-10 160 | FUT: Starting OF | 8E

Bats L Age 17	Year	Lev	Team	AB	R	H	HR	RBI	Avg	OB	Slg	OPS	bb%	ct%	Eye	SB	CS	x/h%	Iso	RC/G
2022 FA (VZ)																				
Pwr +++																				
BAvg +++																				
Spd +++																				
Def +++	2022	Rk	DSL Angels	164	50	51	1	26	311	405	439	844	14	84	1.00	27	6	31	128	6.41

Toolsy LHH OF prospect, signed for $1.7 million in Jan 2022, turned in enticing professional debut in Dominican Summer League at extremely young age. Wiry with room to grow into frame. Linear swing plane, struggled getting to loft. Frame plus swing development time could get to plus power. Disciplined approach with contact foundational skills.

Rafaela,Ceddanne | 68 | Boston | EXP MLB DEBUT: 2024 | H/W: 5-8 152 | FUT: Starting CF | 8C

Bats R Age 22	Year	Lev	Team	AB	R	H	HR	RBI	Avg	OB	Slg	OPS	bb%	ct%	Eye	SB	CS	x/h%	Iso	RC/G
2017 FA (CC)	2019	Rk	GCL Red Sox	153	30	38	6	17	248	311	425	736	8	82	0.50	9	2	29	176	4.55
Pwr +++	2019	A-	Lowell	11	0	2	0	1	182	182	182	364	0	73	0.00	0	0	0	0	-0.75
BAvg +++	2021	A	Salem	394	73	99	10	53	251	296	424	720	6	80	0.32	23	3	39	173	4.32
Spd ++++	2022	A+	Greenville	197	37	65	9	36	330	362	594	956	5	74	0.20	14	2	46	264	7.41
Def +++	2022	AA	Portland	284	45	79	12	50	278	317	500	817	5	78	0.26	14	5	42	222	5.44

Multi-tooled prospect who is developing rapidly. Got off to blistering start and finished 4th in BOS minors in HR and 3rd in SB. Doubled previous high in HR and has bat-to-ball skills and ability to shoot gaps. Can chase breaking balls at times and expand zone. SB would increase with better OBP as he has plus speed. High upside guy who can play SS or CF.

Ramirez,Alex | 89 | New York (N) | EXP MLB DEBUT: 2024 | H/W: 6-3 170 | FUT: Starting OF | 8C

Bats R Age 20	Year	Lev	Team	AB	R	H	HR	RBI	Avg	OB	Slg	OPS	bb%	ct%	Eye	SB	CS	x/h%	Iso	RC/G
2019 FA (DR)																				
Pwr +++																				
BAvg +++	2021	A	St. Lucie	302	41	78	5	35	258	311	384	695	7	66	0.22	16	7	31	126	4.28
Spd +++	2022	A	St. Lucie	271	40	77	6	37	284	351	443	794	9	75	0.41	17	9	32	159	5.51
Def ++++	2022	A+	Brooklyn	227	22	63	5	34	278	325	427	752	7	76	0.30	4	7	37	150	4.78

Twitchy, athletic OF prospect with room for power had a solid 2022 season. Upright stance with a bat wrap in the load. Has toned down pre-pitch movement. Uppercut swing trajectory gets to loft easily with power to all fields. Raw approach, will chase FB up and breakers down. Above-average runner with strong arm. Likely RF.

Ramos,Bryan | 5 | Chicago (A) | EXP MLB DEBUT: 2024 | H/W: 6-2 190 | FUT: Starting 3B | 8D

Bats R Age 21	Year	Lev	Team	AB	R	H	HR	RBI	Avg	OB	Slg	OPS	bb%	ct%	Eye	SB	CS	x/h%	Iso	RC/G
2018 FA (CU)																				
Pwr ++++	2019	Rk	AZL White Sox	188	36	52	4	26	277	343	415	758	9	77	0.43	3	4	31	138	4.97
BAvg +++	2021	A	Kannapolis	431	64	105	13	57	244	324	415	739	11	74	0.46	13	4	40	172	4.78
Spd ++	2022	A+	Winston-Salem	382	64	105	19	74	275	344	471	815	9	81	0.56	1	0	34	196	5.51
Def ++	2022	AA	Birmingham	80	8	18	3	12	225	271	375	646	6	81	0.33	0	1	33	150	3.27

Powerful but streaky, he hit 22 HR across 2 levels. Upright stance with simple load, creates solid power leverage within base. Swing geared towards high EV lofted contact. However, struggles with spin recognition despite solid eye, causing later swing decisions and lighter contact. Improved reactions at 3B; might stick there long-term.

Ramos,Heliot | 789 | San Francisco | EXP MLB DEBUT: 2022 | H/W: 6-1 188 | FUT: Starting OF | 7C

Bats R Age 23	Year	Lev	Team	AB	R	H	HR	RBI	Avg	OB	Slg	OPS	bb%	ct%	Eye	SB	CS	x/h%	Iso	RC/G
2017 (1) HS (PR)	2019	AA	Richmond	95	13	23	3	15	242	314	421	735	10	65	0.30	2	3	43	179	4.94
Pwr ++	2021	AA	Richmond	236	36	56	10	26	237	316	432	748	10	69	0.37	7	2	45	195	4.92
BAvg +++	2021	AAA	Sacramento	213	30	58	4	30	272	320	399	719	7	69	0.23	8	2	29	127	4.46
Spd +++	2022	AAA	Sacramento	427	61	97	11	45	227	295	349	644	9	74	0.37	6	6	30	122	3.37
Def +++	2022	MLB	San Francisco	20	4	2	0	0	100	182	100	282	9	70	0.33	0	0	0	0	-1.72

Strong OF who reached SF, but struggled most of season, including at AAA. Power hasn't developed as much as hoped and makes weak contact. Too many groundballs with erratic approach. Still hope based upon athleticism and batting eye. Has raw power and quickness and is still relatively young. Don't count him out.

Ramos, Jose — 89 — Los Angeles (N)

Bats R **Age** 22
2018 FA (PN)
EXP MLB DEBUT: 2024 | H/W: 6-1 200 | FUT: Starting OF | 7C

		Year	Lev	Team	AB	R	H	HR	RBI	Avg	OB	Slg	OPS	bb%	ct%	Eye	SB	CS	x/h%	Iso	RC/G
Pwr	++	2021	Rk	ACL Dodgers	60	13	23	3	15	383	448	633	1081	10	77	0.50	1	0	39	250	9.17
BAvg	+++	2021	A	Rancho Cuca	195	30	61	8	44	313	365	559	924	8	71	0.28	1	4	48	246	7.34
Spd	++	2022	A	Rancho Cuca	112	20	31	6	23	277	377	518	895	14	68	0.50	2	0	39	241	7.24
Def	+++	2022	A+	Great Lakes	362	63	87	19	74	240	314	467	781	10	63	0.29	2	0	47	227	5.63

Strong, physical OF traded in plate discipline for a more aggressive approach at the plate, reaching career highs in both home runs and strikeouts. Struggles with breaking balls down and away and will need to tighten up as he moves up. Runs well with a plus arm and profiles as an above-average defender in RF.

Reckley, Ryan — 6 — San Francisco

Bats B **Age** 18
2022 FA (BM)
EXP MLB DEBUT: 2027 | H/W: 5-10 160 | FUT: Starting SS | 8E

		Year	Lev	Team	AB	R	H	HR	RBI	Avg	OB	Slg	OPS	bb%	ct%	Eye	SB	CS	x/h%	Iso	RC/G
Pwr	++																				
BAvg	+++																				
Spd	++++																				
Def	+++	2022	Rk	DSL Giants Orange	36	7	7	0	2	194	356	222	578	20	72	0.90	3	1	14	28	2.97

Toolsy, advanced INF who signed for huge bonus. Skills to dream on, but several years away. Plays solid SS with quick hands, smooth actions, and ample range. More hit over power, though should develop at least average power at peak. Knows strike zone well and doesn't chase. Has room to add strength and runs very well.

Redmond, Chandler — 3 — St. Louis

Bats L **Age** 26
2019 (32) Gardner-Webb
EXP MLB DEBUT: 2023 | H/W: 6-1 231 | FUT: Reserve 1B | 6C

		Year	Lev	Team	AB	R	H	HR	RBI	Avg	OB	Slg	OPS	bb%	ct%	Eye	SB	CS	x/h%	Iso	RC/G
		2019	NCAA	Gardner-Webb	191	42	59	18	59	309	411	660	1070	15	77	0.75	1	2	51	351	9.01
Pwr	+++	2019	Rk	Johnson City	181	37	52	12	40	287	374	552	926	12	70	0.45	4	2	46	265	7.43
BAvg	++	2021	A+	Peoria	222	33	52	13	34	234	339	459	798	14	60	0.40	3	1	46	225	6.12
Spd	+	2021	AA	Springfield	122	13	37	5	25	303	361	500	861	8	59	0.22	0	1	38	197	7.33
Def	++	2022	AA	Springfield	327	52	77	21	79	235	317	480	797	11	66	0.35	0	1	45	245	5.64

32nd rounder had mixed results in second stint at AA. More aggressive approach resulted in a career-high in HR, but also leads to plenty of swing-and-miss (32% K rate). Thick frame rather than bat speed generates average to above power. Below-average defender spent most of '22 at 1B and will be hard pressed to carve out a full-time role.

Reimer, Jacob — 5 — New York (N)

Bats R **Age** 19
2022 (4) HS (CA)
EXP MLB DEBUT: 2025 | H/W: 6-2 205 | FUT: Starting 3B | 7D

		Year	Lev	Team	AB	R	H	HR	RBI	Avg	OB	Slg	OPS	bb%	ct%	Eye	SB	CS	x/h%	Iso	RC/G
Pwr	+++																				
BAvg	+++																				
Spd	++																				
Def	+++	2022	Rk	FCL Mets	23	5	6	1	7	261	414	478	892	21	87	2.00	0	0	33	217	7.21

Average build with some athleticism and room to grow. Open stance with slight bat wrap during load. Solid approach, not afraid to let ball travel deep in zone. Will work opposite field. Potential for raw plus power with appropriate body growth. Good hands and reactions at 3B. Average runner.

Rhodes, John — 89 — Baltimore

Bats R **Age** 22
2021 (3) Kentucky
EXP MLB DEBUT: 2024 | H/W: 6-0 200 | FUT: Starting OF | 7C

		Year	Lev	Team	AB	R	H	HR	RBI	Avg	OB	Slg	OPS	bb%	ct%	Eye	SB	CS	x/h%	Iso	RC/G
		2021	Rk	FCL Orioles B	1	0	1	0	2	1000	###	###	2000	0	100		0	0	0	0	16.32
Pwr	+++	2021	Rk	FCL Orioles Orange	13	3	2	0	3	154	313	154	466	19	77	1.00	0	0	0	0	1.52
BAvg	++	2021	A	Delmarva	94	20	25	2	18	266	330	372	702	9	83	0.56	6	0	24	106	4.22
Spd	++++	2022	A+	Aberdeen	201	43	52	5	35	259	369	428	797	15	75	0.70	16	0	42	169	5.80
Def	+++	2022	AA	Bowie	90	12	17	0	9	189	284	267	551	12	76	0.55	0	0	29	78	2.46

(4.26)

Versatile player who roams the OF, can also handle COR IF. No standout tool but does a lot of things well: works counts and knows strike zone, hits for average power, good runner with some SB ability. Can also chase via some wild swings and be beaten by velocity. Gets the most out of his ability; is a hustling, energetic player on the field.

Rincones Jr, Gabriel — 9 — Philadelphia

Bats L **Age** 22
2022 (3) Florida Atlantic
EXP MLB DEBUT: 2026 | H/W: 6-4 225 | FUT: Starting OF | 7D

		Year	Lev	Team	AB	R	H	HR	RBI	Avg	OB	Slg	OPS	bb%	ct%	Eye	SB	CS	x/h%	Iso	RC/G
Pwr	+++																				
BAvg	+++																				
Spd	++																				
Def	++																				

Pure lefty hitter who works counts with solid approach. Power started to show up in 2022 college season with big exit velocities which moved him up draft boards. Still a small sample, has struggled against off-speed and has yet to get into a pro game. Big arm, but size and limited run tool means he's a future corner OF or 1B.

Ritter, Ryan — 6 — Colorado

Bats R **Age** 22
2022 (4) Kentucky
EXP MLB DEBUT: 2025 | H/W: 6-2 200 | FUT: Reserve SS | 6C

		Year	Lev	Team	AB	R	H	HR	RBI	Avg	OB	Slg	OPS	bb%	ct%	Eye	SB	CS	x/h%	Iso	RC/G
Pwr	+																				
BAvg	++																				
Spd	+++	2022	NCAA	Kentucky	226	43	64	8	36	283	344	469	813	9	70	0.31	15	0	38	186	5.81
Def	++++	2022	Rk	ACL Rockies	25	9	8	1	4	320	370	680	1050	7	88	0.67	2	0	75	360	8.41

Glove-first SS shows advanced feel for the position with good range, a quick release, and a plus arm. Showed well at plate in limited pro debut, but projects to be an average hitter and hit just 11 HR in two years at Kentucky and fared poorly in the Cape. Will need to work hard to add power and loft to swing to carve out a big league role.

Rizzo, Joe — 5 — Miami

Bats L **Age** 25
2016 (2) HS (VA)
EXP MLB DEBUT: 2023 | H/W: 5-10 194 | FUT: Starting 3B | 7E

		Year	Lev	Team	AB	R	H	HR	RBI	Avg	OB	Slg	OPS	bb%	ct%	Eye	SB	CS	x/h%	Iso	RC/G
		2017	A+	Modesto	20	1	4	0	1	200	238	300	538	5	60	0.13	0	0	25	100	2.12
Pwr	+++	2018	A+	Modesto	461	46	111	4	55	241	301	321	622	8	77	0.37	6	1	24	80	3.17
BAvg	++	2019	A+	Modesto	518	77	153	10	63	295	352	423	774	8	82	0.48	0	3	28	127	5.08
Spd	++	2021	AA	Arkansas	380	49	96	12	60	253	327	400	727	10	73	0.40	4	4	32	147	4.56
Def	++	2022	AA	Arkansas	488	84	135	21	69	277	341	467	809	9	79	0.47	2	1	38	191	5.47

Late bloomer who posted better numbers across in board in 2nd stint in Double-A. Set easy career high in HR while making excellent contact. Has strong frame to produce pop and could grow into more. Not much value outside of bat. Very slow foot speed and lacks defensive acumen at 3B. Arm is strong, but has limited range.

Rocchio, Brayan — 46 — Cleveland

Bats B **Age** 22
2017 FA (VZ)
EXP MLB DEBUT: 2023 | H/W: 5-10 170 | FUT: Starting SS | 8D

		Year	Lev	Team	AB	R	H	HR	RBI	Avg	OB	Slg	OPS	bb%	ct%	Eye	SB	CS	x/h%	Iso	RC/G
		2019	A-	MahoningVal	268	33	67	5	27	250	302	373	675	7	85	0.50	14	8	30	123	3.88
Pwr	+++	2021	A+	Lake County	257	45	68	9	33	265	318	428	746	7	75	0.31	14	6	34	163	4.64
BAvg	+++	2021	AA	Akron	184	34	54	6	30	293	340	505	846	7	78	0.32	7	4	43	212	5.96
Spd	++++	2022	AA	Akron	373	62	99	13	48	265	340	432	771	10	78	0.52	12	6	35	166	5.10
Def	++++	2022	AAA	Columbus	137	21	32	5	16	234	295	387	682	8	85	0.57	2	3	34	153	3.91

Small-statured, switch-hitting, defensively skilled SS struggled with getting to harder contact in Triple-A sample, especially from RH side. Upright, closed stance with quick trigger, has improved getting to power; there's 25 HR potential in his leveraged swing. Plus runner but struggled with SB% throughout career. Plus SS defensively.

Roden, Alan — 9 — Toronto

Bats L **Age** 23
2022 (3) Creighton
EXP MLB DEBUT: 2024 | H/W: 6-0 215 | FUT: Starting OF | 7D

		Year	Lev	Team	AB	R	H	HR	RBI	Avg	OB	Slg	OPS	bb%	ct%	Eye	SB	CS	x/h%	Iso	RC/G
Pwr	++																				
BAvg	+++																				
Spd	++	2022	NCAA	Creighton	194	48	75	4	45	387	466	598	1064	13	96	3.63	9	4	41	211	8.84
Def	++	2022	A	Dunedin	90	17	21	1	9	233	355	311	666	16	86	1.31	5	1	24	78	4.31

Short, strong OF with extreme contact skills. Very tough to fan due to hand-eye coordination and exemplary barrel control. Lacks present power, though TOR will work to unleash natural strength. Uses entire field and will rack up doubles. Good baserunner despite limited speed. Owns average arm in RF.

Rodriguez, Alberto — 9 — Seattle

Bats L **Age** 22
2017 FA (DR)
EXP MLB DEBUT: 2024 | H/W: 5-11 227 | FUT: Starting OF | 7D

		Year	Lev	Team	AB	R	H	HR	RBI	Avg	OB	Slg	OPS	bb%	ct%	Eye	SB	CS	x/h%	Iso	RC/G
Pwr	++	2019	Rk	GCL Blue Jays	173	19	52	2	29	301	370	422	792	10	82	0.59	13	2	31	121	5.47
BAvg	+++	2021	A	Modesto	370	75	109	10	63	295	380	484	864	12	74	0.54	13	7	41	189	6.61
Spd	+++	2021	A+	Everett	24	5	5	0	2	208	269	250	519	8	71	0.29	2	0	20	42	1.70
Def	+++	2022	A+	Everett	472	59	123	10	46	261	331	396	728	10	71	0.36	6	4	33	136	4.67

Short, strong RF with decent hitting skills and sufficient secondary abilities. Has mature batting eye and good pitch recognition. Smokes doubles to gaps, though may not get to HR without swing adjustments. Exhibits average speed, though not much of basestealing thread. Has good range and strong arm to be adept in RF.

Rodriguez,Carlos — 7 — Milwaukee

EXP MLB DEBUT: 2025 | H/W: 5-10 150 | FUT: Starting OF | 7D

Bats L Age 22	Year	Lev	Team	AB	R	H	HR	RBI	Avg	OB	Slg	OPS	bb%	ct%	Eye	SB	CS	x/h%	Iso	RC/G
2017 FA (VZ)	2018	Rk	AZL Brewers	20	4	7	0	1	350	409	350	759	9	95	2.00	2	1	0	0	5.16
Pwr +	2019	Rk	AZL Brewers Gold	22	5	7	0	1	318	318	364	682	0	91	0.00	1	1	14	45	3.61
BAvg +++	2019	Rk	Rocky Mountain	151	20	50	3	12	331	348	424	772	3	87	0.20	4	6	14	93	4.63
Spd +++	2021	A+	Wisconsin	345	43	92	1	38	267	334	348	682	9	78	0.47	15	6	24	81	4.07
Def +++	2022	A+	Wisconsin	142	23	38	3	21	268	350	415	765	11	75	0.51	10	3	37	148	5.21

Natural-hitting OF who repeated High-A, but season ended in May after tearing ACL. Showed increased gap pop and better hand-eye coordination in limited action. Manages strike zone well and keeps ball on ground where speed plays. Rarely fans. Relegated to LF due to poor arm. Not particularly effective against LHP.

Rodriguez,Edryn — 46 — Seattle

EXP MLB DEBUT: 2026 | H/W: 5-9 150 | FUT: Starting SS | 7E

Bats R Age 19	Year	Lev	Team	AB	R	H	HR	RBI	Avg	OB	Slg	OPS	bb%	ct%	Eye	SB	CS	x/h%	Iso	RC/G
2019 FA (DR)																				
Pwr ++																				
BAvg ++																				
Spd +++	2021	Rk	DSL Mariners	136	28	42	4	28	309	413	515	927	15	74	0.69	5	6	45	206	7.64
Def +++	2022	Rk	ACL Mariners	158	26	38	5	14	241	298	405	703	8	70	0.27	5	4	42	165	4.22

Short, smooth INF who is excellent defender. Moves and ranges well to both sides and has quick, soft hands. Arm strength may be best for 2B, but he has quick release. Offense will take time to develop. Doesn't work counts and has below average strength. Can be pull happy at times. Line drive hitter at present.

Rodriguez,Emmanuel — 8 — Minnesota

EXP MLB DEBUT: 2025 | H/W: 5-10 210 | FUT: Starting CF | 9D

Bats L Age 20	Year	Lev	Team	AB	R	H	HR	RBI	Avg	OB	Slg	OPS	bb%	ct%	Eye	SB	CS	x/h%	Iso	RC/G
2019 FA (DR)																				
Pwr ++++																				
BAvg +++																				
Spd +++	2021	Rk	FCL Twins	126	31	27	10	23	214	336	524	859	15	56	0.41	9	4	63	310	7.59
Def +++	2022	A	Fort Myers	136	35	37	9	25	272	487	551	1039	30	62	1.10	11	5	46	279	10.44

Advanced hitter who ended season in June due to torn meniscus. One of most patient hitters in minors and can put charge into ball with natural strength and bat speed. Possesses potential double-plus power with extreme exit velocity. K rate too high and can flail when behind in count. Plus arm enhances OF play and runs well for SB and range.

Rodriguez,Endy — 24 — Pittsburgh

EXP MLB DEBUT: 2023 | H/W: 6-0 170 | FUT: Starting C | 7B

Bats B Age 22	Year	Lev	Team	AB	R	H	HR	RBI	Avg	OB	Slg	OPS	bb%	ct%	Eye	SB	CS	x/h%	Iso	RC/G
2018 FA (DR)	2019	Rk	GCL Mets	75	14	22	0	6	293	376	453	830	12	83	0.77	4	0	50	160	6.22
Pwr +++	2021	A	Bradenton	377	73	111	15	73	294	377	512	889	12	80	0.65	2	0	41	218	6.71
BAvg ++++	2022	A+	Greensboro	318	63	96	16	55	302	383	544	927	12	76	0.55	3	3	44	242	7.25
Spd ++	2022	AA	Altoona	118	27	42	8	32	356	441	678	1119	13	82	0.86	1	0	52	322	9.51
Def ++	2022	AAA	Indianapolis	22	2	10	1	8	455	455	773	1227	0	86	0.00	0	0	40	318	9.71

One of best success stories in org. Finished 4th in minors in OPS and set highs in HR and BA/OBP/SLG. Versatile defender who played mostly C, but also saw time at 2B, LF and 1B. Hits well from both sides and should hit for high BA with at least average pop. Very athletic behind plate, but a bit raw with release and blocking.

Rodriguez,Gabriel — 6 — Cleveland

EXP MLB DEBUT: 2024 | H/W: 6-2 162 | FUT: Starting 3B | 7D

Bats R Age 21	Year	Lev	Team	AB	R	H	HR	RBI	Avg	OB	Slg	OPS	bb%	ct%	Eye	SB	CS	x/h%	Iso	RC/G
2018 FA (VZ)																				
Pwr +++																				
BAvg +++	2019	Rk	AZL Indians	65	7	14	0	10	215	261	262	522	6	66	0.18	1	1	21	46	1.66
Spd ++	2021	A	Lynchburg	373	44	88	3	34	236	284	314	598	6	70	0.23	3	3	25	78	2.73
Def +++	2022	A+	Lake County	320	45	87	9	38	272	342	416	757	10	78	0.47	4	2	30	144	4.92

Strong, athletic 3B prospect had best year as pro. Open stance with smooth load, delivers quick, linear stroke. Does well to use all fields approach but aggressiveness caps on-base ability. There's power in frame but swing has yet to catch up and doesn't get to consistent hard contact. A strong armed defender, fits best at 3B with solid reactions.

Rodriguez,Hector — 8 — Cincinnati

EXP MLB DEBUT: 2026 | H/W: 5-8 186 | FUT: Starting CF | 7E

Bats R Age 19	Year	Lev	Team	AB	R	H	HR	RBI	Avg	OB	Slg	OPS	bb%	ct%	Eye	SB	CS	x/h%	Iso	RC/G
2021 FA (DR)	2021	Rk	DSL Mets	123	17	37	3	15	301	368	472	839	10	86	0.76	6	8	35	171	5.99
Pwr ++	2022	Rk	ACL Reds	25	7	10	0	4	400	464	720	1184	11	100		3	2	60	320	10.16
BAvg +++	2022	Rk	FCL Mets	106	19	37	3	16	349	384	547	931	5	91	0.60	12	3	30	198	6.72
Spd ++++	2022	A	Daytona	45	7	13	0	6	289	319	467	786	4	78	0.20	1	1	46	178	5.32
Def +++	2022	A	St. Lucie	7	1	1	0	0	143	250	143	393	13	100		0	0	0	0	1.90

Wiry, athletic LHH CF prospect was acquired from NYM mid-season. Shorter statured, but body capable of adding lean muscle. Uber-aggressive approach at the plate. Chases at high rate. Open, upright stance with moderate leg lift. Shorter levers, quick bat. Below average power projected currently. Plus runner; 16 for 22 in SB chances. Potential CF.

Rodriguez,Johnathan — 79 — Cleveland

EXP MLB DEBUT: 2023 | H/W: 6-3 180 | FUT: Reserve OF | 6C

Bats R Age 23	Year	Lev	Team	AB	R	H	HR	RBI	Avg	OB	Slg	OPS	bb%	ct%	Eye	SB	CS	x/h%	Iso	RC/G
2017 (3) HS (PR)	2019	A-	MahoningVal	231	36	57	6	27	247	310	424	734	8	71	0.31	4	2	44	177	4.73
Pwr ++++	2021	A	Lynchburg	220	29	69	5	33	314	360	450	810	7	75	0.30	3	1	28	136	5.51
BAvg ++	2021	A+	Lake County	79	9	17	2	11	215	295	342	637	10	72	0.41	2	1	35	127	3.36
Spd ++	2022	A+	Lake County	295	48	86	21	59	292	341	573	914	7	69	0.24	2	0	45	281	7.04
Def +++	2022	AA	Akron	107	10	22	5	15	206	241	449	690	4	60	0.12	0	1	64	243	4.39

Former 3rd round pick suddenly found power stroke in 6th year as pro. Bulked out frame; at physical projection. Gave up switch hitting, now RHH only. Upright, closed stance with minimal bat wrap. Above-average bat speed and uppercut swing trajectory. Sells out for pull power. Aggressive approach and swing-and-miss play down hit tool.

Rodriguez,Jose — 46 — Chicago (A)

EXP MLB DEBUT: 2023 | H/W: 5-11 175 | FUT: Starting SS | 7C

Bats R Age 21	Year	Lev	Team	AB	R	H	HR	RBI	Avg	OB	Slg	OPS	bb%	ct%	Eye	SB	CS	x/h%	Iso	RC/G
2018 FA (DR)	2019	Rk	AZL White Sox	188	28	55	9	31	293	325	505	830	5	76	0.20	7	1	35	213	5.54
Pwr ++	2021	A	Kannapolis	336	58	95	9	32	283	325	452	777	6	83	0.37	20	5	37	170	4.99
BAvg +++	2021	A+	Winston-Salem	119	19	43	5	19	361	387	538	925	4	89	0.38	10	5	23	176	6.40
Spd +++	2021	AA	Birmingham	14	2	3	0	0	214	214	286	500	0	86	0.00	0	1	33	71	1.55
Def +++	2022	AA	Birmingham	440	75	123	11	68	280	337	430	766	8	85	0.58	40	10	31	150	4.99

Contact-oriented MIF with aggressive approach recovered from slow start to have pleasant season. Hitch in his swing causes late decisions and depresses EV. Struggles getting out in front for contact resulting in lots of inside-out swings. Below average power in frame and swing plane. Near plus defender at SS with average speed.

Rodriguez,Jose — 9 — Minnesota

EXP MLB DEBUT: 2027 | H/W: 6-0 196 | FUT: Starting OF | 8E

Bats R Age 17	Year	Lev	Team	AB	R	H	HR	RBI	Avg	OB	Slg	OPS	bb%	ct%	Eye	SB	CS	x/h%	Iso	RC/G
2022 FA (DR)																				
Pwr +++																				
BAvg ++																				
Spd ++																				
Def ++	2022	Rk	DSL Twins	190	39	55	13	49	289	360	605	965	10	73	0.40	5	0	56	316	7.77

Tall, strong OF who led DSL in HR in first pro experience. Has a lofty ceiling predicated on potential plus hit tool and easy power. Knows strike zone, but can get aggressive when selling out for power. Has exploitable holes in swing. Lack of quickness leads him to OF corner, but has strong enough arm to stick in RF.

Rodriguez,Lizandro — 4 — Kansas City

EXP MLB DEBUT: 2025 | H/W: 5-11 180 | FUT: Starting MIF | 7E

Bats B Age 20	Year	Lev	Team	AB	R	H	HR	RBI	Avg	OB	Slg	OPS	bb%	ct%	Eye	SB	CS	x/h%	Iso	RC/G
2019 FA (DR)																				
Pwr ++																				
BAvg +++	2021	Rk	DSL Royals Blue	97	27	30	6	23	309	432	567	999	18	81	1.17	14	4	40	258	8.28
Spd ++++	2022	Rk	ACL Royals Blue	82	17	26	5	12	317	385	573	958	10	80	0.56	5	3	38	256	7.30
Def +++	2022	A	Columbia	62	13	18	1	5	290	371	435	807	11	82	0.73	1	1	33	145	5.75

Athletic, switch-hitting MIF made full-season debut after starting at the complex. Wiry frame with room to grow. Best present tool is plus speed but hasn't translated to SB yet. Closed stance from both sides, steps in bucket on swing, especially from LH side. It's a longer swing but plus hand/eye has allowed for contact. Fringe average power.

Rodriguez,Nerio — 23 — Houston

EXP MLB DEBUT: 2025 | H/W: 6-2 230 | FUT: Reserve 1B | 6C

Bats R Age 23	Year	Lev	Team	AB	R	H	HR	RBI	Avg	OB	Slg	OPS	bb%	ct%	Eye	SB	CS	x/h%	Iso	RC/G
2016 FA (DR)																				
Pwr +++	2018	Rk	GCL Astros	106	13	20	0	8	189	283	264	547	12	64	0.37	0	0	40	75	2.27
BAvg ++	2019	Rk	GCL Astros	95	17	25	3	13	263	386	442	828	17	69	0.66	0	0	44	179	6.42
Spd +	2021	A	Fayetteville	312	44	77	4	43	247	347	349	697	13	71	0.53	2	1	27	103	4.41
Def ++	2022	A+	Asheville	134	25	39	8	24	291	375	530	905	12	70	0.45	0	0	41	239	7.10

Big-bodied C/1B started season strong but suffered season-ending injury in June. Good receiver behind the plate. Struggles to control run game. May move to 1B where power could play. Upright stance at plate, slowly crouches before pitch arrives. Lots of pre-pitch movement with leg-kick and hitch in swing. Patient approach with decent contact.

Rojas,Johan — 8 — Philadelphia

EXP MLB DEBUT: 2024 | H/W: 6-1 165 | FUT: Starting CF | 8C

Bats R Age 22	Year	Lev	Team	AB	R	H	HR	RBI	Avg	OB	Slg	OPS	bb%	ct%	Eye	SB	CS	x/h%	Iso	RC/G
2018 FA (DR)	2021	Rk	FCL Phillies	4	2	3	1	3	750	750	###	2250	0	100		1	0	33	750	18.22
Pwr +++	2021	A	Clearwater	313	51	75	7	38	240	298	374	672	8	78	0.38	25	6	33	134	3.76
BAvg ++	2021	A+	Jersey Shore	64	16	22	3	11	344	408	563	971	10	88	0.88	8	3	32	219	7.40
4.10 Spd +++++	2022	A+	Jersey Shore	265	40	61	3	22	230	287	325	611	7	79	0.38	33	1	28	94	3.03
Def ++++	2022	AA	Reading	235	42	61	4	16	260	320	387	708	8	81	0.48	29	4	28	128	4.30

Exciting, smaller-framed athlete with some loud tools - foot speed, CF-quality defense, excellent bat-to-ball skills. Very good second half at Double-A, where he worked on hitting the ball in the air more. Won't ever be a slugger; seeking some additional gap power to fill out his game. Can chase at times but not a free swinger. Good bunter.

Rojas,Yendry — 6 — San Diego

EXP MLB DEBUT: 2027 | H/W: 6-0 185 | FUT: Starting SS | 8E

Bats L Age 18	Year	Lev	Team	AB	R	H	HR	RBI	Avg	OB	Slg	OPS	bb%	ct%	Eye	SB	CS	x/h%	Iso	RC/G
2022 FA (CU)																				
Pwr ++																				
BAvg +++																				
Spd +++																				
Def ++	2022	Rk	DSL Padres	154	29	43	0	18	279	383	357	740	14	85	1.13	14	6	19	78	5.20

Pure-hitting INF who has yet to play in US, but has exciting upside. Barrel control and pitch recognition are very advanced for age and rarely chases pitches. Will need to add strength to hit for average pop. Swing mechanics are sound and clean and likes to hit to all fields. Defense will need time to develop, though he has plus arm strength.

Romero,Mikey — 46 — Boston

EXP MLB DEBUT: 2026 | H/W: 6-1 175 | FUT: Starting SS | 7C

Bats L Age 19	Year	Lev	Team	AB	R	H	HR	RBI	Avg	OB	Slg	OPS	bb%	ct%	Eye	SB	CS	x/h%	Iso	RC/G
2022 (1) HS (CA)																				
Pwr ++																				
BAvg +++																				
Spd +++	2022	Rk	FCL Red Sox	36	5	9	1	6	250	372	417	789	16	89	1.75	1	0	44	167	5.83
Def +++	2022	A	Salem	43	6	15	0	11	349	364	581	945	2	74	0.09	1	0	47	233	7.48

Smooth, quick INF with advanced skills for age. May not project to plus tools across board, but knows how to play game. Makes easy contact with bat speed and can catch up to any fastball. Could get to average power in time with swing adjustments. Has frame to add strength. Runs OK and has the hands and feet to be either 2B or SS.

Romo,Drew — 2 — Colorado

EXP MLB DEBUT: 2024 | H/W: 6-1 205 | FUT: Starting C | 8D

Bats B Age 21	Year	Lev	Team	AB	R	H	HR	RBI	Avg	OB	Slg	OPS	bb%	ct%	Eye	SB	CS	x/h%	Iso	RC/G
2020 (1) HS (CA)																				
Pwr ++																				
BAvg +++																				
Spd +	2021	A	Fresno	312	48	98	6	47	314	353	439	793	6	84	0.38	23	6	26	125	5.15
Def ++++	2022	A+	Spokane	374	52	95	5	58	254	318	372	690	9	78	0.43	18	3	31	118	4.09

Defensive backstop took a step back at the plate, posting a pedestrian .693 OPS at A+. Moves well with excellent blocking, receiving, and framing skills and a strong, accurate arm. Improved as a RHH with a contact-over-power approach that limits long-term power development. Defense will get him plenty of ABs once he reaches the majors.

Rosario,Eguy — 456 — San Diego

EXP MLB DEBUT: 2022 | H/W: 5-9 150 | FUT: Starting 2B | 7B

Bats R Age 23	Year	Lev	Team	AB	R	H	HR	RBI	Avg	OB	Slg	OPS	bb%	ct%	Eye	SB	CS	x/h%	Iso	RC/G
2015 FA (DR)	2018	AA	San Antonio	11	2	2	0	2	182	308	182	490	15	55	0.40	1	0	0	0	1.23
Pwr +++	2019	A+	Lake Elsinore	464	60	129	7	72	278	331	412	743	7	78	0.36	21	9	31	134	4.72
BAvg +++	2021	AA	San Antonio	420	65	118	12	61	281	356	455	811	10	74	0.45	30	14	39	174	5.77
Spd +++	2022	AAA	El Paso	490	98	141	22	81	288	364	508	872	11	78	0.54	21	8	43	220	6.44
Def +++	2022	MLB	San Diego	5	0	1	0	0	200	333	200	533	17	60	0.50	0	0	0	0	1.98

Short, strong INF who reached SD after doubling previous career high in HR. Uses short swing to make good contact, yet has patience to work count and reach via walk. Exhibits above average bat speed and can make hard contact for doubles or HR. Has quick wheels for SB, though not enough quickness or range to stick at SS.

Rucker,Jake — 35 — Minnesota

EXP MLB DEBUT: 2024 | H/W: 6-1 195 | FUT: Utility player | 6B

Bats R Age 23	Year	Lev	Team	AB	R	H	HR	RBI	Avg	OB	Slg	OPS	bb%	ct%	Eye	SB	CS	x/h%	Iso	RC/G
2021 (7) Tennessee	2021	NCAA	Tennessee	273	48	90	9	55	330	390	520	910	9	77	0.43	7	3	36	190	6.91
Pwr ++	2021	A	Fort Myers	68	10	18	0	10	265	359	324	683	13	76	0.63	2	1	17	59	4.24
BAvg ++	2022	A	Fort Myers	218	37	49	2	17	225	327	330	657	13	76	0.62	13	7	31	106	3.90
Spd ++	2022	A+	Cedar Rapids	206	29	54	6	35	262	333	447	780	10	75	0.42	5	5	44	184	5.32
Def +++	2022	AAA	St. Paul	26	3	3	1	3	115	179	231	409	7	62	0.20	1	0	33	115	-0.37

Versatile prospect who reached AAA in first full season. Overcame slow start and did OK on three levels. Gets on base with patient approach, but can be beaten with good FB. Power mostly doubles variety and will need to tap into bat speed and strength to reach seats. Plays all over infield and LF with average skills.

Ruiz,Esteury — 789 — Oakland

EXP MLB DEBUT: 2022 | H/W: 6-0 169 | FUT: Starting OF | 7C

Bats R Age 24	Year	Lev	Team	AB	R	H	HR	RBI	Avg	OB	Slg	OPS	bb%	ct%	Eye	SB	CS	x/h%	Iso	RC/G
2015 FA (DR)	2022	AA	San Antonio	180	54	62	9	37	344	443	611	1055	15	78	0.80	37	5	45	267	9.09
Pwr +++	2022	AAA	El Paso	111	30	35	4	9	315	420	477	897	15	77	0.80	23	4	29	162	7.02
BAvg +++	2022	AAA	Nashville	146	30	48	3	19	329	388	459	846	9	80	0.48	25	5	27	130	6.02
Spd ++++	2022	MLB	Milwaukee	8	2	0	0	0	0	111	0	111	11	75	0.50	0	0		0	-3.61
Def +++	2022	MLB	San Diego	27	1	6	0	2	222	222	333	556	0	81	0.00	1	2	33	111	2.15

Made ML debut and led minors in SB while finishing 3rd in BA in breakout campaign. Set highs in both HR and SB while seeing BA and OBP jump considerably. Offers impressive tools, including solid avg power. Terrific baserunner with above avg wheels. Can chase pitches. Could be better defensively. Will get opportunity to win starting OF job in OAK.

Ruiz,Jorge — 89 — Los Angeles (A)

EXP MLB DEBUT: 2026 | H/W: 5-10 164 | FUT: Starting OF | 7E

Bats L Age 18	Year	Lev	Team	AB	R	H	HR	RBI	Avg	OB	Slg	OPS	bb%	ct%	Eye	SB	CS	x/h%	Iso	RC/G
2021 FA (VZ)																				
Pwr ++																				
BAvg ++																				
Spd +++	2021	Rk	DSL Angels	174	32	47	1	14	270	352	362	714	11	86	0.88	19	6	26	92	4.67
Def +++	2022	Rk	ACL Angels	203	36	68	0	23	335	372	414	786	6	90	0.60	8	2	21	79	5.19

Shorter-statured, wiry and athletic LHH posted second consecutive solid season playing across the complex levels. Open stance with noise in the load, struggled with chasing pitches. Plus-plus hand/eye coordination. Posted less than 15% whiff rate despite hear 40% chase rate. Linear swing, does not get to lofted contact.

Rushing,Dalton — 2 — Los Angeles (N)

EXP MLB DEBUT: 2025 | H/W: 6-1 220 | FUT: Starting C | 8D

Bats L Age 22	Year	Lev	Team	AB	R	H	HR	RBI	Avg	OB	Slg	OPS	bb%	ct%	Eye	SB	CS	x/h%	Iso	RC/G
2022 (2) Louisville																				
Pwr +++																				
BAvg ++++	2022	NCAA	Louisville	226	68	70	23	62	310	435	686	1121	18	74	0.86	4	0	56	376	9.99
Spd ++	2022	Rk	ACL Dodgers	5	0	0	0	0	0	167	0	167	17	80	1.00	0	0		0	-2.27
Def ++	2022	A	Rancho Cuca	99	27	42	8	30	424	525	778	1303	18	79	1.00	1	0	45	354	12.28

Offensive-minded backstop might have had the best pro debut of anyone in the 2022 draft, posting a 1.262 OPS. A work-in-progress behind the plate, but shows solid instincts with a strong arm and nailed 31% of baserunners in pro debut. Quick bat speed, compact LH stroke, and advanced plate discipline give him the tools to hit for power and average.

Sabato,Aaron — 3 — Minnesota

EXP MLB DEBUT: 2023 | H/W: 6-2 230 | FUT: Starting 1B | 7E

Bats R Age 23	Year	Lev	Team	AB	R	H	HR	RBI	Avg	OB	Slg	OPS	bb%	ct%	Eye	SB	CS	x/h%	Iso	RC/G
2020 (1) North Carolina	2020	NCAA	North Carolina	65	20	19	7	18	292	471	708	1179	25	75	1.38	0	0	68	415	11.08
Pwr ++++	2021	A	Fort Myers	286	48	54	11	42	189	354	357	710	20	59	0.62	1	0	48	168	4.91
BAvg ++	2021	A+	Cedar Rapids	75	21	19	8	15	253	404	613	1018	20	57	0.59	0	0	58	360	10.03
Spd +	2022	A+	Cedar Rapids	288	50	65	17	57	226	338	448	786	15	61	0.44	2	1	46	222	5.85
Def ++	2022	AA	Wichita	84	13	15	5	18	179	266	405	671	11	63	0.32	2	0	60	226	3.82

Large-framed slugger who hasn't lived up to hype of 1st round pick. Draws walks and can crush balls, but swings and misses often and can be too patient. Can be pull-happy and victim to velocity. Has long struggled to hit for BA. Bat-only prospect who is limited to 1B with poor speed and feet. Focusing on using entire field.

Sabol,Blake — 27 — San Francisco

EXP MLB DEBUT: 2024 | H/W: 6-4 225 | FUT: Utility player | 7E

Bats L Age 25	Year	Lev	Team	AB	R	H	HR	RBI	Avg	OB	Slg	OPS	bb%	ct%	Eye	SB	CS	x/h%	Iso	RC/G
2019 (7) USC	2019	A-	West Virginia	208	26	51	2	22	245	351	351	702	14	71	0.56	5	4	27	106	4.56
Pwr +++	2021	A	Bradenton	46	11	17	2	12	370	500	543	1043	21	74	1.00	0	2	24	174	9.42
BAvg +++	2021	A+	Greensboro	199	39	59	11	33	296	381	553	933	12	64	0.38	6	0	44	256	8.09
Spd ++	2022	AA	Altoona	366	61	103	14	60	281	349	486	835	9	71	0.36	9	2	41	205	6.13
Def ++	2022	AAA	Indianapolis	81	13	24	5	15	296	418	543	962	17	73	0.77	1	0	38	247	8.03

Unheralded prospect who has unusual profile of switching between LF and catcher. Not known for great work behind plate, but is good leader and sufficient receiver. Set highs in 2B, HR and SB while finishing 4th in EL in both BA and OPS. Has plus raw power with keen understanding of strike zone. Limited arm strength holds him back.

Saggese,Thomas — 6 — Texas — EXP MLB DEBUT: 2024 — H/W: 5-11 175 — FUT: Reserve 2B — 7E

Bats R Age 20
2020 (5) HS (CA)

- Pwr ++
- BAvg +++
- Spd ++
- Def +

Year	Lev	Team	AB	R	H	HR	RBI	Avg	OB	Slg	OPS	bb%	ct%	Eye	SB	CS	x/h%	Iso	RC/G
2021	A	Down East	242	44	62	10	37	256	366	463	829	15	65	0.49	11	3	44	207	6.52
2022	A+	Hickory	380	56	117	14	61	308	357	487	844	7	75	0.31	11	3	32	179	5.92
2022	AA	Frisco	21	5	8	1	9	381	409	857	1266	5	86	0.33	1	0	75	476	10.87

Stat line looks like someone who becomes a major leaguer; all he's done is produce. Solid hit with surprising pop and usable speed, but lack of dependable defensive home creates questions. Arm enough for left side but fielding sub-par. Clutch hitter who got better as the year waned. Aggressive in zone but has not hurt yet; solid splits.

Salas,Jose — 456 — Miami — EXP MLB DEBUT: 2024 — H/W: 6-2 191 — FUT: Starting 3B — 8D

Bats B Age 19
2019 FA (VZ)

- Pwr +++
- BAvg +++
- Spd +++
- Def +++

Year	Lev	Team	AB	R	H	HR	RBI	Avg	OB	Slg	OPS	bb%	ct%	Eye	SB	CS	x/h%	Iso	RC/G
2021	Rk	FCL Marlins	92	14	34	1	11	370	437	511	948	11	75	0.48	8	5	32	141	7.71
2021	A	Jupiter	108	12	27	1	8	250	319	315	634	9	74	0.39	6	0	19	65	3.33
2022	A	Jupiter	221	40	59	5	24	267	336	421	757	9	76	0.43	15	1	36	154	5.00
2022	A+	Beloit	191	29	44	4	17	230	303	340	644	9	79	0.49	18	0	27	110	3.47

Switch-hitting IF struggled with discipline across multiple levels in 2022. LH stance is open and upright with minimal trigger. Above-average swing speed, utilizing lower half more, getting to harder contact. RH stance is similar with a bat wrap. It's not as clean of swing plane. Above-average power potential in frame and LH swing. Likely 3B.

Sanchez,Yolbert — 456 — Chicago (A) — EXP MLB DEBUT: 2023 — H/W: 5-11 176 — FUT: Reserve IF — 6C

Bats R Age 25
2019 FA (CU)

- Pwr +
- BAvg +++
- Spd ++
- Def +++

Year	Lev	Team	AB	R	H	HR	RBI	Avg	OB	Slg	OPS	bb%	ct%	Eye	SB	CS	x/h%	Iso	RC/G
2019		Did not play - Injury																	
2021	A+	Salem	217	28	62	5	29	286	340	387	728	8	85	0.55	2	1	19	101	4.45
2021	AA	Birmingham	143	15	49	4	13	343	365	469	833	3	89	0.31	3	0	20	126	5.38
2022	AA	Birmingham	51	7	18	0	6	353	484	373	857	20	86	1.86	0	0	6	20	6.95
2022	AAA	Charlotte	443	44	124	3	40	280	321	341	662	6	84	0.38	11	9	16	61	3.62

Light-hitting MIF moved closer to MLB debut. Contact, up-the-middle approach. It's a linear swing plane with some length, resulting in lots of groundball contact. Doesn't game plan ABs well and can get beat chasing breaking pitches down and away. Power virtually non-existent. A solid defender at either 2B or SS despite below average speed.

Santana,Cristian — 645 — Detroit — EXP MLB DEBUT: 2025 — H/W: 6-0 165 — FUT: Starting 2B — 8D

Bats R Age 19
2021 FA (DR)

- Pwr +++
- BAvg +++
- Spd +++
- Def +++

Year	Lev	Team	AB	R	H	HR	RBI	Avg	OB	Slg	OPS	bb%	ct%	Eye	SB	CS	x/h%	Iso	RC/G
2021	Rk	DSL Tigers	171	40	46	9	27	269	378	520	899	15	73	0.65	12	7	50	251	7.11
2022	Rk	FCL Tigers East	5	3	1	1	2	200	556	800	1356	44	40	1.33	0	1	100	600	20.47
2022	A	Lakeland	265	52	57	9	30	215	348	366	714	17	67	0.61	10	5	39	151	4.70

Stateside debut was mostly a bust. Quick bat speed with a compact stroke give him the potential to be an above-average hitter with power, but is currently undermined by poor pitch recognition against breaking balls down in the zone. Moves well on defense with good hands and a strong arm, but lack of first step quickness could push him to 2B.

Sasaki,Shane — 789 — Tampa Bay — EXP MLB DEBUT: 2025 — H/W: 6-0 165 — FUT: Starting OF — 7E

Bats R Age 22
2019 (3) HS (HI)

- Pwr ++
- BAvg +++
- Spd +++
- Def +++

Year	Lev	Team	AB	R	H	HR	RBI	Avg	OB	Slg	OPS	bb%	ct%	Eye	SB	CS	x/h%	Iso	RC/G
2021	Rk	FCL Rays	124	33	36	2	16	290	380	403	784	13	70	0.49	22	2	22	113	5.63
2022	A	Charleston	346	71	112	9	57	324	408	497	905	12	73	0.53	47	4	35	173	7.21

Athletic OF prospect put up surprising slash line at Low-A. Wiry frame with room to grow. Upright stance with direct path to hit position with hands in load. High BA mostly product of singles approach. Struggled with spin at times and bigger velocity. Below-average power in frame. Above-average runner. Likely best as 4th OF.

Schmitt,Casey — 5 — San Francisco — EXP MLB DEBUT: 2023 — H/W: 6-2 215 — FUT: Starting 3B — 7B

Bats R Age 24
2020 (2) San Diego St

- Pwr +++
- BAvg +++
- Spd +
- Def ++++

Year	Lev	Team	AB	R	H	HR	RBI	Avg	OB	Slg	OPS	bb%	ct%	Eye	SB	CS	x/h%	Iso	RC/G
2020	NCAA	San Diego St	62	6	20	0	9	323	391	452	843	10	79	0.54	1	1	30	129	6.27
2021	A	San Jose	251	36	62	8	29	247	308	406	714	8	82	0.50	2	2	37	159	4.31
2022	A+	Eugene	333	58	91	17	59	273	355	474	829	11	74	0.49	1	2	35	201	5.88
2022	AA	Richmond	120	13	41	3	16	342	373	517	890	5	76	0.21	2	0	34	175	6.47
2022	AAA	Sacramento	15	1	5	1	3	333	333	600	933	0	67	0.00	0	0	40	267	7.17

Underrated INF who finished 2nd in NWL in OPS and SLG in surprise campaign. Added to offensive skills by using entire field and using strength and bat speed to generate power. Plus defense continues to impress and has some time at SS. Doesn't run well, but just enough to leg out doubles. Has developed better hand-eye coordination.

Schobel,Tanner — 4 — Minnesota — EXP MLB DEBUT: 2025 — H/W: 5-10 170 — FUT: Starting 2B — 7D

Bats R Age 21
2022 (2) Virginia Tech

- Pwr ++
- BAvg +++
- Spd +++
- Def +++

Year	Lev	Team	AB	R	H	HR	RBI	Avg	OB	Slg	OPS	bb%	ct%	Eye	SB	CS	x/h%	Iso	RC/G
2022	NCAA	Virginia Tech	235	68	85	19	74	362	444	689	1134	13	83	0.88	7	1	45	328	9.52
2022	Rk	FCL Twins	15	3	3	0	1	200	250	267	517	6	80	0.33	1	0	33	67	1.88
2022	A	Fort Myers	99	11	24	1	10	242	359	303	662	15	77	0.78	6	1	17	61	4.00

Fundamentally-sound INF with limited size, but polished baseball IQ. Puts bat to ball easily and is solid situational hitter who uses all fields. Brings mature approach to plate and gets on base consistently. Offers average power at best, though will be more hit over pop. Likely to stick at 2B where average range and arm work best.

Schuemann,Max — 48 — Oakland — EXP MLB DEBUT: 2023 — H/W: 6-1 186 — FUT: Utility player — 6B

Bats R Age 25
2018 (20) E Michigan

- Pwr ++
- BAvg ++
- Spd +++
- Def ++

Year	Lev	Team	AB	R	H	HR	RBI	Avg	OB	Slg	OPS	bb%	ct%	Eye	SB	CS	x/h%	Iso	RC/G
2021	A+	Lansing	201	43	45	5	20	224	310	363	673	11	75	0.50	34	2	38	139	3.91
2021	AA	Midland	219	38	70	2	21	320	384	416	800	10	79	0.50	17	3	23	96	5.54
2021	AAA	Las Vegas	26	2	6	0	1	231	355	346	701	16	73	0.71	1	0	33	115	4.73
2022	AA	Midland	290	62	84	8	39	290	394	438	832	15	71	0.60	23	5	29	148	6.33
2022	AAA	Las Vegas	35	5	5	1	2	143	268	286	554	15	54	0.38	1	1	60	143	2.35

Instinctual prospect who hit under .200 over last 3 months of season. Set career high in HR, but game is all about OBP and using simple stroke to get on base. Could make more consistent contact with slight swing adjustment. Power more of the gap variety, but can jerk ball out. Plays 2B and OF and likely to play all over.

Schunk,Aaron — 54 — Colorado — EXP MLB DEBUT: 2024 — H/W: 6-2 205 — FUT: Reserve 3B — 6C

Bats R Age 25
2019 (2) Georgia

- Pwr ++
- BAvg ++
- Spd ++
- Def +++

Year	Lev	Team	AB	R	H	HR	RBI	Avg	OB	Slg	OPS	bb%	ct%	Eye	SB	CS	x/h%	Iso	RC/G
2019	NCAA	Georgia	230	49	78	15	58	339	377	604	981	6	87	0.48	3	1	37	265	7.14
2019	A-	Boise	173	31	53	6	23	306	358	503	861	7	86	0.56	4	1	38	197	6.05
2021	A+	Spokane	358	57	80	8	45	223	274	346	621	7	69	0.23	13	5	30	123	3.02
2022	AA	Hartford	450	62	116	14	77	258	313	427	739	7	74	0.31	6	2	41	169	4.62

Strong, athletic OF has above-average raw power, but has been slow to develop. Good bat speed, but struggles to make contact, both in and out of the zone, especially against better velo. Makes hard contact when he finds the barrel, but lacks natural loft needed for HR power. Moves well at 3B with a strong arm.

Sequera,Manuel — 645 — Detroit — EXP MLB DEBUT: 2025 — H/W: 6-1 170 — FUT: Starting 3B — 7D

Bats R Age 20
2019 FA (VZ)

- Pwr +++
- BAvg ++
- Spd +++
- Def ++

Year	Lev	Team	AB	R	H	HR	RBI	Avg	OB	Slg	OPS	bb%	ct%	Eye	SB	CS	x/h%	Iso	RC/G
2021	Rk	FCL Tigers East	171	31	42	11	40	246	306	509	815	8	67	0.26	1	1	55	263	5.83
2022	A	Lakeland	457	59	106	19	64	232	264	422	686	4	76	0.18	4	5	45	190	3.70

Athletic SS has some exciting tools if he can refine his approach at the plate. Can be overly aggressive as he hunts for pitches he can crush to the pull side. Lots of swing-and-miss without drawing many walks raises concerns about whether he will ever hit for enough average. Fringe defender at short and will move to 3B as he fills out and moves up.

Shenton,Austin — 35 — Tampa Bay — EXP MLB DEBUT: 2024 — H/W: 6-0 205 — FUT: Starting 3B — 7D

Bats L Age 25
2019 (5) Fla Intl

- Pwr +++
- BAvg ++
- Spd ++
- Def +++

Year	Lev	Team	AB	R	H	HR	RBI	Avg	OB	Slg	OPS	bb%	ct%	Eye	SB	CS	x/h%	Iso	RC/G
2019	A	West Virginia	119	13	30	5	20	252	315	454	769	8	76	0.38	0	0	43	202	5.01
2021	A+	Everett	224	55	66	11	53	295	404	576	980	15	72	0.66	1	0	58	281	8.40
2021	AA	Arkansas	43	6	14	1	8	326	383	512	895	9	77	0.40	0	0	43	186	6.77
2021	AA	Montgomery	48	5	13	2	9	271	300	458	758	4	69	0.13	0	0	38	188	4.81
2022	AA	Montgomery	195	28	46	8	29	236	332	415	747	13	64	0.40	0	0	39	179	5.16

Strong-bodied CIF struggled with hip injury during 2022 season. Open, upright stance with lots pre-swing movement. Struggled getting bat started, contributing to high in zone whiff rate. Above-average bat speed, gets to hard contact when he connects. Nearly 50% of batted balls were hit hard. Plus raw power, plays above-average to pull field.

Shewmake,Braden — 46 — Atlanta

EXP MLB DEBUT: 2023 | H/W: 6-4 190 | FUT: Utility player | 7C

Bats L Age 25	Year	Lev	Team	AB	R	H	HR	RBI	Avg	OB	Slg	OPS	bb%	ct%	Eye	SB	CS	x/h%	Iso	RC/G
2019 (1) Texas A&M	2019	NCAA	Texas A&M	249	45	78	6	47	313	376	474	850	9	89	0.93	9	3	31	161	6.08
Pwr ++	2019	A	Rome	201	37	64	3	39	318	383	473	856	9	86	0.72	11	3	36	154	6.23
BAvg +++	2019	AA	Mississippi	46	7	10	0	1	217	280	217	497	8	76	0.36	2	0	0	0	1.47
Spd +++	2021	AA	Mississippi	324	40	74	12	40	228	267	401	668	5	77	0.23	4	2	39	173	3.51
Def +++	2022	AAA	Gwinnett	278	37	72	7	25	259	316	399	715	8	79	0.40	9	0	32	140	4.30

Tall, lean former 1st round pick continues to struggle with offensive output in upper minors. Open stance, improved balance and leverage in lower half. Slight bat wrap. Approach got better, chasing less and getting to hard contact more often including pull-side power. Linear swing plane depresses above-average power in frame. Solid defensive SS.

Siani,Michael — 8 — Cincinnati

EXP MLB DEBUT: 2022 | H/W: 6-1 188 | FUT: Reserve OF | 6C

Bats L Age 23	Year	Lev	Team	AB	R	H	HR	RBI	Avg	OB	Slg	OPS	bb%	ct%	Eye	SB	CS	x/h%	Iso	RC/G
2018 (4) HS (PA)	2019	A	Dayton	466	75	118	6	39	253	320	339	659	9	77	0.42	45	15	19	86	3.66
Pwr ++	2021	A+	Dayton	352	60	76	6	26	216	313	327	640	12	71	0.49	30	10	30	111	3.54
BAvg ++	2022	AA	Chattanooga	456	76	115	12	49	252	344	404	748	12	80	0.71	49	12	33	151	4.98
Spd ++++	2022	AAA	Louisville	36	6	9	2	6	250	270	417	687	3	86	0.20	3	0	22	167	3.52
Def ++++	2022	MLB	Cincinnati	24	1	4	0	0	167	167	167	333	0	71	0.00	0	1	0	0	-1.22

Streaky, athletic LHH OF had best season with bat as pro, earning late MLB callup. Wiry frame, maxed out with strength. Contact-oriented bat, struggles getting to consistent hard contact, especially in the air. Best when working all fields with dunks and powering up to below-average pull power. Double-plus runner who is a 70-grade defender in CF.

Simon,Ronny — 45 — Tampa Bay

EXP MLB DEBUT: 2023 | H/W: 5-9 150 | FUT: Utility player | 7D

Bats B Age 22	Year	Lev	Team	AB	R	H	HR	RBI	Avg	OB	Slg	OPS	bb%	ct%	Eye	SB	CS	x/h%	Iso	RC/G
2018 FA (DR)																				
Pwr ++	2021	A	Visalia	301	44	75	15	52	249	343	475	818	13	73	0.53	13	3	47	226	5.87
BAvg +++	2021	A+	Hillsboro	82	8	19	2	11	232	259	378	637	4	76	0.15	6	1	42	146	3.11
Spd ++++	2022	A+	Bowling Green	290	57	74	15	51	255	296	469	765	6	74	0.23	22	6	39	214	4.76
Def +++	2022	AA	Montgomery	144	25	39	7	25	271	323	500	823	7	83	0.44	12	2	44	229	5.52

Short-statured, athletic switch-hitting slasher stood out in AFL stint. Maxed-out frame. Upright stance from both sides of the plate. Utilizes opposite field well in approach and will turn on inside pitch with surprising below average-power. Hacker; hasn't seen a ball he can't hit. Plus runner with solid versatility defensive.

Simpson,Chandler — 78 — Tampa Bay

EXP MLB DEBUT: 2025 | H/W: 6-2 170 | FUT: Starting OF | 8E

Bats L Age 22	Year	Lev	Team	AB	R	H	HR	RBI	Avg	OB	Slg	OPS	bb%	ct%	Eye	SB	CS	x/h%	Iso	RC/G
2022 (2) Georgia Tech																				
Pwr +																				
BAvg ++++																				
Spd +++++	2022	NCAA	Georgia Tech	203	64	88	1	25	433	509	517	1026	13	92	1.94	27	4	14	84	8.41
Def +++	2022	Rk	FCL Rays	27	5	10	0	3	370	485	481	966	18	85	1.50	8	0	30	111	8.23

Long, lean high-waisted MIFer with a wide base stance with no trigger, relies on contact over hard hit. Limited whiffs in profile. Patient approach, works counts. Slasher who uses all fields. No power in swing or frame. Exceptional foot speed makes for high SB output. Candidate to move to CF.

Smith-Njigba,Canaan — 79 — Pittsburgh

EXP MLB DEBUT: 2022 | H/W: 6-0 230 | FUT: Starting OF | 7D

Bats L Age 23	Year	Lev	Team	AB	R	H	HR	RBI	Avg	OB	Slg	OPS	bb%	ct%	Eye	SB	CS	x/h%	Iso	RC/G
2017 (4) HS (TX)	2019	A	Charleston (Sc)	449	67	138	11	74	307	405	465	871	14	76	0.69	16	4	33	158	6.75
Pwr +++	2021	AA	Altoona	219	35	60	6	40	274	398	406	804	17	70	0.68	13	1	28	132	6.04
BAvg ++	2021	AAA	Indianapolis	21	1	2	0	2	95	174	95	269	9	57	0.22	0	0	0	0	-2.66
Spd ++	2022	AAA	Indianapolis	184	31	51	1	19	277	387	408	795	15	72	0.63	8	3	37	130	6.00
Def ++	2022	MLB	Pittsburgh	5	1	1	0	0	200	333	400	733	17	100		0	0	100	200	5.88

Made MLB debut, but season ended early due to fractured wrist. Has very strong frame and excellent bat speed to product loud contact to all fields. Power hasn't yet emerged, though potential is very evident. Hits ball on ground too much. Not blessed with secondary skills. Runs OK, but has sub-par OF with poor routes.

Soderstrom,Tyler — 23 — Oakland

EXP MLB DEBUT: 2023 | H/W: 6-2 200 | FUT: Starting C | 9D

Bats L Age 21	Year	Lev	Team	AB	R	H	HR	RBI	Avg	OB	Slg	OPS	bb%	ct%	Eye	SB	CS	x/h%	Iso	RC/G
2020 (1) HS (CA)																				
Pwr ++++	2021	A	Stockton	222	39	68	12	49	306	382	568	949	11	73	0.44	2	1	49	261	7.65
BAvg +++	2022	A+	Lansing	335	47	87	20	71	260	319	513	832	8	70	0.29	0	0	48	254	5.91
Spd ++	2022	AA	Midland	133	17	37	8	28	278	329	496	825	7	75	0.30	0	1	30	218	5.52
Def ++	2022	AAA	Las Vegas	37	2	11	1	6	297	316	405	721	3	65	0.08	0	0	18	108	4.36

Premium hitter who performed on 3 levels and led OAK prospects in HR despite slow start. Picturesque swing brings ability to hit for BA and power. Hits for pop to all fields and discerning eye enhances batting ability. Needs to improve against LHP. Doesn't run well and has room to grow behind plate. Possesses strong arm, but could move to 1B full time.

Sosa,Lenyn — 456 — Chicago (A)

EXP MLB DEBUT: 2022 | H/W: 6-0 180 | FUT: Starting 2B | 7C

Bats R Age 23	Year	Lev	Team	AB	R	H	HR	RBI	Avg	OB	Slg	OPS	bb%	ct%	Eye	SB	CS	x/h%	Iso	RC/G
2016 FA (VZ)	2021	A+	Salem	334	45	97	10	49	290	319	443	762	4	77	0.18	3	4	31	153	4.67
Pwr +++	2021	AA	Birmingham	117	10	25	1	7	214	227	282	509	2	76	0.07	0	1	24	68	1.37
BAvg +++	2022	AA	Birmingham	257	47	85	14	48	331	381	549	930	8	84	0.53	0	0	31	218	6.73
Spd ++	2022	AAA	Charlotte	226	30	67	9	31	296	348	469	817	7	81	0.42	3	4	31	173	5.46
Def +++	2022	MLB	Chicago (A)	35	3	4	1	1	114	139	229	367	3	66	0.08	0	0	50	114	-0.86

Streaky MIF prospect had exceptional year hurting high minors pitching, earning a MLB callup. Slight open stance with simple load. Drives hands through zone with solid leverage and an uppercut swing trajectory. Added some plate discipline but still aggressive. Above-average raw power plays mostly to pull side gap. Solid defender, best at 2B or 3B.

Soto,Livan — 456 — Los Angeles (A)

EXP MLB DEBUT: 2022 | H/W: 6-0 160 | FUT: Reserve IF | 6B

Bats L Age 22	Year	Lev	Team	AB	R	H	HR	RBI	Avg	OB	Slg	OPS	bb%	ct%	Eye	SB	CS	x/h%	Iso	RC/G
2016 FA (VZ)	2019	A	Burlington	245	24	54	1	20	220	310	253	564	12	84	0.80	6	2	11	33	2.76
Pwr +	2021	A+	Tri-City	360	49	78	7	36	217	293	358	652	10	73	0.39	14	5	37	142	3.63
BAvg +++	2021	AA	Rocket City	40	3	9	0	4	225	279	250	529	7	73	0.27	0	0	11	25	1.80
Spd +++	2022	AA	Rocket City	456	69	128	6	57	281	378	362	739	13	78	0.70	18	8	19	81	4.94
Def ++++	2022	MLB	LA Angels	55	9	22	1	9	400	421	582	1003	4	76	0.15	1	1	32	182	7.88

Light-hitting, defensively skilled MIF prospect parlayed best offensive season into MLB callup. Upright stance. Plus hand/eye coordination allows for plus contact rates. Low chase rate. Has lift in swing but doesn't get to hard contact often enough. It's light power projection, 6 to 10 HR in fulltime role. Slick fielder at 2B/SS. Average runner.

Soularie,Alerick — 47 — Minnesota

EXP MLB DEBUT: 2024 | H/W: 6-0 175 | FUT: Utility player | 6C

Bats R Age 23	Year	Lev	Team	AB	R	H	HR	RBI	Avg	OB	Slg	OPS	bb%	ct%	Eye	SB	CS	x/h%	Iso	RC/G
2020 (2) Tennessee																				
Pwr ++	2020	NCAA	Tennessee	60	16	16	5	17	267	389	533	922	17	87	1.50	2	0	38	267	7.04
BAvg ++	2021	Rk	FCL Twins	20	3	7	1	3	350	458	550	1008	17	70	0.67	0	0	29	200	8.90
Spd +++	2021	A	Fort Myers	105	21	23	2	12	219	339	324	663	15	70	0.61	9	1	26	105	3.93
Def ++	2022	A+	Cedar Rapids	330	68	75	10	39	227	325	382	707	13	68	0.45	18	5	37	155	4.50

Versatile prospect who got off to very slow start. Focuses on leveraging athleticism and solid speed to make impact. Swing mechanics are a bit crude, but can make acceptable contact and exhibit average raw power. Can play any OF position as well as 2B, though master at none. Stands out for quick-twitch movements.

Specht,Tommy — 8 — Texas

EXP MLB DEBUT: 2026 | H/W: 6-3 200 | FUT: Starting OF | 7E

Bats L Age 18	Year	Lev	Team	AB	R	H	HR	RBI	Avg	OB	Slg	OPS	bb%	ct%	Eye	SB	CS	x/h%	Iso	RC/G
2022 (6) HS (IA)																				
Pwr +++																				
BAvg +																				
Spd ++																				
Def +++	2022	Rk	ACL Rangers	10	2	2	0	0	200	333	300	633	17	40	0.33	0	0	50	100	5.92

Another tooled-up '22 draftee, he stands out for power projection and 4th OF defensive floor. Plus bat speed helps mitigate long levers and swing somewhat but development all about the hit tool as everything else here is average or better. Will be a very long stew with considerable upside but ton of risk as he's real windy with the stick.

Spikes,Ryan — 46 — Tampa Bay

EXP MLB DEBUT: 2025 | H/W: 5-9 185 | FUT: Reserve IF | 6C

Bats R Age 20	Year	Lev	Team	AB	R	H	HR	RBI	Avg	OB	Slg	OPS	bb%	ct%	Eye	SB	CS	x/h%	Iso	RC/G
2021 (3) HS (GA)																				
Pwr ++																				
BAvg ++																				
Spd ++++	2021	Rk	FCL Rays	40	9	10	1	5	250	348	400	748	13	68	0.46	4	1	40	150	5.18
Def +++	2022	A	Charleston	290	50	66	10	33	228	291	390	681	8	64	0.25	17	5	36	162	4.05

Short-statured, athletic MIF prospect struggled with swing-and-miss during full-season debut. Open, upright stance. Has developed a bat wrap, causing slower reactions with bat. Average bat speed with slight uppercut trajectory. Struggles pulling hard stuff and chases spin. Uber-aggressive approach. Limited range at SS, fits best at 2B. Plus runner.

teer,Spencer | 456 | Cincinnati | EXP MLB DEBUT: 2022 | H/W: 5-11 185 | FUT: Utility player | 7B

Bats R Age 25
2019 (3) Oregon
Pwr +++
BAvg +++
Spd +++
Def +++

Year	Lev	Team	AB	R	H	HR	RBI	Avg	OB	Slg	OPS	bb%	ct%	Eye	SB	CS	x/h%	Iso	RC/G
2021	AA	Wichita	249	45	60	14	42	241	297	470	767	7	71	0.27	4	0	45	229	4.95
2022	AA	Wichita	137	27	42	8	30	307	371	591	962	9	83	0.61	1	3	52	285	7.33
2022	AAA	Louisville	92	14	27	3	13	293	356	467	824	9	75	0.39	1	0	37	174	5.80
2022	AAA	St. Paul	198	39	48	12	32	242	336	485	821	12	78	0.65	2	0	48	242	5.74
2022	MLB	Cincinnati	95	12	20	2	8	211	292	326	619	10	73	0.42	0	1	35	116	3.13

UT prospect made swing adjustments over last off-season and posted career numbers, earning his MLB callup. Upright, slightly open stance. Has added uppercut trajectory to swing without compromising approach or contact, increasing bat speed and launch angles. Average tools across the board play up due to headiness. Came over from MIN mid-season.

tewart,Sal | 5 | Cincinnati | EXP MLB DEBUT: 2026 | H/W: 6-3 215 | FUT: Starting 3B | 8E

Bats R Age 19
2022 (1) HS (FL)
Pwr +++
BAvg +++
Spd ++
Def +++

Year	Lev	Team	AB	R	H	HR	RBI	Avg	OB	Slg	OPS	bb%	ct%	Eye	SB	CS	x/h%	Iso	RC/G
2022	Rk	ACL Reds	24	5	7	0	5	292	393	458	851	14	79	0.80	0	0	57	167	6.68

Powerful prep prospect made pro debut after successful senior season in high school. Open, upright stance with smooth load. It's a linear swing plane with contact skills. Size and frame suggest power to come. Likely power-over-hit at maturity. A slow runner. Has good reactions, solid footwork and an above-average arm to stay at 3B.

trumpf,Chase | 45 | Chicago (N) | EXP MLB DEBUT: 2023 | H/W: 6-1 170 | FUT: Utility player | 6C

Bats R Age 25
2019 (2) UCLA
Pwr +++
BAvg +
Spd ++
Def ++

Year	Lev	Team	AB	R	H	HR	RBI	Avg	OB	Slg	OPS	bb%	ct%	Eye	SB	CS	x/h%	Iso	RC/G
2019	A-	Eugene	89	17	26	2	14	292	394	449	844	14	69	0.54	2	0	38	157	6.66
2019	A	South Bend	24	3	3	1	2	125	160	292	452	4	71	0.14	0	0	67	167	0.49
2021	A+	South Bend	55	15	17	0	7	309	387	382	769	11	69	0.41	3	1	24	73	5.49
2021	AA	Tennessee	213	25	45	7	29	211	331	380	711	15	69	0.58	1	0	49	169	4.60
2022	AA	Tennessee	393	73	92	21	57	234	354	461	815	16	59	0.45	2	2	49	226	6.64

2nd rounder has yet to click as a pro. Thin wiry frame and average bat speed raised concerns about power upside. Launched a career-high in HR, but sold out for power and whiffed at 33% clip and not likely to hit for average and power. Solid glove on defense, but lack of range and below-average arm limit him to 2B. Looking more and more like a UT.

ugastey,Adrian | 2 | San Francisco | EXP MLB DEBUT: 2025 | H/W: 6-1 170 | FUT: Starting C | 7E

Bats R Age 20
2019 FA (PN)
Pwr ++
BAvg +++
Spd +
Def +++

Year	Lev	Team	AB	R	H	HR	RBI	Avg	OB	Slg	OPS	bb%	ct%	Eye	SB	CS	x/h%	Iso	RC/G
2021	Rk	ACL Giants O	148	23	53	2	25	358	406	439	845	8	82	0.46	1	0	15	81	5.87
2022	Rk	ACL Giants O	26	4	6	0	2	231	333	346	679	13	81	0.80	0	0	33	115	4.37
2022	A	San Jose	300	41	72	5	32	240	309	333	642	9	82	0.57	1	0	24	93	3.52

Agile, athletic C who has upside. Owns double-plus arm strength, but needs work on release and accuracy. Frames well and is adequate receiver, though blocking needs attention. Uses short, compact stroke to make easy contact and is more of a line drive hitter. Needs more strength to realize average power potential.

usac,Daniel | 2 | Oakland | EXP MLB DEBUT: 2025 | H/W: 6-4 218 | FUT: Starting C | 8D

Bats R Age 21
2022 (1) Arizona
Pwr ++++
BAvg +++
Spd +
Def ++

Year	Lev	Team	AB	R	H	HR	RBI	Avg	OB	Slg	OPS	bb%	ct%	Eye	SB	CS	x/h%	Iso	RC/G
2022	NCAA	Arizona	273	50	100	12	61	366	416	582	998	8	81	0.44	0	0	33	216	7.73
2022	Rk	ACL Athletics	6	1	3	0	2	500	500	667	1167	0	100		0	0	33	167	8.73
2022	A	Stockton	98	14	28	1	13	286	333	388	721	7	74	0.28	0	0	29	102	4.42

Tall, strong backstop who has impact with both bat and glove. Owns plus arm strength and enough agility to stick at catcher. Receiving needs attention. Hits ball hard to all fields and has no trouble with premium velocity. Lot of natural power in leveraged stroke and has batting eye to hit for moderate BA. Needs to tone down chasing out of zone.

waggerty,Travis | 789 | Pittsburgh | EXP MLB DEBUT: 2022 | H/W: 5-11 200 | FUT: Starting OF | 7C

Bats L Age 25
2018 (1) So Alabama
Pwr ++
BAvg +++
Spd ++++
Def ++++

Year	Lev	Team	AB	R	H	HR	RBI	Avg	OB	Slg	OPS	bb%	ct%	Eye	SB	CS	x/h%	Iso	RC/G
2018	A	West Virginia	62	6	8	1	5	129	217	226	443	10	71	0.39	0	0	38	97	0.66
2019	A+	Bradenton	457	79	121	9	40	265	346	381	727	11	75	0.49	23	8	26	116	4.65
2021	AAA	Indianapolis	41	6	9	3	7	220	319	439	758	13	80	0.75	3	0	33	220	4.80
2022	AAA	Indianapolis	398	55	101	9	55	254	347	399	747	13	71	0.49	20	5	32	146	5.07
2022	MLB	Pittsburgh	9	0	1	0	0	111	111	111	222	0	56	0.00	0	0	0	0	-3.48

Speedy OF who returned after shoulder surgery in 2021. Matched career high in HR and can differentiate between balls and strikes. However, more about speed and defense than anything else. Can chase breaking balls out of zone and swings and misses too often. Plays all OF positions and has arm and instincts to be asset.

weeney,Trey | 6 | New York (A) | EXP MLB DEBUT: 2024 | H/W: 6-4 200 | FUT: Starting 3B | 8D

Bats L Age 22
2021 (1) Eastern Illinois
Pwr +++
BAvg +++
Spd +++
Def +++

Year	Lev	Team	AB	R	H	HR	RBI	Avg	OB	Slg	OPS	bb%	ct%	Eye	SB	CS	x/h%	Iso	RC/G
2021	NCAA	Eastern Illinois	170	52	65	14	58	382	514	712	1226	21	86	1.92	3	2	40	329	11.12
2021	Rk	FCL Yankees	5	4	3	1	1	600	778	###	1978	44	60	2.00	1	0	33	600	27.61
2021	A	Tampa	110	26	27	6	13	245	352	518	870	14	74	0.62	3	1	52	273	6.67
2022	A+	Hudson Valley	390	70	94	14	51	241	341	415	756	13	72	0.55	29	2	38	174	5.11
2022	AA	Somerset	43	6	10	2	5	233	340	395	735	14	77	0.70	2	1	30	163	4.71

Tall, lean LHH struggled with hit tool split between High-A and Double-A. Upright, open stance. Has developed a bat wrap in load, slowing reactions. Hard contact rate took a hit. Above-average swing speed. Does well to incorporate lower half in swing. Solid uppercut swing trajectory. Has average power potential. Maxed out at SS, arm plays at 3B.

anner,Logan | 2 | Cincinnati | EXP MLB DEBUT: 2025 | H/W: 6-0 215 | FUT: Starting C | 7E

Bats R Age 22
2022 (2) Mississippi St
Pwr +++
BAvg ++
Spd +
Def ++++

Year	Lev	Team	AB	R	H	HR	RBI	Avg	OB	Slg	OPS	bb%	ct%	Eye	SB	CS	x/h%	Iso	RC/G
2022	NCAA	Mississippi St	207	36	59	7	38	285	381	425	806	13	78	0.71	0	0	25	140	5.69
2022	Rk	ACL Reds	3	0	0	0	0	0	0	0	0	0	33	0.00	0	0		0	-9.58
2022	A	Daytona	57	9	12	1	7	211	348	316	664	17	65	0.60	1	0	33	105	4.07

Defensively skilled RHH has solid, catchers frame with plus agility and a double-plus arm. Power over hit approach. Upright, open swing with a small hitch in load. Discerning eye with all-fields approach. Swing has length, thus the high whiff rate. Power mostly to pull side. Average power projection if hit allows. Base clogger.

avarez,Ambioris | 6 | Atlanta | EXP MLB DEBUT: 2026 | H/W: 6-0 168 | FUT: Starting 3B | 7E

Bats R Age 19
2021 FA (DR)
Pwr ++++
BAvg ++
Spd +++
Def +++

Year	Lev	Team	AB	R	H	HR	RBI	Avg	OB	Slg	OPS	bb%	ct%	Eye	SB	CS	x/h%	Iso	RC/G
2022	Rk	FCL Braves	65	12	18	1	8	277	309	385	693	4	57	0.11	3	1	28	108	4.70

Twitchy, athletic SS prospect made professional debut in Florida Complex League. Upright, slight open stance with short trigger and big leg lift. Power driven swing. Power over hit profile with raw plus power. Swing is work-in-progress, needs to be less mechanical. Struggles with strike zone recognition. Average runner with big arm. Likely 3B.

avera,Braylin | 8 | Baltimore | EXP MLB DEBUT: 2027 | H/W: 6-2 175 | FUT: Starting CF | 8E

Bats R Age 18
2022 FA (DR)
Pwr ++
BAvg +++
Spd +++
Def +++

Year	Lev	Team	AB	R	H	HR	RBI	Avg	OB	Slg	OPS	bb%	ct%	Eye	SB	CS	x/h%	Iso	RC/G
2022	Rk	DSL Orioles 2	144	24	35	2	14	243	394	319	714	20	67	0.77	7	4	20	76	4.90

Club's top int'l sign in 2022, he exhibited better than average pitch selection skills even if his quality of contact could improve. With a solid, simple swing presently and a lanky frame to dream on, the power could well come as he gets more physical. Runs well, projects to stay in CF with an average arm. Likely to make stateside debut in 2023.

aylor,Samad | 47 | Kansas City | EXP MLB DEBUT: 2023 | H/W: 5-10 160 | FUT: Utility player | 7C

Bats B Age 24
2016 (10) HS (CA)
Pwr +++
BAvg ++
Spd ++++
Def +++

Year	Lev	Team	AB	R	H	HR	RBI	Avg	OB	Slg	OPS	bb%	ct%	Eye	SB	CS	x/h%	Iso	RC/G
2017	A-	MahoningVal	120	18	36	4	19	300	328	467	795	4	80	0.21	4	2	31	167	5.03
2018	A	Lansing	460	67	105	9	53	228	313	387	700	11	78	0.58	44	16	46	159	4.37
2019	A+	Dunedin	319	48	69	7	38	216	321	364	684	13	66	0.46	26	10	43	147	4.28
2021	AA	New Hampshire	320	69	94	16	52	294	376	503	879	12	66	0.38	30	8	36	209	7.04
2022	AAA	Buffalo	244	41	63	9	45	258	335	426	761	10	75	0.45	23	5	33	168	4.99

Short-statured, athletic UT, acquired in Merrifield deal with TOR, was added to KC 40-man this off-season. Closed, upright stance. Hands are a little long to the trigger. Slight uppercut swing is geared towards pull contact and can cut off the outside part of plate. Has feel for zone and will take walk. Average power to pull side. A 25-SB threat.

ena,Jose — 46 — Cleveland

EXP MLB DEBUT: 2023 | H/W: 5-11 190 | FUT: Utility player | 7C

Bats L Age 22	Year	Lev	Team	AB	R	H	HR	RBI	Avg	OB	Slg	OPS	bb%	ct%	Eye	SB	CS	x/h%	Iso	RC/G
2017 FA (DR)																				
Pwr +++	2019	Rk	AZL Indians 2	191	30	62	1	18	325	345	440	785	3	77	0.14	6	2	23	115	5.06
BAvg +++	2021	A+	Lake County	413	58	116	16	58	281	325	467	792	6	72	0.23	10	5	37	186	5.30
Spd +++	2022	AA	Akron	516	74	136	13	66	264	298	411	708	5	73	0.18	8	5	32	147	4.11
Def +++	2022	AAA	Columbus	19	7	7	1	2	368	478	632	1110	17	79	1.00	0	0	43	263	9.88

Wiry, contact-oriented MIF struggled with aggressiveness against advanced spin. Open, upright stance with minimal load. Linear swing plane produces groundball contact. Aggressive, slasher approach. Previous plus hand/eye took step back due to difficulties with spin. Fringe average power, all to pull field. Range maxed out at SS, likely 2B/UT.

homas,Colby — 9 — Oakland

EXP MLB DEBUT: 2025 | H/W: 6-0 190 | FUT: Starting OF | 7C

Bats R Age 22	Year	Lev	Team	AB	R	H	HR	RBI	Avg	OB	Slg	OPS	bb%	ct%	Eye	SB	CS	x/h%	Iso	RC/G
2022 (3) Mercer																				
Pwr +++																				
BAvg ++																				
Spd +++																				
Def +++																				

Toolsy OF who underwent shoulder surgery in May 2022. OAK will likely modify swing mechanics to leverage natural strength and quickness. Exhibits plus raw power due to bat speed and loft. Owns solid average speed and can steal bases and chase down balls in RF. Good overall player and will need time to develop.

hompson,Sterlin — 59 — Colorado

EXP MLB DEBUT: 2025 | H/W: 6-4 200 | FUT: Starting OF | 7C

Bats L Age 21	Year	Lev	Team	AB	R	H	HR	RBI	Avg	OB	Slg	OPS	bb%	ct%	Eye	SB	CS	x/h%	Iso	RC/G
2022 (1) Florida																				
Pwr +++																				
BAvg +++	2022	NCAA	Florida	254	59	90	11	51	354	436	563	999	13	81	0.79	10	3	32	209	8.07
Spd ++	2022	Rk	ACL Rockies	55	9	15	1	6	273	298	382	680	4	71	0.13	1	0	27	109	3.70
Def ++	2022	A	Fresno	46	9	16	1	4	348	388	500	888	6	74	0.25	2	0	31	152	6.59

Draft-eligible sophomore rode a breakout campaign to 1st round selection. Smooth LH stroke and all-fields approach give him a chance to hit for average. Has the frame and enough bat speed for more power, but can be beat by high heat and for now bat path is more conducive to 2B than HR. Played 2B and 3B in college, but is likely limited to the OF.

oglia,Michael — 3 — Colorado

EXP MLB DEBUT: 2022 | H/W: 6-5 226 | FUT: Starting 1B | 7C

Bats B Age 24	Year	Lev	Team	AB	R	H	HR	RBI	Avg	OB	Slg	OPS	bb%	ct%	Eye	SB	CS	x/h%	Iso	RC/G
2019 (1) UCLA	2021	A+	Spokane	282	50	66	17	66	234	333	465	798	13	68	0.46	7	3	44	230	5.67
Pwr ++++	2021	AA	Hartford	143	16	31	5	18	217	325	406	731	14	64	0.45	3	0	52	189	5.01
BAvg ++	2022	AA	Hartford	363	63	85	23	66	234	329	466	794	12	65	0.40	7	1	44	231	5.68
Spd +	2022	AAA	Albuquerque	66	11	22	7	17	333	413	758	1171	12	67	0.41	0	1	64	424	11.19
Def ++++	2022	MLB	Colorado	111	10	24	2	12	216	275	378	653	8	60	0.20	1	1	50	162	3.97

Plus raw power earned him a late-season callup. Below-average runner and is best suited at 1B where he is a plus defender. Will draw walks with plus power, but all-or-nothing approach makes it unlikely will ever hit for average. But the power and defense could result in a full-time ABs.

olentino,Milan — 456 — Cleveland

EXP MLB DEBUT: 2025 | H/W: 6-0 185 | FUT: Utility player | 7E

Bats L Age 21	Year	Lev	Team	AB	R	H	HR	RBI	Avg	OB	Slg	OPS	bb%	ct%	Eye	SB	CS	x/h%	Iso	RC/G
2020 (4) HS (CA)																				
Pwr +	2021	Rk	ACL Indians	123	27	37	6	31	301	353	496	849	8	67	0.25	3	1	30	195	6.28
BAvg +++	2021	A	Lynchburg	63	6	13	1	9	206	275	286	561	9	65	0.27	0	0	23	79	2.22
Spd +++	2022	A	Lynchburg	168	33	56	1	26	333	440	423	863	16	74	0.73	8	1	23	89	6.88
Def +++	2022	A+	Lake County	244	39	54	3	28	221	340	332	672	15	62	0.48	21	2	39	111	4.30

Bloodlines MIF struggled with mid-season callup to High-A. Open, crouched stance with a slight bat wrap. Added trajectory to swing plane, which compromised contact skills. At best, spray hitter with line drive and groundball tendencies. Power isn't in frame and didn't come through in swing. Solid defender, plays several positions.

olve,Tyler — 2 — Atlanta

EXP MLB DEBUT: 2025 | H/W: 6-1 200 | FUT: Starting C | 7E

Bats L Age 22	Year	Lev	Team	AB	R	H	HR	RBI	Avg	OB	Slg	OPS	bb%	ct%	Eye	SB	CS	x/h%	Iso	RC/G
2021 (17) Kennesaw St	2020	NCAA	Kennesaw St	61	10	16	0	15	262	366	311	678	14	77	0.71	5	0	13	49	4.23
Pwr +++	2021	NCAA	Kennesaw St	207	43	66	7	49	319	387	498	885	10	75	0.44	8	1	29	179	6.67
BAvg ++	2021	Rk	FCL Braves	2	0	0	0	0	0	0	0	0	0	50	0.00	0	0		0	-7.85
Spd +++	2021	A	Augusta	85	12	25	2	10	294	341	447	788	7	67	0.21	2	0	28	153	5.55
Def +++	2022	A+	Rome	287	42	75	12	47	261	331	470	802	9	64	0.29	8	1	41	209	5.99

Athletic, LHH C had encouraging season against High-A competition in 2022. Solid frame with plus athleticism at catcher. Power over hit tool. Upright stance. Drops hands on load. Uppercut swing trajectory, gets to lofted contact. Works counts. Struggles with swings and misses, especially by cutting off plate. Above-average loft. Sticks at C.

oman,Tucker — 5 — Toronto

EXP MLB DEBUT: 2026 | H/W: 6-1 190 | FUT: Starting 3B | 8D

Bats B Age 19	Year	Lev	Team	AB	R	H	HR	RBI	Avg	OB	Slg	OPS	bb%	ct%	Eye	SB	CS	x/h%	Iso	RC/G
2022 (2) HS (SC)																				
Pwr +++																				
BAvg +++																				
Spd +																				
Def ++	2022	Rk	FCL Blue Jays	38	4	11	0	5	289	400	368	768	16	68	0.58	0	0	27	79	5.71

Bat-first 3B who is all about hard contact from both sides of plate. Has plenty of development ahead, but power and BA ability could be exciting. Secondary skills lag far behind. Not much foot speed and defense needs major work. Drives ball to all fields with vicious stroke and has natural leverage and loft to get to plus power soon.

orres,Jose — 46 — Cincinnati

EXP MLB DEBUT: 2024 | H/W: 6-0 171 | FUT: Reserve IF | 6C

Bats R Age 23	Year	Lev	Team	AB	R	H	HR	RBI	Avg	OB	Slg	OPS	bb%	ct%	Eye	SB	CS	x/h%	Iso	RC/G
2021 (3) NC State	2020	NCAA	NC St	60	11	20	3	13	333	365	533	898	5	67	0.15	2	0	30	200	6.92
Pwr +++	2021	NCAA	NC St	197	31	57	10	44	289	333	533	866	6	80	0.33	5	1	44	244	6.03
BAvg ++	2021	Rk	ACL Reds	10	3	3	1	2	300	417	800	1217	17	80	1.00	1	0	67	500	11.02
Spd +++	2021	A	Daytona	95	15	32	4	17	337	388	568	957	8	82	0.47	6	2	34	232	7.24
Def ++++	2022	A+	Dayton	397	53	93	13	46	234	285	378	663	7	71	0.24	26	4	31	144	3.52

Shorter-statured, defensively-skilled SS struggled getting on base in first full season of pro ball. Physically strong despite slight frame. Slightly open, upright stance with a hitch in load. It's an extreme uppercut swing. Lots of popups as a result of below-average bat speed getting under barrel. There is also swing-and-miss present. UT IF upside.

ovar,Ezequiel — 6 — Colorado

EXP MLB DEBUT: 2022 | H/W: 6-0 162 | FUT: Starting SS | 9D

Bats R Age 21	Year	Lev	Team	AB	R	H	HR	RBI	Avg	OB	Slg	OPS	bb%	ct%	Eye	SB	CS	x/h%	Iso	RC/G
2017 FA (VZ)	2021	A	Fresno	298	60	92	11	54	309	340	510	850	4	87	0.37	21	4	38	201	5.70
Pwr +++	2021	A+	Spokane	134	19	32	4	18	239	255	396	651	2	86	0.16	3	2	41	157	3.29
BAvg +++	2022	AA	Hartford	264	39	84	13	47	318	377	545	923	9	76	0.39	17	3	37	227	7.00
Spd +++	2022	AAA	Albuquerque	21	3	7	1	2	333	391	476	867	9	90	1.00	0	0	14	143	6.03
Def ++++	2022	MLB	Colorado	33	2	7	1	2	212	257	333	590	6	73	0.22	0	0	29	121	2.47

Top prospect had a breakout campaign at the plate, posting a .927 OPS and making his MLB debut. Already an elite defender with a plus arm, he showed a more aggressive approach at the plate and sacrificed some plate discipline for power. The trade-off worked as he posted his first .500+ SLG between AA and AAA.

resh,Luca — 2 — Kansas City

EXP MLB DEBUT: 2024 | H/W: 6-0 193 | FUT: Starting C | 7C

Bats R Age 23	Year	Lev	Team	AB	R	H	HR	RBI	Avg	OB	Slg	OPS	bb%	ct%	Eye	SB	CS	x/h%	Iso	RC/G
2021 (17) NC State	2021	NCAA	NC St	229	41	53	15	43	231	304	476	780	9	69	0.34	1	0	47	245	5.21
Pwr +++	2021	Rk	ACL Royals Blue	18	2	7	1	3	389	421	722	1143	5	78	0.25	0	0	57	333	9.64
BAvg +++	2021	A	Columbia	35	0	5	0	5	143	231	171	402	10	69	0.36	0	0	20	29	0.03
Spd +	2022	A+	Quad Cities	300	48	82	14	54	273	361	470	831	12	72	0.48	3	3	37	197	6.05
Def +++	2022	AA	NW Arkansas	91	16	23	5	14	253	346	462	808	13	73	0.52	1	0	39	209	5.66

2021 17th round selection has improved stock immensely in first full pro season. Catcher's body with plus raw power in frame. Open, crouched stance with simple load. Solid eye with pull to pull gap approach. Gets to consistent hard contact with average swing speed. Frame and uppercut trajectory push 20+ HR potential. Improving defender.

riantos,James — 5 — Chicago (N)

EXP MLB DEBUT: 2024 | H/W: 6-1 195 | FUT: Starting 3B | 7C

Bats R Age 20	Year	Lev	Team	AB	R	H	HR	RBI	Avg	OB	Slg	OPS	bb%	ct%	Eye	SB	CS	x/h%	Iso	RC/G
2021 (2) HS (VA)																				
Pwr +++																				
BAvg +++																				
Spd +++	2021	Rk	ACL Cubs	101	27	33	6	19	327	370	594	964	6	82	0.39	3	3	42	267	7.15
Def +++	2022	A	Myrtle Beach	456	74	124	7	50	272	329	386	715	8	82	0.48	20	3	26	114	4.38

Quiet set-up with weight back and a balanced, compact swing and plus bat speed. Good understanding of the strike zone and minimal swing-and-miss. Held his own in full-season debut and just starting to tap into his plus raw power. Runs well, but SBs are not likely to carry over. Solid defender who should stick at 3B.

Triolo,Jared — 5 — Pittsburgh

EXP MLB DEBUT: 2023 | H/W: 6-3 212 | FUT: Starting 3B | 7C

Bats R Age 25
2019 (2) Houston
- Pwr ++
- BAvg +++
- Spd ++
- Def +++

Year	Lev	Team	AB	R	H	HR	RBI	Avg	OB	Slg	OPS	bb%	ct%	Eye	SB	CS	x/h%	Iso	RC/G
2019	NCAA	Houston	217	46	72	7	44	332	415	512	927	13	86	1.03	13	2	35	180	7.15
2019	A-	West Virginia	234	30	56	2	34	239	318	389	707	10	79	0.55	3	1	46	150	4.52
2021	A+	Greensboro	421	74	128	15	78	304	367	480	847	9	78	0.45	25	6	34	176	6.02
2022	AA	Altoona	425	66	120	9	39	282	375	419	794	13	80	0.72	24	5	29	136	5.62

Consistent 3B who finished 2nd in EL in BA. Has proven difficult to K as he uses level swing and hand-eye coordination to put ball in play. Doesn't hit many HR, but lines doubles to gaps in all-fields approach. Could benefit from pulling ball more. Has athletic frame and steals bases more on instincts. Very good 3B with quick hands.

Tucker,Carson — 456 — Cleveland

EXP MLB DEBUT: 2026 | H/W: 6-2 180 | FUT: Starting SS | 7E

Bats R Age 21
2020 (1) HS (AZ)
- Pwr +++
- BAvg ++
- Spd ++++
- Def +++

Year	Lev	Team	AB	R	H	HR	RBI	Avg	OB	Slg	OPS	bb%	ct%	Eye	SB	CS	x/h%	Iso	RC/G
2021	Rk	ACL Indians	20	6	3	1	3	150	320	300	620	20	80	1.25	1	1	33	150	3.45
2022	A	Lynchburg	117	12	16	1	9	137	252	222	474	13	53	0.33	5	0	44	85	1.05

Former 1st rd selection struggled with injuries once again in full-season debut. Has played only 44 games across 2 seasons. Athletic frame; a plus runner with an extra gear. Upright stance produces an uppercut swing trajectory after struggling to get bat going. There's potential average-to-above-average power in bat. Solid defensively at SS.

Turang,Brice — 6 — Milwaukee

EXP MLB DEBUT: 2023 | H/W: 6-0 173 | FUT: Starting SS | 7B

Bats L Age 23
2018 (1) HS (CA)
- Pwr ++
- BAvg ++++
- Spd ++++
- Def +++

Year	Lev	Team	AB	R	H	HR	RBI	Avg	OB	Slg	OPS	bb%	ct%	Eye	SB	CS	x/h%	Iso	RC/G
2019	A	Wisconsin	303	57	87	2	31	287	386	376	763	14	82	0.91	21	4	22	89	5.36
2019	A+	Carolina	170	25	34	1	6	200	333	276	610	17	72	0.72	9	1	26	76	3.33
2021	AA	Biloxi	288	40	76	5	39	264	329	385	715	9	83	0.58	11	7	29	122	4.44
2021	AAA	Nashville	143	19	35	1	14	245	383	315	698	18	76	0.91	9	2	23	70	4.64
2022	AAA	Nashville	532	89	152	13	78	286	363	412	775	11	78	0.55	34	2	26	126	5.22

Consistent, steady SS with plenty of athleticism and defensive skills. Plays CF and 3B, but profiles best at SS where range, hands and feet work well. Makes consistent, hard contact though not power guy. Set highs in both HR and SB in best year of career. Swing is mostly flat and possesses keen eye and barrel control. Owns plus speed.

Urbina,Misael — 8 — Minnesota

EXP MLB DEBUT: 2025 | H/W: 6-0 190 | FUT: Starting CF | 8E

Bats R Age 20
2018 FA (VZ)
- Pwr ++
- BAvg +++
- Spd +++
- Def +++

Year	Lev	Team	AB	R	H	HR	RBI	Avg	OB	Slg	OPS	bb%	ct%	Eye	SB	CS	x/h%	Iso	RC/G
2019		Did not play - Injury																	
2021	A	Fort Myers	367	50	70	5	52	191	295	286	581	13	78	0.66	16	6	30	95	2.85
2022	Rk	FCL Twins	40	3	10	0	5	250	286	350	636	5	78	0.22	1	1	40	100	3.30
2022	A	Fort Myers	191	28	47	5	22	246	327	419	746	11	73	0.45	9	4	47	173	4.95

Promising OF who hasn't yet enjoyed breakout. Repeated Low-A and was better, but not by much. Season started late due to visa issues and faded down stretch. Showed a bit more pop with better knowledge of strike zone and more loft in swing. Can be too pull happy and try to do too much. Could be basestealer with better OBP.

Valdez,Enmanuel — 45 — Boston

EXP MLB DEBUT: 2023 | H/W: 5-9 191 | FUT: Utility player | 7D

Bats L Age 24
2015 FA (DR)
- Pwr +++
- BAvg +++
- Spd ++
- Def +

Year	Lev	Team	AB	R	H	HR	RBI	Avg	OB	Slg	OPS	bb%	ct%	Eye	SB	CS	x/h%	Iso	RC/G
2021	A+	Asheville	283	52	72	21	72	254	315	541	856	8	76	0.37	5	1	53	286	5.94
2021	AA	Corpus Christi	82	11	21	5	18	256	358	512	870	14	73	0.59	0	1	52	256	6.58
2022	AA	Corpus Christi	168	40	60	11	45	357	465	649	1114	17	72	0.72	4	2	45	292	10.26
2022	AAA	Sugar Land	159	26	47	10	32	296	341	560	901	6	82	0.38	1	1	45	264	6.36
2022	AAA	Worcester	173	26	41	7	30	237	313	422	734	10	72	0.40	3	0	41	185	4.64

Acquired from HOU at deadline and struggled after trade. Set career high in HR in breakout. More of bat-first prospect with above average power and ability to get on base. Swings quick bat and doesn't expand zone much. Making more consistent, hard contact. Very limited defense or speed and will need to hit to stick.

Valenzuela,Brandon — 2 — San Diego

EXP MLB DEBUT: 2024 | H/W: 6-0 225 | FUT: Reserve C | 6C

Bats B Age 22
2017 FA (MX)
- Pwr ++
- BAvg ++
- Spd +
- Def +++

Year	Lev	Team	AB	R	H	HR	RBI	Avg	OB	Slg	OPS	bb%	ct%	Eye	SB	CS	x/h%	Iso	RC/G
2019	Rk	AZL Padres	145	21	36	0	20	248	391	290	681	19	78	1.06	0	0	14	41	4.51
2021	A	Lake Elsinore	329	50	101	6	62	307	389	444	833	12	76	0.55	3	2	30	137	6.14
2021	A+	Fort Wayne	49	4	12	1	7	245	422	327	748	23	59	0.75	1	0	17	82	5.74
2022	A+	Fort Wayne	345	39	72	10	47	209	331	348	679	15	72	0.66	0	1	36	139	4.12

Defense-first backstop who is outstanding receiver and blocker. Needs to firm up frame for greater agility. Has strong, accurate arm with average release. Hasn't produced much offensively. Knows value of working counts and drawing walks. BA has been an issue as he lacks hitting instincts. Flat bat path mutes power production.

Valera,George — 789 — Cleveland

EXP MLB DEBUT: 2023 | H/W: 6-0 195 | FUT: Starting OF | 8C

Bats L Age 22
2017 FA (DR)
- Pwr ++++
- BAvg +++
- Spd ++
- Def +++

Year	Lev	Team	AB	R	H	HR	RBI	Avg	OB	Slg	OPS	bb%	ct%	Eye	SB	CS	x/h%	Iso	RC/G
2019	A	Lake County	23	1	2	0	3	87	160	174	334	8	61	0.22	0	2	50	87	-1.20
2021	A+	Lake County	199	45	51	16	43	256	417	548	965	22	71	0.37	10	5	43	291	8.21
2021	AA	Akron	86	6	23	3	22	267	351	407	757	11	65		1	0	26	140	5.23
2022	AA	Akron	330	64	87	15	59	264	364	470	834	14	70	0.52	2	4	40	206	6.26
2022	AAA	Columbus	154	25	34	9	23	221	318	448	766	13	71	0.49	0	0	50	227	5.11

Power-hitting LHH prospect slugged career high 24 HR in solid season, split between upper levels. Open, unorthodox stance with large bat wiggle for timing. Plus-plus bat speed with uppercut swing produces hard EV and loads of loft. Plus-plus power plays to all fields. Patient hitter. Struggles with contact due to holes in zone. COF bat.

Valera,Leonel — 56 — Los Angeles (N)

EXP MLB DEBUT: 2024 | H/W: 6-2 210 | FUT: Reserve OF | 7E

Bats R Age 23
2015 FA (VZ)
- Pwr +++
- BAvg +
- Spd +++
- Def +++

Year	Lev	Team	AB	R	H	HR	RBI	Avg	OB	Slg	OPS	bb%	ct%	Eye	SB	CS	x/h%	Iso	RC/G
2018	Rk	AZL Dodgers	147	23	43	1	13	293	362	367	729	10	69	0.36	13	1	16	75	4.77
2019	A	Great Lakes	449	78	108	5	42	241	315	325	640	10	69	0.36	27	6	22	85	3.47
2021	A+	Great Lakes	362	51	81	16	58	224	290	436	727	9	59	0.23	16	4	47	213	5.08
2022	A+	Great Lakes	147	20	31	5	21	211	284	361	644	9	61	0.26	11	0	32	150	3.59
2022	AA	Tulsa	321	61	93	13	62	290	356	480	836	9	63	0.28	22	1	32	190	6.56

Continues to make steady progress and had his best season as a pro, especially when advanced to AA. Ultra aggressive approach remains a huge red flag and posted a 33% K rate. Does have a quick bat and is willing to use the entire field. Solid defender with good speed and a plus arm gives him a chance.

Valerio,Felix — 4 — Milwaukee

EXP MLB DEBUT: 2023 | H/W: 5-7 165 | FUT: Utility player | 6B

Bats R Age 22
2018 FA (DR)
- Pwr ++
- BAvg ++
- Spd +++
- Def ++

Year	Lev	Team	AB	R	H	HR	RBI	Avg	OB	Slg	OPS	bb%	ct%	Eye	SB	CS	x/h%	Iso	RC/G
2019	Rk	AZL Brewers Gold	157	16	48	0	18	306	374	389	762	10	87	0.81	16	5	27	83	5.19
2021	A	Carolina	309	71	97	6	63	314	416	469	885	15	84	1.10	27	8	34	155	6.91
2021	A+	Wisconsin	118	19	27	5	16	229	316	466	782	11	81	0.68	4	1	67	237	5.34
2022	AA	Biloxi	417	60	95	12	51	228	308	357	665	10	81	0.60	30	9	29	129	3.78

Fast, contact-hitting INF who was cold over last 3 months of season, but finished 3rd in org in SB. Solid hitter overall, but doesn't make enough hard contact to be weapon. Very difficult to fan as he exhibits quick, compact stroke. Rarely chases out of zone. Limited defensive utility with suspect range and arm.

Vaquero,Cristhian — 8 — Washington

EXP MLB DEBUT: 2026 | H/W: 6-3 180 | FUT: Starting CF | 9E

Bats L Age 18
2022 FA (CU)
- Pwr ++
- BAvg +++
- Spd ++++
- Def +++

Year	Lev	Team	AB	R	H	HR	RBI	Avg	OB	Slg	OPS	bb%	ct%	Eye	SB	CS	x/h%	Iso	RC/G
2022	Rk	DSL Nationals	176	33	45	1	22	256	373	341	714	16	78	0.87	17	7	20	85	4.81

Franchise-record int'l bonus ($4M) for teenage outfielder. Every tool is here - power, speed, hit - in an amazingly projectable frame. A switch-hitter with a good feel from both sides, he oozes potential even if only one or two of his skills fully develop. A no-doubt centerfielder for now who could also bring huge value in a corner. Get in.

Vargas,Alexander — 6 — New York (A)

EXP MLB DEBUT: 2025 | H/W: 5-11 148 | FUT: Starting SS | 7E

Bats B Age 21
2018 FA (CU)
- Pwr ++
- BAvg ++
- Spd ++++
- Def ++++

Year	Lev	Team	AB	R	H	HR	RBI	Avg	OB	Slg	OPS	bb%	ct%	Eye	SB	CS	x/h%	Iso	RC/G
2021	Rk	FCL Yankees	150	37	41	3	26	273	359	393	752	12	73	0.50	17	8	27	120	5.05
2022	A	Tampa	389	59	79	8	33	203	269	311	580	8	68	0.28	27	13	30	108	2.49

Former high dollar international signing continues to struggle with hit tool. Wiry frame, struggling to put mass on frame. Switch-hitter with upright, open stance. Simple trigger getting to hit position. Super aggressive approach and long swing length complicates hit tool. Doesn't incorporate speed in profile, trying to hit for power instead.

Vargas,Miguel | 57 | **Los Angeles (N)** | EXP MLB DEBUT: 2022 | H/W: 6-3 205 | FUT: Starting 3B | **8C**

Bats R Age 23	Year	Lev	Team	AB	R	H	HR	RBI	Avg	OB	Slg	OPS	bb%	ct%	Eye	SB	CS	x/h%	Iso	RC/G
2017 FA (CU)	2019	A+	Rancho Cuca	211	23	60	2	32	284	346	408	754	9	81	0.50	4	3	35	123	4.96
Pwr ++++	2021	A+	Great Lakes	156	31	49	7	16	314	352	532	884	5	79	0.28	4	0	39	218	6.21
BAvg +++	2021	AA	Tulsa	327	67	105	16	60	321	388	523	911	10	83	0.63	7	1	31	202	6.71
Spd ++	2022	AAA	Oklahoma City	438	100	133	17	82	304	401	511	912	14	83	0.93	16	5	40	208	7.08
Def +	2022	MLB	Los Angeles	47	4	8	1	8	170	204	255	459	4	72	0.15	1	0	25	85	0.66

Advanced hit tool with a quick bat and excellent bat-to-ball skills. Uptick in power over the past two seasons raised his profile and earned him a big league debut. He's a below average defender split time between 1B, 3B, and LF. He struggled to find consistency in LA but showed signs of a future everyday player.

Vasquez,Willy | 5 | **Tampa Bay** | EXP MLB DEBUT: 2025 | H/W: 6-0 191 | FUT: Starting 3B | **8E**

Bats R Age 21	Year	Lev	Team	AB	R	H	HR	RBI	Avg	OB	Slg	OPS	bb%	ct%	Eye	SB	CS	x/h%	Iso	RC/G
2019 FA (DR)																				
Pwr +++																				
BAvg ++																				
Spd +++	2021	Rk	FCL Rays	146	26	42	2	31	288	373	411	784	12	82	0.74	14	6	26	123	5.50
Def +++	2022	A	Charleston	449	78	115	10	73	256	311	410	721	7	72	0.29	25	3	35	154	4.48

Tall, athletic IF prospect started to get to power in lackluster full-season debut. Bigger than listed size and still has room to grow. Upright stance with toe tap. Struggled with patience, especially against spin. Linear swing plane creates top spin heavy contact. Raw plus power in frame now. Could play with swing change. Likely 3B defensively.

Vazquez,Daniel | 6 | **Kansas City** | EXP MLB DEBUT: 2026 | H/W: 6-0 150 | FUT: Starting SS | **7E**

Bats R Age 19	Year	Lev	Team	AB	R	H	HR	RBI	Avg	OB	Slg	OPS	bb%	ct%	Eye	SB	CS	x/h%	Iso	RC/G
2021 FA (DR)																				
Pwr ++																				
BAvg ++																				
Spd +++	2021	Rk	DSL Royals Blue	102	17	19	1	10	186	284	265	549	12	70	0.45	4	0	26	78	2.23
Def ++++	2022	A	Columbia	293	25	57	0	31	195	265	229	493	9	71	0.33	10	5	18	34	1.36

Defensively skilled SS prospect struggled with hit tool in full-season debut. Contact-oriented approach with feel for the zone struggled mightily with spin. Has solid bat speed on a linear plane but struggles with consistent bat path. Below average power potential in frame and swing. 10-15 HR max. Above-average runner with plus defensive instincts.

Veen,Zac | 79 | **Colorado** | EXP MLB DEBUT: 2024 | H/W: 6-4 190 | FUT: Starting OF | **9D**

Bats L Age 21	Year	Lev	Team	AB	R	H	HR	RBI	Avg	OB	Slg	OPS	bb%	ct%	Eye	SB	CS	x/h%	Iso	RC/G
2020 (1) HS (FL)																				
Pwr +++																				
BAvg +++	2021	A	Fresno	399	83	120	15	75	301	397	501	899	14	68	0.51	36	17	38	201	7.37
Spd +++++	2022	A+	Spokane	342	72	92	11	60	269	362	439	801	13	74	0.56	50	4	36	170	5.72
Def +++	2022	AA	Hartford	124	12	22	1	7	177	261	234	495	10	66	0.33	5	5	23	56	1.30

Some of the best speed in the minors; swiped 55 bases in 2022. Good understanding of the strike zone is mitigated by aggressive approach; needs to be more selective to tap into power. Plus speed and arm strength should play well in RF where and is above-average defender. If speed and OB% stick at the MLB level, plenty of SB await.

Vellojin,Daniel | 2 | **Cincinnati** | EXP MLB DEBUT: 2024 | H/W: 5-11 190 | FUT: Reserve C | **6C**

Bats L Age 23	Year	Lev	Team	AB	R	H	HR	RBI	Avg	OB	Slg	OPS	bb%	ct%	Eye	SB	CS	x/h%	Iso	RC/G
2018 FA (CB)																				
Pwr ++	2021	A	Daytona	283	56	70	7	34	247	400	403	803	20	74	0.99	5	3	41	155	6.13
BAvg ++	2022	A	Daytona	62	7	8	1	4	129	280	177	457	17	66	0.62	3	1	13	48	0.74
Spd ++	2022	A+	Dayton	70	10	19	5	10	271	386	514	900	16	66	0.54	0	2	37	243	7.32
Def ++++	2022	AA	Chattanooga	94	12	18	4	14	191	309	362	671	15	64	0.47	0	1	39	170	3.96

Stocky, defensively skilled C prospect played across 3 levels, struggling with bat in Double-A. Slight open, upright stance. Uppercut swing trajectory maximizes average power in frame. Slower bat speed causes issues with hard contact and whiff rate. Discerning eye, works counts. Double-plus arm, improved receiving skills. Likely plus defender.

Veras,Wilfred | 3 | **Chicago (A)** | EXP MLB DEBUT: 2025 | H/W: 6-2 180 | FUT: Reserve 1B | **7E**

Bats R Age 20	Year	Lev	Team	AB	R	H	HR	RBI	Avg	OB	Slg	OPS	bb%	ct%	Eye	SB	CS	x/h%	Iso	RC/G
2019 FA (DR)																				
Pwr +++																				
BAvg ++	2021	Rk	ACL White Sox	152	25	49	4	26	322	405	533	938	12	72	0.50	3	1	45	211	7.76
Spd ++	2022	A	Kannapolis	394	58	105	17	67	266	314	454	768	6	70	0.23	5	0	36	188	4.99
Def ++	2022	AA	Birmingham	45	5	12	3	5	267	313	533	846	6	69	0.21	0	0	50	267	6.06

Power hitter made full-season debut. Unusual closed upright stance with hands up high; struggles getting bat to hit position. It's a linear swing now but could get to better angles with modification. Strong-bodied frame with room to grow into additional power. Could hit 25+ HR at projection. Better at 1B than 3B.

Viars,Jordan | 7 | **Philadelphia** | EXP MLB DEBUT: 2026 | H/W: 6-4 215 | FUT: Starting OF | **8E**

Bats L Age 19	Year	Lev	Team	AB	R	H	HR	RBI	Avg	OB	Slg	OPS	bb%	ct%	Eye	SB	CS	x/h%	Iso	RC/G
2021 (3) HS (TX)																				
Pwr ++++																				
BAvg ++	2021	Rk	FCL Phillies	47	13	12	3	18	255	397	468	865	19	74	0.92	2	0	33	213	6.61
Spd +++	2022	Rk	FCL Phillies	154	28	37	2	20	240	316	331	647	10	74	0.43	5	0	24	91	3.54
Def ++	2022	A	Clearwater	24	2	5	0	3	208	269	208	478	8	63	0.22	0	0	0	0	0.91

Big-framed power bat who struggled with injuries that marred his first full pro season. Lauded for his good approach, but also takes hefty cuts that make the most of his plus bat speed and plus raw power. Athletic and mobile now, could well lose a step with age that could push him from OF to 1B. Needs a full season to showcase his wares.

Vientos,Mark | 35 | **New York (N)** | EXP MLB DEBUT: 2022 | H/W: 6-4 185 | FUT: Starting 1B | **7C**

Bats R Age 23	Year	Lev	Team	AB	R	H	HR	RBI	Avg	OB	Slg	OPS	bb%	ct%	Eye	SB	CS	x/h%	Iso	RC/G
2017 (2) HS (FL)	2019	A	Columbia	416	48	106	12	62	255	292	411	703	5	74	0.20	1	4	38	156	4.04
Pwr ++++	2021	AA	Binghamton	274	43	77	22	59	281	343	580	924	9	68	0.30	0	1	49	299	7.24
BAvg ++	2021	AAA	Syracuse	36	9	10	3	4	278	395	583	979	16	64	0.54	0	1	50	306	8.71
Spd ++	2022	AAA	Syracuse	378	66	106	24	72	280	355	519	874	10	68	0.36	0	2	39	238	6.68
Def ++	2022	MLB	New York (N)	36	3	6	1	3	167	268	278	546	12	67	0.42	0	0	33	111	2.01

Powerful CIF prospect had good 2022 Triple-A season, earning MLB callup. Long levered physique with room to grow. There is raw plus power in frame. Slight open, upright stance with short trigger. Opposite field approach with power angles playing to opposite field, depressing HR totals. Long levers lead to high in zone whiffs. Likely 1B only.

Vilade,Ryan | 79 | **Pittsburgh** | EXP MLB DEBUT: 2021 | H/W: 6-2 226 | FUT: Utility player | **6B**

Bats R Age 24	Year	Lev	Team	AB	R	H	HR	RBI	Avg	OB	Slg	OPS	bb%	ct%	Eye	SB	CS	x/h%	Iso	RC/G
2017 (2) HS (OK)	2019	A+	Lancaster	509	92	154	12	71	303	372	466	837	10	81	0.59	24	7	32	163	5.99
Pwr +	2021	AAA	Albuquerque	468	82	133	7	44	284	338	410	748	8	80	0.41	12	5	30	126	4.77
BAvg +++	2021	MLB	Colorado	6	0	0	0	0	0	143	0	143	14	83	1.00	0	0		0	-2.27
Spd +++	2022	Rk	ACL Rockies	10	3	3	1	3	300	364	700	1064	9	70	0.33	1	1	67	400	9.13
Def +++	2022	AAA	Albuquerque	369	64	92	5	38	249	342	352	694	12	81	0.75	10	6	26	103	4.36

2nd rounder got a cup of coffee in the bigs in '21, but spent last year at AAA and was claimed off waivers by the Pirates. Patient, mature approach at the plate leads to plenty of contact, but most of it is soft and he now owns a career .410 SLG%. Solid defender and can play off INF or OF. Could be a good fit as UT in PIT.

Vivas,Jorbit | 45 | **Los Angeles (N)** | EXP MLB DEBUT: 2024 | H/W: 5-10 171 | FUT: Utility player | **6C**

Bats L Age 22	Year	Lev	Team	AB	R	H	HR	RBI	Avg	OB	Slg	OPS	bb%	ct%	Eye	SB	CS	x/h%	Iso	RC/G
2017 FA (VZ)	2019	Rk	AZL Dodgers Lasorda	115	18	41	1	20	357	422	513	935	10	87	0.87	5	4	34	157	7.25
Pwr ++	2019	Rk	Ogden	84	13	24	1	12	286	333	417	750	7	81	0.38	5	5	33	131	4.78
BAvg +++	2021	A	Rancho Cuca	328	73	102	13	73	311	363	515	879	8	87	0.64	5	3	36	204	6.23
Spd ++	2021	A+	Great Lakes	85	12	27	1	14	318	408	424	832	13	85	1.00	3	1	26	106	6.15
Def ++	2022	A+	Great Lakes	479	73	129	10	66	269	354	401	755	12	88	1.09	2	1	28	132	5.14

Short, utility type gets the most out of limited physical tools. Advanced bat with surprising pop for his size will be carrying tools. Excellent bat-to-ball skills and walked more than he whiffed in '23. Lack of plus range and speed make 2B his future home on D, but has been used in a variety of roles. Has the potential to hit .280.

Volpe,Anthony | 6 | **New York (A)** | EXP MLB DEBUT: 2023 | H/W: 5-11 180 | FUT: Starting SS | **9C**

Bats R Age 21	Year	Lev	Team	AB	R	H	HR	RBI	Avg	OB	Slg	OPS	bb%	ct%	Eye	SB	CS	x/h%	Iso	RC/G
2019 (1) HS (NJ)	2019	Rk	Pulaski	121	19	26	2	11	215	340	355	696	16	69	0.61	6	1	42	140	4.54
Pwr ++++	2021	A	Tampa	199	56	60	12	49	302	444	623	1067	20	78	1.19	21	5	58	322	9.51
BAvg +++	2021	A+	Hudson Valley	213	57	61	15	37	286	367	587	954	11	73	0.47	12	4	54	300	7.62
Spd +++	2022	AA	Somerset	422	71	106	18	60	251	340	472	812	12	79	0.65	44	6	50	220	5.72
Def +++	2022	AAA	Scranton/WB	89	15	21	3	5	236	299	404	703	8	66	0.27	6	1	38	169	4.33

Shorter-statured, athletic RHH SS recovered from early struggles to post solid returns. Closed, crouched stance with quick trigger to hit position. Plus bat speed with steep launch angle, produces exceptional loft off bat. Will allow pitches to travel deep into zone and take pitches to the opposite field. Solid range at SS, fringe arm.

Vukovich,AJ — 57 — Arizona — EXP MLB DEBUT: 2024 — H/W: 6-5 210 — FUT: Starting OF — 7D

Bats R Age 21
2020 (4) HS (WI)
Pwr +++
BAvg ++
Spd +++
Def +++

Year	Lev	Team	AB	R	H	HR	RBI	Avg	OB	Sig	OPS	bb%	ct%	Eye	SB	CS	x/h%	Iso	RC/G
2021	A	Visalia	247	42	64	10	42	259	312	449	761	7	69	0.25	10	1	41	190	5.01
2021	A+	Hillsboro	121	13	36	3	20	298	315	438	753	2	77	0.11	6	3	25	140	4.48
2022	A+	Hillsboro	424	55	116	15	69	274	303	450	754	4	75	0.17	35	4	37	177	4.59
2022	AA	Amarillo	44	6	13	2	9	295	311	432	743	2	70	0.08	1	0	15	136	4.28

Long-limbed, powerful prospect with super aggressive approach struggled getting on base in 2022. Upright, extremely closed stance with hitch in load. Raw double-plus power, struggles to play due to hit tool limitations. Opposite field approach, struggles pulling the ball with authority. Lots of swing and miss potential. Long stride runner.

Waddell,Luke — 46 — Atlanta — EXP MLB DEBUT: 2024 — H/W: 5-9 180 — FUT: Reserve IF — 6C

Bats L Age 24
2021 (5) Georgia Tech
Pwr +
BAvg +++
Spd +++
Def +++

Year	Lev	Team	AB	R	H	HR	RBI	Avg	OB	Sig	OPS	bb%	ct%	Eye	SB	CS	x/h%	Iso	RC/G
2020	NCAA	Georgia Tech	60	14	18	1	9	300	373	417	790	10	88	1.00	2	0	22	117	5.48
2021	NCAA	Georgia Tech	230	41	71	8	33	309	388	474	862	12	93	1.88	5	3	30	165	6.36
2021	A+	Rome	69	15	21	6	13	304	368	580	948	9	81	0.54	1	1	33	275	6.92
2021	AA	Mississippi	31	3	5	0	2	161	212	161	373	6	87	0.50	1	1	0	0	0.41
2022	AA	Mississippi	162	20	44	2	29	272	362	370	733	12	86	1.05	3	2	27	99	4.93

Contact-oriented MIF prospect went on HR tear to start the season, settled into his contact-over-power ways the rest of the season. Open stance with simple trigger, maximizes contact over exit velocity. All fields, slasher approach. Below-average power to the pull side only. Less than 10 HR power at projection. Versatile athlete. Solid defensively.

Wagner,Max — 5 — Baltimore — EXP MLB DEBUT: 2024 — H/W: 6-0 215 — FUT: Starting 3B — 8D

Bats R Age 21
2022 (2) Clemson
Pwr ++++
BAvg ++
Spd ++
Def +++

Year	Lev	Team	AB	R	H	HR	RBI	Avg	OB	Sig	OPS	bb%	ct%	Eye	SB	CS	x/h%	Iso	RC/G
2022	NCAA	Clemson	203	66	75	27	76	369	484	852	1336	18	75	0.88	2	1	57	483	12.78
2022	Rk	FCL Orioles B	4	0	2	0	2	500	500	750	1250	0	100		1	0	50	250	9.68
2022	A	Delmarva	48	9	12	1	8	250	368	438	806	16	73	0.69	0	0	42	188	6.09
2022	A+	Aberdeen	18	3	3	0	1	167	167	167	333	0	72	0.00	1	0	0	0	-1.16

Medium build from a strong frame, starts partially open and showed hard contact to all fields. Some swing and miss, but also worked ABs with good plate disciple and strike-zone recognition. Can be a tough out. Smart and heady defender despite non-premium athleticism; may need to move across the diamond. Full pro season will reveal a lot.

Wagner,Will — 345 — Houston — EXP MLB DEBUT: 2024 — H/W: 6-0 210 — FUT: Utility player — 6B

Bats L Age 23
2021 (18) Liberty
Pwr +
BAvg +++
Spd +++
Def +++

Year	Lev	Team	AB	R	H	HR	RBI	Avg	OB	Sig	OPS	bb%	ct%	Eye	SB	CS	x/h%	Iso	RC/G
2020	NCAA	Liberty	12	0	1	0	0	83	154	83	237	8	67	0.25	0	0	0	0	-2.61
2021	NCAA	Liberty	210	32	70	7	52	333	402	538	940	10	83	0.67	6	1	37	205	7.22
2021	A	Fayetteville	117	22	35	2	14	299	383	436	819	12	72	0.48	5	0	31	137	6.09
2022	A+	Asheville	163	22	45	4	25	276	395	405	800	16	75	0.78	3	1	27	129	5.87
2022	AA	Corpus Christi	251	40	63	6	28	251	343	386	729	12	77	0.61	5	1	32	135	4.72

INF prospect is no pushover in the box with some of the best pure contact skills in the system. Quiet setup with direct swing and slight leg kick. Rarely swings and misses. Mostly gap power with and has the speed to leg out XBH. Capable base stealer. Can play adequate defense all around infield.

Walker,Jordan — 59 — St. Louis — EXP MLB DEBUT: 2023 — H/W: 6-5 220 — FUT: Starting OF — 9B

Bats R Age 20
2020 (1) HS (GA)
Pwr ++++
BAvg +++
Spd ++
Def ++

Year	Lev	Team	AB	R	H	HR	RBI	Avg	OB	Sig	OPS	bb%	ct%	Eye	SB	CS	x/h%	Iso	RC/G
2021	A	Palm Beach	99	24	37	6	21	374	470	687	1157	15	79	0.86	1	0	49	313	10.36
2021	A+	Peoria	226	39	66	8	27	292	336	487	823	6	71	0.23	13	2	38	195	5.81
2022	AA	Springfield	461	100	141	19	68	306	383	510	893	11	75	0.50	22	5	38	204	6.82

Big, physical player with plus bat speed, pitch recognition, and plus raw power. Slightly open RH stance and finds the barrel regularly with elite exit velo, but can get beat by breaking balls away. Runs surprisingly well and is being transitioned to LF where he has enough arm to be a solid defender. Only shortcoming is a sub-optimal GB rate.

Wallace,Cayden — 5 — Kansas City — EXP MLB DEBUT: 2025 — H/W: 6-1 205 — FUT: Starting 3B — 8D

Bats R Age 21
2022 (2) Arkansas
Pwr ++++
BAvg +++
Spd +++
Def +++

Year	Lev	Team	AB	R	H	HR	RBI	Avg	OB	Sig	OPS	bb%	ct%	Eye	SB	CS	x/h%	Iso	RC/G
2022	NCAA	Arkansas	275	62	82	16	60	298	383	553	936	12	80	0.68	12	1	45	255	7.22
2022	Rk	ACL Royals Blue	7	3	2	0	1	286	500	429	929	30	86	3.00	0	0	50	143	8.52
2022	A	Columbia	109	15	32	2	16	294	364	468	832	10	80	0.55	8	1	38	174	6.01

Athletic, strong-bodied 3B prospect who is close to physical projection. Power and arm strength carry profile. Upright stance with limited load. Works counts and gets to hard contact consistently. Plus power in frame, hasn't gotten to it with wood bat yet. Above-average runner. Sticks at 3B.

Wallner,Matt — 9 — Minnesota — EXP MLB DEBUT: 2022 — H/W: 6-5 220 — FUT: Starting OF — 7C

Bats L Age 25
2019 (1) Southern Miss
Pwr ++++
BAvg ++
Spd +
Def ++

Year	Lev	Team	AB	R	H	HR	RBI	Avg	OB	Sig	OPS	bb%	ct%	Eye	SB	CS	x/h%	Iso	RC/G
2021	Rk	FCL Twins	6	2	2	0	0	333	333	333	667	0	67	0.00	0	0	0	0	3.37
2021	A+	Cedar Rapids	258	39	68	15	47	264	336	508	843	10	62	0.29	0	1	46	244	6.69
2022	AA	Wichita	268	61	80	21	64	299	430	597	1027	19	60	0.58	8	5	46	299	10.08
2022	AAA	St. Paul	190	29	47	6	31	247	364	463	828	16	67	0.56	1	0	55	216	6.54
2022	MLB	Minnesota	57	4	13	2	10	228	302	386	688	10	56	0.24	1	0	38	158	4.64

Slugging OF with prototypical RF arm and pop. Thrived with big increase in walk rate and culminated with 57 AB in majors. Drawback to power is ton of swing and miss - led org in Ks. Few can match power output and uppercut, vicious swing. Posted career high in HR and doubles. Breaking balls have proven difficult and is sub-par defender.

Ward,Ryan — 7 — Los Angeles (N) — EXP MLB DEBUT: 2024 — H/W: 5-11 200 — FUT: Reserve OF — 6C

Bats L Age 25
2019 (8) Bryant
Pwr +++
BAvg ++
Spd +
Def +

Year	Lev	Team	AB	R	H	HR	RBI	Avg	OB	Sig	OPS	bb%	ct%	Eye	SB	CS	x/h%	Iso	RC/G
2019	NCAA	Bryant Univ	249	59	95	13	51	382	448	614	1062	11	93	1.76	12	4	32	233	8.42
2019	Rk	Ogden	188	35	51	4	23	271	338	415	753	9	84	0.63	7	4	33	144	4.92
2021	A+	Great Lakes	439	91	122	27	84	278	348	524	872	10	73	0.40	8	6	42	246	6.39
2022	AA	Tulsa	459	62	117	28	78	255	313	486	799	8	75	0.34	5	1	41	231	5.25

Undersized OF has an ability to find the barrel with above-average power that makes up for funky mechanics and a lack of athleticism. Has mashed 55 HR over the past two seasons between A+ and AA, but doesn't draw a ton of walks and will need to continue to mash to carve out a 4th OF role. Below average speed and defense, but everything on the bat.

Warren,Zavier — 35 — Milwaukee — EXP MLB DEBUT: 2024 — H/W: 6-1 215 — FUT: Utility player — 6C

Bats B Age 24
2020 (3) C Michigan
Pwr ++
BAvg ++
Spd +++
Def +++

Year	Lev	Team	AB	R	H	HR	RBI	Avg	OB	Sig	OPS	bb%	ct%	Eye	SB	CS	x/h%	Iso	RC/G
2020	NCAA	Central Michigan	64	17	21	1	9	328	456	406	862	19	86	1.67	0	2	14	78	6.84
2021	A	Carolina	191	34	48	10	30	251	362	471	833	15	74	0.67	1	0	42	220	6.11
2021	A+	Wisconsin	135	21	36	3	18	267	353	400	753	12	76	0.56	5	0	31	133	5.02
2022	A+	Wisconsin	373	48	82	10	46	220	290	381	671	9	78	0.46	6	1	46	161	3.83
2022	AA	Biloxi	92	9	23	2	11	250	337	348	684	12	71	0.44	3	0	22	98	4.06

Quick, versatile INF who caught some in 2021, but no games in 2022. Suffered thru challenging season as swing mechanics got out of whack and started to chase more in hopes of pop production. Better from left side of plate. Has enough strength for gap power and can pull ball out of park. Runs well and has enough arm for 3B.

Watson,Kahlil — 46 — Miami — EXP MLB DEBUT: 2025 — H/W: 5-9 178 — FUT: Starting SS — 8E

Bats L Age 19
2021 (1) HS (NC)
Pwr ++++
BAvg ++
Spd ++++
Def ++++

Year	Lev	Team	AB	R	H	HR	RBI	Avg	OB	Sig	OPS	bb%	ct%	Eye	SB	CS	x/h%	Iso	RC/G
2021	Rk	FCL Marlins	33	13	13	0	5	394	512	606	1118	20	79	1.14	4	1	38	212	10.58
2022	Rk	FCL Marlins	11	4	3	1	3	273	500	727	1227	31	55	1.00	0	0	100	455	14.96
2022	A	Jupiter	324	50	75	9	44	231	291	395	686	8	61	0.21	16	3	40	164	4.35

Twitchy, athletic LHH SS prospect struggled during full-season debut. Shorter frame with room to grow. Open stance with easy trigger. Super aggressive approach and present swing-and-miss dampen profile. Plus-plus bat speed powers plus HR potential, could get to 30+ HR. Plus runner. Has the ability to stick at SS and steal bases.

Wells,Austin — 2 — New York (A) — EXP MLB DEBUT: 2023 — H/W: 6-2 220 — FUT: Starting C — 8C

Bats L Age 23
2020 (1) Arizona
Pwr ++++
BAvg +++
Spd ++
Def ++

Year	Lev	Team	AB	R	H	HR	RBI	Avg	OB	Sig	OPS	bb%	ct%	Eye	SB	CS	x/h%	Iso	RC/G
2021	A	Tampa	236	61	61	9	54	258	390	479	869	18	74	0.82	11	0	49	220	6.91
2021	A+	Hudson Valley	146	21	40	7	22	274	361	473	834	12	62	0.36	5	0	35	199	6.60
2022	A	Tampa	26	5	6	2	6	231	412	538	950	24	81	1.60	0	0	67	308	7.87
2022	A+	Hudson Valley	99	21	32	6	16	323	432	576	1008	16	73	0.70	9	0	41	253	8.65
2022	AA	Somerset	211	34	55	12	43	261	350	479	829	12	73	0.50	7	0	38	218	5.93

Offensive-first LHH C prospect showcased plus power output after Double-A promotion. Strong, power driven frame. Upright, open stance with leg lift. Above-average bat speed. Has knack for creating loft off bat. Works counts, works up the middle with approach. Could get to 30+ HR potential with more pull added to profile. Improved arm behind plate.

Westburg,Jordan
456 | Baltimore | EXP MLB DEBUT: 2023 | H/W: 6-3 203 | FUT: Starting 3B | 8B

Bats R Age 24	Year	Lev	Team	AB	R	H	HR	RBI	Avg	OB	Slg	OPS	bb%	ct%	Eye	SB	CS	x/h%	Iso	RC/G
2020 (1) Mississippi St	2021	A	Delmarva	71	18	26	3	24	366	458	592	1049	14	66	0.50	5	1	35	225	9.86
Pwr ++++	2021	A+	Aberdeen	241	41	69	8	41	286	377	469	846	13	71	0.49	9	4	38	183	6.45
BAvg +++	2021	AA	Bowie	112	15	26	4	14	232	317	429	746	11	71	0.44	3	0	46	196	4.94
Spd +++	2022	AA	Bowie	182	32	45	9	32	247	341	473	814	13	69	0.46	3	0	51	225	5.96
Def +++	2022	AAA	Norfolk Tides	362	64	99	18	74	273	352	508	861	11	75	0.49	9	3	46	235	6.33

Took a liking to the high minors and hit the most HR of his career as he was able to pull the ball more. Short/quick swing with minimal stride; doesn't chase and high exit velocity comes easy. High baseball IQ that serves him well on the bases and in the field. A premium athlete, he can handle SS/2B but probably 3B is his best long-term position.

Whitaker,Tyler
569 | Houston | EXP MLB DEBUT: 2026 | H/W: 6-4 190 | FUT: Starting OF | 7E

Bats R Age 20	Year	Lev	Team	AB	R	H	HR	RBI	Avg	OB	Slg	OPS	bb%	ct%	Eye	SB	CS	x/h%	Iso	RC/G
2021 (3) HS (NV)																				
Pwr +++																				
BAvg +																				
Spd +++	2021	Rk	FCL Astros	104	16	21	3	6	202	265	327	592	8	62	0.23	8	1	29	125	2.71
Def +++	2022	A	Fayetteville	460	48	86	11	54	187	253	313	567	8	61	0.23	16	4	38	126	2.38

Young, athletic OF boasts plus speed and defensive chops but struggled extensively with subpar hit tool in full-season debut. Prone to chasing pitches away and struggles with timing. Above-average power potential with some projection remaining in frame. Contact skills need refinement in order for any success at next level.

White,Lonnie
89 | Pittsburgh | EXP MLB DEBUT: 2026 | H/W: 6-3 212 | FUT: Starting OF | 8D

Bats R Age 20	Year	Lev	Team	AB	R	H	HR	RBI	Avg	OB	Slg	OPS	bb%	ct%	Eye	SB	CS	x/h%	Iso	RC/G
2021 (2) HS (PA)																				
Pwr +++																				
BAvg ++																				
Spd ++++	2021	Rk	FCL Pirates Black	31	6	8	2	5	258	303	516	819	6	55	0.14	0	0	50	258	6.95
Def +++	2022	Rk	FCL Pirates Black	7	1	2	1	3	286	286	857	1143	0	57	0.00	0	0	100	571	11.87

Missed most of season with elbow injury. Very exciting upside based upon athleticism, power and speed. Has the wheels to steal bases and patrol CF with above average range. Still raw with bat as he can lunge at pitches and be beaten with breaking balls. May take time to get to pop as he curtails aggressiveness.

White,TJ
7 | Washington | EXP MLB DEBUT: 2026 | H/W: 6-2 210 | FUT: Starting OF | 7D

Bats B Age 19	Year	Lev	Team	AB	R	H	HR	RBI	Avg	OB	Slg	OPS	bb%	ct%	Eye	SB	CS	x/h%	Iso	RC/G
2021 (5) HS (SC)																				
Pwr +++																				
BAvg ++																				
4.51 Spd +	2021	Rk	FCL Nationals	53	11	15	4	12	283	345	547	892	9	74	0.36	1	0	40	264	6.48
Def ++	2022	A	Fredericksburg	329	55	85	11	52	258	346	432	777	12	68	0.42	8	1	39	173	5.49

Improving in-game power led to double-digit HR in first full season. A switch hitter, most of his damage in 2022 came from the left side. Has a strong lower half and body is at projection, though is young for his draft class. Contact/hit tool lags behind pop, and doesn't run well. Defense also a question; LF now, but may need to move to 1B later.

Wiemer,Joey
9 | Milwaukee | EXP MLB DEBUT: 2023 | H/W: 6-5 215 | FUT: Starting OF | 7B

Bats R Age 24	Year	Lev	Team	AB	R	H	HR	RBI	Avg	OB	Slg	OPS	bb%	ct%	Eye	SB	CS	x/h%	Iso	RC/G
2020 (4) Cincinnati	2020	NCAA	Cincinnati	48	16	14	1	12	292	452	438	889	23	81	1.56	5	1	36	146	7.40
Pwr ++++	2021	A	Carolina	268	53	74	13	44	276	380	478	858	14	74	0.65	22	4	35	201	6.45
BAvg ++	2021	A+	Wisconsin	128	33	43	14	33	336	418	719	1137	12	72	0.50	8	2	49	383	10.03
Spd +++	2022	AA	Biloxi	334	57	81	15	47	243	313	440	753	9	66	0.30	25	1	43	198	5.04
Def +++	2022	AAA	Nashville	150	24	43	6	30	287	374	520	894	12	77	0.62	6	2	51	233	6.89

Large, athletic OF who has posted 20/20 output in each of last two years. Double plus raw power is highlight. Very strong, fast swing enhanced by leverage and loft. Runs well for size - finished 2nd in org in SB. Big concern is K rate and struggles with spin. Best attribute may be cannon arm which fits well in RF. BA projects low.

Williams,Alika
6 | Tampa Bay | EXP MLB DEBUT: 2024 | H/W: 6-2 180 | FUT: Starting SS | 7D

Bats R Age 24	Year	Lev	Team	AB	R	H	HR	RBI	Avg	OB	Slg	OPS	bb%	ct%	Eye	SB	CS	x/h%	Iso	RC/G
2020 (1) Arizona St	2021	A+	Bowling Green	61	12	17	3	9	279	302	475	777	3	80	0.17	1	1	35	197	4.68
Pwr ++	2021	AAA	Durham	9	1	2	1	3	222	222	556	778	0	89	0.00	0	0	50	333	4.25
BAvg +++	2022	A+	Bowling Green	323	59	82	10	58	254	349	390	739	13	79	0.69	6	3	27	136	4.81
Spd +++	2022	AA	Montgomery	21	1	5	0	2	238	333	286	619	13	62	0.38	1	0	20	48	3.41
Def ++++	2022	AAA	Durham	17	1	3	0	2	176	333	235	569	19	59	0.57	0	1	33	59	2.72

Athletic, glove-first SS prospect played across 3 levels in 2022. Upright RHH stance with bat wrap in load. all-fields approach. Works counts and grinds at AB. Average bat speed, Will allow pitches to travel and slap the other way. Limited power projection. Doesn't achieve solid leverage in lower half. Plus defender at SS, carries profile.

Williams,Carson
6 | Tampa Bay | EXP MLB DEBUT: 2025 | H/W: 6-2 180 | FUT: Starting SS | 8D

Bats R Age 19	Year	Lev	Team	AB	R	H	HR	RBI	Avg	OB	Slg	OPS	bb%	ct%	Eye	SB	CS	x/h%	Iso	RC/G
2021 (1) HS (CA)																				
Pwr ++++																				
BAvg +++																				
Spd +++	2021	Rk	FCL Rays	39	8	11	0	8	282	378	436	814	13	67	0.46	2	2	45	154	6.51
Def ++++	2022	A	Charleston	452	81	114	19	70	252	336	471	807	11	63	0.34	28	10	45	219	6.22

Wiry, athletic SS prospect hit 19 HRs in full-season debut. Open, upright stance with hands moving direct to hit position. Plus-plus bat speed with upper-cut trajectory. Fringe hit tool courtesy of chasing spin and cutting off the plate. Raw plus power in frame and swing. Could play up higher with more contact. Plus defender with strong arm at SS.

Williams,Jett
6 | New York (N) | EXP MLB DEBUT: 2025 | H/W: 5-8 175 | FUT: Starting SS | 8C

Bats R Age 19	Year	Lev	Team	AB	R	H	HR	RBI	Avg	OB	Slg	OPS	bb%	ct%	Eye	SB	CS	x/h%	Iso	RC/G
2022 (1) HS (TX)																				
Pwr +++																				
BAvg ++++																				
Spd +++																				
Def +++	2022	Rk	FCL Mets	32	7	8	1	6	250	333	438	771	11	81	0.67	6	0	38	188	5.22

Short-statured, athletic SS prospect, taken in 1st round of 2022 draft, made pro debut. Short limbed physique, allows for compact swing, has room for added bulk. Upright, closed stance. Present contact skills with uppercut swing trajectory. Achieves great angles off the bat. Average power potential. Plus runner.

Wilson,Ethan
9 | Philadelphia | EXP MLB DEBUT: 2024 | H/W: 6-1 210 | FUT: Starting OF | 7D

Bats L Age 23	Year	Lev	Team	AB	R	H	HR	RBI	Avg	OB	Slg	OPS	bb%	ct%	Eye	SB	CS	x/h%	Iso	RC/G
2021 (2) So Alabama	2020	NCAA	South Alabama	71	13	20	3	12	282	320	465	785	5	72	0.20	6	0	35	183	5.11
Pwr ++	2021	NCAA	South Alabama	209	38	66	8	34	316	409	531	940	14	90	1.57	9	4	38	215	7.38
BAvg +++	2021	A	Clearwater	107	15	23	3	17	215	282	374	656	9	77	0.40	2	2	39	159	3.59
4.44 Spd +	2022	A+	Jersey Shore	424	39	101	7	45	238	285	344	630	6	78	0.30	25	7	29	106	3.16
Def ++	2022	AA	Reading	70	7	15	1	3	214	267	286	552	7	70	0.24	1	2	20	71	2.03

Seen as a high-floor collegian, he's neither been able to hit for much power nor get on base at a good clip in his year and a half as a pro. Did steal 26 bases in 2022, but not necessarily a burner, and that fact that got less patient at the plate is concerning. Power hasn't shown up yet; limited athleticism in the field though has a strong arm.

Wilson,Peyton
48 | Kansas City | EXP MLB DEBUT: 2024 | H/W: 5-9 180 | FUT: Starting CF | 7C

Bats B Age 23	Year	Lev	Team	AB	R	H	HR	RBI	Avg	OB	Slg	OPS	bb%	ct%	Eye	SB	CS	x/h%	Iso	RC/G
2021 (2) Alabama	2021	NCAA	Alabama	248	46	72	9	31	290	348	460	808	8	83	0.54	10	3	32	169	5.41
Pwr +++	2021	Rk	ACL Royals Blue	3	0	0	0	0	0	250	0	250	25	67	1.00	0	0		0	-2.42
BAvg ++	2021	Rk	ACL Royals Gold	32	7	7	1	7	219	324	469	793	14	69	0.50	2	2	71	250	5.93
Spd ++++	2021	A	Columbia	39	6	9	0	1	231	302	359	661	9	74	0.40	5	0	44	128	3.91
Def ++++	2022	A+	Quad Cities	340	60	91	14	44	268	346	456	802	11	71	0.42	23	2	36	188	5.64

Athletic, switch-hitting MIF started transition to CF during '22 season. Shorter stature with minimal room to grow. Power over hit tool at the plate. Upright stance with some length in the load but a fairly compact, uppercut swing. Gets to average power by using leverage in lower half. Plus run with speed to cover CF. Plus arm too.

Wilson,Will
46 | San Francisco | EXP MLB DEBUT: 2023 | H/W: 6-0 184 | FUT: Starting 2B | 7D

Bats R Age 24	Year	Lev	Team	AB	R	H	HR	RBI	Avg	OB	Slg	OPS	bb%	ct%	Eye	SB	CS	x/h%	Iso	RC/G
2019 (1) NC State	2021	A+	Eugene	195	37	49	10	26	251	333	497	831	11	71	0.43	7	1	53	246	6.06
Pwr +++	2021	AA	Richmond	196	20	37	5	22	189	271	306	577	10	59	0.27	1	0	35	117	2.60
BAvg ++	2022	Rk	ACL Giants O	28	6	14	1	9	500	563	750	1313	13	71	0.50	0	0	36	250	13.12
Spd ++	2022	AA	Richmond	191	35	43	12	27	225	324	445	769	13	66	0.43	2	2	42	220	5.25
Def +++	2022	AAA	Sacramento	33	2	6	0	2	182	229	242	471	6	58	0.14	0	1	33	61	0.98

Missed time with broken hand. Still shows glimpses of first round talent, though not consistently. Struggles to hit for BA as breaking balls give him hits and can pull ball too much. Hits for good power and can also tone down swing to go gap to gap. Plays both middle INF spots with 2B the better of two. Lacks ideal foot speed.

Winn,Masyn | 6 | St. Louis | EXP MLB DEBUT: 2024 | H/W: 5-11 180 | FUT: Starting SS | 8C

Bats R Age 21	Year	Lev	Team	AB	R	H	HR	RBI	Avg	OB	Slg	OPS	bb%	ct%	Eye	SB	CS	x/h%	Iso	RC/G
2020 (2) HS (TX)																				
Pwr ++	2021	A	Palm Beach	237	50	62	3	34	262	368	388	756	14	75	0.67	16	2	34	127	5.30
BAvg +++	2021	A+	Peoria	148	26	31	2	10	209	240	304	544	4	73	0.15	16	3	26	95	1.90
Spd ++++	2022	A+	Peoria	129	22	45	1	15	349	408	566	974	9	78	0.45	15	0	42	217	8.02
Def +++++	2022	AA	Springfield	345	69	89	11	48	258	352	432	784	13	75	0.58	28	5	42	174	5.46

Breakout campaign with improved production across the board. Was a two-way player when drafted and has the tools to be an elite defender at short with plus-plus arm. Uptick in power changed his profile from a glove-first prospect. Questions about his ability to hit premium velocity remain, but the speed and defense are major league ready right now.

Wisely,Brett | 3456 | San Francisco | EXP MLB DEBUT: 2023 | H/W: 5-10 180 | FUT: Utility player | 7C

Bats L Age 23	Year	Lev	Team	AB	R	H	HR	RBI	Avg	OB	Slg	OPS	bb%	ct%	Eye	SB	CS	x/h%	Iso	RC/G
2019 (15) Gulf Coast CC	2019	Rk	Princeton	179	30	49	5	25	274	337	441	778	9	84	0.59	3	2	35	168	5.17
Pwr ++	2021	A	Charleston	274	50	80	11	44	292	358	467	825	9	75	0.41	28	7	31	175	5.77
BAvg +++	2021	A+	Bowling Green	112	28	36	8	30	321	424	589	1014	15	74	0.69	3	1	39	268	8.51
Spd +++	2022	AA	Montgomery	430	84	118	15	56	274	366	460	826	13	76	0.60	31	11	37	186	6.01
Def +++	2022	AAA	Durham	21	3	5	0	2	238	273	333	606	5	71	0.17	1	0	40	95	2.89

Versatile, contact-oriented LHH had fantastic '22 season, mostly in AA. Short-statured, near physical projection with above-average athleticism. Shorter limbs add with keeping swing compact. Uppercut trajectory swing, mostly pull pop. Will work all fields with spray approach. Power tapped at 15-20 HR range. Natural 2B. Will play all IF & LF.

Wong,Connor | 2 | Boston | EXP MLB DEBUT: 2021 | H/W: 6-1 181 | FUT: Reserve C | 6B

Bats R Age 26	Year	Lev	Team	AB	R	H	HR	RBI	Avg	OB	Slg	OPS	bb%	ct%	Eye	SB	CS	x/h%	Iso	RC/G
2017 (3) Houston	2019	AA	Tulsa	149	17	52	9	31	349	394	604	998	7	66	0.22	2	1	37	255	8.53
Pwr +++	2021	AAA	Worcester	199	22	51	8	26	256	288	442	731	4	71	0.16	7	1	41	186	4.38
BAvg ++	2021	MLB	Boston	13	3	4	0	1	308	357	538	896	7	46	0.14	0	0	50	231	11.16
Spd ++	2022	AAA	Worcester	323	47	93	15	44	288	343	489	832	8	75	0.34	7	3	38	201	5.75
Def +++	2022	MLB	Boston	48	8	9	1	7	188	264	313	577	9	67	0.31	0	0	44	125	2.51

Athletic, defensive-oriented backstop who has value by playing multiple positions. Limited size, but has decent strength and leverages quick release to enhance average arm. Good receiver with excellent agility. Can play 2B and 3B. Not much offensive production. Lot of Ks with average power.

Wood,James | 8 | Washington | EXP MLB DEBUT: 2024 | H/W: 6-7 240 | FUT: Starting CF | 9D

Bats L Age 20	Year	Lev	Team	AB	R	H	HR	RBI	Avg	OB	Slg	OPS	bb%	ct%	Eye	SB	CS	x/h%	Iso	RC/G
2021 (2) HS (FL)																				
Pwr ++++	2021	Rk	ACL Padres	86	18	32	3	22	372	455	535	989	13	63	0.41	10	0	25	163	9.20
BAvg +++	2022	Rk	ACL Padres	16	1	2	0	0	125	263	125	388	16	56	0.43	1	0	0	0	-0.65
Spd +++	2022	A	Fredericksburg	82	14	24	2	17	293	370	463	833	11	68	0.38	4	0	42	171	6.37
Def +++	2022	A	Lake Elsinore	193	55	65	10	45	337	443	601	1045	16	78	0.88	15	5	46	264	8.98

Massively-built, talented teenager posted MLB-level exit velocity in first full season of Low-A across two orgs. Mix of explosive bat speed and timing for heaters, and uncanny balance to wait on off speed. It's a potential 30+ HR talent who could stay in CF. Some swing and miss, but long strides will lead to SB and there's still room to grow.

Workman,Gage | 65 | Detroit | EXP MLB DEBUT: 2024 | H/W: 6-3 202 | FUT: Starting 3B | 7E

Bats B Age 23	Year	Lev	Team	AB	R	H	HR	RBI	Avg	OB	Slg	OPS	bb%	ct%	Eye	SB	CS	x/h%	Iso	RC/G
2020 (4) Arizona St																				
Pwr +++	2020	NCAA	Arizona St	68	12	17	3	14	250	301	471	772	7	69	0.24	3	1	47	221	5.16
BAvg +	2021	A	Lakeland	195	26	50	3	19	256	356	426	781	13	69	0.50	22	3	46	169	5.77
Spd +++	2021	A+	West Michigan	257	42	61	9	39	237	300	440	740	8	62	0.24	9	5	52	202	5.15
Def +++	2022	AA	Erie	475	61	107	14	68	225	277	415	692	7	57	0.17	30	9	50	189	4.79

Has struggled to translate above-average raw tools into success on the diamond. Uses a slightly open stance from both sides and has above-average bat speed and impressive raw power. Inability to identify spin or catch up to high heat results in an alarming amount of swing-and-miss and will need to be corrected. Moves well defensively and can play both SS and 3B.

Yorke,Nick | 4 | Boston | EXP MLB DEBUT: 2024 | H/W: 6-0 200 | FUT: Starting 2B | 8D

Bats R Age 21	Year	Lev	Team	AB	R	H	HR	RBI	Avg	OB	Slg	OPS	bb%	ct%	Eye	SB	CS	x/h%	Iso	RC/G
2020 (1) HS (CA)																				
Pwr +++																				
BAvg +++	2021	A	Salem	294	59	95	10	47	323	406	500	906	12	84	0.87	11	8	29	177	6.88
Spd +++	2021	A+	Greenville	84	17	28	4	15	333	411	571	982	12	74	0.50	2	1	39	238	8.09
Def +++	2022	A+	Greenville	337	48	78	11	45	231	300	365	665	9	72	0.35	8	4	28	134	3.62

Strong 2B who suffered thru poor season, though ended well. Still possesses high BA potential, but became too pull-happy in bid to increase pop. Sees lot of pitches and can read spin. Swing mechanics are sound and can put ball in play. Bat will have to carry him. Defense has been average and has the footwork and arm strength to thrive.

Young,Carter | 6 | Baltimore | EXP MLB DEBUT: 2026 | H/W: 6-0 180 | FUT: Starting SS | 7D

Bats B Age 22	Year	Lev	Team	AB	R	H	HR	RBI	Avg	OB	Slg	OPS	bb%	ct%	Eye	SB	CS	x/h%	Iso	RC/G
2022 (17) Vanderbilt																				
Pwr ++																				
BAvg +++	2022	NCAA	Vanderbilt	188	34	39	7	26	207	317	383	699	14	65	0.45	2	2	41	176	4.45
4.55 Spd ++	2022	Rk	FCL Orioles B	14	0	4	0	1	286	333	286	619	7	71	0.25	0	0	0	0	2.95
Def +++	2022	A	Delmarva	65	11	16	1	7	246	300	400	700	7	80	0.38	0	0	44	154	4.21

Inconsistent college career with the bat; showed some power but early batted-ball metrics in the pros are tepid. Average run times but solid instincts on the bases, fringe-average hit tool and raw pop from a switch hitter. Capable shortstop with good range and a strong arm; looks like utility player but could be more if bat becomes more reliable.

Young,Cole | 6 | Seattle | EXP MLB DEBUT: 2025 | H/W: 6-0 180 | FUT: Starting SS | 8D

Bats L Age 19	Year	Lev	Team	AB	R	H	HR	RBI	Avg	OB	Slg	OPS	bb%	ct%	Eye	SB	CS	x/h%	Iso	RC/G
2022 (1) HS (PA)																				
Pwr ++																				
BAvg ++++																				
Spd +++	2022	Rk	ACL Mariners	21	6	7	0	5	333	440	476	916	16	81	1.00	3	0	29	143	7.56
Def +++	2022	A	Modesto	39	11	15	2	9	385	442	538	980	9	90	1.00	1	2	13	154	7.31

Natural-hitting SS who makes easy, loud contact with simple, direct swing. Controls barrel with aplomb and uses whole field in approach. Lacks present power, but should get to at least average with more strength. Owns above average speed which enhances defense at SS. Ranges well to both sides and has quality fundamental glovework.

Zamora,Freddy | 6 | Milwaukee | EXP MLB DEBUT: 2024 | H/W: 6-1 190 | FUT: Starting SS | 7D

Bats R Age 24	Year	Lev	Team	AB	R	H	HR	RBI	Avg	OB	Slg	OPS	bb%	ct%	Eye	SB	CS	x/h%	Iso	RC/G
2020 (2) Miami																				
Pwr +																				
BAvg ++	2021	A	Carolina	268	58	77	5	40	287	390	399	789	14	79	0.79	9	5	25	112	5.63
Spd +++	2021	A+	Wisconsin	79	12	27	1	9	342	429	494	922	13	76	0.63	1	0	37	152	7.49
Def ++++	2022	AA	Biloxi	91	10	19	1	5	209	250	286	536	5	76	0.23	4	0	26	77	1.87

Dislocated left shoulder in May and underwent surgery. Quick, fast SS who can make routine and highlight plays. Ranges well to both sides and has textbook footwork. Profiles to hit at bottom of lineup. Not much power production with limited bat speed. Has compact swing to make acceptable contact and will get on base.

Zavala,Aaron | 9 | Texas | EXP MLB DEBUT: 2024 | H/W: 6-0 193 | FUT: Starting OF | 8C

Bats L Age 22	Year	Lev	Team	AB	R	H	HR	RBI	Avg	OB	Slg	OPS	bb%	ct%	Eye	SB	CS	x/h%	Iso	RC/G
2021 (2) Oregon	2021	NCAA	Oregon	199	64	78	9	38	392	514	628	1142	20	84	1.61	11	2	33	236	10.29
Pwr ++	2021	Rk	ACL Rangers	22	5	6	0	2	273	360	318	678	12	68	0.43	2	0	17	45	4.17
BAvg ++++	2021	A	Down East	53	13	16	1	7	302	413	434	847	16	75	0.77	7	0	31	132	6.54
Spd ++	2022	A+	Hickory	299	61	83	11	41	278	411	441	853	19	74	0.86	10	5	29	164	6.66
Def ++	2022	AA	Frisco	112	28	31	5	21	277	391	482	873	16	74	0.72	4	1	42	205	6.78

Another Rangers premium hit tool guy also showing platoon splits, albeit strong-side. He had a breakout 2022 before going down in the AFL with a UCL injury. Ate RHP alive across two levels, but exceptional zone awareness led to passivity at the plate. Average power and run tools, definite LF-fit in this org with 4th OF floor. Clutch hitter.

Zavala,Samuel | 8 | San Diego | EXP MLB DEBUT: 2027 | H/W: 6-1 175 | FUT: Starting OF | 8D

Bats L Age 18	Year	Lev	Team	AB	R	H	HR	RBI	Avg	OB	Slg	OPS	bb%	ct%	Eye	SB	CS	x/h%	Iso	RC/G
2021 FA (VZ)																				
Pwr +++																				
BAvg +++	2021	Rk	DSL Padres	195	44	58	3	40	297	396	487	884	14	82	0.89	11	7	43	190	6.94
Spd +++	2022	Rk	ACL Padres	29	6	10	1	6	345	424	621	1045	12	62	0.36	0	0	50	276	10.38
Def +++	2022	A	Lake Elsinore	122	24	31	7	26	254	355	508	863	13	70	0.51	5	3	48	254	6.64

Aggressive, toolsy OF with immense upside. Very young for Low-A and held his own due to advanced skills. Added more strength and loft to short stroke and starting to hit for power. Has struggled with pitch recognition, but should get better with more AB. Has potential to hit for BA and power. Plays a true CF with strong arm and instincts.

Pitchers are classified as Starters (SP) or Relievers (RP).

THROWS: Handedness — right (RH) or left (LH).

AGE: Pitcher's age, as of April 1, 2023.

DRAFTED: The year, round, and school that the pitcher performed at as an amateur if drafted, or the year and country where the player was signed from, if a free agent.

EXP MLB DEBUT: The year a player is expected to debut in the major leagues.

H/W: The player's height and weight.

FUT: The role that the pitcher is expected to have for the majority of his major league career, not necessarily his greatest upside.

PITCHES: Each pitch that a pitcher throws is graded and designated with a "+", indicating the quality of the pitch, taking into context the pitcher's age and level pitched. Pitches are graded for their velocity, movement, and command. An average pitch will receive three "+" marks. If known, a pitcher's velocity for each pitch is indicated.

FB	fastball
CB	curveball
SP	split-fingered fastball
SL	slider
CU	change-up
CT	cut-fastball
KC	knuckle-curve
KB	knuckle-ball
SC	screwball
SU	slurve

PLAYER STAT LINES: Pitcher's statistics for the last five teams that he played for (if applicable), including college and the major leagues.

TEAM DESIGNATIONS: Each team that the pitcher performed for during a given year is included.

LEVEL DESIGNATIONS: The level for each team a player performed is included. "AAA" means Triple-A, "AA" means Double-A, "A+" means high Class-A, "A" means full-season low Class-A, and "Rk" means rookie level. Prior to 2020, an "A-" referred to short-season Class-A, a level between rookie level and full-season low-A. Starting in 2021, that level no longer exists.

SABERMETRIC CATEGORIES: Descriptions of all the sabermetric categories appear in the glossary.

CAPSULE COMMENTARIES: For each pitcher, a brief analysis of their skills/statistics, and their future potential is provided.

ELIGIBILITY: Eligibility for inclusion is the standard for which Major League Baseball adheres to; less than 50 innings pitched and less than 45 days in the 26-man roster.

POTENTIAL RATINGS: The Potential Ratings are a two-part system in which a player is assigned a number rating based on his upside potential (1-10) and a letter rating based on the probability of reaching that potential (A-E).

Potential

10:	Hall of Famer	5:	MLB reserve
9:	Elite player	4:	Top minor leaguer
8:	Solid regular	3:	Average minor leaguer
7:	Average regular	2:	Minor league reserve
6:	Platoon player	1:	Minor league roster filler

Probability Rating

A:	90% probability of reaching potential
B:	70% probability of reaching potential
C:	50% probability of reaching potential
D:	30% probability of reaching potential
E:	10% probability of reaching potential

FASTBALL: Scouts grade a fastball in terms of both velocity and movement. Movement of a pitch is purely subjective, but one can always watch the hitter to see how he reacts to a pitch or if he swings and misses. Pitchers throw four types of fastballs with varying movement. A two-seam fastball is often referred to as a sinker. A four-seam fastball appears to maintain its plane at high velocities. A cutter can move in different directions and is caused by the pitcher both cutting-off his extension out front and by varying the grip. A split-fingered fastball (forkball) is thrown with the fingers spread apart against the seams and demonstrates violent downward movement. Velocity is often graded on the 20-80 scale and is indicated by the chart below.

Scout Grade	Velocity (mph)
80	96+
70	94-95
60	92-93
50 (avg)	89-91
40	87-88
30	85-86
20	82-84

PITCHER RELEASE TIMES: The speed (in seconds) that a pitcher releases a pitch from the stretch is extremely important in terms of halting the running game and establishing good pitching mechanics. Pitchers are timed from the movement of the front leg until the baseball reaches the catcher's mitt. The phrases "slow to the plate" or "quick to the plate" may appear in the capsule commentary box.

1.0-1.2	+
1.3-1.4	MLB average
1.5+	−

Abbott,Andrew — SP — Cincinnati

EXP MLB DEBUT: 2023 | H/W: 6-0 180 | FUT: #4 starter | 8D

Thrws L Age 23 — 2021 (2) Virginia

Velo	Pitch	Grade
90-94	FB	++++
78-81	CB	+++
84-86	CU	+++
80-82	SL	++

Year	Lev	Team	W	L	Sv	IP	K	ERA	WHIP	BF/G	OBA	H%	S%	xERA	Ctl	Dom	Cmd	hr/9	BPV
2021	NCAA	Virginia	9	6	0	106	162	2.88	1.14	22.1	229	36	81	3.22	2.7	13.7	5.1	1.1	192
2021	Rk	ACL Reds	0	0	0	2	3	0.00	0.50	3.3	151	27	100		0.0	13.5		0.0	261
2021	A	Daytona	0	0	0	11	19	4.91	1.36	11.5	262	43	69	4.70	3.3	15.5	4.8	1.6	209
2022	A+	Dayton	3	0	0	27	40	0.67	0.85	19.8	174	29	95	1.13	2.3	13.3	5.7	0.3	195
2022	AA	Chattanooga	7	7	0	91	119	4.75	1.37	19.1	247	36	65	3.68	4.1	11.8	2.9	0.7	120

3/4s pitchability LHP struggled with command but racked up whiffs with 3 average-to-above offerings. It's a repeatable delivery with solid extension. 4-seam FB sits low 90s with solid riding profile from lower arm slot. CB is best secondary offering with plus sweeping action. Throws deceptive CU. SL is newer wrinkle but looks similar to CB.

Abel,Mick — SP — Philadelphia

EXP MLB DEBUT: 2024 | H/W: 6-5 190 | FUT: #3 starter | 9C

Thrws R Age 21 — 2020 (1) HS (OR)

Velo	Pitch	Grade
94-97	FB	++++
83-85	SL	++++
78-81	CB	++
86-89	CU	+++

Year	Lev	Team	W	L	Sv	IP	K	ERA	WHIP	BF/G	OBA	H%	S%	xERA	Ctl	Dom	Cmd	hr/9	BPV
2021	A	Clearwater	1	3	0	44	66	4.48	1.22	12.8	178	27	65	2.75	5.5	13.4	2.4	1.0	111
2022	A+	Jersey Shore	7	8	0	85	103	4.02	1.33	19.6	238	33	70	3.40	4.0	10.9	2.7	0.6	106
2022	AA	Reading	1	3	0	23	27	3.52	1.35	19.2	227	27	85	4.55	4.7	10.6	2.3	2.0	81

Lean starter continues to fill out and put together a very good season over two levels. Four-pitch mix highlighted by FB/SL combo that he can both land for strikes and gets whiffs/chases on. CU can sometimes gets too firm, but ahead of CB right now. Great arm speed; still some projectability, impeccable mound presence and intangibles. High floor.

Acker,Dane — SP — Texas

EXP MLB DEBUT: 2025 | H/W: 6-2 189 | FUT: #4 starter | 7E

Thrws R Age 24 — 2020 (4) Oklahoma

Velo	Pitch	Grade
93-96	FB	+++
77-81	CB	++
85-88	CU	+

Year	Lev	Team	W	L	Sv	IP	K	ERA	WHIP	BF/G	OBA	H%	S%	xERA	Ctl	Dom	Cmd	hr/9	BPV
2020	NCAA	Oklahoma	1	1	0	25	28	3.57	0.79	22.8	174	23	56	1.38	1.8	10.0	5.6	0.7	150
2021	A	Down East	0	1	0	6	11	2.95	0.82	11.1	189	39	60	0.87	1.5	16.2	11.0	0.0	270
2022	Rk	ACL Rangers	0	0	0	13	14	2.08	0.92	9.7	160	21	82	1.54	3.5	9.7	2.8	0.7	99
2022	A+	Hickory	0	3	0	12	17	11.07	2.13	15.1	317	43	48	8.04	7.4	12.5	1.7	2.2	45

Mulligan '22 stats due to Tommy John recovery; just back into game action after looking like he was breaking out in '21. FF predicated on past 99-mph velo returning, topped 96 in '22 and plus variables still here. SL shelved for CB, CU distant third but not enough data to discern future value. Wildcard who may get pushed to bullpen.

Acton,Garrett — RP — Oakland

EXP MLB DEBUT: 2023 | H/W: 6-2 215 | FUT: Setup reliever | 6B

Thrws R Age 24 — 2020 NDFA (Illinois)

Velo	Pitch	Grade
94-97	FB	++++
85-87	SL	+++
	CU	+

Year	Lev	Team	W	L	Sv	IP	K	ERA	WHIP	BF/G	OBA	H%	S%	xERA	Ctl	Dom	Cmd	hr/9	BPV
2020	NCAA	Illinois	0	0	6	6	8	0.00	0.97	3.9	103	17	100	0.41	5.8	11.6	2.0	0.0	70
2021	A	Stockton	2	0	0	36	53	3.74	1.25	7.3	233	34	77	3.93	3.5	13.2	3.8	1.5	162
2021	A+	Lansing	1	0	2	17	34	3.68	0.82	4.4	172	33	64	2.15	2.1	17.9	8.5	1.6	283
2022	AA	Midland	1	3	6	27	42	4.30	1.58	6.3	274	43	75	4.84	4.6	13.9	3.0	1.0	143
2022	AAA	Las Vegas	2	6	3	42	50	5.56	1.45	5.6	279	33	71	6.09	3.2	10.7	3.3	2.6	124

Career RP who had 2nd highest K rate in org. Operates with essentially two pitches in quick FB and SL that flashes plus. Subject to flyballs and HR and has limited success with FB command. LHH have also hit him hard. Misses bats by using fast arm and velocity, particularly up in zone. Rarely changes speeds.

Acuna,Jose — SP — Cincinnati

EXP MLB DEBUT: 2026 | H/W: 6-2 175 | FUT: #4 starter | 7D

Thrws R Age 20 — 2019 FA (VZ)

Velo	Pitch	Grade
90-93	FB	+++
79-82	SL	+++
81-84	CU	+++

Year	Lev	Team	W	L	Sv	IP	K	ERA	WHIP	BF/G	OBA	H%	S%	xERA	Ctl	Dom	Cmd	hr/9	BPV
2021	Rk	FCL Mets	1	0	0	7	7	3.86	0.86	6.4	132	7	75	2.86	3.9	9.0	2.3	2.6	76
2022	Rk	FCL Mets	3	0	0	25	36	3.21	0.99	16.0	202	31	70	2.17	2.5	12.9	5.1	0.7	182
2022	A	Daytona	0	1	0	31	35	3.18	0.87	16.4	162	23	62	1.04	2.9	10.1	3.5	0.3	122
2022	A	St. Lucie	0	0	0	8	12	1.13	1.13	15.8	151	27	89	1.26	5.6	13.5	2.4	0.0	109

Three-quarters slot RHP, acquired mid-season from NYM, has advanced feel for pitching. Repeatable delivery with some timing variations. 3-pitch pitcher. 4-seam FB plays up with flat-angled approach and combination of ride/run. Needs to tighten up 2-plane SL to get to above-average outcome. Sells tumbling CU well. Strike thrower.

Allan,Matt — SP — New York (N)

EXP MLB DEBUT: 2024 | H/W: 6-3 225 | FUT: #3 starter | 8E

Thrws R Age 21 — 2019 (3) HS (FL)

Velo	Pitch	Grade
93-96	FB	++++
77-81	CB	++++
85-88	CU	+++

Year	Lev	Team	W	L	Sv	IP	K	ERA	WHIP	BF/G	OBA	H%	S%	xERA	Ctl	Dom	Cmd	hr/9	BPV
2019	Rk	GCL Mets	1	0	0	8	11	1.11	1.11	6.4	180	30	89	1.55	4.4	12.2	2.8	0.0	118
2019	A-	Brooklyn	0	0	0	2	3	9.00	3.00	11.6	470	65	67	11.29	4.5	13.5	3.0	0.0	140

Advanced, strike-throwing RHP prospect lost 2nd straight season recovering from spring 2021 Tommy John surgery. Solid, athletic pitcher's build. High 3/4 slot with above-average extension and repeatable mechanics. Mid 90s FB has plus carry and some arm-side run. 12-to-6 CB is a whiff inducer with late downward action. Fading CU is above-avg.

Allen,Logan — SP — Cleveland

EXP MLB DEBUT: 2023 | H/W: 6-1 190 | FUT: #3 starter | 8C

Thrws L Age 24 — 2020 (2) Florida Intl

Velo	Pitch	Grade
90-93	FB	+++
78-80	SL	+++
82-84	SP	++++
84-87	CT	+++

Year	Lev	Team	W	L	Sv	IP	K	ERA	WHIP	BF/G	OBA	H%	S%	xERA	Ctl	Dom	Cmd	hr/9	BPV
2020	NCAA	Florida Intl	2	1	0	25	41	2.50	0.91	23.5	193	33	76	1.85	2.1	14.6	6.8	0.7	224
2021	A+	Lake County	5	0	0	51	67	1.59	0.98	21.6	204	31	87	2.00	2.3	11.8	5.2	0.5	169
2021	AA	Akron	4	0	0	60	76	2.85	0.88	18.5	191	25	77	2.38	2.0	11.4	5.8	1.4	171
2022	AA	Akron	5	3	0	73	104	3.33	1.10	22.0	220	32	75	3.02	2.7	12.8	4.7	1.1	176
2022	AAA	Columbus	4	4	0	59	73	6.54	1.57	18.6	277	37	59	5.09	4.4	11.1	2.5	1.2	99

Shorter-statured LHP inched closer to MLB debut with solid '22 campaign. Repeatable, crossfire, low 3/4s delivery with four pitches. 4-seam FB has excellent riding profile from a lower arm slot, playing up average pitch. SP is best pitch with great deception off FB. Hitters love chasing sweeping SL. CT a solid new offering.

Alvarado,Elvis — RP — Detroit

EXP MLB DEBUT: 2023 | H/W: 6-4 183 | FUT: Setup reliever | 7C

Thrws R Age 24 — 2015 FA (DR)

Velo	Pitch	Grade
95-97	FB	++++
89-92	SL	+++
87-90	CU	+

Year	Lev	Team	W	L	Sv	IP	K	ERA	WHIP	BF/G	OBA	H%	S%	xERA	Ctl	Dom	Cmd	hr/9	BPV
2019	A	West Virginia	0	0	0	1	2	7.50	0.83	4.4	228	0		8.44	0.0	15.0		7.5	288
2021	A	Modesto	0	2	0	45	33	6.60	2.04	7.1	321	38	66	6.42	6.4	6.6	1.0	0.6	-36
2022	A	Lakeland	0	1	1	8	8	2.25	1.38	5.6	237	32	82	2.93	4.5	9.0	2.0	0.0	59
2022	A+	West Michigan	3	1	7	29	32	1.86	1.10	4.9	234	33	84	2.49	2.2	9.9	4.6	0.3	138
2022	AA	Erie	5	1	2	22	23	4.05	1.04	4.3	204	26	62	2.42	2.8	9.3	3.3	0.8	109

Strong-armed RP had his best season as a pro, posting a 2.72 ERA with 10 saves across 3 levels. FB sits at 95-97, topping out at 100 mph with good late sink. Backs up the FB with a power SL that sits in the low-90s and generates plenty of swing-and-miss and weak contact. CU can be a bit firm and is seldom used. Effective against both RHH and LHH.

Arrighetti,Spencer — SP — Houston

EXP MLB DEBUT: 2024 | H/W: 6-2 186 | FUT: #3 starter | 8C

Thrws R Age 23 — 2021 (6) Louisiana-Lafayette

Velo	Pitch	Grade
93-98	FB	++++
82-86	SL	+++
78-84	CB	+++
86-89	CU	++

Year	Lev	Team	W	L	Sv	IP	K	ERA	WHIP	BF/G	OBA	H%	S%	xERA	Ctl	Dom	Cmd	hr/9	BPV
2021	NCAA	Louisiana-Lafayette	7	6	2	83	91	3.14	1.18	20.8	227	31	73	2.61	3.1	9.8	3.1	0.3	110
2021	Rk	FCL Astros	1	1	0	4	6	2.25	1.75	9.1	383	57	86	6.15	0.0	13.5		0.0	261
2021	A	Fayetteville	2	1	0	9	16	2.93	0.54	7.7	104	17	50	0.23	2.0	15.7	8.0	1.0	247
2022	A+	Asheville	6	5	2	85	124	5.07	1.57	17.0	268	41	67	4.40	4.9	13.1	2.7	0.6	123
2022	AA	Corpus Christi	1	1	0	21	28	3.43	1.05	16.2	180	24	74	2.60	3.9	12.0	3.1	1.3	130

Right-handed starter attacks hitters with four-pitch mix. FB-heavy approach but mixes in effective SL and CB against RHB and LHB, respectively. Both breaking balls show good late action to miss bats. Occasionally struggles with command. Change-up lags behind other pitches.

Askew,Keyshawn — RP — Tampa Bay

EXP MLB DEBUT: 2024 | H/W: 6-4 190 | FUT: Middle reliever | 6C

Thrws L Age 23 — 2021 (10) Clemson

Velo	Pitch	Grade
89-92	FB	+++
75-78	SL	++++
82-84	CU	++

Year	Lev	Team	W	L	Sv	IP	K	ERA	WHIP	BF/G	OBA	H%	S%	xERA	Ctl	Dom	Cmd	hr/9	BPV
2020	NCAA	Clemson	0	0	0	12	12	3.69	1.89	11.5	259	31	86	5.89	8.1	8.9	1.1	1.5	-42
2021	NCAA	Clemson	1	2	0	57	69	5.84	1.39	20.0	297	40	59	4.97	1.7	10.9	6.3	1.3	167
2021	Rk	FCL Mets	2	0	0	9	14	1.00	0.78	8.1	106	15	100	0.88	4.0	14.0	3.5	1.0	162
2022	A	St. Lucie	4	0	1	46	64	1.95	1.02	13.6	177	27	84	1.83	3.7	12.5	3.4	0.6	142
2022	A+	Brooklyn	1	0	0	19	28	3.75	1.25	15.6	217	36	67	2.32	4.2	13.1	3.1	0.0	140

Sidearm RHP, acquired in off-season trade with NYM, pitched well across lower level affiliates. Long, lean frame. Lots of limbs going different directions in delivery. Does well to stick to slot. Two-seam FB is average pitch with solid sinking profile. Sweeping SL is best pitch with long break profile. Can also stick for called strikes. Flashes CU.

Atencio,Javier — SP — New York (N)

EXP MLB DEBUT: 2025 | H/W: 6-0 160 | FUT: #5 SP/swingman | 6C

Thrws L Age 21 — 2018 FA (VZ)

Velo	Pitch	Grade
90-92	FB	+++
76-78	SL	+++
82-84	CU	++

Year	Lev	Team	W	L	Sv	IP	K	ERA	WHIP	BF/G	OBA	H%	S%	xERA	Ctl	Dom	Cmd	hr/9	BPV
2021	Rk	DSL Mets	1	3	0	48	76	2.44	0.98	12.2	171	31	74	1.28	3.6	14.3	4.0	0.2	178
2022	Rk	FCL Mets	0	0	0	4	8	0.00	1.50	5.8	262	55	100	3.49	4.5	18.0	4.0	0.0	221
2022	A	St. Lucie	2	0	1	39	48	2.30	1.35	16.4	213	32	83	2.77	5.3	11.0	2.1	0.2	74

Shorter-statured, low 3/4s LHP pitched well across lower level affiliates. Room to add strength to frame. Control issues product of vary release points. 4-seam FB has natural arm-side ride and solid run, especially from the lower slot. SL is sweeper profile. Sometimes drops down to sidearm slot to get frisbee movement. CU lacks firmness.

Bachman,Sam — SP — Los Angeles (A)

EXP MLB DEBUT: 2024 | H/W: 6-1 235 | FUT: Closer | 8E

Thrws R Age 23 — 2021 (1) Miami (OH)

Velo	Pitch	Grade
92-95	FB	++++
86-88	SL	++++
84-87	CU	+++

Year	Lev	Team	W	L	Sv	IP	K	ERA	WHIP	BF/G	OBA	H%	S%	xERA	Ctl	Dom	Cmd	hr/9	BPV
2020	NCAA	Miami	1	2	0	23	31	3.49	1.34	24.1	276	41	73	3.70	2.3	12.0	5.2	0.4	172
2021	NCAA	Miami	4	4	0	59	93	1.82	0.78	17.7	148	27	76	0.49	2.6	14.1	5.5	0.2	203
2021	A+	Tri-City	0	2	0	14	15	3.83	1.21	11.4	246	33	69	3.22	2.6	9.6	3.8	0.6	121
2022	AA	Rocket City	1	1	0	43	30	3.96	1.53	15.7	252	29	76	4.32	5.2	6.3	1.2	0.8	-10

Strong-bodied, low 3/4s RHP struggled with command and whiffs in limited duty. Stiff delivery with jerky leg lift and little deception. 3-pitch pitcher. 2-seam FB has double-plus movement but lacks control, with extremely low called strike rate. SL is best pitch with tight, two-plane break. CU has an average-to-above-average potential.

Baker,Andrew — RP — Philadelphia

EXP MLB DEBUT: 2023 | H/W: 6-3 190 | FUT: Setup reliever | 8C

Thrws R Age 23 — 2021 (11) Chipola

Velo	Pitch	Grade
89-99	FB	+++
82-84	CB	++++

Year	Lev	Team	W	L	Sv	IP	K	ERA	WHIP	BF/G	OBA	H%	S%	xERA	Ctl	Dom	Cmd	hr/9	BPV
2020	NCAA	Auburn	0	0	0	5	11	10.38	3.27	5.3	429	75	65	10.89	10.4	19.0	1.8	0.0	80
2021	Rk	FCL Phillies	0	0	0	2	4	0.00	0.50	3.3	151	38	100		0.0	18.0		0.0	342
2021	A	Clearwater	1	2	0	10	16	11.70	2.10	7.0	124	20	40	4.29	15.3	14.4	0.9	0.9	-136
2022	A+	Jersey Shore	3	1	0	43	61	4.79	1.50	4.7	252	37	70	4.39	5.0	12.7	2.5	1.0	112
2022	AA	Reading	1	0	0	10	11	0.88	0.78	6.1	94	14	88		4.4	9.7	2.2	0.0	74

Improving relief prospect who could move quickly due to reducing his walk rate. Stuff is not bad, either: high-spin, high-90s FB that works up in the zone, and big vertical power breaking ball that gets tons of whiffs and soft contact. Packs a solid frame and has tenacity for the late innings. Consistency is the final hurdle.

Balazovic,Jordan — SP — Minnesota

EXP MLB DEBUT: 2023 | H/W: 6-5 215 | FUT: #4 starter | 7C

Thrws R Age 24 — 2016 (5) HS (ON)

Velo	Pitch	Grade
91-96	FB	+++
81-83	CB	++
87-89	CU	++

Year	Lev	Team	W	L	Sv	IP	K	ERA	WHIP	BF/G	OBA	H%	S%	xERA	Ctl	Dom	Cmd	hr/9	BPV
2019	A	Cedar Rapids	2	1	0	20		2.23	0.94	19.0	208	37	78	1.84	1.8	14.7	8.3	0.4	235
2019	A+	Fort Myers	6	4	0	73	96	2.84	1.00	18.6	202	31	71	1.87	2.6	11.8	4.6	0.4	161
2021	AA	Wichita	5	4	0	97	102	3.62	1.40	20.5	264	34	76	4.14	3.5	9.5	2.7	0.8	93
2022	A	Fort Myers	0	0	0	2	1	18.00	3.00	11.6	415	39	40	14.29	9.0	4.5	0.5	4.5	-144
2022	AAA	St. Paul	0	7	0	70	76	7.44	1.95	15.2	340	40	68	8.32	4.5	9.7	2.2	2.6	72

Big, physical SP who suffered through awful year, though finished strong. Became far too hittable as FB became straight and LHH killed him. Hasn't found consistency with split CU, but it has average potential. Control regressed due to erratic release point. FB has plus potential with good velocity. CB also could become go-to pitch.

Barclay,Edgar — RP — New York (A)

EXP MLB DEBUT: 2024 | H/W: 5-10 200 | FUT: #4 starter | 7D

Thrws L Age 24 — 2019 (15) Cal St Bakersfield

Velo	Pitch	Grade
88-91	FB	+++
76-79	SL	++++
77-79	CU	+++

Year	Lev	Team	W	L	Sv	IP	K	ERA	WHIP	BF/G	OBA	H%	S%	xERA	Ctl	Dom	Cmd	hr/9	BPV
2021	A	Tampa	3	1	2	48	73	2.24	0.85	9.8	150	27	73	0.73	3.2	13.6	4.3	0.2	178
2021	A+	Hudson Valley	1	3	0	28	39	5.74	1.31	10.6	267	36	61	4.94	2.6	12.4	4.9	1.9	173
2022	A+	Hudson Valley	7	4	1	67	86	1.74	0.91	8.9	178	28	79	1.03	2.7	11.5	4.3	0.0	153

Stocky frame, LHP dominated younger competition across lower level affiliates. Low 3/4s slot delivery. Alters slot for deception but continually repeats delivery. Mix/matches profile of 4-seam FB, achieving premium arm-side run. Sweeping SL is best offering with a big break profile, especially from a side-arm slot. Creates separation with CU.

Barco,Hunter — SP — Pittsburgh

EXP MLB DEBUT: 2025 | H/W: 6-4 210 | FUT: #4 starter | 7C

Thrws L Age 22 — 2022 (2) Florida

Velo	Pitch	Grade
90-93	FB	+++
79-81	SL	+++
83-85	CU	+++

Did not pitch upon draft due to Tommy John surgery in May. When healthy, has solid stuff enhanced by natural deception. Delivery is tough to read and makes FB and sweeping SL tough to hit. Likes to move ball around zone with varying velocities and shapes. Average velocity with FB, though spots to all quadrants.

Barnett,Mason — SP — Kansas City

EXP MLB DEBUT: 2025 | H/W: 6-0 218 | FUT: #4 starter | 7D

Thrws R Age 22 — 2022 (3) Auburn

Velo	Pitch	Grade
93-96	FB	++++
82-84	SL	+++
75-77	CB	++
83-85	CU	+++

Year	Lev	Team	W	L	Sv	IP	K	ERA	WHIP	BF/G	OBA	H%	S%	xERA	Ctl	Dom	Cmd	hr/9	BPV
2022	NCAA	Auburn	3	3	0	63	83	4.41	1.50	14.4	261	38	71	4.22	4.6	11.8	2.6	0.7	108
2022	Rk	ACL Royals Blue	0	0	0	1	1	0.00	0.00	2.8	0	0			0.0	9.0		0.0	180
2022	A	Columbia	1	0	0	7	11	0.00	0.14	6.9	0	0	100		1.3	14.1	11.0	0.0	238

Athletic, 3/4s RHP has long arm path in delivery and doesn't always maintain release point. At physical projection, he's a 4-pitch pitcher. 4-seam FB has solid ride/run profile, but slightly below average strike percentage. SL has short, average break profile. Has feel for CU, could be effective 3rd pitch.

Barriera,Brandon — SP — Toronto

EXP MLB DEBUT: 2025 | H/W: 6-2 180 | FUT: #2 starter | 9D

Thrws L Age 19 — 2022 (1) HS (FL)

Velo	Pitch	Grade
90-94	FB	+++
81-84	SL	+++
82-85	CU	+++

Pure, athletic SP with immense upside based on electric arm and potential, dazzling pitch mix. Fast arm speed produces FB that exhibits plenty of movement. Combo of FB/SL has potential to be double-plus given both miss bats. Lot of bite on sharp SL and delivery adds to effectiveness. Will need to use CU more. Will see his first pro innings in 2023.

Batista,Edinson — SP — Houston

EXP MLB DEBUT: 2025 | H/W: 6-2 185 | FUT: #5 SP/swingman | 7D

Thrws R Age 20 — 2019 FA (DR)

Velo	Pitch	Grade
92-95	FB	+++
80-85	SL	+++
78-86	CB	+++
87-91	CU	++

Year	Lev	Team	W	L	Sv	IP	K	ERA	WHIP	BF/G	OBA	H%	S%	xERA	Ctl	Dom	Cmd	hr/9	BPV
2021	Rk	FCL Astros	1	2	1	24	33	7.84	2.12	10.8	320	47	60	6.32	7.1	12.3	1.7	0.4	48
2021	A	Fayetteville	0	0	0	1	0	0.00	0.00	2.8	0	0			0.0	0.0		0.0	18
2022	A	Fayetteville	8	3	0	93	113	2.61	1.10	17.4	183	27	76	1.84	4.2	10.9	2.6	0.3	102
2022	A+	Asheville	1	0	0	14	14	3.19	1.28	19.3	185	21	81	3.25	5.7	8.9	1.6	1.3	24

Young RHP prospect handled first extended look in full-season ball. Tends to work FB up and plays secondaries off it down low. Some effort to delivery with slight head whack. Room on frame to add a couple ticks of velo to mid-90s FB. FB is effective but has spotty command. Shows good bat-missing ability and can get batter to chase outside the zone.

Battenfield,Peyton — SP — Cleveland

EXP MLB DEBUT: 2023 | H/W: 6-4 224 | FUT: #5 SP/swingman | 6B

Thrws R Age 25 — 2019 (9) Oklahoma St

Velo	Pitch	Grade
90-93	FB	+++
84-87	SL	+++
88-91	CT	++
78-80	CB	+++

Year	Lev	Team	W	L	Sv	IP	K	ERA	WHIP	BF/G	OBA	H%	S%	xERA	Ctl	Dom	Cmd	hr/9	BPV
2019	A-	Tri City	2	1	0	39	46	1.61	0.97	10.6	173	26	82	1.13	3.5	10.6	3.1	0.0	115
2021	A+	Bowling Green	2	0	0	31	49	1.45	0.74	15.8	171	29	86	1.04	1.5	14.2	9.8	0.6	235
2021	AA	Akron	2	1	0	35	36	3.32	0.88	18.6	195	24	67	2.13	1.8	9.2	5.1	1.0	135
2021	AA	Montgomery	3	0	0	36	46	2.74	0.86	19.0	191	25	77	2.22	1.7	11.5	6.6	1.2	177
2022	AAA	Columbus	8	6	0	153	109	3.64	1.27	22.4	242	27	75	3.70	3.3	6.4	1.9	1.0	43

Over-the-top RHP closed in on MLB debut with solid Triple-A season. 5-pitch arsenal. Flat-angled 4-seam FB is workhorse offering with natural ride and some arm/side run. Throws CT from same tunnel with slight cutting action. SL is best offering with tight gyro spin. CB is a solid eye level changing pitch. Also features an arm-side running CU.

Baumler,Carter — SP — Baltimore

EXP MLB DEBUT: 2026 | H/W: 6-2 195 | FUT: #3 starter | 8E

Thrws R Age 21 — 2020 (5) HS (IA)

Velo	Pitch	Grade
90-93	FB	+++
78-80	CB	+++
84-86	CU	++

Year	Lev	Team	W	L	Sv	IP	K	ERA	WHIP	BF/G	OBA	H%	S%	xERA	Ctl	Dom	Cmd	hr/9	BPV
2022	A	Delmarva	0	0	0	11	20	1.61	1.25	11.4	181	38	86	1.88	5.6	16.1	2.9	0.0	155

Missed two full seasons due to pandemic and Tommy John surgery. Made Low-A debut in May and flashed the athleticism, FB with life, and big-breaking CB that had club excited after his 2020 draft year. Then a shoulder injury shelved him in 2022 after four starts. Upside due to pedigree and pitch movement, but needs to stay healthy and perform.

Beck,Brendan — SP — New York (A)

EXP MLB DEBUT: 2025 | H/W: 6-2 205 | FUT: #4 starter | 7D

Thrws R Age 24 — 2021 (2) Stanford

Velo	Pitch	Grade
90-93	FB	+++
81-84	SL	++++
76-78	CB	++
83-85	CU	+++

Pitchability RHP missed 2022 recovering from Tommy John surgery. Longer arm path needed to get to 3/4s slot. Does well repeating delivery. Sits low-90s with FB. Plays up FB due to plus command. SL is best offering with tight breaking profile. CU has FB arm-speed and solid fading action. CB is solid but unspectacular offering.

Bedell,Ian

SP | St. Louis | EXP MLB DEBUT: 2024 | H/W: 6-2 198 | FUT: #5 SP/swingman | 6C

Thrws R Age 23
2020 (4) Missouri

Velo	Pitch	Grade
90-93	FB	++
77-79	CB	+++
	CT	+++
80-83	CU	+++

Year	Lev	Team	W	L	Sv	IP	K	ERA	WHIP	BF/G	OBA	H%	S%	xERA	Ctl	Dom	Cmd	hr/9	BPV
2020	NCAA	Missouri	2	2	0	24	35	3.73	1.00	23.0	227	31	74	3.57	1.5	13.1	8.8	1.9	213
2021	A+	Peoria	0	1	0	2	4	12.27	4.09	7.6	530	76	67	15.82	8.2	16.4	2.0	0.0	92
2022	Rk	FCL Cardinals	0	0	0	3	6	0.00	1.67	4.5	262	55	100	3.91	6.0	18.0	3.0	0.0	180
2022	A	Palm Beach	0	0	0	2	4	8.18	3.18	4.4	492	73	71	12.33	4.1	16.4	4.0	0.0	202

Went under the knife for Tommy John surgery in 2021 and finally returned to action at the end of 2022. Prior to the injury featured a low-90s 2- and 4-seam FB and velo was back in that range when he returned. Still has SP upside due to 4-pitch mix that includes above-average CB, CU, and CT. Should be fully healthy and pounds the strike. Possible back-end starter.

Bednar,Will

SP | San Francisco | EXP MLB DEBUT: 2024 | H/W: 6-2 230 | FUT: #4 starter | 7C

Thrws R Age 22
2021 (1) Mississippi St

Velo	Pitch	Grade
90-94	FB	+++
76-79	CB	++
82-85	SL	+++
83-85	CU	++

Year	Lev	Team	W	L	Sv	IP	K	ERA	WHIP	BF/G	OBA	H%	S%	xERA	Ctl	Dom	Cmd	hr/9	BPV
2020	NCAA	Mississippi St	0	0	1	15	23	1.79	0.99	14.4	174	31	80	1.18	3.6	13.7	3.8	0.0	168
2021	NCAA	Mississippi St	9	1	0	92	139	3.13	1.06	18.8	217	33	77	2.95	2.5	13.6	5.3	1.2	194
2021	Rk	ACL Giants O	0	0	0	2	3	0.00	0.50	3.3	0	0	100		4.5	13.5	3.0	0.0	140
2021	A	San Jose	0	0	0	5	3	1.80	1.20	10.1	299	35	83	3.39	0.0	5.4		0.0	115
2022	A	San Jose	1	3	0	43	51	4.19	1.09	14.0	171	20	68	2.80	4.6	10.7	2.3	1.5	86

Strong, physical RHP who ended season in June due to back issue. Owns quality pitch mix and could get better in time. Mix is highlighted by excellent FB/SL combo. FB shows good riding life in up zone while SL serves as swing-and-miss pitch. Sequences occasional CB and fading CU, but neither dependable yet. Developing command.

Beeter,Clayton

SP | New York (A) | EXP MLB DEBUT: 2023 | H/W: 6-2 220 | FUT: Setup reliever | 7D

Thrws R Age 24
2020 (2) Texas Tech

Velo	Pitch	Grade
93-96	FB	++++
83-85	SL	++++

Year	Lev	Team	W	L	Sv	IP	K	ERA	WHIP	BF/G	OBA	H%	S%	xERA	Ctl	Dom	Cmd	hr/9	BPV
2020	NCAA	Texas Tech	2	1	0	21		2.14	0.81	19.1	180	28	86	1.98	1.7	14.1	8.3	1.3	226
2021	A+	Great Lakes	0	4	0	37	55	3.15	1.16	6.4	211	34	75	2.71	3.6	13.3	3.7	0.7	160
2021	AA	Tulsa	0	2	0	15	23	4.20	1.13	11.9	191	29	67	2.85	4.2	13.8	3.3	1.2	153
2022	AA	Somerset	0	0	0	25	41	2.15	1.08	14.0	184	33	81	1.82	3.9	14.7	3.7	0.4	176
2022	AA	Tulsa	0	3	0	51	88	5.80	1.62	12.6	250	40	68	5.30	6.2	15.5	2.5	1.8	130

Hard-throwing, over-the-top RHP, acquired in mid-season trade with LA, piled whiffs in Double-A. Physical strong frame at projection. Struggles landing over-the-top delivery release. 2-pitch pitcher. 4-seam FB is naturally flat-angled but suffers from poor control. SL generates late wicked downward break, a potential plus-plus pitch. Likely RP outcome.

Bennett,Jake

SP | Washington | EXP MLB DEBUT: 2025 | H/W: 6-6 234 | FUT: #3 starter | 8E

Thrws L Age 22
2022 (2) Oklahoma

Velo	Pitch	Grade
91-93	FB	+++
82-85	SL	++
82-84	CU	++++

Year	Lev	Team	W	L	Sv	IP	K	ERA	WHIP	BF/G	OBA	H%	S%	xERA	Ctl	Dom	Cmd	hr/9	BPV

Tall lefty comes from a low slot and brings polished, mature way of working through lineups honed at University of Oklahoma. Heavy NCAA workload kept him from his pro debut, but efficient FB and the best CU in the system are the headliners. SL can still use some work, but maturity and athleticism give him a great shot.

Bergert,Ryan

SP | San Diego | EXP MLB DEBUT: 2024 | H/W: 6-1 210 | FUT: #4 starter | 7C

Thrws R Age 23
2021 (6) West Virginia

Velo	Pitch	Grade
92-96	FB	+++
77-80	CB	+++
81-83	SL	+++
82-86	CU	+++

Year	Lev	Team	W	L	Sv	IP	K	ERA	WHIP	BF/G	OBA	H%	S%	xERA	Ctl	Dom	Cmd	hr/9	BPV
2020	NCAA	West Virginia	2	1	0	24	30	2.98	1.03	23.3	170	25	71	1.61	4.1	11.2	2.7	0.4	108
2021	Rk	ACL Padres	1	0	1	11	14	0.00	0.27	4.9	88	15	100		0.0	11.5		0.0	224
2022	A+	Fort Wayne	4	10	0	103	129	5.85	1.61	19.0	299	40	67	5.85	3.7	11.3	3.1	1.6	122

Strong-armed SP who bypassed Low-A and finished 4th in MWL in K. Solid pitch mix with good velocity and two breaking balls. Struggles in longer outings and has been subject to HR and poor performance against LHH. Needs to upgrade CU to be mid-rotation guy. Misses bats with pitch movement and big spinning CB.

Bergner,Austin

SP | Detroit | EXP MLB DEBUT: 2023 | H/W: 6-5 210 | FUT: #5 SP/swingman | 6C

Thrws R Age 25
2019 (25) North Carolina

Velo	Pitch	Grade
92-95	FB	+++
74-78	CB	+++
77-83	SL	+
84-86	CU	++

Year	Lev	Team	W	L	Sv	IP	K	ERA	WHIP	BF/G	OBA	H%	S%	xERA	Ctl	Dom	Cmd	hr/9	BPV
2021	A	Lakeland	2	2	1	24	34	4.48	0.95	9.1	181	26	55	2.21	3.0	12.7	4.3	1.1	166
2021	A+	West Michigan	4	0	0	59	76	2.90	1.27	14.2	231	32	84	3.71	3.8	11.6	3.0	1.2	124
2022	AA	Erie	4	2	0	90	93	2.39	1.06	18.4	204	25	86	2.86	3.1	9.3	3.0	1.2	102
2022	AAA	Toledo	1	3	0	28	28	7.02	1.49	15.2	246	29	54	4.84	5.1	8.9	1.8	1.6	41

Tall, lean hurler flies under the radar, but continues to put up respectable numbers. Short stride with tall-and-fall cross-fire action. FB sits at 92-95 with solid carry up in the zone. Best offering is an above-average 11-to-5 CB and is complemented by a hard mid-80s CU. Added a SL to round out his arsenal.

Berroa,Prelander

SP | Seattle | EXP MLB DEBUT: 2024 | H/W: 5-11 170 | FUT: Setup reliever | 7C

Thrws R Age 22
2016 FA (DR)

Velo	Pitch	Grade
93-96	FB	++++
82-86	SL	+++
86-88	CU	++

Year	Lev	Team	W	L	Sv	IP	K	ERA	WHIP	BF/G	OBA	H%	S%	xERA	Ctl	Dom	Cmd	hr/9	BPV
2019	A-	Salem-Keizer	0	1	0	16	11	9.56	1.63	17.8	274	31	38	5.14	5.1	6.2	1.2	1.1	-7
2021	A	San Jose	5	6	0	98	135	3.57	1.34	17.0	222	32	78	3.75	4.9	12.4	2.5	1.2	110
2022	A+	Eugene	0	0	0	13	16	0.69	0.84	12.0	119	19	91	0.25	4.1	11.0	2.7	0.0	105
2022	A+	Everett	2	2	0	52	81	2.42	1.17	16.0	165	29	80	1.84	5.5	14.0	2.5	0.3	121
2022	AA	Arkansas	2	1	0	35	53	4.37	1.29	16.0	168	27	67	2.58	6.4	13.6	2.1	0.8	90

Short, powerful arm acquired from SF in May. Has trouble hitting spots with below average command and control. Max-effort delivery may require move to pen to leverage strengths. FB has velocity and riding life up in zone. SL can also miss bats, but usually as chaser. Lack of CU hinders upside, but could be intriguing RP.

Bibee,Tanner

SP | Cleveland | EXP MLB DEBUT: 2023 | H/W: 6-2 205 | FUT: #3 starter | 9D

Thrws R Age 24
2021 (5) Cal St Fullerton

Velo	Pitch	Grade
93-96	FB	+++
82-85	SL	++++
75-78	CB	++
83-86	CU	++++

Year	Lev	Team	W	L	Sv	IP	K	ERA	WHIP	BF/G	OBA	H%	S%	xERA	Ctl	Dom	Cmd	hr/9	BPV
2022	A+	Lake County	2	1	0	59	86	2.59	1.07	19.1	231	34	84	3.19	2.0	13.1	6.6	1.2	201
2022	AA	Akron	6	1	0	73	81	1.84	0.89	20.9	198	27	82	1.68	1.7	10.0	5.8	0.5	151

Known for pitchability and command, took an enormous step up in stuff in 2022. 4-pitch arsenal of average-or-better offerings. 4-seam FB sits mid-90s with an average spin profile. Commands a fading CU, with late drop out of the zone. It's a plus pitch and could be more. High-spinning, sweeping SL also projects as plus. CB is solid.

Bitsko,Nick

SP | Tampa Bay | EXP MLB DEBUT: 2026 | H/W: 6-4 225 | FUT: #3 starter | 8E

Thrws R Age 20
2020 (1) HS (PA)

Velo	Pitch	Grade
90-94	FB	+++
79-82	SL	+++
	SP	

Year	Lev	Team	W	L	Sv	IP	K	ERA	WHIP	BF/G	OBA	H%	S%	xERA	Ctl	Dom	Cmd	hr/9	BPV
2021	--	*Injured, DNP*																	
2022	Rk	FCL Rays	1	2	0	17	15	7.41	2.00	8.2	226	30	59	4.38	10.6	7.9	0.8	0.0	-125
2022	A	Charleston	0	0	0	9	5	4.00	1.67	10.1	240	28	73	3.74	7.0	5.0	0.7	0.0	-81

Former 1st round pick returned from 2021 Tommy John surgery with down stuff. High 3/4s delivery wasn't repeatable and seemingly went through bout with the yips. FB sat in low 90s with limited feel for zone. Had more success with SL but pitch struggled mightily with consistency. Did not throw his split during Complex League action.

Black,Mason

SP | San Francisco | EXP MLB DEBUT: 2024 | H/W: 6-3 230 | FUT: #3 starter | 8D

Thrws R Age 23
2021 (3) Lehigh

Velo	Pitch	Grade
92-97	FB	++++
83-86	SL	+++
81-84	CU	++

Year	Lev	Team	W	L	Sv	IP	K	ERA	WHIP	BF/G	OBA	H%	S%	xERA	Ctl	Dom	Cmd	hr/9	BPV
2022	A	San Jose	1	1	0	34	44	1.58	0.97	16.1	206	32	84	1.75	2.1	11.6	5.5	0.3	170
2022	A+	Eugene	5	3	0	77	92	3.96	1.27	19.7	243	32	74	3.93	3.3	10.7	3.3	1.3	123

High-upside arm who finished 4th in org in Ks. Very good in Low-A in first pro season. Can dominate at times by leveraging height and extension. Uses both 4-seam and 2-seam FB and features velocity and armside run. Mixes in sharp SL that hitters can chase. CU needs work, though has shown glimpses of becoming at least average.

Bolton,Cody

SP | Pittsburgh | EXP MLB DEBUT: 2023 | H/W: 6-3 230 | FUT: #4 starter | 7D

Thrws R Age 24
2017 (6) HS (CA)

Velo	Pitch	Grade
91-95	FB	+++
82-85	SL	+++
81-84	CU	++

Year	Lev	Team	W	L	Sv	IP	K	ERA	WHIP	BF/G	OBA	H%	S%	xERA	Ctl	Dom	Cmd	hr/9	BPV
2017	Rk	GCL Pirates	0	2	0	25	22	3.21	1.23	11.3	245	31	73	3.01	2.9	7.9	2.8	0.4	82
2018	A	West Virginia	3	3	0	44	45	3.67	1.13	19.4	257	32	73	3.74	1.4	9.2	6.4	1.2	145
2019	A+	Bradenton	6	3	0	61	69	1.62	0.87	18.8	184	27	81	1.14	2.1	10.1	4.9	0.1	145
2019	AA	Altoona	2	3	0	40	33	5.85	1.33	18.4	247	28	57	4.22	3.6	7.4	2.1	1.4	54
2022	AAA	Indianapolis	4	2	0	75	82	3.11	1.29	10.3	212	29	76	2.84	4.8	9.8	2.1	0.5	65

Returned after missing last two seasons (knee surgery and pandemic). Was on strict pitch/inning count whether as SP or RP. Generates good velocity despite long arm action. Mechanics are aligned. Induces groundballs with quality sinker. Might be more effective as RP who can miss bats and throw hard in short stints.

Bonnin,Bryce — SP — Cincinnati

EXP MLB DEBUT: 2025 | H/W: 6-2 190 | FUT: Closer | 7C

Thrws R	Age 24		Year	Lev	Team	W	L	Sv	IP	K	ERA	WHIP	BF/G	OBA	H%	S%	xERA	Ctl	Dom	Cmd	hr/9	BPV
2020 (3) Texas Tech			2020	NCAA	Texas Tech	2	0	0	14	27	7.61	1.76	16.3	322	57	57	6.24	3.8	17.1	4.5	1.3	223
94-96	FB	++++	2021	Rk	ACL Reds	0	0	0	4	7	2.25	0.75	14.3	151	32	67	0.29	2.3	15.8	7.0	0.0	241
85-88	SL	++++	2021	A	Daytona	4	0	0	32	44	1.41	0.81	16.6	166	28	81	0.65	2.3	12.4	5.5	0.0	180
			2021	A+	Dayton	0	2	0	11	20	7.36	1.36	15.3	184	21	55	5.27	6.5	16.4	2.5	3.3	136
			2022	A+	Dayton	1	1	0	25	28	2.52	0.92	15.6	135	12	89	2.31	4.3	10.1	2.3	1.8	83

Hard-throwing, 3/4s RHP missed most of '22 due to shoulder impingement. It's an athletic, long limbed delivery with solid extension. 2-pitch mix in '22. 4-seam FB sits mid-90s with near elite riding profile, whiff rate near 40%. Tight, gyro spinning SL is a plus offering. Continued injury issues murky overall outlook.

Bowlan,Jonathan — SP — Kansas City

EXP MLB DEBUT: 2023 | H/W: 6-6 240 | FUT: #4 starter | 7C

Thrws R	Age 26		Year	Lev	Team	W	L	Sv	IP	K	ERA	WHIP	BF/G	OBA	H%	S%	xERA	Ctl	Dom	Cmd	hr/9	BPV
2018 (2) Memphis			2019	A+	Wilmington	5	3	0	76	76	2.96	1.04	22.6	235	31	73	2.61	1.5	9.0	5.8	0.6	138
91-93	FB	+++	2021	AA	NW Arkansas	2	0	0	17	25	1.59	0.94	16.0	213	36	81	1.50	1.6	13.2	8.3	0.0	213
82-85	SL	+++	2022	Rk	ACL Royals Blue	0	1	0	19	26	5.18	1.73	12.4	350	50	69	5.94	1.9	12.3	6.5	0.5	188
86-88	CU	++	2022	A+	Quad Cities	0	0	0	4	6	0.00	1.75	18.3	347	53	100	5.49	2.3	13.5	6.0	0.0	200
			2022	AA	NW Arkansas	1	3	0	39	30	6.92	1.74	19.8	317	35	62	6.55	3.9	6.9	1.8	1.6	37

Big-bodied, pitchability RHP returned from Tommy John with mixed results. Low 3/4s slot; repeatable delivery despite height and girth. FB velocity was down compared to pre-injury. Command was also not back. Took steps forward in development prior to surgery. Still, it's a 3-pitch mix with the 4-seam FB and SL both above-average offerings.

Boyle,Joe — SP — Cincinnati

EXP MLB DEBUT: 2024 | H/W: 6-7 240 | FUT: Setup reliever | 7C

Thrws R	Age 23		Year	Lev	Team	W	L	Sv	IP	K	ERA	WHIP	BF/G	OBA	H%	S%	xERA	Ctl	Dom	Cmd	hr/9	BPV
2020 (5) Notre Dame			2021	NCAA	Notre Dame	1	1	2	8		3.33	1.98	6.5	116	34	81	3.00	14.4	18.9	1.3	0.0	-32
95-97	FB	++++	2021	Rk	ACL Reds	0	0	0	7	13	0.00	0.57	5.9	132	31	100		1.3	16.7	13.0	0.0	284
87-90	CT	++++	2021	A	Daytona	0	0	0	12	28	3.69	1.56	13.4	149	44	78	2.95	9.6	20.7	2.2	0.7	131
84-86	SL	+++	2022	A+	Dayton	3	4	0	74	122	2.18	1.13	17.2	107	20	81	1.17	7.2	14.8	2.1	0.4	91
			2022	AA	Chattanooga	0	2	0	26	31	4.85	1.77	19.9	223	30	74	4.70	8.7	10.7	1.2	1.0	-23

Tall, big-bodied RHP struggled with consistency despite some of the best stuff in system. High 3/4s delivery with effort and head whack. Utilizes frame well extending towards plate. 3-pitch pitcher. Exceptional FB profile when finding zone. CT is also plus offering, especially against LHP. SL is tightly wound. Below-average command overall.

Bradley,Taj — SP — Tampa Bay

EXP MLB DEBUT: 2023 | H/W: 6-2 190 | FUT: #1 starter | 8B

Thrws R	Age 22		Year	Lev	Team	W	L	Sv	IP	K	ERA	WHIP	BF/G	OBA	H%	S%	xERA	Ctl	Dom	Cmd	hr/9	BPV
2018 (5) HS (GA)			2019	Rk	Princeton	2	5	0	51	57	3.18	1.20	17.1	226	30	75	2.99	3.4	10.1	3.0	0.7	109
94-96	FB	++++	2021	A	Charleston	9	3	0	66	81	1.77	0.86	16.2	165	24	83	1.28	2.7	11.0	4.1	0.5	143
86-88	SL	+++	2021	A+	Bowling Green	3	0	0	36	42	1.99	1.08	17.6	215	29	89	2.83	2.7	10.4	3.8	1.0	132
87-89	SP	++	2022	AA	Montgomery	3	1	0	74	88	1.70	0.92	17.3	193	28	84	1.68	2.2	10.7	4.9	0.5	151
76-79	CB	++	2022	AAA	Durham	4	3	0	59	53	3.66	1.19	19.7	248	28	77	4.05	2.3	8.1	3.5	1.5	102

Hard-throwing high 3/4s RHP pushed closer to MLB debut. Long, physical athletic frame. Repeats delivery with plus extension. 4-seam FB is overpowering with flat-angled approach and plus ride. It's a double-plus pitch. Hard SL is CT like. It's an above-average offering. Struggled with feel for CU. Working with splitter grip; CB is eye-level changer only.

Bratt,Mitch — SP — Texas

EXP MLB DEBUT: 2025 | H/W: 6-1 190 | FUT: #4 starter | 7B

Thrws L	Age 19		Year	Lev	Team	W	L	Sv	IP	K	ERA	WHIP	BF/G	OBA	H%	S%	xERA	Ctl	Dom	Cmd	hr/9	BPV
2021 (5) HS (GA)																						
91-95	FB	+++																				
79-85	SL	++																				
75-79	CB	++	2021	Rk	ACL Rangers	0	0	0	6	13	0.00	0.67	5.2	191	51	100	0.49	0.0	19.5		0.0	369
84-87	CU	+++	2022	A	Down East	5	5	0	80	99	2.47	1.17	16.9	226	33	80	2.68	3.1	11.1	3.5	0.4	133

The '22 Wayne Norton Award winner (look it up) shook off bumpy May to mow 'em down rest of way. Cold-weather arm, remaining frame projection, athleticism, and precocious zone feel makes average arsenal play up from left side. Ate RHB up; FF and CU lead way. Fringe-average breakers need to bump but FB command is advanced.

Bright,Trace — SP — Baltimore

EXP MLB DEBUT: 2025 | H/W: 6-4 199 | FUT: #5 SP/swingman | 7D

Thrws R	Age 22		Year	Lev	Team	W	L	Sv	IP	K	ERA	WHIP	BF/G	OBA	H%	S%	xERA	Ctl	Dom	Cmd	hr/9	BPV
2022 (5) Auburn																						
91-93	FB	+++																				
75-77	CB	+++	2022	NCAA	Auburn	5	4	0	80	94	5.16	1.45	19.0	256	35	65	4.20	4.3	10.5	2.5	0.9	93
83-85	SL	++	2022	Rk	FCL Orioles B	0	0	0	2	4	0.00	0.00	5.6	0	0			0.0	18.0		0.0	342
84-86	CU	++	2022	A	Delmarva	0	0	1	7	5	2.50	0.83	8.8	90	12	67	0.01	5.0	6.3	1.3	0.0	-5

Upright and tall in delivery with 3/4s slot, struggles with tempo and consistent release point despite notable athleticism. Current command wavers but could improve over time. Four-pitch mix led by low-90s FB that he can run inside. Nothing overpowering; 12-to-6 CB flashes good shape; SL a bit ahead of the CU but both need work.

Brito,Jhony — SP — New York (A)

EXP MLB DEBUT: 2023 | H/W: 6-2 160 | FUT: #5 SP/swingman | 6C

Thrws R	Age 25		Year	Lev	Team	W	L	Sv	IP	K	ERA	WHIP	BF/G	OBA	H%	S%	xERA	Ctl	Dom	Cmd	hr/9	BPV
2016 FA (DR)			2019	A	Charleston (Sc)	6	4	2	100	79	3.59	1.05	17.6	244	30	65	2.63	1.3	7.1	5.6	0.4	112
93-97	FB	+++	2021	A+	Hudson Valley	4	4	0	70	73	2.57	1.01	19.2	230	31	74	2.17	1.5	9.4	6.1	0.3	145
85-88	CU	+++	2021	AA	Somerset	3	3	0	46	45	5.06	1.28	23.7	277	33	65	4.70	1.8	8.8	5.0	1.6	128
78-81	SL	++	2022	AA	Somerset	5	2	0	42	38	2.36	1.12	20.7	233	28	84	3.05	2.4	8.1	3.5	0.9	101
84-88	CT	++	2022	AAA	Scranton/WB	6	2	0	70	53	3.33	1.18	15.6	230	27	73	2.98	3.1	6.8	2.2	0.6	57

3/4s RHP was added to 40-man roster this off-season. Slight frame with room to grow. Crossfire delivery is repeatable from a variable slot. Strike thrower. Varys FB angles between 2-seam and 4-seam FB. Also throws CT from similar tunnel. Fading CU features late tumble action. Also has SL with short break profile.

Brown,Aaron — SP — Houston

EXP MLB DEBUT: 2025 | H/W: 6-4 220 | FUT: Setup reliever | 6C

Thrws R	Age 24		Year	Lev	Team	W	L	Sv	IP	K	ERA	WHIP	BF/G	OBA	H%	S%	xERA	Ctl	Dom	Cmd	hr/9	BPV
2021 (9) Middle Tenn St			2020	NCAA	Middle Tenn St	1	3	0	17	11	3.68	1.75	19.6	272	29	85	5.87	6.3	5.8	0.9	1.6	-48
91-95	FB	+++	2021	NCAA	Middle Tenn St	7	5	0	85	113	4.01	0.96	23.0	218	30	64	2.91	1.6	11.9	7.5	1.4	190
83-89	SL	++	2021	Rk	FCL Astros	0	0	0	2	4	0.00	1.00	7.6	151	38	100	0.90	4.5	18.0	4.0	0.0	221
79-84	CU	+++	2021	A	Fayetteville	1	3	0	19	28	6.09	1.20	15.4	270	38	53	4.65	1.4	13.1	9.3	1.9	216
77-81	CB	++	2022	A+	Asheville	4	9	2	109	95	5.28	1.50	18.8	296	34	70	5.69	2.8	7.8	2.8	1.7	83

Large righty pitched to mixed results for High-A Asheville. Park environment, low strand rate at least partly to blame for bloated ERA, as he showed good ability to generate whiffs. Gets good separation between FB and CU, but other secondaries tend to lack spin, shape. Likely best suited for long relief.

Brown,Ben — SP — Chicago (N)

EXP MLB DEBUT: 2024 | H/W: 6-6 210 | FUT: #3 starter | 8D

Thrws R	Age 23		Year	Lev	Team	W	L	Sv	IP	K	ERA	WHIP	BF/G	OBA	H%	S%	xERA	Ctl	Dom	Cmd	hr/9	BPV
2017 (33) HS (NY)			2019	A	Lakewood	0	0	0	13	20	0.00	1.06	12.8	228	39	100	1.98	2.0	13.6	6.7	0.0	208
94-96	FB	++++	2021	Rk	FCL Phillies	1	0	0	4	3	2.25	0.75	4.8	151	19	67	0.38	2.3	6.8	3.0	0.0	79
84-86	CB	++	2021	A+	Jersey Shore	0	0	0	12	14	7.50	1.58	13.2	262	34	53	5.18	5.3	10.5	2.0	1.5	65
86-89	SL	++	2022	A+	Jersey Shore	3	5	0	73	105	3.08	1.04	17.6	205	31	74	2.46	2.8	12.9	4.6	0.9	174
			2022	AA	Tennessee	3	0	0	31	44	4.06	1.48	19.1	274	41	74	4.49	3.8	12.8	3.4	0.9	146

Acquired in the D. Robertson deal, he had his best season as a pro, posting a 3.38 ERA. Uses his large frame to pitch downhill and attacks hitters with a plus 4-seam FB that sits at 94-96 with nice arm-side run. Improved slurvy CB and power SL give him a chance to develop into a solid mid-rotation arm.

Brown,Hunter — SP — Houston

EXP MLB DEBUT: 2022 | H/W: 6-2 212 | FUT: #3 starter | 8C

Thrws R	Age 24		Year	Lev	Team	W	L	Sv	IP	K	ERA	WHIP	BF/G	OBA	H%	S%	xERA	Ctl	Dom	Cmd	hr/9	BPV
2019 (5) Wayne St			2019	A-	Tri City	2	2	0	23	33	4.66	1.34	8.0	166	29	61	1.96	7.0	12.8	1.8	0.0	60
96-100	FB	++++	2021	AA	Corpus Christi	1	4	1	49	76	4.22	1.51	16.3	245	38	75	4.36	5.3	13.9	2.6	1.1	125
92-96	SL	+++	2021	AAA	Sugar Land	5	1	0	51	55	3.88	1.33	19.3	246	32	74	3.94	3.7	9.7	2.6	1.1	93
82-87	CB	++++	2022	AAA	Sugar Land	9	4	1	106	134	2.55	1.08	18.0	190	28	77	2.00	3.8	11.4	3.0	0.4	120
88-92	CU	++	2022	MLB	Houston	2	0	0	20	22	0.90	1.09	11.2	209	30	91	1.87	3.1	9.9	3.1	0.0	111

Hard-throwing righty features 4-pitch mix headlined by plus FB. Added velocity to reach triple digits. FB plays well off plus curveball which helps generate high GB%. Repeats delivery well but continues to struggle inducing swings and limiting walks.

Brown,McCade — SP — Colorado

EXP MLB DEBUT: 2024 | H/W: 6-6 225 | FUT: #5 SP/swingman | 6C

Thrws R	Age 22		Year	Lev	Team	W	L	Sv	IP	K	ERA	WHIP	BF/G	OBA	H%	S%	xERA	Ctl	Dom	Cmd	hr/9	BPV
2021 (3) Indiana																						
90-94	FB	+++	2020	NCAA	Indiana	0	1	1	4	9	13.50	2.25	5.1	262	47	43	9.58	11.3	20.3	1.8	4.5	79
77-80	CB	+++	2021	NCAA	Indiana	5	4	0	61	97	3.39	1.28	20.8	169	29	75	2.53	6.3	14.3	2.3	0.7	104
83-85	SL	++	2021	Rk	ACL Rockies	0	0	0	8	9	6.75	1.63	8.9	307	37	64	6.66	3.4	10.1	3.0	2.3	109
86-88	CU	++	2022	A	Fresno	4	4	0	89	118	5.25	1.27	20.3	264	37	59	3.93	2.3	11.9	5.1	1.0	170

Back injury cost him most of two years in college, but a had a solid 2022. Tall RHP has a 4-pitch mix that features a 90-94 FB that tops at 97. Best offering is a power an upper-70s power CB that has good spin and sharp, late break. CU and SL are fringe-average. Generates plenty of swing and miss, but also struggles with command.

Bruns,Maddux

SP | Los Angeles (N) | EXP MLB DEBUT: 2025 | H/W: 6-2 205 | FUT: #2 SP/closer | 8E

Thrws L Age 20
2021 (1) HS (AL)

Velo	Pitch	Grade
93-96	FB	++++
73-76	CB	+++
81-83	SL	+++

Year	Lev	Team	W	L	Sv	IP	K	ERA	WHIP	BF/G	OBA	H%	S%	xERA	Ctl	Dom	Cmd	hr/9	BPV
2021	Rk	ACL Dodgers	0	2	0	5	5	16.20	3.00	7.3	362	40	46	12.33	12.6	9.0	0.7	3.6	-160
2022	A	Rancho Cuca	0	3	0	44	67	5.71	1.84	9.8	224	38	66	4.08	9.2	13.7	1.5	0.2	16

Continues to struggle to harness his above-average stuff. Crossfire action in delivery creates deception combined with mid-90s FB that hits 99. Lowered arm slot from HS days, which helps generate more east-west action on SL and CB, both of which flash as plus. Inability to command any of the three offerings raises concerns about reaching his potential.

Burhenn,Garrett

SP | Detroit | EXP MLB DEBUT: 2025 | H/W: 6-3 215 | FUT: #5 SP/swingman | 6C

Thrws R Age 23
2021 (9) Ohio St

Velo	Pitch	Grade
91-94	FB	++
73-76	CB	++
80-83	SL	+++
78-83	CU	+++

Year	Lev	Team	W	L	Sv	IP	K	ERA	WHIP	BF/G	OBA	H%	S%	xERA	Ctl	Dom	Cmd	hr/9	BPV
2022	A	Lakeland	4	5	0	78	103	3.45	1.19	17.4	251	35	78	3.92	2.2	11.9	5.4	1.4	172
2022	A+	West Michigan	0	1	0	13	9	7.56	2.14	16.2	362	40	65	8.10	4.8	6.2	1.3	1.4	-1

Comes after hitters with a 4-pitch mix, but lacks a dominant offering, relying instead on command and control. FB sits in the 91-94 range with arm-side ride while SL and CB are fringe-average. CU is his best offering, generating swing-and-miss fade and sink. Short arm action with a high 3/4 arm slot offers some deception without sacrificing command.

Burke,Sean

SP | Chicago (A) | EXP MLB DEBUT: 2023 | H/W: 6-6 230 | FUT: #4 starter | 7B

Thrws R Age 23
2021 (3) Maryland

Velo	Pitch	Grade
92-95	FB	+++
81-85	SL	+++
75-79	CB	+++

Year	Lev	Team	W	L	Sv	IP	K	ERA	WHIP	BF/G	OBA	H%	S%	xERA	Ctl	Dom	Cmd	hr/9	BPV
2021	Rk	ACL White Sox	0	0	0	3		0.00	0.67	5.2	106	22	100		3.0	15.0	5.0	0.0	207
2021	A	Kannapolis	0	1	0	14	20	3.21	1.36	11.7	186	32	74	2.23	6.4	12.9	2.0	0.0	76
2022	A+	Winston-Salem	2	1	0	28	31	2.89	1.29	19.2	233	30	82	3.55	3.9	10.0	2.6	1.0	93
2022	AA	Birmingham	2	7	0	73	99	4.81	1.44	16.4	259	36	70	4.63	4.1	12.2	3.0	1.4	128
2022	AAA	Charlotte	0	2	0	7	7	11.57	2.14	17.4	378	46	43	8.30	3.9	9.0	2.3	1.3	76

Tall, big-bodied 3-pitch RHP struggled putting away hitters and gave up too much hard contact. Pitches off a good foundation with strike-throwing tendencies. 4-seam FB has ride profile but struggles keeping barrel of it. Lacks consistency with 12-to-6 CB, which isn't a trusted out pitch. SL is a short breaker with a downward profile.

Burkhalter,Blake

RP | Atlanta | EXP MLB DEBUT: 2024 | H/W: 6-0 204 | FUT: Setup reliever | 7D

Thrws R Age 22
2022 (2) Auburn

Velo	Pitch	Grade
92-95	FB	++++
88-90	CT	+++
82-85	CU	++

Year	Lev	Team	W	L	Sv	IP	K	ERA	WHIP	BF/G	OBA	H%	S%	xERA	Ctl	Dom	Cmd	hr/9	BPV
2022	NCAA	Auburn	4	2	16	46	71	3.71	0.91	5.7	212	31	70	3.05	1.4	13.9	10.1	1.8	231
2022	Rk	FCL Braves	0	0	0	0	0		40.00	4.3	914	91	50	#####	90.0	0.0	0.0	0.0	-2412
2022	A	Augusta	1	0	0	4	7	0.00	0.24	6.3	80	18	100		0.0	15.4		0.0	295

Over-the-top college closer is shorter in stature and close to physical projection. Quick reliever delivery with below-average extension. 3-pitch pitcher. Flat-angled 4-seam FB explodes late up in zone. Plays up due to low release height. CT Has short, late break profile. Also, works in fringe CU.

Burns,Tanner

SP | Cleveland | EXP MLB DEBUT: 2024 | H/W: 6-0 210 | FUT: #4 starter | 7C

Thrws R Age 24
2020 (1) Auburn

Velo	Pitch	Grade
90-93	FB	+++
85-87	SL	+++
76-79	CB	+++
82-86	CU	++

Year	Lev	Team	W	L	Sv	IP	K	ERA	WHIP	BF/G	OBA	H%	S%	xERA	Ctl	Dom	Cmd	hr/9	BPV
2020	NCAA	Auburn	3	1	0	22	32	2.44	1.00	21.1	194	30	80	2.18	2.9	13.0	4.6	0.8	176
2021	A+	Lake County	2	5	0	75	91	3.59	1.24	16.9	232	31	76	3.62	3.5	10.9	3.1	1.2	120
2022	AA	Akron	3	7	0	88	92	3.57	1.36	17.6	232	28	80	4.17	4.6	9.4	2.0	1.4	63

Pitchability RHP struggled with command in '22. Easy mechanics with smooth high 3/4s delivery. Struggled to corral flat-angled FB with arm-side ride and above-average run. Secondary pitches also took a step back. SL continues to best secondary with late vertical break. CB is a good eye level changer. Struggled getting whiffs with CU.

Burrows,Michael

SP | Pittsburgh | EXP MLB DEBUT: 2023 | H/W: 6-2 195 | FUT: #4 starter | 7B

Thrws R Age 23
2018 (11) HS (CT)

Velo	Pitch	Grade
93-96	FB	++++
77-80	CB	++++
82-86	CU	++

Year	Lev	Team	W	L	Sv	IP	K	ERA	WHIP	BF/G	OBA	H%	S%	xERA	Ctl	Dom	Cmd	hr/9	BPV
2018	Rk	GCL Pirates	0	0	0	14	9	0.00	0.71	12.4	132	16	100	0.11	2.6	5.8	2.3	0.0	53
2019	A-	West Virginia	2	3	0	43	43	4.38	1.48	16.9	265	35	69	3.97	4.2	9.0	2.2	0.4	67
2021	A+	Greensboro	2	2	0	49	66	2.20	0.90	14.0	148	23	78	1.19	3.7	12.1	3.3	0.6	137
2022	AA	Altoona	4	2	0	52	69	2.94	1.10	17.0	206	31	74	2.30	3.3	11.9	3.6	0.5	144
2022	AAA	Indianapolis	1	4	0	42	42	5.34	1.35	14.6	275	34	62	4.39	2.6	9.0	3.5	1.1	110

Breakout SP who took big leap forward on two levels. Not as strong in AAA, but can dominate with two top offerings in FB and CB. Has confidence to use any pitch in any count. FB features riding life up in zone while CB has plenty of bend and break. CU lags behind and needs to upgrade. Also subject to flyballs.

Bush,Ky

SP | Los Angeles (A) | EXP MLB DEBUT: 2023 | H/W: 6-6 240 | FUT: #3 starter | 7A

Thrws L Age 23
2021 (2) St. Mary's (CA)

Velo	Pitch	Grade
91-93	FB	+++
81-84	SL	+++
83-86	CU	+++
74-76	CB	++

Year	Lev	Team	W	L	Sv	IP	K	ERA	WHIP	BF/G	OBA	H%	S%	xERA	Ctl	Dom	Cmd	hr/9	BPV
2020	NJCA	Central Ariz Coll	5	1	0	33	43	2.45	1.18	18.9	176	28	77	1.69	5.2	11.7	2.3	0.0	89
2021	NCAA	St. Mary's (CA)	7	5	0	78	112	3.00	1.13	22.0	239	38	73	2.61	2.2	12.9	5.9	0.3	191
2021	A+	Tri-City	0	2	0	12	20	4.50	1.58	10.6	293	50	68	4.17	3.8	15.0	4.0	0.0	187
2022	AA	Rocket City	7	4	0	103	101	3.67	1.18	19.6	243	29	74	3.67	2.5	8.8	3.5	1.2	108

Big-bodied, command/control 3/4s LHP pitched solidly in first full pro season. Repeatable crossfire delivery with plus extension and a deceptive angle. 4-pitch pitcher. Commands 4-seam FB well with solid carry profile, enhanced by arm slot. SL is best offering with tight gyro spin profile. CU features arm-side fade and tumble. CB is seldom used.

Butto,Jose

SP | New York (N) | EXP MLB DEBUT: 2022 | H/W: 6-1 202 | FUT: #5 SP/swingman | 6B

Thrws R Age 25
2017 FA (VZ)

Velo	Pitch	Grade
92-94	FB	+++
81-83	CU	+++
77-79	CB	++
80-82	SL	+++

Year	Lev	Team	W	L	Sv	IP	K	ERA	WHIP	BF/G	OBA	H%	S%	xERA	Ctl	Dom	Cmd	hr/9	BPV
2021	A+	Brooklyn	1	4	0	58	60	4.34	1.14	19.2	237	28	69	3.93	2.3	9.3	4.0	1.7	123
2021	AA	Binghamton	3	2	0	40	50	3.14	1.05	19.4	226	30	78	3.21	2.0	11.2	5.6	1.3	165
2022	AA	Binghamton	6	5	0	92	108	4.01	1.31	19.0	249	32	75	4.20	3.4	10.6	3.1	1.4	116
2022	AAA	Syracuse	1	1	0	36	30	2.49	0.97	17.1	203	24	78	2.20	2.2	7.5	3.3	0.7	92
2022	MLB	New York (N)	0	0	0	4	5	15.75	2.75	22.3	444	53	44	14.25	4.5	11.3	2.5	4.5	99

Solid 3/4s RHP made MLB debut in 2022 continues to struggle with FB command. Solid frame with a little more growth possible. 4-pitch pitcher. 4-seam FB is flat-angled with solid ride and run, especially commanded up. SL is best pitch, especially with late vertical drop. CU is solid with arm/side fading profile. CB is eye-level changer.

Cabrera,Jean

SP | Philadelphia | EXP MLB DEBUT: 2026 | H/W: 6-0 145 | FUT: #4 starter | 7D

Thrws R Age 21
2019 FA (VZ)

Velo	Pitch	Grade
92-95	FB	+++
78-81	CB	++
80-82	SL	++
84-86	CU	+++

Year	Lev	Team	W	L	Sv	IP	K	ERA	WHIP	BF/G	OBA	H%	S%	xERA	Ctl	Dom	Cmd	hr/9	BPV
2021	Rk	DSL Phillies White	3	2	0	52	61	1.55	0.84	14.7	188	28	81	1.14	1.7	10.5	6.1	0.2	161
2022	A	Clearwater	2	4	0	46	51	5.27	1.78	17.7	293	37	74	6.19	5.5	10.0	1.8	1.6	50

Low-$ international sign with more promise than expected. Throws four pitches; commands a low-90s FB; two breakers in similar velocity band with good chase/whiff rates. Best secondary is CU thrown with great arm action. Advanced feel for pitching; frame still filling out; club has had success with adding velocity. Worth keeping tabs on.

Cameron,Noah

SP | Kansas City | EXP MLB DEBUT: 2024 | H/W: 6-3 220 | FUT: #5 SP/swingman | 7D

Thrws L Age 23
2021 (7) Central Arkansas

Velo	Pitch	Grade
89-92	FB	+++
78-82	CB	+++
78-82	CU	++++

Year	Lev	Team	W	L	Sv	IP	K	ERA	WHIP	BF/G	OBA	H%	S%	xERA	Ctl	Dom	Cmd	hr/9	BPV
2022	Rk	ACL Royals Blue	0	1	0	5	7	3.46	1.73	7.9	380	51	88	7.69	0.0	12.1		1.7	236
2022	A	Columbia	0	1	0	29	39	3.72	1.07	16.1	212	31	68	2.69	2.8	12.1	4.3	0.9	160
2022	A+	Quad Cities	2	1	0	31	53	3.48	1.10	13.5	236	42	69	2.70	2.0	15.4	7.6	0.6	240

Tall, 3/4 slot pitchability LHP enjoyed solid pro debut across 3 levels. Repeatable delivery with little deception. 3-pitch mix. 4-seam FB sits 89-92 with good command. Complements arm-side fading CU with excellent separation off FB. It also drops off the table. CB is a fringe-average offering with solid shape.

Campbell,Isaiah

RP | Seattle | EXP MLB DEBUT: 2023 | H/W: 6-4 230 | FUT: Setup reliever | 7D

Thrws R Age 25
2019 (2) Arkansas

Velo	Pitch	Grade
94-97	FB	+++
84-88	SL	+++

Year	Lev	Team	W	L	Sv	IP	K	ERA	WHIP	BF/G	OBA	H%	S%	xERA	Ctl	Dom	Cmd	hr/9	BPV
2021	A+	Everett	3	1	0	19	20	2.36	0.99	14.6	194	25	82	2.34	2.8	9.4	3.3	0.9	111
2022	A+	Everett	1	0	10	33	35	0.82	0.85	6.4	162	22	96	1.23	2.7	9.5	3.5	0.5	116
2022	AA	Arkansas	0	4	1	13	24	3.46	1.15	3.7	262	46	77	3.93	1.4	16.6	12.0	1.4	280

Tall, power-armed RP who stayed healthy after missing most of 2021 due to elbow issues. Converted to RP full-time in '22 and had save opps. Operates with two pitches that can flash plus. FB effective, but needs better command, especially early in count. Puts away hitters with SL that has great sweeping action. No pitch against LHH.

Campbell,Justin — SP — Cleveland

EXP MLB DEBUT: 2025 | H/W: 6-7 219 | FUT: #3 starter | 8E

Thrws R Age 22 — 2022 (1) Oklahoma St

Velo	Pitch	Grade
90-93	FB	++++
75-78	CB	+++
78-81	CU	+++
81-83	SL	++

Year	Lev	Team	W	L	Sv	IP	K	ERA	WHIP	BF/G	OBA	H%	S%	xERA	Ctl	Dom	Cmd	hr/9	BPV

Tall, lean 2022 draft pick had excellent college season. High 3/4s delivery will need pro refinement but gets to plus extension. Mostly 3-pitch pitcher. 4-seam FB sits low-90s with solid ride/run profile and plus command. Late-fading CU is best secondary with plus separation off FB. 12-to-6 CB is potentially best secondary long term.

Cannon,Jonathan — SP — Chicago (A)

EXP MLB DEBUT: 2024 | H/W: 6-6 213 | FUT: #4 starter | 7C

Thrws R Age 22 — 2022 (3) Georgia

Velo	Pitch	Grade
92-95	FB	+++
80-84	SL	+++
88-90	CT	+++
83-86	CU	++

Year	Lev	Team	W	L	Sv	IP	K	ERA	WHIP	BF/G	OBA	H%	S%	xERA	Ctl	Dom	Cmd	hr/9	BPV
2022	NCAA	Georgia	9	4	0	78	68	4.03	1.01	23.0	233	27	64	3.06	1.4	7.8	5.7	1.2	122
2022	Rk	ACL White Sox	0	0	1	1	1	0.00	1.00	3.8	0	0	100		9.0	9.0	1.0	0.0	-63
2022	A	Kannapolis	0	0	0	6	3	1.48	0.98	7.7	189	22	83	1.41	3.0	4.4	1.5	0.0	18

Tall, big-bodied strike throwing RHP made full-season debut. It's an easy operation featuring plus extension and repeatable mechanics. Three pitches, all average-or-better. 2-seam FB has solid arm-side run but doesn't miss many bats. Tunnels CT off 2-seam FB, creating different angles. SL has solid 2-plane break.

Canterino,Matt — SP — Minnesota

EXP MLB DEBUT: 2024 | H/W: 6-2 222 | FUT: #3 starter | 8D

Thrws R Age 25 — 2019 (2) Rice

Velo	Pitch	Grade
93-97	FB	+++
81-83	SL	+++
80-83	CU	+++
82-84		+++

Year	Lev	Team	W	L	Sv	IP	K	ERA	WHIP	BF/G	OBA	H%	S%	xERA	Ctl	Dom	Cmd	hr/9	BPV
2019	A	Cedar Rapids	1	1	0	20		1.35	0.65	13.9	96	16	77		3.2	11.3	3.6	0.0	135
2021	A	Fort Myers	0	0	0	2	2	0.00	0.00	5.6	0	0			0.0	9.0		0.0	180
2021	A+	Cedar Rapids	1	0	0	21	43	0.86	0.67	14.6	144	36	92	0.39	1.7	18.4	10.8	0.4	303
2022	Rk	FCL Twins	0	0	0	2	4	4.09	1.82	5.1	326	48	100	9.11	4.1	16.4	4.0	4.1	202
2022	AA	Wichita	0	1	0	34	50	1.85	1.14	12.3	150	26	84	1.55	5.8	13.2	2.3	0.3	99

Injury-prone RHP who underwent Tommy John surgery in July. When healthy, has pitch mix and production to be top prospect. Has been difficult to make hard contact against with multiple above average offerings. Has lot of effort in delivery, but provides deception. Impressive spin rates, but has trouble commanding zone.

Cantillo,Joey — SP — Cleveland

EXP MLB DEBUT: 2023 | H/W: 6-4 225 | FUT: #4 starter | 7B

Thrws L Age 23 — 2017 (16) HS (HI)

Velo	Pitch	Grade
90-93	FB	+++
77-80	CU	++++
83-86	SL	++
71-74	CB	+++

Year	Lev	Team	W	L	Sv	IP	K	ERA	WHIP	BF/G	OBA	H%	S%	xERA	Ctl	Dom	Cmd	hr/9	BPV
2019	A	Fort Wayne	9	3	0	98	128	1.93	0.87	19.0	173	27	78	1.13	2.5	11.8	4.7	0.3	163
2019	A+	Lake Elsinore	1	1	0	13	16	4.77	1.44	18.7	244	32	71	4.44	4.8	10.9	2.3	1.4	86
2021	Rk	ACL Indians	0	0	0	5	7	0.00	0.60	8.6	124	22	100		1.8	12.6	7.0	0.0	196
2021	AA	Akron	0	2	0	8	12	4.50	2.25	8.1	262	43	78	5.42	11.3	13.5	1.2	0.0	-43
2022	AA	Akron	4	3	0	60	87	1.94	1.10	16.8	183	30	83	1.82	4.2	13.0	3.1	0.3	139

Crafty, low 3/4s LHP had best season as pro despite late shoulder injury. Added velocity to entire pitch mix while also improving spin of CB. 4-seam FB sits low-90s with natural ride up in zone. Best pitch is arm-side fading CU with late drop. Has improved spin profile of CB to get greater break profile. SL is below-average offering.

Carela,Juan — SP — New York (A)

EXP MLB DEBUT: 2025 | H/W: 6-3 186 | FUT: #4 starter | 7E

Thrws R Age 21 — 2018 FA (DR)

Velo	Pitch	Grade
90-93	FB	+++
79-82	SL	+++
83-86	CT	++
84-87	CU	++

Year	Lev	Team	W	L	Sv	IP	K	ERA	WHIP	BF/G	OBA	H%	S%	xERA	Ctl	Dom	Cmd	hr/9	BPV
2021	Rk	FCL Yankees	2	0	0	22	27	1.64	0.86	13.5	184	29	79	0.99	2.0	11.0	5.4	0.0	162
2021	A	Tampa	0	2	0	20	22	11.64	2.49	17.8	361	46	51	8.89	8.1	9.9	1.2	1.3	-22
2022	A	Tampa	7	2	0	79	110	2.96	1.06	19.2	180	28	73	1.97	4.0	12.5	3.1	0.6	136
2022	A+	Hudson Valley	1	4	0	28	21	7.71	1.50	17.3	240	27	47	4.52	5.5	6.8	1.2	1.3	-8

Low 3/4 RHP pitched well in well in first half at Low-A. Athletic, wiry build with room to add strength. Achieves solid extension with delivery. Struggles commanding arm-side boring 2-seam FB with high spin rate. Two-plane sweeping SL is best pitch. Has plus SL command. Also commands CT with movement too early in pitch progression.

Carrillo,Gerardo — RP — Washington

EXP MLB DEBUT: 2024 | H/W: 5-11 163 | FUT: Middle reliever | 7C

Thrws R Age 24 — 2017 FA (MX)

Velo	Pitch	Grade
90-93	FB	++
85-87	SL	+++
82-85	CU	++

Year	Lev	Team	W	L	Sv	IP	K	ERA	WHIP	BF/G	OBA	H%	S%	xERA	Ctl	Dom	Cmd	hr/9	BPV
2021	AA	Harrisburg	0	5	0	37	38	5.59	1.65	20.7	277	35	68	5.31	5.1	9.2	1.8	1.2	46
2021	AA	Tulsa	3	2	0	59	70	4.26	1.32	16.3	227	29	72	3.94	4.4	10.7	2.4	1.4	91
2022	Rk	FCL Nationals	0	0	0	3	1	3.00	1.67	6.7	371	40	80	5.83	0.0	3.0		0.0	72
2022	A+	Wilmington	1	0	2	10	10	3.60	1.20	4.5	199	25	73	2.87	4.5	9.0	2.0	0.9	59
2022	AA	Harrisburg	1	1	0	10	17	11.58	2.18	5.0	330	53	43	7.09	7.1	15.1	2.1	0.9	98

Short-statured RHP lost some ticks off fastball and effectiveness in 2022; likely related to shoulder problems that cost him two months. Without his boring mid-90s two-seamer, leaned on SL more, but stuff is rather ordinary and setup potential is replaced by a middle reliever. If health + velo returns in 2023, could be a different story.

Carter,Irv — SP — Toronto

EXP MLB DEBUT: 2026 | H/W: 6-4 210 | FUT: #3 starter | 8D

Thrws R Age 20 — 2021 (5) HS (FL)

Velo	Pitch	Grade
91-94	FB	+++
81-85	SL	+++
83-85	CU	++

Year	Lev	Team	W	L	Sv	IP	K	ERA	WHIP	BF/G	OBA	H%	S%	xERA	Ctl	Dom	Cmd	hr/9	BPV
2022	Rk	FCL Blue Jays	1	3	0	33	42	5.96	1.42	15.6	278	35	64	5.60	3.0	11.4	3.8	2.2	142
2022	A	Dunedin	0	1	0	14	11	4.50	1.29	14.4	262	30	69	4.26	2.6	7.1	2.8	1.3	76

Large, durable SP with high-maintenance delivery and arm action, but posted high K rate in first pro experience. Good upside and could break out with added polish to SL and CU. Allows lot of HR and will need to more effectively sequence and spot FB down in zone. Has some reliever risk, but stuff too good to convert now.

Carver,Ross — SP — Cleveland

EXP MLB DEBUT: 2024 | H/W: 6-2 191 | FUT: #5 SP/swingman | 6C

Thrws R Age 23 — 2021 (20) Dallas Baptist

Velo	Pitch	Grade
91-93	FB	+++
82-84	SL	+++
77-80	CB	++
80-82	CU	+++

Year	Lev	Team	W	L	Sv	IP	K	ERA	WHIP	BF/G	OBA	H%	S%	xERA	Ctl	Dom	Cmd	hr/9	BPV
2021	A	Visalia	0	2	1	22	33	4.09	1.45	11.8	253	42	69	3.29	4.5	13.5	3.0	0.0	140
2022	A+	Hillsboro	2	5	0	81	97	3.11	1.01	20.7	194	26	73	2.31	3.0	10.8	3.6	0.9	131
2022	AA	Amarillo	2	5	0	36	31	9.50	1.75	18.3	321	32	52	8.63	3.8	7.8	2.1	3.8	56

Serviceable, backend SP acquired in off-season trade with Arizona. 3/4s slot delivery with solid extension. 4 pitch repertoire. Flat-angled FB has ride/run profile. Tightly wound SL has a solid two-plane movement profile. CB has short, downward break profile. CU lacks firmness but features late fading action and deception off FB.

Castaneda,Victor — SP — Milwaukee

EXP MLB DEBUT: 2023 | H/W: 6-1 185 | FUT: #4 starter | 7D

Thrws R Age 24 — 2017 FA (MX)

Velo	Pitch	Grade
90-94	FB	+++
78-80	CB	++
83-86	SP	+++

Year	Lev	Team	W	L	Sv	IP	K	ERA	WHIP	BF/G	OBA	H%	S%	xERA	Ctl	Dom	Cmd	hr/9	BPV
2019	A	Wisconsin	4	2	6	44	53	4.50	1.32	5.7	262	36	67	3.87	2.9	10.8	3.8	0.8	136
2021	A+	Wisconsin	5	7	0	97	114	5.20	1.31	20.0	248	31	65	4.46	3.4	10.6	3.1	1.7	116
2021	AAA	Nashville	1	1	0	12	17	2.25	1.42	16.9	210	35	82	2.66	6.0	12.8	2.1	0.0	86
2022	AA	Biloxi	4	6	0	106	110	3.98	1.36	19.3	245	30	76	4.25	4.0	9.3	2.3	1.4	78
2022	AAA	Nashville	2	0	0	14	8	5.14	1.36	19.5	262	29	61	3.86	3.2	5.1	1.6	0.6	24

Steadily-rising SP who has never had standout season, but consistently gets job done. K rate has fallen as upper levels, but effectively mixes three potential average to above average offerings. Struggles with LHH and can elevate ball when overthrowing. Uses good arm speed to enhance FB with arm-side run. Needs more punch to SL.

Cavalli,Cade — SP — Washington

EXP MLB DEBUT: 2022 | H/W: 6-4 240 | FUT: #2 starter | 9C

Thrws R Age 24 — 2020 (1) Oklahoma

Velo	Pitch	Grade
94-98	FB	+++++
84-87	CB	++++
87-90	SL	+++
86-89	CU	+++

Year	Lev	Team	W	L	Sv	IP	K	ERA	WHIP	BF/G	OBA	H%	S%	xERA	Ctl	Dom	Cmd	hr/9	BPV
2021	A+	Wilmington	3	1	0	40	71	1.79	0.90	21.3	175	35	80	1.12	2.7	15.9	5.9	0.2	232
2021	AA	Harrisburg	3	3	0	58	80	2.79	1.28	21.6	193	31	78	2.40	5.4	12.4	2.3	0.3	95
2021	AAA	Rochester	1	5	0	24	24	7.44	1.90	19.0	326	41	59	6.25	4.8	8.9	1.8	0.7	48
2022	AAA	Rochester	6	4	0	97	104	3.71	1.18	19.4	215	30	67	2.41	3.6	9.6	2.7	0.3	94
2022	MLB	Washington	0	1	0	4	6	15.37	1.95	19.6	342	52	13	5.90	4.4	13.2	3.0	0.0	137

Made MLB debut in Aug after spending all season in AAA. Power arsenal can overwhelm lesser bats: High-90s FB gets by more on velo than movement; vertical swing-and-miss CB slightly ahead of shorter, tighter SL, and CU flashes as well. Command has improved; won't ever be pristine but array of pitches and knowing how to use them will lead to success.

Cecconi,Slade — SP — Arizona

EXP MLB DEBUT: 2023 | H/W: 6-4 219 | FUT: #4 starter | 7C

Thrws R Age 23 — 2020 (1) Miami

Velo	Pitch	Grade
92-94	FB	+++
80-83	SL	++++
70-73	CB	+++
80-83	CU	++

Year	Lev	Team	W	L	Sv	IP	K	ERA	WHIP	BF/G	OBA	H%	S%	xERA	Ctl	Dom	Cmd	hr/9	BPV
2020	NCAA	Miami	2	1	0	21	30	3.84	1.04	20.4	201	31	65	2.42	3.0	12.8	4.3	0.9	168
2021	A+	Hillsboro	4	2	0	59	63	4.12	1.24	19.9	242	32	68	3.35	3.1	9.6	3.2	0.8	109
2022	AA	Amarillo	7	6	0	129	127	4.39	1.32	20.6	276	33	72	4.77	2.2	8.8	4.0	1.5	117

Tall, strong RHP struggled with overall command in '22 season spent in Double-A. 3/4s delivery; fights with flying open. Throws strikes with riding/running 4-seam FB, struggles with in-zone command. Tight two-plane breaking SL has late horizontal movement. Struggles throwing 11-to-5 CB from slot. Doesn't sell late fading CU.

Champlain, Chandler — SP — Kansas City
EXP MLB DEBUT: 2025 | H/W: 6-5 220 | FUT: Middle reliever | 6C
Thrws R   Age 23
2021 (9) USC

Pitch	Grade
93-95 FB	+++
82-85 SL	++
77-80 CB	+++

Year	Lev	Team	W	L	Sv	IP	K	ERA	WHIP	BF/G	OBA	H%	S%	xERA	Ctl	Dom	Cmd	hr/9	BPV
2022	A	Tampa	2	5	0	73	94	4.31	1.24	18.6	259	35	70	4.14	2.3	11.6	4.9	1.4	163
2022	A+	Quad Cities	1	3	0	32	22	9.84	2.16	19.9	391	45	52	8.21	3.1	6.2	2.0	0.8	46

Big-bodied, former college RHP added velocity and was traded by NYY in '22. Repeats high 3/4s delivery well. Controls 3-pitch arsenal. Touched 98 MPH with riding 4-seam FB. Struggled with in-zone command after trade. Has more confidence in one-plane breaking SL than 12-to-6 CB but CB is better overall pitch with solid depth and shape.

Chandler, Bubba — SP — Pittsburgh
EXP MLB DEBUT: 2025 | H/W: 6-2 200 | FUT: #3 starter | 9E
Thrws R   Age 20
2021 (3) HS (GA)

Pitch	Grade
91-96 FB	+++
77-79 CB	+++
82-85 SL	++
81-82 CU	+++

Year	Lev	Team	W	L	Sv	IP	K	ERA	WHIP	BF/G	OBA	H%	S%	xERA	Ctl	Dom	Cmd	hr/9	BPV
2022	Rk	FCL Pirates	0	0	0	15	27	0.00	0.86	9.3	66	16	100		6.0	16.1	2.7	0.0	147
2022	A	Bradenton	1	1	0	26	33	4.15	1.46	13.9	214	30	74	3.82	6.2	11.4	1.8	1.0	55

Two-way player who saw time at SS and DH. One of top athletes in sport with premium arm strength and feel to pitch. Delivery is a bit crude and has inconsistent arm slot. Has potential for 4 average to plus pitches, led by dominant FB. Mixes in two breaking balls with CB ahead of SL. CU shows flashes of brilliance but inconsistent.

Church, Marc — RP — Texas
EXP MLB DEBUT: 2024 | H/W: 6-3 189 | FUT: Setup reliever | 7C
Thrws R   Age 22
2019 (18) HS (GA)

Pitch	Grade
95-98 FB	+++++
86-91 SL	+++

Year	Lev	Team	W	L	Sv	IP	K	ERA	WHIP	BF/G	OBA	H%	S%	xERA	Ctl	Dom	Cmd	hr/9	BPV
2021	A	Down East	3	1	3	27	49	4.32	1.11	5.6	224	40	65	3.26	2.7	16.3	6.1	1.3	239
2022	A+	Hickory	2	2	4	34	57	2.91	1.03	5.7	226	35	86	3.60	1.9	15.1	8.1	1.9	240
2022	AA	Frisco	1	3	1	15	21	7.20	1.67	4.8	299	40	62	6.75	4.2	12.6	3.0	2.4	131

Sleeper alert—he has a disgusting plus-plus FB with velocity, rise, angle and the ability to consistently rip it past batters at shoulder level. SL tunnels well off FB and his command of both is advanced. Delivery is violent but team is going to tinker with starting him in '23 so CU development is critical. Closer-worthy stuff otherwise.

Coleman, Carson — RP — New York (A)
EXP MLB DEBUT: 2023 | H/W: 6-2 190 | FUT: Middle reliever | 6C
Thrws R   Age 25
2020 (NDFA) Kentucky

Pitch	Grade
94-96 FB	++++
79-82 SL	+++
88-90 CU	+++

Year	Lev	Team	W	L	Sv	IP	K	ERA	WHIP	BF/G	OBA	H%	S%	xERA	Ctl	Dom	Cmd	hr/9	BPV
2020	NCAA	Kentucky	0	0	0	5	13	3.46	0.96	3.3	214	71	60	1.47	1.7	22.5	13.0	0.0	376
2021	A	Tampa	2	3	5	35	49	6.15	1.74	5.2	261	40	63	4.61	6.7	12.6	1.9	0.5	64
2022	A+	Hudson Valley	0	0	4	19	26	0.47	0.84	7.8	115	18	100	0.63	4.2	12.3	2.9	0.5	124
2022	AA	Somerset	2	3	15	44	69	2.86	0.91	4.7	195	34	68	1.57	2.0	14.1	6.9	0.4	217

Tall, low 3/4s RP-only prospect pitched well across High-A and Double-A. Quick delivery with solid extension. Will adjust slot to cause deception. Flat-angled FB has solid ride, which plays up due to lower slot. Sweeping SL does struggle with consistency but pairs awesomely with FB trajectory. CU has fading profile, keeps LHH at bay.

Contreras, Efrain — SP — San Diego
EXP MLB DEBUT: 2024 | H/W: 5-10 225 | FUT: #4 starter | 7E
Thrws R   Age 23
2017 FA (MX)

Pitch	Grade
92-95 FB	+++
78-82 CB	+++
83-86 CU	+++

Year	Lev	Team	W	L	Sv	IP	K	ERA	WHIP	BF/G	OBA	H%	S%	xERA	Ctl	Dom	Cmd	hr/9	BPV
2018	Rk	AZL Padres	1	3	0	43	44	2.72	1.05	18.5	229	30	76	2.59	1.9	9.2	4.9	0.6	133
2018	Rk	DSL Padres	0	0	1	19	25	1.41	0.79	13.8	182	28	86	1.20	1.4	11.8	8.3	0.5	192
2018	A-	Tri-City	1	0	0	6	7	0.00	0.50	10.0	56	9	100		3.0	10.5	3.5	0.0	126
2019	A	Fort Wayne	6	6	0	109	121	3.63	1.18	17.5	240	31	73	3.40	2.6	10.0	3.8	1.0	126
2022	A+	Fort Wayne	0	5	0	53	64	5.76	1.68	14.0	299	40	67	5.66	4.2	10.8	2.6	1.2	99

Returned in May after Tommy John surgery; had not pitched since 2019. Short, stocky frame produces quality CB that features sharp breaking action. CB is one of best in org and effective due to consistent release point and arm speed. Control regressed upon return, but shows flashes of prior status. Owns clean delivery and FB with good carry.

Corry, Seth — SP — San Francisco
EXP MLB DEBUT: 2025 | H/W: 6-2 195 | FUT: #4 starter | 7E
Thrws L   Age 24
2017 (3) HS (UT)

Pitch	Grade
90-95 FB	+++
78-82 CB	+++
81-84 CU	++

Year	Lev	Team	W	L	Sv	IP	K	ERA	WHIP	BF/G	OBA	H%	S%	xERA	Ctl	Dom	Cmd	hr/9	BPV
2017	Rk	AZL Giants O	3	1	0	38	42	2.61	1.45	18.0	262	36	81	3.66	4.0	9.9	2.5	0.2	88
2018	A-	Salem-Keizer	1	2	0	19	17	5.63	1.51	16.6	205	26	61	3.33	7.0	8.0	1.1	0.5	-28
2019	A	Augusta	9	3	0	122	172	1.77	1.07	17.6	175	29	84	1.67	4.3	12.7	3.0	0.3	131
2021	A+	Eugene	3	3	0	67	100	6.03	1.73	16.1	219	35	63	4.04	8.4	13.4	1.6	0.5	31
2022	A+	Eugene	0	0	0	2	1	4.29	2.86	6.0	336	38	83	8.18	12.9	4.3	0.3	0.0	-252

Missed most of season after shoulder surgery. Injury came on heels of miserable 2021 which depressed prospect status. Normally has electric stuff. FB can be sneaky quick with filthy movement when bending CB can be K pitch. Control has been major issue and he can slow arm speed when aiming. Long road back, but hope remains.

Cox, Jackson — SP — Colorado
EXP MLB DEBUT: 2026 | H/W: 6-1 185 | FUT: #4 starter | 7E
Thrws R   Age 19
2022 (2) HS (WA)

Pitch	Grade
90-94 FB	+++
79-82 CB	+++
82-85 CU	+

Small RHP hides the ball well, but exaggerated shoulder rotation and max effort delivery raises concerns about injuries. FB sits in the low 90s, topping at 96 with some nice arm-side run and ride. Best offering is a tight power slurve that has plus spin and late break. Also shows some feel for a CU, but rarely used it in HS. Shows solid FB command.

Crawford, Reggie — SP — San Francisco
EXP MLB DEBUT: 2025 | H/W: 6-4 235 | FUT: #3 starter | 8D
Thrws L   Age 22
2022 (1) Connecticut

Pitch	Grade
94-98 FB	++++
83-87 SL	+++
82-86 CU	+

First round pick who didn't pitch due to Tommy John surgery. Has limited pitching experience, but is strong and athletic that lead to intriguing ceiling. Uses high effort delivery and quick arm action to produce easy velocity with plus FB. Likes to pitch up and inside. SL serves a different look, though CU is poor at present.

Criswell, Jeff — SP — Colorado
EXP MLB DEBUT: 2023 | H/W: 6-4 225 | FUT: #4 starter | 7C
Thrws R   Age 24
2020 (2) Michigan

Pitch	Grade
92-95 FB	+++
78-80 CB	++
82-84 SL	+++
81-84 CU	+++

Year	Lev	Team	W	L	Sv	IP	K	ERA	WHIP	BF/G	OBA	H%	S%	xERA	Ctl	Dom	Cmd	hr/9	BPV
2020	NCAA	Michigan	0	1	0	24	26	4.50	1.13	23.7	210	29	58	2.31	3.4	9.8	2.9	0.4	102
2021	A+	Lansing	0	0	0	12	12	4.50	1.08	9.4	210	27	58	2.57	3.0	9.0	3.0	0.8	99
2022	A+	Lansing	2	3	0	50	58	3.78	1.10	19.6	208	27	71	3.05	3.2	10.4	3.2	1.3	118
2022	AA	Midland	2	6	0	57	57	4.25	1.49	20.5	274	35	73	4.60	3.8	9.0	2.4	0.9	77
2022	AAA	Las Vegas	0	1	0	10	4	4.41	1.27	20.9	258	29	62	3.01	2.6	3.5	1.3	0.0	10

Strong-armed RHP who pitched on 3 levels and had 2nd most Ks in org. Successful in High-A thanks to effective mixing of four pitches, highlighted by FB and CU. Has effort in delivery and needs to smoothen mechanics for better command. FB could add a few more mph while SL and CU could continue upward trajectory.

Crouse, Hans — RP — Philadelphia
EXP MLB DEBUT: 2021 | H/W: 6-4 180 | FUT: Middle reliever | 7D
Thrws R   Age 24
2017 (2) HS (CA)

Pitch	Grade
90-93 FB	+++
83-85 SL	+++
81-85 CU	++

Year	Lev	Team	W	L	Sv	IP	K	ERA	WHIP	BF/G	OBA	H%	S%	xERA	Ctl	Dom	Cmd	hr/9	BPV
2021	AA	Frisco	3	2	0	51	54	3.35	0.90	14.6	158	20	66	1.64	3.4	9.5	2.8	0.9	99
2021	AA	Reading	2	2	0	29	38	2.77	1.23	19.7	226	32	82	3.27	3.7	11.7	3.2	0.9	129
2021	AAA	Lehigh Valley	0	0	0	4	6	6.59	1.95	19.6	302	42	71	7.32	6.6	13.2	2.0	2.2	77
2021	MLB	Philadelphia	0	2	0	7	2	5.14	1.57	15.4	168	10	78	5.10	9.0	2.6	0.3	2.6	-179
2022	AAA	Lehigh Valley	0	3	0	12	13	13.39	2.23	12.2	381	47	36	8.76	4.5	9.7	2.2	1.5	72

Health issues flared up again in 2022 (COVID, bicepts tendinitis) and forced him to miss most of the season. When back, his FB/SL-led arsenal had backed up, losing velocity and effectiveness and reinforcing his reliever profile. Has energy, deceptive delivery and breaking ball to thrive in a bullpen role, but will need to reestablish it all in AAA.

Crow, Coleman — SP — Los Angeles (A)
EXP MLB DEBUT: 2023 | H/W: 6-0 175 | FUT: Middle reliever | 6B
Thrws R   Age 22
2019 (28) HS (GA)

Pitch	Grade
88-92 FB	++
83-86 SL	++
76-78 CB	+++
82-84 CU	++

Year	Lev	Team	W	L	Sv	IP	K	ERA	WHIP	BF/G	OBA	H%	S%	xERA	Ctl	Dom	Cmd	hr/9	BPV
2021	A	Inland Empire	4	3	0	62	62	4.20	1.56	20.9	280	35	76	4.94	4.2	9.0	2.1	1.0	66
2022	AA	Rocket City	9	3	0	128	128	4.85	1.31	22.0	269	33	67	4.53	2.5	9.0	3.7	1.4	114

3/4s slot RHP with feel for spin had ups and downs in Double-A. Repeatable delivery. Strike thrower. Variates between two breaking pitches at higher rate than FB. CB is a sweeping variety with above-average potential. SL is mostly a horizontal breaker. Throws 2-seam FB at high rate but is a below-average offering. Also mixes in 4-seam FB & CU.

Curet,Yoniel — SP — Tampa Bay

EXP MLB DEBUT: 2024 | H/W: 6-2 190 | FUT: #3 starter | 8E

Thrws R Age 20	Year	Lev	Team	W	L	Sv	IP	K	ERA	WHIP	BF/G	OBA	H%	S%	xERA	Ctl	Dom	Cmd	hr/9	BPV
2019 FA (DR)																				
94-97 FB ++++																				
75-78 CB +++	2021	Rk	DSL Rays 2	2	4	0	51	63	3.71	1.25	14.8	205	31	67	2.21	4.8	11.1	2.3	0.0	89
85-87 CU ++	2022	Rk	FCL Rays	2	1	0	36	48	1.75	1.11	10.9	158	23	89	2.02	5.3	12.0	2.3	0.8	92
	2022	A	Charleston	0	0	0	6	10	4.50	2.17	15.0	262	46	77	5.20	10.5	15.0	1.4	0.0	5

Raw, athletic RHP flashed dominance pitching at the complex before moving up to Low-A in 2022. Low 3/4s delivery with some effort at release point. Repeats well for age/level. Frame has room to add mass. Sits mid-90s with average arm-side run and late giddy-up. Complements with sweeping CB in mid-70s range. Doesn't have a feel for CU.

Curry,Xzavion — SP — Cleveland

EXP MLB DEBUT: 2022 | H/W: 6-0 195 | FUT: #5 SP/swingman | 6A

Thrws R Age 24	Year	Lev	Team	W	L	Sv	IP	K	ERA	WHIP	BF/G	OBA	H%	S%	xERA	Ctl	Dom	Cmd	hr/9	BPV
2019 (7) Georgia Tech	2021	A+	Lake County	5	1	0	67	80	2.68	0.97	19.6	219	28	82	2.91	1.6	10.7	6.7	1.3	167
90-94 FB +++	2021	AA	Akron	0	0	0	4	5	4.29	1.43	17.8	336	37	100	8.54	0.0	10.7		4.3	211
83-86 SL ++++	2022	AA	Akron	5	3	0	69	80	3.65	1.09	20.7	223	29	71	3.12	2.5	10.4	4.2	1.2	139
73-76 CB ++	2022	AAA	Columbus	4	1	0	53	54	4.58	1.38	18.5	251	30	72	4.55	3.9	9.2	2.3	1.5	78
84-87 CU ++	2022	MLB	Cleveland	0	1	0	9	3	5.93	2.09	22.3	336	35	72	7.18	5.9	3.0	0.5	1.0	-89

Shorter-statured, over-the-top RHP pitched well in upper levels, earning MLB promotion. Height plus release point creates deceptive slot. 4-seam FB features below-average velocity but exceptional riding profile. Does well to work up and down with pitch. SL is best secondary with a slurvy profile. Other offerings help keep hitters off balance.

Cushing,Jack — SP — Oakland

EXP MLB DEBUT: 2023 | H/W: 6-3 195 | FUT: #5 SP/swingman | 7E

Thrws R Age 26	Year	Lev	Team	W	L	Sv	IP	K	ERA	WHIP	BF/G	OBA	H%	S%	xERA	Ctl	Dom	Cmd	hr/9	BPV
2019 (22) Georgetown	2021	A	Stockton	1	1	0	40		2.91	1.17	20.0	246	31	81	3.58	2.2	9.6	4.3	1.1	131
90-93 FB +++	2021	A+	Lansing	6	1	0	46	48	2.74	1.11	22.6	240	32	77	2.85	2.0	9.4	4.8	0.6	134
79-84 SL ++	2021	AA	Midland	0	5	0	25	20	4.68	1.68	22.5	332	40	71	5.45	2.5	7.2	2.9	0.4	80
82-84 CU ++	2022	AA	Midland	11	3	0	110	95	3.68	1.31	23.9	265	33	73	3.76	2.6	7.8	3.0	0.7	87
	2022	AAA	Las Vegas	1	3	0	21	20	14.14	2.38	18.2	421	45	44	13.01	3.0	8.6	2.9	4.7	91

Tall, projectable SP who got lit up in AAA and was sent back to AA in June. Command-oriented pitcher with consistent arm speed and delivery. Lacks out pitch, but is effective sequencer who can change speeds and eye levels. Very limited upside and needs to hit spots to be successful. Has allowed too many HR.

Cusick,Ryan — SP — Oakland

EXP MLB DEBUT: 2024 | H/W: 6-6 235 | FUT: #3 starter | 8D

Thrws R Age 23	Year	Lev	Team	W	L	Sv	IP	K	ERA	WHIP	BF/G	OBA	H%	S%	xERA	Ctl	Dom	Cmd	hr/9	BPV
2021 (1) Wake Forest	2020	NCAA	Wake Forest	0	2	0	22	43	3.26	1.86	25.8	270	54	80	4.49	7.3	17.5	2.4	0.0	135
94-97 FB ++++	2021	NCAA	Wake Forest	3	5	0	70	108	4.24	1.39	24.5	248	39	73	4.14	4.1	13.9	3.4	1.2	157
82-84 CB ++	2021	A	Augusta	0	1	0	16	34	2.80	1.18	10.7	248	55	78	3.01	2.2	19.0	8.5	0.6	300
85-87 SL +++	2022	Rk	ACL Athletics	0	0	0	2	3	9.00	1.50	8.6	347	53	33	4.86	0.0	13.5		0.0	261
85-88 CU ++	2022	AA	Midland	1	6	0	41	43	7.02	2.02	16.6	314	40	65	6.49	6.6	9.4	1.4	0.9	10

Acquired from ATL in Olson trade and missed time with oblique injury. Owns big, strong frame and can light up radar gun when healthy. FB features high spin rate with riding life up in zone. SL has makings of taking step forward and being true out pitch. Throwing strikes has been obstacle thus far. Not much separation between FB and CU.

Dabovich,R.J. — RP — San Francisco

EXP MLB DEBUT: 2023 | H/W: 6-3 208 | FUT: Closer | 7B

Thrws R Age 24	Year	Lev	Team	W	L	Sv	IP	K	ERA	WHIP	BF/G	OBA	H%	S%	xERA	Ctl	Dom	Cmd	hr/9	BPV
2020 (4) Arizona St	2020	NCAA	Arizona St	0	0	4	11	17	0.80	1.07	4.8	87	17	92	0.50	7.2	13.7	1.9	0.0	69
92-97 FB ++++	2021	A+	Eugene	0	0	4	12	28	1.48	0.66	3.9	55	0	100	0.50	4.4	20.7	4.7	1.5	270
83-87 CB ++++	2021	AA	Richmond	1	1	6	19	34	3.75	1.04	3.7	194	37	63	1.93	3.3	15.9	4.9	0.5	216
	2022	AA	Richmond	4	1	5	26	38	2.75	0.92	4.4	196	32	70	1.55	2.1	13.1	6.3	0.3	197
	2022	AAA	Sacramento	2	0	1	24	31	4.46	1.49	4.5	190	29	69	2.97	7.4	11.5	1.6	0.4	25

Career RP whose control regressed upon promotion to AAA. Very tough to hit on basis on two plus offerings in high octane FB and hard CB. Throws from high arm slot to add deception and unique angle to plate. Spots CB in zone and can induce weak contact. K rate fell, but still very high in short stints.

Danner,Hagen — RP — Toronto

EXP MLB DEBUT: 2023 | H/W: 6-1 210 | FUT: Setup reliever | 7C

Thrws R Age 24	Year	Lev	Team	W	L	Sv	IP	K	ERA	WHIP	BF/G	OBA	H%	S%	xERA	Ctl	Dom	Cmd	hr/9	BPV
2017 (2) HS (CA)																				
94-98 FB ++++																				
85-88 SL ++																				
CU +	2021	A+	Vancouver	2	1	3	35	42	2.05	0.94	5.3	175	25	81	1.55	3.1	10.7	3.5	0.5	128
	2022	AA	New Hampshire	0	0	2	3	1	5.63	2.50	4.3	357	38	75	7.65	8.4	2.8	0.3	0.0	-159

Converted C who moved to mound in 2021. Ended season in April due to elbow, but returned in AFL. Owns one of most electric arms in org. Has good FB command despite inexperience as pitcher and features both velocity and carry up in zone. Key will be to find 2nd pitch between hard SL, occasional CB and CU.

Devers,Luis — SP — Chicago (N)

EXP MLB DEBUT: 2024 | H/W: 6-3 178 | FUT: #5 SP/swingman | 6B

Thrws R Age 22	Year	Lev	Team	W	L	Sv	IP	K	ERA	WHIP	BF/G	OBA	H%	S%	xERA	Ctl	Dom	Cmd	hr/9	BPV
2017 FA (DR)																				
88-92 FB ++	2021	Rk	ACL Cubs	2	4	0	51	54	3.35	1.21	17.2	250	33	73	3.18	2.5	9.5	3.9	0.5	123
73-75 SL ++	2021	A	Myrtle Beach	0	0	0	3	5	6.00	3.00	8.7	415	63	78	9.95	9.0	15.0	1.7	0.0	45
80-83 CU ++++	2022	A	Myrtle Beach	9	3	0	66	75	2.59	1.07	17.2	234	33	76	2.51	1.9	10.2	5.4	0.4	150
	2022	A+	South Bend	4	0	0	51	47	1.06	0.80	16.8	168	22	88	0.84	2.1	8.3	3.9	0.2	110

Lean, athletic hurler had a breakout season between Low and High-A going 13-3 with a 1.91 ERA. Thrives despite the lack of elite velocity. FB sits at 88-92 with good sink and is well located. Best offering is a plus CU that he will throw in any count and induces swing-and-miss and weak contact. Below-average SL keeps hitters honest.

Diaz,Joel — SP — New York (N)

EXP MLB DEBUT: 2025 | H/W: 6-2 208 | FUT: #4 starter | 7D

Thrws R Age 19	Year	Lev	Team	W	L	Sv	IP	K	ERA	WHIP	BF/G	OBA	H%	S%	xERA	Ctl	Dom	Cmd	hr/9	BPV
2021 FA (DR)																				
92-95 FB +++																				
76-78 CB +++	2021	Rk	DSL Mets 2	0	2	0	49	62	0.55	0.77	12.6	173	27	92	0.63	1.6	11.4	6.9	0.0	178
84-87 CU +++	2021	Rk	DSL Mets	0	0	0	1	1	0.00	0.00	2.8	0	0			0.0	9.0		0.0	180
	2022	A	St. Lucie	3	2	0	55	51	5.88	1.58	15.1	285	35	64	5.19	4.1	8.3	2.0	1.1	58

Projectable RHP with solid control struggled in full-season debut. Athletic build with room to grow. 3/4s repeatable delivery with solid extension. 3-pitch pitcher. Struggles with in-zone command of flat-angled FB. 11-to-5 breaker has a slurvy profile but is capable of becoming an out pitch. CU has solid fading action with late bore.

Dion,Will — SP — Cleveland

EXP MLB DEBUT: 2024 | H/W: 5-10 180 | FUT: #5 SP/swingman | 6C

Thrws L Age 22	Year	Lev	Team	W	L	Sv	IP	K	ERA	WHIP	BF/G	OBA	H%	S%	xERA	Ctl	Dom	Cmd	hr/9	BPV
2021 (9) McNeese St	2021	NCAA	McNeese St	9	4	1	99	121	3.08	0.99	22.2	220	32	68	2.07	1.7	11.0	6.4	0.4	169
86-89 FB +++	2021	Rk	ACL Indians	0	0	0	9	18	0.00	0.44	7.3	38	12	100		3.0	18.0	6.0	0.0	261
83-84 SL ++	2021	A	Lynchburg	0	0	0	3	3	0.00	0.67	10.5	0	0	100		6.0	9.0	1.5	0.0	18
72-76 CB ++	2022	A	Lynchburg	8	4	0	115	142	2.27	1.03	19.3	213	30	81	2.34	2.4	11.1	4.6	0.6	152
77-80 CU ++++	2022	A+	Lake County	0	1	0	12	15	0.74	0.82	22.2	169	24	100	1.40	2.2	11.1	5.0	0.7	157

Soft-tossing LHP with nearly identical delivery to Clayton Kershaw enjoyed spectacular success in low minors. Shorter-statured, near physical projection. 4-seam FB is flat angled with solid ride up in zone. Best pitch is a low-spin CU with plus arm-side fade and late drop. SL is a fringe offering and the CB is fair at best.

Dodd,Dylan — SP — Atlanta

EXP MLB DEBUT: 2023 | H/W: 6-2 210 | FUT: #4 starter | 7D

Thrws L Age 24	Year	Lev	Team	W	L	Sv	IP	K	ERA	WHIP	BF/G	OBA	H%	S%	xERA	Ctl	Dom	Cmd	hr/9	BPV
2021 (3) SE Missouri St	2021	A	Augusta	0	1	0	11	14	4.91	1.18	14.7	244	37	54	2.51	2.5	11.5	4.7	0.0	158
88-93 FB +++	2021	A+	Rome	0	1	0	3	6	24.00	3.00	17.5	515	67	20	23.86	0.0	18.0		12.0	342
81-84 SL +++	2022	A+	Rome	9	5	0	89	91	3.44	1.15	22.1	253	33	71	3.13	1.7	9.2	5.4	0.6	137
80-83 CU +++	2022	AA	Mississippi	2	4	0	46	55	3.12	1.28	21.0	261	36	77	3.55	2.5	10.7	4.2	0.6	143
	2022	AAA	Gwinnett	1	0	0	6	7	4.35	0.97	23.5	222	28	60	3.07	1.5	10.2	7.0	1.5	162

Made it up to Triple-A in first full pro season. 3/4 pitchability LHP with repeatable mechanics and solid extension in delivery. Mixes 4-seam and 2-seam FB well with plus command of 3 pitches. Utilizes angles and tunneling to play up arsenal. SL is short, tight breaker. CU has late arm-side run and some late fade.

Dollard,Taylor — SP — Seattle

EXP MLB DEBUT: 2023 | H/W: 6-3 195 | FUT: #4 starter | 7C

Thrws R Age 24	Year	Lev	Team	W	L	Sv	IP	K	ERA	WHIP	BF/G	OBA	H%	S%	xERA	Ctl	Dom	Cmd	hr/9	BPV
2020 (5) Cal Poly																				
90-94 FB +++	2020	NCAA	Cal Poly	1	0	0	27	36	1.67	0.89	25.0	208	33	79	1.32	1.3	12.0	9.0	0.0	198
77-79 CB ++	2021	A	Modesto	3	2	0	37	59	3.39	1.34	22.1	276	45	75	3.78	2.4	14.3	5.9	0.5	210
80-83 SL +++	2021	A+	Everett	6	2	0	67	74	6.17	1.37	23.4	292	36	58	5.19	1.9	9.9	5.3	1.6	146
82-86 CU +++	2022	AA	Arkansas	16	2	0	144	131	2.25	0.95	20.1	207	26	79	2.03	1.9	8.2	4.2	0.6	113

Tall, athletic SP who led Texas League in ERA and minors in wins. Not blessed with great velocity or knockout pitch, but mixes well and hits spots in strike zone. All about command and control and rarely beats himself. Has tremendous pitchability and likes to use sinker for groundballs. Could add more velocity with more strength.

Drohan,Shane | SP | Boston | EXP MLB DEBUT: 2023 | H/W: 6-3 195 | FUT: #5 SP/swingman | 7D

Thrws L Age 24	Year	Lev	Team	W	L	Sv	IP	K	ERA	WHIP	BF/G	OBA	H%	S%	xERA	Ctl	Dom	Cmd	hr/9	BPV
2020 (5) Florida St																				
88-93 FB +++	2020	NCAA	Florida St	0	1	0	17	27	4.19	1.51	18.6	236	41	69	3.21	5.8	14.1	2.5	0.0	117
74-78 CB ++	2021	A	Salem	7	4	0	88	86	3.98	1.43	16.3	246	32	71	3.47	4.6	8.8	1.9	0.3	52
80-83 CU +++	2022	A+	Greenville	6	7	0	105	136	4.02	1.25	19.4	235	32	72	3.75	3.4	11.6	3.4	1.3	135
	2022	AA	Portland	1	1	0	24	21	3.38	1.33	19.9	237	26	85	4.60	4.1	7.9	1.9	1.9	48

Tall, athletic SP who is steadily rising thru system. Finished 2nd in SAL in K with deceptive delivery and natural pitch movement. Good spin enhances rudimentary FB and mixes in slow CB with depth. CU effective due to separation in velocity from FB. Has more of back-end profile and will need to add strength.

Duran,Carlos | SP | Los Angeles (N) | EXP MLB DEBUT: 2025 | H/W: 6-7 230 | FUT: #4 starter | 7D

Thrws R Age 21	Year	Lev	Team	W	L	Sv	IP	K	ERA	WHIP	BF/G	OBA	H%	S%	xERA	Ctl	Dom	Cmd	hr/9	BPV
2017 FA (DR)	2019	Rk	AZL Dodgers/L	0	4	0	19	16	8.48	2.51	12.7	414	48	67	10.10	4.7	7.5	1.6	1.4	26
92-95 FB +++	2021	A	Rancho Cuca	2	4	0	73	109	5.29	1.43	15.6	282	42	65	4.69	3.0	13.4	4.5	1.1	180
83-85 SL ++++	2021	A+	Great Lakes	0	1	0	7	6	8.87	2.25	18.0	333	42	56	6.57	7.6	7.6	1.0	0.0	-50
86-88 CU +	2022	Rk	ACL Dodgers	0	0	0	1	1	0.00	0.00	2.8	0	0			0.0	9.0		0.0	180
	2022	A+	Great Lakes	1	3	0	48	68	4.29	1.39	14.5	240	35	72	4.03	4.5	12.7	2.8	1.1	126

Huge RHP comes after hitters with an above-average 2-seam 92-95 FB with good late sink. Arm action and size creates deception and allows stuff to play up. Best offering is a plus to plus-plus mid-80s SL that misses plenty of bats. CU is below-average and will need to improve if he is to remain a SP. Had Tommy John surgery in Nov and will miss 2023.

Eder,Jake | SP | Miami | EXP MLB DEBUT: 2023 | H/W: 6-4 215 | FUT: #3 starter | 8D

Thrws L Age 24	Year	Lev	Team	W	L	Sv	IP	K	ERA	WHIP	BF/G	OBA	H%	S%	xERA	Ctl	Dom	Cmd	hr/9	BPV
2020 (4) Vanderbilt																				
91-95 FB ++++																				
79-83 SL ++++																				
82-86 CU +++	2020	NCAA	Vanderbilt	1	1	0	20	27	3.60	1.45	21.4	262	39	75	3.84	4.1	12.2	3.0	0.5	127
	2021	AA	Pensacola	3	5	0	71	99	1.77	0.98	18.0	177	28	84	1.55	3.4	12.5	3.7	0.4	151

High-effort 3/4s LHP, missed the entire 2022 season recovering and rehabbing from Tommy John surgery. Deceptive delivery plays up pitch mix. Late-running FB features solid command and control. Varies between tighter two-plane SL and sweeping SL with deeper break; both potentially plus . Cu has solid separation off FB and late-fading action.

Englert,Mason | SP | Detroit | EXP MLB DEBUT: 2024 | H/W: 6-4 206 | FUT: #4 starter | 7C

Thrws R Age 23	Year	Lev	Team	W	L	Sv	IP	K	ERA	WHIP	BF/G	OBA	H%	S%	xERA	Ctl	Dom	Cmd	hr/9	BPV
2018 (4) HS (TX)																				
92-95 FB ++																				
84-88 CU +++	2021	A	Down East	6	3	0	80	90	4.38	1.23	17.1	244	34	63	3.08	2.9	10.1	3.5	0.4	121
75-79 CB ++	2022	A+	Hickory	7	5	0	103	116	3.58	0.96	18.6	201	25	69	2.66	2.3	10.1	4.5	1.3	139
82-89 SL ++	2022	AA	Frisco	1	1	0	15	20	4.17	1.26	20.5	247	37	67	3.30	3.0	11.9	4.0	0.6	152

After 2019 Tommy John, 2021 was first pro action. Got better as 2022 season went on, and pushed CU now to plus offering. Extreme release angle helps average-shaped FF play, but CB better that fools batters to not offer at despite hitting bottom of zone. 15.7% SwK says there's a major league role here as #4 or maybe setup.

Enlow,Blayne | SP | Minnesota | EXP MLB DEBUT: 2024 | H/W: 6-3 170 | FUT: #4 starter | 7D

Thrws R Age 24	Year	Lev	Team	W	L	Sv	IP	K	ERA	WHIP	BF/G	OBA	H%	S%	xERA	Ctl	Dom	Cmd	hr/9	BPV
2017 (3) HS (LA)	2019	A	Cedar Rapids	4	3	0	41	44	4.60	1.39	21.6	266	35	68	4.17	3.3	9.6	2.9	0.9	103
91-95 FB +++	2019	A+	Fort Myers	4	4	0	69	51	3.39	1.22	21.5	238	28	73	3.06	3.0	6.6	2.2	0.5	57
81-84 CB +++	2021	A+	Cedar Rapids	1	1	0	14	23	1.90	1.34	19.7	245	41	89	3.48	3.8	14.6	3.8	0.6	178
88-89 SL +++	2022	A	Fort Myers	0	0	0	1	1	22.50	5.00	9.4	596	63	60	27.87	7.5	7.5	1.0	7.5	-50
85-87 CU ++	2022	AA	Wichita	1	3	3	57	64	4.41	1.58	10.5	271	37	72	4.48	4.7	10.1	2.1	0.6	72

Returned in May after 2021 Tommy John surgery. Had promising season despite rust and velocity most of way back. Mixes four quality offerings, though firm CU has lost some luster. Best pitch is still FB with late movement down in zone. SL with CT-like action can be effective against hitters from both sides. CB showed improvement.

Enright,Nic | RP | Miami | EXP MLB DEBUT: 2023 | H/W: 6-3 205 | FUT: Middle reliever | 6C

Thrws R Age 26	Year	Lev	Team	W	L	Sv	IP	K	ERA	WHIP	BF/G	OBA	H%	S%	xERA	Ctl	Dom	Cmd	hr/9	BPV
2019 (20) Virginia Tech																				
90-93 FB ++++	2021	A+	Lake County	1	0	3	18	32	1.49	0.83	6.0	190	39	80	0.92	1.5	15.9	10.7	0.0	264
74-76 CB +++	2021	AA	Akron	3	4	2	39	56	4.36	0.97	6.5	202	30	58	2.52	2.3	12.9	5.6	1.1	187
81-83 SL +++	2022	AA	Akron	1	1	10	28	37	3.19	0.96	5.6	193	29	68	1.91	2.6	11.8	4.6	0.6	162
83-85 CU ++	2022	AAA	Columbus	4	0	1	37	50	2.68	0.97	4.8	223	32	81	2.86	1.5	12.2	8.3	1.2	198

Middle RP prospect came over from CLE in Rule 5 draft this off-season. Tall, lean build, near physical projection. Over-the-top delivery with solid extension, repeats well. Flat-angled low-90s FB lives up with plus riding action. 12-to-6 CB has solid depth. SL has overtaken CB as best secondary with solid breaking profile. Keeps LHH honest with CU.

Erla,Mason | SP | Los Angeles (A) | EXP MLB DEBUT: 2024 | H/W: 6-4 200 | FUT: #5 SP/swingman | 6B

Thrws R Age 25	Year	Lev	Team	W	L	Sv	IP	K	ERA	WHIP	BF/G	OBA	H%	S%	xERA	Ctl	Dom	Cmd	hr/9	BPV
2021 (17) Michigan St	2020	NCAA	Michigan St	2	0	0	26	42	1.04	1.00	24.8	214	38	92	1.97	2.1	14.5	7.0	0.3	224
92-95 FB +++	2021	NCAA	Michigan St	5	6	0	79	80	3.52	1.34	25.3	254	34	73	3.38	3.4	9.1	2.7	0.3	90
83-86 SL ++	2021	Rk	ACL Angels	1	0	0	5	9	0.00	0.40	8.1	124	28	100		0.0	16.2		0.0	310
85-88 CU +++	2021	A+	Tri-City	0	1	0	2	2	4.29	0.95	7.9	252	34	50	2.07	0.0	8.6		0.0	172
	2022	AA	Rocket City	5	6	0	82	64	4.28	1.30	21.1	276	32	69	4.23	2.1	7.0	3.4	1.0	88

Low 3/4s RHP with innings eater frame pitched to mix results in Double-A. Repeatable delivery with limited extension. Varies between two distinctive FB. 2-seam is ground ball inducing offering while 4-seam FB gets whiffs. Improved executing CU with fading action. Commands frisbee SL well. It's hittable due to inconsistency with spin profile.

Espino,Daniel | SP | Cleveland | EXP MLB DEBUT: 2023 | H/W: 6-2 225 | FUT: #1 starter | 9C

Thrws R Age 22	Year	Lev	Team	W	L	Sv	IP	K	ERA	WHIP	BF/G	OBA	H%	S%	xERA	Ctl	Dom	Cmd	hr/9	BPV
2019 (1) HS (GA)	2019	Rk	AZL Indians	0	1	0	13	16	2.05	0.91	8.2	158	22	82	1.46	3.4	10.9	3.2	0.7	122
96-98 FB +++++	2019	A-	MahoningVal	0	2	0	10	18	6.30	1.40	14.1	242	44	54	3.83	4.5	16.2	3.6	0.9	188
85-89 SL ++++	2021	A	Lynchburg	1	2	0	42	64	3.41	1.35	17.6	222	37	75	3.04	4.9	13.6	2.8	0.4	131
74-75 CB ++	2021	A+	Lake County	2	6	0	49	88	4.04	0.94	18.4	178	31	62	2.27	2.9	16.2	5.5	1.3	230
88-90 CU +++	2022	AA	Akron	1	0	0	18	35	2.49	0.72	16.0	150	24	89	2.06	2.0	17.4	8.8	2.0	278

Short-statured, athletic RHP made only 4 starts due to right knee injury. Utilizes lower half like no other pitcher, allowing for high-octane arsenal. 4-seam FB combines velocity, ride and run with elite, near 40% whiff rate. SL flashes double-plus; sells CU well with a bit of run; may have scrapped CB. Commands FB/SL combination well.

Estanista,Jaydenn | SP | Philadelphia | EXP MLB DEBUT: 2026 | H/W: 6-3 180 | FUT: #4 starter | 7D

Thrws R Age 21	Year	Lev	Team	W	L	Sv	IP	K	ERA	WHIP	BF/G	OBA	H%	S%	xERA	Ctl	Dom	Cmd	hr/9	BPV
2019 FA (Curacao)																				
93-97 FB +++																				
74-78 CB ++																				
83-86 CU +	2021	Rk	DSL Phillies White	1	1	1	30	33	3.28	1.26	12.3	182	26	73	2.25	5.7	9.8	1.7	0.3	42
	2022	Rk	FCL Phillies	3	0	0	31	35	2.03	0.96	9.8	138	17	85	1.57	4.6	10.1	2.2	0.9	75

Loose athlete with very projectable frame, showed some intriguing tools in his first stateside innings. Fastball easily sits mid-90s with life; fair amount of swings/misses in rookie ball. Curve ball is ahead of the seldom-used change-up, but team is encouraged his pitching acumen along with skills and athleticism. Full season ball comes next.

Estes,Joey | SP | Oakland | EXP MLB DEBUT: 2024 | H/W: 6-2 190 | FUT: #4 starter | 7C

Thrws R Age 21	Year	Lev	Team	W	L	Sv	IP	K	ERA	WHIP	BF/G	OBA	H%	S%	xERA	Ctl	Dom	Cmd	hr/9	BPV
2019 (16) HS (CA)																				
91-95 FB +++																				
81-84 SL +++																				
82-85 CU ++	2021	A	Augusta	3	6	0	99	127	2.91	0.96	18.7	191	28	72	1.90	2.6	11.5	4.4	0.6	155
	2022	A+	Lansing	3	7	0	91	92	4.55	1.27	18.6	251	30	71	4.44	3.0	9.1	3.1	1.7	102

Consistent, steady SP with no dominate pitch, but changes speeds and spots FB well to all quadrants. Was very good the last two months of season with improving SL and CU. SL features varying velocity and can be used as chase pitch. Some effort in delivery may mean move to bullpen, but has potential for three solid-average offerings.

Estrada,Jeremiah | RP | Chicago (N) | EXP MLB DEBUT: 2022 | H/W: 6-1 185 | FUT: Setup reliever | 6B

Thrws R Age 24	Year	Lev	Team	W	L	Sv	IP	K	ERA	WHIP	BF/G	OBA	H%	S%	xERA	Ctl	Dom	Cmd	hr/9	BPV
2017 (6) HS (CA)	2021	A	Myrtle Beach	1	1	0	23	38	1.57	1.04	8.1	217	37	91	2.52	2.3	14.9	6.3	0.8	222
94-97 FB ++++	2022	A+	South Bend	2	2	5	23	39	1.17	1.04	5.9	178	33	91	1.69	3.9	15.3	3.9	0.4	187
80-83 SL +++	2022	AA	Tennessee	1	0	2	19	27	1.88	1.05	5.7	170	29	80	1.27	4.2	12.7	3.0	0.0	133
73-75 CB +	2022	AAA	Iowa	0	0	2	6	12	0.00	1.17	4.0	262	55	100	2.65	1.5	18.0	12.0	0.0	302
83-85 CU +	2022	MLB	Chicago (N)	0	0	0	5	8	3.46	1.73	4.7	290	43	88	6.14	5.2	13.8	2.7	1.7	127

Reliever is fully recovered from a serious case of COVID and made his MLB debut in 2022. Struggles with command at times, but logged a 48% K rate thanks for a plus upper-90s heater and a wipeout SL that replaced below average CB and CU. That 1-2 combo proved lethal and should start 2023 in the Cubs pen.

Ferrer,Jose

RP | Washington | EXP MLB DEBUT: 2023 | H/W: 6-1 215 | FUT: Setup reliever | 8D

Thrws L Age 23
2017 FA (DR)

95-97	FB	++++
84-88	SL	++
86-89	CU	+++

Year	Lev	Team	W	L	Sv	IP	K	ERA	WHIP	BF/G	OBA	H%	S%	xERA	Ctl	Dom	Cmd	hr/9	BPV
2019	Rk	GCL Nationals	2	3	0	21	24	2.97	1.23	9.5	179	27	73	1.85	5.5	10.2	1.8	0.0	52
2021	Rk	FCL Nationals	0	4	2	35	47	2.81	1.14	8.2	238	36	74	2.55	2.3	12.0	5.2	0.3	172
2022	A	Fredericksburg	1	0	2	19	24	1.42	0.68	5.1	183	27	83	0.96	0.5	11.4	24.0	0.5	210
2022	A+	Wilmington	2	1	9	38	43	2.59	1.07	5.3	229	29	86	3.39	2.1	10.1	4.8	1.4	143
2022	AA	Harrisburg	0	1	0	7	11	5.00	1.53	4.5	330	49	70	5.81	1.3	13.8	11.0	1.3	232

Hard-throwing, crossfire FB/CU reliever who emerged quickly in 2022. High-90s heat from a low slot and more control in the zone than most fireballer prospects. Gets tons of whiffs on disappearing CU that can sport a ~10 mph difference off FB. Also mixes in occasional SL, but might not need it in relief. Setup reliever ceiling.

Ferris,Jackson

SP | Chicago (N) | EXP MLB DEBUT: 2026 | H/W: 6-4 195 | FUT: #3 starter | 8D

Thrws L Age 19
2022 (2) HS (FL)

92-95	FB	++++
75-78	CB	+++
83-85	CU	+++

Year	Lev	Team	W	L	Sv	IP	K	ERA	WHIP	BF/G	OBA	H%	S%	xERA	Ctl	Dom	Cmd	hr/9	BPV

Lanky HS LHP was inked to an above-slot $3 million deal. FB already sits at 92-95 with room for more as he matures. Backs up the heater with a high-spin 12-to-6 CB and a potentially above-average CU. Will see first pro action in 2023.

Festa,David

SP | Minnesota | EXP MLB DEBUT: 2024 | H/W: 6-6 185 | FUT: #4 starter | 7C

Thrws R Age 23
2021 (13) Seton Hall

92-97	FB	++++
83-86	SL	+++
84-86	CU	++

Year	Lev	Team	W	L	Sv	IP	K	ERA	WHIP	BF/G	OBA	H%	S%	xERA	Ctl	Dom	Cmd	hr/9	BPV
2021	NCAA	Seton Hall	6	4	0	72		2.00	1.07	18.7	178	22	85	2.05	4.1	8.4	2.0	0.6	57
2021	Rk	FCL Twins	1	0	0	5	8	0.00	0.20	7.6	66	14	100		0.0	14.4		0.0	277
2021	A	Fort Myers	0	0	0	3	4	11.61	1.94	7.4	186	30	33	3.70	11.6	11.6	1.0	0.0	-87
2022	A	Fort Myers	2	1	0	24	33	1.50	0.75	17.1	151	24	82	0.68	2.3	12.4	5.5	0.4	180
2022	A+	Cedar Rapids	7	3	0	79	75	2.73	1.20	19.9	231	29	79	2.95	3.2	8.5	2.7	0.6	86

Improving prospect with breakout campaign. Uses lean frame and cleaner delivery to throw consistent strikes and add both velocity and spin to mix. Knows how to pitch with feel for sequencing. Fast arm produces quality FB where he spots to both sides. SL serves as chase pitch, but CU needs work.

Fitterer,Evan

SP | Miami | EXP MLB DEBUT: 2024 | H/W: 6-3 192 | FUT: #5 SP/swingman | 6C

Thrws R Age 22
2019 (5) HS (CA)

91-93	FB	++
83-85	SL	+++
77-80	CB	+++
81-83	CU	+++

Year	Lev	Team	W	L	Sv	IP	K	ERA	WHIP	BF/G	OBA	H%	S%	xERA	Ctl	Dom	Cmd	hr/9	BPV
2021	Rk	FCL Marlins	0	0	0	4	6	2.14	1.43	8.9	144	25	83	1.97	8.6	12.9	1.5	0.0	18
2021	A	Jupiter	0	1	0	25	27	4.64	1.43	15.3	297	40	66	4.23	2.1	9.6	4.5	0.4	134
2022	A+	Beloit	4	7	0	107	80	4.29	1.38	20.5	252	30	69	3.81	3.9	6.7	1.7	0.7	35

Athletic 3/4 RHP struggled during stint in High-A. Innings count jumped to 107.1 after just 29 in 2021. Crossfire delivery with solid extension. 4-pitch pitcher. 4-seam FB has poor spin profile. All 3 secondary pitches projects as average or better offerings. SL has short, tighter break profile. 11-to-5 CB is best with vertical sweep.

Flores,Wilmer

SP | Detroit | EXP MLB DEBUT: 2024 | H/W: 6-4 225 | FUT: #3 starter | 8C

Thrws R Age 22
2020 FA (VZ)

93-95	FB	++++
78-82	CB	++++
84-86	CT	++
85-87	CU	+

Year	Lev	Team	W	L	Sv	IP	K	ERA	WHIP	BF/G	OBA	H%	S%	xERA	Ctl	Dom	Cmd	hr/9	BPV
2021	Rk	FCL Tigers West	2	1	0	13	18	4.85	1.31	17.9	290	45	59	3.46	1.4	12.5	9.0	0.0	205
2021	A	Lakeland	4	3	0	53	72	3.40	1.30	19.9	239	37	72	2.90	3.7	12.2	3.3	0.2	137
2022	A+	West Michigan	1	0	0	19	35	1.88	0.83	11.7	205	39	86	1.98	0.9	16.4	17.5	0.9	288
2022	AA	Erie	6	4	0	83	95	3.03	1.06	17.0	222	30	75	2.74	2.3	10.3	4.5	0.9	142

Younger brother of MLBer of the same name had a breakout season. Worked hard to get stronger and showed improved command and velocity. FB sits in the mid-90s, topping at 98 with good spin and late life. Best offering is a plus 12-to-6 CB that generates plenty of swing-and-miss. CU shows potential, but needs work to remain a starter.

Ford,Walter

SP | Seattle | EXP MLB DEBUT: 2027 | H/W: 6-3 198 | FUT: #1 starter | 9E

Thrws R Age 18
2022 (2) HS (FL)

90-95	FB	++++
81-82	SL	++
80-84	CU	++

Year	Lev	Team	W	L	Sv	IP	K	ERA	WHIP	BF/G	OBA	H%	S%	xERA	Ctl	Dom	Cmd	hr/9	BPV

Young, projectable SP with extreme upside, but lot of work ahead. Blessed with natural athleticism and fast arm to produce excellent velocity. Delivery will need to be refined to improve command as well as prevent injury. FB is plus pitch presently and SL could join it down line. SL has huge spin and break. CU also needs work.

Franklin,Kohl

SP | Chicago (N) | EXP MLB DEBUT: 2024 | H/W: 6-4 195 | FUT: #4 starter | 7E

Thrws R Age 23
2018 (6) HS (OK)

94-97	FB	++++
77-80	CB	+++
82-84	CU	+++

Year	Lev	Team	W	L	Sv	IP	K	ERA	WHIP	BF/G	OBA	H%	S%	xERA	Ctl	Dom	Cmd	hr/9	BPV
2018	Rk	AZL Cubs 2	0	1	0	8	8	6.59	1.34	6.8	178	25	45	2.14	6.6	8.8	1.3	0.0	-2
2019	A-	Eugene	1	3	0	39	49	2.31	1.15	15.5	220	32	81	2.57	3.2	11.3	3.5	0.5	134
2019	A	South Bend	0	0	0	3	3	3.00	1.67	13.5	0	0	80	1.34	15.0	9.0	0.6	0.0	-225
2022	A+	South Bend	3	7	0	69	75	6.90	1.64	13.4	270	35	57	5.00	5.3	9.8	1.8	1.0	50

Long, lanky RHP has added velo to his FB since being drafted. Has been limited by oblique and shoulder injuries and hadn't pitched since 2019. The layoff showed with a disastrous showing at A+. FB now sits at 94-97 up to 99 and CB and CU are average to above, but lack consistency. With improved control, could be something worth waiting for.

Frasso,Nick

SP | Los Angeles (N) | EXP MLB DEBUT: 2023 | H/W: 6-5 200 | FUT: #2 SP/closer | 8D

Thrws R Age 24
2020 (4) Loyola Marymount

94-98	FB	+++++
83-86	SL	+++
83-85	CU	++

Year	Lev	Team	W	L	Sv	IP	K	ERA	WHIP	BF/G	OBA	H%	S%	xERA	Ctl	Dom	Cmd	hr/9	BPV
2021	A	Dunedin	0	0	0	5	8	0.00	1.00	6.4	175	33	100	1.20	3.6	14.4	4.0	0.0	180
2022	A	Dunedin	0	0	0	25	42	0.71	0.83	13.2	155	31	90	0.55	2.9	15.0	5.3	0.0	211
2022	A+	Great Lakes	0	0	0	5	9	1.73	0.96	9.8	254	47	80	2.05	0.0	15.6		0.0	298
2022	A+	Vancouver	0	0	0	11	15	0.82	0.45	12.0	88	11	100		1.6	12.3	7.5	0.8	195
2022	AA	Tulsa	0	0	0	11	10	5.63	1.70	12.6	275	34	67	5.02	5.6	8.0	1.4	0.8	11

Was sent to the Dodgers as part of the Mitch White deal. Thin frame and long levers and crossfire action. Fastball sits in the 94-98 range, topping at 101. He also has an above-average SL and a CU that flashes above-average at times. Could be a hidden gem.

Fulton,Dax

SP | Miami | EXP MLB DEBUT: 2024 | H/W: 6-7 225 | FUT: #4 starter | 7C

Thrws L Age 21
2020 (2) HS (OK)

91-93	FB	+++
79-81	SL	+++
86-88	CU	++

Year	Lev	Team	W	L	Sv	IP	K	ERA	WHIP	BF/G	OBA	H%	S%	xERA	Ctl	Dom	Cmd	hr/9	BPV
2021	A	Jupiter	2	4	0	58	66	4.33	1.37	16.3	234	32	68	3.31	4.6	10.2	2.2	0.5	76
2021	A+	Beloit	0	1	0	19	18	5.63	1.51	16.6	279	33	65	5.18	3.8	8.4	2.3	1.4	69
2022	A+	Beloit	5	6	0	97	120	4.08	1.43	20.6	275	39	71	4.09	3.2	11.1	3.4	0.6	131
2022	AA	Pensacola	1	1	0	21	30	2.57	0.76	18.8	132	19	71	0.97	3.0	12.9	4.3	0.9	168

Tall 3/4s RHP performed well against advanced competition in 2022. Solid frame, at physical projection. Repeats crossfire delivery with plus extension. 3-pitch arsenal. 4-seam FB with some ride plays up due to delivery. Needs to improve FB shape. Sweeping SL has long break profile, best diving down late. Struggles commanding fading CU for strikes.

Gaddis,Hunter

SP | Cleveland | EXP MLB DEBUT: 2022 | H/W: 6-6 260 | FUT: #4 starter | 8D

Thrws R Age 24
2019 (5) Georgia St

91-95	FB	+++
83-86	SL	++++
76-80	CU	++++
72-75	CB	++

Year	Lev	Team	W	L	Sv	IP	K	ERA	WHIP	BF/G	OBA	H%	S%	xERA	Ctl	Dom	Cmd	hr/9	BPV
2019	A-	MahoningVal	0	1	0	15	27	2.37	0.99	9.6	204	41	73	1.48	2.4	16.0	6.8	0.0	242
2021	A+	Lake County	4	11	0	97	127	4.17	1.14	19.2	233	30	73	4.01	2.6	11.8	4.5	1.9	160
2022	AA	Akron	4	3	0	76	102	4.26	1.17	20.2	227	31	69	3.59	3.1	12.1	3.9	1.4	152
2022	AAA	Columbus	4	3	0	45	56	3.60	0.93	18.8	175	24	65	2.00	3.0	11.2	3.7	1.0	139
2022	MLB	Cleveland	0	2	0	7	5	19.01	2.54	19.0	428	35	27	17.51	3.8	6.3	1.7	8.9	29

Hard-throwing, XXL RHP improved pitch mix on route to making MLB debut. High 3/4s delivery with double-plus extension, falls off mound follow through. 4-pitch arsenal. FB has near elite ride but struggles to command within zone. CU is best secondary with plus arm-side run and late drop. SL is short, two-plane breaker. CB vastly improved.

Garcia,Deivi

SP | New York (A) | EXP MLB DEBUT: 2020 | H/W: 5-9 163 | FUT: #5 SP/swingman | 6C

Thrws R Age 23
2015 FA (DR)

93-95	FB	+++
80-82	SL	++
77-80	CB	+++
84-86	CU	++

Year	Lev	Team	W	L	Sv	IP	K	ERA	WHIP	BF/G	OBA	H%	S%	xERA	Ctl	Dom	Cmd	hr/9	BPV
2020	MLB	New York	3	2	0	34	33	5.01	1.20	22.9	267	31	63	4.39	1.6	8.7	5.5	1.6	132
2021	AAA	Scranton/WB	3	7	0	90	97	6.88	1.88	17.7	286	34	68	6.85	6.8	9.7	1.4	2.1	9
2021	MLB	New York	0	2	0	8	7	6.67	1.48	17.4	259	31	55	4.55	4.4	7.8	1.8	1.1	38
2022	AA	Somerset	2	1	0	26	37	5.50	1.07	17.0	213	28	55	3.76	2.7	12.7	4.6	2.1	173
2022	AAA	Scranton/WB	2	4	0	37	39	8.01	1.73	12.0	277	33	54	5.94	5.8	9.5	1.6	1.7	31

Former HQ100 prospect continued spiral of ineffectiveness with upper level stints. High 3/4 slot, struggles keeping on-time with release. Flat-angled 4-seam FB has solid ride but lacks in-zone command. Also, incorporates CT with quick break. Both breakers continue to back up, with CB over SL. Slows arm throwing CU, curbing effectiveness.

Gasser,Robert — SP — Milwaukee

EXP MLB DEBUT: 2023 | H/W: 6-1 185 | FUT: #4 starter | 7C

Thrws L Age 23
2021 (2) Houston

Velo	Pitch	Grade
90-94	FB	+++
80-84	SL	+++
84-85	CU	+++

Year	Lev	Team	W	L	Sv	IP	K	ERA	WHIP	BF/G	OBA	H%	S%	xERA	Ctl	Dom	Cmd	hr/9	BPV
2021	Rk	ACL Padres	0	0	0	1	1	0.00	0.00	2.8	0	0			0.0	9.0		0.0	180
2021	A	Lake Elsinore	0	0	0	14	13	1.29	0.93	10.5	218	27	92	2.18	1.3	8.4	6.5	0.6	134
2022	A+	Fort Wayne	4	9	0	90	115	4.20	1.27	20.4	253	36	68	3.59	2.8	11.5	4.1	0.8	149
2022	AA	Biloxi	1	1	0	20	26	2.24	1.09	19.7	198	28	85	2.56	3.6	11.6	3.3	0.9	131
2022	AAA	Nashville	2	2	0	26	31	4.48	1.61	23.1	261	37	71	4.15	5.5	10.7	1.9	0.3	61

Acquired from SD at deadline. Pitched at three levels in 2022 and finished 5th in minors in Ks. Leverages 3 quality offerings and ability to spot to all quadrants. Uses SL as K pitch and particularly effective against LHH. Lacks frontline velocity and size, but relies on changing speeds and locating pitches. CU features late drop.

Gaston,Sandy — RP — Tampa Bay

EXP MLB DEBUT: 2025 | H/W: 6-3 200 | FUT: Setup reliever | 7E

Thrws R Age 21
2018 FA (CU)

Velo	Pitch	Grade
94-97	FB	++++
82-84	SL	+++
88-91	CU	+

Year	Lev	Team	W	L	Sv	IP	K	ERA	WHIP	BF/G	OBA	H%	S%	xERA	Ctl	Dom	Cmd	hr/9	BPV
2019	Rk	GCL Rays	1	2	0	27	31	6.00	1.85	11.5	232	33	65	4.37	9.0	10.3	1.1	0.3	-39
2021	Rk	FCL Rays	1	0	0	19	32	3.28	1.04	10.6	114	21	68	1.11	6.1	15.0	2.5	0.5	123
2021	A	Charleston	2	1	0	30	38	3.89	1.46	18.4	206	30	74	3.30	6.6	11.4	1.7	0.6	45
2022	A	Charleston	2	4	3	54	77	4.65	1.64	7.8	178	28	71	3.32	9.3	12.8	1.4	0.5	-3

Strong, hard-throwing 3/4s RHP converted to RP in 2022. Physically strong body, near physical projection. Struggles maintaining release point with straight-on delivery. FB touched 101 but sat 94-97 on the season. It has plus carry, inducing whiffs. Struggles with control and with consistency of short breaking SL. CU isn't very deceptive.

German,Franklin — RP — Boston

EXP MLB DEBUT: 2022 | H/W: 6-2 195 | FUT: Setup reliever | 7D

Thrws R Age 25
2018 (4) North Florida

Velo	Pitch	Grade
95-98	FB	++++
81-85	SL	+++
83-87	SP	++

Year	Lev	Team	W	L	Sv	IP	K	ERA	WHIP	BF/G	OBA	H%	S%	xERA	Ctl	Dom	Cmd	hr/9	BPV
2019	A+	Tampa	4	4	0	76		3.79	1.38	20.0	246	32	76	4.06	4.1	9.7	2.3	1.1	81
2021	AA	Portland	3	9	2	84	72	5.14	1.53	15.3	295	35	69	5.35	3.2	7.7	2.4	1.3	70
2022	AA	Portland	3	1	0	11	18	3.24	0.81	3.7	161	31	56	0.56	2.4	14.6	6.0	0.0	215
2022	AAA	Worcester	2	1	7	38	46	2.60	0.94	4.5	157	23	74	1.34	3.8	10.9	2.9	0.5	112
2022	MLB	Boston	0	0	0	4	4	18.00	2.75	4.5	383	41	33	12.95	9.0	9.0	1.0	4.5	-63

Improving RP who converted to bullpen full-time in 2022. Owns electric FB thrown from quick arm action and brute strength. Posted very low oppBA, which was big turnaround from previous season. Hard splitter operates as off-speed pitch to LHH and SL shows flashes of improvement. Limited control mutes reliability at present.

Gil,Luis — SP — New York (A)

EXP MLB DEBUT: 2021 | H/W: 6-2 185 | FUT: Setup reliever | 7C

Thrws R Age 24
2015 FA (DR)

Velo	Pitch	Grade
95-97	FB	++++
84-86	SL	+++
90-92	CU	+++

Year	Lev	Team	W	L	Sv	IP	K	ERA	WHIP	BF/G	OBA	H%	S%	xERA	Ctl	Dom	Cmd	hr/9	BPV
2021	AA	Somerset	1	1	0	30	50	2.68	1.23	17.5	220	38	80	2.84	3.9	14.9	3.8	0.6	182
2021	AAA	Scranton/WB	4	0	1	48	67	4.85	1.39	15.6	205	29	68	3.76	6.0	12.5	2.1	1.3	82
2021	MLB	New York	1	1	0	29	38	3.09	1.34	20.2	196	27	83	3.48	5.9	11.8	2.0	1.2	71
2022	AAA	Scranton/WB	0	3	0	21	31	8.07	1.70	16.0	260	34	57	6.40	6.4	13.2	2.1	2.5	83
2022	MLB	New York (A)	0	0	0	4	5	9.00	1.75	18.3	307	44	43	4.85	4.5	11.3	2.5	0.0	99

Strong, 3/4s RHP with SP-quality stuff continued to struggle with command; had Tommy John surgery in May. Cross delivery with solid extension. Struggles to repeat. 3-pitch pitcher. FB has plus carry and solid arm-side run profile. Misses bats. SL is a mostly horizontal breaker, best down in zone. Sells FB arm speed with fading CU.

Ginn,J.T. — SP — Oakland

EXP MLB DEBUT: 2024 | H/W: 6-2 200 | FUT: #3 starter | 8D

Thrws R Age 23
2020 (2) Mississippi St

Velo	Pitch	Grade
90-94	FB	+++
81-84	SL	++++
83-86	CU	++

Year	Lev	Team	W	L	Sv	IP	K	ERA	WHIP	BF/G	OBA	H%	S%	xERA	Ctl	Dom	Cmd	hr/9	BPV
2020	NCAA	Mississippi St	0	0	0	3	4	6.00	1.67	13.5	262	40	60	3.97	6.0	12.0	2.0	0.0	72
2021	A	St. Lucie	2	1	0	38	35	2.59	0.94	18.0	194	24	76	1.99	2.4	8.2	3.5	0.7	103
2021	A+	Brooklyn	3	4	0	53	46	3.39	1.15	21.1	247	32	67	2.50	2.0	7.8	3.8	0.0	103
2022	Rk	ACL Athletics	0	0	0	7	5	0.00	0.57	11.9	168	21	100	0.12	0.0	6.4		0.0	134
2022	AA	Midland	1	4	0	35	41	6.15	1.48	15.1	277	38	57	4.46	3.6	10.5	2.9	0.8	110

Athletic SP who missed a lot of time with forearm issue. Injury history is concern, but has ingredients to be mid-rotation arm. K rate and walk rate both rose in 2022 and needs to regain feel. SL is best pitch with extreme two-plane break. Throws it for strikes and used as K pitch. Dynamic FB has average velocity, but late sinking action.

Gomez,Yoendrys — SP — New York (A)

EXP MLB DEBUT: 2024 | H/W: 6-3 175 | FUT: #4 starter | 7C

Thrws R Age 23
2016 FA (VZ)

Velo	Pitch	Grade
92-95	FB	++++
80-83	SL	+++
87-90	CU	++

Year	Lev	Team	W	L	Sv	IP	K	ERA	WHIP	BF/G	OBA	H%	S%	xERA	Ctl	Dom	Cmd	hr/9	BPV
2019	A	Charleston (Sc)	0	3	0	26	25	6.18	1.41	18.5	275	35	54	4.19	3.1	8.6	2.8	0.7	89
2021	A	Tampa	0	0	0	23	29	3.49	0.99	9.8	176	23	70	2.31	3.5	11.3	3.2	1.2	126
2022	Rk	FCL Yankees	0	0	0	2	3	0.00	1.36	9.2	326	48	100	4.16	0.0	12.3		0.0	239
2022	A+	Hudson Valley	0	0	0	28	27	1.93	1.14	11.1	202	28	81	1.92	3.9	8.7	2.3	0.0	70
2022	AA	Somerset	1	0	0	16	19	3.91	1.24	16.4	236	33	68	3.09	3.4	10.6	3.2	0.6	119

Tall, projectable oft-injured RHP struggled again to pitch healthy innings in 2022. Has gotten stronger with some room to still grow. Easy, repeatable 3/4s delivery. 3-pitch arsenal remains unchanged. High spin rate 4-seam FB is best pitch with solid ride and variating run to either side. Tight spinning SL has above-average capabilities. Solid CU.

Gonzalez,Wikelman — SP — Boston

EXP MLB DEBUT: 2025 | H/W: 6-0 167 | FUT: #3 starter | 8D

Thrws R Age 21
2018 FA (VZ)

Velo	Pitch	Grade
92-95	FB	++++
77-80	CB	+++
83-85	CU	+++

Year	Lev	Team	W	L	Sv	IP	K	ERA	WHIP	BF/G	OBA	H%	S%	xERA	Ctl	Dom	Cmd	hr/9	BPV
2021	Rk	FCL Red Sox	4	2	0	35	46	3.60	1.06	17.0	227	35	64	2.22	2.1	11.8	5.8	0.3	175
2021	A	Salem	0	0	0	17	20	1.57	1.22	17.4	211	30	90	2.70	4.2	10.5	2.5	0.5	93
2022	A	Salem	4	3	0	81	98	4.55	1.37	16.2	216	32	64	2.84	5.3	10.9	2.0	0.2	70
2022	A+	Greenville	0	0	0	17	23	2.65	1.12	16.7	213	34	74	1.96	3.2	12.2	3.8	0.0	151

Loose-armed SP who enjoyed first full season as pro. Doesn't have great size or strength, but generates excellet arm speed to deliver three solid offerings. Repeats simple delivery, though has trouble with command. CB has its moments and features depth. CU is key to future. Shows flashes of plus action and can be difficult to hit.

Gordon,Colton — SP — Houston

EXP MLB DEBUT: 2024 | H/W: 6-4 225 | FUT: #3 starter | 8E

Thrws L Age 24
2021 (8) Central Florida

Velo	Pitch	Grade
91-94	FB	++++
80-85	SL	+++
75-79	CB	+++
84-87	CU	++

Year	Lev	Team	W	L	Sv	IP	K	ERA	WHIP	BF/G	OBA	H%	S%	xERA	Ctl	Dom	Cmd	hr/9	BPV
2022	Rk	FCL Astros O	0	0	0	6	11	4.50	1.17	12.0	262	46	67	4.07	1.5	16.5	11.0	1.5	275
2022	Rk	FCL Astros	0	1	0	7	11	0.00	0.57	5.9	132	26	100		1.3	14.1	11.0	0.0	238
2022	A	Fayetteville	0	0	0	20	27	2.24	0.80	14.5	187	29	73	1.25	1.3	12.1	9.0	0.4	199
2022	A+	Asheville	2	0	1	20	29	2.69	0.80	18.2	187	28	71	1.67	1.3	13.0	9.7	0.9	215

Big-bodied southpaw returned from Tommy John surgery and dominated across low minors in second-half stint. Works quickly, getting good extension down the mound throwing from 3/4 arm slot. FB is plus pitch that he locates to both sides of the plate. SL and CB both show good shape and plus potential. Change-up is distant fourth pitch.

Gordon,Tanner — SP — Atlanta

EXP MLB DEBUT: 2024 | H/W: 6-5 215 | FUT: #5 SP/swingman | 6C

Thrws R Age 25
2019 (6) Indiana

Velo	Pitch	Grade
91-93	FB	+++
83-86	SL	+++
83-85	CU	+++

Year	Lev	Team	W	L	Sv	IP	K	ERA	WHIP	BF/G	OBA	H%	S%	xERA	Ctl	Dom	Cmd	hr/9	BPV
2019	Rk	Danville	2	1	0	24	36	2.24	1.04	7.2	161	26	83	1.84	4.5	13.4	3.0	0.7	139
2021	A	Augusta	4	4	0	57	65	3.46	0.93	19.5	210	28	65	2.20	1.6	10.2	6.5	0.8	160
2021	A+	Rome	2	4	1	50	44	4.48	1.35	19.1	287	33	72	4.93	2.0	7.9	4.0	1.4	107
2022	A+	Rome	3	1	0	22	36	1.64	0.82	20.0	225	39	82	1.70	0.0	14.7		0.4	283
2022	AA	Mississippi	9	6	0	98	97	5.32	1.46	20.0	277	33	67	5.06	3.4	8.9	2.6	1.5	87

Command/control RHP struggled after Double-A callup. Tall frame, close to physical projection. Repeatable, high 3/4s delivery with solid extention. 4-seam FB is an arm-side runner with ride when thrown up in the zone. SL is best offering with a gyro movement profile. Utilizes a CU with solid fade and occasional tumble. Near 70% strike rate.

Goss,J.J. — SP — Tampa Bay

EXP MLB DEBUT: 2025 | H/W: 6-3 185 | FUT: #4 starter | 7D

Thrws R Age 22
2019 (1) HS (TX)

Velo	Pitch	Grade
90-92	FB	++
78-81	CB	+++
84-87	CU	+++
84-87	SL	++

Year	Lev	Team	W	L	Sv	IP	K	ERA	WHIP	BF/G	OBA	H%	S%	xERA	Ctl	Dom	Cmd	hr/9	BPV
2019	Rk	GCL Rays	1	3	0	17	16	5.82	1.24	7.7	284	36	50	3.72	1.1	8.5	8.0	0.5	142
2021	Rk	FCL Rays	1	0	0	10	12	6.24	1.49	10.9	345	48	53	4.81	0.0	10.7		0.0	210
2022	A	Charleston	4	5	0	101	101	4.01	1.17	16.1	254	33	66	3.21	1.9	9.0	4.8	0.6	129

Former high round pick struggled early in season, coming on late to post solid 2nd half stats. Command/control profile. Repeatable 3/4s delivery with solid extension. 4-pitch pitcher. Commands poor performing 4-seam FB well enough to be effective. Slurvy CB is best pitch with above-average potential. Has a feel for late-fading CU. SL is 4th pitch.

Graceffo,Gordon — SP — St. Louis

EXP MLB DEBUT: 2024 | H/W: 6-4 210 | FUT: #3 starter | 8D

Thrws R Age 23
2021 (5) Villanova

Velo	Pitch	Grade
94-96	FB	++++
85-88	SL	+++
76-80	CB	+++
80-83	CU	+++

Year	Lev	Team	W	L	Sv	IP	K	ERA	WHIP	BF/G	OBA	H%	S%	xERA	Ctl	Dom	Cmd	hr/9	BPV
2020	NCAA	Villanova	4	0	0	25	12	1.43	1.12	24.7	229	25	89	2.56	2.5	4.3	1.7	0.4	28
2021	NCAA	Villanova	7	2	0	82	86	1.54	0.96	28.2	222	31	82	1.70	1.4	9.4	6.6	0.0	149
2021	A	Palm Beach	1	0	1	26	37	1.73	1.42	10.0	276	43	89	3.87	3.1	12.8	4.1	0.3	164
2022	A+	Peoria	3	2	0	45	56	1.00	0.69	19.8	175	27	87	0.62	0.8	11.2	14.0	0.2	197
2022	AA	Springfield	7	4	0	93	83	3.96	1.07	20.2	224	25	70	3.47	2.3	8.0	3.5	1.5	100

Uses an advanced 4-pitch mix to keep hitters off balance and induce weak contact. Spike in FB velo from college gives him ability to miss bats; good sinking action allows other offerings to play up. FB now sits at 94-96; SL and 12-to-6 CB are above-average and CU flashes plus with late fade and sink. The FB/CU combo should play.

Granillo,Andre — RP — St. Louis
EXP MLB DEBUT: 2024 | H/W: 6-4 245 | FUT: Setup reliever | 6C

Thrws R Age 22 — 2021 (14) UC Riverside

Pitch	Grade	Year	Lev	Team	W	L	Sv	IP	K	ERA	WHIP	BF/G	OBA	H%	S%	xERA	Ctl	Dom	Cmd	hr/9	BPV
94-96 FB	+++	2021	NCAA	UC Riverside	2	0	0	1	4	81.00	17.00	2.5	780	115	50	74.72	63.0	36.0	0.6	9.0	-1035
78-81 SL	+++	2021	A	Palm Beach	2	3	2	18	23	1.50	1.06	5.0	165	24	89	1.72	4.5	11.5	2.6	0.5	104
		2022	A	Palm Beach	3	1	2	15	26	2.96	1.25	6.2	189	32	82	3.09	5.3	15.4	2.9	1.2	151
		2022	A+	Peoria	1	4	5	34	51	3.68	1.35	5.5	219	35	74	3.32	5.0	13.4	2.7	0.8	125
		2022	AA	Springfield	0	1	1	2	5	22.50	4.50	4.9	554	92	44	17.64	9.0	22.5	2.5	0.0	180

Big bodied RH reliever has a max-effort delivery and poor front-side mechanics that result in plus velocity but below-average control. FB lives in 94-96 range with arm-side run up in the zone. Pairs the heater with an above-average to plus low-80s SL with good depth and downward break. With improved control, has stuff to be an effective reliever.

Gray,Drew — SP — Chicago (N)
EXP MLB DEBUT: 2025 | H/W: 6-3 190 | FUT: #4 starter | 7D

Thrws L Age 19 — 2021 (3) HS (FL)

Pitch	Grade	Year	Lev	Team	W	L	Sv	IP	K	ERA	WHIP	BF/G	OBA	H%	S%	xERA	Ctl	Dom	Cmd	hr/9	BPV
90-94 FB	++																				
74-76 CB	+++																				
80-83 SL	+																				
		2021	Rk	ACL Cubs	0	1	0	4	9	0.00	1.00	7.6	210	57	100	1.54	2.3	20.3	9.0	0.0	322

Athletic lefty blew out elbow in 2nd pro start and missed all of 2022 recovering from Tommy John surgery. Prior to the injury, he showed a promising low-90s FB and a potentially plus CB. SL lags behind the other offerings. Good hip turn and arm speed, but needs to work on finding release point, frequently overthrowing and missing down.

Greene,Zach — RP — New York (N)
EXP MLB DEBUT: 2023 | H/W: 6-1 215 | FUT: Setup reliever | 7D

Thrws R Age 26 — 2019 (8) South Alabama

Pitch	Grade	Year	Lev	Team	W	L	Sv	IP	K	ERA	WHIP	BF/G	OBA	H%	S%	xERA	Ctl	Dom	Cmd	hr/9	BPV
90-93 FB	++++																				
77-80 SL	+++	2021	A+	Hudson Valley	2	2	1	20	33	2.24	0.70	7.9	96	14	75	0.47	3.6	14.8	4.1	0.9	187
85-88 CU	++	2021	AA	Somerset	2	5	2	39	58	3.68	1.18	6.3	230	36	71	3.17	3.0	13.4	4.5	0.9	178
		2022	AAA	Scranton/WB	9	0	0	68	96	3.44	1.22	5.7	210	29	79	3.53	4.2	12.7	3.0	1.5	132

Rule 5 pick had great year pitching in Triple-A. 3/4s RHP with repeatable delivery and solid extension. Delivers pitch late in delivery progression. 3-pitch pitcher. Flat-angled FB has plus ride and late cutting action with nearly 40% whiff rate. Slow sweeping SL is solid offering, plays up due to FB. CU keeps LHH off FB but doesn't do much else.

Groome,Jay — SP — San Diego
EXP MLB DEBUT: 2023 | H/W: 6-6 262 | FUT: #3 starter | 8E

Thrws L Age 24 — 2016 (1) HS (NJ)

Pitch	Grade	Year	Lev	Team	W	L	Sv	IP	K	ERA	WHIP	BF/G	OBA	H%	S%	xERA	Ctl	Dom	Cmd	hr/9	BPV
		2021	A+	Greenville	3	8	0	81	108	5.32	1.33	18.7	249	35	63	4.20	3.5	12.0	3.4	1.3	138
90-95 FB	+++	2021	AA	Portland	2	0	0	15	26	2.37	1.05	19.6	219	42	75	1.82	2.4	15.4	6.5	0.0	231
77-79 CB	+++	2022	AA	Portland	3	4	0	76	81	3.54	1.26	19.4	213	26	78	3.55	4.5	9.6	2.1	1.3	69
83-86 SL	+++	2022	AAA	El Paso	3	2	0	51	44	3.17	1.39	21.5	265	32	79	4.02	3.3	7.7	2.3	0.7	67
84-85 CU	+++	2022	AAA	Worcester	1	1	0	16	15	3.94	1.50	23.0	274	33	77	4.80	3.9	8.4	2.1	1.1	64

Huge-framed SP acquired from BOS at deadline. Declining stock, but has been healthy last two years after limited time due to injuries. K rate has declined as CB has regressed to average. SL may be best offering with sharp break and flashes plus. Has posted reverse splits. Struggles to repeat delivery due to lack of athleticism.

Grove,Michael — SP — Los Angeles (N)
EXP MLB DEBUT: 2022 | H/W: 6-3 200 | FUT: #4 starter | 7C

Thrws R Age 26 — 2018 (2) West Virginia

Pitch	Grade	Year	Lev	Team	W	L	Sv	IP	K	ERA	WHIP	BF/G	OBA	H%	S%	xERA	Ctl	Dom	Cmd	hr/9	BPV
		2019	A+	Rancho Cuca	0	5	0	51	73	6.15	1.56	10.7	297	43	62	5.36	3.3	12.8	3.8	1.2	159
93-96 FB	++++	2021	AA	Tulsa	1	4	0	71	88	7.86	1.79	15.6	298	37	60	7.07	5.3	11.2	2.1	2.4	75
83-86 SL	+++	2022	AA	Tulsa	0	1	0	16	22	2.80	0.99	12.3	195	30	73	1.95	2.8	12.3	4.4	0.6	164
78-80 CB	+++	2022	AAA	Oklahoma City	1	4	0	59	68	4.10	1.30	17.4	251	32	75	4.34	3.2	10.3	3.2	1.5	118
		2022	MLB	Los Angeles	1	0	0	29	24	4.64	1.44	17.7	281	31	75	5.46	3.1	7.4	2.4	1.9	68

Has been slow to develop, but finally made MLB debut. Simple, repeatable mechanics and improved 12-to-6 power CB give him a chance to stick in MLB rotation. Plus mid-90s FB tops out at 98 with arm-side run and sink. Mid-80s SL is above-average and gives him three above-average offerings. Control has been an issue in the past, but has improved.

Hajjar,Steven — SP — Cincinnati
EXP MLB DEBUT: 2025 | H/W: 6-5 240 | FUT: #4 starter | 7C

Thrws L Age 22 — 2021 (2) Michigan

Pitch	Grade	Year	Lev	Team	W	L	Sv	IP	K	ERA	WHIP	BF/G	OBA	H%	S%	xERA	Ctl	Dom	Cmd	hr/9	BPV
89-92 FB	+++																				
80-83 SL	++++	2022	Rk	FCL Twins	0	0	0	1	2	30.00	5.83	10.4	470	68	43	18.42	30.0	15.0	0.5	0.0	-522
76-79 CB	++	2022	A	Fort Myers	2	2	0	43	71	2.50	1.09	14.1	170	30	80	1.95	4.6	14.8	3.2	0.6	161
81-84 CU	+++	2022	A+	Dayton	0	1	0	7	10	6.43	1.43	14.9	168	29	50	2.22	7.7	12.9	1.7	0.0	41

Tall, projectable LHP made pro debut and was traded mid-season by MIN. 3/4s deceptive delivery. Stays balanced despite jerky leg lift. High whiff rate FB plays up due to flat-angled ride profile with run. SL is best secondary with short, tight break late. CU has plus tumble but struggles mimicking FB delivery. Also throws CB with decent shape.

Hall,DL — SP — Baltimore
EXP MLB DEBUT: 2022 | H/W: 6-2 195 | FUT: #2 SP/closer | 9D

Thrws L Age 24 — 2017 (1) HS (GA)

Pitch	Grade	Year	Lev	Team	W	L	Sv	IP	K	ERA	WHIP	BF/G	OBA	H%	S%	xERA	Ctl	Dom	Cmd	hr/9	BPV
		2021	AA	Bowie	2	0	0	31	56	3.17	1.03	17.1	154	27	75	2.10	4.6	16.2	3.5	1.2	184
95-98 FB	+++++	2022	A+	Aberdeen	0	0	0	4	6	0.00	0.50	13.3	151	27	100		0.0	13.5		0.0	261
85-89 SL	++++	2022	AA	Bowie	0	1	0	3	6	5.63	1.25	13.0	250	50	50	2.70	2.8	16.9	6.0	0.0	246
83-86 CU	++	2022	AAA	Norfolk Tides	3	7	0	76	125	4.72	1.46	14.8	224	37	70	4.02	5.8	14.8	2.6	1.2	127
78-80 CB	++	2022	MLB	Baltimore	1	1	1	13	19	6.14	1.74	5.5	314	48	61	4.91	4.1	13.0	3.2	0.0	141

One of the best swing-and-miss FBs from the left side in MiLB; overpowers both lefty and righty bats. A sweeping, plus SL is a second plus pitch; darting in and down to RHH. CU and CB are average, but sketchy command and health history need to be overcome. Walked too many in AAA and his MLB debut, but potential difference maker in any role.

Hamel,Dominic — SP — New York (N)
EXP MLB DEBUT: 2024 | H/W: 6-2 206 | FUT: #4 starter | 7C

Thrws R Age 24 — 2021 (3) Dallas Baptist

Pitch	Grade	Year	Lev	Team	W	L	Sv	IP	K	ERA	WHIP	BF/G	OBA	H%	S%	xERA	Ctl	Dom	Cmd	hr/9	BPV
		2020	NCAA	Dallas Baptist	2	0	0	19	27	4.69	1.04	18.5	194	29	56	2.41	3.3	12.7	3.9	0.9	157
90-93 FB	+++	2021	NCAA	Dallas Baptist	13	2	1	91	136	4.24	1.12	20.0	209	30	69	3.38	3.4	13.4	4.0	1.6	169
81-84 SL	++++	2021	Rk	FCL Mets	0	0	0	3	7	0.00	0.00	4.2	0	0			0.0	21.0		0.0	396
81-84 CU	+++	2022	A	St. Lucie	5	2	0	63	71	3.85	1.22	18.2	212	29	69	2.89	4.1	10.1	2.4	0.7	89
71-74 CB	+++	2022	A+	Brooklyn	5	1	0	55	74	2.61	1.09	19.6	184	30	73	1.53	4.1	12.1	3.0	0.0	125

Tall, high 3/4s RHP pitched well across lower level affiliates in 2022. Repeats straight-on delivery well with solid extension. Presently, at physical projection. 4-pitch repertoire. Utilizes flatter plane FB with deceptive riding action. Needs to throw FB for strikes. Tight, high-spin rate SL is best pitch. CB and CU could be average offerings.

Hancock,Emerson — SP — Seattle
EXP MLB DEBUT: 2023 | H/W: 6-4 213 | FUT: #2 starter | 8B

Thrws R Age 23 — 2020 (1) Georgia

Pitch	Grade	Year	Lev	Team	W	L	Sv	IP	K	ERA	WHIP	BF/G	OBA	H%	S%	xERA	Ctl	Dom	Cmd	hr/9	BPV
92-96 FB	++++	2020	NCAA	Georgia	2	0	0	24	34	3.75	1.04	23.2	245	37	65	2.87	1.1	12.8	11.3	0.8	217
77-82 CB	+++	2021	A+	Everett	2	0	0	31	30	2.32	1.03	13.3	179	24	77	1.64	3.8	8.7	2.3	0.3	73
79-84 SL	+++	2021	AA	Arkansas	1	1	0	13	13	3.41	1.06	17.1	212	29	64	1.83	2.7	8.9	3.3	0.0	104
83-87 CU	++++	2022	AA	Arkansas	7	4	0	98	92	3.76	1.20	18.8	224	26	75	3.72	3.5	8.4	2.4	1.5	76

Polished, durable SP who hasn't yet dominated, but has the ingredients to be special. Has average to plus stuff across board. Control tends to wane and is more of a flyball guy. Plus FB is the standout pitch with power and riding life up in zone. Features two quality breaking balls with sweeping SL ahead of CB. CU can become plus.

Hankins,Ethan — SP — Cleveland
EXP MLB DEBUT: 2024 | H/W: 6-6 200 | FUT: #3 starter | 8E

Thrws R Age 22 — 2018 (1) HS (GA)

Pitch	Grade	Year	Lev	Team	W	L	Sv	IP	K	ERA	WHIP	BF/G	OBA	H%	S%	xERA	Ctl	Dom	Cmd	hr/9	BPV
92-96 FB	++++																				
81-85 SL	+++	2019	A-	MahoningVal	0	0	0	38	43	1.41	1.07	16.5	176	25	88	1.65	4.2	10.1	2.4	0.2	86
76-80 CB	+++	2019	A	Lake County	0	3	0	21	28	4.69	1.52	18.3	252	35	72	4.65	5.1	11.9	2.3	1.3	95
88-91 CU	+++	2022	Rk	ACL Indians	0	0	0	1	1	0.00	0.00	2.8	0	0			0.0	9.0		0.0	180

Hard-throwing former 1st round pick spent most of the season rehabbing from '21 Tommy John surgery. Only pitched 1-inning on 8/1 in ACL and didn't appear again. FB touches high 90s with solid run/ride profile. All 3 secondary pitches flash above-average-or-better. SL has always been secondary closest to a plus offering. Hard to know what to expect.

Hansen,Pete — SP — St. Louis
EXP MLB DEBUT: 2025 | H/W: 6-2 205 | FUT: #4 starter | 7C

Thrws L Age 22 — 2022 (3) Texas

Pitch	Grade	Year	Lev	Team	W	L	Sv	IP	K	ERA	WHIP	BF/G	OBA	H%	S%	xERA	Ctl	Dom	Cmd	hr/9	BPV
87-90 FB	++																				
72-76 CB	+++																				
78-82 SL	++++																				
80-83 CU	+++																				

Command and control lefty was a workhorse in college and was able to thrive despite a FB that rarely breaks 90 mph. Secondary offerings are all above-average with late breaking CB and plus SL generating swing-and-miss and weak contact. Average CU is a solid 4th offering. Repeats mechanics well and pounds the strike zone. Potential back-end starter.

Harrington,Thomas — SP — Pittsburgh

EXP MLB DEBUT: 2024 | H/W: 6-2 185 | FUT: #3 starter | 8C

Thrws R Age 21 — 2022 (1) Campbell

90-93	FB	+ + +
77-78	CB	+ + +
81-83	SL	+ + +
83-85	CU	+ + +

Year	Lev	Team	W	L	Sv	IP	K	ERA	WHIP	BF/G	OBA	H%	S%	xERA	Ctl	Dom	Cmd	hr/9	BPV

Athletic, projectable SP who has good upside thanks to deep repertoire and ability to repeat delivery. Lacks put away pitch now, but plenty of room to enhance package. Changes speeds very well and FB results in swing and miss due to late carry. CU could be one of best in org and features late tumbling action.

Harris,Ben — RP — Los Angeles (N)

EXP MLB DEBUT: 2024 | H/W: 6-1 195 | FUT: Closer | 6B

Thrws L Age 23 — 2021 (8) Georgia

92-95	FB	+ + + +
80-83	SL	+ +

Year	Lev	Team	W	L	Sv	IP	K	ERA	WHIP	BF/G	OBA	H%	S%	xERA	Ctl	Dom	Cmd	hr/9	BPV
2021	NCAA	Georgia	4	2	3	38	66	2.36	1.15	7.6	129	25	81	1.53	6.6	15.5	2.4	0.5	120
2021	Rk	ACL Dodgers	0	0	0	1	2	8.18	3.64	3.6	244	48	75	8.64	24.5	16.4	0.7	0.0	-350
2021	A	Rancho Cuca	0	0	0	4	7	6.75	2.25	5.1	347	54	75	8.84	6.8	15.8	2.3	2.3	119
2022	A	Rancho Cuca	1	1	3	27	59	5.63	1.65	5.5	231	55	64	3.76	7.3	19.5	2.7	0.3	173
2022	A+	Great Lakes	3	0	4	28	48	1.93	0.86	4.7	102	21	78	0.39	4.8	15.4	3.2	0.3	166

Lefty reliever started to harness his stuff more effectively with uptick in velo. FB is now in the 92-95 range, topping at 98 with plus spin. Highest K% of anyone in the minors - 17.8 K/9. Was a two-way player until junior year at Georgia, so low mileage on his arm. Hides the ball exceptionally well. Potential future closer.

Harris,Hogan — SP — Oakland

EXP MLB DEBUT: 2024 | H/W: 6-3 230 | FUT: #4 starter | 7D

Thrws L Age 26 — 2018 (3) Louisiana-Lafayette

91-94	FB	+ + +
72-75	CB	+ + +
80-84	SL	+ +
78-82	CU	+ +

Year	Lev	Team	W	L	Sv	IP	K	ERA	WHIP	BF/G	OBA	H%	S%	xERA	Ctl	Dom	Cmd	hr/9	BPV
2019	A-	Vermont	1	3	0	26		3.12	0.88	12.0	160	24	67	1.42	3.1	12.5	4.0	0.7	158
2019	A+	Stockton	0	2	0	28	29	2.55	0.99	15.4	185	24	77	1.93	3.2	9.3	2.9	0.6	98
2022	A+	Lansing	0	1	0	13	18	1.38	0.92	7.0	120	21	83	0.45	4.8	12.5	2.6	0.0	111
2022	AA	Midland	1	0	0	32	48	1.68	1.06	15.6	142	26	82	1.01	5.3	13.5	2.5	0.0	116
2022	AAA	Las Vegas	1	3	0	28	39	6.41	1.71	15.9	281	38	67	6.15	5.4	12.5	2.3	1.9	96

Returned from Tommy John surgery; hadn't pitched since 2019. Posted highest K rate in org while continuing to mute oppBA with top-notch sinker. Likes to work FB to all of strike zone and has developed CU with effective, late drop. Uses two distinct breaking balls to keep hitters off guard. Too inefficient and control has been a big issue.

Harrison,Kyle — SP — San Francisco

EXP MLB DEBUT: 2023 | H/W: 6-2 200 | FUT: #2 starter | 8B

Thrws L Age 21 — 2020 (3) HS (CA)

92-95	FB	+ + + +
81-85	SL	+ + + +
80-84	CU	+ + +

Year	Lev	Team	W	L	Sv	IP	K	ERA	WHIP	BF/G	OBA	H%	S%	xERA	Ctl	Dom	Cmd	hr/9	BPV
2021	A	San Jose	4	3	0	98	157	3.21	1.41	18.0	237	41	76	3.21	4.8	14.4	3.0	0.3	148
2022	A+	Eugene	0	1	0	29	59	1.55	1.00	15.8	189	43	89	1.89	3.1	18.3	5.9	0.6	264
2022	AA	Richmond	4	2	0	84	127	3.11	1.18	18.7	202	31	80	3.07	4.2	13.6	3.3	1.2	150

Dominant LHP who continues to register high K rates regardless of level. Has among best pure stuff in minors with all offerings at least solid-average to double-plus. Creates deception from low arm slot and all pitches can miss bats. CU sometimes lacks movement and command needs work. SL is one of best breaking balls in baseball.

Hartwig,Grant — RP — New York (N)

EXP MLB DEBUT: 2023 | H/W: 6-5 235 | FUT: Middle reliever | 6C

Thrws R Age 25 — 2021 NDFA (Miami-OH)

93-95	FB	+ + +
81-84	SL	+ + + +
85-87	CU	+ +

Year	Lev	Team	W	L	Sv	IP	K	ERA	WHIP	BF/G	OBA	H%	S%	xERA	Ctl	Dom	Cmd	hr/9	BPV
2021	A	St. Lucie	0	0	3	4	3	2.14	0.95	4.0	202	25	75	1.46	2.1	6.4	3.0	0.0	76
2022	A	St. Lucie	3	0	3	14	21	4.44	1.41	6.0	273	44	65	3.45	3.2	13.3	4.2	0.0	172
2022	A+	Brooklyn	1	0	7	15	24	0.60	0.99	5.2	174	30	100	1.73	3.6	14.3	4.0	0.6	179
2022	AA	Binghamton	0	2	3	23	34	1.16	1.08	5.7	176	31	88	1.42	4.3	13.2	3.1	0.0	140
2022	AAA	Syracuse	2	0	0	3	4	0.00	0.67	5.2	0	0	100		6.0	12.0	2.0	0.0	72

Sidearm throwing RHP pitched across 4 levels during superb 2022 season. Tall and thin. Frame is at physical projection. Achieves solid extension in delivery. 4-seam FB has natural arm-side running action, lives down in zone. Well commanded frisbee SL is best offering, flashing plus horizontal movement. Also features arm-side fading CU.

Hawkins,Garrett — SP — San Diego

EXP MLB DEBUT: 2024 | H/W: 6-5 230 | FUT: #4 starter | 7D

Thrws R Age 23 — 2021 (9) British Columbia

91-94	FB	+ + +
80-83	SL	+ +
82-85	CU	+ + +

Year	Lev	Team	W	L	Sv	IP	K	ERA	WHIP	BF/G	OBA	H%	S%	xERA	Ctl	Dom	Cmd	hr/9	BPV
2020	NAIA	British Columbia	3	1	0	32	46	3.66	1.25	21.7	274	40	75	4.13	1.7	12.9	7.7	1.1	205
2021	Rk	ACL Padres	3	1	0	15	27	2.38	1.13	8.5	260	47	81	3.10	1.2	16.1	13.5	0.6	275
2022	A	Lake Elsinore	5	5	0	77	108	3.96	1.20	18.3	251	37	70	3.64	2.3	12.6	5.4	1.0	182
2022	A+	Fort Wayne	0	3	0	15	12	8.94	2.12	18.6	341	34	65	9.73	6.0	7.2	1.2	3.6	-14

Large-framed SP who uses height and extension well to make average pitch mix play up. Throws with average velocity, but FB effective up in zone with pitch movement and ride. Operates with above average control, though could get better within zone. Subject to flyballs and lacks true swing-and-miss offering. SL is third pitch.

Haynes,Jagger — SP — San Diego

EXP MLB DEBUT: 2026 | H/W: 6-3 170 | FUT: #3 starter | 8E

Thrws L Age 20 — 2020 (5) HS (NC)

87-93	FB	+ + +
81-83	SL	+ +
84-85	CU	+ + +

Year	Lev	Team	W	L	Sv	IP	K	ERA	WHIP	BF/G	OBA	H%	S%	xERA	Ctl	Dom	Cmd	hr/9	BPV

Tall and projectable arm who hasn't yet pitched as pro due to Tommy John surgery. Outstanding athlete with potential for plus velocity with hard-charging FB and intriguing SL that can get slurvy. Has raw feel for changing speeds which has resulted in struggles with LHH. Has ingredients to become quite strong and needs innings.

Headrick,Brent — SP — Minnesota

EXP MLB DEBUT: 2024 | H/W: 6-6 235 | FUT: #5 SP/swingman | 7E

Thrws L Age 25 — 2019 (9) Illinois St

89-93	FB	+ + +
85-87	CT	+ +
82-85	CU	+ +

Year	Lev	Team	W	L	Sv	IP	K	ERA	WHIP	BF/G	OBA	H%	S%	xERA	Ctl	Dom	Cmd	hr/9	BPV
2019	Rk	Elizabethton	0	0	0	3	2	0.00	2.19	5.3	181	22	100	4.35	14.1	5.6	0.4	0.0	-260
2021	Rk	FCL Twins	0	0	0	1	2	0.00	2.50	6.4	228	42	100	5.59	15.0	15.0	1.0	0.0	-117
2021	A	Fort Myers	3	5	0	61	86	3.83	1.59	18.0	271	41	77	4.58	4.9	12.7	2.6	0.7	115
2022	A+	Cedar Rapids	8	2	0	65	77	2.35	0.89	16.1	197	26	80	2.11	1.8	10.6	5.9	1.0	161
2022	AA	Wichita	2	3	0	43	59	4.81	1.37	18.0	279	37	75	5.63	2.5	12.3	4.9	2.3	172

Tall, durable SP who was 2nd in org in Ks. More of a command-oriented pitcher than power as margin for error is slim. Added a few ticks to FB and continues to throw consistent strikes. K rate may not last as he lacks true put-away pitch. CU and CT have moments, but more for weak contact. Added splitter to mix.

Hence,Tink — SP — St. Louis

EXP MLB DEBUT: 2025 | H/W: 6-1 175 | FUT: #3 starter | 9E

Thrws R Age 20 — 2020 (2) HS (AR)

95-97	FB	+ + + +
77-79	CB	+ + + +
82-86	CU	+ +

Year	Lev	Team	W	L	Sv	IP	K	ERA	WHIP	BF/G	OBA	H%	S%	xERA	Ctl	Dom	Cmd	hr/9	BPV
2021	Rk	FCL Cardinals	0	1	1	8	14	9.00	1.75	4.6	328	54	46	6.19	3.4	15.8	4.7	1.1	210
2022	A	Palm Beach	0	1	0	52	81	1.38	0.88	12.1	174	31	84	1.06	2.6	14.0	5.4	0.2	200

STL continue to limit workload due to concerns about durability, but was dominant when on the mound. Electric FB sits at 95-97, maxing at 99. Backs up the heater with a plus upper-70s CB with good spin and late action. CU showed improvement, but remains a work in progress. Quick arm action, slender frame, and solid command makes him worth the wait.

Henderson,Layne — RP — Detroit

EXP MLB DEBUT: 2025 | H/W: 6-4 200 | FUT: Setup reliever | 6C

Thrws R Age 26 — 2018 (30) Azusa Pacific

90-94	FB	+ + +
82-85	CU	+ + +
78-81	SL	+ +

Year	Lev	Team	W	L	Sv	IP	K	ERA	WHIP	BF/G	OBA	H%	S%	xERA	Ctl	Dom	Cmd	hr/9	BPV
2019	AA	Corpus Christi	1	2	0	13	13	7.62	2.08	8.0	290	35	64	6.74	8.3	9.0	1.1	1.4	-44
2021	A+	Asheville	0	0	0	3	6	0.00	0.32	3.2	103	27	100		0.0	17.4		0.0	332
2021	AA	Corpus Christi	5	2	0	49	61	3.84	1.40	8.0	224	31	75	3.67	5.3	11.2	2.1	0.9	76
2022	AA	Corpus Christi	5	4	0	44	56	3.89	1.23	6.4	205	29	70	2.91	4.5	11.5	2.5	0.8	103
2022	AAA	Sugar Land	0	0	0	9	12	1.98	0.88	5.6	190	27	86	2.01	2.0	11.9	6.0	1.0	178

Large righty with an unorthodox, over-the-top delivery that includes a huge leg lift and then downhill release point. Gets good separation between FB and CU, but other secondaries tend to lack spin, shape. Likely best suited for long relief.

Henderson,Logan — SP — Milwaukee

EXP MLB DEBUT: 2025 | H/W: 5-11 194 | FUT: #3 starter | 8E

Thrws R Age 21 — 2021 (4) McLennan CC

89-94	FB	+ + +
75-77	CB	+ +
82-85	CU	+ + + +

Year	Lev	Team	W	L	Sv	IP	K	ERA	WHIP	BF/G	OBA	H%	S%	xERA	Ctl	Dom	Cmd	hr/9	BPV
2022	Rk	ACL Brewers Blue	0	0	0	2	5	0.00	0.50	3.3	151	61	100		0.0	22.5		0.0	423
2022	A	Carolina	0	1	0	11	18	4.82	1.79	10.3	307	51	70	4.90	4.8	14.5	3.0	0.0	148

Short, strong RHP who returned from elbow surgery in August. May not have much experience or projection due to size and short arm action, but throws strikes and has deceptive CU to fool hitters from both sides. Gets great spin on FB and plays up as it is never straight. Particularly stingy against RHH, though will need better breaking ball.

Henriquez,Edgardo

SP | Los Angeles (N) | EXP MLB DEBUT: 2025 | H/W: 6-4 200 | FUT: #2 SP/closer | 8E

Thrws R Age 20
2018 FA (VZ)

Velo	Pitch	Grade
96-98	FB	++++
83-86	SL	+++
74-76	CB	++
83-85	CU	++

Year	Lev	Team	W	L	Sv	IP	K	ERA	WHIP	BF/G	OBA	H%	S%	xERA	Ctl	Dom	Cmd	hr/9	BPV
2021	Rk	ACL Dodgers	2	3	0	32	47	4.19	1.30	11.1	180	28	69	2.82	6.1	13.1	2.1	0.8	88
2021	A	Rancho Cuca	0	0	0	2	3	18.00	2.50	10.6	347	53	20	7.38	9.0	13.5	1.5	0.0	18
2022	A	Rancho Cuca	2	3	0	35	44	4.60	1.62	11.2	282	40	71	4.62	4.6	11.3	2.4	0.5	96

Venezuelan hurler has a big time FB that sits at 96-98 and has been as high at 101. Power SL is best secondary offering and both CB and CU show potential but lack consistency. Uses tall frame to pitch north/south and has some arm-side run to FB. Struggles to repeat mechanics, leading to bouts of wildness. Tommy John surgery in Dec; will miss 2023.

Henriquez,Ronny

SP | Minnesota | EXP MLB DEBUT: 2022 | H/W: 5-10 155 | FUT: #4 starter | 7C

Thrws R Age 22
2017 FA (DR)

Velo	Pitch	Grade
92-96	FB	++++
84-87	SL	+++
85-88	CU	+++

Year	Lev	Team	W	L	Sv	IP	K	ERA	WHIP	BF/G	OBA	H%	S%	xERA	Ctl	Dom	Cmd	hr/9	BPV
2019	A	Hickory	6	6	0	82	99	4.50	1.44	16.6	282	39	69	4.31	3.0	10.9	3.7	0.7	134
2021	A+	Hickory	1	3	0	24	27	3.75	0.88	17.7	161	21	58	1.48	3.0	10.1	3.4	0.8	119
2021	AA	Frisco	4	4	0	69	78	5.07	1.18	17.3	250	30	64	4.44	2.2	10.1	4.6	2.0	141
2022	AAA	St. Paul	3	4	1	95	106	5.68	1.39	16.7	270	33	64	5.08	3.1	10.0	3.2	1.8	114
2022	MLB	Minnesota	0	1	0	11	9	2.41	0.98	14.2	202	24	80	2.28	2.4	7.2	3.0	0.8	83

Short, fast-armed RHP with incredible stuff. Despite limited size, produces plus velocity and movement to all pitches. Pitches up in zone with carry and repeats low effort delivery well. Struggles with HR allowed and can be around fat part of plate too often. Production hasn't lived up to potential, but still young and raw.

Henry,Cole

SP | Washington | EXP MLB DEBUT: 2023 | H/W: 6-4 215 | FUT: #4 starter | 7D

Thrws R Age 23
2020 (2) LSU

Velo	Pitch	Grade
93-96	FB	+++
78-82	CB	++
84-87	CU	+++

Year	Lev	Team	W	L	Sv	IP	K	ERA	WHIP	BF/G	OBA	H%	S%	xERA	Ctl	Dom	Cmd	hr/9	BPV
2020	NCAA	LSU	2	1	0	19		1.89	1.11	18.6	219	31	85	2.45	2.8	10.9	3.8	0.5	137
2021	Rk	FCL Nationals	0	2	0	4	7	6.75	1.50	8.6	307	54	50	4.17	2.3	15.8	7.0	0.0	241
2021	A+	Wilmington	3	3	0	43	63	1.88	0.79	17.3	159	26	81	1.10	2.3	13.2	5.7	0.6	193
2022	AA	Harrisburg	0	0	0	23	28	0.78	0.60	11.3	71	10	92		3.5	10.9	3.1	0.4	119
2022	AAA	Rochester	1	0	0	8	6	4.50	1.38	16.8	285	33	70	4.67	2.3	6.8	3.0	1.1	79

Arm has promise but battled injuries—thoracic outlet syndrome shut him down in June and required surgery in August. It means best-case is a late start to 2023, but now has considerable long-term risk. CU had taken a step forward in 2022 to pair with mid-90s FB; CB is also average pitch. Lots of questions now; bullpen may be his future destination.

Heredia,Nathanael

RP | St. Louis | EXP MLB DEBUT: 2024 | H/W: 6-3 190 | FUT: Setup reliever | 7E

Thrws L Age 22
2018 FA (DR)

Velo	Pitch	Grade
93-96	FB	+++
78-81	SL	++

Year	Lev	Team	W	L	Sv	IP	K	ERA	WHIP	BF/G	OBA	H%	S%	xERA	Ctl	Dom	Cmd	hr/9	BPV
2019	Rk	GCL Cardinals	5	4	0	49	48	3.85	1.59	18.0	237	31	75	3.82	6.4	8.8	1.4	0.4	3
2019	A-	State College	0	0	0	0	1	90.00	25.00	5.6	780	177	75	#####		45.0	0.3	45.0	-2817
2021	A	Palm Beach	1	1	0	37	49	4.85	1.56	10.2	223	35	66	3.20	6.8	11.9	1.8	0.0	49
2021	A+	Peoria	1	2	0	18	21	7.91	2.64	7.1	249	35	68	6.72	15.3	10.4	0.7	0.5	-209
2022	A+	Peoria	4	4	0	74	86	4.13	1.57	7.9	229	32	74	3.86	6.6	10.4	1.6	0.6	29

Hard-throwing LH reliever from the DR is a work in progress. Quick, athletic delivery from a low 3/4 arm slot creates movement and deception, but struggles to find a consistent release point, leading to well-below average control. FB sits at 93-96 with late life and an above-average SL. If strikethrowing improves, his FB/SL combo can get MLB hitters out.

Hermann,Sean

SP | New York (A) | EXP MLB DEBUT: 2025 | H/W: 6-0 160 | FUT: #4 starter | 7D

Thrws R Age 19
2021 (14) HS (FL)

Velo	Pitch	Grade
90-92	FB	+++
82-84	SL	+++
84-87	CU	+++
86-88	CT	++

Year	Lev	Team	W	L	Sv	IP	K	ERA	WHIP	BF/G	OBA	H%	S%	xERA	Ctl	Dom	Cmd	hr/9	BPV
2022	Rk	FCL Yankees	2	0	0	33	41	2.45	1.03	21.2	231	32	81	2.72	1.6	11.1	6.8	0.8	175
2022	A	Tampa	0	0	0	20	16	2.69	1.29	20.7	251	26	95	5.03	3.1	7.2	2.3	2.2	62

Smaller statured, low 3/4s RHP pitched solidly in pro debut. Athletic frame with room to grow. Limited extension in delivery, struggles maintaining slot in outing. Flat-angled FB features solid riding profile, which plays up due to low arm slot. Has advanced command of tight, two-plane SL. Needs to improve firmness of fading CU. Also throws CT.

Hernandez,Adrian

RP | Toronto | EXP MLB DEBUT: 2023 | H/W: 5-8 190 | FUT: Setup reliever | 6B

Thrws R Age 23
2017 FA (MX)

Velo	Pitch	Grade
89-91	FB	++
79-85	SL	++
80-83	CU	++++

Year	Lev	Team	W	L	Sv	IP	K	ERA	WHIP	BF/G	OBA	H%	S%	xERA	Ctl	Dom	Cmd	hr/9	BPV
2021	AA	New Hampshire	0	0	4	15	27	2.37	0.72	5.4	104	16	78	0.88	3.6	16.0	4.5	1.2	210
2022	Rk	FCL Blue Jays	1	0	0	2	2	4.09	2.27	5.6	326	42	80	6.50	8.2	8.2	1.0	0.0	-56
2022	A	Dunedin	0	0	0	3	7	0.00	0.65	5.4	186	53	100	0.37	0.0	20.3		0.0	384
2022	AA	New Hampshire	1	0	1	4	6	2.25	1.25	5.4	151	27	80	1.57	6.8	13.5	2.0	0.0	79
2022	AAA	Buffalo	3	0	7	32	44	5.03	1.27	4.3	216	29	66	3.95	4.5	12.3	2.8	1.7	119

Very short RP who bypassed High-A and reached Triple-A, though missed time mid-year. Spent most of career in bullpen and has leveraged CU to considerable success. Registers ton of Ks with CU regardless of whether LHH or RHH. FB and SL, however, fall short of average. Has trouble with walks.

Herz,D.J.

SP | Chicago (N) | EXP MLB DEBUT: 2024 | H/W: 6-2 175 | FUT: #4 starter | 7E

Thrws L Age 22
2019 (8) HS (NC)

Velo	Pitch	Grade
90-94	FB	++
78-82	CB	++
80-83	CU	++++

Year	Lev	Team	W	L	Sv	IP	K	ERA	WHIP	BF/G	OBA	H%	S%	xERA	Ctl	Dom	Cmd	hr/9	BPV
2021	A	Myrtle Beach	3	4	0	65	105	3.45	1.07	14.9	148	25	70	1.87	5.2	14.5	2.8	0.8	137
2021	A+	South Bend	1	0	0	16	26	2.81	1.00	20.4	181	32	73	1.79	3.4	14.6	4.3	0.6	190
2022	A+	South Bend	2	2	0	63	99	2.28	1.11	14.6	156	27	81	1.67	5.3	14.1	2.7	0.4	130
2022	AA	Tennessee	1	4	0	31	42	8.37	1.83	16.1	214	29	54	5.11	9.5	12.1	1.3	1.4	-21

Athletic lefty started the season well, but imploded when moved up to Double-A. Comes at hitters from the 1st base side of rubber with crossfire action that allows fringe FB to play up. Best secondary is plus CU that drops off the table, while CB is just average. Command has always been an issue, but walked more than a batter per nine at Double-A.

Hidalgo,Alejandro

SP | Minnesota | EXP MLB DEBUT: 2025 | H/W: 6-1 160 | FUT: #4 starter | 7C

Thrws R Age 19
2019 FA (VZ)

Velo	Pitch	Grade
90-93	FB	++++
77-80	SL	++
81-84	CU	++++

Year	Lev	Team	W	L	Sv	IP	K	ERA	WHIP	BF/G	OBA	H%	S%	xERA	Ctl	Dom	Cmd	hr/9	BPV
2021	Rk	ACL Angels	3	2	0	27	31	4.67	1.30	15.9	255	31	72	4.83	3.0	10.3	3.4	2.0	123
2022	A	Inland Empire	0	3	0	39	58	4.62	1.36	16.3	236	37	66	3.49	4.4	13.4	3.1	0.7	141

Athletic, shorter-statured RHP features one of the best CU in lower minors. Long arm circle in delivery, struggles with on-time release. 4-seam FB has significant riding action, coupled with run away & is difficult to command. CU has solid fade and late drop, but inconsistent firmness. SL has very short break profile and is rarely used.

Hill,Jaden

SP | Colorado | EXP MLB DEBUT: 2024 | H/W: 6-4 234 | FUT: #2 SP/closer | 8D

Thrws R Age 24
2021 (2) Lousiana St

Velo	Pitch	Grade
93-96	FB	++++
81-84	SL	++
80-83	CU	++++

Year	Lev	Team	W	L	Sv	IP	K	ERA	WHIP	BF/G	OBA	H%	S%	xERA	Ctl	Dom	Cmd	hr/9	BPV
2022	Rk	ACL Rockies	0	0	0	10	11	3.56	1.49	6.2	279	39	73	3.77	3.6	9.8	2.8	0.0	98
2022	A	Fresno	0	0	0	7	14	2.54	1.27	9.7	259	54	78	2.86	2.5	17.7	7.0	0.0	269

Had Tommy John surgery early in 2021, but was still selected at #44 overall. He finally made his pro debut in August and looked sharp in his return. FB was back in the mid-90s with late life up in the zone and CU still has plus late fade and sink. SL needs consistency, but gives him three potential above-average to plus offerings.

Hjerpe,Cooper

SP | St. Louis | EXP MLB DEBUT: 2024 | H/W: 6-3 200 | FUT: #4 starter | 7C

Thrws L Age 22
2022 (1) Oregon St

Velo	Pitch	Grade
92-94	FB	++++
77-80	SL	+
80-82	CU	+++

Year	Lev	Team	W	L	Sv	IP	K	ERA	WHIP	BF/G	OBA	H%	S%	xERA	Ctl	Dom	Cmd	hr/9	BPV

LHP is more a sum of his parts. Relies heavily on deception and an above-average 3-pitch mix. Attacks hitters from a low 3/4s, almost side-arm slot with a FB that sits at 92-94, topping at 96 mph. Low-80s CU is his best secondary offering and velo difference from the FB creates swing-and-miss. Below-average SL will need to improve.

Hodge,Porter

SP | Chicago (N) | EXP MLB DEBUT: 2024 | H/W: 6-4 230 | FUT: #5 SP/swingman | 7D

Thrws R Age 22
2019 (13) HS (UT)

Velo	Pitch	Grade
92-94	FB	+++
77-79	CB	++
82-85	SL	++++
86-88	CU	+

Year	Lev	Team	W	L	Sv	IP	K	ERA	WHIP	BF/G	OBA	H%	S%	xERA	Ctl	Dom	Cmd	hr/9	BPV
2021	Rk	ACL Cubs	1	2	0	29	35	7.45	1.55	18.1	306	40	53	5.79	2.8	10.9	3.9	1.6	138
2021	A	Myrtle Beach	1	1	0	21	29	3.82	1.27	12.4	241	38	67	2.70	3.4	12.3	3.6	0.0	148
2022	A	Myrtle Beach	4	2	0	69	90	3.00	1.35	16.9	217	34	76	2.71	5.1	11.7	2.3	0.1	92
2022	A+	South Bend	3	3	0	40	51	2.02	1.05	19.4	187	27	85	2.11	3.6	11.4	3.2	0.7	127

Tall RHP had a breakout season, punching out a ton with just 4 HR over two levels. Tall, athletic frame and fluid delivery with a FB that sits 92-94, topping at 97 with late arm-side run. Best offering is a plus two-plane break SL that results in lots of swing-and-miss and is MLB ready. Below-average CU and poor command could push him into a relief role.

Hoeing,Bryan

SP | **Miami** | EXP MLB DEBUT: 2022 | H/W: 6-6 210 | FUT: #5 SP/swingman | **6C**

Thrws R Age 26
2019 (7) Louisville

Velo	Pitch	Grade
90-93	FB	+++
77-80	CB	+++
82-84	CU	+++
80-83	SL	++

Year	Lev	Team	W	L	Sv	IP	K	ERA	WHIP	BF/G	OBA	H%	S%	xERA	Ctl	Dom	Cmd	hr/9	BPV
2021	A+	Beloit	7	6	0	121	96	4.83	1.27	22.5	276	32	63	4.13	1.8	7.1	4.0	1.0	98
2022	AA	Pensacola	2	1	0	25	26	0.36	0.95	23.8	220	31	96	1.64	1.4	9.3	6.5	0.0	147
2022	AAA	Jacksonville	7	5	0	94	49	5.07	1.44	22.2	274	28	68	4.89	3.4	4.7	1.4	1.3	12
2022	MLB	Miami	1	1	0	12	6	12.54	1.97	7.3	356	33	37	9.75	3.7	4.4	1.2	3.7	-2

Dependable inning-eating RHP pitched across two minor league levels and found himself pitching for MIA. Low 3/4s slot delivery with plus extension. 4-pitch pitcher, all fringe-to-average offerings. FB has plus arm-side run profile but is easily read out of hand. Doesn't miss bats. CB and SL are best pitches, both lacking consistency.

Hoffmann,Andrew

SP | **Kansas City** | EXP MLB DEBUT: 2024 | H/W: 6-5 210 | FUT: Setup reliever | **7C**

Thrws R Age 23
2021 (12) Illinois

Velo	Pitch	Grade
91-94	FB	+++
81-84	SL	++++
83-85	CU	++

Year	Lev	Team	W	L	Sv	IP	K	ERA	WHIP	BF/G	OBA	H%	S%	xERA	Ctl	Dom	Cmd	hr/9	BPV
2020	NJCA	Logan College	5	0	0	26	46	2.08	0.88	19.3	179	34	81	1.58	2.4	15.9	6.6	0.7	239
2021	NCAA	Illinois	3	0	0	62	64	2.89	1.03	21.8	218	29	72	2.23	2.2	9.3	4.3	0.4	126
2021	A	Augusta	2	2	0	29	37	2.77	0.99	15.9	203	30	74	2.11	2.5	11.4	4.6	0.6	157
2022	A+	Rome	7	2	0	80	90	2.36	1.05	20.6	218	28	84	2.82	2.4	10.1	4.3	1.0	136
2022	AA	NW Arkansas	2	4	0	39	30	6.68	1.79	20.0	312	36	63	6.15	4.6	6.9	1.5	1.2	18

Tall high 3/4s slot RHP was acquired mid-season in trade with ATL. Unorthodox pacing with delivery, including an slight back turn, creates deception. Best pitch clearly is double-plus SL with 2-plane late break and a hard, sweepy profile. Alternates between both a 4-seam and 2-seam FB. 4-seam is relatively new. Throws CU lacking deception.

Hoglund,Gunnar

SP | **Oakland** | EXP MLB DEBUT: 2024 | H/W: 6-4 220 | FUT: #3 starter | **8C**

Thrws R Age 23
2021 (1) Mississippi

Velo	Pitch	Grade
91-96	FB	+++
79-84	CB	+++
81-85	SL	+++
81-83	CU	++

Year	Lev	Team	W	L	Sv	IP	K	ERA	WHIP	BF/G	OBA	H%	S%	xERA	Ctl	Dom	Cmd	hr/9	BPV
2022	Rk	ACL Athletics	0	1	0	5	7	0.00	0.80	9.1	221	36	100	1.24	0.0	12.6		0.0	245
2022	A	Stockton	0	0	0	3	1	0.00	1.33	12.5	262	29	100	3.22	3.0	3.0	1.0	0.0	-9

Durable-framed SP who missed most of 2022 after Tommy John surgery in May 2021. Acquired in Chapman trade, he has big upside, but needs to prove health. Delivery is easy and free and consistently repeats arm speed and slot. Commands FB to both sides of plate and tight SL has plus potential. Throws strikes and sequences well.

Horton,Cade

SP | **Chicago (N)** | EXP MLB DEBUT: 2024 | H/W: 6-1 211 | FUT: #3 starter | **8D**

Thrws R Age 21
2022 (1) Oklahoma

Velo	Pitch	Grade
94-96	FB	++++
86-89	SL	++++
77-79	CB	++
85-86	CU	+

Year	Lev	Team	W	L	Sv	IP	K	ERA	WHIP	BF/G	OBA	H%	S%	xERA	Ctl	Dom	Cmd	hr/9	BPV

Impressive NCAA postseason run vaulted him into the 1st round of 2022 draft. Attacks hitters with a plus 94-96 FB that tops at 98 with late life up in the zone. Refined power SL that now results in swing-and-miss two plane break. Athletic hurler has boom-or-bust potential and development of a usable CU or CB will be essential.

Hubbart,Bryce

SP | **Cincinnati** | EXP MLB DEBUT: 2025 | H/W: 6-1 181 | FUT: Setup reliever | **7D**

Thrws L Age 21
2022 (3) Florida St

Velo	Pitch	Grade
88-92	FB	+++
76-80	CB	++++
80-83	CU	+

Year	Lev	Team	W	L	Sv	IP	K	ERA	WHIP	BF/G	OBA	H%	S%	xERA	Ctl	Dom	Cmd	hr/9	BPV
2022	NCAA	Florida St	8	3	0	76	96	3.32	1.16	20.2	238	32	78	3.60	2.5	11.4	4.6	1.3	155
2022	Rk	ACL Reds	0	0	0	1	2	7.50	4.17	4.2	371	59	80	12.01	22.5	15.0	0.7	0.0	-320
2022	A	Daytona	1	0	0	5	10	0.00	0.77	6.2	64	18	100		5.2	17.3	3.3	0.0	189

Athletic high 3/4s RHP had solid year as #2 SP for Florida State. Athletic, crossfire delivery with slight head whack. Mostly 2-pitch mix. 88-92 mph has a solid ride profile with late arm-side run. Pounds FB for strikes. Sweeping CB is best offering with 1-to-7 break profile. 30% plus CB whiff rate in college. Rarely throws CU.

Hughes,Gabriel

SP | **Colorado** | EXP MLB DEBUT: 2025 | H/W: 6-4 220 | FUT: #3 starter | **8D**

Thrws R Age 21
2022 (1) Gonzaga

Velo	Pitch	Grade
93-96	FB	++++
88-91	SL	+++
83-86	CU	++

Year	Lev	Team	W	L	Sv	IP	K	ERA	WHIP	BF/G	OBA	H%	S%	xERA	Ctl	Dom	Cmd	hr/9	BPV
2022	NCAA	Gonzaga	8	3	0	98	138	3.21	1.14	25.9	213	34	72	2.45	3.4	12.7	3.7	0.5	154
2022	A	Fresno	0	0	0	3	1	0.00	0.67	10.5	106	12	100		3.0	3.0	1.0	0.0	-9

Surprise 10th overall pick had a breakout season for the Zags and is an intriguing arm. 4-seam FB sits at 93-96 and is well located up in the zone. 2-seamer has good late action and sink. SL shows above-average to plus potential and he commanded it better in 2022. CU is too firm and needs work for him to reach his potential as a mid-rotation SP.

Hurt,Kyle

SP | **Los Angeles (N)** | EXP MLB DEBUT: 2024 | H/W: 6-3 240 | FUT: #5 SP/swingman | **7E**

Thrws R Age 24
2020 (5) USC

Velo	Pitch	Grade
93-96	FB	++++
86-90	SL	+++
78-81	CB	++
85-88	CU	++

Year	Lev	Team	W	L	Sv	IP	K	ERA	WHIP	BF/G	OBA	H%	S%	xERA	Ctl	Dom	Cmd	hr/9	BPV
2020	NCAA	USC	2	1	0	17	25	3.71	1.12	16.7	187	28	71	2.63	4.2	13.2	3.1	1.1	142
2021	Rk	ACL Dodgers	1	0	0	4	8	6.43	1.43	4.5	336	57	60	6.47	0.0	17.1		2.1	327
2021	A	Rancho Cuca	1	2	1	16	28	5.59	1.37	8.4	209	39	57	3.02	5.6	15.7	2.8	0.6	149
2022	A+	Great Lakes	4	2	0	40	64	2.24	1.07	12.0	156	29	79	1.38	4.9	14.3	2.9	0.2	143
2022	AA	Tulsa	1	5	0	31	45	9.29	2.32	13.3	286	43	58	6.77	10.7	13.1	1.2	0.9	-37

Acquired by the Dodgers in the Dylan Floro trade and 2022 was a tale of two seasons. Started well at A+, but got obliterated when moved up to AA. Above-average FB sits at 93-96, topping at 99 with good arm-side run. Backs up the FB with a potentially plus CU and above-average SL and CB. Control is the biggest obstacle to future success.

Hurter,Brant

SP | **Detroit** | EXP MLB DEBUT: 2024 | H/W: 6-6 250 | FUT: #5 SP/swingman | **6B**

Thrws L Age 24
2021 (7) Georgia Tech

Velo	Pitch	Grade
91-94	FB	+++
81-83	SL	++++
82-85	CU	++

Year	Lev	Team	W	L	Sv	IP	K	ERA	WHIP	BF/G	OBA	H%	S%	xERA	Ctl	Dom	Cmd	hr/9	BPV
2022	A	Lakeland	3	3	0	42	57	2.99	0.95	15.9	223	33	72	2.45	1.3	12.2	9.5	0.9	203
2022	A+	West Michigan	4	1	0	50	62	3.23	1.10	17.9	237	35	70	2.54	2.0	11.1	5.6	0.4	165
2022	AA	Erie	0	2	0	13	17	8.18	1.89	15.6	361	50	54	6.75	2.7	11.6	4.3	0.7	153

Tall lefty had Tommy John surgery in 2019 and finally made his MiLB debut, holding his own at three different levels. Comes after hitters from low 3/4s arm slot with low-90s FB that tops out at 95 mph with good late sink and boring action vs RHB. High spin SL is best secondary and CU that shows potential. Pounds the zone with good command.

Iriarte,Jairo

SP | **San Diego** | EXP MLB DEBUT: 2025 | H/W: 6-2 160 | FUT: #3 starter | **8D**

Thrws R Age 21
2018 FA (VZ)

Velo	Pitch	Grade
92-96	FB	+++
82-86	SL	++
85-87	CU	++++

Year	Lev	Team	W	L	Sv	IP	K	ERA	WHIP	BF/G	OBA	H%	S%	xERA	Ctl	Dom	Cmd	hr/9	BPV
2021	Rk	ACL Padres	0	1	0	21	25	4.71	1.19	10.5	233	33	58	2.80	3.0	10.7	3.6	0.4	130
2021	A	Lake Elsinore	0	4	0	9	9	27.00	3.44	14.1	496	55	15	17.90	6.0	9.0	1.5	5.0	18
2022	A	Lake Elsinore	4	7	0	91	109	5.14	1.37	18.2	244	32	65	4.21	4.1	10.8	2.6	1.3	100

Intriguing and unheralded SP who has continued to grow into body and add velocity to solid FB. Still room to add durability and weight to frame. FB may be good, but CU is even better. CU thrown with same arm speed and features nifty fade and drop. Tough to make hard contact against. Lack of trustworthy SL needs to be addressed.

Jacob,Alek

RP | **San Diego** | EXP MLB DEBUT: 2023 | H/W: 6-3 190 | FUT: Setup reliever | **6B**

Thrws R Age 24
2021 (16) Gonzaga

Velo	Pitch	Grade
85-89	FB	++
72-75	SL	+++
72-76	CU	+++

Year	Lev	Team	W	L	Sv	IP	K	ERA	WHIP	BF/G	OBA	H%	S%	xERA	Ctl	Dom	Cmd	hr/9	BPV
2021	Rk	ACL Padres	0	0	0	1	3	0.00	2.00	4.8	415	110	100	7.31	0.0	27.0		0.0	504
2021	A	Lake Elsinore	2	0	2	18	26	0.00	0.77	5.4	190	32	100	0.79	1.0	12.9	13.0	0.0	223
2022	A+	Fort Wayne	3	0	0	9	16	0.00	0.44	7.3	136	30	100		0.0	16.0		0.0	306
2022	AA	San Antonio	1	0	2	34	43	1.85	1.09	5.8	219	33	83	2.20	2.6	11.3	4.3	0.3	151
2022	AAA	El Paso	1	1	2	13	18	6.82	1.74	3.8	326	42	68	7.68	3.4	12.3	3.6	2.7	147

Deceptive RP who has spent entire career in bullpen. Attacks hitters with low slot delivery which adds plenty of sink and run to all pitches in mix. Rarely touches 90 mph with FB, but features late sinking action that hitters bury in ground. Very stingy against RHH. Slow, sweeping SL is best pitch while CU is OK and both thrown for strikes.

Jameson,Drey

SP | **Arizona** | EXP MLB DEBUT: 2022 | H/W: 6-0 165 | FUT: #3 starter | **8D**

Thrws R Age 25
2019 (1) Ball St

Velo	Pitch	Grade
94-98	FB	++++
84-86	SL	++++
86-89	CU	++
75-78	CB	++

Year	Lev	Team	W	L	Sv	IP	K	ERA	WHIP	BF/G	OBA	H%	S%	xERA	Ctl	Dom	Cmd	hr/9	BPV
2021	A+	Hillsboro	2	4	0	64	77	3.93	1.22	19.9	249	33	72	3.86	2.5	10.8	4.3	1.3	144
2021	AA	Amarillo	3	2	0	46	68	4.10	1.21	23.3	226	34	70	3.45	3.5	13.3	3.8	1.2	162
2022	AA	Amarillo	2	1	0	18	23	2.47	0.93	17.1	202	31	71	1.37	2.0	11.4	5.8	0.0	169
2022	AAA	Reno	5	12	0	114	109	6.95	1.59	22.8	302	36	58	5.94	3.3	8.6	2.6	1.7	83
2022	MLB	Arizona	3	0	0	24	24	1.49	1.12	23.7	227	29	92	2.87	2.6	9.0	3.4	0.7	109

Hard-throwing, 3/4s RHP pitched well in his big league debut. Shorter-statured, lacks extension in delivery. It's a 5-pitch mix. Throws both variations of FB, both plus offerings, playing up tunnels and angles. SL is best offering with horizontal and late vertical break. CU acts more like 2-seam FB than fading CU. Lacks command of slurvy CB.

Jarvis,Bryce — SP — Arizona
EXP MLB DEBUT: 2024 | H/W: 6-2 195 | FUT: #5 SP/swingman | 6C

Thrws R Age 25	Year	Lev	Team	W	L	Sv	IP	K	ERA	WHIP	BF/G	OBA	H%	S%	xERA	Ctl	Dom	Cmd	hr/9	BPV
2020 (1) Duke	2020	NCAA	Duke	3	1	0	27	40	0.67	0.48	22.3	126	23	85		0.7	13.3	20.0	0.0	240
93-95 FB ++	2021	Rk	ACL DBacks	0	0	0	3	7	0.00	0.33	9.5	106	41	100		0.0	21.0		0.0	396
84-86 SL +++	2021	A+	Hillsboro	1	2	0	37	42	3.64	1.16	21.1	223	29	72	3.11	3.2	10.2	3.2	1.0	116
85-87 CU +++	2021	AA	Amarillo	1	2	0	35	40	5.66	1.40	18.5	245	29	66	5.02	4.4	10.3	2.4	2.1	85
78-81 CB +++	2022	AA	Amarillo	3	6	0	106	110	8.31	1.89	20.0	320	38	59	7.58	5.1	9.3	1.8	2.3	49

Former 1st rd pick had one of the worst statistical seasons in baseball last season. Arm slot has dropped since pro debut, playing down arsenal. Arm-side running FB has solid ride but is easy to identify out of delivery. Two-plane breaking SL is best offering with tight spin profile. Fading CU has chance to be whiff maker. CB changes eye levels.

Jensen,Ryan — SP — Chicago (N)
EXP MLB DEBUT: 2023 | H/W: 6-0 190 | FUT: Setup reliever | 7D

Thrws R Age 25	Year	Lev	Team	W	L	Sv	IP	K	ERA	WHIP	BF/G	OBA	H%	S%	xERA	Ctl	Dom	Cmd	hr/9	BPV
2019 (1) Fresno St																				
94-96 FB ++++	2019	A-	Eugene	0	0	0	12	19	2.25	1.75	9.1	171	32	86	3.05	10.5	14.3	1.4	0.0	-9
87-90 CB +++	2021	A+	South Bend	2	7	0	62	75	4.50	1.06	15.1	194	25	60	2.69	3.5	10.9	3.1	1.2	120
80-83 SL +++	2021	AA	Tennessee	1	0	0	18	15	3.00	1.17	17.9	216	25	79	3.10	3.5	7.5	2.1	1.0	59
88-90 CU +	2022	AA	Tennessee	2	4	0	59	60	4.26	1.40	14.7	209	27	71	3.37	5.9	9.1	1.5	0.8	22

Added to 40-man roster because of upside. Is a work-in-progress as he tweaks mechanics. Short, athletic hurler has a solid 4-pitch mix highlighted by a plus 2-seam mid-90s fastball that tops at 99 with late sink. Power SL and CB give him two above-average breaking balls, while CU lacks separation and movement. Likely to be moved to a relief role.

Jimenez,Antonio — SP — Tampa Bay
EXP MLB DEBUT: 2025 | H/W: 5-11 145 | FUT: #4 starter | 7E

Thrws L Age 21	Year	Lev	Team	W	L	Sv	IP	K	ERA	WHIP	BF/G	OBA	H%	S%	xERA	Ctl	Dom	Cmd	hr/9	BPV
2018 FA (DR)																				
89-93 FB ++																				
78-80 SL ++++	2021	Rk	FCL Rays	2	0	1	32	44	1.68	0.93	15.1	202	32	83	1.61	2.0	12.3	6.3	0.3	187
79-81 CU +++	2021	A	Charleston	1	1	0	15	20	4.77	1.32	15.6	234	33	67	3.85	4.2	11.9	2.9	1.2	120
	2022	A	Charleston	11	5	0	108	123	3.75	1.36	17.4	239	33	73	3.54	4.2	10.2	2.4	0.7	88

Shorter-statured, low 3/4s LHP enjoyed solid full-season debut. Body has room to grow but is limited due to height. It's a repeatable delivery with below-average extension, hurting his FB especially. 3-pitch arsenal. Best pitch is slower SL with varying break profile. 4-seam FB has flattened approach but limited command. Also throws fading CU.

Jobe,Jackson — SP — Detroit
EXP MLB DEBUT: 2024 | H/W: 6-2 190 | FUT: #1 starter | 9C

Thrws R Age 20	Year	Lev	Team	W	L	Sv	IP	K	ERA	WHIP	BF/G	OBA	H%	S%	xERA	Ctl	Dom	Cmd	hr/9	BPV
2021 (1) HS (TX)																				
94-96 FB ++++																				
79-82 SL +++++																				
80-83 CB +++	2022	A	Lakeland	2	5	0	61	71	4.56	1.37	14.3	255	32	74	4.80	3.7	10.4	2.8	1.8	107
86-89 CU +++	2022	A+	West Michigan	2	0	0	15	10	1.18	0.99	19.3	189	20	100	2.52	3.0	5.9	2.0	1.2	45

Solid pro debut with elite arsenal, but struggles with command and HR issues. FB sits 94-96 with improved spin, and late life up in the zone. Plus SL remains best offering with high spin and late break resulting in swing-and-miss. Slurvy CB gives him two above-average breaking balls. CU also flashes plus with arm-side sink.

Johnson,M.D. — SP — Miami
EXP MLB DEBUT: 2024 | H/W: 6-5 190 | FUT: Setup reliever | 7D

Thrws R Age 25	Year	Lev	Team	W	L	Sv	IP	K	ERA	WHIP	BF/G	OBA	H%	S%	xERA	Ctl	Dom	Cmd	hr/9	BPV
2019 (6) Dallas Baptist	2019	NCAA	Dallas Baptist	10	2	0	98	110	2.76	1.02	23.5	204	27	78	2.49	2.7	10.1	3.8	0.9	128
89-92 FB ++	2019	A-	Batavia	1	0	0	19	22	4.26	1.68	5.7	282	39	74	4.75	5.2	10.4	2.0	0.5	65
82-84 SL ++++	2021	A	Jupiter	3	4	0	42	48	3.21	1.40	17.8	156	21	79	2.65	7.9	10.3	1.3	0.6	-11
74-76 CB ++++	2021	A+	Beloit	3	4	0	59	59	2.59	1.07	20.9	182	22	82	2.49	4.0	9.0	2.3	1.1	73
82-85 CU ++	2022	A+	Beloit	9	9	0	112	125	3.46	1.04	21.6	220	29	70	2.78	2.3	10.0	4.5	1.0	138

Long, lean over-the-top RHP performed solidly in age-appropriate environment. Quick delivery, doesn't always maintain balance. Has advanced feel for spin with both SL and CB possibly plus offerings. Spike CB is a high spin rate pitch. Maintains tight SL mostly but will sometimes sweep it. Throws FB on downhill trajectory, backing up effectiveness.

Johnson,Seth — SP — Baltimore
EXP MLB DEBUT: 2026 | H/W: 6-1 200 | FUT: Setup reliever | 8E

Thrws R Age 24	Year	Lev	Team	W	L	Sv	IP	K	ERA	WHIP	BF/G	OBA	H%	S%	xERA	Ctl	Dom	Cmd	hr/9	BPV
2019 (1) Campbell																				
94-96 FB ++++	2019	Rk	GCL Rays	0	0	0	10	7	0.00	0.90	7.4	199	25	100	1.29	1.8	6.3	3.5	0.0	83
84-86 SL +++	2019	Rk	Princeton	0	1	0	7	9	5.14	1.57	7.7	336	48	64	4.87	1.3	11.6	9.0	0.0	192
76-78 CB ++	2021	A	Charleston	6	6	0	93	115	2.90	1.28	16.6	247	35	79	3.42	3.2	11.1	3.5	0.7	132
83-85 CU ++	2022	A+	Bowling Green	1	1	0	27	41	3.00	1.26	15.7	232	35	83	3.78	3.7	13.7	3.7	1.3	165

A key piece of the Trey Mancini trade, he underwent Tommy John surgery shortly after and will miss most if not all of 2023. Arsenal highlighted by plus fastball that he can command and get whiffs from. Also throws mid-80s SL for strikes; it's his best secondary. CB/CU lags behind; injury history now points towards a possible bullpen future.

Jones,Jared — SP — Pittsburgh
EXP MLB DEBUT: 2024 | H/W: 6-1 180 | FUT: #3 starter | 8D

Thrws R Age 21	Year	Lev	Team	W	L	Sv	IP	K	ERA	WHIP	BF/G	OBA	H%	S%	xERA	Ctl	Dom	Cmd	hr/9	BPV
2020 (2) HS (CA)																				
93-97 FB ++++																				
81-83 CB ++																				
85-87 SL +++	2021	A	Bradenton	3	6	0	66	103	4.64	1.47	15.7	253	41	69	4.10	4.6	14.0	3.0	0.8	146
85-89 CU ++	2022	A+	Greensboro	5	7	0	122	142	4.64	1.36	19.6	250	32	70	4.36	3.8	10.5	2.8	1.4	105

Live-armed SP who led both SAL and org in Ks. Struggles with consistency and command at times, though has toned down delivery. Excellent athleticism on mound and throws with great arm speed. FB has potential to be double plus and has seen success with hard SL. All pitches exhibit movement, but tough to control.

Joyce,Ben — RP — Los Angeles (A)
EXP MLB DEBUT: 2023 | H/W: 6-5 225 | FUT: Closer | 8E

Thrws R Age 22	Year	Lev	Team	W	L	Sv	IP	K	ERA	WHIP	BF/G	OBA	H%	S%	xERA	Ctl	Dom	Cmd	hr/9	BPV
2022 (3) Tennessee																				
00-102 FB +++++																				
82-84 SL +++																				
	2022	NCAA	Tennessee	2	1	0	32	53	2.24	1.00	4.5	166	26	89	2.40	3.9	14.9	3.8	1.4	179
	2022	AA	Rocket City	1	0	1	13	20	2.08	1.15	4.0	231	40	80	2.25	2.8	13.8	5.0	0.0	192

Hard-throwing, low 3/4s RHP's need for speed captivated the college baseball world. Loose, whippy arm action delivery with solid extension. Exceptional FB sits in triple digits with plus arm-side run. SL can be wildly inconsistent. It's a two-plane breaker with natural horizontal tilt from low 3/4s release point. It flashes plus.

Juan,Jorge — SP — Oakland
EXP MLB DEBUT: 2024 | H/W: 6-8 200 | FUT: Setup reliever | 7D

Thrws R Age 24	Year	Lev	Team	W	L	Sv	IP	K	ERA	WHIP	BF/G	OBA	H%	S%	xERA	Ctl	Dom	Cmd	hr/9	BPV
2017 FA (DR)	2019	Rk	AZL A's Green	1	5	0	33	36	7.34	1.96	12.2	255	35	59	4.90	9.0	9.8	1.1	0.3	-48
94-98 FB ++++	2021	A	Stockton	1	1	0	21	31	3.86	1.05	13.5	202	32	65	2.44	3.0	13.3	4.4	0.9	176
85-87 SL +++	2021	A+	Lansing	0	2	0	5	9	12.12	2.50	13.8	323	47	55	10.20	10.4	15.6	1.5	3.5	18
88-91 CU +	2022	Rk	ACL Athletics	1	0	0	4	8	0.00	0.50	6.6	81	23	100		2.3	18.0	8.0	0.0	281
	2022	A+	Lansing	0	0	0	16	20	5.00	1.11	10.6	180	21	60	3.12	4.4	11.1	2.5	1.7	98

Large-framed SP with significant injury history. Only 47 IP over last two seasons and was on limited pitch count in 2022. Has dazzling FB thrown from steep angle to plate and features electric life. FB enhanced by average command. SL operates as out pitch and wipes out hitters from right side. Lacks CU and likely to move to RP.

Juarez,Victor — SP — Colorado
EXP MLB DEBUT: 2025 | H/W: 6-0 173 | FUT: #4 starter | 7D

Thrws R Age 19	Year	Lev	Team	W	L	Sv	IP	K	ERA	WHIP	BF/G	OBA	H%	S%	xERA	Ctl	Dom	Cmd	hr/9	BPV
2019 FA (MX)																				
89-92 FB ++																				
78-82 SL ++	2021	Rk	DSL Colorado	2	0	0	26	34	0.69	0.65	13.0	130	22	88		2.1	11.7	5.7	0.0	173
76-78 CB +++	2021	Rk	ACL Rockies	0	1	0	10	13	6.30	1.40	14.1	316	42	58	5.78	0.9	11.7	13.0	1.8	204
82-84 CU +	2022	A	Fresno	6	5	0	103	100	4.98	1.31	20.3	260	31	65	4.31	2.9	8.7	3.0	1.3	97

Short RHP out of Mexico looked promising after a strong debut in the DSL, but has failed to duplicate those results. FB sits at 89-92 with good late riding action up in the zone. Upper-70s power CB is his best secondary and can generate swing-and-miss. Solid control, but frequently finds too much of the plate and needs better command in the zone.

Juenger,Hayden — SP — Toronto
EXP MLB DEBUT: 2023 | H/W: 6-0 180 | FUT: #3 starter | 8C

Thrws R Age 22	Year	Lev	Team	W	L	Sv	IP	K	ERA	WHIP	BF/G	OBA	H%	S%	xERA	Ctl	Dom	Cmd	hr/9	BPV
2021 (6) Missouri St	2020	NCAA	Missouri St	1	0	4	9	13	2.00	1.44	4.8	262	42	85	3.40	4.0	13.0	3.3	0.0	144
93-96 FB ++++	2021	NCAA	Missouri St	2	2	6	21	31	3.86	1.24	5.3	252	38	74	3.95	2.6	13.3	5.2	1.3	188
84-87 SL +++	2021	A+	Vancouver	2	0	0	20	34	2.70	0.75	6.5	163	33	60	0.43	1.8	15.3	8.5	0.0	245
83-88 CU +++	2022	AA	New Hampshire	0	5	0	56	67	4.02	1.09	10.9	202	24	73	3.58	3.4	10.8	3.2	1.9	121
	2022	AAA	Buffalo	3	2	2	32	33	3.35	1.21	7.2	202	23	82	3.66	4.5	9.2	2.1	1.7	63

SP in AA before move to bullpen in AAA. Has seen quick ascent up the ladder and takes advantage of stuff that is hard to hit. Every pitch comes out quick and hard, though size and slot could be susceptible to flyballs and HR. Misses bats with both heavy FB and sweeping SL with arm-side run. Likely to return to rotation for 2023.

Junk,Janson — SP — Milwaukee

EXP MLB DEBUT: 2021 | H/W: 6-1 177 | FUT: #5 SP/swingman | 6B

Thrws R Age 27	Year	Lev	Team	W	L	Sv	IP	K	ERA	WHIP	BF/G	OBA	H%	S%	xERA	Ctl	Dom	Cmd	hr/9	BPV
2017 (22) Seattle	2021	AA	Rocket City	2	2	0	27	29	5.31	1.44	23.1	295	36	68	5.46	2.3	9.6	4.1	1.7	129
91-94 FB +++	2021	AA	Somerset	4	1	1	65	68	1.79	0.97	17.6	190	24	88	2.10	2.8	9.4	3.4	0.8	112
80-83 SL ++++	2021	MLB	Los Angeles	0	1	0	16	10	3.91	1.37	16.9	306	30	88	6.54	1.1	5.6	5.0	2.8	88
78-80 CB ++	2022	AAA	Salt Lake	1	7	0	73	69	4.67	1.30	18.8	272	33	66	4.25	2.2	8.5	3.8	1.1	111
87-89 CU ++	2022	MLB	LA Angels	1	1	0	8	11	6.67	1.60	11.9	304	43	58	5.47	3.3	12.2	3.7	1.1	148

High 3/4s RHP struggled in Triple-A despite quality pitch mix, highlighted by FB/SL. Repeatable delivery with solid extension. Acquired in Hunter Renfroe deal with LAA. 4-pitch pitcher. Low-90s 4-seam FB has natural ride and history of strikes. SL breaks on two planes with a late movement profile and plus command. CU is workable MLB offering.

Kauffman,Karl — SP — Colorado

EXP MLB DEBUT: 2023 | H/W: 6-2 200 | FUT: Setup reliever | 7E

Thrws R Age 25	Year	Lev	Team	W	L	Sv	IP	K	ERA	WHIP	BF/G	OBA	H%	S%	xERA	Ctl	Dom	Cmd	hr/9	BPV
2019 (2) Michigan																				
90-93 FB ++	2021	A+	Spokane	1	1	0	9	6	2.97	0.77	16.3	163	20	57	0.57	2.0	5.9	3.0	0.0	71
82-84 SL ++	2021	AA	Hartford	2	11	0	82	65	7.35	2.00	20.8	347	39	66	8.04	4.5	7.1	1.6	2.0	25
83-86 CU ++	2022	AA	Hartford	5	4	0	77	84	4.08	1.36	21.5	246	32	73	3.99	4.0	9.8	2.5	1.0	87
	2022	AAA	Albuquerque	4	5	0	64	60	6.05	1.80	22.7	279	33	69	6.03	6.3	8.4	1.3	1.5	-1

2nd rounder has yet to find sustained success as a pro. Works from 1b side of the mound with simple mechanics, but max effort delivery results in well below-average Cmd. Low-90s 2-seam power sinker is best offering with 4-seamer touching 95. SL and CU are average at best. With improved command, he could still work effectively as a back-end starter.

Kelley,Jared — SP — Chicago (A)

EXP MLB DEBUT: 2024 | H/W: 6-3 230 | FUT: Setup reliever | 7C

Thrws R Age 21	Year	Lev	Team	W	L	Sv	IP	K	ERA	WHIP	BF/G	OBA	H%	S%	xERA	Ctl	Dom	Cmd	hr/9	BPV
2020 (2) HS (TX)																				
93-96 FB +++	2021	Rk	ACL White Sox	0	2	0	2	2	16.36	3.18	6.6	326	19	60	16.48	16.4	8.2	0.5	8.2	-277
85-88 SL ++++	2021	A	Kannapolis	0	5	0	21	25	6.86	2.05	10.2	262	37	64	5.34	9.4	10.7	1.1	0.4	-44
80-84 CU ++	2022	A	Kannapolis	1	4	0	64	59	3.36	1.43	15.2	223	27	79	3.70	5.6	8.3	1.5	0.8	15
	2022	AA	Birmingham	0	2	0	12	12	4.50	1.67	17.9	278	33	78	5.63	5.3	9.0	1.7	1.5	38

Beefy, hard-throwing RHP with plus stuff continues struggle with zone. XXL frame. Struggles finishing on-time during delivery. 3-pitch mix with heavy 2-seam FB usage. It's arm-side heavy boring action entices groundball contact. Short, hard SL is out pitch. Has feel for CU with fade/drop profile. Less than 60% strike rate will push profile to RP.

Kelly,Antoine — SP — Texas

EXP MLB DEBUT: 2025 | H/W: 6-5 205 | FUT: Setup reliever | 7D

Thrws L Age 23	Year	Lev	Team	W	L	Sv	IP	K	ERA	WHIP	BF/G	OBA	H%	S%	xERA	Ctl	Dom	Cmd	hr/9	BPV
2019 (2) Wabash Valley CC	2021	Rk	ACL Brewers Blue	0	0	0	1	0	0.00	0.00	2.8	0	0			0.0	0.0		0.0	18
95-98 FB ++	2021	A	Carolina	0	1	0	17	24	6.88	1.71	11.0	213	35	55	3.43	8.5	12.7	1.5	0.0	18
83-87 SL +++	2021	A+	Wisconsin	0	1	0	1	3	65.45	5.45	9.1	492	97		17.97	24.5	24.5	1.0	0.0	-203
88-90 CU +	2022	A+	Wisconsin	2	4	0	91	119	3.86	1.23	19.4	190	28	69	2.52	5.1	11.8	2.3	0.6	91
	2022	AA	Frisco	0	0	0	18	24	7.42	1.70	11.8	190	31	52	3.15	9.4	11.9	1.3	0.0	-22

Can't seem to stay healthy enough to develop considerable tools. FF licks 98 early but sits at lowest end of band for majority of starts. SL has good two-plane break and his main swing-and-miss offering. CU gets mentioned like he's working on it but tallied just 116 tosses in '22. Modest 12.8% SwK and poor command doesn't inspire rotation future.

Kennedy,Michael — SP — Pittsburgh

EXP MLB DEBUT: 2026 | H/W: 6-1 205 | FUT: #3 starter | 8E

Thrws L Age 18	Year	Lev	Team	W	L	Sv	IP	K	ERA	WHIP	BF/G	OBA	H%	S%	xERA	Ctl	Dom	Cmd	hr/9	BPV
2022 (4) HS (NY)																				
87-93 FB +++																				
78-80 SL +++																				
78-82 CU +++																				

Young, advanced SP who lacks ideal size and projection, but has solid pitch mix with nice feel. Repeats easy delivery which leads to excellent control. Pitches play up due to natural deception. Effectively sequences three pitches and will need to hit spots as FB mostly average. Pitch movement is also key.

Kent,Zak — SP — Texas

EXP MLB DEBUT: 2023 | H/W: 6-3 208 | FUT: #5 SP/swingman | 6C

Thrws R Age 25	Year	Lev	Team	W	L	Sv	IP	K	ERA	WHIP	BF/G	OBA	H%	S%	xERA	Ctl	Dom	Cmd	hr/9	BPV
2019 (9) VMI	2019	A-	Spokane	0	1	0	18	16	5.47	1.77	8.3	329	40	70	6.21	3.5	8.0	2.3	1.0	67
93-97 FB ++	2021	A+	Hickory	6	2	0	60	78	2.85	1.01	16.5	213	31	75	2.41	2.2	11.7	5.2	0.7	168
85-90 SL +++	2021	AA	Frisco	0	4	0	28	39	5.43	1.52	20.4	299	38	76	6.85	2.9	12.4	4.3	2.9	164
79-82 CB ++	2022	AA	Frisco	2	3	0	82	87	4.71	1.37	18.1	264	33	69	4.41	3.3	9.5	2.9	1.2	101
86-90 SP ++	2022	AAA	Round Rock	1	1	0	27	23	1.67	1.11	21.2	183	22	89	2.25	4.3	7.7	1.8	0.7	39

Backend arm kept head above water through high minors and offers swingman viability this season. Throws both a FF and FS in mid 90s but SL almost used more and his best offering. SP and CU also here and everything is roughly fringe-to-average. Will get SP shot but pedestrian SwK might improve with bullpen conversion if he can't hack it every five.

Kerr,Ray — RP — San Diego

EXP MLB DEBUT: 2022 | H/W: 6-3 185 | FUT: Setup reliever | 6B

Thrws L Age 28	Year	Lev	Team	W	L	Sv	IP	K	ERA	WHIP	BF/G	OBA	H%	S%	xERA	Ctl	Dom	Cmd	hr/9	BPV
2017 NDFA (Lassen JC)	2019	AAA	Tacoma	1	0	0	2	2	0.00	0.00	5.9	0	0			0.0	8.6		0.0	172
95-99 FB ++++	2021	AA	Arkansas	2	1	3	28	43	2.87	0.99	4.5	185	30	73	1.89	3.2	13.7	4.3	0.6	179
81-84 SL ++	2021	AAA	Tacoma	0	0	2	11	17	4.09	1.27	3.8	205	36	64	2.23	4.9	13.9	2.8	0.0	136
	2022	AAA	El Paso	5	0	3	44	67	5.10	1.84	4.5	266	42	73	5.20	7.3	13.7	1.9	0.8	66
	2022	MLB	San Diego	0	0	0	5	3	9.00	1.40	3.0	175	15	33	3.99	7.2	5.4	0.8	1.8	-79

Flamethrowing RP who reached SD in 2022 with rest of season in Triple-A. Generates plenty of velocity with minimal effort and athletic delivery. Throws with lower arm slot which gives unique look. Mostly works off FB, but will mix in occasional, late-breaking SL. Struggles to command plate and walks far too many.

Kilian,Caleb — SP — Chicago (N)

EXP MLB DEBUT: 2022 | H/W: 6-4 180 | FUT: #4 starter | 7D

Thrws R Age 25	Year	Lev	Team	W	L	Sv	IP	K	ERA	WHIP	BF/G	OBA	H%	S%	xERA	Ctl	Dom	Cmd	hr/9	BPV
2019 (8) Texas Tech	2021	A+	Eugene	3	0	0	21	32	1.27	0.47	17.4	131	24	70		0.4	13.6	32.0	0.0	251
92-95 FB +++	2021	AA	Richmond	3	2	0	63	64	2.43	0.94	21.5	223	30	74	1.92	1.1	9.1	8.0	0.3	152
87-89 CT ++	2021	AA	Tennessee	1	2	0	15	16	4.14	1.25	15.5	259	31	75	4.58	2.4	9.5	4.0	1.8	125
74-77 CB ++	2022	AAA	Iowa	5	4	0	106	125	4.24	1.57	17.9	265	37	73	4.34	5.0	10.6	2.1	0.6	74
85-86 CU +	2022	MLB	Chicago (N)	0	2	0	11	9	10.54	2.07	18.1	260	33	43	5.01	9.7	7.3	0.8	0.0	-113

Showed improved velocity and made three big-league starts, but improved velo was offset by surprising struggles with command. FB now at 93-95, topping out at 97 and throws a cutter as well. Also mixes in a couple of fringe off-speed pitches with CB and CU, but he works primarily off the heater. Will likely be used in a swing role.

Kindreich,Larson — SP — Texas

EXP MLB DEBUT: 2025 | H/W: 6-4 210 | FUT: #5 SP/swingman | 6C

Thrws L Age 23	Year	Lev	Team	W	L	Sv	IP	K	ERA	WHIP	BF/G	OBA	H%	S%	xERA	Ctl	Dom	Cmd	hr/9	BPV
2021 (8) Biola	2020	NCAA	Biola	3	1	0	30	48	0.00	0.67	20.9	151	29	100	0.09	1.5	14.4	9.6	0.0	237
91-95 FB ++	2021	NCAA	Biola	5	2	0	54	79	3.33	1.19	24.0	220	33	77	3.30	3.5	13.2	3.8	1.2	161
82-85 CU +++	2021	Rk	ACL Rangers	0	0	1	8	18	1.13	1.00	5.1	181	52	88	1.21	3.4	20.3	6.0	0.0	291
77-81 CB +	2022	A	Down East	3	2	0	38	55	2.37	1.18	16.9	189	32	78	1.83	4.7	13.0	2.8	0.0	125
	2022	A+	Hickory	1	1	0	26	36	5.50	1.64	13.0	196	27	69	4.36	8.6	12.4	1.4	1.4	9

Drafted with hopes of developing LHP velocity and stuff, command woes dropped him and remain prominent in profile at 23. FB remains average with CU doing the heavy work and giving him leash to continue to figure things out in a rotation. Without more pitch life, may end up in bullpen where a few more ticks and fringe command is a lesser issue.

Kloffenstein,Adam — SP — Toronto

EXP MLB DEBUT: 2024 | H/W: 6-5 243 | FUT: #4 starter | 7E

Thrws R Age 22	Year	Lev	Team	W	L	Sv	IP	K	ERA	WHIP	BF/G	OBA	H%	S%	xERA	Ctl	Dom	Cmd	hr/9	BPV
2018 (3) HS (TX)																				
90-93 FB +++	2019	A	Vancouver	4	4	0	64	64	2.25	1.09	19.3	206	27	82	2.37	3.2	9.0	2.8	0.6	93
81-84 SL +++	2021	A+	Vancouver	7	7	0	101	107	6.23	1.55	19.2	252	33	59	4.41	5.4	9.5	1.8	0.9	43
78-80 CB ++	2022	A+	Vancouver	0	2	0	26	30	3.81	1.46	18.6	276	36	79	4.97	3.5	10.4	3.0	1.4	111
83-85 CU ++	2022	AA	New Hampshire	2	5	0	86	88	6.07	1.66	20.3	288	36	65	5.53	4.7	9.2	2.0	1.3	57

Tall, durable SP who suffered thru horrific season for 2nd straight year. Finished 2nd in org in K, though has been hit hard due to flat pitches and inability to consistently change speeds. Hasn't developed as much velocity as expected despite large frame. Has potential for 4 average pitches. All hope not lost.

Knack,Landon — SP — Los Angeles (N)

EXP MLB DEBUT: 2024 | H/W: 6-2 220 | FUT: #4 starter | 7D

Thrws R Age 25	Year	Lev	Team	W	L	Sv	IP	K	ERA	WHIP	BF/G	OBA	H%	S%	xERA	Ctl	Dom	Cmd	hr/9	BPV
2020 (2) East Tennessee St																				
93-95 FB +++	2020	NCAA	East Tennessee St	4	0	0	25	51	1.08	0.52	20.9	145	34	91	0.31	0.4	18.4	51.0	0.7	339
85-86 SL +	2021	A+	Great Lakes	5	0	0	39	55	2.53	0.92	14.7	219	34	74	1.95	1.1	12.6	11.0	0.5	214
77-79 CB +	2021	AA	Tulsa	2	1	0	22	27	4.46	0.99	14.1	233	27	69	4.18	1.2	10.9	9.0	2.4	182
81-83 CU +++	2022	AA	Tulsa	2	10	0	64	80	5.05	1.42	16.0	261	36	66	4.39	3.8	11.2	3.0	1.1	118

Struggled to replicate his impressive pro debut. FB velocity ticked up and now sits at 93-95 with some arm-side run, but struggled to consistently keep the pitch in the zone. Above-average CU is the best secondary offering to go along with SL and upper-70s CB. Injury delayed his 2022.

Kopp,Ronan

SP | **Los Angeles (N)** | EXP MLB DEBUT: 2024 | H/W: 6-7 250 | FUT: Setup reliever | **7E**

Thrws L Age 20
2021 (12) South Mtn CC

Velo	Pitch	Grade
94-97	FB	++++
83-86	SL	+++
73-76	CB	+

Year	Lev	Team	W	L	Sv	IP	K	ERA	WHIP	BF/G	OBA	H%	S%	xERA	Ctl	Dom	Cmd	hr/9	BPV
2021	Rk	ACL Dodgers	0	0	0	2	5	0.00	1.50	2.9	262	76	100	3.44	4.5	22.5	5.0	0.0	302
2022	A	Rancho Cuca	5	2	1	57	102	2.83	1.28	9.8	182	36	79	2.40	5.8	16.0	2.8	0.5	150
2022	A+	Great Lakes	0	1	0	4	6	2.14	2.14	6.9	202	34	89	4.40	12.9	12.9	1.0	0.0	-98

Huge framed LH hurler had a breakout full-season debut, punching out almost 16 batters per nine. Spent most of the year working in relief, but did make 11 starts. Plus FB sits at 94-97, topping at 99 with glove-side run and carry up in the zone. SL flashes plus, but needs consistency. Often struggles to find the strike zone and could derail promising upside.

Kopps,Kevin

RP | **San Diego** | EXP MLB DEBUT: 2023 | H/W: 6-0 200 | FUT: Setup reliever | **6B**

Thrws R Age 26
2021 (3) Arkansas

Velo	Pitch	Grade
87-92	FB	++
74-77	CB	++
80-85	CT	++++
82-84	CU	++

Year	Lev	Team	W	L	Sv	IP	K	ERA	WHIP	BF/G	OBA	H%	S%	xERA	Ctl	Dom	Cmd	hr/9	BPV
2021	NCAA	Arkansas	12	1	11	89	131	0.91	0.76	9.7	166	27	94	0.98	1.8	13.2	7.3	0.5	207
2021	Rk	ACL Padres	0	0	0	4	10	2.14	0.95	4.0	202	62	75	1.31	2.1	21.4	10.0	0.0	346
2021	A+	Fort Wayne	1	0	3	8	10	0.00	0.75	3.6	81	14	100		4.5	11.3	2.5	0.0	99
2021	AA	San Antonio	0	0	0	2	2	0.00	0.50	3.3	0	0	100		4.5	9.0	2.0	0.0	59
2022	AA	San Antonio	1	2	4	54	60	4.16	1.44	5.5	224	30	72	3.55	5.7	10.0	1.8	0.7	45

Strong RP who spent entire first pro season in Double-A. Has multiple pitches in repertoire, but mostly works off of dynamite CT that has vicious bite. Commands CT fairly well, but gets into trouble when behind in count. Lacks ideal velocity and CB is well below average. FB command also not up to snuff.

Kouba,Rhett

SP | **Houston** | EXP MLB DEBUT: 2025 | H/W: 6-0 180 | FUT: Setup reliever | **6C**

Thrws R Age 23
2021 (12) Dallas Baptist

Velo	Pitch	Grade
91-94	FB	+++
81-85	SL	++
83-86	CU	++
77-83	CB	++

Year	Lev	Team	W	L	Sv	IP	K	ERA	WHIP	BF/G	OBA	H%	S%	xERA	Ctl	Dom	Cmd	hr/9	BPV
2021	NCAA	Dallas Baptist	6	2	0	74		2.79	1.12	18.3	223	31	78	2.77	2.8	10.6	3.8	0.7	133
2021	Rk	FCL Astros	0	0	0	5	7	5.40	1.40	10.6	299	41	67	5.51	1.8	12.6	7.0	1.8	196
2021	A	Fayetteville	0	0	0	13	13	1.37	0.92	12.2	229	29	91	2.32	0.7	8.9	13.0	0.7	160
2022	A	Fayetteville	1	0	0	15	20	2.40	1.07	14.6	206	31	80	2.31	3.0	12.0	4.0	0.6	153
2022	A+	Asheville	5	3	0	55	65	4.57	1.39	16.6	261	34	71	4.51	3.6	10.6	3.0	1.3	112

RHP pitched well but ran into bad luck in hitter-friendly Asheville. Fiery competitor. Four-pitch mix headlined by FB with feel for spin. Gets good movement on secondaries but struggles to locate them consistently, perhaps due to inconsistent release points in delivery. Sub-60% strand% likely root of high ERA. Best suited for long-relief role.

Kudrna,Ben

SP | **Kansas City** | EXP MLB DEBUT: 2025 | H/W: 6-3 175 | FUT: #3 starter | **8D**

Thrws R Age 20
2021 (2) HS (KS)

Velo	Pitch	Grade
90-94	FB	+++
80-83	SL	++++
82-85	CU	+++

Year	Lev	Team	W	L	Sv	IP	K	ERA	WHIP	BF/G	OBA	H%	S%	xERA	Ctl	Dom	Cmd	hr/9	BPV
2022	A	Columbia	2	5	0	72	61	3.50	1.36	17.7	245	30	74	3.48	4.0	7.6	1.9	0.5	47

Strong-armed RHP pitched well in professional debut; has room to add bulk. Repeatable high 3/4s delivery. Commands 4-seam FB with riding action well. Will need to clean up spin efficiency to reach above-average projection. Tight, short-spinning SL is best pitch. Has feel for CU, flashing solid arm-side run and late plus sink.

Lacy,Asa

SP | **Kansas City** | EXP MLB DEBUT: 2025 | H/W: 6-4 215 | FUT: #3 starter | **8E**

Thrws L Age 23
2020 (1) Texas A&M

Velo	Pitch	Grade
93-96	FB	+++
87-90	SL	++++
84-87	CU	++++

Year	Lev	Team	W	L	Sv	IP	K	ERA	WHIP	BF/G	OBA	H%	S%	xERA	Ctl	Dom	Cmd	hr/9	BPV
2020	NCAA	Texas A&M	3	0	0	24	46	0.75	0.71	21.2	117	29	88		3.0	17.3	5.8	0.0	248
2021	A+	Quad Cities	2	5	0	52	79	5.19	1.58	16.3	219	35	68	3.97	7.1	13.7	1.9	0.9	73
2022	Rk	ACL Royals Blue	1	0	0	8	10	9.00	2.25	10.1	151	19	59	5.17	15.8	11.3	0.7	1.1	-205
2022	AA	NW Arkansas	1	2	0	20	25	11.25	1.85	8.5	138	18	34	3.82	12.6	11.3	0.9	0.9	-120

Hard-thrower continued to struggle with command in injury-plagued season that required Tommy John surgery in July. Has struggled repeating release within 3/4s delivery. 3-pitch arsenal. Touches 98 MPH with FB but missed zone badly. SL is still best pitch with solid gyro spin profile. Scrapped CB. CU features fade and sudden late drop.

Lara,Andry

SP | **Washington** | EXP MLB DEBUT: 2025 | H/W: 6-4 180 | FUT: #3 starter | **7C**

Thrws R Age 20
2019 FA (VZ)

Velo	Pitch	Grade
92-95	FB	+++
82-85	SL	+++
86-89	CU	++

Year	Lev	Team	W	L	Sv	IP	K	ERA	WHIP	BF/G	OBA	H%	S%	xERA	Ctl	Dom	Cmd	hr/9	BPV
2021	Rk	FCL Nationals	3	2	0	39	47	4.59	1.22	17.6	240	32	65	3.66	3.0	10.8	3.6	1.1	132
2021	A	Fredericksburg	0	1	0	8	5	5.49	1.71	18.6	206	18	75	5.48	8.8	5.5	0.6	2.2	-120
2022	A	Fredericksburg	3	8	0	101	105	5.52	1.45	18.8	265	34	62	4.34	3.9	9.3	2.4	0.9	80

Met some bumps in first full season. Even though velocity ticked up a bit, fastball was tough to control, and was hit hard in the zone. Moved from CB to harder SL for his breaking pitch, got whiffs on it but command of it was suspect; still searching for good feel of CU. Athletic, repeatable delivery and young make it too early to write him off.

Leftwich,Jack

SP | **Cleveland** | EXP MLB DEBUT: 2024 | H/W: 6-4 220 | FUT: #4 starter | **7C**

Thrws R Age 24
2021 (7) Florida

Velo	Pitch	Grade
91-94	FB	+++
78-82	SL	++++
85-87	CU	+++

Year	Lev	Team	W	L	Sv	IP	K	ERA	WHIP	BF/G	OBA	H%	S%	xERA	Ctl	Dom	Cmd	hr/9	BPV
2022	A	Lynchburg	4	2	0	60	84	2.40	0.88	15.9	202	33	71	1.37	1.5	12.6	8.4	0.1	204
2022	A+	Lake County	4	0	0	49	56	3.12	0.96	18.5	193	26	70	2.02	2.6	10.3	4.0	0.7	134

Tall, athletic hurler enjoyed success after tweaks to pitch design and delivery. 3-pitch pitcher with better than average command of each pitch. 4-seam FB sits low-90s with solid ride and run. Does well hitting quadrants of zone. Has exceptional feel for deep horizontally breaking SL. It is clearly best pitch. Late-fading CU is solid 3rd pitch.

Legumina,Casey

SP | **Cincinnati** | EXP MLB DEBUT: 2023 | H/W: 6-2 195 | FUT: #4 starter | **7D**

Thrws R Age 25
2019 (8) Gonzaga

Velo	Pitch	Grade
91-95	FB	+++
82-85	SL	+++
77-79	CB	++
	CU	++

Year	Lev	Team	W	L	Sv	IP	K	ERA	WHIP	BF/G	OBA	H%	S%	xERA	Ctl	Dom	Cmd	hr/9	BPV
2021	A	Fort Myers	4	2	0	44	56	3.05	1.02	12.1	199	28	73	2.31	2.9	11.4	4.0	0.8	146
2021	A+	Cedar Rapids	0	0	0	4	7	6.43	1.90	19.8	336	55	63	5.67	4.3	15.0	3.5	0.0	172
2022	A+	Cedar Rapids	0	1	0	13	16	4.12	1.07	17.0	213	32	57	1.84	2.7	11.0	4.0	0.0	142
2022	AA	Wichita	2	5	3	73	76	4.93	1.51	10.5	275	34	71	5.05	3.9	9.4	2.4	1.4	80

Quick-armed pitcher who spent last 2 months in bullpen. Works with deep repertoire and particularly stingy against RHH. Can live in fat part of plate too often and get hit hard. Command needs to improve to stick as SP. Uses quick, clean arm action to produce easy velocity and has SL that would work well in any role.

Leiter,Jack

SP | **Texas** | EXP MLB DEBUT: 2024 | H/W: 6-1 205 | FUT: #2 SP/closer | **9D**

Thrws R Age 22
2021 (1) Vanderbilt

Velo	Pitch	Grade
95-100	FB	++++
85-89	SL	++++
77-83	CB	++
86-90	CU	+

Year	Lev	Team	W	L	Sv	IP	K	ERA	WHIP	BF/G	OBA	H%	S%	xERA	Ctl	Dom	Cmd	hr/9	BPV
2022	AA	Frisco	3	10	0	92	109	5.56	1.56	17.6	253	34	65	4.60	5.5	10.6	1.9	1.1	62

This is why we play the games. Consensus industry Top 50 prospect despite 0 pro IP ended up more raw than anticipated. FB not as crisp, CB and CU really lagged to fringe-average. LHB hit him well. Command also big issue, though SL was a monster and CT manifested late. Enough concerns to question SP future.

Lesko,Dylan

SP | **San Diego** | EXP MLB DEBUT: 2026 | H/W: 6-2 195 | FUT: #1 starter | **9E**

Thrws R Age 19
2022 (1) HS (GA)

Velo	Pitch	Grade
91-95	FB	+++
78-80	CB	+++
81-84	CU	++++

Year	Lev	Team	W	L	Sv	IP	K	ERA	WHIP	BF/G	OBA	H%	S%	xERA	Ctl	Dom	Cmd	hr/9	BPV

Young, projectable arm with as much upside as any in minors. Underwent Tommy John surgery and missed all 2022. When healthy, has three dynamic offerings and all miss bats consistently. Has advanced feel for changing speeds as well as sequencing. Clean, quick arm produces velocity and movement. Locates all pitches for strikes.

Liberatore,Matt

SP | **St. Louis** | EXP MLB DEBUT: 2022 | H/W: 6-4 200 | FUT: #4 starter | **7C**

Thrws L Age 23
2018 (1) HS (AZ)

Velo	Pitch	Grade
92-94	FB	++
86-87	SL	+++
74-77	CB	+++
84-86	CU	+++

Year	Lev	Team	W	L	Sv	IP	K	ERA	WHIP	BF/G	OBA	H%	S%	xERA	Ctl	Dom	Cmd	hr/9	BPV
2018	Rk	GCL Rays	1	2	0	27	32	0.99	0.99	13.0	173	26	89	1.19	3.6	10.6	2.9	0.0	110
2019	A	Bowling Green	6	2	0	78	76	3.11	1.29	20.1	241	32	75	3.00	3.6	8.8	2.5	0.2	79
2021	AAA	Memphis	9	9	0	124	123	4.06	1.26	23.0	260	31	73	4.23	2.4	8.9	3.7	1.4	114
2022	AAA	Memphis	7	9	0	115	116	5.17	1.38	22.0	267	33	65	4.52	3.2	9.1	2.8	1.3	95
2022	MLB	St. Louis	2	2	0	34	28	6.05	1.75	17.4	303	35	67	6.07	4.7	7.4	1.6	1.3	23

Big lefty has taken a step back, both in terms of stuff and results, over the past two years. FB sits at a pedestrian 92-94, but lacks spin or run. Secondary stuff remains above-average highlighted by high spin mid-70 CB and above-average SL and CU. Command is not what it was and struggled with consistency in MLB debut. Still too early to give up.

Lin,Yu-Min — SP — Arizona
EXP MLB DEBUT: 2025 | H/W: 5-11 160 | FUT: #3 starter | 8E

Thrws L Age 19 — 2021 FA (TW)

Velo	Pitch	Grade
88-90	FB	+++
79-82	CU	++++
75-78	SL	+++
73-75	CB	++

Year	Lev	Team	W	L	Sv	IP	K	ERA	WHIP	BF/G	OBA	H%	S%	xERA	Ctl	Dom	Cmd	hr/9	BPV
2022	Rk	ACL Dbacks	0	2	0	23	41	2.35	0.65	11.4	122	27	60		2.3	16.0	6.8	0.0	243
2022	A	Visalia	2	0	0	33	50	2.99	1.42	20.0	249	40	80	3.67	4.4	13.6	3.1	0.5	145

Shorter-statured, deceptive LHP alternates slot, pacing and hesitation to keep hitters off balance. Mostly 3/4s slot. 4-seam FB has solid ride/run profile. Late-fading CU is go to offering. Has tremendous feel and ability to take off from pitch. Sweeping SL lives down with horizontal break profile. 1-to-7 CB is an eye changing pitch.

Little,Luke — SP — Chicago (N)
EXP MLB DEBUT: 2024 | H/W: 6-8 220 | FUT: Setup reliever | 7D

Thrws L Age 22 — 2020 (4) San Jacinto

Velo	Pitch	Grade
94-97	FB	+++++
80-82	SL	++
85-88	CU	+

Year	Lev	Team	W	L	Sv	IP	K	ERA	WHIP	BF/G	OBA	H%	S%	xERA	Ctl	Dom	Cmd	hr/9	BPV
2022	A	Myrtle Beach	1	4	0	52	84	2.93	1.32	10.8	201	37	75	2.30	5.5	14.5	2.6	0.0	130
2022	A+	South Bend	0	1	0	13	17	0.69	0.92	12.2	141	23	92	0.66	4.2	11.8	2.8	0.0	118

Huge JuCo lefty uses his size to generate easy gas and had an impressive full-season debut at Low and High-A. FB sits in the mid-90s and has been clocked at 100 mph. Other offerings lag behind, though low-80s SL shows promise. Will need to find a quality third offering to remain a starter, but has the stuff to be an impact reliever.

Lizarraga,Victor — SP — San Diego
EXP MLB DEBUT: 2025 | H/W: 6-3 180 | FUT: #3 starter | 8D

Thrws R Age 19 — 2021 FA (MX)

Velo	Pitch	Grade
90-94	FB	+++
76-79	CB	++
81-84	CU	+++

Year	Lev	Team	W	L	Sv	IP	K	ERA	WHIP	BF/G	OBA	H%	S%	xERA	Ctl	Dom	Cmd	hr/9	BPV
2021	Rk	ACL Padres	0	4	0	30	35	5.10	1.33	11.3	228	29	66	4.11	4.5	10.5	2.3	1.5	86
2022	A	Lake Elsinore	8	3	0	94	95	3.44	1.29	19.3	247	32	73	3.28	3.3	9.1	2.8	0.5	94

Tall, lean SP who had terrific first full year as pro despite being young for Low-A. Athletic and smooth delivery enhances pitch mix and has potential to throw harder. Command comes and goes, though should get to average in time. FB can be straight, but learning how to manipulate ball. CB and CU both could get to above average status.

Lopez,Jacob — SP — Tampa Bay
EXP MLB DEBUT: 2023 | H/W: 6-4 220 | FUT: Middle reliever | 6C

Thrws L Age 25 — 2018 (26) Coll of Canyons

Velo	Pitch	Grade
90-93	FB	+++
80-85	SL	++++
83-87	CU	+++

Year	Lev	Team	W	L	Sv	IP	K	ERA	WHIP	BF/G	OBA	H%	S%	xERA	Ctl	Dom	Cmd	hr/9	BPV
2018	Rk	AZL Giants O	1	1	0	25	34	1.43	0.96	10.5	203	30	91	2.10	2.2	12.2	5.7	0.7	179
2019	A-	Hudson Valley	2	0	0	15	18	2.40	0.80	18.1	159	20	80	1.68	2.4	10.8	4.5	1.2	148
2019	A-	Salem-Keizer	2	3	0	41	39	3.06	1.17	18.2	261	34	74	3.13	1.5	8.5	5.6	0.4	130
2021	A+	Bowling Green	3	1	2	54	88	2.32	1.05	15.0	207	34	84	2.63	2.8	14.6	5.2	1.0	205
2021	AA	Montgomery	0	0	0	5	8	3.60	0.80	18.1	175	33	50	0.69	1.8	14.4	8.0	0.0	229

Tall, big-bodied LHP missed entire season after 2021 Tommy John surgery. 3/4s slot with repeatable mechanics. Features 4-seam FB with solid carry and late running action. Pairs FB with plus SL that variates between a sweeper and a tighter break. Both produce swings and misses. Has feel for arm-side fading CU, which is effective tool against RHH.

Loutos,Ryan — SP — St. Louis
EXP MLB DEBUT: 2023 | H/W: 6-5 215 | FUT: Setup reliever | 6C

Thrws R Age 24 — 2021 FA (Wash/St. Louis)

Velo	Pitch	Grade
94-96	FB	++++
80-83	SL	++

Year	Lev	Team	W	L	Sv	IP	K	ERA	WHIP	BF/G	OBA	H%	S%	xERA	Ctl	Dom	Cmd	hr/9	BPV
2021	NCAA	Wash U/St. Louis	11	1	1	94	116	1.34	0.83	24.5	199	30	84	1.25	1.1	11.1	9.7	0.2	187
2021	A	Palm Beach	1	2	0	22	26	5.68	1.53	8.1	309	43	59	4.33	2.4	10.5	4.3	0.0	142
2022	A+	Peoria	2	2	4	14	17	3.19	0.99	6.0	217	31	69	2.29	1.9	10.9	5.7	0.6	162
2022	AA	Springfield	1	1	3	22	26	1.63	1.09	5.8	183	28	83	1.54	4.1	10.6	2.6	0.0	99
2022	AAA	Memphis	0	3	2	27	29	6.33	2.07	6.0	366	46	71	7.94	4.0	9.7	2.4	1.3	84

DIII NDFA signed for $20,000 and had a breakout season working mostly in relief and pitching at three different stops. Tall, high 3/4s arm slot and max effort delivery allows him to work north and south. Plus FB sits at 94-96, topping out at 98 along with an improved low-80s SL allows him to miss bats, but struggles with command caught up to him at AAA.

Love,Austin — SP — St. Louis
EXP MLB DEBUT: 2025 | H/W: 6-3 232 | FUT: #5 SP/swingman | 7D

Thrws R Age 24 — 2021 (3) North Carolina

Velo	Pitch	Grade
90-93	FB	++
80-83	CB	++
86-88	SL	+++
85-88	CU	+++

Year	Lev	Team	W	L	Sv	IP	K	ERA	WHIP	BF/G	OBA	H%	S%	xERA	Ctl	Dom	Cmd	hr/9	BPV
2020	NCAA	North Carolina	1	0	1	14	14	6.97	1.34	7.4	216	23	50	4.36	5.1	8.9	1.8	1.9	41
2021	NCAA	North Carolina	10	4	0	102	129	3.71	1.15	23.8	228	32	69	2.97	2.8	11.4	4.0	0.8	147
2021	Rk	FCL Cardinals	0	0	0	5	9	1.80	0.40	3.2	124	16	100	0.83	0.0	16.2		1.8	310
2021	A	Palm Beach	0	0	0	3	4	0.00	0.67	5.2	106	18	100		3.0	12.0	4.0	0.0	153
2022	A+	Peoria	7	12	0	125	151	5.75	1.53	20.9	282	38	63	4.93	3.7	10.9	2.9	1.1	112

Took a huge step back and struggled with an aggressive assignment at A+ after just 2G at A. FB velocity sits at 90-93 as a starter but can regularly get to 96-98 in shorter stints. Also features an above-average power SL, CB, and a potentially plus 85-88 mph CU. That 4-pitch mix can be effective and he did whiff lots, but was doomed by BB and HR.

Lugo,Moises — RP — San Diego
EXP MLB DEBUT: 2023 | H/W: 6-1 185 | FUT: Middle reliever | 7D

Thrws R Age 24 — 2017 FA (DR)

Velo	Pitch	Grade
92-97	FB	++++
81-85	SL	+++

Year	Lev	Team	W	L	Sv	IP	K	ERA	WHIP	BF/G	OBA	H%	S%	xERA	Ctl	Dom	Cmd	hr/9	BPV
2019	A	Fort Wayne	0	1	0	5	3	16.20	2.20	8.4	362	35	22	10.35	5.4	5.4	1.0	3.6	-31
2021	A+	Fort Wayne	4	3	0	75	93	3.48	1.12	17.4	197	27	73	2.79	3.8	11.1	2.9	1.1	115
2021	AA	San Antonio	0	1	0	15	22	1.80	1.27	10.2	206	33	89	2.80	4.8	13.2	2.8	0.6	126
2022	AA	San Antonio	6	0	2	62	85	2.75	1.21	8.9	190	29	79	2.45	4.9	12.3	2.5	0.6	107
2022	AAA	El Paso	2	0	0	10	12	6.24	1.58	4.0	279	35	64	5.68	4.5	10.7	2.4	1.8	90

Converted to RP in 2022 due to two-pitch mix. Both offerings are quite good, particularly explosive FB. Heater exhibits plenty of ride and carry up in zone. Misses bats with both FB and SL, though SL is more of average offering. Doesn't have effective pitch to battle LHH. Control comes and goes.

Mace,Tommy — SP — Cleveland
EXP MLB DEBUT: 2024 | H/W: 6-6 230 | FUT: #5 SP/swingman | 7D

Thrws R Age 24 — 2021 (1) Florida

Velo	Pitch	Grade
90-93	FB	+++
82-85	SL	++++
74-77	CB	++
82-84	CU	+++

Year	Lev	Team	W	L	Sv	IP	K	ERA	WHIP	BF/G	OBA	H%	S%	xERA	Ctl	Dom	Cmd	hr/9	BPV
2022	A+	Lake County	1	5	0	85	75	4.55	1.32	16.0	236	27	70	4.08	4.0	7.9	2.0	1.4	52

Struggled in pro debut. Pro coaching moved arm slot up and changed up FB grip to lackluster results. Throws 4-seam FB with better movement profile than 2-seam FB. Struggled commanding FB. Best secondary remains 2-plane SL, which induces a lot of hitters to chase. CU is a solid 3rd offering with the CB being a distant 4th.

Macko,Adam — SP — Toronto
EXP MLB DEBUT: 2024 | H/W: 6-0 170 | FUT: #3 starter | 8D

Thrws L Age 22 — 2019 (7) HS (AB)

Velo	Pitch	Grade
92-96	FB	+++
72-77	CB	+++
83-85	SL	+++
81-83	CU	++

Year	Lev	Team	W	L	Sv	IP	K	ERA	WHIP	BF/G	OBA	H%	S%	xERA	Ctl	Dom	Cmd	hr/9	BPV
2019	Rk	AZL Mariners	0	3	0	21	31	3.41	1.42	11.2	242	39	76	3.47	4.7	13.2	2.8	0.4	129
2019	A-	Everett	0	0	0	2	1	0.00	0.50	6.6	0	0	100		4.5	4.5	1.0	0.0	-23
2021	A	Modesto	2	2	0	33	56	4.62	1.51	15.9	237	43	67	3.47	5.7	15.2	2.7	0.3	138
2022	A+	Everett	0	2	0	38	60	4.02	1.39	20.1	235	38	73	3.78	4.7	14.2	3.0	0.9	146

Injury-prone SP who hasn't pitched much the last 3 years; ended season in May. Other than fringy CU, has exemplary stuff. Hasn't yet mastered control, but lack of innings plays a role. Can dominate with FB/CB combo. Knows how to vary velocity and angles to keep hitters off guard. Posts very high K rate.

Madden,Ty — SP — Detroit
EXP MLB DEBUT: 2024 | H/W: 6-3 215 | FUT: #3 starter | 8C

Thrws R Age 23 — 2021 (1) Texas

Velo	Pitch	Grade
94-96	FB	+++
84-86	SL	++++
75-78	CB	++
80-83	CU	++

Year	Lev	Team	W	L	Sv	IP	K	ERA	WHIP	BF/G	OBA	H%	S%	xERA	Ctl	Dom	Cmd	hr/9	BPV
2022	A+	West Michigan	6	4	0	87	84	3.10	1.09	17.9	220	27	76	2.97	2.7	8.7	3.2	1.0	102
2022	AA	Erie	2	2	0	35	49	2.81	1.14	19.9	220	30	85	3.52	3.1	12.5	4.1	1.5	161

Reworked high 3/4 arm-slot to a more traditional 3/4 to get more vertical movement on mid-90s FB that now works better up in the zone. Handled the jump to AA with ease. Plus SL is best offering and generates plenty of swing-and-miss. Used CB and CU effectively and four-pitch mix should continue to play.

Maier,Adam — SP — Atlanta
EXP MLB DEBUT: 2025 | H/W: 6-0 203 | FUT: #4 starter | 7D

Thrws R Age 21 — 2022 (7) Oregon

Velo	Pitch	Grade
90-93	FB	+++
80-83	SL	+++
83-85	CU	++

Year	Lev	Team	W	L	Sv	IP	K	ERA	WHIP	BF/G	OBA	H%	S%	xERA	Ctl	Dom	Cmd	hr/9	BPV

Fell in draft due to elbow injury requiring surgery. Repeats 3/4s delivery with above-average arm speed. 3-pitch pitcher. 4-seam FB is mostly an arm-side runner with limited ride. Two-plane SL has above-average potential, especially if tightened up and thrown harder. Feel for changing speeds with CU but lacks movement consistency.

Marceaux,Landon — SP — Los Angeles (A)

EXP MLB DEBUT: 2024 | H/W: 6-0 199 | FUT: #5 SP/swingman | 6B

Thrws R		Age 23	Year	Lev	Team	W	L	Sv	IP	K	ERA	WHIP	BF/G	OBA	H%	S%	xERA	Ctl	Dom	Cmd	hr/9	BPV
2021 (3) LSU			2020	NCAA	LSU	2	0	0	23	22	2.73	1.13	22.8	226	28	79	2.90	2.7	8.6	3.1	0.8	99
90-93	FB	+++	2021	NCAA	LSU	7	7	0	102	116	2.55	1.15	22.6	242	33	81	3.09	2.3	10.2	4.5	0.7	140
83-85	SL	+++	2021	Rk	ACL Angels	0	1	0	3	6	16.88	2.19	8.0	437	70	14	8.38	0.0	16.9		0.0	322
80-82	CB	+++	2022	A+	Tri-City	4	5	0	85	69	2.65	0.92	19.9	211	26	73	1.97	1.5	7.3	4.9	0.5	109
84-87	CU	+++	2022	AA	Rocket City	0	1	0	5	4	8.65	1.54	11.3	290	32	43	5.73	3.5	6.9	2.0	1.7	49

Pitchability high 3/4s RHP put together solid results in High-A. Repeatable, high 3/4s slot delivery. 2-seam FB is workhorse offering with arm-side bore. Mixes in 4-seam to keep hitters off balance. SL is best pitch with above-average potential. CB was most effective pitch but lacks upper level whiff markers. Solid CU with inconsistent tumble.

Marsh,Alec — SP — Kansas City

EXP MLB DEBUT: 2023 | H/W: 6-2 220 | FUT: #4 starter | 7C

Thrws R		Age 24	Year	Lev	Team	W	L	Sv	IP	K	ERA	WHIP	BF/G	OBA	H%	S%	xERA	Ctl	Dom	Cmd	hr/9	BPV
2019 (2) Arizona St			2019	NCAA	Arizona St	9	4	0	101	99	3.47	1.26	24.2	242	30	76	3.62	3.2	8.8	2.8	1.0	90
92-95	FB	+++	2019	Rk	Idaho Falls	0	1	0	33	38	4.08	1.03	9.8	243	31	66	3.40	1.1	10.3	9.5	1.4	175
86-90	SL	++++	2021	AA	NW Arkansas	1	3	0	25	42	5.02	1.31	17.3	220	36	66	3.86	4.7	15.1	3.2	1.4	163
77-80	CB	++	2022	AA	NW Arkansas	1	15	0	114	147	7.34	1.67	20.5	299	39	60	6.52	4.3	11.6	2.7	2.1	112
85-87	CU	+++	2022	AAA	Omaha	1	1	0	10	9	1.80	1.00	19.1	151	17	89	1.84	4.5	8.1	1.8	0.9	42

Projectable mid-rotation SP returned from '21 arm trouble to post terrible season in Double-A. 3/4s delivery. 4-pitch pitcher; lost release point at times in '22 and struggled to command riding 4-seam FB. Bad in-zone FB command contributed to alarming HR rate. Gyro SL most consistent offering, contributing to high whiff and high called strike rate.

Martin,Trevor — RP — Tampa Bay

EXP MLB DEBUT: 2025 | H/W: 6-5 238 | FUT: Setup reliever | 7D

Thrws R		Age 22	Year	Lev	Team	W	L	Sv	IP	K	ERA	WHIP	BF/G	OBA	H%	S%	xERA	Ctl	Dom	Cmd	hr/9	BPV
2022 (3) Oklahoma St																						
92-95	FB	+++																				
82-85	SL	+++																				
76-80	CB	++	2022	NCAA	Oklahoma St	4	3	9	47	79	4.78	1.32	6.5	231	35	73	4.63	4.2	15.1	3.6	2.1	176
			2022	Rk	FCL Rays	0	0	0	1	2	0.00	2.00	4.8	262	55	100	4.75	9.0	18.0	2.0	0.0	99

Big-bodied, hard-throwing RHP was taken in 3rd round of 2022 draft. College closer. 3/4s delivery with solid extension. Primarily, two-pitch RP. Low-to-mid 90s FB has above-average ride with plus control. Lost SL early in 2022 season. It has solid two-plane depth and movement. Doesn't have feel for CU. Rumors swirl for possible SP conversion.

Mata,Bryan — SP — Boston

EXP MLB DEBUT: 2023 | H/W: 6-3 238 | FUT: #3 starter | 8D

Thrws R		Age 23	Year	Lev	Team	W	L	Sv	IP	K	ERA	WHIP	BF/G	OBA	H%	S%	xERA	Ctl	Dom	Cmd	hr/9	BPV
2016 FA (VZ)			2019	AA	Portland	4	6	0	53	59	5.08	1.47	20.7	265	35	67	4.47	4.1	10.0	2.5	1.0	88
93-98	FB	++++	2022	A	Salem	0	0	0	2	2	0.00	1.00	7.6	0	0	100		9.0	9.0	1.0	0.0	-63
78-81	CB	++	2022	A+	Greenville	0	1	0	9	15	4.00	1.33	12.5	191	33	73	3.15	6.0	15.0	2.5	1.0	126
85-87	SL	+++	2022	AA	Portland	5	2	0	48	58	1.87	1.20	19.4	205	28	89	2.78	4.3	10.8	2.5	0.7	97
84-86	CU	+++	2022	AAA	Worcester	2	0	0	23	30	3.51	1.47	19.8	226	35	74	3.01	5.8	11.7	2.0	0.0	71

Big, durable SP who returned after missing all 2021 due to Tommy John surgery. Hasn't pitched since 2019. Performed well, but walk rate concerning. Has electric offerings when healthy led by dazzling FB with crazy sink. Induces GB and can fan hitters with hard SL. Health history is iffy, yet could be solid mid rotation guy.

Mattison,Tyler — RP — Detroit

EXP MLB DEBUT: 2024 | H/W: 6-4 235 | FUT: Setup reliever | 7D

Thrws R		Age 23	Year	Lev	Team	W	L	Sv	IP	K	ERA	WHIP	BF/G	OBA	H%	S%	xERA	Ctl	Dom	Cmd	hr/9	BPV
2021 (4) Bryant																						
93-95	FB	+++																				
84-87	CB	++																				
84-86	SL	+	2022	Rk	FCL Tigers East	0	1	1	7	8	1.29	0.86	8.6	168	25	83	0.80	2.6	10.3	4.0	0.0	134
84-86	CU	+++	2022	A	Lakeland	7	0	1	32	46	5.31	1.30	5.5	216	34	58	2.98	4.8	12.9	2.7	0.6	121

Imposing reliever is better than numbers indicate. Uses strong lower half and quick arm action to rush his FB in at the mid-90s, topping out at 97 mph with some arm-side run, but high 3/4 arm slot limits spin and deception. Mid-80s CU is best secondary offering and will mix in SL/CT and CB, both of which are fringe at best. Struggles with control.

Mautz,Brycen — SP — St. Louis

EXP MLB DEBUT: 2025 | H/W: 6-3 190 | FUT: #5 SP/swingman | 7D

Thrws L		Age 21	Year	Lev	Team	W	L	Sv	IP	K	ERA	WHIP	BF/G	OBA	H%	S%	xERA	Ctl	Dom	Cmd	hr/9	BPV
2022 (2) San Diego																						
92-94	FB	+++																				
80-83	SL	++																				
84-86	CU	+																				

Attacks hitters from a deceptive low 3/4s arm slot that allows his 92-94 mph FB to play up. Heater has good sink and run and misses bats. Worked both as a starter and reliever in college and can hit 97 in shorter stints. Low-80s SL is best secondary, while CU is below-average. Will need to develop a viable 3rd offering to remain in a SP role.

Mazur,Adam — SP — San Diego

EXP MLB DEBUT: 2024 | H/W: 6-2 180 | FUT: #3 starter | 8C

Thrws R		Age 21	Year	Lev	Team	W	L	Sv	IP	K	ERA	WHIP	BF/G	OBA	H%	S%	xERA	Ctl	Dom	Cmd	hr/9	BPV
2022 (2) Iowa																						
91-96	FB	+++																				
75-80	CB	+++																				
81-85	SL	++++																				
81-84	CU	+++																				

Quick-armed hurler with clean, athletic delivery. Knows how to pitch and has excellent control of deep pitch mix. SL can be outstanding with velocity and vicious, late break. Throws strikes with FB and can get hitters to chase two breakers. CU is already good, but has tendency to slow arm. Good ability now with projection.

McCambley,Zach — SP — Miami

EXP MLB DEBUT: 2023 | H/W: 6-2 220 | FUT: Middle reliever | 6C

Thrws R		Age 23	Year	Lev	Team	W	L	Sv	IP	K	ERA	WHIP	BF/G	OBA	H%	S%	xERA	Ctl	Dom	Cmd	hr/9	BPV
2020 (3) Coastal Carolina																						
91-94	FB	+++	2020	NCAA	Coastal Carolina	3	1	0	25	32	1.80	1.08	24.4	221	32	88	2.64	2.5	11.5	4.6	0.7	157
78-81	SL	+++	2021	A+	Beloit	2	4	0	57	73	3.79	1.02	19.9	244	32	71	3.59	0.9	11.5	12.2	1.6	200
84-87	CU	++	2021	AA	Pensacola	1	6	0	40	47	5.18	1.53	19.3	267	31	76	6.02	4.5	10.6	2.4	2.5	87
			2022	AA	Pensacola	6	8	0	94	101	5.65	1.44	21.1	238	30	62	4.18	5.0	9.7	1.9	1.1	58

Solid 3/4s RHP continues to struggle with high walk rate. Struggles flying open and repeating delivery. 3-pitch pitcher. 4-seam FB has solid ride up in zone. It is poorly located and could play up in shorter spirts. Tight SL is best secondary. Even when doesn't hold onto tightness, SL gets whiffs. Armside fading CU has too much hump.

McDermott,Chayce — SP — Baltimore

EXP MLB DEBUT: 2024 | H/W: 6-3 197 | FUT: Setup reliever | 7D

Thrws R		Age 24	Year	Lev	Team	W	L	Sv	IP	K	ERA	WHIP	BF/G	OBA	H%	S%	xERA	Ctl	Dom	Cmd	hr/9	BPV
2021 (4) Ball St			2021	Rk	FCL Astros	0	0	0	3	7	0.00	0.67	10.5	106	41	100		3.0	21.0	7.0	0.0	315
92-95	FB	+++	2021	A	Fayetteville	0	0	0	18	33	3.48	1.16	12.0	177	31	78	3.01	5.0	16.4	3.3	1.5	179
82-84	SL	+++	2022	A+	Aberdeen	0	1	0	5	10	3.60	0.80	9.1	175	33	67	2.35	1.8	18.0	10.0	1.8	293
75-78	CB	++	2022	A+	Asheville	6	1	0	72	114	5.50	1.39	15.9	219	35	62	3.75	5.4	14.3	2.7	1.1	129
85-87	CU	+	2022	AA	Bowie	1	1	0	26	36	6.18	1.41	18.5	187	21	63	4.65	6.9	12.4	1.8	2.4	55

Well-framed RHP throws hard, but consistently poor ball% across his arsenal limits his upside. Both SL and CB are good for whiffs, chases and Ks, but struggles to get strike one. SL has moved past CB as most effective breaker; rarely throws CU. Traded from HOU for Mancini; may be time to limit his offerings and try him in relief.

McDougal,Tanner — SP — Chicago (A)

EXP MLB DEBUT: 2026 | H/W: 6-5 185 | FUT: #5 SP/swingman | 7E

Thrws R		Age 20	Year	Lev	Team	W	L	Sv	IP	K	ERA	WHIP	BF/G	OBA	H%	S%	xERA	Ctl	Dom	Cmd	hr/9	BPV
2021 (5) HS (NV)																						
90-95	FB	+++																				
75-79	CB	+++																				
85-89	CU	+++																				
			2021	Rk	ACL White Sox	1	2	0	9	17	9.78	1.63	6.8	278	47	38	5.90	4.9	16.6	3.4	2.0	185

Slim, athletic RHP missed all of '22 after Tommy John surgery. It's a high 3/4s delivery with effort and a noticeable head whack, lending itself to command concerns. 3-pitch pitcher with average-to-above-average potential. 4-seam FB sits low-to-mid 90s with ride. CB is a 12-to-6 tumbler and CU is firm with some fade to it.

McGarry,Griff — SP — Philadelphia

EXP MLB DEBUT: 2023 | H/W: 6-2 190 | FUT: #2 SP/closer | 9C

Thrws R		Age 23	Year	Lev	Team	W	L	Sv	IP	K	ERA	WHIP	BF/G	OBA	H%	S%	xERA	Ctl	Dom	Cmd	hr/9	BPV
2021 (5) Virginia			2021	A	Clearwater	0	0	1	11	22	3.27	1.18	8.8	162	40	69	1.48	5.7	18.0	3.1	0.0	187
94-98	FB	+++++	2021	A+	Jersey Shore	1	0	0	13	21	2.75	1.07	17.0	159	31	71	1.20	4.8	14.4	3.0	0.0	148
82-86	SL	+++	2022	A+	Jersey Shore	3	3	0	46	82	3.90	1.23	15.6	202	36	73	3.17	4.7	16.0	3.4	1.2	179
84-88	CT	++++	2022	AA	Reading	1	3	0	32	39	2.24	1.02	15.5	125	19	78	1.04	5.6	10.9	2.0	0.3	63
79-81	CB		2022	AAA	Lehigh Valley	0	2	0	8	9	9.00	2.00	5.5	237	27	57	6.61	10.1	10.1	1.0	2.3	-73

Took a huge step forward in 2022 in terms of both throwing enough strikes, but also in pitch development. New mid-80s cutter had striking whiff and chase rates; adding to his riding, high-spin FB and developing SL, CB and even CU. The raw, powerful stuff papers over only middling present command, though can also go wrong quickly. About ready.

McGowan,Christian — SP — Philadelphia

EXP MLB DEBUT: 2026 | H/W: 6-3 205 | FUT: #3 starter | 8E

Thrws R Age 23			Year	Lev	Team	W	L	Sv	IP	K	ERA	WHIP	BF/G	OBA	H%	S%	xERA	Ctl	Dom	Cmd	hr/9	BPV
2021 (7) Eastern OK St			2020	NJCA	Eastern OK St	4	0	0	35	58	3.33	0.91	21.8	154	29	61	0.98	3.6	14.9	4.1	0.3	189
92-95	FB	++++	2021	NJCA	Eastern OK St	9	0	0	74	109	2.55	1.28	25.3	238	36	86	3.69	3.6	13.3	3.6	1.1	158
82-85	SL	++	2021	Rk	FCL Phillies	0	0	0	1	3	0.00	0.00	2.8	0	0			0.0	27.0		0.0	504
86-89	CU	+++	2021	A	Clearwater	0	0	0	4	5	0.00	0.75	4.8	151	24	100	0.34	2.3	11.3	5.0	0.0	160
			2022	A+	Jersey Shore	0	1	0	7	7	5.07	1.41	15.0	285	35	67	4.87	2.5	8.9	3.5	1.3	109

Over-slot sign from 2021 draft with great present size and three pitches with at least average potential. It will all need to be reset after early-2022 Tommy John surgery. Pre-injury, two-seamer had downhill plane in the mid-90s; slider flashed good bite, and change-up had some plus characteristics. Command needs work, but raw ingredients are there.

McGreevy,Michael — SP — St. Louis

EXP MLB DEBUT: 2024 | H/W: 6-4 215 | FUT: #5 SP/swingman | 7D

Thrws R Age 22			Year	Lev	Team	W	L	Sv	IP	K	ERA	WHIP	BF/G	OBA	H%	S%	xERA	Ctl	Dom	Cmd	hr/9	BPV
2021 (1) UC Santa Barbara			2021	NCAA	UC Santa Barbara	9	2	0	101	115	2.93	1.19	25.3	276	38	76	3.48	1.0	10.2	10.5	0.5	176
	FB	+++	2021	Rk	FCL Cardinals	0	2	0	1	3	15.00	4.17	4.2	542	91	60	16.36	7.5	22.5	3.0	0.0	221
	SL	+++	2021	A	Palm Beach	0	0	0	6	4	9.00	1.83	5.6	371	41	50	7.63	1.5	6.0	4.0	1.5	86
	CB	++	2022	A+	Peoria	3	1	0	45	41	2.59	1.00	21.5	244	32	73	2.26	0.8	8.2	10.3	0.2	144
	CU	++	2022	AA	Springfield	6	4	0	99	76	4.64	1.36	20.7	281	32	69	4.72	2.4	6.9	2.9	1.3	79

Strike-throwing machine lacks a true swing-and-miss pitch, but an uptick in velocity gives him a chance to work as a back-end starter. Quick tempo and plus command of 4-pitch mix. FB now sits at 90-93 with sink and arm-side run. SL is most heavily used secondary offering and is a tick above average with CB and CU rounding out his arsenal.

McMahon,Chris — SP — Colorado

EXP MLB DEBUT: 2024 | H/W: 6-2 217 | FUT: #4 starter | 6C

Thrws R Age 24			Year	Lev	Team	W	L	Sv	IP	K	ERA	WHIP	BF/G	OBA	H%	S%	xERA	Ctl	Dom	Cmd	hr/9	BPV
2020 (2) Miami																						
88-92	FB	+++	2020	NCAA	Miami	3	0	0	25	38	1.07	0.95	23.8	211	36	88	1.50	1.8	13.6	7.6	0.0	214
77-81	SL	++	2021	A+	Spokane	10	3	0	114	119	4.18	1.32	21.5	270	34	71	4.20	2.5	9.4	3.7	1.0	119
78-82	CU	+++	2022	Rk	ACL Rockies	0	0	0	10	9	2.65	1.96	12.2	371	45	89	7.35	2.6	7.9	3.0	0.9	89
			2022	A+	Spokane	1	0	0	18	16	7.00	1.78	20.7	371	43	64	7.94	1.0	8.0	8.0	2.0	135

Lat injury delayed his 2022 campaign and kept him out of action until late July. Prior to the injury featured a good three-pitch mix highlighted by a 91-95 FB, but velo was down across the board when he returned. Shows good feel for spin on SL and a potentially plus CU that keeps hitters off-balance. Will need to prove he's healthy.

McFarlane,Alex — SP — Philadelphia

EXP MLB DEBUT: 2026 | H/W: 6-4 215 | FUT: #3 starter | 8D

Thrws R Age 21			Year	Lev	Team	W	L	Sv	IP	K	ERA	WHIP	BF/G	OBA	H%	S%	xERA	Ctl	Dom	Cmd	hr/9	BPV
2022 (4) Miami																						
94-97	FB	++++																				
84-87	SL	+++																				
84-86	CU	++	2022	NCAA	Miami	3	2	0	45	68	4.00	1.36	7.0	244	39	71	3.49	4.0	13.6	3.4	0.6	155
			2022	A	Clearwater	0	3	0	8	12	9.00	1.88	12.5	347	51	50	6.86	3.4	13.5	4.0	1.1	170

Mainly a college RP, has enough of a pitch mix and present SP's build that the team is giving him a rotation look. Long arm action contributes to shaky command, but possesses a high-90s sinker with run that doesn't quite miss enough bats, along with a SL and CU that both show promise. Will need to prove he can throw enough strikes.

Medina,Brayan — SP — Minnesota

EXP MLB DEBUT: 2026 | H/W: 6-1 180 | FUT: #3 starter | 8E

Thrws R Age 20			Year	Lev	Team	W	L	Sv	IP	K	ERA	WHIP	BF/G	OBA	H%	S%	xERA	Ctl	Dom	Cmd	hr/9	BPV
2019 FA (VZ)																						
93-96	FB	++++																				
83-87	SL	+++	2021	Rk	DSL Padres	0	2	0	28	42	3.83	1.52	11.1	217	36	74	3.31	6.7	13.4	2.0	0.3	78
86-88	CU	++	2021	Rk	ACL Padres	0	1	0	5	7	18.00	2.80	9.4	438	53	36	15.08	5.4	12.6	2.3	5.4	99
			2022	Rk	FCL Twins	1	0	0	23	24	6.59	1.68	10.4	225	30	58	3.91	7.8	9.3	1.2	0.4	-24

Athletic SP who was acquired from SD in April. Throws with a lot of effort, but has lightning quick arm to produce velocity and late life to FB. Still growing into frame and needs to add good muscle. Can overthrow, leaving FB too straight. Sharp SL is quality secondary offering, but walk rate needs significant improvement.

Medina,Luis — SP — Oakland

EXP MLB DEBUT: 2023 | H/W: 6-1 175 | FUT: #3 starter | 8D

Thrws R Age 23			Year	Lev	Team	W	L	Sv	IP	K	ERA	WHIP	BF/G	OBA	H%	S%	xERA	Ctl	Dom	Cmd	hr/9	BPV
2015 FA (DR)			2019	A+	Tampa	0	0	0	10	12	0.88	0.98	19.4	196	29	90	1.42	2.6	10.6	4.0	0.0	137
96-100	FB	+++++	2021	A+	Hudson Valley	2	1	0	32	50	2.80	1.15	18.3	165	26	82	2.52	5.3	14.0	2.6	1.1	126
81-83	CB	+++	2021	AA	Somerset	4	3	0	73	83	3.69	1.45	20.8	239	32	77	3.94	5.0	10.2	2.0	0.9	66
87-90	CU	++	2022	AA	Midland	1	4	0	20	26	12.03	2.82	16.3	381	51	56	10.08	9.8	11.6	1.2	1.3	-38
			2022	AA	Somerset	4	3	0	72	81	3.38	1.19	17.0	185	26	72	2.31	5.0	10.1	2.0	0.5	65

Live-armed SP acquired from NYY in Montas deal. Repeated AA and got shelled after trade. Elite FB is headliner with velocity and natural cut. Due to erratic delivery, has trouble keeping in zone. Complements heater with hard CB and flat, firm CU. Misses bats with both FB and CB, but will need CU to last as SP. Control will dictate future.

Melean,Alejandro — SP — Toronto

EXP MLB DEBUT: 2024 | H/W: 6-0 175 | FUT: #4 starter | 7D

Thrws R Age 22			Year	Lev	Team	W	L	Sv	IP	K	ERA	WHIP	BF/G	OBA	H%	S%	xERA	Ctl	Dom	Cmd	hr/9	BPV
2017 FA (VZ)			2019	Rk	Bluefield	1	1	0	21	25	5.57	1.67	13.5	252	34	67	4.66	6.4	10.7	1.7	0.9	37
91-95	FB	+++	2021	A	Dunedin	3	5	1	63	75	5.29	1.57	14.6	280	36	70	5.33	4.3	10.7	2.5	1.4	95
80-82	SL	+++	2021	A+	Vancouver	1	1	0	19	17	4.74	1.74	21.6	335	41	74	6.19	2.8	8.1	2.8	0.9	86
81-84	CU	+++	2022	A+	Vancouver	2	1	1	32	35	1.69	0.88	13.1	181	25	85	1.52	2.3	9.8	4.4	0.6	134
			2022	AA	New Hampshire	0	4	0	30	24	5.10	1.43	16.0	235	26	68	4.48	5.1	7.2	1.4	1.5	10

Stout SP who relies more on ability to hit spots than natural stuff. Lives in lower half of zone with sinking FB and tumbling CU. FB has excellent late action that is tough to elevate. CU and SL are two best pitches in mix. Likes to change arm slots and velocities with both. Lacks projection and likely to end up in bullpen.

Melton,Troy — SP — Detroit

EXP MLB DEBUT: 2025 | H/W: 6-4 210 | FUT: #4 starter | 7D

Thrws R Age 22			Year	Lev	Team	W	L	Sv	IP	K	ERA	WHIP	BF/G	OBA	H%	S%	xERA	Ctl	Dom	Cmd	hr/9	BPV
2022 (4) San Diego St																						
92-95	FB	+++																				
84-86	SL	++																				
	CB	++	2022	NCAA	San Diego St	5	2	0	65	67	2.07	1.11	23.2	237	32	81	2.51	2.1	9.3	4.5	0.3	129
86-88	CU	+	2022	A	Lakeland	0	0	0	5	5	0.00	0.60	8.6	175	25	100	0.25	0.0	9.0		0.0	180

Projectable RHP added bulk and reworked his delivery and now features a mid-90s heater that tops out at 97 mph. Improved mechanics also resulted in better command. Mid-80s SL shows potential, but lacks depth and added a CB that has average to above potential. CU is too firm and will need to show more separation to remain a starter.

Mena,Cristian — SP — Chicago (A)

EXP MLB DEBUT: 2024 | H/W: 6-2 170 | FUT: #5 SP/swingman | 7D

Thrws R Age 20			Year	Lev	Team	W	L	Sv	IP	K	ERA	WHIP	BF/G	OBA	H%	S%	xERA	Ctl	Dom	Cmd	hr/9	BPV
2019 FA (DR)																						
90-93	FB	+++	2021	Rk	ACL White Sox	1	4	0	48	62	7.86	1.87	17.4	337	45	59	7.04	3.9	11.6	3.0	1.5	121
83-85	SL	++++	2022	A	Kannapolis	1	2	0	53	66	2.71	1.13	19.1	231	34	76	2.52	2.5	11.2	4.4	0.3	150
80-83	CB	++	2022	A+	Winston-Salem	1	3	0	40	47	4.70	1.52	17.4	256	35	70	4.37	4.9	10.5	2.1	0.9	74
86-88	CU	++	2022	AA	Birmingham	0	1	0	10	13	6.30	1.70	15.1	362	50	63	6.49	0.9	11.7	13.0	0.9	204

High 3/4s RHP with plus SL made it up to Double-A in '22. Repeatable delivery, struggles with consistent FB release point. 4-seam FB has below average spin characteristics and struggles to miss bats and stay in the zone. Plus SL has plus 2-plane break profile; overwhelmingly his best offering. CB works as a solid eye level changer. CU lags behind.

Mercedes,Juan — SP — Seattle

EXP MLB DEBUT: 2024 | H/W: 6-2 190 | FUT: #4 starter | 7D

Thrws R Age 23			Year	Lev	Team	W	L	Sv	IP	K	ERA	WHIP	BF/G	OBA	H%	S%	xERA	Ctl	Dom	Cmd	hr/9	BPV
2017 FA (DR)			2019	A+	Modesto	0	1	0	4	2	2.25	0.75	7.1	210	24	67	1.07	0.0	4.5	####	0.0	99
91-95	FB	+++	2021	A	Modesto	7	4	0	63	88	5.56	1.33	7.7	274	39	60	4.48	2.4	12.6	5.2	1.3	178
82-86	SL	++	2022	A	Modesto	0	1	0	4	7	2.25	1.25	16.3	210	41	80	2.21	4.5	15.8	3.5	0.0	180
77-79	CB	++	2022	A+	Everett	7	8	0	107	124	4.53	1.20	19.6	247	32	66	3.79	2.5	10.4	4.1	1.3	137
82-85	CU	+++	2022	AAA	Tacoma	0	2	0	10	6	6.30	1.80	15.4	332	39	61	5.43	3.6	5.4	1.5	0.0	18

Improving SP who is starting to put entire pitch mix together. Continues to control plate well with all offerings, though FB command still needs work. Has increased K rate in last 2 years by adding more punch to FB and using CU to keep hitters off guard. Uses to breaking balls that aren't consistent. More polish needed.

Mercedes,Manuel — RP — San Francisco

EXP MLB DEBUT: 2025 | H/W: 6-4 190 | FUT: Setup reliever | 8E

Thrws R Age 20			Year	Lev	Team	W	L	Sv	IP	K	ERA	WHIP	BF/G	OBA	H%	S%	xERA	Ctl	Dom	Cmd	hr/9	BPV
2019 FA (DR)																						
93-97	FB	++++																				
82-85	SL	++																				
83-88	CU	+	2021	Rk	ACL Giants O	3	3	0	56	62	5.13	1.53	17.4	278	37	67	4.63	4.0	9.9	2.5	0.8	89
			2022	A	San Jose	4	6	2	80	67	5.16	1.62	14.2	229	27	68	4.20	7.1	7.5	1.1	0.8	-38

Tall, power-armed pitcher who was moved to RP in July. Everything out of hand is hard, highlighted by electric FB with riding life up in zone. FB serves as go-to pitch to get outs. K rate hasn't been that high despite stuff. Needs to find consistency with SL and LHH have field day off off-speed stuff. Struggles with command.

Messick,Parker

SP | Cleveland | EXP MLB DEBUT: 2025 | H/W: 6-0 225 | FUT: #5 SP/swingman | 7D

Thrws L Age 22 — 2022 (2) Florida St

Velo	Pitch	Grade
90-92	FB	+++
81-84	CU	++++
78-81	SL	+++
74-77	CB	++

Year	Lev	Team	W	L	Sv	IP	K	ERA	WHIP	BF/G	OBA	H%	S%	xERA	Ctl	Dom	Cmd	hr/9	BPV

Stocky 2022 draft pick relies more heavily on finesse than stuff. Repeats 3/4s delivery well. It's a 4-pitch mix. The FB sits in the low-90s with plus carry and solid arm-side run. It gets a fair amount of whiffs but mostly sets up his plus CU with solid arm-side run, plus velocity separation and late drop. Both breaking pitches need refinement.

Meyer,Max

SP | Miami | EXP MLB DEBUT: 2022 | H/W: 6-0 196 | FUT: #1 starter | 9D

Thrws R Age 24 — 2020 (1) Minnesota

Velo	Pitch	Grade
94-96	FB	+++
88-90	SL	++++
86-89	CU	++++

Year	Lev	Team	W	L	Sv	IP	K	ERA	WHIP	BF/G	OBA	H%	S%	xERA	Ctl	Dom	Cmd	hr/9	BPV
2021	AA	Pensacola	6	3	0	101	113	2.41	1.23	20.4	228	31	83	3.02	3.6	10.1	2.8	0.6	103
2021	AAA	Jacksonville	0	1	0	10	17	0.90	0.80	18.1	175	31	100	1.53	1.8	15.3	8.5	0.9	245
2022	A	Jupiter	0	0	0	3	4	3.00	0.33	9.5	106	18	0		0.0	12.0		0.0	234
2022	AAA	Jacksonville	3	4	0	58	65	3.72	1.00	18.5	193	26	64	2.16	2.9	10.1	3.4	0.8	120
2022	MLB	Miami	0	1	0	6	6	7.50	1.50	13.0	293	31	57	6.84	3.0	9.0	3.0	3.0	99

Hard-throwing RHP made MLB debut but suffered arm injury, resulting in Tommy John surgery. Athletic, 3/4s delivery; solid extension despite shorter frame. 3-pitch pitcher. 4-seam FB regressed in shape since college. Horizontal breaker has inconsistent command in zone. Short, tight SL is best pitch. Improved feel for CU has added additional plus pitch.

Mikulski,Matt

SP | San Francisco | EXP MLB DEBUT: 2025 | H/W: 6-4 205 | FUT: #4 starter | 7D

Thrws L Age 23 — 2021 (2) Fordham

Velo	Pitch	Grade
89-92	FB	+++
81-83	CB	++
80-84	SL	+++
82-85	CU	++

Year	Lev	Team	W	L	Sv	IP	K	ERA	WHIP	BF/G	OBA	H%	S%	xERA	Ctl	Dom	Cmd	hr/9	BPV
2020	NCAA	Fordham	2	1	0	21	18	1.29	1.33	21.8	243	32	89	2.92	3.9	7.7	2.0	0.0	53
2021	NCAA	Fordham	9	0	0	68	124	1.45	0.82	22.5	131	28	85	0.64	3.6	16.4	4.6	0.4	217
2021	Rk	ACL Giants B	0	0	0	5	5	1.80	1.40	5.3	221	31	86	2.79	5.4	9.0	1.7	0.0	34
2022	A	San Jose	4	5	0	79	96	6.95	1.58	15.8	297	39	57	5.55	3.5	10.9	3.1	1.4	120

Tall, durable SP who had poor year and atrocious August as all offerings regressed. Operates with short arm action which gives him deception, but can't solely rely on secondary stuff. Lost velocity across board and lost confidence in CU, though shows flashes. Needs to refine breaking balls and regain velocity. Still has some upside.

Milbrant,Karson

SP | Miami | EXP MLB DEBUT: 2026 | H/W: 6-2 190 | FUT: #4 starter | 7D

Thrws R Age 18 — 2022 (3) HS (MO)

Velo	Pitch	Grade
89-93	FB	++++
75-77	CB	+++
77-80	SL	++
79-83	CU	+++

Year	Lev	Team	W	L	Sv	IP	K	ERA	WHIP	BF/G	OBA	H%	S%	xERA	Ctl	Dom	Cmd	hr/9	BPV
2022	A	Jupiter	0	0	0	2	1	9.00	1.50	8.6	262	30	33	3.62	4.5	4.5	1.0	0.0	-23

Athletic 3/4s RHP has frame with room to add 15-20 pounds of bulk. Repeats delivery with solid extension well. 4-pitch pitcher. 4-seam FB features plus carry, consistently on flatter plane. 11-to-5 CB has late vertical break and could be above-average offering. Has a feel for CU. Sweepy SL lacks consistency.

Miller,Bobby

SP | Los Angeles (N) | EXP MLB DEBUT: 2023 | H/W: 6-5 220 | FUT: #1 starter | 9C

Thrws R Age 24 — 2020 (1) Louisville

Velo	Pitch	Grade
97-98	FB	+++++
86-88	SL	++++
80-82	CB	++
85-87	CU	++++

Year	Lev	Team	W	L	Sv	IP	K	ERA	WHIP	BF/G	OBA	H%	S%	xERA	Ctl	Dom	Cmd	hr/9	BPV
2020	NCAA	Louisville	2	0	0	23	34	2.34	1.04	22.3	187	29	82	2.17	3.5	13.2	3.8	0.8	162
2021	A+	Great Lakes	2	2	0	47	56	1.91	0.87	12.4	185	27	78	1.20	2.1	10.7	5.1	0.2	154
2021	AA	Tulsa	0	0	0	9	14	4.95	1.32	12.6	280	44	64	4.26	2.0	13.8	7.0	1.0	214
2022	AA	Tulsa	6	6	0	91	117	4.45	1.20	18.3	233	33	63	3.15	3.1	11.6	3.8	0.8	144
2022	AAA	Oklahoma City	1	1	0	21	28	3.41	1.09	20.6	222	29	79	3.60	2.6	11.9	4.7	1.7	164

Top arm in a deep LA system and should be up in 2023. Has two plus FB: 4-seamer sits at 97-98, topping out at 102 mph and 2-seamer works in the mid-90s. Also has a plus hard SL at 86-88, a plus CU with late fade and sink, and low-80s CB that show potential. He still needs to harness his full arsenal, but has ideal power pitching frame.

Miller,Bryce

SP | Seattle | EXP MLB DEBUT: 2024 | H/W: 6-2 180 | FUT: #3 starter | 8D

Thrws R Age 24 — 2021 (4) Texas A&M

Velo	Pitch	Grade
92-96	FB	++++
78-80	CB	++
82-85	SL	+++
82-85	CU	++

Year	Lev	Team	W	L	Sv	IP	K	ERA	WHIP	BF/G	OBA	H%	S%	xERA	Ctl	Dom	Cmd	hr/9	BPV
2021	NCAA	Texas A&M	3	2	0	56	70	4.48	1.51	18.7	232	31	74	4.40	5.9	11.2	1.9	1.3	60
2021	A	Modesto	0	0	0	9	15	4.95	1.87	8.5	369	58	71	6.17	2.0	14.8	7.5	0.0	232
2022	A	Modesto	0	0	0	5	3	1.76	1.37	21.4	258	31	86	3.24	3.5	5.3	1.5	0.0	18
2022	A+	Everett	3	3	0	77	99	3.26	1.02	18.5	199	28	71	2.32	2.9	11.5	4.0	0.8	147
2022	AA	Arkansas	4	1	0	50	61	3.23	1.06	19.5	194	28	70	2.08	3.4	10.9	3.2	0.5	123

Consistently good SP who has flown under radar despite high K rate (led the org in Ks). Posted very low oppBA due to plus FB with late movement and hard SL. Hitters have trouble squaring him up. Lack of ability to change speeds could force move to RP. Lot of movement in delivery along with long arm action. Keep an eye on him.

Miller,Erik

RP | San Francisco | EXP MLB DEBUT: 2023 | H/W: 6-5 240 | FUT: Setup reliever | 8E

Thrws L Age 25 — 2019 (4) Stanford

Velo	Pitch	Grade
93-97	FB	+++
86-89	SL	++++
83-86	CU	+++

Year	Lev	Team	W	L	Sv	IP	K	ERA	WHIP	BF/G	OBA	H%	S%	xERA	Ctl	Dom	Cmd	hr/9	BPV
2021	Rk	FCL Phillies	0	0	0	3	2	0.00	1.25	6.5	100	12	100	1.15	8.4	5.6	0.7	0.0	-109
2021	A	Clearwater	0	0	0	5	10	3.46	1.73	11.8	214	46	78	3.46	8.7	17.3	2.0	0.0	96
2021	A+	Jersey Shore	0	0	0	3	4	0.00	1.94	14.7	255	39	100	4.56	8.7	11.6	1.3	0.0	-8
2022	AA	Reading	1	0	0	36	44	2.24	1.16	6.5	197	30	79	1.89	4.2	11.0	2.6	0.0	101
2022	AAA	Lehigh Valley	0	1	0	12	18	7.50	2.33	6.2	293	39	75	8.89	10.5	13.5	1.3	3.0	-23

Injury-prone, big-bodied southpaw was converted to full-time RP mid-2022. Stuff has not been the question; owns a plus velo FB, and two secondaries in SL and CU that get both whiffs and chases. But struggles with command profile that has led to elevated walk rates, which he'll need to overcome in the new role. Also must stay healthy.

Miller,Jacob

SP | Miami | EXP MLB DEBUT: 2026 | H/W: 6-2 180 | FUT: #3 starter | 8E

Thrws R Age 19 — 2022 (2) HS (OH)

Velo	Pitch	Grade
91-94	FB	+++
76-80	CB	++++
80-83	SL	+++
83-85	CU	++

Year	Lev	Team	W	L	Sv	IP	K	ERA	WHIP	BF/G	OBA	H%	S%	xERA	Ctl	Dom	Cmd	hr/9	BPV
2022	Rk	FCL Marlins	0	1	0	3	3	8.44	1.88	5.0	307	33	60	7.83	5.6	8.4	1.5	2.8	18
2022	A	Jupiter	0	1	0	2	3	0.00	0.50	6.6	151	27	100		0.0	13.5		0.0	261

Prep RHP, selected in 2nd round of 2022 draft, made pro debut. Athletic build with lots of room to grow. High 3/4s with solid extension. 4-seam FB has plus ride profile with solid arm-side run profile. Has advanced FB command. Hard SL has tight spin and late vertical break. 12-to-6 CB is best pitch; plus shape/depth.

Miller,Mason

SP | Oakland | EXP MLB DEBUT: 2023 | H/W: 6-5 200 | FUT: #3 starter | 8D

Thrws R Age 24 — 2021 (3) Gardner-Webb

Velo	Pitch	Grade
93-96	FB	++++
80-85	SL	+++
84-86	CU	+

Year	Lev	Team	W	L	Sv	IP	K	ERA	WHIP	BF/G	OBA	H%	S%	xERA	Ctl	Dom	Cmd	hr/9	BPV
2021	NCAA	Gardner-Webb	8	1	0	92	121	3.32	1.12	24.2	219	33	71	2.58	2.9	11.8	4.0	0.6	152
2021	Rk	ACL Athletics	0	1	0	6	9	1.50	1.17	8.0	191	34	86	1.81	4.5	13.5	3.0	0.0	140
2022	Rk	ACL Athletics	0	0	0	2	5	0.00	0.00	5.6	0	0			0.0	22.5		0.0	423
2022	A+	Lansing	0	1	0	7	13	3.86	0.71	8.2	132	23	50	1.21	2.6	16.7	6.5	1.3	249
2022	AAA	Las Vegas	0	1	0	5	7	5.40	1.20	10.1	262	30	75	6.17	1.8	12.6	7.0	3.6	196

Live-armed SP with limited time as pro due to injuries, including shoulder. Can touch triple digits with brute arm strength. Delivery is clean and repeatable. Control quite good for velocity and has SL with potential to be true out pitch at any level. CU has its moments, but can slow arm speed. Would be intriguing RP option if can't prove stamina.

Mills,Zane

SP | St. Louis | EXP MLB DEBUT: 2025 | H/W: 6-4 220 | FUT: #5 SP/swingman | 6C

Thrws R Age 22 — 2021 (4) Washington St

Velo	Pitch	Grade
89-92	FB	+++
80-83	SL	+++
83-85	CU	+++

Year	Lev	Team	W	L	Sv	IP	K	ERA	WHIP	BF/G	OBA	H%	S%	xERA	Ctl	Dom	Cmd	hr/9	BPV
2020	NCAA	Washington St	3	0	0	25	32	1.44	1.00	23.9	175	28	84	1.23	3.6	11.5	3.2	0.0	128
2021	NCAA	Washington St	5	5	0	80	83	4.16	1.35	25.7	276	36	68	3.81	2.5	9.3	3.8	0.4	119
2021	Rk	FCL Cardinals	0	0	0	7	9	1.25	0.56	3.5	165	26	75		0.0	11.3		0.0	221
2022	A	Palm Beach	1	2	0	41	35	3.50	1.24	23.8	275	34	73	3.74	1.5	7.7	5.0	0.7	115
2022	A+	Peoria	4	6	0	102	69	4.05	1.37	22.5	280	32	72	4.36	2.5	6.1	2.5	0.9	61

RHP built like a 3B with good size and a strong frame. Short stride and lacks athleticism, but pounds the strike zone with a solid 3-pitch mix. FB sits in the low-90s, topping out at 94 and he pairs it with an above-average SL and CU. While nothing jumps out as plus, has good command of all three offerings and has easy, repeatable mechanics.

Misiorowski,Jacob

SP | Milwaukee | EXP MLB DEBUT: 2025 | H/W: 6-7 190 | FUT: #2 starter | 9E

Thrws R Age 21 — 2022 (2) Crowder JC

Velo	Pitch	Grade
94-98	FB	++++
85-87	SL	+++
	CU	++

Year	Lev	Team	W	L	Sv	IP	K	ERA	WHIP	BF/G	OBA	H%	S%	xERA	Ctl	Dom	Cmd	hr/9	BPV
2022	NJCA	Crowder	10	0	0	76	136	2.72	1.25	20.6	189	38	78	2.30	5.3	16.1	3.0	0.4	164
2022	A	Carolina	0	0	0	1	3	7.50	6.67	5.7	228	72	88	16.02	52.5	22.5	0.4	0.0	-995

Tall, lean SP with lot of development time ahead. Has ingredients to be frontline SP or back-end RP. FB touches 100+ on gun with plenty of spin and carry up in zone. Gets swings and misses with both plus FB and hard SL. Has yet to feature ideal offspeed pitch and control needs major attention. With velocity and SL, upside abounds.

Mlodzinski,Carmen

SP | Pittsburgh | EXP MLB DEBUT: 2023 | H/W: 6-2 225 | FUT: #4 starter | 7C

Thrws R Age 24
2020 (1) South Carolina

Velo	Pitch	Grade
93-96	FB	+++
81-84	SL	+++
82-85	CU	+++

Year	Lev	Team	W	L	Sv	IP	K	ERA	WHIP	BF/G	OBA	H%	S%	xERA	Ctl	Dom	Cmd	hr/9	BPV
2020	NCAA	South Carolina	2	1	0	25	22	2.87	1.31	25.9	261	31	83	4.12	2.9	7.9	2.8	1.1	83
2021	A+	Greensboro	2	3	0	50	64	3.95	1.30	14.7	242	33	74	3.95	3.6	11.5	3.2	1.3	128
2021	AAA	Indianapolis	0	1	0	2	2	4.50	2.50	10.6	347	45	80	7.42	9.0	9.0	1.0	0.0	-63
2022	AA	Altoona	6	8	0	105	111	4.80	1.42	16.5	269	35	67	4.27	3.4	9.5	2.8	0.9	97

Steady performer who gives unique look to hitters with deceptive delivery and arm action. Peppers strike zone with all pitches, but not a dominant one. Has deep enough mix to thrive in any role and could eventually move to bullpen. Lacks stamina and durability with injury history. Best pitch is FB and has impressive SL with cutting action.

Montes de Oca,Bryce

RP | New York (N) | EXP MLB DEBUT: 2022 | H/W: 6-7 265 | FUT: Setup reliever | 7E

Thrws R Age 26
2018 (9) Missouri

Velo	Pitch	Grade
97-99	FB	++++
91-93	CT	+++
84-86	SL	++++
80-82	CB	+

Year	Lev	Team	W	L	Sv	IP	K	ERA	WHIP	BF/G	OBA	H%	S%	xERA	Ctl	Dom	Cmd	hr/9	BPV
2021	A+	Brooklyn	1	3	6	32	42	4.77	1.53	5.4	196	30	67	3.04	7.6	11.8	1.6	0.3	26
2021	AA	Binghamton	0	0	0	1	5	0.00	0.83	2.2	228		100	1.17	0.0	37.5		0.0	693
2022	AA	Binghamton	1	1	3	17	24	3.16	1.46	5.2	186	31	76	2.50	7.4	12.6	1.7	0.0	46
2022	AAA	Syracuse	2	2	8	34	56	3.44	1.41	4.8	200	38	73	2.51	6.4	14.8	2.3	0.0	113
2022	MLB	New York (N)	0	0	0	3	6	11.61	2.90	5.9	445	72	56	10.37	5.8	17.4	3.0	0.0	175

Tall, XXL frame RHP made MLB debut late in 2022 season. Low 3/4 slot delivery with double-plus extension. Struggles repeating delivery, especially slot. Plus stuff across the board, struggles to play up due to poor command. Throws both 4-seam and 2-seam FB. Sweeping SL is most consistent breaker with plus movement. Angles CT well off FB.

Montgomery,Mason

SP | Tampa Bay | EXP MLB DEBUT: 2024 | H/W: 6-2 195 | FUT: #3 starter | 8D

Thrws L Age 22
2021 (6) Texas Tech

Velo	Pitch	Grade
89-94	FB	++++
83-86	SL	+++
82-84	CU	++

Year	Lev	Team	W	L	Sv	IP	K	ERA	WHIP	BF/G	OBA	H%	S%	xERA	Ctl	Dom	Cmd	hr/9	BPV
2020	NCAA	Texas Tech	3	1	0	18		3.00	1.06	17.4	191	26	72	2.03	3.5	10.0	2.9	0.5	104
2021	NCAA	Texas Tech	5	3	0	63	84	3.84	1.19	18.1	212	30	72	3.19	3.8	12.0	3.1	1.1	130
2021	Rk	FCL Rays	1	0	0	10	20	0.88	0.49	6.8	122	31	80		0.9	17.6	20.0	0.0	312
2022	A+	Bowling Green	3	2	0	69	118	1.82	1.10	16.9	201	36	89	2.46	3.5	15.3	4.4	0.8	199
2022	AA	Montgomery	3	1	0	54	53	2.50	1.04	19.0	208	26	80	2.50	2.7	8.8	3.3	0.8	105

3/4s LHP mowed down batters across 2 levels on back of plus FB. Cross-fire delivery, hides pitch well in hand and body. Repeats well. 4-seam FB has plus carry from lower slot, playing up average velocity to plus. Can add and subtract within FB mph range. Has solid command of two-plane SL. Struggles mimicking FB delivery with CU.

Mooney,Sean

SP | Minnesota | EXP MLB DEBUT: 2024 | H/W: 6-1 200 | FUT: #4 starter | 7D

Thrws R Age 25
2019 (12) St. John's

Velo	Pitch	Grade
90-95	FB	+++
79-82	SL	++
83-84	CT	++
	CU	+++

Year	Lev	Team	W	L	Sv	IP	K	ERA	WHIP	BF/G	OBA	H%	S%	xERA	Ctl	Dom	Cmd	hr/9	BPV
2021	A	Fort Myers	0	1	0	29	52	1.24	1.07	11.3	146	30	90	1.34	5.3	16.1	3.1	0.3	166
2021	A+	Cedar Rapids	0	1	0	13	19	6.23	1.08	16.9	179	28	38	2.10	4.2	13.2	3.2	0.7	143
2022	A+	Cedar Rapids	2	3	0	60	82	3.30	1.25	13.6	210	30	78	3.24	4.5	12.3	2.7	1.1	118

Sleeper SP who posted 2nd highest K% in org. Very tough on RHH with combo on spinning FB and solid CU. FB is rarely straight and effective up in zone. Adept at sequencing and misses bats as a result. Extreme flyballer with sub-par control. Will need to hit spots to be effective at upper levels.

Moore,Andrew

RP | Cincinnati | EXP MLB DEBUT: 2024 | H/W: 6-5 205 | FUT: Closer | 8E

Thrws R Age 23
2021 (14) Chipola JC

Velo	Pitch	Grade
95-98	FB	++++
85-88	SL	++++
79-81	CB	+++

Year	Lev	Team	W	L	Sv	IP	K	ERA	WHIP	BF/G	OBA	H%	S%	xERA	Ctl	Dom	Cmd	hr/9	BPV
2021	Rk	ACL Mariners	0	0	0	1	0	9.00	2.00	4.8	262	26	50	4.93	9.0	0.0	0.0	0.0	-225
2021	A	Modesto	0	1	0	18	16	6.96	1.88	6.5	250	30	63	5.31	8.5	8.0	0.9	1.1	-67
2022	Rk	ACL Reds	0	0	0	0	1	0.00	0.00	0.3	0	0			0.0	90.0		0.0	1638
2022	A	Daytona	0	0	0	9	14	12.86	2.64	8.3	319	49	48	8.17	11.9	13.8	1.2	1.0	-53
2022	A	Modesto	2	1	1	32	58	1.96	1.31	5.3	216	43	83	2.43	4.8	16.3	3.4	0.0	182

Hard-throwing RP-only prospect, acquired from SEA mid-season, blazed low-A with 3 pitch mix. Athletic, low 3/4s delivery. Achieves flat-angled riding profile with 4-seam FB from lower slot. Features two above-average-or-better breakers. A tight, 2-plane breaking SL best the 11-to-5 CB with sweeper break. Over 40% whiff rate with each pitch.

Moore,McKinley

RP | Philadelphia | EXP MLB DEBUT: 2024 | H/W: 6-6 225 | FUT: Middle reliever | 6C

Thrws R Age 24
2019 (14) Arkansas-LR

Velo	Pitch	Grade
95-99	FB	+++
86-88	SL	+++
90-92	CU	++

Year	Lev	Team	W	L	Sv	IP	K	ERA	WHIP	BF/G	OBA	H%	S%	xERA	Ctl	Dom	Cmd	hr/9	BPV
2019	Rk	AZL White Sox	2	1	3	19	27	5.65	1.99	4.6	281	44	68	5.04	8.0	12.7	1.6	0.0	31
2019	Rk	Great Falls	0	0	0	3	5	0.00	0.67	5.2	191	37	100	0.53	0.0	15.0		0.0	288
2021	A	Kannapolis	1	1	6	22	35	4.46	1.44	5.0	223	37	70	3.64	5.7	14.2	2.5	0.8	120
2021	A+	Salem	1	1	3	18	24	4.00	1.44	4.3	272	39	75	4.49	3.5	12.0	3.4	1.0	140
2022	AA	Reading	4	5	0	49	71	4.39	1.54	5.5	265	41	71	4.21	4.8	13.0	2.7	0.5	123

Hard-throwing relief prospect come over in the Adam Haseley trade. Plenty of velocity and carry on his FB, but it can get hit hard. Can locate SL, but doesn't miss many bats with it; CU is firm and lacks separation off fastball. Overall strike-throwing ability is below average which limits his ceiling. Good size but only marginal athleticism.

Morales,Francisco

RP | Philadelphia | EXP MLB DEBUT: 2022 | H/W: 6-4 185 | FUT: Setup reliever | 8D

Thrws R Age 23
2017 FA (VZ)

Velo	Pitch	Grade
93-97	FB	+++
85-88	SL	++++

Year	Lev	Team	W	L	Sv	IP	K	ERA	WHIP	BF/G	OBA	H%	S%	xERA	Ctl	Dom	Cmd	hr/9	BPV
2021	AA	Reading	4	13	0	83	110	6.94	1.64	16.8	245	34	58	4.79	6.5	11.9	1.8	1.2	57
2021	AAA	Lehigh Valley	0	1	0	8	7	0.00	1.59	18.1	206	27	100	3.09	7.7	7.7	1.0	0.0	-51
2022	AA	Reading	2	0	1	30	54	1.50	0.86	4.8	96	23	81	0.04	5.1	16.1	3.2	0.0	171
2022	AAA	Lehigh Valley	3	3	2	20	16	9.80	2.57	5.0	296	36	59	7.22	12.5	7.1	0.6	0.4	-191
2022	MLB	Philadelphia	0	0	1	5	3	7.20	1.60	7.4	124	8	57	3.96	10.8	5.4	0.5	1.8	-176

Moved to full-time relief in 2022 after the organization finally ditched a long search for effective CU. Two-pitch arsenal led by dominant swing-and-miss SL that he threw more than his FB for the first time. Has the physical qualities of a late-inning reliever, but struggles mightily with control, which will be the key to any future success.

Morales,Michael

SP | Seattle | EXP MLB DEBUT: 2025 | H/W: 6-2 205 | FUT: #3 starter | 8E

Thrws R Age 20
2021 (3) HS (PA)

Velo	Pitch	Grade
87-93	FB	+++
77-81	CB	+++
81-83	CU	++

Year	Lev	Team	W	L	Sv	IP	K	ERA	WHIP	BF/G	OBA	H%	S%	xERA	Ctl	Dom	Cmd	hr/9	BPV
2021	Rk	ACL Mariners	0	0	0	1	1	18.00	3.00	5.8	415	52	33	10.01	9.0	9.0	1.0	0.0	-63
2022	A	Modesto	5	7	0	120	125	5.92	1.61	20.4	297	38	64	5.33	3.7	9.4	2.5	1.0	85

Athletic, smooth SP who spent all 2022 in Low-A. Got hit consistently hard all year, but many highlights to build upon. Has clean delivery with repeatable arm action which allow him to pitch with average control. Command should continue to improve in time, particularly as he finds consistency with CB. Needs CU to combat LHH.

Morris,Cody

SP | Cleveland | EXP MLB DEBUT: 2022 | H/W: 6-4 205 | FUT: #3 starter | 8D

Thrws R Age 26
2018 (7) South Carolina

Velo	Pitch	Grade
93-96	FB	+++
87-89	CT	++
80-83	CU	++++
78-81	CB	+++

Year	Lev	Team	W	L	Sv	IP	K	ERA	WHIP	BF/G	OBA	H%	S%	xERA	Ctl	Dom	Cmd	hr/9	BPV
2021	AA	Akron	0	0	0	20	29	1.35	1.05	15.5	199	32	90	2.03	3.2	13.1	4.1	0.5	168
2021	AAA	Columbus	2	2	0	36	52	1.74	1.02	15.5	197	32	83	1.74	3.0	12.9	4.3	0.2	170
2022	Rk	ACL Indians	0	0	0	6	9	0.00	0.67	7.0	191	34	100	0.54	0.0	13.5		0.0	261
2022	AAA	Columbus	0	0	1	15	30	2.38	0.73	8.9	105	19	78	0.89	3.6	17.9	5.0	1.2	243
2022	MLB	Cleveland	1	2	0	23	23	2.33	1.42	14.1	243	30	90	4.22	4.7	8.9	1.9	1.2	53

Promising rookie SP struggled with shoulder injury in spring but pitched for MLB club during pennant chase. Repeatable 3/4s delivery. Flashed plus command of FB, CT & CB in minors. 4-seam FB has an average movement profile with ride and arm-side run. Fading CU with late drop is best whiff inducer. CB is solid eye level changing pitch.

Mozzicato,Frank

SP | Kansas City | EXP MLB DEBUT: 2025 | H/W: 6-3 175 | FUT: #2 starter | 8D

Thrws L Age 19
2021 (1) HS (CT)

Velo	Pitch	Grade
89-92	FB	+++
75-82	CB	++++
83-85	CU	+++

Year	Lev	Team	W	L	Sv	IP	K	ERA	WHIP	BF/G	OBA	H%	S%	xERA	Ctl	Dom	Cmd	hr/9	BPV
2022	A	Columbia	2	6	0	69	89	4.30	1.54	15.8	220	32	73	3.84	6.7	11.6	1.7	0.8	47

Took to pro strength conditioning and coaching and added strength to frame. 4-seam FB velocity ticked up 3 mph from 2021 instructs. Repeatable, low 3/4s delivery. Struggled to command 3-pitch mix in debut. Flat-angled FB features late ride and arm-side run. 1-to-7 CB is best pitch, especially diving towards RHH leg. Has feel for CU.

Mule,Nazier

SP | Chicago (N) | EXP MLB DEBUT: 2026 | H/W: 6-3 210 | FUT: #2 SP/closer | 8E

Thrws R Age 18
2022 (4) HS (NJ)

Velo	Pitch	Grade
94-96	FB	++++
80-83	SL	++
	CU	+

Year	Lev	Team	W	L	Sv	IP	K	ERA	WHIP	BF/G	OBA	H%	S%	xERA	Ctl	Dom	Cmd	hr/9	BPV

Two-way prep player was drafted by the Cubs as a RHP but has yet to make his pro debut due to a sore arm. A bit of a project on the mound, has a plus mid-90s FB that was clocked at 100 last summer. Low-80s SL and nascent CU need refinement, but flash potential. Athletic frame and played SS in HS with good speed and good bat-to-ball skills.

Muller,Kyle — SP — Oakland

EXP MLB DEBUT: 2021 | H/W: 6-7 250 | FUT: Setup reliever | **7A**

Thrws L Age 25 — 2016 (2) HS (TX)

Velo	Pitch	Grade
93-95	FB	++++
85-87	SL	++++
79-82	CB	+++
87-89	CU	++

Year	Lev	Team	W	L	Sv	IP	K	ERA	WHIP	BF/G	OBA	H%	S%	xERA	Ctl	Dom	Cmd	hr/9	BPV
2019	AA	Mississippi	7	6	0	111	120	3.16	1.34	21.0	205	28	76	2.82	5.5	9.7	1.8	0.4	44
2021	AAA	Gwinnett	5	4	0	79	93	3.41	1.36	19.5	228	30	79	3.73	4.8	10.6	2.2	1.0	79
2021	MLB	Atlanta	2	4	0	36	37	4.23	1.27	16.5	203	27	66	2.71	5.0	9.2	1.9	0.5	49
2022	AAA	Gwinnett	6	8	0	134	159	3.42	1.18	23.4	239	32	74	3.35	2.7	10.7	4.0	0.9	138
2022	MLB	Atlanta	1	1	0	12	12	8.18	1.74	18.4	276	33	53	5.77	6.0	8.9	1.5	1.5	18

Big-bodied, imposing LHP made cameo in the big leagues in route to a solid 2022. Repeatable, 3/4s delivery with plus extension. Improved strike throwing ability with mid-90s 4-seam FB. A hard, tightly spun 2-plane SL is best secondary with near 40% chase and whiff rate. CB has solid shape with eye-level changing movement. CU is below average.

Munoz,Roddery — SP — Atlanta

EXP MLB DEBUT: 2024 | H/W: 6-2 210 | FUT: Setup reliever | **7D**

Thrws R Age 22 — 2018 FA (DR)

Velo	Pitch	Grade
94-97	FB	++++
88-91	SL	++++
88-91	CU	++

Year	Lev	Team	W	L	Sv	IP	K	ERA	WHIP	BF/G	OBA	H%	S%	xERA	Ctl	Dom	Cmd	hr/9	BPV
2021	A	Augusta	1	2	0	29	33	6.78	1.51	15.8	286	38	54	4.80	3.4	10.2	3.0	0.9	110
2022	A+	Rome	8	4	0	89	105	4.04	1.37	19.6	253	34	73	3.96	3.7	10.6	2.8	0.9	108
2022	AA	Mississippi	0	0	0	11	14	9.82	1.55	16.0	279	35	36	6.21	4.1	11.5	2.8	2.5	114

Hard-throwing 3/4s RHP with wicked SL was added to 40-man roster this off-season. Upright delivery with plus arm speed. Struggles with release point due to longer arm path. FB has plus ride/run profile. Inconsistent control. Tight, hard breaker is plus offering now. Commands SL better than any pitch. Slows arm and alters slot throwing fading CU.

Murphy,Chris — SP — Boston

EXP MLB DEBUT: 2023 | H/W: 6-1 175 | FUT: #4 starter | **7C**

Thrws L Age 24 — 2019 (6) San Diego

Velo	Pitch	Grade
92-95	FB	+++
78-79	CB	++
82-84	SL	+++
80-84	CU	+++

Year	Lev	Team	W	L	Sv	IP	K	ERA	WHIP	BF/G	OBA	H%	S%	xERA	Ctl	Dom	Cmd	hr/9	BPV
2019	A-	Lowell	0	1	0	33		1.09	0.91	12.3	198	27	90	1.52	1.9	9.2	4.9	0.3	133
2021	A+	Greenville	5	3	0	68	81	4.23	1.25	19.8	244	29	78	4.80	3.0	10.7	3.5	2.2	129
2021	AA	Portland	3	2	0	33	47	5.45	1.30	19.4	244	36	59	3.82	3.5	12.8	3.6	1.1	153
2022	AA	Portland	4	5	0	76	91	2.60	1.01	19.5	176	24	77	1.94	3.7	10.7	2.9	0.7	113
2022	AAA	Worcester	3	6	0	75	58	5.51	1.57	22.0	267	31	65	4.74	4.9	7.0	1.4	1.0	10

Deceptive LHP with solid ability to sequence four pitch mix. Lacks knockout offering and can be susceptible to hard contact and HR. Finished 2nd in org in K due to ability to mix and provide difficult angle to plate. Needs to command zone with FB to have success at upper levels. Stingy against LHH which could lead to RP role.

Murphy,Luke — RP — Los Angeles (A)

EXP MLB DEBUT: 2023 | H/W: 6-5 190 | FUT: Setup reliever | **7D**

Thrws R Age 23 — 2021 (4) Vanderbilt

Velo	Pitch	Grade
92-95	FB	++++
82-85	SL	++

Year	Lev	Team	W	L	Sv	IP	K	ERA	WHIP	BF/G	OBA	H%	S%	xERA	Ctl	Dom	Cmd	hr/9	BPV
2020	NCAA	Vanderbilt	0	0	0	2	4	13.50	5.50	4.2	262	55	73	13.57	40.5	18.0	0.4	0.0	-752
2021	NCAA	Vanderbilt	4	1	9	41	61	2.41	0.95	5.7	172	25	85	2.27	3.3	13.4	4.1	1.3	170
2021	A+	Tri-City	0	1	2	9	15	3.00	0.89	4.8	216	40	63	1.39	1.0	15.0	15.0	0.0	261
2022	AA	Rocket City	7	2	1	44	52	2.65	1.15	4.7	167	26	75	1.53	5.3	10.6	2.0	0.0	66

Hard-throwing college RP has struggled to find top velocity since becoming pro. Long-limbed, crossfire 3/4s delivery. Has tendency to fly open, effecting strike rate. Two pitches: FB sits mid-90s, touching 97, with ride and run profile; SL wildly inconsistent, struggles to miss bats. Balls are an issue with both.

Murphy,Owen — SP — Atlanta

EXP MLB DEBUT: 2025 | H/W: 6-1 190 | FUT: #2 starter | **9E**

Thrws R Age 19 — 2022 (1) HS (IL)

Velo	Pitch	Grade
90-94	FB	++++
75-77	CB	++++
82-84	SL	+++
79-81	CU	+

Year	Lev	Team	W	L	Sv	IP	K	ERA	WHIP	BF/G	OBA	H%	S%	xERA	Ctl	Dom	Cmd	hr/9	BPV
2022	Rk	FCL Braves	0	0	0	5	7	0.00	0.40	8.1	124	22	100		0.0	12.6		0.0	245
2022	A	Augusta	0	1	0	7	10	7.71	1.57	10.2	202	34	45	2.96	7.7	12.9	1.7	0.0	41

Two-sport, two-way RHP taken by ATL in 1st round. Athletic build with room to grow. Repeatable 3/4s delivery with solid extension. 4-seam FB has natural ride/run in profile. FB carry is plus-plus. Power CB has 11-to-5 break and misses bats. SL is a short breaker with inconsistent downward finish. Showed CU as prep pitcher but likely not a pro pitch.

Murphy,Ryan — SP — San Francisco

EXP MLB DEBUT: 2024 | H/W: 6-1 190 | FUT: #4 starter | **7C**

Thrws R Age 23 — 2020 (5) Le Moyne

Velo	Pitch	Grade
90-94	FB	+++
78-80	CB	++
82-84	SL	+++
80-85	CU	++

Year	Lev	Team	W	L	Sv	IP	K	ERA	WHIP	BF/G	OBA	H%	S%	xERA	Ctl	Dom	Cmd	hr/9	BPV
2021	A+	Eugene	2	2	0	31	48	1.45	0.68	18.1	129	23	80	0.17	2.3	13.9	6.0	0.3	206
2022	Rk	ACL Giants B	0	0	0	1	0	9.00	2.00	4.8	415	26	100	16.04	0.0	0.0		9.0	18
2022	A	San Jose	0	0	0	1	3	15.00	3.33	7.4	470	84	67	19.09	7.5	22.5	3.0	7.5	221
2022	A+	Eugene	1	0	0	31	47	2.90	1.03	17.1	186	32	71	1.68	3.5	13.6	3.9	0.3	170
2022	AA	Richmond	1	1	0	8	7	9.88	2.32	21.1	280	30	59	7.97	11.0	7.7	0.7	2.2	-140

Aggressive RHP who had limited time after May due to back and elbow issues. Stuff is better than stats indicate, though lacks put-away pitch. Pitches with deceptive slot and angle, but tough to repeat consistently. Lot of spin on average FB gives it good life and uses both SL and CB of varying velocities and shapes.

Mushinski,Parker — RP — Houston

EXP MLB DEBUT: 2022 | H/W: 6-0 218 | FUT: Middle reliever | **6B**

Thrws L Age 27 — 2017 (7) Texas Tech

Velo	Pitch	Grade
89-91	CT	+++
92-94	FB	+++
80-82	CB	++
81-83	SL	++

Year	Lev	Team	W	L	Sv	IP	K	ERA	WHIP	BF/G	OBA	H%	S%	xERA	Ctl	Dom	Cmd	hr/9	BPV
2019	A+	Fayetteville	0	1	1	52	63	3.79	1.21	19.1	242	34	69	3.20	2.8	10.9	3.9	0.7	139
2021	AA	Corpus Christi	0	4	1	52	66	3.80	1.38	14.6	261	38	72	3.74	3.5	11.4	3.3	0.5	130
2021	AAA	Sugar Land	0	0	0	12	18	2.95	1.39	6.4	289	40	93	5.74	2.2	13.3	6.0	2.2	197
2022	AAA	Sugar Land	2	2	0	40	41	2.69	1.17	4.2	198	26	80	2.57	4.3	9.2	2.2	0.7	68
2022	MLB	Houston	0	0	0	7	8	3.80	1.13	4.0	200	29	63	1.84	3.8	10.1	2.7	0.0	98

Lefty reliever rode Triple-A performance to major league debut. Deep pitch mix for reliever, but relies heavily on FB/CT combo with good shape. Some notable effort in delivery confirms bullpen role. Lack of high-end velocity limits strikeout upside but does good job of missing barrels, keeping ball on the ground.

Nastrini,Nick — SP — Los Angeles (N)

EXP MLB DEBUT: 2023 | H/W: 6-3 215 | FUT: #3 starter | **8E**

Thrws R Age 23 — 2021 (4) UCLA

Velo	Pitch	Grade
93-96	FB	++++
84-88	SL	+++
77-80	CB	++
85-87	CU	+

Year	Lev	Team	W	L	Sv	IP	K	ERA	WHIP	BF/G	OBA	H%	S%	xERA	Ctl	Dom	Cmd	hr/9	BPV
2021	NCAA	UCLA	2	2	0	31	48	6.95	1.83	12.1	178	29	61	4.15	11.0	13.9	1.3	0.9	-29
2021	Rk	ACL Dodgers	0	0	0	1	2	0.00	1.00	3.8	262	55	100	2.23	0.0	18.0		0.0	342
2021	A	Rancho Cuca	0	0	0	13	30	2.08	1.00	8.3	141	38	91	2.07	4.8	20.8	4.3	1.4	261
2022	A+	Great Lakes	5	3	0	86	127	3.87	1.16	16.3	201	30	72	3.08	4.1	13.3	3.3	1.3	147
2022	AA	Tulsa	1	1	0	30	42	4.19	1.00	19.1	142	17	64	2.26	4.8	12.6	2.6	1.5	115

Has three potentially above-average pitches including a mid-90s fastball with good carry and life up in the zone, a short slider, and a sweeping curveball. He struggled with control in college and can still be wild (4 BB/9), but on the year posted 3.93 ERA and 169 punchouts in 116.2 IP between High-A and Double-A.

Nelson,Ryne — SP — Arizona

EXP MLB DEBUT: 2022 | H/W: 6-3 184 | FUT: #4 starter | **7B**

Thrws R Age 25 — 2019 (2) Oregon

Velo	Pitch	Grade
92-94	FB	+++
80-83	SL	+++
74-77	CB	++++
80-82	CU	++

Year	Lev	Team	W	L	Sv	IP	K	ERA	WHIP	BF/G	OBA	H%	S%	xERA	Ctl	Dom	Cmd	hr/9	BPV
2019	A-	Hillsboro	0	1	0	18	26	2.97	1.37	7.6	226	36	79	3.22	4.9	12.9	2.6	0.5	116
2021	A+	Hillsboro	4	1	0	39	59	2.53	0.90	18.2	160	26	75	1.43	3.2	13.6	4.2	0.7	175
2021	AA	Amarillo	3	3	0	77	104	3.51	1.19	22.1	233	32	78	3.82	3.0	12.2	4.0	1.5	155
2022	AAA	Reno	10	5	0	136	128	5.43	1.39	22.0	270	31	65	4.97	3.1	8.5	2.7	1.7	86
2022	MLB	Arizona	1	1	0	18	16	1.49	0.83	22.0	150	17	92	1.49	3.0	8.0	2.7	1.0	81

Tall, athletic high 3/4s RHP pitched well in brief MLB stint. Repeatable delivery with plus extension, operates exclusively out of stretch. Flatter plane 4-seam FB sits low 90s plays up due to extension. SL potential plus pitch, especially incorporating late vertical drop. CB changes eye levels well. Fading CU struggles with consistency.

Nicolas,Kyle — SP — Pittsburgh

EXP MLB DEBUT: 2023 | H/W: 6-4 223 | FUT: #4 starter | **7C**

Thrws R Age 24 — 2020 (2) Ball State

Velo	Pitch	Grade
93-96	FB	++++
80-83	CB	++
83-85	SL	+++
83-86	CU	++

Year	Lev	Team	W	L	Sv	IP	K	ERA	WHIP	BF/G	OBA	H%	S%	xERA	Ctl	Dom	Cmd	hr/9	BPV
2020	NCAA	Ball St	0	1	0	23	37	2.74	0.96	21.7	188	33	71	1.60	2.7	14.5	5.3	0.4	205
2021	A+	Beloit	3	2	0	59	86	5.32	1.37	19.1	255	35	68	4.96	3.6	13.1	3.6	2.0	155
2021	AA	Pensacola	3	2	0	39	50	2.53	1.23	19.8	173	25	82	2.42	5.8	11.5	2.0	0.7	70
2022	AA	Altoona	2	4	0	90	101	3.99	1.31	15.5	218	29	72	3.36	4.7	10.1	2.1	0.9	73

Power SP with arm strength and excellent velocity. Repertoire among best in org. FB is best pitch with high spin rate and heavy life. SL can be K pitch, but likes to use CB to keep hitters off guard. Too many flyballs and has trouble with sequencing. May be better off with one breaking ball and enhancing below average CU.

Nikhazy,Doug — SP — Cleveland

EXP MLB DEBUT: 2024 | H/W: 6-0 205 | FUT: #4 starter | **8D**

Thrws L Age 23 — 2021 (2) Mississippi

Velo	Pitch	Grade
90-94	FB	+++
86-88	SL	+++
79-82	CB	+++
82-85	CU	++

Year	Lev	Team	W	L	Sv	IP	K	ERA	WHIP	BF/G	OBA	H%	S%	xERA	Ctl	Dom	Cmd	hr/9	BPV
2022	A+	Lake County	4	4	0	93	118	3.19	1.37	18.5	184	26	79	2.97	6.6	11.4	1.7	0.8	46
2022	AA	Akron	0	2	0	9	10	11.87	2.75	16.9	353	45	54	9.07	10.9	9.9	0.9	1.0	-98

Over-the-top 2021 pick advanced to Double-A after solid High-A campaign. Athletic delivery with solid extension for size. 4-pitch arsenal. 4-seam FB lives up with natural riding action but struggles with strikes. SL is a two-plane breaker, becoming most consistent offering. CB is 12-to-6, high-spin rate pitch that lacks consistency.

Oliveraz,Helcris — SP — Colorado

EXP MLB DEBUT: 2025 | H/W: 6-2 192 | FUT: Setup reliever | 7E

Thrws L Age 22 — 2017 FA (DR)

Velo	Pitch	Grade
93-95	FB	+++
76-79	CB	++
82-84	CU	+

Year	Lev	Team	W	L	Sv	IP	K	ERA	WHIP	BF/G	OBA	H%	S%	xERA	Ctl	Dom	Cmd	hr/9	BPV
2018	Rk	DSL Colorado	2	0	0	19	24	1.42	0.79	17.1	170	27	80	0.64	1.9	11.4	6.0	0.0	171
2018	Rk	DSL Rockies	4	1	0	35	36	2.81	1.34	16.3	201	28	78	2.63	5.6	9.2	1.6	0.3	32
2019	Rk	Grand Junction	3	4	0	46	61	4.87	1.54	18.3	265	35	74	5.33	4.7	11.9	2.5	1.8	106
2021	A+	Spokane	4	9	0	99	112	6.08	1.58	19.9	241	32	61	4.35	6.2	10.2	1.6	0.9	34
2022	Rk	ACL Rockies	0	0	0	2	1	0.00	0.00	5.6	0	0			0.0	4.5		0.0	99

Projectable frame owns a mid-90s FB that touches 97, but missed most of 2022 with a shoulder strain. Coils with a high leg kick and a long stride. High 3/4s arm angle creates downhill tilt, but puts strain on shoulder. Upper-70s CB can generate swing-and-miss action and CU shows potential. At 22, he's likely destined to a relief role.

Olson,Reese — SP — Detroit

EXP MLB DEBUT: 2023 | H/W: 6-1 160 | FUT: #4 starter | 7C

Thrws R Age 23 — 2018 (13) HS (GA)

Velo	Pitch	Grade
93-95	FB	+++
75-77	CB	+++
85-87	SL	+++
	CU	+++

Year	Lev	Team	W	L	Sv	IP	K	ERA	WHIP	BF/G	OBA	H%	S%	xERA	Ctl	Dom	Cmd	hr/9	BPV
2019	A	Wisconsin	4	7	0	94	84	4.68	1.60	15.4	281	35	71	4.84	4.5	8.0	1.8	0.8	41
2021	A+	West Michigan	1	0	0	11	14	0.00	0.73	19.5	162	26	100	0.40	1.6	11.5	7.0	0.0	180
2021	A+	Wisconsin	5	4	0	69	79	4.30	1.35	20.5	230	31	68	3.37	4.6	10.3	2.3	0.7	80
2021	AA	Erie	2	1	0	24	21	4.83	1.32	20.0	209	26	61	2.81	5.2	7.8	1.5	0.4	18
2022	AA	Erie	8	6	0	119	168	4.15	1.23	18.6	245	36	70	3.70	2.9	12.7	4.4	1.1	169

Not the flashiest arm in the system, but gets the job done with four-pitch mix. FB sits at 92-95 with some late life. CB, SL, and CU all profile as above-average offerings, leading to a career K/9 of 10.2. Improved CU and command in 2022 raised his profile, but max-effort delivery has led to inconsistent results in the past.

Ortiz,Luis — SP — Pittsburgh

EXP MLB DEBUT: 2022 | H/W: 6-2 240 | FUT: #3 starter | 8D

Thrws R Age 24 — 2018 FA (DR)

Velo	Pitch	Grade
94-98	FB	++++
83-87	SL	+++
85-88	CU	+

Year	Lev	Team	W	L	Sv	IP	K	ERA	WHIP	BF/G	OBA	H%	S%	xERA	Ctl	Dom	Cmd	hr/9	BPV
2019	Rk	Bristol	2	2	0	50		4.12	1.43	19.4	253	30	72	3.99	4.3	6.6	1.5	0.7	21
2021	A	Bradenton	5	3	0	87	113	3.10	1.26	16.2	250	37	76	3.28	2.9	11.7	4.0	0.5	150
2022	AA	Altoona	5	9	0	114	126	4.65	1.17	19.0	237	29	65	3.83	2.7	9.9	3.7	1.5	124
2022	AAA	Indianapolis	0	0	0	10	12	3.60	0.80	18.1	124	16	57	1.05	3.6	10.8	3.0	0.9	115
2022	MLB	Pittsburgh	0	2	0	16	17	4.50	1.13	15.8	151	20	59	1.83	5.6	9.6	1.7	0.6	38

Large-bodied RHP who reached PIT after exceeding expectations in minors. Was terrific late in season and finished 2nd in org in Ks. Hitters have trouble barreling heavy FB that looks even quicker than mid-to-high 90s. Both FB and SL miss bats and only needs more consistency with SL to be plus offering. CU is distant 3rd pitch.

Orze,Eric — RP — New York (N)

EXP MLB DEBUT: 2023 | H/W: 6-4 195 | FUT: Middle reliever | 6C

Thrws R Age 25 — 2020 (5) New Orleans

Velo	Pitch	Grade
92-94	FB	+++
81-83	SP	++++
83-85	SL	+++

Year	Lev	Team	W	L	Sv	IP	K	ERA	WHIP	BF/G	OBA	H%	S%	xERA	Ctl	Dom	Cmd	hr/9	BPV
2021	A+	Brooklyn	1	2	1	20	26	4.05	1.25	6.3	252	36	70	3.63	2.7	11.7	4.3	0.9	156
2021	AA	Binghamton	2	0	4	17	25	2.63	0.76	5.6	199	30	73	1.87	0.5	13.2	25.0	1.1	241
2021	AAA	Syracuse	1	0	0	12	16	2.23	1.16	4.8	170	25	85	2.26	5.2	11.9	2.3	0.7	92
2022	A	St. Lucie	0	0	0	3	5	0.00	0.67	5.2	191	37	100	0.53	0.0	15.0		0.0	288
2022	AAA	Syracuse	4	3	1	47	64	5.16	1.19	5.9	240	31	64	4.45	2.7	12.2	4.6	2.1	166

Tall, 3/4s RHP with reliever delivery struggled mightily giving up bombs in Triple-A. 3-pitch pitcher. High spin rate FB has plus carry and solid run. Struggles with in-zone command, leading to high flyball rate. Two-plane breaking, tight SL is best whiff offering. SP features solid ride and plus tumble. Struggles with CU control.

Ottenbreit,Micah — SP — Philadelphia

EXP MLB DEBUT: 2026 | H/W: 6-4 190 | FUT: #4 starter | 7E

Thrws R Age 19 — 2021 (4) HS (MI)

Velo	Pitch	Grade
91-94	FB	++
76-79	CB	+++
81-84	CU	++

Year	Lev	Team	W	L	Sv	IP	K	ERA	WHIP	BF/G	OBA	H%	S%	xERA	Ctl	Dom	Cmd	hr/9	BPV
2021	Rk	FCL Phillies	1	0	0	6	4	4.50	1.50	5.2	262	32	67	3.61	4.5	6.0	1.3	0.0	5
2022	A	Clearwater	0	1	0	5	4	8.65	2.12	12.8	290	32	60	7.18	8.7	6.9	0.8	1.7	-91

RHP went down with Tommy John surgery in mid-2022, but has some characteristics worth waiting on. Had gained some velo in Fall 2021 instructs and made his mark with a high-spin CB. Also dabbled with a CU and showed some feel to pitch. With a classic SP body, youth and arsenal, an interesting name to tuck away should TJS recovery go smoothly.

Pacheco,Freddy — RP — St. Louis

EXP MLB DEBUT: 2023 | H/W: 5-11 203 | FUT: Setup reliever | 7C

Thrws R Age 24 — 2018 FA (VZ)

Velo	Pitch	Grade
95-97	FB	++++
82-85	SL	+++

Year	Lev	Team	W	L	Sv	IP	K	ERA	WHIP	BF/G	OBA	H%	S%	xERA	Ctl	Dom	Cmd	hr/9	BPV
2021	A+	Peoria	0	0	8	31	57	5.21	1.29	5.3	186	33	63	3.37	5.8	16.5	2.9	1.4	159
2021	AA	Springfield	1	0	3	19	33	1.88	0.78	4.6	114	22	79	0.45	3.8	15.5	4.1	0.5	195
2021	AAA	Memphis	0	0	0	3	5	0.00	0.67	5.2	106	22	100		3.0	15.0	5.0	0.0	207
2022	AA	Springfield	1	5	8	28	41	3.84	1.28	4.8	202	29	75	3.42	5.1	13.1	2.6	1.3	116
2022	AAA	Memphis	2	2	4	33	43	2.44	0.87	4.7	154	23	74	1.18	3.3	11.7	3.6	0.5	140

Best reliever in the system. Short RHP comes after hitters with an aggressive two-pitch mix. Quick arm action and max effort delivery generate plenty of velo on a plus mid-90s heater with 2500 rpm that maxes out at 99 mph. Backs up the heat with a power SL that generates swing-and-miss. Control is only red flag; should be up in 2023.

Painter,Andrew — SP — Philadelphia

EXP MLB DEBUT: 2023 | H/W: 6-7 215 | FUT: #1 starter | 9B

Thrws R Age 19 — 2021 (1) HS (FL)

Velo	Pitch	Grade
96-99	FB	+++++
81-84	SL	++++
87-89	CU	++++
77-79	CB	++

Year	Lev	Team	W	L	Sv	IP	K	ERA	WHIP	BF/G	OBA	H%	S%	xERA	Ctl	Dom	Cmd	hr/9	BPV
2021	Rk	FCL Phillies	0	0	0	6	12	0.00	0.67	5.2	191	45	100	0.50	0.0	18.0		0.0	342
2022	A	Clearwater	1	1	0	38	69	1.41	0.86	15.6	136	31	82	0.43	3.8	16.3	4.3	0.0	209
2022	A+	Jersey Shore	3	0	0	36	49	0.99	0.88	16.8	197	30	93	1.64	1.7	12.2	7.0	0.5	190
2022	AA	Reading	2	1	0	28	37	2.56	0.96	21.2	240	34	79	2.80	0.6	11.9	18.5	1.0	214

High-90s FB from simple mechanics and 3/4s release. Throws all pitches for strikes; can finish off ABs with FB, SL, CU. Tall, strong build commands the game and has poise for days. Steals strikes and gets chases from low-80s SL; CU doesn't move a ton, but tunnels from FB slot and velo difference results in huge whiff rates. A teenager, but ready.

Palencia,Daniel — SP — Chicago (N)

EXP MLB DEBUT: 2024 | H/W: 5-11 160 | FUT: #2 SP/closer | 8E

Thrws R Age 23 — 2020 FA (VZ)

Velo	Pitch	Grade
96-100	FB	++++
88-92	SL	+++
86-89	CU	+

Year	Lev	Team	W	L	Sv	IP	K	ERA	WHIP	BF/G	OBA	H%	S%	xERA	Ctl	Dom	Cmd	hr/9	BPV
2021	A	Stockton	0	2	0	14	14	7.02	1.63	10.5	299	35	60	6.25	3.8	8.9	2.3	1.9	75
2021	A	Myrtle Beach	1	0	0	27	38	3.67	1.30	15.9	183	28	73	2.67	6.0	12.7	2.1	0.7	84
2022	A+	South Bend	1	3	0	75	98	3.95	1.21	14.4	209	30	69	2.93	4.2	11.7	2.8	0.8	116

Came over in the Chafin deal and has some of the best pure velo in the system. Uses athletic frame, thick, powerful lower half, and high 3/4 arm slot to generate easy 100+ velo, topping at 102 with arm-side run. Backs up the heater with a nasty 11-to-5 power SL that sits in the low-90s. CU is below-average and will need to improve to remain a starter.

Pallette,Peyton — SP — Chicago (A)

EXP MLB DEBUT: 2025 | H/W: 6-1 180 | FUT: #3 starter | 8D

Thrws R Age 21 — 2022 (2) Arkansas

Velo	Pitch	Grade
92-96	FB	+++
77-81	CB	++++
86-89	CU	+++

Year	Lev	Team	W	L	Sv	IP	K	ERA	WHIP	BF/G	OBA	H%	S%	xERA	Ctl	Dom	Cmd	hr/9	BPV

Missed all of 2022 due to Tommy John surgery. Low-effort 3/4s delivery but doesn't use height well. Three-pitch arsenal; 4-seam FB sits mid-90s and misses enough bats. Lack of deception may cause FB to back up. CB clearly best pitch with plus 2-plane 11-to-5 break. Has feel for firm CU with arm-side run and occasional late drop.

Palmer,Trent — SP — Toronto

EXP MLB DEBUT: 2023 | H/W: 6-1 230 | FUT: #3 starter | 8D

Thrws R Age 24 — 2020 (3) Jacksonville

Velo	Pitch	Grade
90-93	FB	+++
78-80	CB	++
81-83	SL	+++
82-83	CU	+++

Year	Lev	Team	W	L	Sv	IP	K	ERA	WHIP	BF/G	OBA	H%	S%	xERA	Ctl	Dom	Cmd	hr/9	BPV
2020	NCAA	Jacksonville	2	1	0	27	41	1.32	0.63	23.4	135	25	76		1.7	13.6	8.2	0.0	218
2021	A	Dunedin	4	2	0	63	83	3.00	1.19	15.8	157	26	72	1.50	6.0	11.9	2.0	0.0	69
2022	A+	Vancouver	1	2	0	23	36	4.27	1.55	16.9	300	44	81	6.03	3.1	14.0	4.5	1.9	186
2022	AA	New Hampshire	1	1	0	31	33	3.75	1.19	17.9	200	26	71	2.81	4.3	9.5	2.2	0.9	73

Strongly-built SP who didn't pitch in 2nd half of season due to injury. Arm strength produces average velocity from low arm slot. Thrives from pitch movement which makes it tough for hitters to barrel balls. Control dramatically improved, particularly with FB. Uses both CB and SL with SL better of two. Could be intriguing RP.

Palmquist,Carson — SP — Colorado

EXP MLB DEBUT: 2025 | H/W: 6-3 185 | FUT: Setup reliever | 6B

Thrws L Age 22 — 2022 (3) Miami

Velo	Pitch	Grade
90-93	FB	++
77-80	SL	+++
	CU	+

Year	Lev	Team	W	L	Sv	IP	K	ERA	WHIP	BF/G	OBA	H%	S%	xERA	Ctl	Dom	Cmd	hr/9	BPV
2022	NCAA	Miami	9	4	0	84	118	2.89	1.21	21.2	228	32	85	3.79	3.4	12.6	3.7	1.5	153
2022	Rk	ACL Rockies	0	0	0	1	1	0.00	2.00	4.8	0	0	100	2.18	18.0	9.0	0.5	0.0	-306

Lanky collegiate lefty attacks hitters from a low 3/4s sidearm slot creating excellent movement and deception. FB sits in the low-to-mid 90s and can be sneaky fast and up to 96 mph with good command. Two-plane break SL is best offering and is tough vs LHB, while CU will need to improve to remain a starter. Most likely he ends up as a setup reliever.

Paniagua,Inohan

SP | St. Louis | EXP MLB DEBUT: 2025 | H/W: 6-1 148 | FUT: #5 SP/swingman | 7D

Thrws R Age 23 — 2017 FA (DR)

Velo	Pitch	Grade
90-93	FB	+++
75-78	CB	+++
82-84	CU	+

Year	Lev	Team	W	L	Sv	IP	K	ERA	WHIP	BF/G	OBA	H%	S%	xERA	Ctl	Dom	Cmd	hr/9	BPV
2019	Rk	GCL Cardinals	2	5	0	49	47	6.04	1.52	19.4	298	38	58	4.69	2.9	8.6	2.9	0.5	94
2019	A-	State College	0	0	0	5	1	10.59	2.55	13.7	327	34	54	7.28	10.6	1.8	0.2	0.0	-236
2021	A	Palm Beach	4	1	2	46	62	3.90	1.21	11.6	222	33	68	2.85	3.7	12.1	3.3	0.6	136
2022	A	Palm Beach	6	4	0	99	107	2.18	0.96	22.0	205	28	78	1.82	2.1	9.7	4.7	0.4	137
2022	A+	Peoria	2	2	0	38	38	4.48	1.31	19.7	240	27	74	4.57	3.8	9.0	2.4	1.9	77

Older international prospect signed for $160,000. Is able to generate arm speed and velo despite slender frame. FB sits at 90-93, but can get to 95 on occasion with good late sink. Slurvy CB is best secondary with sweeping two-plane break and high spin and low-80s CU that shows potential, but needs refinement. Solid command of all 3 offerings.

Parrish,Drew

SP | Kansas City | EXP MLB DEBUT: 2023 | H/W: 5-11 200 | FUT: #5 SP/swingman | 6C

Thrws L Age 25 — 2019 (8) Florida St

Velo	Pitch	Grade
88-92	FB	++
70-74	CB	+++
78-81	CU	+++

Year	Lev	Team	W	L	Sv	IP	K	ERA	WHIP	BF/G	OBA	H%	S%	xERA	Ctl	Dom	Cmd	hr/9	BPV
2021	A+	Quad Cities	1	0	1	15	23	0.00	0.53	12.7	104	20	100		1.8	13.6	7.7	0.0	215
2021	AA	NW Arkansas	5	4	0	83	95	3.36	1.08	18.0	217	29	72	2.75	2.7	10.3	3.8	0.9	130
2022	AA	NW Arkansas	4	3	0	55	48	2.13	0.82	20.0	167	20	80	1.48	2.3	7.9	3.4	0.8	98
2022	AAA	Omaha	3	8	0	73	51	5.66	1.54	18.8	251	26	68	5.29	5.4	6.3	1.2	1.8	-15

Short-statured 3/4s LHP who relies on command/control struggled after Triple-A callup. Repeatable, crossfire delivery with limited extension. 3-pitch pitcher; throws strikes with 4-seam FB. FB spin profile doesn't lend itself to success. Best pitch is fading CU with drop-off-the-table late sink. CB has solid shape but is 3rd pitch.

Peluse,Colin

SP | Oakland | EXP MLB DEBUT: 2023 | H/W: 6-3 230 | FUT: #4 starter | 7D

Thrws R Age 24 — 2019 (9) Wake Forest

Velo	Pitch	Grade
92-96	FB	+++
83-86	SL	+++
80-85	CU	++

Year	Lev	Team	W	L	Sv	IP	K	ERA	WHIP	BF/G	OBA	H%	S%	xERA	Ctl	Dom	Cmd	hr/9	BPV
2019	A-	Vermont	2	1	0	24		2.25	1.13	11.8	237	32	81	2.64	2.3	9.8	4.3	0.4	133
2021	A+	Lansing	7	3	0	86	92	3.66	1.21	19.3	253	32	73	3.70	2.3	9.6	4.2	1.0	129
2021	AA	Midland	2	0	0	15	17	1.80	0.87	18.4	175	24	83	1.47	2.4	10.2	4.3	0.6	137
2022	AA	Midland	10	6	1	118	92	5.41	1.36	21.5	285	32	63	4.80	2.1	7.0	3.3	1.3	87
2022	AAA	Las Vegas	0	1	0	1	1	52.50	6.67	11.4	674	68	17	43.54	7.5	7.5	1.0	15.0	-50

Tall, durable SP with exceptional control and ability to locate FB to both sides of plate. Doesn't have plus offering, but all work well in tandem. Pitches aggressively with FB and complements with hard SL and improving CU. Allows flyballs and K rate has fallen as he climbs. May be too hittable to stick as SP.

Pepiot,Ryan

SP | Los Angeles (N) | EXP MLB DEBUT: 2022 | H/W: 6-3 215 | FUT: #2 starter | 9D

Thrws R Age 25 — 2019 (3) Butler

Velo	Pitch	Grade
94-96	FB	++++
86-88	SL	++
84-86	CU	+++++

Year	Lev	Team	W	L	Sv	IP	K	ERA	WHIP	BF/G	OBA	H%	S%	xERA	Ctl	Dom	Cmd	hr/9	BPV
2019	A	Great Lakes	0	0	0	18	21	2.49	1.22	8.1	203	30	77	2.10	4.5	10.4	2.3	0.0	85
2021	AA	Tulsa	3	4	0	59	81	2.89	0.95	14.9	152	21	76	1.84	4.0	12.3	3.1	1.1	133
2021	AAA	Oklahoma City	2	5	0	41	46	7.21	1.82	17.4	317	37	67	7.66	4.6	10.0	2.2	2.6	75
2022	AAA	Oklahoma City	9	1	0	91	114	2.57	1.08	18.7	194	27	82	2.56	3.6	11.3	3.2	1.0	125
2022	MLB	Los Angeles	3	0	0	36	42	3.49	1.47	17.2	203	25	83	4.14	6.7	10.5	1.6	1.5	25

Spent much of the year on the shuttle between OKC and LA but it all added up to a breakout campaign. Mid-90s FB tops at 98 with plus late life. CU is widely considered the best in the minors. SL lags behind as his third pitch and his struggles with control will need to improve to reach full potential as a #2 starter.

Perales,Luis

SP | Boston | EXP MLB DEBUT: 2026 | H/W: 6-1 160 | FUT: #3 starter | 8E

Thrws R Age 19 — 2019 FA (VZ)

Velo	Pitch	Grade
91-96	FB	++++
76-78	CB	++
81-82	CU	++

Year	Lev	Team	W	L	Sv	IP	K	ERA	WHIP	BF/G	OBA	H%	S%	xERA	Ctl	Dom	Cmd	hr/9	BPV
2021	Rk	DSL Red Sox	0	0	0	2	3	4.50	1.00	7.6	151	27	50	0.94	4.5	13.5	3.0	0.0	140
2022	Rk	FCL Red Sox	0	1	0	25	34	1.08	0.76	9.9	124	22	84	0.08	3.2	12.2	3.8	0.0	151
2022	A	Salem	0	1	0	10	16	3.53	2.06	12.4	258	41	85	5.71	9.7	14.1	1.5	0.9	10

Young, power- arm who may not have much projection remaining, but has quick action to produce velocity and life. CB features lot of spin, but tough to drop in zone for strikes. Throws with little effort and three-pitch mix difficult for hitters to barrel. FB is best pitch and will need more consistency with CB and more trust in CU to succeed.

Perez,Eury

SP | Miami | EXP MLB DEBUT: 2023 | H/W: 6-8 220 | FUT: #1 starter | 9C

Thrws R Age 19 — 2019 FA (DR)

Velo	Pitch	Grade
95-97	FB	++++
80-83	SL	++++
85-87	CT	++++
88-91	CU	++++

Year	Lev	Team	W	L	Sv	IP	K	ERA	WHIP	BF/G	OBA	H%	S%	xERA	Ctl	Dom	Cmd	hr/9	BPV
2021	A	Jupiter	2	3	0	56	82	1.61	0.95	14.1	168	28	84	1.30	3.4	13.2	3.9	0.3	164
2021	A+	Beloit	1	2	0	22	26	2.86	0.73	15.6	151	14	82	2.21	2.0	10.6	5.2	2.0	154
2022	A	Jupiter	0	0	0	2	4	0.00	0.50	6.6	151	38	100		0.0	18.0		0.0	342
2022	AA	Pensacola	3	3	0	75	106	4.08	1.16	17.6	227	33	68	3.24	3.0	12.7	4.2	1.1	166

Tall, projectable athletic RHP is inching closer to his big league debut. Super tall, lean muscular frame with room to grow. Repeats low 3/4s delivery with plus-plus extension extremely well. 4-pitch pitcher, all potentially plus offerings. FB has plus ride profile. SL and CB have distinctive movement profiles. Late-tumbling CU is best pitch.

Petty,Chase

SP | Cincinnati | EXP MLB DEBUT: 2025 | H/W: 6-1 190 | FUT: #2 starter | 9E

Thrws R Age 20 — 2021 (1) HS (NJ)

Velo	Pitch	Grade
92-95	FB	++++
82-86	SL	++++
85-88	CU	+++

Year	Lev	Team	W	L	Sv	IP	K	ERA	WHIP	BF/G	OBA	H%	S%	xERA	Ctl	Dom	Cmd	hr/9	BPV
2021	Rk	FCL Twins	0	0	0	5	6	5.40	1.40	10.6	299	43	57	3.84	1.8	10.8	6.0	0.0	164
2022	A	Daytona	0	4	0	67	63	3.08	1.21	15.0	231	29	76	3.06	3.2	8.4	2.6	0.7	83
2022	A+	Dayton	1	2	0	30	33	4.47	1.13	17.0	241	32	59	2.90	2.1	9.8	4.7	0.6	139

Short-statured, hard-throwing RHP was acquired mid-season in trade with MIN. Double plus arm speed and athletic delivery propels velocity. Sits low-to-mid 90s with 2-seam FB with excellent arm-side run and inconsistent sink. Sink is plus when maintaining 3/4s slot. Tight SL is a whiff maker. Improved feel of CU.

Pfaadt,Brandon

SP | Arizona | EXP MLB DEBUT: 2023 | H/W: 6-4 220 | FUT: #2 starter | 8C

Thrws R Age 24 — 2020 (5) Bellarmine

Velo	Pitch	Grade
92-95	FB	++++
81-83	SL	++++
77-80	CB	+++
85-88	CU	+++

Year	Lev	Team	W	L	Sv	IP	K	ERA	WHIP	BF/G	OBA	H%	S%	xERA	Ctl	Dom	Cmd	hr/9	BPV
2021	A	Visalia	2	2	0	40	57	3.14	0.90	21.3	204	30	71	2.34	1.6	12.8	8.1	1.1	206
2021	A+	Hillsboro	5	4	0	58	67	2.48	0.91	24.1	193	26	77	1.94	2.2	10.4	4.8	0.8	146
2021	AA	Amarillo	1	1	0	33	36	4.62	1.33	22.9	284	30	84	6.52	1.9	9.8	5.1	3.3	143
2022	AA	Amarillo	6	6	0	105	144	4.54	1.26	22.5	276	38	70	4.66	1.6	12.3	7.6	1.6	196
2022	AAA	Reno	5	1	0	61	74	2.65	1.00	23.4	214	28	83	2.92	2.1	10.9	5.3	1.3	158

Tall, strike-throwing 3/4s RHP continued march to big league debut. Athletic build. Deceptive delivery, messes with hitters timing. 4-pitch arsenal. High spin rate 4-seam FB features ride and arm-side run from lower slot. SL flashes plus with 2-plane movement, especially late horizontal break out of the zone. CU and CB average-or-better.

Phillips,Cole

SP | Atlanta | EXP MLB DEBUT: 2026 | H/W: 6-3 200 | FUT: #2 starter | 8E

Thrws R Age 19 — 2022 (2) HS (TX)

Velo	Pitch	Grade
95-98	FB	++++
80-83	SL	+++
74-78	CB	+++
85-87	CU	

Year	Lev	Team	W	L	Sv	IP	K	ERA	WHIP	BF/G	OBA	H%	S%	xERA	Ctl	Dom	Cmd	hr/9	BPV

Top Texas prep RHP dropped to the 2nd round in 2022 draft due to Tommy John surgery. Lean, athletic frame with room to mature. Refined 3/4s delivery last off-season, picking up velocity. 3-pitch pitcher. 4-seam FB has ride and run, exploding late up in the zone. Tight, 2-plane SL has late vertical movement, contributing to high whiff potential. Solid CU.

Phillips,Connor

SP | Cincinnati | EXP MLB DEBUT: 2024 | H/W: 6-2 190 | FUT: #3 starter | 8E

Thrws R Age 21 — 2020 (2) McLennan CC

Velo	Pitch	Grade
95-97	FB	++++
82-85	SL	++++
77-80	CB	+++

Year	Lev	Team	W	L	Sv	IP	K	ERA	WHIP	BF/G	OBA	H%	S%	xERA	Ctl	Dom	Cmd	hr/9	BPV
2020	NJCA	McLennan CC	3	1	0	25	27	3.21	1.19	16.8	174	21	78	2.72	5.4	9.6	1.8	1.1	47
2021	A	Modesto	7	3	0	72	104	4.75	1.47	19.3	234	38	65	3.21	5.5	13.0	2.4	0.1	104
2021	A+	Everett	0	1	0	4	7	2.25	1.00	15.3	151	19	100	3.04	4.5	15.8	3.5	2.3	180
2022	A+	Dayton	4	3	0	64	90	2.95	1.11	21.0	178	27	76	2.18	4.5	12.7	2.8	0.7	124
2022	AA	Chattanooga	1	5	0	45	60	4.98	1.81	17.5	274	40	72	5.06	6.8	11.9	1.8	0.6	50

Hard-throwing, high 3/4s RHP features 3 pitches with swing-and-miss potential. Quick, whippy arm action with above-average extensions plays up arsenal. Flat-angled mid-90s FB has explosive ride/run action up in the zone. Two-plane SL is whiff magnet. Hammer CB has plus depth and late bite. Present control is fair, at best.

Porter,Brock

SP | Texas | EXP MLB DEBUT: 2027 | H/W: 6-4 208 | FUT: #2 starter | 9E

Thrws R Age 19 — 2022 (4) HS (MI)

Velo	Pitch	Grade
94-98	FB	+++
79-82	CU	++++
82-85	SL	++
74-77	CB	+

Year	Lev	Team	W	L	Sv	IP	K	ERA	WHIP	BF/G	OBA	H%	S%	xERA	Ctl	Dom	Cmd	hr/9	BPV

Texas' class prize in 4th round has massive stuff and huge upside, but yet to throw a pro pitch and thus lower on the list than the stuff grades. A future plus mid-90s FF with life and ride isn't the star, it's his 70-grade CU that looks like his FF but drops entirely off the table. Needs breaking ball but projects towards front of rotation.

Povich,Cade | SP | Baltimore | EXP MLB DEBUT: 2024 | H/W: 6-3 185 | FUT: #4 starter | 7C

Thrws L Age 22	Year	Lev	Team	W	L	Sv	IP	K	ERA	WHIP	BF/G	OBA	H%	S%	xERA	Ctl	Dom	Cmd	hr/9	BPV
2021 (3) Nebraska	2021	Rk	FCL Twins	0	0	0	2	3	0.00	0.50	6.6	151	27	100		0.0	13.5		0.0	261
90-93 FB +++	2021	A	Fort Myers	0	0	0	8	16	1.13	1.00	10.2	210	48	88	1.56	2.3	18.0	8.0	0.0	281
79-82 SL ++++	2022	A+	Aberdeen	2	0	0	12	15	0.00	0.50	19.9	106	18	100		1.5	11.3	7.5	0.0	180
74-76 CB ++	2022	A+	Cedar Rapids	6	8	0	78	107	4.49	1.24	19.8	244	35	66	3.62	3.0	12.3	4.1	1.0	159
82-84 CU ++	2022	AA	Bowie	2	2	0	23	26	7.01	1.39	16.2	244	29	52	4.86	4.3	10.1	2.4	1.9	85

Lefty from the Lopez trade brings a deep four-pitch arsenal. Best pitch is a sweeping low-80s slider that gets chases and whiffs. Also features a mid-70s CB whose velocity difference messes with hitters' timing. FB velo wavers, but settles in low-90s and commands it well. Also has CU. Strike-thrower, strong frame; could get to mid-rotation outcome.

Prielipp,Connor | SP | Minnesota | EXP MLB DEBUT: 2025 | H/W: 6-2 210 | FUT: #3 starter | 8C

Thrws L Age 22	Year	Lev	Team	W	L	Sv	IP	K	ERA	WHIP	BF/G	OBA	H%	S%	xERA	Ctl	Dom	Cmd	hr/9	BPV
2022 (2) Alabama																				
91-94 FB +++																				
85-89 SL ++++																				
82-85 CU ++																				

Did not pitch in 2022 due to Tommy John surgery; could have been top draft pick. Exhibits quick arm action and athleticism to pepper strike zone with exquisite offerings. Operates mostly with FB and SL combo while using arm angle and release point to throw downhill. SL may be best breaking ball in org while FB also misses bats.

Priester,Quinn | SP | Pittsburgh | EXP MLB DEBUT: 2023 | H/W: 6-3 210 | FUT: #2 starter | 8B

Thrws R Age 22	Year	Lev	Team	W	L	Sv	IP	K	ERA	WHIP	BF/G	OBA	H%	S%	xERA	Ctl	Dom	Cmd	hr/9	BPV
2019 (1) HS (IL)	2021	A+	Greensboro	7	4	0	97		3.06	1.24	19.8	230	30	78	3.21	3.6	9.1	2.5	0.7	84
92-95 FB ++++	2022	A	Bradenton	0	0	0	3	1	0.00	0.00	8.5	0	0			0.0	3.0		0.0	72
79-83 CB ++++	2022	A+	Greensboro	0	0	0	2	3	20.45	3.18	13.2	492	61	33	16.21	4.1	12.3	3.0	4.1	128
83-85 SL +++	2022	AA	Altoona	4	4	0	75	75	2.88	1.20	20.1	243	32	77	3.01	2.6	9.0	3.4	0.5	109
82-86 CU +++	2022	AAA	Indianapolis	1	1	0	9	10	3.96	1.32	18.8	163	20	73	2.84	6.9	9.9	1.4	1.0	9

Strong SP who began season late due to oblique. Has the repertoire, athleticism and moxie to thrive in upper levels. Likes to establish plate with plus FB, whether 4-seamer or sinker. Induces ton of groundballs. Terrific CB is legit swing-and-miss pitch and could get better with more consistent arm slot. SL and CU both are solid average.

Ragsdale,Carson | SP | San Francisco | EXP MLB DEBUT: 2024 | H/W: 6-8 225 | FUT: #4 starter | 7D

Thrws R Age 24	Year	Lev	Team	W	L	Sv	IP	K	ERA	WHIP	BF/G	OBA	H%	S%	xERA	Ctl	Dom	Cmd	hr/9	BPV
2020 (4) South Florida																				
90-95 FB +++																				
81-84 CB +++	2020	NCAA	South Florida	1	0	0	19	37	2.84	1.00	18.1	183	42	68	1.25	3.3	17.5	5.3	0.0	244
86-88 CT ++	2021	A	San Jose	8	6	0	113	167	4.45	1.34	19.6	251	38	69	3.96	3.6	13.3	3.7	1.0	160
82-85 CU ++	2022	Rk	ACL Giants B	1	0	0	5	9	0.00	1.15	4.1	170	35	100	1.51	5.2	15.6	3.0	0.0	158

Only pitched 5 innings due to thoracic outlet syndrome. Should be healthy for spring training. Very tall frame and uses to his advantage by throwing on downhill plane. Possesses inconsistent control but has slot and delivery are tough to repeat. Uses FB effectively and mixes in effective CB and new CT. K rate likely to drop without better mix.

Rajcic,Max | SP | St. Louis | EXP MLB DEBUT: 2025 | H/W: 6-0 210 | FUT: #4 starter | 7D

Thrws R Age 21	Year	Lev	Team	W	L	Sv	IP	K	ERA	WHIP	BF/G	OBA	H%	S%	xERA	Ctl	Dom	Cmd	hr/9	BPV
2022 (6) UCLA																				
89-92 FB ++																				
76-78 CB ++																				
80-83 SL ++																				
79-83 CU +																				

Comes at hitters from a high 3/4s arm slot that creates some deception and works mostly north to south in the zone. FB sits in the low-90s occasionally up to 94 to go along with 12-to-6 power CB, SL and fringe CU. No projection left, but pounds strikes.

Ramirez,Aldo | SP | Washington | EXP MLB DEBUT: 2026 | H/W: 6-0 191 | FUT: #4 starter | 7D

Thrws R Age 21	Year	Lev	Team	W	L	Sv	IP	K	ERA	WHIP	BF/G	OBA	H%	S%	xERA	Ctl	Dom	Cmd	hr/9	BPV
2018 FA (MX)																				
92-95 FB +++																				
77-79 CB +++	2019	A-	Lowell	2	3	0	61	63	3.97	1.23	17.7	255	33	69	3.48	2.4	9.3	3.9	0.7	121
87-90 CU ++++	2021	Rk	FCL Nationals	1	1	0	7	3	8.75	1.81	8.3	307	34	46	5.06	5.0	3.8	0.8	0.0	-50
	2021	A	Salem	1	1	0	31	32	2.03	1.13	15.3	236	32	82	2.57	2.3	9.3	4.0	0.3	123

Missed entire 2022 season with elbow injury that clouds his future a bit—at the very least pushing back his MLB timeline. When healthy, it's a back-end rotation starter kit. Smaller-framed, he's a pitch-to-contact arm with some feel for a change-up who throws strikes. Young enough to improve, but getting elbow healthy is his priority.

Ramirez,Luis | SP | Texas | EXP MLB DEBUT: 2026 | H/W: 6-2 200 | FUT: #4 starter | 7D

Thrws R Age 22	Year	Lev	Team	W	L	Sv	IP	K	ERA	WHIP	BF/G	OBA	H%	S%	xERA	Ctl	Dom	Cmd	hr/9	BPV
2022 (7) Long Beach																				
91-94 FB +++																				
79-81 SL ++																				
83-87 CU ++																				

2022 draftee down with shoulder woes but when healthy has a strong FS that eats bats alive and elicits a huge GB tilt. Shows the makings of a quality SL and CU, earning roughly average grades across the arsenal with average command; there's a ton of developmental clay here. But injury concerns will need monitoring; shoulder isn't the first.

Raya,Marco | SP | Minnesota | EXP MLB DEBUT: 2025 | H/W: 6-1 170 | FUT: #3 starter | 8D

Thrws R Age 20	Year	Lev	Team	W	L	Sv	IP	K	ERA	WHIP	BF/G	OBA	H%	S%	xERA	Ctl	Dom	Cmd	hr/9	BPV
2020 (4) HS (TX)																				
92-96 FB +++																				
78-80 CB +++																				
82-85 SL +++																				
CU ++	2022	A	Fort Myers	3	2	0	65	76	3.05	1.08	13.3	204	27	77	2.80	3.2	10.5	3.3	1.1	121

Advanced, athletic SP who thrived in first pro experience. Missed all 2021 due to shoulder issues, but returned with aplomb. Has all ingredients to be top prospect in org. Not blessed with size, but generates velocity with clean, repeatable delivery. Uses two breaking balls with SL better than CB, though both good. CU is distant 4th pitch.

Ridings,Stephen | RP | New York (N) | EXP MLB DEBUT: 2021 | H/W: 6-8 220 | FUT: Setup reliever | 7D

Thrws R Age 27	Year	Lev	Team	W	L	Sv	IP	K	ERA	WHIP	BF/G	OBA	H%	S%	xERA	Ctl	Dom	Cmd	hr/9	BPV
2016 (8) Haverford	2021	AA	Somerset	4	0	2	19	30	0.47	0.53	4.5	130	25	90		0.9	14.2	15.0	0.0	248
95-98 FB ++++	2021	AAA	Scranton/WB	1	0	1	10	12	2.70	1.00	4.8	221	27	88	3.46	1.8	10.8	6.0	1.8	164
84-87 SL ++++	2021	MLB	New York	0	0	0	5	7	1.80	1.20	4.0	221	36	83	2.25	3.6	12.6	3.5	0.0	148
	2022	AA	Somerset	0	0	0	1	2	0.00	1.00	3.8	262	55	100	2.23	0.0	18.0		0.0	342
	2022	AAA	Scranton/WB	0	0	0	1	2	0.00	1.00	3.8	262	55	100	2.23	0.0	18.0		0.0	342

Tall, big-bodied RHP struggled with shoulder issues in 2022, limiting to 2 games. Acquired via waivers by NYM. 3/4 delivery with double-plus extension. Throws both 4-seam and 2-seam FB. 4-seam FB has solid ride/run profile and big velocity. 2-seam FB has classic arm-side bore profile. SL features tight spinning profile. Late vertical break is plus.

Ritchie,JR | SP | Atlanta | EXP MLB DEBUT: 2026 | H/W: 6-2 185 | FUT: #3 starter | 8D

Thrws R Age 19	Year	Lev	Team	W	L	Sv	IP	K	ERA	WHIP	BF/G	OBA	H%	S%	xERA	Ctl	Dom	Cmd	hr/9	BPV
2022 (1) HS (WA)																				
90-94 FB +++																				
81-84 SL +++																				
83-86 CU +++	2022	Rk	FCL Braves	0	0	0	4	4	0.00	0.73	7.3	147	21	100	0.28	2.2	8.8	4.0	0.0	117
	2022	A	Augusta	0	0	0	10	10	2.70	1.10	13.1	199	25	80	2.62	3.6	9.0	2.5	0.9	83

High 2022 HS draft pick made pro debut. Projectable frame, looked smaller than listed. Low 3/4s delivery is repeatable with solid extension. Flatter angled 4-seam FB struggles with overall shape, flashes plus arm-side run. Sweeping SL is best pitch with solid command. High spin rate CU with 2-seam movement profile projects as above-average.

Roa,Christian | SP | Cincinnati | EXP MLB DEBUT: 2024 | H/W: 6-4 220 | FUT: #5 SP/swingman | 7C

Thrws R Age 24	Year	Lev	Team	W	L	Sv	IP	K	ERA	WHIP	BF/G	OBA	H%	S%	xERA	Ctl	Dom	Cmd	hr/9	BPV
2020 (2) Texas A&M	2021	Rk	ACL Reds	1	0	0	6	9	0.00	0.49	10.1	55	11	100		3.0	13.3	4.5	0.0	177
90-94 FB +++	2021	A	Daytona	1	1	0	17	21	3.66	1.57	15.1	271	37	80	4.84	4.7	11.0	2.3	1.0	89
80-84 SL +++	2021	A+	Dayton	2	2	0	34	37	4.21	1.37	17.9	249	32	72	4.07	3.9	9.7	2.5	1.1	87
74-77 CB +++	2022	A+	Dayton	4	3	0	74	83	4.14	1.45	18.6	220	30	72	3.46	5.8	10.1	1.7	0.6	42
83-86 CT +++	2022	AA	Chattanooga	2	0	0	17	19	1.06	0.71	20.0	94	12	91	0.19	3.7	10.1	2.7	0.5	99

Injury-prone, pitchability RHP employs kitchen sink-like arsenal. Repeatable 3/4s delivery. Features 5 offerings. 4-seam FB improved as usage rate declined, mixing in CT more often. SL has solid sweeping break profile and CB works as an 11-to-5 offering. Throws a firm CU with some fade. Below average command improved as season wore on.

Robberse,Sem
SP | Toronto | EXP MLB DEBUT: 2024 | H/W: 6-1 160 | FUT: #3 starter | 8C

Thrws R Age 21
2019 FA (NT)

Velo	Pitch	Grade
88-93	FB	+++
78-82	CB	+++
83-85	SL	+++
82-86	CU	++

Year	Lev	Team	W	L	Sv	IP	K	ERA	WHIP	BF/G	OBA	H%	S%	xERA	Ctl	Dom	Cmd	hr/9	BPV
2021	A	Dunedin	5	4	0	57	61	3.93	1.15	16.2	222	30	66	2.77	3.1	9.6	3.1	0.6	106
2021	A+	Vancouver	0	3	0	31	29	5.23	1.84	20.6	308	38	72	5.94	5.2	8.4	1.6	0.9	28
2022	A+	Vancouver	4	4	0	86	78	3.13	1.16	20.2	238	29	75	3.10	2.5	8.1	3.3	0.7	97
2022	AA	New Hampshire	0	3	0	24	19	3.72	1.20	19.4	218	23	76	3.66	3.7	7.1	1.9	1.5	45

Young, advanced SP who was promoted to AA in August. Arm action and delivery are advanced while he continues to command plate. Not overpowering, but has the lean build to add muscle mass and potential velocity. Effortless delivery provides some deception and gets plenty of groundballs. Varies velocity and shape of CB and SL.

Robinson,Cam
RP | Milwaukee | EXP MLB DEBUT: 2023 | H/W: 6-1 194 | FUT: Setup reliever | 7D

Thrws R Age 23
2017 (23) HS (FL)

Velo	Pitch	Grade
91-95	FB	+++
77-79	CB	+++
85-87	CT	++

Year	Lev	Team	W	L	Sv	IP	K	ERA	WHIP	BF/G	OBA	H%	S%	xERA	Ctl	Dom	Cmd	hr/9	BPV
2021	A+	Wisconsin	2	1	1	15	21	4.74	1.91	6.0	296	45	72	5.06	6.5	12.4	1.9	0.0	66
2021	AA	Biloxi	0	0	0	1	2	0.00	1.00	3.8	262	55	100	2.23	0.0	18.0		0.0	342
2022	A+	Wisconsin	3	1	19	37	52	1.46	1.02	5.1	167	29	84	1.19	4.1	12.6	3.1	0.0	134
2022	AA	Biloxi	0	0	6	14	16	1.27	0.92	4.1	167	25	85	0.93	3.2	10.1	3.2	0.0	115
2022	AAA	Nashville	0	0	0	13	16	6.92	1.85	5.5	304	42	61	5.69	5.5	11.1	2.0	0.7	68

Fast-moving RP who led minors in saves. Spent most of career in bullpen and thrives by keeping hitters off balance, though no plus offerings. Misses bats with unique delivery and slot despite lack of size. Also keeps ball on ground and rarely allows HR. Needs to address command and control. Very tough on RHH with FB and CB.

Roby,Tekoah
SP | Texas | EXP MLB DEBUT: 2024 | H/W: 6-1 185 | FUT: #4 starter | 7C

Thrws R Age 21
2020 (3) HS (FL)

Velo	Pitch	Grade
94-97	FB	++
78-82	CB	+++
80-86	CU	++

Year	Lev	Team	W	L	Sv	IP	K	ERA	WHIP	BF/G	OBA	H%	S%	xERA	Ctl	Dom	Cmd	hr/9	BPV
2021	A	Down East	2	2	0	22	35	2.45	0.95	13.8	184	32	75	1.57	2.9	14.3	5.0	0.4	198
2022	A+	Hickory	3	11	0	104	126	4.66	1.25	19.3	244	31	68	4.23	3.0	10.9	3.6	1.6	132

Moderate-body-projection guy with raw average stuff kept churning and stayed at High-A all year post '21 injury that dulled repertoire spin. 94 mph FF and big-spin CB front arsenal, great velo delta on CU which is coming along well. Strong reverse splits suggest as much but finished strong down stretch, really limiting previous FB/HR alarms.

Rock,Joe
SP | Colorado | EXP MLB DEBUT: 2024 | H/W: 6-6 200 | FUT: #4 starter | 7D

Thrws L Age 22
2021 (2) Ohio

Velo	Pitch	Grade
91-94	FB	+++
82-84	SL	+++
83-86	CU	+

Year	Lev	Team	W	L	Sv	IP	K	ERA	WHIP	BF/G	OBA	H%	S%	xERA	Ctl	Dom	Cmd	hr/9	BPV
2021	NCAA	Ohio	8	3	0	88	117	2.35	1.07	24.5	212	33	77	2.01	2.8	11.9	4.3	0.2	159
2021	Rk	ACL Rockies	1	0	0	8	11	1.13	0.75	7.1	181	30	83	0.66	1.1	12.4	11.0	0.0	210
2022	A+	Spokane	7	8	0	107	109	4.45	1.23	21.7	223	28	65	3.19	3.8	9.2	2.4	0.8	81
2022	AA	Hartford	0	0	0	8	11	10.13	1.75	18.3	285	38	42	6.62	5.6	12.4	2.2	2.3	89

Mixed full-season debut. Tall LHP uses a tall and fall low 3/4s delivery with a surprisingly short stride. Quick arm action leads to low-90s FB that gets on hitters quickly and tops at 97. Late breaking SL is best secondary and a CU that still needs refinement and separation from FB. Command was an issue in 2022 and will have to improve to remain a SP.

Rocker,Kumar
SP | Texas | EXP MLB DEBUT: 2025 | H/W: 6-5 245 | FUT: #3 starter | 8D

Thrws R Age 23
2022 (1) Vanderbilt

Velo	Pitch	Grade
92-97	FB	+++
81-85	SL	++++
86-89	CT	++
83-87	CU	++

Year	Lev	Team	W	L	Sv	IP	K	ERA	WHIP	BF/G	OBA	H%	S%	xERA	Ctl	Dom	Cmd	hr/9	BPV

XL-framed slider-master reentered draft after Mets concerns over arm and showed up to the AFL fairly raw; walked nearly a batter an inning but the cheese was apparent. Devastating SL does the heavy lifting with a mid-90s plus FB, and two average secondaries in CT and CU. FB velo back up but injury concerns follow profile since Vandy days.

Rodriguez,Carlos
SP | Milwaukee | EXP MLB DEBUT: 2024 | H/W: 6-0 180 | FUT: #4 starter | 7D

Thrws R Age 21
2021 (6) Florida SW JC

Velo	Pitch	Grade
91-95	FB	+++
82-85	SL	++
83-85	CU	+++

Year	Lev	Team	W	L	Sv	IP	K	ERA	WHIP	BF/G	OBA	H%	S%	xERA	Ctl	Dom	Cmd	hr/9	BPV
2022	A	Carolina	3	4	1	71	84	3.54	1.13	14.8	209	28	71	2.77	3.4	10.6	3.1	0.9	117

Interesting SP who had very good first pro experience. May not have frontline velocity or dominant pitch mix, but sequences well and adds touch of movement to all offerings. Arm action is quite smooth and gets good spin to riding FB and CU with drop. Not much success with breaking ball, but throws with conviction.

Rodriguez,Dionys
SP | St. Louis | EXP MLB DEBUT: 2024 | H/W: 6-0 188 | FUT: #5 SP/swingman | 6C

Thrws R Age 22
2018 FA (DR)

Velo	Pitch	Grade
92-94	FB	+++
80-85	SL	++
85-88	CU	+

Year	Lev	Team	W	L	Sv	IP	K	ERA	WHIP	BF/G	OBA	H%	S%	xERA	Ctl	Dom	Cmd	hr/9	BPV
2021	A	Palm Beach	4	5	0	69	88	3.38	1.07	12.2	210	30	70	2.42	2.9	11.4	4.0	0.7	147
2022	A+	Peoria	3	11	0	121	119	4.60	1.34	18.7	243	30	68	3.92	3.9	8.8	2.2	1.0	71

Short, athletic hurler failed to duplicate breakout in 2021. Broad shoulders and strong frame with a high leg kick and long stride but can get out of sync and fly open leading to below-average control. FB sits at 92-94, topping at 97 with good carry up in the zone. Low-80s SL is best secondary, but flattens when overthrown. CU is a work-in-progress.

Rodriguez,Grayson
SP | Baltimore | EXP MLB DEBUT: 2023 | H/W: 6-5 220 | FUT: #1 starter | 9B

Thrws R Age 23
2018 (1) HS (TX)

Velo	Pitch	Grade
94-96	FB	+++++
80-83	SL	++++
81-84	CU	+++
76-79	CB	+++

Year	Lev	Team	W	L	Sv	IP	K	ERA	WHIP	BF/G	OBA	H%	S%	xERA	Ctl	Dom	Cmd	hr/9	BPV
2021	A+	Aberdeen	3	0	0	23	40	1.56	0.69	16.2	144	26	86	0.82	1.9	15.6	8.0	0.8	246
2021	AA	Bowie	6	1	0	79	121	2.61	0.87	16.2	174	28	75	1.72	2.5	13.8	5.5	0.9	198
2022	A+	Aberdeen	0	0	0	1	1	0.00	2.73	6.1	244	32	100	6.43	16.4	8.2	0.5	0.0	-277
2022	AA	Bowie	0	1	0	4	11	10.71	1.67	9.4	144	70	29	2.46	10.7	23.6	2.2	0.0	153
2022	AAA	Norfolk Tides	6	1	0	69	97	2.21	0.94	18.6	184	30	76	1.40	2.7	12.6	4.6	0.3	171

Game's best pitching prospect missed three months with lat strain and returned to dominate Triple-A. Exquisite FB command at 94-96 and can touch 99; has four other pitches in his arsenal. Pounds the strike zone with them all; features CU and SL for whiffs and chases. Has mound presence, physicality and toolbox to be an ace.

Rodriguez,Randy
SP | San Francisco | EXP MLB DEBUT: 2023 | H/W: 6-0 166 | FUT: Setup reliever | 7C

Thrws R Age 23
2017 FA (DR)

Velo	Pitch	Grade
93-97	FB	++++
81-83	SL	+++
83-85	CU	++

Year	Lev	Team	W	L	Sv	IP	K	ERA	WHIP	BF/G	OBA	H%	S%	xERA	Ctl	Dom	Cmd	hr/9	BPV
2019	Rk	AZL Giants	2	6	2	25	29	5.40	1.68	7.0	269	38	66	4.46	5.8	10.4	1.8	0.4	50
2021	A	San Jose	6	3	2	62	101	1.74	1.08	7.6	201	37	82	1.69	3.3	14.7	4.4	0.0	192
2022	A+	Eugene	2	3	0	50	71	3.41	1.18	12.5	198	30	74	2.76	4.3	12.7	3.0	0.9	131
2022	AA	Richmond	0	1	0	10	19	6.30	1.50	7.2	199	35	62	4.39	7.2	17.1	2.4	1.8	131
2022	AAA	Sacramento	0	1	0	6	7	10.50	2.33	6.2	151	23	50	4.33	16.5	10.5	0.6	0.0	-239

Converted to SP, but mostly RP prior to 2022. Has two outstanding pitches in electric FB and SL. Throws from lower release point to provide sweeping action to SL. FB features good riding life up in zone and is tough for hitters to square up. Generates plenty of whiffs, though short frame and angle make him susceptible to flyballs and HR.

Rodriguez,Yerry
RP | Texas | EXP MLB DEBUT: 2022 | H/W: 6-2 198 | FUT: Middle reliever | 7E

Thrws R Age 25
2015 FA (DR)

Velo	Pitch	Grade
97-100	FB	+++
83-88	SL	+++
85-89	CU	+

Year	Lev	Team	W	L	Sv	IP	K	ERA	WHIP	BF/G	OBA	H%	S%	xERA	Ctl	Dom	Cmd	hr/9	BPV
2019	A	Hickory	7	3	0	73	85	2.09	0.90	21.0	179	25	80	1.61	2.6	10.5	4.0	0.6	136
2021	AA	Frisco	1	1	0	51	63	2.64	1.15	14.5	209	30	79	2.50	3.7	11.1	3.0	0.5	118
2021	AAA	Round Rock	3	3	0	30	37	8.07	1.63	10.3	304	40	50	5.89	3.6	11.1	3.1	1.5	120
2022	AAA	Round Rock	4	1	4	59	73	4.27	1.56	5.3	265	35	77	5.04	4.9	11.1	2.3	1.4	87
2022	MLB	Texas	0	0	0	1	1	0.00	1.00	3.8	262	35	100	2.32	0.0	9.0		0.0	180

Finally, mercifully transitioned to bullpen where he was still far too hittable despite absolute gas. Hit 101 with the FF but batters found barrels and he gave up tons of contact. Formerly advanced CU regressed and SL now primary secondary. Still has stuff to pitch in leverage but command consistently holds him back. 11.9% SwK won't close games.

Rodriguez-Cruz,Elmer
SP | Boston | EXP MLB DEBUT: 2026 | H/W: 6-3 160 | FUT: #3 starter | 8E

Thrws R Age 19
2021 (4) HS (PR)

Velo	Pitch	Grade
92-94	FB	+++
78-81	CB	+++
83-86	SL	++
84-87	CU	++

Year	Lev	Team	W	L	Sv	IP	K	ERA	WHIP	BF/G	OBA	H%	S%	xERA	Ctl	Dom	Cmd	hr/9	BPV
2022	Rk	FCL Red Sox	0	3	0	32	36	1.96	1.25	11.9	236	34	83	2.59	3.4	10.1	3.0	0.0	109
2022	A	Salem	0	0	0	6	6	1.50	1.00	11.5	151	22	83	0.99	4.5	9.0	2.0	0.0	59

Young, projectable arm who had solid pro debut in low minors. Very unpolished repertoire with crude mechanics and arm action. Present pitch mix is sound for age, but needs more deception or pitch movement to get by at upper levels. FB features arm-side run and carry up in zone. Best secondary is bendy CB.

Rolison,Ryan — SP — Colorado — EXP MLB DEBUT: 2024 — H/W: 6-2 213 — FUT: #5 SP/swingman — 6C

Thrws L	Age 25		Year	Lev	Team	W	L	Sv	IP	K	ERA	WHIP	BF/G	OBA	H%	S%	xERA	Ctl	Dom	Cmd	hr/9	BPV
2018 (1) Mississippi			2019	A+	Lancaster	6	7	0	116	118	4.88	1.44	22.5	283	34	72	5.32	2.9	9.1	3.1	1.7	103
90-93	FB	+++	2021	Rk	ACL Rockies	0	0	0	6	9	7.38	1.97	14.6	368	55	58	6.41	3.0	13.3	4.5	0.0	177
77-81	CB	++++	2021	A+	Spokane	0	0	0	5	3	3.60	1.20	20.1	221	21	80	4.02	3.6	5.4	1.5	1.8	18
82-85	SL	++	2021	AA	Hartford	2	1	0	14	20	3.17	0.92	17.7	216	33	67	2.06	1.3	12.7	10.0	0.6	212
84-86	CU	++	2021	AAA	Albuquerque	2	2	0	45	45	5.97	1.48	19.4	286	35	62	5.18	3.2	9.0	2.8	1.4	93

Injuries derailed a once-promising career. Broken hand and appendectomy limited in 2021 and a shoulder surgery in 2022. Should be healthy heading into spring, but will need to regain his form. Prior to the injuries, featured a low-90s FB with good command, plus CB, and usable SL and CU. 4-pitch mix gives him a chance to carve out a role as a SP.

Rom,Drew — SP — Baltimore — EXP MLB DEBUT: 2023 — H/W: 6-2 170 — FUT: #4 starter — 7C

Thrws L	Age 23		Year	Lev	Team	W	L	Sv	IP	K	ERA	WHIP	BF/G	OBA	H%	S%	xERA	Ctl	Dom	Cmd	hr/9	BPV
2018 (4) HS (KY)			2019	A	Delmarva	6	3	1	95	122	2.93	1.22	18.3	236	35	77	2.95	3.1	11.5	3.7	0.5	142
89-91	FB	+++	2021	A+	Aberdeen	8	0	0	67	73	2.81	1.15	19.0	240	32	79	3.15	2.3	9.8	4.3	0.8	133
79-81	SL	+++	2021	AA	Bowie	3	1	0	40	47	3.83	1.10	17.4	237	31	71	3.49	2.0	10.6	5.2	1.4	154
76-78	CB	+	2022	AA	Bowie	7	2	0	82	101	4.38	1.47	18.6	284	39	72	4.74	3.2	11.1	3.5	1.0	131
80-83	SP	++	2022	AAA	Norfolk Tides	1	1	0	37	43	4.60	1.51	23.0	266	37	67	3.86	4.4	10.4	2.4	0.2	88

Strikeouts translated to high minors, but walked more batters and gave up more hits. Low-90s FB plays up because of location and deception, SL plays well against both sides, and new split-change registered tons of whiffs and chases. Compact, efficient delivery. Close to debut but needs to limit AAA baserunners.

Roupp,Landen — SP — San Francisco — EXP MLB DEBUT: 2024 — H/W: 6-2 205 — FUT: #4 starter — 7C

Thrws R	Age 24		Year	Lev	Team	W	L	Sv	IP	K	ERA	WHIP	BF/G	OBA	H%	S%	xERA	Ctl	Dom	Cmd	hr/9	BPV
2021 (12) UNC Wilmington			2021	Rk	ACL Giants B	0	0	0	6		3.00	1.00	5.7	228	50	67	1.78	1.5	18.0	12.0	0.0	302
90-95	FB	+++	2021	A	San Jose	0	0	0	2	2	0.00	0.50	6.6	151	22	100		0.0	9.0		0.0	180
84-86	CB	+++	2022	A	San Jose	5	2	0	48	69	2.61	1.04	13.3	195	32	75	1.88	3.2	12.9	4.1	0.4	164
82-84	SL	++++	2022	A+	Eugene	3	0	0	32	52	1.68	0.87	16.9	173	32	81	1.12	2.5	14.6	5.8	0.3	212
80-85	CU	++	2022	AA	Richmond	2	1	0	26	31	3.79	1.15	20.7	205	27	70	2.92	3.8	10.7	2.8	1.0	108

Versatile arm who enjoyed breakout season on three levels. Finished 3rd in org in K and was tough against hitters from both sides. Natural stuff isn't that great, but sequences well and throws with modicum of deception. Plus SL is put-away pitch and has ability to locate FB anywhere in zone. Good arm speed and angle on all pitches.

Rutledge,Jackson — SP — Washington — EXP MLB DEBUT: 2024 — H/W: 6-8 243 — FUT: #4 starter — 8D

Thrws R	Age 24		Year	Lev	Team	W	L	Sv	IP	K	ERA	WHIP	BF/G	OBA	H%	S%	xERA	Ctl	Dom	Cmd	hr/9	BPV
2019 (1) San Jacinto JC			2019	A	Hagerstown	2	0	0	27	31	2.32	0.92	16.9	155	24	72	0.82	3.7	10.3	2.8	0.0	105
93-96	FB	++++	2021	Rk	FCL Nationals	0	1	0	3	5	8.44	1.56	7.0	250	33	50	6.16	5.6	14.1	2.5	2.8	119
86-89	SL	+++	2021	A	Fredericksburg	1	2	0	22	26	5.32	1.32	13.0	244	35	57	3.24	3.7	10.6	2.9	0.4	110
86-88	CU	++	2021	A+	Wilmington	0	3	0	10	10	13.24	2.55	13.7	371	48	42	7.99	7.9	8.8	1.1	0.0	-38
75-80	CB	++	2022	A	Fredericksburg	8	6	0	97	99	4.91	1.39	20.4	279	36	64	4.15	2.7	9.2	3.4	0.6	111

Took big strides forward in 2022 in terms of control and durability that will determine his future role. Plenty of velo on both 2- and 4-seam fastballs, newfound ability to spot those pitches sets the stage for a wipeout, high-80s SL. Also has CB and CU that flash, but are overall inconsistent so far. Reversed likely bullpen future for now.

Ryan,River — RP — Los Angeles (N) — EXP MLB DEBUT: 2024 — H/W: 6-2 195 — FUT: Setup reliever — 7D

Thrws R	Age 24		Year	Lev	Team	W	L	Sv	IP	K	ERA	WHIP	BF/G	OBA	H%	S%	xERA	Ctl	Dom	Cmd	hr/9	BPV
2021 (11) UNC Pembroke																						
94-96	FB	++++	2020	NCAA	UNC Pembroke	1	0	4	16	24	0.56	0.44	6.5	100	19	86		1.1	13.5	12.0	0.0	231
88-91	CT	++	2021	NCAA	UNC Pembroke	5	1	6	51	68	3.69	1.11	11.8	213	31	69	2.76	3.2	12.0	3.8	0.9	148
86-89	CU	++	2022	A	Rancho Cuca	1	3	0	33	48	2.71	1.27	13.6	236	37	80	3.12	3.5	13.0	3.7	0.5	157
			2022	A+	Great Lakes	1	1	0	14	22	1.93	1.21	11.3	186	29	93	3.06	5.1	14.1	2.8	1.3	134

RH reliever came over in the Matt Beaty deal. Started pro career as position player and transitioned to the mound this year with impressive results. Best offering is an above-average mid-90s FB that tops at 99 with late life up in the zone. Backs up the FB with a CT and CU, both of which are fringe-average. FB has plus spin and vertical break.

alinas,Royber — SP — Oakland — EXP MLB DEBUT: 2024 — H/W: 6-3 205 — FUT: Setup reliever — 8E

Thrws R	Age 21		Year	Lev	Team	W	L	Sv	IP	K	ERA	WHIP	BF/G	OBA	H%	S%	xERA	Ctl	Dom	Cmd	hr/9	BPV
2018 FA (VZ)																						
92-96	FB	+++	2021	Rk	FCL Braves	1	3	1	25	49	3.23	1.39	10.6	212	41	84	3.93	5.7	17.6	3.1	1.4	179
81-85	SL	++++	2021	A	Augusta	2	0	0	14	18	0.64	1.00	17.8	132	22	93	0.77	5.1	11.6	2.3	0.0	87
75-80	CB	++++	2022	A	Augusta	0	1	0	23	52	1.55	0.95	17.5	133	40	86	0.93	4.7	20.2	4.3	0.4	255
			2022	A+	Rome	5	7	0	85	123	4.12	1.34	17.7	208	33	69	3.04	5.4	13.0	2.4	0.6	107

XXL frame, 3/4s RHP struck out a lot of batter but also walked a lot of batters too in 2023. Herky-jerky delivery with varied arm slot. Struggles commanding riding 4-seam FB up in the zone. Both secondary offerings flash plus-to-double-plus potential. SL is a tight, two-plane breaker while CB has a deeper vertical break.

anchez,Franklin — SP — Miami — EXP MLB DEBUT: 2025 — H/W: 6-6 183 — FUT: Setup reliever — 7D

Thrws R	Age 22		Year	Lev	Team	W	L	Sv	IP	K	ERA	WHIP	BF/G	OBA	H%	S%	xERA	Ctl	Dom	Cmd	hr/9	BPV
2019 FA (DR)																						
95-97	FB	+++	2021	Rk	FCL Mets	2	3	0	24	31	7.44	1.49	7.4	227	35	44	3.06	6.0	11.5	1.9	0.0	65
89-91	SL	++++	2021	A	St. Lucie	0	0	1	3	4	0.00	2.00	4.8	106	18	100	3.04	15.0	12.0	0.8	0.0	-171
			2022	A	St. Lucie	1	1	0	30	37	3.90	1.30	9.5	206	31	68	2.62	5.1	11.1	2.2	0.3	80
			2022	A+	Brooklyn	1	1	0	5	5	3.46	1.92	6.2	290	38	80	5.05	6.9	8.7	1.3	0.0	-13

Long, lanky RHP, acquired in off-season trade with NYM, performed well across lower level affiliates. Low 3/4s delivery provides difficult angles for hitters, especially with plus extension. Two-pitch pitcher. FB is flat-angled 4-seamer with plus carry late in pitch progression. Plus SL varies between tighter break and sweeper action.

anchez,Sixto — SP — Miami — EXP MLB DEBUT: 2020 — H/W: 6-0 234 — FUT: #2 starter — 8D

Thrws R	Age 24		Year	Lev	Team	W	L	Sv	IP	K	ERA	WHIP	BF/G	OBA	H%	S%	xERA	Ctl	Dom	Cmd	hr/9	BPV
2015 FA (DR)			2017	A+	Clearwater	0	4	0	27	20	4.63	1.32	22.5	260	31	63	3.45	3.0	6.6	2.2	0.3	57
96-100	FB	+++++	2018	A+	Clearwater	4	3	0	46	45	2.53	1.08	22.5	230	31	76	2.29	2.1	8.8	4.1	0.2	118
88-90	CT	+++	2019	A+	Jupiter	0	2	0	11	6	4.91	1.45	23.5	311	34	67	4.99	1.6	4.9	3.0	0.8	62
84-87	SL	+++	2019	AA	Jacksonville	8	4	0	103	97	2.53	1.03	22.0	230	30	76	2.39	1.7	8.5	5.1	0.4	126
87-92	CU	++++	2020	MLB	Miami	3	2	0	39	33	3.46	1.21	22.4	247	30	73	3.29	2.5	7.6	3.0	0.7	87

Electric, hard-throwing RHP missed a 2nd straight season due to shoulder issues. In 2021, it was surgery to repair a right shoulder capsule tear. In Oct 2022, it was an arthroscopic procedure on the same shoulder. When healthy, 96-100 MPH FB is elite offering. CU is plus-plus offering with late arm-side fade and tumble. Expected ready for ST.

anders,Cam — SP — Chicago (N) — EXP MLB DEBUT: 2023 — H/W: 6-2 175 — FUT: Middle reliever — 6C

Thrws R	Age 26		Year	Lev	Team	W	L	Sv	IP	K	ERA	WHIP	BF/G	OBA	H%	S%	xERA	Ctl	Dom	Cmd	hr/9	BPV
2018 (12) LSU			2018	A-	Eugene	1	2	0	16	22	4.50	1.50	4.6	181	30	67	2.55	7.9	12.4	1.6	0.0	28
95-97	FB	++++	2019	A	South Bend	8	4	0	101	84	2.94	1.23	19.5	200	24	78	2.79	4.7	7.5	1.6	0.7	25
80-83	SL	+++	2021	AA	Tennessee	4	7	0	89	107	5.35	1.32	20.5	227	29	64	4.18	4.4	10.8	2.4	1.6	92
70-73	CB	++	2022	AA	Tennessee	1	1	0	24	36	3.38	1.00	15.3	161	24	71	2.11	4.1	13.5	3.3	1.1	150
84-86	CU	++	2022	AAA	Iowa	1	8	0	74	75	5.47	1.42	10.8	211	26	63	3.74	6.0	9.1	1.5	1.1	21

Son of former major leaguer Scott Sanders started the season well, but scuffled when moved up. Uptick in velo gives him a chance and moved to a relief role. FB now sits at 95-97 and 2-seamer has good late sink while 4-seam rides up in the zone. Above-average SL pairs well with FB, but CB and CU are avg, likely making the bullpen move lasting.

ands,Cole — SP — Minnesota — EXP MLB DEBUT: 2022 — H/W: 6-3 215 — FUT: #4 starter — 7D

Thrws R	Age 25		Year	Lev	Team	W	L	Sv	IP	K	ERA	WHIP	BF/G	OBA	H%	S%	xERA	Ctl	Dom	Cmd	hr/9	BPV
2018 (5) Florida St			2019	A+	Fort Myers	5	2	0	52	53	2.25	0.83	21.1	197	25	77	1.71	1.2	9.2	7.6	0.7	150
92-95	FB	+++	2019	AA	Pensacola	0	0	0	4	6	4.50	1.25	16.3	262	43	60	2.90	2.3	13.5	6.0	0.0	200
78-82	CB	+++	2021	AA	Wichita	4	2	0	80	96	2.47	1.17	16.8	207	29	82	2.67	3.9	10.8	2.7	0.7	106
82-85	CU	+++	2022	AAA	St. Paul	3	6	0	61	72	5.59	1.67	14.5	311	41	69	5.95	3.5	10.6	3.0	1.3	113
			2022	MLB	Minnesota	0	3	1	30	28	5.96	1.59	12.1	291	35	64	5.35	3.9	8.3	2.2	1.2	64

Durable SP who made debut with MIN. Didn't throw as many strikes and got hit hard. Operates with three good pitches, but worked behind in count too often. Gets good armside movement with FB and slower CB features plentiful bend. Sufficient separation between FB and CU. May be best in pen where velocity could tick up.

antos II,Alex — SP — Houston — EXP MLB DEBUT: 2026 — H/W: 6-4 194 — FUT: #5 SP/swingman — 7E

Thrws R	Age 21		Year	Lev	Team	W	L	Sv	IP	K	ERA	WHIP	BF/G	OBA	H%	S%	xERA	Ctl	Dom	Cmd	hr/9	BPV
2020 (2) HS (NY)																						
90-93	FB	++++																				
81-87	SL	+++																				
82-85	CU	++	2021	A	Fayetteville	2	2	1	41	48	3.50	1.48	14.8	211	30	76	3.26	6.6	10.5	1.6	0.4	30
76-88	CB	++	2022	A	Fayetteville	0	11	1	82	104	6.02	1.35	14.9	242	32	58	4.45	4.1	11.4	2.8	1.6	114

Tall RHP shows good bat-missing ability but struggles with command. Get goods extension but tends to fall off the mound, seems to struggle with balance in delivery. Best pitch is plus FB with great command and life. Gets good spin on SL. Lack of command, effort in delivery may send him down reliever track. Youth buys him time to work through it.

Santos,Dahian

SP | Toronto | EXP MLB DEBUT: 2025 | H/W: 5-11 160 | FUT: #3 starter | 8D

Thrws R Age 20	Year	Lev	Team	W	L	Sv	IP	K	ERA	WHIP	BF/G	OBA	H%	S%	xERA	Ctl	Dom	Cmd	hr/9	BPV
2019 FA (VZ)																				
90-94 FB ++++	2021	Rk	FCL Blue Jays	1	2	0	35	53	4.62	1.20	14.1	233	35	65	3.58	3.1	13.6	4.4	1.3	180
80-83 SL ++	2021	A	Dunedin	0	2	0	5	5	12.60	2.40	13.1	362	43	45	9.13	7.2	9.0	1.3	1.8	-14
81-85 CU ++	2022	A	Dunedin	4	5	0	73	120	3.45	1.12	15.2	186	31	73	2.54	4.3	14.8	3.4	1.0	168
	2022	A+	Vancouver	0	2	0	12	22	11.07	2.13	15.1	331	53	48	8.22	6.6	16.2	2.4	2.2	131

Short, lanky SP who led org in K with 2nd highest K%. Has tremendous arm strength with whip-like delivery and has projectable frame to add a few ticks to already plus FB. Gets incredible movement to both FB and SL, though both difficult to command. Will need to have greater separation between FB to CU to battle LHH.

Santos,Gregory

RP | Chicago (A) | EXP MLB DEBUT: 2021 | H/W: 6-2 190 | FUT: Setup reliever | 8E

Thrws R Age 23	Year	Lev	Team	W	L	Sv	IP	K	ERA	WHIP	BF/G	OBA	H%	S%	xERA	Ctl	Dom	Cmd	hr/9	BPV
2015 FA (DR)	2021	AAA	Sacramento	1	1	0	15	15	5.33	1.64	4.8	272	35	67	4.64	5.3	8.9	1.7	0.6	34
93-98 FB ++++	2021	MLB	San Francisco	0	2	0	2	3	22.50	3.50	4.2	470	43	50	25.24	9.0	13.5	1.5	13.5	18
87-90 SL ++++	2022	Rk	ACL Giants B	0	0	0	2	3	0.00	1.00	3.8	262	43	100	2.27	0.0	13.5		0.0	261
	2022	AAA	Sacramento	1	2	1	33	34	4.91	1.48	4.3	238	30	69	4.24	5.5	9.3	1.7	1.1	38
	2022	MLB	San Francisco	0	0	0	3	2	5.63	1.88	7.5	250	30	67	4.39	8.4	5.6	0.7	0.0	-109

Physical, hard-throwing RP with time in majors last two years. Has dynamite FB that misses bats, but can also be straight when overthrown. Good hitters can sit on FB as he doesn't have average command. Can be intimidating presence due to large frame. Likes to flash plus SL at times, but tough to rein in for strikes.

Santos,Junior

SP | New York (N) | EXP MLB DEBUT: 2024 | H/W: 6-7 244 | FUT: Setup reliever | 7D

Thrws R Age 21	Year	Lev	Team	W	L	Sv	IP	K	ERA	WHIP	BF/G	OBA	H%	S%	xERA	Ctl	Dom	Cmd	hr/9	BPV
2018 FA (DR)	2018	Rk	DSL Mets	1	1	0	45		2.80	0.91	15.3	216	27	68	1.71	1.2	7.2	6.0	0.2	115
93-95 FB ++++	2018	Rk	GCL Mets	0	0	0	5	3	0.00	0.80	6.0	221	26	100	1.32	0.0	5.4		0.0	115
82-85 SL ++++	2019	Rk	Kingsport	0	5	0	40	36	5.15	1.77	13.2	289	35	72	5.48	5.6	8.1	1.4	0.9	12
85-88 CU +	2021	A	St. Lucie	6	6	0	96	79	4.59	1.52	19.8	285	34	70	4.68	3.6	7.4	2.1	0.8	55
	2022	A+	Brooklyn	8	13	0	116	105	4.49	1.46	19.1	278	35	67	4.01	3.4	8.1	2.4	0.3	72

Big physical RHP improved pitch shape and strike throwing ability at High-A. Low 3/4s delivery with plus extension. Repeatable mechanics. Near physical projection. 2-seam FB is high spin rate with plus arm-side run and heavy boring action. Doesn't miss bats. SL has tight spin profile with chance at plus outcome. Doesn't have feel for CU.

Santos,Winston

SP | Texas | EXP MLB DEBUT: 2024 | H/W: 6-0 160 | FUT: #4 starter | 7D

Thrws R Age 20	Year	Lev	Team	W	L	Sv	IP	K	ERA	WHIP	BF/G	OBA	H%	S%	xERA	Ctl	Dom	Cmd	hr/9	BPV
2019 FA (DR)																				
93-97 FB +++																				
86-89 CU +++	2021	Rk	ACL Rangers	2	2	0	29	32	3.10	0.93	10.9	180	25	65	1.42	2.8	9.9	3.6	0.3	121
82-88 SL +	2021	Rk	DSL Rangers	0	0	0	4	4	4.50	1.50	17.3	347	45	67	4.90	0.0	9.0		0.0	180
	2022	A	Down East	7	6	0	108	108	3.50	1.10	19.3	226	29	69	2.73	2.5	9.0	3.6	0.7	112

Undersized RHP has quietly flown under the radar and produced with roughly average stuff. CU is the prize with hard dropping action, alongside an inconsistent SL that flashes above-average but is more consistently fringe. SL tunnels off FF and the heater now regularly sits mid-90s hinting at more due to his unique slot. Intriguing watch piece.

Sauer,Matt

SP | New York (A) | EXP MLB DEBUT: 2024 | H/W: 6-4 195 | FUT: #5 SP/swingman | 6C

Thrws R Age 24	Year	Lev	Team	W	L	Sv	IP	K	ERA	WHIP	BF/G	OBA	H%	S%	xERA	Ctl	Dom	Cmd	hr/9	BPV
2017 (2) HS (CA)	2019	A	Charleston (Sc)	0	1	0	8	8	2.20	1.46	17.6	206	28	83	2.77	6.6	8.8	1.3	0.0	-2
90-93 FB +++	2021	A	Tampa	2	4	0	66	76	4.36	1.36	18.4	237	32	69	3.66	4.4	10.3	2.4	0.8	87
82-84 SL +++	2021	A+	Hudson Valley	3	2	0	45	51	5.20	1.11	22.1	216	27	56	3.31	3.0	10.2	3.4	1.4	121
76-78 CB +++	2022	A+	Hudson Valley	5	3	0	88	100	3.78	1.25	19.9	232	31	72	3.30	3.6	10.2	2.9	0.8	105
85-87 CU ++	2022	AA	Somerset	0	2	0	20	34	8.02	1.44	21.5	279	43	46	5.68	3.1	15.1	4.9	2.2	206

Former 2nd round pick with extensive injury history continued slow trek towards big leagues. 3/4s delivery with longer arm path. Average across-the-board arsenal of pitches with solid overall command. 4-seam FB has average run profile with some late arm-side run. Tighter SL is better than 12-to-6 CB. SL is above-average offering. Has feel for CU.

Savino,Nate

SP | Arizona | EXP MLB DEBUT: 2025 | H/W: 6-3 210 | FUT: #4 starter | 7D

Thrws L Age 21	Year	Lev	Team	W	L	Sv	IP	K	ERA	WHIP	BF/G	OBA	H%	S%	xERA	Ctl	Dom	Cmd	hr/9	BPV
2022 (3) Virginia																				
91-93 FB +++																				
81-84 SL +++																				
83-86 CU +++																				

Tall, crossfire low 3/4s LHP was 3rd round pick after successful career at UVA. Deceptive delivery with solid extension messes with timing of hitters. 4-seam FB features arm-side running profile. Needs to improve FB spin efficiency. Sweeping SL is best pitch, living down, in and out of the zone. CU lacks firmness but features fade and tumble.

Schultz,Noah

SP | Chicago (A) | EXP MLB DEBUT: 2026 | H/W: 6-9 220 | FUT: #2 starter | 9E

Thrws L Age 19	Year	Lev	Team	W	L	Sv	IP	K	ERA	WHIP	BF/G	OBA	H%	S%	xERA	Ctl	Dom	Cmd	hr/9	BPV
2022 (1) HS (IL)																				
89-93 FB ++++																				
79-84 SL ++++																				
80-82 CU ++																				

Extra tall, lean projectable LHP missed most of draft season due to mono. Low 3/4s delivery with lots of moving parts, doesn't always get fully extended. Easy, low-90s velocity with room for much more. FB has late running action. SL is best present pitch with sweeping, 2-plane break profile. Has feel for CU but lacks consistency.

Schwellenbach,Spencer

SP | Atlanta | EXP MLB DEBUT: 2025 | H/W: 6-1 200 | FUT: #4 starter | 7E

Thrws R Age 22	Year	Lev	Team	W	L	Sv	IP	K	ERA	WHIP	BF/G	OBA	H%	S%	xERA	Ctl	Dom	Cmd	hr/9	BPV
2021 (2) Nebraska																				
93-96 FB ++++																				
81-84 SL +++																				
81-84 CU +++																				

Athletic, hard-throwing RHP with knack for piling strikes remained shelved in 2022 due to Tommy John surgery recovery. Two-way player in college, could have made run as pro as SS. 3-pitch arsenal. Mid-90s FB has plus carry profile, especially up in the zone. SL has inconsistent break profile but will likely be refined into a gyro SL. Rarely uses CU.

Scott,Christian

SP | New York (N) | EXP MLB DEBUT: 2024 | H/W: 6-4 215 | FUT: #5 SP/swingman | 6D

Thrws R Age 23	Year	Lev	Team	W	L	Sv	IP	K	ERA	WHIP	BF/G	OBA	H%	S%	xERA	Ctl	Dom	Cmd	hr/9	BPV
2021 (5) Florida	2020	NCAA	Florida	2	0	0	15	16	1.20	1.13	8.5	206	29	88	1.94	3.6	9.6	2.7	0.0	94
92-95 FB +++	2021	NCAA	Florida	4	2	2	54	51	3.00	1.02	8.0	232	28	77	3.07	1.5	8.5	5.7	1.2	131
82-84 SL +++	2021	Rk	FCL Mets	0	0	0	3	1	3.00	1.33	4.2	262	29	75	3.22	3.0	3.0	1.0	0.0	-9
81-83 CU +	2022	A	St. Lucie	3	3	0	37	52	4.85	1.40	13.1	277	42	64	3.95	2.9	12.6	4.3	0.5	166
	2022	A+	Brooklyn	0	0	0	21	25	3.84	1.47	15.1	261	38	71	3.47	4.3	10.7	2.5	0.0	95

Command/control, pitchability RHP is a serviceable performer. Long body. Repeats 3/4s delivery with solid extension. 3-pitch pitcher. 4-seam FB has solid ride profile but lacks deception out of slot. Two-plane breaking SL is tight. Commands SL extremely well in and out of zone. Struggles with maintaining FB arm speed with CU, lacking firmness.

Seabold,Connor

SP | Boston | EXP MLB DEBUT: 2021 | H/W: 6-2 190 | FUT: #4 starter | 7D

Thrws R Age 27	Year	Lev	Team	W	L	Sv	IP	K	ERA	WHIP	BF/G	OBA	H%	S%	xERA	Ctl	Dom	Cmd	hr/9	BPV
2017 (3) Cal St Fullerton	2021	Rk	FCL Red Sox	0	0	0	5	12	3.46	1.15	10.3	170	53	67	1.46	5.2	20.8	4.0	0.0	252
89-92 FB ++	2021	AAA	Worcester	4	3	0	54	52	3.50	1.15	19.5	220	27	73	3.09	3.2	8.7	2.7	1.0	89
74-78 CB ++	2021	MLB	Boston	0	0	0	3	0	6.00	1.67	13.5	262	19	75	6.91	6.0	0.0	0.0	3.0	-144
82-84 SL ++	2022	AAA	Worcester	8	2	0	86	89	3.34	1.14	18.0	245	32	73	3.12	2.0	9.3	4.7	0.7	132
82-84 CU ++++	2022	MLB	Boston	0	4	0	18	19	11.44	2.38	18.8	407	48	53	10.59	4.0	9.4	2.4	2.5	81

Control-oriented SP who lacks dynamite pitch mix, but can spot ball to all quadrants of zone. K rate higher than stuff suggests as he sequences well and changes eye levels. Has been more of a flyball pitcher, particularly with fringy breaking balls. Fools hitters with solid-average CU that he trusts in critical situations.

Segura,Enrique

SP | Philadelphia | EXP MLB DEBUT: 2027 | H/W: 6-3 175 | FUT: #3 starter | 8E

Thrws R Age 18	Year	Lev	Team	W	L	Sv	IP	K	ERA	WHIP	BF/G	OBA	H%	S%	xERA	Ctl	Dom	Cmd	hr/9	BPV
2022 FA (DR)																				
90-93 FB +++																				
77-79 CB +++																				
82-86 CU ++																				
	2022	Rk	DSL Phillies Red	5	1	0	42	39	2.35	1.37	13.6	232	30	82	3.08	4.7	8.3	1.8	0.2	41

Teenager from the 2022 class who stood out in first DSL season. Already tall with a projectable frame, he showed a solid delivery and a low-90s FB with a ground ball tilt. A swing-and-miss breaking ball is his best secondary; occasionally throws a change-up. With added strength/growth and more reps, could take a step forward in the coming years.

Selvidge,Brock — SP — New York (A)

EXP MLB DEBUT: 2026 | H/W: 6-3 205 | FUT: #4 starter | **7E**

Thrws L Age 20
2021 (3) HS (AZ)

Velo	Pitch	Grade
88-91	FB	+++
81-83	SL	++++
80-82	CU	++

Year	Lev	Team	W	L	Sv	IP	K	ERA	WHIP	BF/G	OBA	H%	S%	xERA	Ctl	Dom	Cmd	hr/9	BPV
2021	Rk	FCL Yankees	0	0	0	3	4	2.81	0.94	4.0	181	28	67	1.14	2.8	11.3	4.0	0.0	145
2022	Rk	FCL Yankees	3	1	0	42	53	2.99	1.28	15.7	237	35	77	3.07	3.6	11.3	3.1	0.4	124

Athletic LHP SP prospect pitched well in Complex League. Low 3/4s upright delivery with solid action. Has longer arm path but does well to stay on time at release. 3-pitch pitcher. 4-seam FB has high spin rate but doesn't maintain shape well. Plus SL has tight, quick late break profile. Rarely features arm-side running CU.

Serna,Luis — SP — New York (A)

EXP MLB DEBUT: 2026 | H/W: 5-11 162 | FUT: #3 starter | **8E**

Thrws R Age 18
2021 FA (MX)

Velo	Pitch	Grade
89-93	FB	+++
77-80	SL	++++
72-75	CU	+++

Year	Lev	Team	W	L	Sv	IP	K	ERA	WHIP	BF/G	OBA	H%	S%	xERA	Ctl	Dom	Cmd	hr/9	BPV
2021	Rk	DSL Yankees	1	5	0	40	46	2.25	1.05	12.9	181	27	76	1.43	3.8	10.4	2.7	0.0	101
2022	Rk	FCL Yankees	0	0	0	41	56	1.97	1.22	15.1	222	36	82	2.30	3.7	12.3	3.3	0.0	138

Projectable, shorter statured RHP showed advance feel for 3-pitch mix. 3/4 crossfire delivery. Repeats delivery well. Athletic frame with good room to add strength to. 2400 rpm spinning 4-seam FB has solid ride/run profile. High spin rate CU has extreme velocity separation off FB and plus movement. Sweeper SL could be 3rd average pitch.

Seymour,Carson — SP — San Francisco

EXP MLB DEBUT: 2024 | H/W: 6-6 260 | FUT: #4 starter | **7C**

Thrws R Age 24
2021 (6) Kansas St

Velo	Pitch	Grade
92-96	FB	+++
80-82	CB	+++
85-88	SL	+++
85-87	CB	++

Year	Lev	Team	W	L	Sv	IP	K	ERA	WHIP	BF/G	OBA	H%	S%	xERA	Ctl	Dom	Cmd	hr/9	BPV
2021	NCAA	Kansas St	3	4	0	56		6.25	1.60	17.7	268	33	61	4.97	5.1	9.1	1.8	1.1	44
2021	Rk	FCL Mets	0	0	0	4	4	2.20	2.20	5.1	206	28	89	4.62	13.2	8.8	0.7	0.0	-180
2022	A	St. Lucie	4	0	0	30	27	1.20	1.06	16.7	213	28	88	1.86	2.7	8.1	3.0	0.0	91
2022	A+	Brooklyn	1	5	0	51	65	3.70	1.12	18.3	238	32	73	3.59	2.1	11.4	5.4	1.4	167
2022	A+	Eugene	2	3	0	29	43	4.02	1.20	19.5	234	38	65	2.70	3.1	13.3	4.3	0.3	174

Extreme groundball pitcher who uses height to advantage. Acquired from NYM at deadline. Throws downhill and uses sinker to keep ball down. K rate has been high at lower levels, though expected to decline as he advances. Likely to benefit more from weak contact than Ks. No one pitch stands out, though SL/CT can be good.

Seymour,Ian — SP — Tampa Bay

EXP MLB DEBUT: 2025 | H/W: 6-0 210 | FUT: #4 starter | **7D**

Thrws L Age 24
2020 (2) Virginia Tech

Velo	Pitch	Grade
88-91	FB	++++
80-82	SL	++
78-81	CU	+++

Year	Lev	Team	W	L	Sv	IP	K	ERA	WHIP	BF/G	OBA	H%	S%	xERA	Ctl	Dom	Cmd	hr/9	BPV
2020	NCAA	Virginia Tech	3	0	0	20	40	2.24	0.90	18.7	187	44	72	1.02	2.2	17.9	8.0	0.0	280
2021	A	Charleston	2	0	0	35	59	2.56	0.83	12.8	139	25	73	1.09	3.3	15.1	4.5	0.8	200
2021	A+	Bowling Green	1	0	0	10	19	1.80	0.80	18.1	175	35	86	1.51	1.8	17.1	9.5	0.9	277
2021	AAA	Durham	1	0	0	10	9	0.00	0.80	18.1	124	17	100	0.23	3.6	8.1	2.3	0.0	67
2022	AA	Montgomery	0	2	0	16	23	8.33	2.10	15.9	325	47	59	7.04	6.7	12.8	1.9	1.1	68

High effort, high 3/4s LHP struggled mightily during 5 game Double-A stint, resulting in eventual Tommy John surgery. Deceptive, crossfire delivery. Always repeated getting to slot well in the past, completely fell apart, likely pitching through injury. 4-seam FB features plus carry. Has significant velocity separation off FB with late moving CU.

Sheehan,Emmet — SP — Los Angeles (N)

EXP MLB DEBUT: 2024 | H/W: 6-5 220 | FUT: #3 starter | **8D**

Thrws R Age 23
2021 (6) Boston College

Velo	Pitch	Grade
95-97	FB	++++
83-85	SL	++
80-83	CU	+++

Year	Lev	Team	W	L	Sv	IP	K	ERA	WHIP	BF/G	OBA	H%	S%	xERA	Ctl	Dom	Cmd	hr/9	BPV
2021	Rk	ACL Dodgers	0	0	0	1	3	0.00	0.00	2.8	0	0			0.0	27.0		0.0	504
2021	A	Rancho Cuca	3	0	0	13	27	4.15	1.15	10.3	214	45	69	3.29	3.5	18.7	5.4	1.4	261
2021	A+	Great Lakes	0	0	0	1	4	22.50	2.50	6.4	0	0	0	3.23	22.5	30.0	1.3	0.0	-50
2022	A+	Great Lakes	7	2	0	63	101	2.85	1.09	13.7	187	34	73	1.83	4.0	14.4	3.6	0.3	169
2022	AA	Tulsa	0	0	0	4	5	4.39	1.22	8.3	147	13	75	3.55	6.6	11.0	1.7	2.2	38

Long strider with low 3/4s arm slot and athletic delivery. Up-tick in FB velocity fueled breakout and heater now sits at 95-97 topping at 99 with good spin and life up in the zone. Some cross-fire in delivery creates deception, but also bouts of wildness. Potentially plus CU and below-average SL round out his repertoire.

Shuster,Jared — SP — Atlanta

EXP MLB DEBUT: 2023 | H/W: 6-3 210 | FUT: #5 SP/swingman | **6A**

Thrws L Age 24
2020 (1) Wake Forest

Velo	Pitch	Grade
89-91	FB	++
81-83	SL	++++
79-81	CU	+++

Year	Lev	Team	W	L	Sv	IP	K	ERA	WHIP	BF/G	OBA	H%	S%	xERA	Ctl	Dom	Cmd	hr/9	BPV
2020	NCAA	Wake Forest	2	1	0	26	43	3.79	0.96	24.7	222	40	58	1.96	1.4	14.8	10.8	0.3	248
2021	A+	Rome	2	0	0	58	73	3.72	1.07	15.1	223	29	73	3.41	2.3	11.3	4.9	1.5	159
2021	AA	Mississippi	0	0	0	14	17	7.61	1.69	21.3	322	38	63	7.91	3.2	10.8	3.4	3.2	126
2022	AA	Mississippi	6	7	0	90	106	2.79	0.96	20.1	204	28	75	2.22	2.2	10.6	4.8	0.8	149
2022	AAA	Gwinnett	1	3	0	48	39	4.29	1.22	19.5	240	25	73	4.37	3.0	7.3	2.4	1.9	68

Over-the-top LHP enjoyed success after increase in overall velocity. Has improved incorporating lower half in delivery. Does well to repeat. Low 90s FB has ride/run profile but struggles with in zone command. Achieves great velocity separation with late tumbling CU. A plus pitch. SL is near average with tight, short break. Steals strikes.

Sikkema,T.J. — SP — Kansas City

EXP MLB DEBUT: 2024 | H/W: 6-0 221 | FUT: #4 starter | **7C**

Thrws L Age 24
2019 (1) Missouri

Velo	Pitch	Grade
89-92	FB	+++
77-82	SL	++++
82-85	CU	+++

Year	Lev	Team	W	L	Sv	IP	K	ERA	WHIP	BF/G	OBA	H%	S%	xERA	Ctl	Dom	Cmd	hr/9	BPV
2019	A-	Staten Island	0	0	0	10	13	0.88	0.69	8.9	173	28	86	0.41	0.9	11.5	13.0	0.0	201
2022	A+	Hudson Valley	1	1	0	36	54	2.49	0.83	12.0	171	27	74	1.44	2.2	13.5	6.0	0.7	200
2022	AA	NW Arkansas	0	5	0	32	29	7.55	1.77	18.5	316	37	59	6.65	4.2	8.1	1.9	1.7	51

Deceptive, oft-injured crafty LHP enjoyed solid season. Was acquired in mid-season trade with NYY. Utilizes crossfire, side-armed delivery with solid extension. Sweeping SL is best pitch with plus movement and command. Late dropping CU projects as above-average offering. Commands fringe average FB well despite its lower strike rate.

Silseth,Chase — SP — Los Angeles (A)

EXP MLB DEBUT: 2022 | H/W: 6-0 217 | FUT: #4 starter | **7B**

Thrws R Age 22
2021 (11) Arizona

Velo	Pitch	Grade
93-97	FB	+++
82-85	SL	+++
85-88	SP	+++
78-81	CB	++

Year	Lev	Team	W	L	Sv	IP	K	ERA	WHIP	BF/G	OBA	H%	S%	xERA	Ctl	Dom	Cmd	hr/9	BPV
2021	NCAA	Arizona	8	1	0	97	105	5.56	1.45	23.0	290	39	60	4.38	2.7	9.7	3.6	0.6	121
2021	Rk	ACL Angels	0	0	0	2	4	4.50	1.00	7.6	151	38	50	0.90	4.5	18.0	4.0	0.0	221
2021	AA	Rocket City	0	2	0	3	3	14.52	1.94	7.4	407	47	20	9.89	0.0	8.7		2.9	175
2022	AA	Rocket City	7	0	0	83	110	2.28	0.95	20.9	182	25	85	2.29	2.9	11.9	4.1	1.2	154
2022	MLB	LA Angels	1	3	0	28	24	6.70	1.60	17.8	293	32	63	6.38	3.8	7.7	2.0	2.2	52

Short, big-bodied RHP was forced into big league action a year early. Repeatable 3/4s delivery with limited extension. Strike thrower. Mixes 4 pitches. Flat-angled 4-seam FB has solid ride profile. Above-average two-plane SL is best pitch with late vertical drop. SP could get to above-average. CB is a 12-to-6 offering with solid depth.

Silva,Eric — SP — San Francisco

EXP MLB DEBUT: 2025 | H/W: 6-1 185 | FUT: #3 starter | **8D**

Thrws R Age 20
2021 (4) HS (CA)

Velo	Pitch	Grade
90-95	FB	+++
78-80	CB	+++
81-84	SL	+++
82-84	CU	++

Year	Lev	Team	W	L	Sv	IP	K	ERA	WHIP	BF/G	OBA	H%	S%	xERA	Ctl	Dom	Cmd	hr/9	BPV
2021	Rk	ACL Giants O	0	1	0	1	2	36.00	7.00	4.9	587	83	43	25.31	27.0	18.0	0.7	0.0	-387
2022	A	San Jose	3	7	0	85	99	5.92	1.36	16.2	243	32	57	4.05	4.1	10.5	2.5	1.2	95

Quick-armed RHP who didn't have great year, but shows flashes of mid-rotation upside. Generates power from live arm and owns two breaking balls that could evolve into plus offerings. Has feel for pitching and simply needs consistently. Size could be problematic for durability. Development of CU to combat LHH will be key to future.

Simas,Kohl — SP — Chicago (A)

EXP MLB DEBUT: 2024 | H/W: 6-1 190 | FUT: #4 starter | **7C**

Thrws R Age 23
2021 FA (San Diego St)

Velo	Pitch	Grade
89-93	FB	+++
82-84	SL	+++
74-77	CB	+++
83-86	CU	+++

Year	Lev	Team	W	L	Sv	IP	K	ERA	WHIP	BF/G	OBA	H%	S%	xERA	Ctl	Dom	Cmd	hr/9	BPV
2021	NCAA	San Diego St	0	1	0	16	25	9.00	2.50	5.7	347	53	62	7.90	9.0	14.1	1.6	0.6	28
2021	Rk	ACL White Sox	0	1	0	3	2	3.00	1.33	4.2	262	32	75	3.19	3.0	6.0	2.0	0.0	45
2021	A	Kannapolis	2	0	1	18	23	1.50	0.72	6.4	151	22	83	0.73	2.0	11.5	5.8	0.5	171
2022	A	Kannapolis	2	2	0	61	76	3.68	1.24	15.5	228	31	74	3.43	3.7	11.2	3.0	1.0	120
2022	AA	Birmingham	0	0	0	6	6	10.33	2.30	5.2	368	38	64	11.44	5.9	8.9	1.5	4.4	18

Former RP with MLB bloodlines spent 2022 as fulltime SP. Pitched well overall despite low FB strike rate. 4-pitch pitcher. 4-seam FB features below average velocity but plays up due to plus ride and run. Best secondary is an sweeping CB with two-plane break. Generates gyro spin with SL and has a firm CU with solid fading action.

Simpson,Josh — RP — Miami

EXP MLB DEBUT: 2023 | H/W: 6-2 190 | FUT: Setup reliever | **7D**

Thrws L Age 25
2019 (32) Columbia

Velo	Pitch	Grade
93-96	FB	++++
78-80	CB	++++

Year	Lev	Team	W	L	Sv	IP	K	ERA	WHIP	BF/G	OBA	H%	S%	xERA	Ctl	Dom	Cmd	hr/9	BPV
2021	Rk	FCL Marlins	0	0	0	2	4	12.86	1.43	8.9	336	61	0	4.45	0.0	17.1		0.0	327
2021	A+	Beloit	0	2	0	43	58	5.64	1.30	9.9	233	33	58	3.84	4.0	12.1	3.1	1.3	129
2022	AA	Pensacola	5	2	2	55	89	3.91	1.09	5.4	166	28	65	2.08	4.7	14.5	3.1	0.8	152
2022	AAA	Jacksonville	2	0	0	12	23	4.46	1.24	4.9	227	47	60	2.38	3.7	17.1	4.6	0.0	226

Hard-throwing LHP struck out bunches of hitters, split between upper level affiliates. Low 3/4s crossfire delivery with solid extension creates deception. Primarily 2-pitch pitcher. FB has solid carry coming from lower arm slot, contributing to high whiff rate. Needs to feature better in-zone FB command. A plus sweeping CB maintains consistency.

Sims, Landon — SP — Arizona

EXP MLB DEBUT: 2025 | H/W: 6-2 227 | FUT: #3 starter | 8D

Thrws R | Age 22
2022 (1) Mississippi St
91-94 FB ++++
82-84 SL ++++

Year	Lev	Team	W	L	Sv	IP	K	ERA	WHIP	BF/G	OBA	H%	S%	xERA	Ctl	Dom	Cmd	hr/9	BPV

Strong-bodied, former College World Series star had spring Tommy John surgery. High 3/4 slot delivery with solid extension. Primarily two pitches: 4-seam FB has flat-angled approach, missing bats with late riding action. 2-plane SL is nasty, especially with late vertical break. Commands both offerings well.

[S]mall, Ethan — SP — Milwaukee

EXP MLB DEBUT: 2022 | H/W: 6-4 215 | FUT: #4 starter | 7B

Thrws L | Age 26
2019 (1) Mississippi St
90-93 FB +++
78-80 CB +
81-82 SL ++
81-84 CU ++++

Year	Lev	Team	W	L	Sv	IP	K	ERA	WHIP	BF/G	OBA	H%	S%	xERA	Ctl	Dom	Cmd	hr/9	BPV
2021	Rk	ACL Brewers-G	0	0	0	1	1	0.00	2.00	4.8	415	52	100	7.49	0.0	9.0		0.0	
2021	AA	Biloxi	2	2	0	41	67	1.97	1.14	20.4	183	34	83	1.85	4.6	14.7	3.2	0.0	158
2021	AAA	Nashville	2	0	0	35	24	2.06	1.37	16.3	215	24	89	3.40	5.4	6.2	1.1	0.8	-17
2022	AAA	Nashville	7	6	0	103	114	4.46	1.36	15.9	220	30	67	3.33	5.1	10.0	2.0	0.7	60
2022	MLB	Milwaukee	0	0	0	6	7	7.38	2.62	16.6	317	41	73	8.61	11.8	10.3	0.9	1.5	-115

Tall, durable SP who started 2 games with MIL. Keeps ball in yard as groundball guy and no pitch is straight. Plus CU is dynamite offering with quick arm speed similar to FB. Lot of spin on FB gives it carry and can add sink at bottom. Neither breaking ball is average and may shelve CB in favor of SL. Has to throw strikes.

Smith, Dylan — SP — Detroit

EXP MLB DEBUT: 2024 | H/W: 6-2 180 | FUT: #4 starter | 7C

Thrws R | Age 22
2021 (3) Alabama
93-95 FB +++
82-84 SL +++
76-78 CB +++
CU ++

Year	Lev	Team	W	L	Sv	IP	K	ERA	WHIP	BF/G	OBA	H%	S%	xERA	Ctl	Dom	Cmd	hr/9	BPV
2022	A	Lakeland	0	0	0	5	3	0.00	0.60	8.6	175	21	100	0.28	0.0	5.4		0.0	115
2022	A+	West Michigan	8	6	0	83	86	4.01	1.19	16.7	250	33	67	3.24	2.3	9.3	4.1	0.6	124

Attacks hitters with an above-average four-pitch mix and held his own in debut. FB sits at 93-95 but lacks spin and movement. Plus SL sits at 82-84 and results in plenty of swing-and-miss; inconsistent CB and a split-change show potential and round out arsenal. Aggressive approach; pounds the strike zone.

Smith, Russell — SP — Milwaukee

EXP MLB DEBUT: 2024 | H/W: 6-7 255 | FUT: #4 starter | 7D

Thrws L | Age 24
2021 (2) Texas Christian
89-94 FB +++
80-83 SL ++
83-85 CU +++

Year	Lev	Team	W	L	Sv	IP	K	ERA	WHIP	BF/G	OBA	H%	S%	xERA	Ctl	Dom	Cmd	hr/9	BPV
2022	A+	Wisconsin	2	5	0	68	62	4.89	1.32	18.8	247	30	65	3.93	3.6	8.2	2.3	1.1	69

Large-framed SP who ended first pro season in July. Height and slot give tough angle to plate along with extension, making FB more than gun reading. Inconsistent command has been issue and slows arm speed on CU at times. Not overpowering but could be unique RP if starting doesn't work out.

[S]mith-Shawver, AJ — SP — Atlanta

EXP MLB DEBUT: 2024 | H/W: 6-3 205 | FUT: #2 starter | 9E

Thrws R | Age 20
2021 (7) HS (TX)
93-96 FB ++++
86-89 SL ++++
86-88 CU +++

Year	Lev	Team	W	L	Sv	IP	K	ERA	WHIP	BF/G	OBA	H%	S%	xERA	Ctl	Dom	Cmd	hr/9	BPV
2021	Rk	FCL Braves	0	1	0	8	16	8.89	1.73	9.2	149	23	50	4.81	11.1	17.8	1.6	2.2	38
2022	A	Augusta	3	4	0	68	103	5.15	1.36	16.8	219	36	61	3.13	5.1	13.6	2.6	0.5	124

Tall, projectable hard-throwing RHP experienced growing pains during his full-season debut. Athletic build; was a 2-way performer. High 3/4s delivery with plus extension struggles with release point. Mid-90s 4-seam FB features plus carry and solid run. Tight spinning SL has late vertical break profile. Struggles keeping late fading CU firm.

[S]nelling, Robby — SP — San Diego

EXP MLB DEBUT: 2026 | H/W: 6-3 210 | FUT: #2 starter | 9E

Thrws L | Age 19
2022 (1) HS (NV)
90-94 FB +++
77-83 CB ++++
81-84 CU +

Year	Lev	Team	W	L	Sv	IP	K	ERA	WHIP	BF/G	OBA	H%	S%	xERA	Ctl	Dom	Cmd	hr/9	BPV

Big, strong lefty who produces velocity thanks to natural strength and clean delivery. Has advanced ability to spin ball and has wipeout CB that serves as K pitch against hitters from both sides. Hasn't used CU much and will get instruction as pro. All pitches have different speed and movement to give him added deception.

[S]olometo, Anthony — SP — Pittsburgh

EXP MLB DEBUT: 2025 | H/W: 6-5 220 | FUT: #3 starter | 8D

Thrws L | Age 20
2021 (2) HS (NJ)
91-94 FB +++
82-85 SL +++
79-84 CU ++

Year	Lev	Team	W	L	Sv	IP	K	ERA	WHIP	BF/G	OBA	H%	S%	xERA	Ctl	Dom	Cmd	hr/9	BPV
2022	A	Bradenton	5	1	0	47	51	2.67	1.06	14.1	189	27	72	1.55	3.6	9.7	2.7	0.0	95

Tall, projectable SP who began season in May and is being brought along slowly. Has ability to dominate hitters with lively pitches and very deceptive delivery. Long arm action tough to read, but leads to command issues. Didn't allow HR as he lives in lower half of zone. Uses FB frequently and has SL to miss bats. CU needs work.

[S]oriano, George — RP — Miami

EXP MLB DEBUT: 2023 | H/W: 6-2 210 | FUT: Setup reliever | 7C

Thrws R | Age 24
2015 FA (DR)
94-97 FB ++++
82-84 SL ++++
88-90 CU +++

Year	Lev	Team	W	L	Sv	IP	K	ERA	WHIP	BF/G	OBA	H%	S%	xERA	Ctl	Dom	Cmd	hr/9	BPV
2019	A	Clinton	4	7	1	119	99	3.93	1.33	21.5	243	30	71	3.47	3.8	7.5	2.0	0.6	51
2021	A	Jupiter	3	0	0	34	47	2.91	1.29	20.0	213	32	80	3.14	4.8	12.4	2.6	0.8	113
2021	A+	Beloit	4	1	0	55	67	3.76	1.40	21.1	272	37	75	4.20	3.1	10.9	3.5	0.8	131
2022	AA	Pensacola	0	2	0	29	36	3.10	1.45	15.5	234	33	80	3.64	5.3	11.2	2.1	0.6	77
2022	AAA	Jacksonville	4	2	8	47	49	2.49	1.15	5.8	190	26	79	2.14	4.4	9.4	2.1	0.4	68

Hard-thrower former SP moved to pen early in the season and is close to contributing. Strong frame, at physical projection. Low 3/4s delivery provides solid deception. Flat-angled 4-seam FB has plus ride from lower slot. SL has above-average horizontal slide with late vertical break, a plus pitch. CU is a usable weapon against LHH.

[S]piers, Carson — SP — Cincinnati

EXP MLB DEBUT: 2023 | H/W: 6-3 205 | FUT: #5 SP/swingman | 6C

Thrws R | Age 25
2020 FA (Clemson)
91-94 FB +++
78-82 SL +++
86-89 CT ++
84-86 CU +

Year	Lev	Team	W	L	Sv	IP	K	ERA	WHIP	BF/G	OBA	H%	S%	xERA	Ctl	Dom	Cmd	hr/9	BPV
2020	NCAA	Clemson	3	0	4	15	17	0.00	0.53	5.6	105	16	100		1.8	10.1	5.7	0.0	152
2021	A	Daytona	2	0	1	22	27	3.24	1.08	17.3	233	34	70	2.50	2.0	10.9	5.4	0.4	160
2021	A+	Dayton	6	4	0	89	103	3.64	1.09	17.4	213	29	69	2.66	2.9	10.4	3.6	0.8	126
2022	AA	Chattanooga	2	5	0	104	90	5.01	1.47	20.3	280	31	74	5.71	3.4	7.8	2.3	2.1	67
2022	AAA	Louisville	2	1	0	17	15	7.41	1.88	16.0	352	41	62	7.45	3.2	7.9	2.5	1.6	75

Low 3/4s RHP had an up and down 2022 season split between upper level affiliates. Repeatable delivery with limited extension, relies heavily on tunneling pitches off of flat angled 4-seam FB. Throws strikes, struggles with in-zone command. Best secondary is sweeping SL with two-plane break. Also throws 2-seam FB, CT & CU.

Staine, Connor — SP — Colorado

EXP MLB DEBUT: 2025 | H/W: 6-4 200 | FUT: #5 SP/swingman | 6C

Thrws R | Age 22
2022 (5) Central Florida
93-95 FB +++
SL +++
CB ++
CU +

Year	Lev	Team	W	L	Sv	IP	K	ERA	WHIP	BF/G	OBA	H%	S%	xERA	Ctl	Dom	Cmd	hr/9	BPV

Projectable RHP had a breakout season for Central Florida that landed him in the 5th round. Uptick in FB velo fueled the breakout and heater now sits at 93-95 topping at 97. Sits low on the back side before driving to the plate with a quick athletic delivery. Secondaries include above-average SL with late downward tilt and a below-average CU.

Stone, Gavin — SP — Los Angeles (N)

EXP MLB DEBUT: 2023 | H/W: 6-1 175 | FUT: #3 starter | 8D

Thrws R | Age 24
2020 (5) Central Arkansas
93-96 FB +++
84-86 SL +++
84-87 CU +++
79-81 CB +

Year	Lev	Team	W	L	Sv	IP	K	ERA	WHIP	BF/G	OBA	H%	S%	xERA	Ctl	Dom	Cmd	hr/9	BPV
2021	A	Rancho Cuca	1	2	0	70	101	3.73	1.27	15.9	259	40	71	3.53	2.6	13.0	5.1	0.6	182
2021	A+	Great Lakes	1	0	0	21	37	3.86	1.10	16.4	233	42	67	2.91	2.1	15.9	7.4	0.9	246
2022	A+	Great Lakes	1	1	0	25	28	1.44	1.00	15.9	212	30	88	2.01	2.2	10.1	4.7	0.4	141
2022	AA	Tulsa	6	4	0	73	107	1.60	1.22	21.1	223	37	86	2.43	3.7	13.2	3.6	0.1	155
2022	AAA	Oklahoma City	2	1	0	23	33	1.17	0.95	14.5	177	29	90	1.48	3.1	12.9	4.1	0.4	165

Dominated across three levels due to spike in velo and now features an above-avg 93-96 mph FB that is well located. Best offering is a mid-80 CU that he will throw in any count and mixes in a SL that works well against RHH. Advanced ability to pound the zone and hit his spots with the 3-pitch mix and above-average command.

toudt,Levi

SP | Cincinnati | EXP MLB DEBUT: 2023 | H/W: 6-1 195 | FUT: #4 starter | 7C

Thrws R Age 25
2019 (3) Lehigh

Velo	Pitch	Grade
93-95	FB	+++
82-84	SL	++++
74-77	CB	++
84-87	CU	+++

Year	Lev	Team	W	L	Sv	IP	K	ERA	WHIP	BF/G	OBA	H%	S%	xERA	Ctl	Dom	Cmd	hr/9	BPV
2021	A+	Everett	6	1	0	64	67	3.52	1.19	21.4	207	27	73	2.87	4.1	9.4	2.3	0.8	77
2021	AA	Arkansas	1	2	0	17	19	2.62	1.28	23.5	224	29	85	3.50	4.2	9.9	2.4	1.0	84
2022	AA	Arkansas	6	6	0	87	82	5.28	1.31	20.0	273	33	62	4.52	2.3	8.5	3.7	1.3	109
2022	AA	Chattanooga	1	0	0	5	6	0.00	0.40	16.1	124	20	100		0.0	10.8		0.0	212
2022	AAA	Louisville	0	2	0	19	15	3.32	1.42	13.4	241	31	74	3.12	4.7	7.1	1.5	0.0	18

Hard-throwing, athletic RHP struggled with zone command split between upper levels. It's a repeatable 3/4s delivery with minimal deception, especially with the FB. 4-seam FB sits mid-90s with flat-angled approach. A late tumbling CU battles a two-plane breaking SL as the best secondary. SL command gives it an edge. CB is a low spin rate offering.

usana,Jarlin

SP | Washington | EXP MLB DEBUT: 2026 | H/W: 6-6 235 | FUT: #2 SP/closer | 9D

Thrws R Age 19
2022 FA (DR)

Velo	Pitch	Grade
96-99	FB	++++
86-89	SL	++++
90-93	CU	++

Year	Lev	Team	W	L	Sv	IP	K	ERA	WHIP	BF/G	OBA	H%	S%	xERA	Ctl	Dom	Cmd	hr/9	BPV
2022	Rk	ACL Padres	0	0	0	29	44	2.47	0.89	13.5	155	27	72	1.00	3.4	13.6	4.0	0.3	171
2022	Rk	FCL Nationals	0	0	0	5	9	1.76	1.57	11.2	218	43	88	3.11	7.1	15.9	2.3	0.0	113
2022	A	Fredericksburg	0	0	0	10	13	2.67	1.39	14.2	240	34	85	3.81	4.5	11.6	2.6	0.9	106

Teenage prodigy from the Soto deal whose exploits include touching 103 on his four-seamer and a high-80s, swing-and-miss SL. Current command is raw, and gets fewer whiffs on the heater than one would think. But has less than 50 IP in pro ball and his build/arm strength at his age has scouts buzzing. Also features CU as a distant third pitch.

winey,Nick

SP | San Francisco | EXP MLB DEBUT: 2024 | H/W: 6-3 185 | FUT: #4 starter | 7C

Thrws L Age 24
2020 (2) North Carolina St

Velo	Pitch	Grade
88-93	FB	+++
77-79	CB	+++
78-80	CU	++++

Year	Lev	Team	W	L	Sv	IP	K	ERA	WHIP	BF/G	OBA	H%	S%	xERA	Ctl	Dom	Cmd	hr/9	BPV
2020	NCAA	NC St	4	0	0	28	42	1.29	0.68	24.5	141	23	88	0.64	1.9	13.5	7.0	0.6	209
2021	Rk	ACL Giants B	0	0	0	8	16	1.13	1.63	7.1	237	52	92	3.47	6.8	18.0	2.7	0.0	160
2021	A	San Jose	0	0	0	24	42	0.75	1.16	13.7	191	38	93	1.76	4.5	15.7	3.5	0.0	179
2022	A+	Eugene	4	6	0	89	105	3.84	1.21	17.1	201	28	69	2.73	4.6	10.6	2.3	0.7	86

Tall SP who has erratic control, but continually befuddles hitters with deception and pitch movement. Lacks frontline velocity, but likes to use big-breaking CB to advantage. Best pitch is CU that has natural drop and fade and is true weapon against RHH. Has focused on streamlining delivery for better command. Too many flyballs.

Tamarez,Misael

SP | Houston | EXP MLB DEBUT: 2023 | H/W: 6-1 206 | FUT: Setup reliever | 7C

Thrws R Age 23
2019 FA (DR)

Velo	Pitch	Grade
94-98	FB	+++
85-90	SL	++++
87-91	CU	++

Year	Lev	Team	W	L	Sv	IP	K	ERA	WHIP	BF/G	OBA	H%	S%	xERA	Ctl	Dom	Cmd	hr/9	BPV
2021	A	Fayetteville	4	2	1	43	64	3.98	1.30	14.8	188	30	70	2.70	5.9	13.4	2.3	0.6	101
2021	A+	Asheville	2	1	0	33	39	3.52	1.20	19.1	243	32	75	3.58	2.7	10.6	3.9	1.1	135
2022	AA	Corpus Christi	3	6	1	103	122	4.63	1.27	17.6	207	26	69	3.76	4.8	10.6	2.2	1.6	80
2022	AAA	Sugar Land	1	1	0	18	20	2.50	1.17	17.9	106	12	84	1.90	7.5	10.0	1.3	1.0	-5

Tall right-hander uses potent FB/SL combo to wrack up whiffs and strikeouts outside the zone. Some effort and inconsistency in delivery leads to poor fastball command. Mixes in occasional changeup. Two-pitch mix, command issues suggest bullpen trajectory.

'arnok,Freddy

SP | Oakland | EXP MLB DEBUT: 2022 | H/W: 6-3 185 | FUT: #5 SP/swingman | 7C

Thrws R Age 24
2017 (3) HS (FL)

Velo	Pitch	Grade
92-95	FB	++++
79-82	CB	+++
82-85	CU	+++
82-84	SL	++

Year	Lev	Team	W	L	Sv	IP	K	ERA	WHIP	BF/G	OBA	H%	S%	xERA	Ctl	Dom	Cmd	hr/9	BPV
2021	A+	Rome	3	2	0	28	48	4.80	1.21	16.2	209	32	68	3.92	4.2	15.4	3.7	1.9	182
2021	AA	Mississippi	3	2	0	45	61	2.60	1.11	19.7	216	33	77	2.35	3.0	12.2	4.1	0.4	157
2022	AA	Mississippi	2	2	0	62	75	4.34	1.30	17.1	235	31	70	3.80	3.9	10.9	2.8	1.2	108
2022	AAA	Gwinnett	2	1	0	44	49	3.68	1.25	17.9	234	29	77	3.92	3.5	10.0	2.9	1.4	105
2022	MLB	Atlanta	0	0	0	0	1	0.00	5.00	1.6	639	177	100	22.66	0.0	45.0		0.0	828

Tall, strong-bodied RHP had solid season in upper minors resulting in MLB debut. High 3/4s delivery with a long arm circle. Stays on time at release point. 4-pitch pitcher. FB has above-average ride profile but struggles keeping offering flat. CU flashes plus with arm-side run and late fade. CB has backed up and no longer plus pitch. SL is mediocre.

'averas,Diosmerky

SP | Houston | EXP MLB DEBUT: 2024 | H/W: 6-5 256 | FUT: Setup reliever | 6C

Thrws R Age 23
2017 FA (DR)

Velo	Pitch	Grade
94-97	FB	+++
87-92	SL	++
81-85	CB	++
86-88	CU	++

Year	Lev	Team	W	L	Sv	IP	K	ERA	WHIP	BF/G	OBA	H%	S%	xERA	Ctl	Dom	Cmd	hr/9	BPV
2018	Rk	DSL Astros Blue	2	3	3	37	35	4.14	1.49	10.6	212	29	69	2.90	6.6	8.5	1.3	0.0	-6
2019	Rk	GCL Astros	1	2	2	24	28	5.58	1.98	9.7	227	33	69	4.32	10.4	10.4	1.0	0.0	-76
2021	A	Fayetteville	3	4	0	60	72	5.23	1.59	15.6	238	35	64	3.62	6.4	10.8	1.7	0.1	38
2021	A+	Asheville	3	0	0	17	23	1.57	0.87	15.9	157	22	92	1.68	3.1	12.0	3.8	1.0	150
2022	A+	Asheville	5	3	0	75	92	4.79	1.52	14.2	235	34	67	3.57	5.9	11.0	1.9	0.4	58

Imposing RHP split time between starting and relieving at High-A. FB sits mid-to-high 90s, has good life and garners whiffs in the zone. Shows decent SL but struggles to get batters to chase it out of the zone. Poor command likely result of inconsistent delivery. Very good at avoiding hard contact, doesn't give up many HR.

'eodo,Emiliano

SP | Texas | EXP MLB DEBUT: 2025 | H/W: 6-1 165 | FUT: Setup reliever | 7D

Thrws R Age 22
2020 FA (DR)

Velo	Pitch	Grade
96-101	FB	+++
85-93	SL	++++
88-92	CU	+

Year	Lev	Team	W	L	Sv	IP	K	ERA	WHIP	BF/G	OBA	H%	S%	xERA	Ctl	Dom	Cmd	hr/9	BPV
2021	Rk	ACL Rangers	4	2	0	29	48	3.40	1.44	6.5	226	41	74	2.91	5.6	14.8	2.7	0.0	135
2022	A	Down East	3	6	0	84	115	3.10	1.13	15.1	177	26	75	2.27	4.7	12.3	2.6	0.7	112

Weird that a 101-mph FB isn't main attraction but pitch shape is average and command shaky. SL a monster plus plus offering, with CU far distant and thrown only 71 times, so the trend is towards relief unless he really pushes it. SwK highlights K ability alongside 59% GB and youth will give him time but in the pen he's got leveraged upside.

Then,Juan

RP | Seattle | EXP MLB DEBUT: 2023 | H/W: 6-1 200 | FUT: Setup reliever | 7D

Thrws R Age 23
2016 FA (DR)

Velo	Pitch	Grade
92-97	FB	+++
84-86	SL	++
81-85	CU	

Year	Lev	Team	W	L	Sv	IP	K	ERA	WHIP	BF/G	OBA	H%	S%	xERA	Ctl	Dom	Cmd	hr/9	BPV
2019	A-	Everett	0	3	0	30	32	3.59	1.10	16.8	220	30	66	2.30	2.7	9.6	3.6	0.3	118
2019	A	West Virginia	1	2	0	16	14	2.25	0.69	18.7	134	16	70	0.57	2.3	7.9	3.5	0.6	99
2021	A+	Everett	2	5	0	54	59	6.49	1.61	17.1	308	37	64	6.40	3.2	9.8	3.1	2.0	109
2022	Rk	ACL Mariners	0	0	0	2	2	0.00	2.00	4.8	262	35	100	4.84	9.0	9.0	1.0	0.0	-63
2022	AA	Arkansas	0	1	0	10	14	5.40	1.40	4.2	281	39	67	5.24	2.7	12.6	4.7	1.8	172

Injury-prone prospect who pitched out of pen upon return in August. Most of career as SP. Limited time due to variety of injuries, including shoulder. Has impressive, raw stuff including high-octane FB thrown with lightning quick arm action. Mixes in strong SL and CU. Control getting better with more time. Could be hard-throwing RP.

Thomas,Connor

SP | St. Louis | EXP MLB DEBUT: 2023 | H/W: 5-11 173 | FUT: #5 SP/swingman | 6C

Thrws L Age 24
2019 (5) Georgia Tech

Velo	Pitch	Grade
87-89	FB	++
80-83	SL	+++
81-84	CU	++

Year	Lev	Team	W	L	Sv	IP	K	ERA	WHIP	BF/G	OBA	H%	S%	xERA	Ctl	Dom	Cmd	hr/9	BPV
2019	A-	State Coll	2	0	0	15		4.14	1.18	12.2	284	40	61	3.08	0.6	10.1	17.0	0.0	183
2019	A	Peoria	2	1	1	27	19	3.65	1.25	11.0	246	29	72	3.40	3.0	6.3	2.1	0.7	51
2021	AA	Springfield	0	2	0	20	24	4.93	1.44	21.4	314	39	75	6.30	1.3	10.7	8.0	2.2	175
2021	AAA	Memphis	6	4	1	101	92	3.11	1.36	19.2	275	33	81	4.34	2.7	8.2	3.1	1.0	93
2022	AAA	Memphis	6	12	0	135	110	5.47	1.57	21.2	311	37	66	5.50	2.7	7.3	2.8	1.1	78

Short LHP struggled to repeat success from 2021 and found AAA tough sledding. Below-average FB rarely breaks 90 but does have good sink generating plenty of ground ball outs. Plus SL and above-average CU gives him a chance and command allows stuff to play up. Likely destined to a spot starter/swing role and should get his shot in 2023.

Thompson,Matthew

SP | Chicago (A) | EXP MLB DEBUT: 2023 | H/W: 6-3 195 | FUT: Setup reliever | 7C

Thrws R Age 22
2019 (2) HS (TX)

Velo	Pitch	Grade
91-95	FB	+++
76-81	CB	+++
81-84	SL	+++
84-87	CU	++

Year	Lev	Team	W	L	Sv	IP	K	ERA	WHIP	BF/G	OBA	H%	S%	xERA	Ctl	Dom	Cmd	hr/9	BPV
2019	Rk	AZL White Sox	0	0	0	2	2	0.00	1.00	3.8	262	35	100	2.32	0.0	9.0		0.0	180
2021	Rk	ACL White Sox	0	1	0	2	1	9.00	1.50	8.6	347	30	50	9.18	0.0	4.5		4.5	99
2021	A	Kannapolis	2	8	0	71	77	5.94	1.70	16.9	292	38	65	5.34	4.8	9.7	2.0	0.9	64
2022	A+	Winston-Salem	4	5	0	84	73	4.71	1.32	19.3	257	30	68	4.37	3.1	7.8	2.5	1.4	75
2022	AA	Birmingham	0	2	0	25	31	5.38	1.47	15.4	269	37	65	4.59	3.9	11.1	2.8	1.1	112

Tall RHP had pedestrian 2022. Athletic build with some room for growth. Has improved 4-seam FB command, improving strike rate and limiting barrels but doesn't miss bats. 12-to-6 CB is best secondary, but struggles with consistency. Brought back SL grip to better results, 2nd most dependable pitch. Lacks out pitch.

Thompson,Riley

SP | Chicago (N) | EXP MLB DEBUT: 2023 | H/W: 6-4 210 | FUT: #4 starter | 7D

Thrws R Age 26
2018 (11) Louisville

Velo	Pitch	Grade
93-96	FB	++++
90-92	CT	++
77-80	CB	++
84-86	CU	+

Year	Lev	Team	W	L	Sv	IP	K	ERA	WHIP	BF/G	OBA	H%	S%	xERA	Ctl	Dom	Cmd	hr/9	BPV
2018	NCAA	Louisville	1	3	0	33	35	6.82	1.76	13.7	262	36	58	4.48	6.8	9.5	1.4	0.3	6
2018	A-	Eugene	0	2	0	25	25	2.87	1.31	11.5	253	33	78	3.33	3.2	9.0	2.8	0.4	92
2019	A	South Bend	8	6	0	94	87	3.06	1.23	18.1	243	30	79	3.47	3.0	8.3	2.8	0.9	88
2022	AA	Tennessee	2	5	0	57	64	4.42	1.39	12.6	226	29	72	4.00	5.1	10.1	2.0	1.3	63

Was finally back on the mound after recovering from Tommy John surgery and a shoulder injury. Held his own in 19 AA starts; team was careful managing his workload. Tall RHP generates mid-90s heat on his plus FB and has been up to 98 with high spin and late life. Backs it up with a potentially plus CB, CT, and an inconsistent CU.

Thorpe,Drew — SP — New York (A)

EXP MLB DEBUT: 2024 | H/W: 6-4 190 | FUT: #3 starter | 8D

Thrws R Age 21
2022 (2) Cal Poly

Velo	Pitch	Grade
89-92	FB	+ + +
80-82	CU	+ + + +
81-84	SL	+ + +

Year	Lev	Team	W	L	Sv	IP	K	ERA	WHIP	BF/G	OBA	H%	S%	xERA	Ctl	Dom	Cmd	hr/9	BPV

Tall, athletic over-the-top RHP SP with some room to grow into frame. Balanced, repeatable delivery with plus extension. Does well to keep pitch release on-time. 3-pitch pitcher. Flat-angled FB doesn't miss bats but is well commanded. Fading CU has late plus tumble. Can get whiffs up and down. SL is above-average.

Tidwell,Blade — SP — New York (N)

EXP MLB DEBUT: 2024 | H/W: 6-4 207 | FUT: #3 starter | 8D

Thrws R Age 21
2022 (2) Tennessee

Velo	Pitch	Grade
94-96	FB	+ + + +
82-85	SL	+ + + +
85-88	CU	+ + +

Year	Lev	Team	W	L	Sv	IP	K	ERA	WHIP	BF/G	OBA	H%	S%	xERA	Ctl	Dom	Cmd	hr/9	BPV
2022	NCAA	Tennessee	3	2	0	39	51	3.00	1.08	11.7	220	30	81	3.24	2.5	11.8	4.6	1.4	161
2022	Rk	FCL Mets	0	0	0	1	2	0.00	1.00	3.8	0	0	100		9.0	18.0	2.0	0.0	99
2022	A	St. Lucie	0	1	0	8	9	2.22	1.23	8.2	149	22	80	1.55	6.7	10.0	1.5	0.0	18

3/4 slot RHP made professional debut after 2nd round selection in 2022. Athletic frame with room for added bulk. Deceptive delivery with plus extension; repeatable. 3-pitch pitcher. Altered 4-seam FB usage as pro, taking advantage of natural ride profile to good results. High spin rate SL has late two-plane break profile. Has feel for CU.

Tiedemann,Ricky — SP — Toronto

EXP MLB DEBUT: 2023 | H/W: 6-4 220 | FUT: #1 starter | 9C

Thrws L Age 20
2021 (3) Golden West Coll

Velo	Pitch	Grade
92-96	FB	+ + + +
81-84	SL	+ + + +
83-85	CU	+ + +

Year	Lev	Team	W	L	Sv	IP	K	ERA	WHIP	BF/G	OBA	H%	S%	xERA	Ctl	Dom	Cmd	hr/9	BPV
2022	A	Dunedin	3	1	0	30	49	1.80	0.80	18.1	115	22	78	0.35	3.9	14.7	3.8	0.3	177
2022	A+	Vancouver	2	2	0	37	54	2.42	0.94	17.5	180	29	76	1.57	2.9	13.1	4.5	0.5	175
2022	AA	New Hampshire	0	1	0	11	14	2.45	0.82	10.0	139	23	67	0.38	3.3	11.5	3.5	0.0	136

Breakout SP in first pro experience. Pitched on 3 levels and posted miniscule oppBA at all stops. Had highest K% in org while also throwing consistent strikes. Has found success with arm slot and clean delivery and has confidence to use any pitch in any count. FB and SL took big steps forward and currently plus to double-plus.

Tokar,Heitor — SP — Houston

EXP MLB DEBUT: 2025 | H/W: 6-6 276 | FUT: #5 SP/swingman | 7E

Thrws R Age 22
2018 FA (BR)

Velo	Pitch	Grade
90-94	FB	+ +
83-88	SL	+ + +
83-86	CU	+ + +
75-83	CB	+ +

Year	Lev	Team	W	L	Sv	IP	K	ERA	WHIP	BF/G	OBA	H%	S%	xERA	Ctl	Dom	Cmd	hr/9	BPV
2019	Rk	GCL Astros	1	0	2	35	29	2.83	1.17	11.6	233	29	77	2.87	2.8	7.5	2.6	0.5	76
2021	Rk	FCL Astros	2	1	0	14	18	3.86	1.07	9.1	186	25	69	2.73	3.9	11.6	3.0	1.3	122
2021	A	Fayetteville	3	3	2	40	37	4.73	1.18	14.5	257	32	59	3.33	1.8	8.3	4.6	0.7	119
2022	A+	Asheville	3	4	0	76	64	8.04	1.76	17.4	322	37	55	6.60	3.8	7.6	2.0	1.5	52

Pitching prospect split time between starting and bullpen duties. Struggled all year with inconsistent outings, sky-high ERA. Large stature and long limbs make repeating delivery difficult. Gets good separation on CU from FB. Sub-50 strand% not supported by batted ball, plate discipline, contact metrics. Could take big step up with consistency.

Torres,Eric — RP — Los Angeles (A)

EXP MLB DEBUT: 2023 | H/W: 6-0 195 | FUT: Middle reliever | 6B

Thrws L Age 23
2021 (14) Kansas St

Velo	Pitch	Grade
89-92	FB	+ + +
78-81	SL	+ + + +
83-86	CU	+ +

Year	Lev	Team	W	L	Sv	IP	K	ERA	WHIP	BF/G	OBA	H%	S%	xERA	Ctl	Dom	Cmd	hr/9	BPV
2020	NCAA	Kansas St	0	1	0	5	9	6.92	0.77	3.1	64	15	0		5.2	15.6	3.0	0.0	158
2021	NCAA	Kansas St	4	0	1	39	58	2.76	1.02	6.0	219	35	76	2.43	2.1	13.4	6.4	0.7	202
2021	A+	Tri-City	0	1	0	8	13	5.56	1.36	4.2	235	38	60	3.85	4.4	14.4	3.3	1.1	158
2022	AA	Rocket City	2	2	22	51	81	1.59	0.94	4.6	148	26	87	1.26	4.1	14.3	3.5	0.5	166

Side-armed LHP, closer in Double-A, inched closer to the big leagues. Deceptive delivery with solid extension. Mostly 2-pitch mix. Workhorse is 88-92 mph 2-seam FB with an arm-side boring profile. Commands frisbee SL extremely well. Borderline plus movement profile. Uses below-average arm-side running CU as show me pitch to RHH.

Urena,Walbert — SP — Los Angeles (A)

EXP MLB DEBUT: 2025 | H/W: 6-0 170 | FUT: Setup reliever | 7E

Thrws R Age 19
2021 FA (DR)

Velo	Pitch	Grade
95-98	FB	+ + + +
86-88	CU	+ + +
80-84	SL	+ + +

Year	Lev	Team	W	L	Sv	IP	K	ERA	WHIP	BF/G	OBA	H%	S%	xERA	Ctl	Dom	Cmd	hr/9	BPV
2022	Rk	ACL Angels	3	4	0	37	45	3.88	1.54	13.5	193	28	75	3.24	7.8	10.9	1.4	0.5	5

Hard-throwing, short-statured RHP averaged 97 mph with FB in professional debut. Double-plus arm speed propels velocity. Mechanically risky delivery. 3-pitch pitcher; 4-seam FB has dominant running profile and will need to work on spin efficiency. Has better feel for CU than SL. CU has arm-side boring action. Struggles spinning SL effectively.

Uribe,Abner — RP — Milwaukee

EXP MLB DEBUT: 2024 | H/W: 6-2 200 | FUT: Closer | 8E

Thrws R Age 22
2018 FA (DR)

Velo	Pitch	Grade
97-102	FB	+ + + +
87-89	SL	+ + +
85-86	CU	+

Year	Lev	Team	W	L	Sv	IP	K	ERA	WHIP	BF/G	OBA	H%	S%	xERA	Ctl	Dom	Cmd	hr/9	BPV
2019	Rk	AZL Brewers Blue	1	1	0	2	2	17.14	3.81	4.6	403	50	50	11.80	17.1	8.6	0.5	0.0	-291
2019	Rk	Rocky Mountain	2	1	0	7	5	9.00	2.57	9.4	358	40	65	9.03	9.0	6.4	0.7	1.3	-109
2021	A	Carolina	1	0	3	33	52	4.07	1.48	8.4	204	35	72	3.24	6.8	14.1	2.1	0.5	89
2022	AA	Biloxi	0	0	0	3	4	0.00	2.00	7.2	191	31	100	3.92	12.0	12.0	1.0	0.0	-90

Big, strong RP who ended season in April after knee surgery. Has best FB in org with big-time heat and rising action. Hard SL features cutting action and tough to elevate. Big issue has been inability to throw strikes. Can slow arm to aim ball, leaving him susceptible to hard hit balls. Rarely changes speeds.

Van Eyk,CJ — SP — Toronto

EXP MLB DEBUT: 2024 | H/W: 6-1 198 | FUT: #4 starter | 7D

Thrws R Age 24
2020 (2) Florida State

Velo	Pitch	Grade
90-94	FB	+ + +
80-83	CB	+ + +
84-87	SL	+ +
	CU	+ +

Year	Lev	Team	W	L	Sv	IP	K	ERA	WHIP	BF/G	OBA	H%	S%	xERA	Ctl	Dom	Cmd	hr/9	BPV
2020	NCAA	Florida St	1	1	0	20	25	1.34	1.14	20.0	162	26	87	1.43	5.3	11.1	2.1	0.0	74
2021	A+	Vancouver	4	6	0	80	100	5.84	1.37	17.7	239	33	57	3.88	4.4	11.2	2.6	1.0	102

Advanced SP who missed all of season after Tommy John surgery. Has the pitch mix and deception to be a solid starter, but health is concern. Effortful delivery can by hindrance to throwing strikes, but arm action is deceptive. Fast arm produces quality FB and hard CB. Mixes in a SL with cutter action and rarely used CU.

Vanasco,Ricky — SP — Texas

EXP MLB DEBUT: 2024 | H/W: 6-3 180 | FUT: Middle reliever | 7E

Thrws R Age 24
2017 (15) HS (FL)

Velo	Pitch	Grade
94-98	FB	+ + +
81-87	CB	+ + +
85-91	CU	+
87-91	SL	+

Year	Lev	Team	W	L	Sv	IP	K	ERA	WHIP	BF/G	OBA	H%	S%	xERA	Ctl	Dom	Cmd	hr/9	BPV
2018	Rk	AZL Rangers	3	3	0	24	25	4.46	1.57	15.2	268	36	70	4.19	4.8	9.3	1.9	0.4	55
2019	A-	Spokane	3	1	0	39	59	1.85	1.15	17.2	173	29	86	2.00	5.1	13.6	2.7	0.5	126
2019	A	Hickory	0	0	0	10	16	1.76	0.78	18.4	148	28	75	0.37	2.6	14.1	5.3	0.0	201
2022	A+	Hickory	3	5	0	84	111	4.49	1.49	17.2	247	34	73	4.53	5.0	11.9	2.4	1.3	96
2022	AA	Frisco	0	0	0	8	7	6.75	2.00	19.3	328	37	71	7.96	5.6	7.9	1.4	2.3	8

Tommy John return season went about as well as it could, though FB velocity not back and sat low-90s deeper into starts. CB is best offering which he can bury when on but return rust made things harder to discern. SL and CU remain distant and he'll really need to push the CU to remain in the rotation, as he's already 40-manned and clock suggests relief.

Vargas,Jordy — SP — Colorado

EXP MLB DEBUT: 2026 | H/W: 6-3 153 | FUT: #5 SP/swingman | 7D

Thrws R Age 19
2021 FA (DR)

Velo	Pitch	Grade
90-94	FB	+ + +
83-86	CB	+ +
73-75	CU	+ +

Year	Lev	Team	W	L	Sv	IP	K	ERA	WHIP	BF/G	OBA	H%	S%	xERA	Ctl	Dom	Cmd	hr/9	BPV
2021	Rk	DSL Colorado	2	0	0	34	46	1.32	0.99	11.9	157	26	85	1.01	4.2	12.1	2.9	0.0	122
2022	Rk	ACL Rockies	2	1	0	26	40	2.40	0.65	13.0	150	28	59	0.05	1.4	13.7	10.0	0.0	228
2022	A	Fresno	2	0	0	24	24	3.72	1.36	16.9	227	25	82	4.52	4.8	8.9	1.8	1.9	48

Long-limbed, lanky hurler is all about projection at this point and impressed in his state-side debut. FB sits in the lows-90s with good vertical action and late life. 11-to-6 power CB is best secondary, but struggles with command will need to be addressed (3.5 BB/9). Shows some feel for mid-80s CU, but it is a work in progress.

Varland,Louie — SP — Minnesota

EXP MLB DEBUT: 2022 | H/W: 6-1 205 | FUT: #4 starter | 7B

Thrws R Age 25
2019 (15) Concordia

Velo	Pitch	Grade
93-96	FB	+ + +
82-85	CB	+ +
84-87	SL	+ +
82-85	CU	+ + +

Year	Lev	Team	W	L	Sv	IP	K	ERA	WHIP	BF/G	OBA	H%	S%	xERA	Ctl	Dom	Cmd	hr/9	BPV
2021	A	Fort Myers	4	2	0	47	76	2.10	1.21	19.0	236	41	84	2.80	3.1	14.5	4.8	0.4	197
2021	A+	Cedar Rapids	6	2	0	55	66	2.12	1.00	21.1	208	29	82	2.22	2.3	10.8	4.7	0.7	150
2022	AA	Wichita	7	4	0	105	119	3.34	1.34	21.9	256	33	80	4.22	3.3	10.2	3.1	1.2	111
2022	AAA	St. Paul	1	1	0	21	27	1.71	0.85	19.4	201	30	82	1.55	1.3	11.5	9.0	0.4	191
2022	MLB	Minnesota	1	2	0	26	21	3.81	1.23	21.1	262	30	75	4.22	2.1	7.3	3.5	1.4	93

Steady SP who led org in Ks and made big league debut. Added a few ticks to FB and now features four offerings. Can pitch up in zone and add sink for groundballs. CU continues to improve and may be near plus status with impeccable drop. Doesn't yet have reliable breaking ball. Hard SL could be cultivated while CB lags behind.

Vasil,Mike | SP | New York (N) | EXP MLB DEBUT: 2024 | H/W: 6-5 225 | FUT: #4 starter | 7C

Thrws R Age 23	Year	Lev	Team	W	L	Sv	IP	K	ERA	WHIP	BF/G	OBA	H%	S%	xERA	Ctl	Dom	Cmd	hr/9	BPV
2021 (8) Virginia	2021	NCAA	Virginia	7	5	0	81	73	4.54	1.47	20.5	306	36	74	5.50	2.0	8.1	4.1	1.4	110
92-95 FB +++	2021	Rk	FCL Mets	0	0	0	7	10	1.29	0.43	7.6	132	24	67		0.0	12.9		0.0	249
86-88 SL +++	2022	Rk	FCL Mets	0	0	0	1	2	0.00	1.00	3.8	262	55	100	2.23	0.0	18.0		0.0	342
79-81 CB +++	2022	A	St. Lucie	3	1	0	37	39	2.19	1.00	15.7	199	28	78	1.75	2.7	9.5	3.5	0.2	117
83-86 CU +++	2022	A+	Brooklyn	1	1	0	33	44	5.17	1.18	16.5	205	30	56	2.77	4.1	12.0	2.9	0.8	123

Big-bodied 2021 draft pick enjoyed solid season and excelled during fall AFL stint. Body is workhorse-like frame. Repeats 3/4s delivery well with above-average extension. 4-pitch pitcher with average-to-above-average stuff. FB has solid arm/side run profile and some ride. Struggles with in-zone command. SL has tight, 2-plane break. CB and CU solid.

Vasquez,Randy | SP | New York (A) | EXP MLB DEBUT: 2023 | H/W: 6-0 165 | FUT: #4 starter | 7C

Thrws R Age 24	Year	Lev	Team	W	L	Sv	IP	K	ERA	WHIP	BF/G	OBA	H%	S%	xERA	Ctl	Dom	Cmd	hr/9	BPV
2018 FA (DR)	2019	Rk	Pulaski	4	1	0	54	53	3.32	1.18	19.7	191	23	76	2.82	4.6	8.8	1.9	1.0	51
92-94 FB +++	2021	A	Tampa	3	3	0	50	58	2.34	1.16	15.3	199	28	80	2.25	4.1	10.4	2.5	0.4	94
80-83 SL ++++	2021	A+	Hudson Valley	3	0	0	36	53	1.75	1.14	23.8	245	40	83	2.40	2.0	13.3	6.6	0.0	203
87-89 CU +++	2021	AA	Somerset	2	1	0	21	19	4.27	1.42	22.4	279	34	71	4.43	3.0	8.1	2.7	0.9	83
86-88 CT +++	2022	AA	Somerset	2	7	0	115	120	3.91	1.28	18.9	246	32	71	3.61	3.2	9.4	2.9	0.9	100

Command/control RHP struggled bringing high whiff rate to Double-A. Lean frame. Struggled maintaining low 3/4s slot, changing shape of pitches. Throws to variations of FB. 2-seam FB has plus command and solid bore. 4-seam FB has regressed. CB is horizontal breaker. It's a plus pitch but looked more like a SL from lower slot. Also throws CU and CT.

Vela,Noel | SP | San Diego | EXP MLB DEBUT: 2024 | H/W: 6-1 185 | FUT: #4 starter | 7C

Thrws L Age 23	Year	Lev	Team	W	L	Sv	IP	K	ERA	WHIP	BF/G	OBA	H%	S%	xERA	Ctl	Dom	Cmd	hr/9	BPV
2017 (28) HS (TX)	2019	Rk	AZL Padres	0	3	0	10		10.69	2.87	8.2	387	52	59	9.09	9.8	10.7	1.1	0.0	-54
90-95 FB +++	2021	A	Lake Elsinore	1	8	0	54	63	3.99	1.33	17.3	216	29	72	3.32	5.0	10.5	2.1	0.8	72
81-83 CB +++	2021	A+	Fort Wayne	0	3	0	33	44	3.81	1.42	17.5	249	37	73	3.69	4.4	12.0	2.8	0.5	116
83-85 CU +++	2022	A+	Fort Wayne	6	7	0	87	101	3.83	1.39	18.3	232	32	73	3.47	4.9	10.4	2.1	0.6	75
	2022	AA	San Antonio	1	3	0	22	24	6.49	2.03	12.0	285	38	66	5.61	8.1	9.7	1.2	0.4	-26

Unheralded LHP who had most walks in org, but has positive attributes to build on. Has swing and miss stuff, led by outstanding CB that flashes plus. Very tough on LHH and operates in all quadrants of zone. Mostly a groundball guy who hasn't allowed many HR. Delivery has been inconsistent, but uses all pitches in arsenal.

Ventura,Jordany | SP | New York (N) | EXP MLB DEBUT: 2025 | H/W: 6-0 162 | FUT: #4 starter | 7E

Thrws R Age 22	Year	Lev	Team	W	L	Sv	IP	K	ERA	WHIP	BF/G	OBA	H%	S%	xERA	Ctl	Dom	Cmd	hr/9	BPV
2018 FA (DR)																				
92-95 FB +++	2019	Rk	GCL Mets	2	1	0	33	34	4.36	1.06	14.2	225	30	58	2.50	2.2	9.3	4.3	0.5	126
78-80 CB ++	2019	Rk	Kingsport	0	1	0	8	9	1.13	1.13	15.8	117	18	89	0.96	6.8	10.1	1.5	0.0	18
85-87 CU ++++	2022	Rk	FCL Mets	0	0	0	2	3	0.00	0.00	5.6	0	0			0.0	13.5		0.0	261
	2022	A	St. Lucie	0	0	0	6	10	5.81	1.45	8.8	286	48	56	3.74	2.9	14.5	5.0	0.0	201

Oft-injured, athletic RHP returned from long absence due to Tommy John surgery recovery to be put back on IL to miss last 3 months of season. Loose 3/4s crossfire delivery. Frame near physical projection. 3-pitch arsenal. 4-seam FB has solid run and ride profile. Late-fading CU is best pitch, featuring occasional drop and plus command. 11-to-5 CB is fringe.

Vera,Norge | SP | Chicago (A) | EXP MLB DEBUT: 2024 | H/W: 6-4 185 | FUT: #3 starter | 8D

Thrws R Age 22	Year	Lev	Team	W	L	Sv	IP	K	ERA	WHIP	BF/G	OBA	H%	S%	xERA	Ctl	Dom	Cmd	hr/9	BPV
2021 FA (CU)																				
91-96 FB ++++	2021	Rk	DSL White Sox	1	0	0	19	34	0.00	0.74	8.4	144	31	100	0.18	2.4	16.1	6.8	0.0	244
79-83 SL +++	2022	A	Kannapolis	0	2	0	24	35	1.88	1.13	11.8	151	25	85	1.61	5.6	13.1	2.3	0.4	102
78-82 CU +++	2022	A+	Winston-Salem	0	1	0	3	5	8.71	1.94	7.4	186	35	50	3.68	11.6	14.5	1.3	0.0	-34
	2022	AA	Birmingham	0	0	0	8	12	5.63	2.13	13.2	181	32	71	4.11	13.5	13.5	1.0	0.0	-104

Physical, high 3/4s RHP struggled in full-season debut with inability to throw strikes. Tall, lean frame with developed lower half that powers delivery. Athletic, but struggles to maintain release point. FB is best pitch with plus potential. Gyro-spinning SL and firm, fading CU have above-average markers but lack consistency.

Vines,Darius | SP | Atlanta | EXP MLB DEBUT: 2023 | H/W: 6-1 190 | FUT: #4 starter | 7C

Thrws R Age 24	Year	Lev	Team	W	L	Sv	IP	K	ERA	WHIP	BF/G	OBA	H%	S%	xERA	Ctl	Dom	Cmd	hr/9	BPV
2019 (7) Cal St Bakersfield																				
90-93 FB +++	2021	A	Augusta	2	0	0	36	48	2.25	0.94	16.9	191	28	81	1.97	2.5	12.0	4.8	0.8	167
80-84 SL +++	2021	A+	Rome	4	4	0	75	81	3.24	1.05	20.8	221	27	78	3.26	2.3	9.7	4.3	1.4	131
80-82 CU ++++	2022	AA	Mississippi	7	4	0	107	127	3.95	1.21	21.6	249	32	73	3.93	2.5	10.7	4.2	1.3	142
73-75 CB ++	2022	AAA	Gwinnett	1	0	0	33	29	3.25	1.30	19.5	236	30	74	2.99	3.8	7.9	2.1	0.3	57

Durable high 3/4s RHP inched closer to big league debut with solid 2022. Near physical projection. Stays on time in delivery despite longer arm circle. 4-pitch pitcher. Controls 4-seam FB in zone, best up where ride comes alive. CU is best secondary. Sells well with late tumble. SL has short break profile, best with late downward movement.

Vodnik,Victor | RP | Atlanta | EXP MLB DEBUT: 2023 | H/W: 6-0 200 | FUT: Middle reliever | 6C

Thrws R Age 23	Year	Lev	Team	W	L	Sv	IP	K	ERA	WHIP	BF/G	OBA	H%	S%	xERA	Ctl	Dom	Cmd	hr/9	BPV
2018 (14) HS (CA)	2018	Rk	GCL Braves	1	1	0	4	9	10.71	2.14	5.2	403	71	50	9.51	2.1	19.3	9.0	2.1	307
94-97 FB ++++	2019	A	Rome	1	3	3	67	69	2.95	1.18	11.7	225	31	73	2.41	3.2	9.3	2.9	0.1	98
87-89 CU +++	2021	AA	Mississippi	1	4	0	33	41	5.42	1.63	13.4	255	34	69	5.05	6.0	11.1	1.9	1.4	57
SL ++	2022	AA	Mississippi	0	0	1	7	14	0.00	1.00	3.8	168	41	100	1.09	3.9	18.0	4.7	0.0	238
	2022	AAA	Gwinnett	2	0	2	27	33	2.98	1.54	4.9	253	35	83	4.17	5.3	10.9	2.1	0.7	72

Hard-throwing, max effort 3/4s RHP inched closer to the big leagues, performing at both upper levels. Struggles repeating release point in a longer arm circle delivery. Primarily 2-pitch pitcher. FB best up in the zone, where it misses bats. Struggles with in-zone command. Fading CU has late rumble but doesn't get enough velocity separation.

Vrieling,Trystan | SP | New York (A) | EXP MLB DEBUT: 2024 | H/W: 6-4 200 | FUT: #4 starter | 7D

Thrws R Age 22	Year	Lev	Team	W	L	Sv	IP	K	ERA	WHIP	BF/G	OBA	H%	S%	xERA	Ctl	Dom	Cmd	hr/9	BPV
2022 (3) Gonzaga																				
90-93 FB +++																				
83-86 SL +++																				
79-82 CB ++++																				
85-88 CT ++																				

Tall RHP was drafted in 3rd round of 2022 draft. Solid physical build with room to grow. 3/4 crossfire delivery with above-average delivery. Struggles repeating release/slot. 4-seam FB is arm-side runner, lacking consistent ride. 12-to-6 CB is best pitch. It features high spin rate, plus depth and solid movement. SL is tight breaker. Also throws CT.

Waites,Cole | RP | San Francisco | EXP MLB DEBUT: 2022 | H/W: 6-3 180 | FUT: Setup reliever | 7C

Thrws R Age 24	Year	Lev	Team	W	L	Sv	IP	K	ERA	WHIP	BF/G	OBA	H%	S%	xERA	Ctl	Dom	Cmd	hr/9	BPV
2019 (18) West Alabama	2021	A	San Jose	1	0	2	10	24	0.89	0.50	3.3	34	18	80		3.6	21.4	6.0	0.0	307
94-99 FB ++++	2022	A+	Eugene	1	1	1	12	27	3.69	1.15	3.7	225	55	69	2.79	3.0	19.9	6.8	0.7	297
84-88 SL +++	2022	AA	Richmond	2	2	4	21	38	1.71	1.29	4.8	168	36	85	1.82	6.4	16.3	2.5	0.0	138
	2022	AAA	Sacramento	1	0	1	8	11	0.00	0.75	4.1	117	21	100		3.4	12.4	3.7	0.0	150
	2022	MLB	San Francisco	0	0	0	5	4	3.46	1.92	3.5	290	32	89	6.70	6.9	6.9	1.0	1.7	-44

Career RP who reached majors based on improved command and control. Big-time K rate a byproduct of potential double-plus FB and knockout SL with amazing depth. Focuses mostly on FB with interesting boring action. Pitches very aggressively, but lacks touch and feel for changing speeds. Has trouble with LHH.

Waldichuk,Ken | SP | Oakland | EXP MLB DEBUT: 2022 | H/W: 6-4 220 | FUT: #4 starter | 8C

Thrws L Age 25	Year	Lev	Team	W	L	Sv	IP	K	ERA	WHIP	BF/G	OBA	H%	S%	xERA	Ctl	Dom	Cmd	hr/9	BPV
2019 (5) St. Mary's (CA)	2021	AA	Somerset	4	3	0	79	108	4.21	1.29	20.3	223	31	73	3.90	4.3	12.3	2.8	1.5	122
93-96 FB ++++	2022	AA	Somerset	4	0	0	28	46	1.28	0.92	17.6	167	29	92	1.51	3.2	14.7	4.6	0.6	196
77-79 CB ++	2022	AAA	Las Vegas	0	1	0	18	21	3.46	1.26	18.6	280	36	80	4.62	1.5	10.4	7.0	1.5	165
83-87 SL +++	2022	AAA	Scranton/WB	2	3	0	47	70	3.62	1.29	17.6	222	34	75	3.39	4.4	13.3	3.0	1.0	140
81-85 CU +++	2022	MLB	Oakland	2	2	0	34	33	5.00	1.23	19.8	249	30	62	3.96	2.6	8.7	3.3	1.3	103

Funky, deceptive LHP who reached majors after trade with NYY. Posts very high K rate due to ability to vary angles and slots to plate. Low 3/4s slot adds terrific action to both FB and SL. Can get on side of CB and be hit hard, but is dominant against LHH. FB has average velocity, but so much movement and tail that hitters can't barrel.

Waldron,Matt | SP | San Diego | EXP MLB DEBUT: 2023 | H/W: 6-2 185 | FUT: #4 starter | 7D

Thrws R Age 26	Year	Lev	Team	W	L	Sv	IP	K	ERA	WHIP	BF/G	OBA	H%	S%	xERA	Ctl	Dom	Cmd	hr/9	BPV
2019 (18) Nebraska	2019	A-	MahoningVal	3	0	1	35	40	3.58	0.94	13.2	226	31	61	2.16	1.0	10.2	10.0	0.5	174
90-92 FB ++	2021	A+	Fort Wayne	3	4	0	72	72	3.25	1.22	22.4	253	32	76	3.46	2.4	9.0	3.8	0.7	116
75-79 SL ++	2021	AA	San Antonio	0	4	0	31	31	6.66	1.64	19.8	285	37	57	4.80	4.6	9.0	1.9	0.6	54
71-79 KB +++	2022	AA	San Antonio	2	1	0	44	38	2.86	1.18	19.6	252	32	76	3.04	2.0	7.8	3.8	0.4	102
	2022	AAA	El Paso	3	9	0	69	58	8.47	1.75	19.7	321	37	51	6.57	3.8	7.6	2.0	1.6	52

Knuckleballer who throws consistent strikes. Got lit up in Triple-A after success in Double-A. KB is most used pitch, but also throws FB with decent velocity. Tough to rely entirely on KB as it can be hit or show inconsistent movement. Does nice job of pitching backwards, using KB to set up low-90s FB and middling SL.

Walsh,Jake — RP — St. Louis

EXP MLB DEBUT: 2022 | H/W: 6-1 192 | FUT: Middle reliever | 6C

Thrws R Age 27 — 2017 (16) Florida Southern

Velo	Pitch	Grade
93-96	FB	+++
79-82	CB	+++
	CU	+

Year	Lev	Team	W	L	Sv	IP	K	ERA	WHIP	BF/G	OBA	H%	S%	xERA	Ctl	Dom	Cmd	hr/9	BPV
2019	Rk	GCL Cardinals	0	0	0	1	4	15.00	2.50	3.2	371	145	33	7.66	7.5	30.0	4.0	0.0	356
2021	AA	Springfield	2	1	0	18	25	1.50	0.89	5.1	178	30	81	0.97	2.5	12.5	5.0	0.0	176
2021	AAA	Memphis	0	1	1	4	9	9.00	1.25	4.1	151	0	33	5.74	6.8	20.3	3.0	4.5	200
2022	AAA	Memphis	1	0	6	15	22	1.19	1.19	4.7	205	33	94	2.60	4.2	13.1	3.1	0.6	141
2022	MLB	St. Louis	0	1	0	2	5	16.36	2.27	3.7	326	71	20	6.37	8.2	20.5	2.5	0.0	165

Walsh missed almost two years of action due illness and Tommy John surgery in 2019 and continues to be plagued by elbow soreness and has been moved into a relief role. When healthy uses simple repeatable mechanics and features a mid-90s 4-seam heater, an above-average CB, and a usable CU. A return to health could have him in the majors in 2023.

Walston,Blake — SP — Arizona

EXP MLB DEBUT: 2024 | H/W: 6-5 175 | FUT: #3 starter | 8D

Thrws L Age 21 — 2019 (1) HS (NC)

Velo	Pitch	Grade
90-92	FB	+++
79-83	SL	+++
72-76	CB	++
86-88	CU	++++

Year	Lev	Team	W	L	Sv	IP	K	ERA	WHIP	BF/G	OBA	H%	S%	xERA	Ctl	Dom	Cmd	hr/9	BPV
2021	A	Visalia	2	2	0	43	60	3.34	1.18	21.6	219	33	74	2.97	3.5	12.5	3.5	0.8	148
2021	A+	Hillsboro	2	3	0	52	57	4.15	1.31	19.5	261	31	79	5.02	2.8	9.8	3.6	2.1	121
2022	A+	Hillsboro	1	0	0	17	27	2.62	1.16	17.1	211	38	75	2.03	3.7	14.1	3.9	0.0	173
2022	AA	Amarillo	7	3	0	106	110	5.17	1.45	21.6	278	34	67	4.95	3.3	9.3	2.8	1.4	97

Tall, projectable low-3/4s LHP struggled to compete against older competition. Lean wiry build. Repeatable delivery with longer arm circle and plus extension. 4-seam FB has low spin rate and mostly operates with only arm-side run. Late-fading CU is well commanded with tumble presently. SL is a tight, two-plane breaker. CB is eye-level changer.

Walter,Brandon — SP — Boston

EXP MLB DEBUT: 2023 | H/W: 6-2 200 | FUT: #4 starter | 7C

Thrws L Age 26 — 2019 (26) Delaware

Velo	Pitch	Grade
92-95	FB	+++
80-83	SL	++++
81-83	CU	++

Year	Lev	Team	W	L	Sv	IP	K	ERA	WHIP	BF/G	OBA	H%	S%	xERA	Ctl	Dom	Cmd	hr/9	BPV
2021	A	Salem	1	1	2	31	46	1.45	0.87	8.8	194	34	81	1.09	1.7	13.4	7.7	0.0	211
2021	A+	Greenville	4	3	0	58	86	3.72	1.03	18.7	219	34	67	2.67	2.2	13.3	6.1	0.9	199
2022	AA	Portland	2	2	0	50	68	2.88	0.78	20.0	203	29	70	2.00	0.5	12.2	22.7	1.1	224
2022	AAA	Worcester	1	1	0	7	7	8.75	1.81	16.7	307	40	46	5.01	5.0	8.8	1.8	0.0	41

Control-oriented SP who had good season before ending in June due to disc issue in upper back. Led org in lowest BB/9 and posted 3rd highest K rate. Keeps ball on ground with heavy-sinking FB and low 3/4s slot. Best pitch is slider that sweeps away from LHH. Numbers exceed natural stuff and will need to polish CU to combat RHH.

Ward,Thaddeus — SP — Washington

EXP MLB DEBUT: 2023 | H/W: 6-3 192 | FUT: #4 starter | 7D

Thrws R Age 26 — 2018 (5) Central Florida

Velo	Pitch	Grade
92-96	FB	+++
81-85	SL	+++
84-87	CU	++

Year	Lev	Team	W	L	Sv	IP	K	ERA	WHIP	BF/G	OBA	H%	S%	xERA	Ctl	Dom	Cmd	hr/9	BPV
2021	AA	Portland	0	0	0	8	11	5.63	2.00	19.3	328	49	69	5.80	5.6	12.4	2.2	0.0	89
2022	Rk	FCL Red Sox	0	0	0	5	9	0.00	0.20	7.6	66	16	100		0.0	16.2		0.0	310
2022	A	Salem	0	0	0	6	10	0.00	0.50	10.0	106	22	100		1.5	15.0	10.0	0.0	248
2022	A+	Greenville	0	1	0	7	6	5.14	1.86	16.4	313	40	69	5.25	5.1	7.7	1.5	0.0	18
2022	AA	Portland	0	1	0	33	41	2.45	1.27	19.3	231	32	85	3.33	3.8	11.1	2.9	0.8	116

Athletic sinkerballer who returned in July after Tommy John surgery. Achieved success with polished pitch mix and ability to get groundball outs. Command still not all the way back and needs more polish to CU. Likes to pair sinker with SL that features late bite and cutting action. Can use CT as chase pitch before spotting FB down. Rule 5 pick from BOS.

Warren,Will — SP — New York (A)

EXP MLB DEBUT: 2023 | H/W: 6-2 175 | FUT: #3 starter | 8D

Thrws R Age 23 — 2021 (8) SE Louisiana

Velo	Pitch	Grade
91-95	FB	+++
82-85	SL	++++
78-80	CB	++
85-88	CU	+++

Year	Lev	Team	W	L	Sv	IP	K	ERA	WHIP	BF/G	OBA	H%	S%	xERA	Ctl	Dom	Cmd	hr/9	BPV
2022	A+	Hudson Valley	2	3	0	35	42	3.60	1.11	17.2	233	33	68	2.69	2.3	10.8	4.7	0.5	150
2022	AA	Somerset	7	6	0	94	83	4.02	1.30	21.5	251	31	70	3.65	3.2	7.9	2.5	0.8	76

Low 3/4s slot 2021 draft pick 8th round pick emerged as organization's best pitching prospect. High waist, lean body with some room left to grow. Low 3/4s slot delivery with effort and below-average extension. Works horizontally with pitch mix. Added 2-seam FB with above-average potential. Sweeping SL is best pitch with deep break. CT is solid too.

Watters,Jacob — SP — Oakland

EXP MLB DEBUT: 2024 | H/W: 6-4 230 | FUT: Setup reliever | 7C

Thrws R Age 22 — 2022 (4) West Virginia

Velo	Pitch	Grade
93-95	FB	+++
83-84	CB	+++
83-85	CU	++

Year	Lev	Team	W	L	Sv	IP	K	ERA	WHIP	BF/G	OBA	H%	S%	xERA	Ctl	Dom	Cmd	hr/9	BPV
2022	NCAA	West Virginia	3	7	1	59	75	6.24	1.78	15.1	277	38	66	5.61	6.2	11.4	1.8	1.2	55
2022	Rk	ACL Athletics	0	0	0	1	1	0.00	1.00	3.8	0	0	100		9.0	9.0	1.0	0.0	-63
2022	A+	Lansing	0	0	0	3	2	0.00	1.33	6.2	106	13	100	1.42	9.0	6.0	0.7	0.0	-117

Large-framed SP with intriguing upside if he can harness power FB. Generates heat with lot of effort in delivery that has been difficult to repeat. Exhibits sub-par control and command and can be guilty of aiming ball. Has chance to develop knockout CB with power and break. Leverages deception on CU, but only average potential.

Way,Beck — SP — Kansas City

EXP MLB DEBUT: 2024 | H/W: 6-4 200 | FUT: #4 starter | 7C

Thrws R Age 23 — 2020 (4) NW Florida St

Velo	Pitch	Grade
93-95	FB	+++
81-85	SL	++++
86-89	CU	+++

Year	Lev	Team	W	L	Sv	IP	K	ERA	WHIP	BF/G	OBA	H%	S%	xERA	Ctl	Dom	Cmd	hr/9	BPV
2020	NJCA	NW Florida St	5	0	0	40	58	0.68	0.65	19.8	131	24	88		2.0	13.1	6.4	0.0	198
2021	A	Tampa	3	1	0	47	54	2.68	1.11	12.3	148	21	76	1.57	5.6	10.3	1.9	0.4	54
2021	A+	Hudson Valley	1	2	0	16	29	7.83	1.68	18.1	284	48	54	5.84	5.0	16.2	3.2	1.7	174
2022	A+	Hudson Valley	5	5	0	72	80	3.74	1.12	19.0	213	27	71	3.04	3.2	10.0	3.1	1.1	110
2022	A+	Quad Cities	3	3	0	35	47	3.84	1.16	20.0	195	31	65	2.10	4.3	12.0	2.8	0.3	117

Tall, projectable RHP enjoyed solid season in high-A, split between NYY & KC. Crossfire 3/4s delivery. Struggles to maintain release point and throwing FB for strikes. Primary FB is sinking 2-seam FB but also throws 4-seam variety. Commands sweeping SL, which is borderline plus pitch. Has feel for solid arm-side running CU.

Weatherly,Sam — SP — Colorado

EXP MLB DEBUT: 2024 | H/W: 6-4 205 | FUT: #4 starter | 7E

Thrws L Age 23 — 2020 (3) Clemson

Velo	Pitch	Grade
90-93	FB	+++
79-83	SL	+++
	CU	+

Year	Lev	Team	W	L	Sv	IP	K	ERA	WHIP	BF/G	OBA	H%	S%	xERA	Ctl	Dom	Cmd	hr/9	BPV
2020	NCAA	Clemson	2	0	0	22	43	0.81	0.95	20.9	101	26	90	0.28	5.7	17.4	3.1	0.0	179
2021	A	Fresno	4	6	0	69	96	4.83	1.32	19.0	233	35	64	3.56	4.2	12.5	3.0	0.9	131
2022	Rk	ACL Rockies	0	1	0	7	18	3.75	1.25	7.3	283	75	75	4.28	1.3	22.5	18.0	1.3	389
2022	A+	Spokane	0	0	0	4	5	4.50	1.75	18.3	347	44	83	7.63	2.3	11.3	5.0	2.3	160

Lat and shoulder issues have limited him to just 80 pro innings and he missed almost all of 2022. When healthy comes after hitters from a high 3/4s arm slot with a plus low-to-mid-90s heater that has good spin and late life. Best secondary is a tight, late-breaking, swing-and-miss SL. Fringe CU and health will need to improve to remain a starter.

Weems,Avery — RP — Texas

EXP MLB DEBUT: 2024 | H/W: 6-2 205 | FUT: Middle reliever | 6D

Thrws L Age 25 — 2019 (6) Arizona

Velo	Pitch	Grade
91-97	FB	+
86-90	SL	+++
84-89	CU	+
77-81	CB	++

Year	Lev	Team	W	L	Sv	IP	K	ERA	WHIP	BF/G	OBA	H%	S%	xERA	Ctl	Dom	Cmd	hr/9	BPV
2019	NCAA	Arizona	4	5	2	61	47	7.21	1.70	10.2	330	38	57	6.10	2.8	6.9	2.5	1.0	67
2019	Rk	AZL White Sox	1	1	0	13	14	0.69	1.00	12.4	214	31	92	1.70	2.1	9.7	4.7	0.0	136
2019	Rk	Great Falls	4	3	0	47	60	2.48	1.06	18.3	245	37	76	2.39	1.3	11.5	8.6	0.2	188
2021	A+	Hickory	4	6	0	85	124	5.08	1.22	17.2	243	34	64	4.17	2.9	13.1	4.6	1.7	177
2022	AA	Frisco	2	6	0	91	107	5.14	1.41	14.8	272	35	67	4.77	3.2	10.6	3.3	1.4	123

Velo band belies poor FB shape and command, playing it down to well below-average with regular launchpad activity (21% HR/FB). SL is real write-home offering, and CB also promising, but CU remains distant. Without a dependable FB, nor off-speed, it's unlikely the SL can hold serve. Without more FB oomph, not even a RP.

Weissert,Greg — RP — New York (A)

EXP MLB DEBUT: 2022 | H/W: 6-2 215 | FUT: Setup reliever | 7C

Thrws R Age 28 — 2016 (18) Fordham

Velo	Pitch	Grade
93-96	FB	++++
79-82	SL	++++
84-86	CU	++

Year	Lev	Team	W	L	Sv	IP	K	ERA	WHIP	BF/G	OBA	H%	S%	xERA	Ctl	Dom	Cmd	hr/9	BPV
2019	AA	Trenton	1	2	1	24	28	1.88	0.96	6.5	129	20	78	0.65	4.9	10.5	2.2	0.0	75
2021	AA	Somerset	1	2	4	12	20	0.74	1.15	4.0	207	38	93	1.93	3.7	14.8	4.0	0.0	184
2021	AAA	Scranton/WB	3	1	2	36	40	1.99	1.16	5.1	164	22	85	1.99	5.5	9.9	1.8	0.5	49
2022	AAA	Scranton/WB	2	1	18	48	70	1.69	0.90	4.2	151	24	85	1.21	3.6	13.1	3.7	0.6	158
2022	MLB	New York (A)	3	0	0	11	11	5.68	0.99	3.5	161	20	40	1.84	4.1	8.9	2.2	0.8	69

Hard-throwing, low 3/4s RHP made MLB debut after solid 2022 season in Triple-A. Quick delivery, cuts off extension with slot creating some deception. Primarily 2-pitch guy. Flat-angled 4-seam FB has explosive ride from slot and includes plus ride too. Frisbee SL achieves incredible horizontal break. Can also get to tighter SL break too.

Wentz,Joey — SP — Detroit

EXP MLB DEBUT: 2022 | H/W: 6-5 220 | FUT: #4 starter | 7C

Thrws L Age 25 — 2016 (1) HS (KS)

Velo	Pitch	Grade
92-94	FB	+++
82-85	CT	+++
73-75	CB	+++
83-85	CU	++++

Year	Lev	Team	W	L	Sv	IP	K	ERA	WHIP	BF/G	OBA	H%	S%	xERA	Ctl	Dom	Cmd	hr/9	BPV
2021	A	Lakeland	0	3	0	18	24	6.92	1.70	16.5	309	40	65	7.08	4.0	11.9	3.0	2.5	125
2021	AA	Erie	0	4	0	53	58	3.73	1.39	17.2	215	27	78	3.81	5.6	9.8	1.8	1.2	44
2022	A+	West Michigan	0	0	0	5	4	1.80	0.80	9.1	124	17	75	0.24	3.6	7.2	2.0	0.0	50
2022	AAA	Toledo	2	2	0	48	53	3.18	1.19	16.1	214	27	78	3.21	3.7	9.9	2.7	1.1	95
2022	MLB	Detroit	2	2	0	32	27	3.07	1.12	18.1	202	25	74	2.39	3.6	7.5	2.1	0.6	56

Fully recovered from Tommy John surgery; made MLB debut. Lacks elite stuff, but 4-pitch mix gives him tools to be effective back-end SP. Improved FB sits low-90s with high spin and run up in the zone. Plus 82-84 CU is well located and effective vs RHB. Added an effective CT to go along with CB. The whole is more than the sum of his parts.

Wesneski,Hayden

SP | Chicago (N) | EXP MLB DEBUT: 2022 | H/W: 6-3 210 | FUT: #4 starter | 7D

Thrws R Age 25
2019 (6) Sam Houston St
92-94 FB ++++
87-88 CT +++
79-83 SL ++
83-86 CU ++

Year	Lev	Team	W	L	Sv	IP	K	ERA	WHIP	BF/G	OBA	H%	S%	xERA	Ctl	Dom	Cmd	hr/9	BPV
2021	AA	Somerset	8	4	0	83	92	4.01	1.18	22.1	245	31	70	3.66	2.4	10.0	4.2	1.2	133
2021	AAA	Scranton/WB	2	1	0	11	12	3.27	1.36	15.3	244	34	73	2.98	4.1	9.8	2.4	0.0	84
2022	AAA	Iowa	0	2	0	20	23	5.79	1.24	16.4	230	32	50	2.90	3.6	10.2	2.9	0.4	106
2022	AAA	Scranton/WB	6	7	0	89	83	3.53	1.15	18.7	230	28	72	3.14	2.8	8.4	3.0	0.9	92
2022	MLB	Chicago (N)	3	2	0	33	33	2.18	0.94	20.7	205	26	82	2.21	1.9	9.0	4.7	0.8	128

Strike-throwing machine; attacks hitters with a diverse arsenal highlighted by a 92-94 FB and a low-90s sinker with late break. Also mixes in a plus SL, a CU, and a recently added CT. Used the 4-seamer and SL to great effect in his MLB debut. 4-pitch mix keeps hitters off balance, but lack of velo likely makes him a back-end starter.

Whisenhunt,Carson

SP | San Francisco | EXP MLB DEBUT: 2024 | H/W: 6-3 209 | FUT: #3 starter | 8D

Thrws L Age 22
2022 (2) East Carolina
90-95 FB +++
76-79 CB +++
81-84 CU ++++

Year	Lev	Team	W	L	Sv	IP	K	ERA	WHIP	BF/G	OBA	H%	S%	xERA	Ctl	Dom	Cmd	hr/9	BPV
2022	Rk	ACL Giants O	0	0	0	3	7	0.00	0.33	4.7	106	41	100		0.0	21.0		0.0	396
2022	A	San Jose	0	0	0	4	7	0.00	1.43	8.9	297	51	100	3.84	2.1	15.0	7.0	0.0	230

Tall, athletic SP who missed college season to PED suspension. Possesses mix and durability to be quality pitcher. Few can match his arm speed and dynamic CU that features late drop. Tough for hitters to elevate pitches. Has good separation between FB and CU while mixing in solid average CB. Very tough on LHH.

White,Brendan

RP | Detroit | EXP MLB DEBUT: 2024 | H/W: 5-11 185 | FUT: Setup reliever | 7C

Thrws R Age 24
2019 (26) Siena
91-95 FB +++
80-83 SL ++++

Year	Lev	Team	W	L	Sv	IP	K	ERA	WHIP	BF/G	OBA	H%	S%	xERA	Ctl	Dom	Cmd	hr/9	BPV
2021	A+	West Michigan	3	9	0	101	107	4.18	1.29	16.0	265	35	69	3.83	2.4	9.5	4.0	0.8	125
2022	AA	Erie	6	5	9	67	73	2.68	0.91	5.2	189	26	71	1.54	2.3	9.8	4.3	0.4	133

26th round pick had a breakout campaign after switching to a relief role. Move to the pen allows him to focus on plus 3,000+ rpm slider and mid-90s fastball to play up. Strong, athletic frame and low 3/4s arm slot and is able to repeat mechanics consistently. Above-average command and should be able to carve out a nice role in relief.

White,Colby

RP | Tampa Bay | EXP MLB DEBUT: 2024 | H/W: 6-0 190 | FUT: Setup reliever | 7D

Thrws R Age 24
2019 (6) Mississippi St
94-97 FB ++++
81-87 SL +++
79-82 CU +++

Year	Lev	Team	W	L	Sv	IP	K	ERA	WHIP	BF/G	OBA	H%	S%	xERA	Ctl	Dom	Cmd	hr/9	BPV
2019	A-	Hudson Valley	1	0	1	19	29	2.83	1.26	5.2	129	17	86	2.70	7.5	13.7	1.8	1.4	60
2021	A	Charleston	1	1	4	16	36	0.00	0.56	4.9	150	43	113	0.28	0.6	20.1	36.0	0.6	365
2021	A+	Bowling Green	2	2	3	23	35	2.34	0.65	5.3	109	14	75	0.75	2.7	13.6	5.0	1.2	190
2021	AA	Montgomery	0	0	2	13	19	1.38	0.54	5.5	98	18	71		2.1	13.2	6.3	0.0	199
2021	AAA	Durham	1	0	2	9	14	1.96	1.09	4.0	188	33	80	1.56	3.9	13.7	3.5	0.0	159

Shorter-statured, high 3/4s RHP missed 2022 season after Tommy John surgery. RP only; varies angles of pitches to create deception. Primarily two-pitch pitcher. 4-seam FB has plus carry and late life. Throws strikes and lives with flat-angled approach up. SL has late downward action, piling up whiffs. Solid CU with arm-side fade profile.

White,Owen

SP | Texas | EXP MLB DEBUT: 2024 | H/W: 6-3 199 | FUT: #2 SP/closer | 9E

Thrws R Age 23
2018 (2) HS (NC)
93-98 FB +++
85-89 SL ++++
79-84 CB +++
88-91 CU ++

Year	Lev	Team	W	L	Sv	IP	K	ERA	WHIP	BF/G	OBA	H%	S%	xERA	Ctl	Dom	Cmd	hr/9	BPV
2021	Rk	ACL Rangers	1	0	0	2	2	0.00	0.50	6.6	151	22	100		0.0	9.0		0.0	180
2021	A	Down East	3	1	0	33	54	3.26	1.12	16.3	211	37	71	2.42	3.3	14.7	4.5	0.5	194
2022	A+	Hickory	6	2	0	58	81	4.02	1.20	21.3	237	35	70	3.48	2.9	12.5	4.3	1.1	164
2022	AA	Frisco	3	0	0	21	23	2.55	1.08	20.7	241	33	77	2.64	1.7	9.8	5.8	0.4	148

Oft-injured SP returns and shortly thereafter reinjures self by punching wall. Seemed to put behind him in 2022, dominated across two levels, eclipsing 80 IP and then July forearm fatigue shut him down, clouding future role. FF, SL, CB, CU all at least average, headlined by plus SL he can really land. A starter if health cooperates.

Whitley,Forrest

SP | Houston | EXP MLB DEBUT: 2023 | H/W: 6-7 238 | FUT: #5 SP/swingman | 7C

Thrws R Age 25
2016 (1) HS (TX)
95-99 FB ++
86-90 CU +++
86-90 SL +++
88-93 CT +++

Year	Lev	Team	W	L	Sv	IP	K	ERA	WHIP	BF/G	OBA	H%	S%	xERA	Ctl	Dom	Cmd	hr/9	BPV
2019	AA	Corpus Christi	2	2	0	22	36	5.68	1.67	16.6	223	38	66	4.20	7.7	14.6	1.9	0.8	73
2019	AAA	Round Rock	0	3	0	24	29	12.32	2.07	14.7	340	40	41	9.37	5.6	10.8	1.9	3.4	62
2022	Rk	FCL Astros	0	0	0	2	2	13.50	2.50	10.6	347	45	40	7.42	9.0	9.0	1.0	0.0	-63
2022	A	Fayetteville	0	0	0	5	7	0.00	0.20	7.6	66	12	100		0.0	12.6		0.0	245
2022	AAA	Sugar Land	0	2	0	33	36	7.09	1.73	15.0	256	34	56	4.57	6.8	9.8	1.4	0.5	11

Former star prospect made 40-inning return from Tommy John surgery. Retained velocity and deep repertoire but untenable command/control issues persist. Has real trouble locating FB consistently to all parts of zone, and will spike breaking balls in dirt. Still owns plus stuff, as hopes that he could be impactful major league starter persist.

Wicks,Jordan

SP | Chicago (N) | EXP MLB DEBUT: 2024 | H/W: 6-3 220 | FUT: #4 starter | 7C

Thrws L Age 23
2021 (1) Kansas St
92-94 FB +++
75-78 CB +++
80-82 SL +++
80-83 CU ++++

Year	Lev	Team	W	L	Sv	IP	K	ERA	WHIP	BF/G	OBA	H%	S%	xERA	Ctl	Dom	Cmd	hr/9	BPV
2020	NCAA	Kansas St	3	0	0	26	26	0.35	0.65	22.6	151	22	94	0.12	1.4	9.0	6.5	0.0	143
2021	NCAA	Kansas St	6	3	0	92	118	3.71	1.28	25.2	257	36	73	3.76	2.7	11.5	4.2	0.9	152
2021	A+	South Bend	0	0	0	7	5	5.14	1.43	7.4	262	32	60	3.42	3.9	6.4	1.7	0.0	30
2022	A+	South Bend	4	3	0	66	86	3.67	1.25	16.9	261	38	72	3.56	2.3	11.7	5.1	0.7	166
2022	AA	Tennessee	0	3	0	28	35	4.18	1.25	14.2	233	30	73	4.05	3.5	11.3	3.2	1.6	125

Solid full-season debut, posting a sub 4.00 ERA in 24 starts between A+/AA. Low-90s FB that bumps 95 on occasion, but best offering is a plus CU with late fade and sink that he is willing to throw in any count. Above-average SL and CB round out arsenal.

Wilcox,Cole

SP | Tampa Bay | EXP MLB DEBUT: 2024 | H/W: 6-5 232 | FUT: #3 starter | 8E

Thrws R Age 23
2020 (3) Georgia
91-93 FB ++++
84-87 SL ++++
86-88 CU ++
83-85

Year	Lev	Team	W	L	Sv	IP	K	ERA	WHIP	BF/G	OBA	H%	S%	xERA	Ctl	Dom	Cmd	hr/9	BPV
2020	NCAA	Georgia	3	0	0	23	32	1.57	0.87	21.2	217	33	89	2.11	0.8	12.5	16.0	0.8	222
2021	A	Charleston	1	0	0	44	52	2.04	0.86	16.2	210	31	76	1.47	1.0	10.6	10.4	0.2	181
2022	Rk	FCL Rays	0	1	0	5	9	7.20	1.80	7.7	332	58	56	5.32	3.6	16.2	4.5	0.0	212
2022	A	Charleston	0	1	0	11	15	2.45	0.91	10.3	205	30	78	2.10	1.6	12.3	7.5	0.8	195

Tall, big-bodied RHP spent most of the season rehabbing from 2021 Tommy John surgery. 3/4s delivery with jerky leg kick and longer arm path. Does well staying on time. Stuff backed up in late 2022 outings. Two-seam FB velocity was down and command was out of whack. Same goes for SL, even though the short break profile still got whiffs. Rarely threw CU.

Williams ,Gavin

SP | Cleveland | EXP MLB DEBUT: 2023 | H/W: 6-6 255 | FUT: #2 starter | 9C

Thrws R Age 23
2021 (1) East Carolina
94-96 FB ++++
83-87 SL ++++
75-78 CB +++
85-88 CU +++

Year	Lev	Team	W	L	Sv	IP	K	ERA	WHIP	BF/G	OBA	H%	S%	xERA	Ctl	Dom	Cmd	hr/9	BPV
2022	A+	Lake County	2	1	0	45	67	1.40	0.87	18.4	165	29	82	0.76	2.8	13.4	4.8	0.0	184
2022	AA	Akron	3	3	0	70	82	2.31	1.00	16.7	182	23	85	2.40	3.3	10.5	3.2	1.2	118

Strong-bodied, hard-throwing RHP enjoyed breakout pro debut. Pro coaching streamlined high 3/4s delivery, improving FB command. Mid-to-high 90s 4-seam FB has plus ride with solid run, lots of whiffs. Best secondary is two-plane SL with late vertical drop. 12-to-6 CB and late fading CU are both viable 3rd and 4th offerings in arsenal.

Williams,Henry

SP | San Diego | EXP MLB DEBUT: 2025 | H/W: 6-5 200 | FUT: #3 starter | 8E

Thrws R Age 21
2022 (3) Duke
89-94 FB +++
80-84 SL +++
83-86 CU ++

Year	Lev	Team	W	L	Sv	IP	K	ERA	WHIP	BF/G	OBA	H%	S%	xERA	Ctl	Dom	Cmd	hr/9	BPV

Tall SP who underwent Tommy John surgery in December 2021. Has the frame that orgs crave as he could add more power and velocity. Lives in lower half of zone with quality stuff and can dominate hitters with sharp SL. Key will be development of CU. Has tendency to telegraph CU and can be too firm. Delivery needs work.

Williamson,Brandon

SP | Cincinnati | EXP MLB DEBUT: 2023 | H/W: 6-6 210 | FUT: #3 starter | 8D

Thrws L Age 25
2019 (2) Texas Christian
91-93 FB +++
81-85 SL ++++
71-75 CB +++
81-84 CU +++

Year	Lev	Team	W	L	Sv	IP	K	ERA	WHIP	BF/G	OBA	H%	S%	xERA	Ctl	Dom	Cmd	hr/9	BPV
2019	A-	Everett	0	0	0	15	25	2.38	0.93	5.7	174	34	71	1.00	3.0	14.9	5.0	0.0	206
2021	A+	Everett	2	1	0	31	59	3.19	1.00	19.7	194	37	74	2.47	2.9	17.1	5.9	1.2	248
2021	AA	Arkansas	2	5	0	67	94	3.49	1.27	21.1	247	37	76	3.63	3.1	12.6	4.1	0.9	162
2022	AA	Chattanooga	5	2	0	67	74	4.16	1.51	20.7	244	33	73	3.97	5.4	9.9	1.9	0.7	52
2022	AAA	Louisville	1	5	0	55	49	4.08	1.63	18.9	254	32	76	4.43	6.0	8.0	1.3	0.7	-1

Long-limbed, projectable LHP struggled with command in sideways 2022 season. Low 3/4s delivery with plus extension, struggled with release point consistency. 4-pitch mix. Low 90s 4-seam FB features carry from lower slot. Struggled with feel for CB most of the season. SL took step ahead in development with tight two-plane break profile.

Willis,Alec — SP — St. Louis

EXP MLB DEBUT: 2025 | H/W: 6-5 220 | FUT: #4 starter | 7D

Thrws R Age 20 — 2021 (7) HS (CO)

Velo	Pitch	Grade
90-94	FB	+++
79-82	SL	++
74-76	CB	++
	CU	+

Year	Lev	Team	W	L	Sv	IP	K	ERA	WHIP	BF/G	OBA	H%	S%	xERA	Ctl	Dom	Cmd	hr/9	BPV
2021	Rk	FCL Cardinals	0	0	0	1	1	0.00	0.00	2.8	0	0			0.0	9.0		0.0	180
2022	Rk	FCL Cardinals	0	1	0	11	16	1.62	0.72	6.6	161	25	86	1.11	1.6	13.0	8.0	0.8	208

Projectable frame; could add more velo as he matures. Has been slow to recover from elbow surgery in 2020. FB sits at 90-94 with late life up in the zone. Improved SL is best secondary with solid CB and shows some feel for a serviceable CU. Needs to refine his mechanics and build up arm strength, but the raw tools are exciting

Winn,Cole — SP — Texas

EXP MLB DEBUT: 2023 | H/W: 6-2 190 | FUT: #3 starter | 8C

Thrws R Age 23 — 2018 (1) HS (CA)

Velo	Pitch	Grade
94-99	FB	+++
85-90	CU	+++
79-93	CB	++++
84-88	SL	++

Year	Lev	Team	W	L	Sv	IP	K	ERA	WHIP	BF/G	OBA	H%	S%	xERA	Ctl	Dom	Cmd	hr/9	BPV
2019	A	Hickory	4	4	0	68	65	4.49	1.44	16.1	235	30	69	3.68	5.1	8.6	1.7	0.7	33
2021	AA	Frisco	3	3	0	78	97	2.31	0.82	14.9	147	21	76	1.13	3.0	11.2	3.7	0.7	138
2021	AAA	Round Rock	1	0	0	8	10	3.38	1.25	16.3	181	24	78	2.98	5.6	11.3	2.0	1.1	69
2022	AAA	Round Rock	9	8	0	121	123	6.53	1.75	19.8	268	34	62	5.19	6.5	9.1	1.4	1.0	8

Everything on paper looks high-end starter: Great frame, athletic, repeatable delivery, four quality pitches—three nearly or plus in FF, CB and unicorn CU—near-average command. Took comebacker off ankle in April and subsequent delivery changes sank everything, surface- and underlying metrics-wise. Command fell apart but Ks remained.

Wolf,Jackson — SP — San Diego

EXP MLB DEBUT: 2023 | H/W: 6-7 205 | FUT: #4 starter | 7D

Thrws L Age 23 — 2021 (4) West Virginia

Velo	Pitch	Grade
86-89	FB	++
80-82	SL	+++
77-82	CB	+++
80-83	CU	+

Year	Lev	Team	W	L	Sv	IP	K	ERA	WHIP	BF/G	OBA	H%	S%	xERA	Ctl	Dom	Cmd	hr/9	BPV
2021	NCAA	West Virginia	6	5	0	89		3.03	1.16	25.3	208	30	74	2.39	3.7	10.5	2.8	0.4	106
2021	Rk	ACL Padres	0	0	0	3	5	0.00	0.67	5.2	106	22	100		3.0	15.0	5.0	0.0	207
2021	A	Lake Elsinore	0	0	0	12	19	3.75	1.50	10.4	262	43	76	4.23	4.5	14.3	3.2	0.8	153
2022	A+	Fort Wayne	7	8	0	119	134	4.01	1.13	20.5	213	27	69	3.16	3.3	10.1	3.0	1.2	111
2022	AA	San Antonio	0	2	0	10	8	8.82	1.76	23.4	294	35	47	5.56	5.3	7.1	1.3	0.9	2

Tall, lean SP who had most Ks in org and 2nd in MWL. High Ks due more to unique delivery and angle than natural stuff. Low arm slot has proven difficult for LHH as ball comes at them quickly. Sweeping SL is solid offering and pairs well with CB. FB is nothing special and CU is well below average. Extreme flyball pitcher.

Woo,Bryan — SP — Seattle

EXP MLB DEBUT: 2024 | H/W: 6-2 205 | FUT: #3 starter | 8D

Thrws R Age 23 — 2021 (6) Cal Poly

Velo	Pitch	Grade
94-96	FB	+++
85-88	SL	+++
87-89	CU	+++

Year	Lev	Team	W	L	Sv	IP	K	ERA	WHIP	BF/G	OBA	H%	S%	xERA	Ctl	Dom	Cmd	hr/9	BPV
2022	Rk	ACL Mariners	0	0	0	4	9	0.00	0.71	4.9	202	51	100	0.73	0.0	19.3		0.0	365
2022	A	Modesto	0	1	0	20	29	4.03	1.19	13.4	241	37	68	3.33	2.7	13.0	4.8	0.9	179
2022	A+	Everett	1	3	0	32	46	4.78	1.50	19.7	262	40	67	4.06	4.5	12.9	2.9	0.6	129

Sleeper prospect who has been brought along slowly since Tommy John surgery in 2021. Could have as much electric stuff as any in org. FB thrown with great velocity, but tends to be flat and hittable and upper 90s. Hard SL is a true out pitch and will need time to find consistency with solid average CU. Could be a quick mover if healthy.

Woods-Richardson,Sime — SP — Minnesota

EXP MLB DEBUT: 2022 | H/W: 6-3 210 | FUT: #3 starter | 8C

Thrws R Age 22 — 2018 (2) HS (TX)

Velo	Pitch	Grade
91-94	FB	+++
78-80	CB	+++
81-82	SL	++
82-84	CU	++++

Year	Lev	Team	W	L	Sv	IP	K	ERA	WHIP	BF/G	OBA	H%	S%	xERA	Ctl	Dom	Cmd	hr/9	BPV
2021	AA	New Hampshire	2	4	0	45	67	5.79	1.51	17.7	248	38	62	4.31	5.2	13.4	2.6	1.0	119
2021	AA	Wichita	1	1	0	8	10	6.75	1.75	9.1	210	32	57	3.52	9.0	11.3	1.3	0.0	-23
2022	AA	Wichita	3	3	0	70	77	3.08	1.17	17.5	221	30	74	2.67	3.3	9.9	3.0	0.5	106
2022	AAA	St. Paul	2	0	0	36	38	2.24	0.86	19.0	171	23	76	1.30	2.5	9.4	3.8	0.5	121
2022	MLB	Minnesota	0	1	0	5	3	3.60	1.00	19.1	175	15	75	2.98	3.6	5.4	1.5	1.8	18

Production starting to improve for young SP and enjoyed best pro season that ended in majors. Possesses good control and command and still has delivery and arm strength to potentially add velocity to above average FB. Exhibits best CU in system with great fade. Mixes in both CB and SL. Deceptive delivery enhances package.

Workman,Logan — SP — Tampa Bay

EXP MLB DEBUT: 2024 | H/W: 6-4 215 | FUT: #4 starter | 7C

Thrws R Age 24 — 2021 (7) Lee

Velo	Pitch	Grade
93-96	FB	++++
82-84	CU	+++
81-84	SL	+++
88-91	CT	

Year	Lev	Team	W	L	Sv	IP	K	ERA	WHIP	BF/G	OBA	H%	S%	xERA	Ctl	Dom	Cmd	hr/9	BPV
2020	NCAA	Lee	5	0	0	42	53	0.21	0.67	24.4	92	15	96		3.4	11.4	3.3	0.0	130
2021	NCAA	Lee	8	1	0	79	110	1.82	0.93	24.8	174	28	83	1.46	3.1	12.5	4.1	0.5	160
2021	Rk	FCL Rays	1	0	0	10	14	0.89	1.09	6.6	174	29	91	1.43	4.5	12.5	2.8	0.0	122
2022	A	Charleston	1	0	0	23	34	0.78	0.78	13.9	187	33	89	0.79	1.2	13.2	11.3	0.0	225
2022	A+	Bowling Green	5	3	0	90	81	3.50	1.21	18.2	246	29	77	3.86	2.6	8.1	3.1	1.3	94

Strike-throwing, former D2 college RHP, popped up as a prospect with performance across 2 levels. 3/4s delivery with jerky leg lift and kick out of the windup at the balance point. 3-pitch pitcher. Mid-90s 4-seam FB features plus carry and run, especially up. Has plus command of SL with slurvy break. Improved feel for fading CU.

Zerpa,Angel — SP — Kansas City

EXP MLB DEBUT: 2021 | H/W: 6-0 220 | FUT: #5 SP/swingman | 6B

Thrws L Age 23 — 2017 FA (VZ)

Velo	Pitch	Grade
92-95	FB	++
82-86	SL	++++
84-87	CU	++

Year	Lev	Team	W	L	Sv	IP	K	ERA	WHIP	BF/G	OBA	H%	S%	xERA	Ctl	Dom	Cmd	hr/9	BPV
2021	AAA	Omaha	0	1	0	1	1	24.55	2.73	6.1	392	32	0	16.54	8.2	8.2	1.0	8.2	-56
2021	MLB	Kansas City	0	1	0	5	4	0.00	0.80	18.1	175	23	100	0.77	1.8	7.2	4.0	0.0	99
2022	AA	NW Arkansas	2	5	0	64	69	4.36	1.42	20.9	279	36	71	4.55	3.0	9.7	3.3	1.0	113
2022	AAA	Omaha	0	0	0	7	0	1.25	0.83	4.4	90	9	83	0.07	5.0	0.0	0.0	0.0	-117
2022	MLB	Kansas City	2	1	0	11	3	1.64	1.09	14.3	225	20	100	3.67	2.5	2.5	1.0	1.6	-4

Short-statured, pudgy low 3/4s slot LHP made 3 MLB starts. Repeatable delivery with limited extension relies heavily on SL to get hitters out. Mid-90s 4-seam FB is unique for run/ride profile from lower arm slot but doesn't command enough to thrive. Sweeping SL is best pitch with downward movement coming late. Also mixes 2-seam FB and CU.

Zibin,Jacob — SP — Cleveland

EXP MLB DEBUT: 2026 | H/W: 6-4 218 | FUT: #3 starter | 8E

Thrws R Age 18 — 2022 (10) HS (FL)

Velo	Pitch	Grade
91-94	FB	++++
78-81	SL	++
82-84	CU	++++

Year	Lev	Team	W	L	Sv	IP	K	ERA	WHIP	BF/G	OBA	H%	S%	xERA	Ctl	Dom	Cmd	hr/9	BPV

Low 3/4s RHP; slim build with room to add bulk to physique. Repeatable mechanics. Mostly FB/CU pitcher. FB sits low 90s, touching 97 with solid ride profile from lower slot. Maintains arm speed with late-fading CU. CU has late bite too. Sweeping SL does not look like pro quality pitch.

Ziegler,Calvin — SP — New York (N)

EXP MLB DEBUT: 2025 | H/W: 6-0 205 | FUT: #3 starter | 8E

Thrws R Age 20 — 2021 (2) HS (FL)

Velo	Pitch	Grade
91-94	FB	+++
80-83	CB	+++
82-85	SP	++++

Year	Lev	Team	W	L	Sv	IP	K	ERA	WHIP	BF/G	OBA	H%	S%	xERA	Ctl	Dom	Cmd	hr/9	BPV
2022	A	St. Lucie	0	6	0	46	70	4.48	1.32	12.0	166	28	66	2.46	6.8	13.6	2.0	0.6	79

Athletic, high 3/4s RHP struggled with walks in pro debut. Near physical projection despite youth. Struggles maintaining slot, causing command issues. 3-pitch pitcher. Flat-angled FB features plus ride and some run. SP has arm-side fading action and late, drop off the table movement. A plus pitch. Turns over 12-to-6 CB well from slot.

Zulueta,Yosver — SP — Toronto

EXP MLB DEBUT: 2023 | H/W: 6-1 190 | FUT: #3 starter | 8C

Thrws R Age 25 — 2019 FA (CU)

Velo	Pitch	Grade
94-99	FB	+++++
83-87	CB	+++
77-80	SL	+++
84-87	CU	+++

Year	Lev	Team	W	L	Sv	IP	K	ERA	WHIP	BF/G	OBA	H%	S%	xERA	Ctl	Dom	Cmd	hr/9	BPV
2021	A	Dunedin	0	0	0	0	0			0.0									
2022	A	Dunedin	0	0	0	12	23	3.00	1.00	15.3	210	45	67	1.57	2.3	17.3	7.7	0.0	268
2022	A+	Vancouver	1	3	0	23	31	3.88	1.25	15.7	216	33	68	2.68	4.3	12.0	2.8	0.4	119
2022	AA	New Hampshire	1	1	0	15	25	4.17	1.59	7.4	190	34	74	3.40	8.3	14.9	1.8	0.6	61
2022	AAA	Buffalo	0	1	0	4	5	4.29	1.67	6.3	202	30	71	3.22	8.6	10.7	1.3	0.0	-21

Injury-prone SP who pitched on 4 levels. Generates Ks and groundballs with elite FB and complements with heavy CU with run and drop. High walk rate is concern, but has delivery to improve. Uses two breaking balls and both have very high spin rates. Had Tommy John surgery in 2019, torn ACL in 2021 and additional ailments in 2022.

Zwack,Nick — SP — San Francisco

EXP MLB DEBUT: 2024 | H/W: 6-3 230 | FUT: #4 starter | 7D

Thrws L Age 24 — 2021 (17) Xavier

Velo	Pitch	Grade
90-94	FB	+++
81-84	SL	+++
82-85	CU	++

Year	Lev	Team	W	L	Sv	IP	K	ERA	WHIP	BF/G	OBA	H%	S%	xERA	Ctl	Dom	Cmd	hr/9	BPV
2021	NCAA	Xavier	6	5	1	80	75	3.15	1.28	21.8	234	30	76	3.07	3.7	8.4	2.3	0.5	70
2021	Rk	FCL Mets	1	0	0	7	13	0.00	1.14	5.5	233	47	100	2.22	2.6	16.7	6.5	0.0	249
2022	A	St. Lucie	1	1	0	12	24	5.16	1.31	12.6	289	56	60	4.10	1.5	17.7	12.0	0.7	297
2022	A+	Brooklyn	5	1	1	63	72	1.85	0.95	17.0	198	28	81	1.64	2.3	10.3	4.5	0.3	141
2022	A+	Eugene	1	1	0	29	36	4.02	1.34	20.2	219	30	72	3.47	4.9	11.1	2.3	0.9	85

Big, strong SP who was acquired from NYM in August. Not blessed with plus stuff, but knows how to pitch and keep hitters guessing. FB features natural sinking action while sweeping SL is very difficult for LHH to hit. Sinking CU has moments, but not enough velocity separation from FB. Throws strikes and could be multi-inning RP.

In his 1985 *Baseball Abstract,* Bill James introduced the concept of major league equivalencies. His assertion was that, with the proper adjustments, a minor leaguer's statistics could be converted to an equivalent major league level performance with a great deal of accuracy.

Because of wide variations in the level of play among different minor leagues, it is difficult to get a true reading on a player's potential. For instance, a .300 batting average achieved in the high-offense Triple-A West is not nearly as much of an accomplishment as a similar level in the Double-A Northeast. MLEs normalize these types of variances, for all statistical categories.

The actual MLEs are not projections. They represent how a player's previous performance might look at the major league level. However, the MLE stat line can be used in forecasting future performance in just the same way as a major league stat line would.

The model we use contains a few variations to James' version and updates all of the minor league and ballpark factors. In addition, we designed a module to convert pitching statistics, which is something James did not originally do.

Do MLEs really work?

Used correctly, MLEs are excellent indicators of potential. But just like we cannot take traditional major league statistics at face value, the same goes for MLEs. The underlying measures of base skill—batting eye ratios, pitching command ratios, etc.—are far more accurate in evaluating future talent than raw home runs, batting averages or ERAs.

The charts we present here also provide the unique perspective of looking at up to five years' worth of data. Ironically, the longer the history, the less likely the player is a legitimate prospect—he should have made it to the majors before compiling a long history in AA and/or AAA ball. Of course, the shorter trends

are more difficult to read despite them often belonging to players with higher ceilings. But even here we can find small indications of players improving their skills, or struggling, as they rise through more difficult levels of competition. Since players—especially those with any talent—are promoted rapidly through major league systems, a two or three-year scan is often all we get to spot any trends.

Here are some things to look for as you scan these charts:

Target players who...

- spent a full year in AA and then a full year in AAA
- had consistent playing time from one year to the next
- improved their base skills as they were promoted

Raise the warning flag for players who...

- were stuck at a level for multiple seasons, or regressed
- displayed marked changes in playing time from one year to the next
- showed large drops in BPIs from one year to the next

Players are listed on the charts if they spent at least part of 2018-2022 in AAA or AA and had at least 100 AB or 30 IP within those two levels. Each is listed with the organization with which they finished the season.

Only statistics accumulated in AAA and AA ball are included (players who split a season are indicated as a/a); Single-A stats are excluded.

Each player's actual AB and IP totals are used as the base for the conversion. However, it is more useful to compare performances using common levels, so rely on the ratios and sabermetric gauges. Complete explanations of these formulas appear in the Glossary.

BATTER	B	Yr	Age	Pos	Lvl	Tm	AB	R	H	D	T	HR	RBI	BB	K	SB	CS	BA	OB	Slg	OPS	bb%	ct%	Eye	PX	SX	RC/G	BPV
Abreu,Wilyer	L	22	23	CF	aa	BOS	457	72	98	28	0	12	49	77	167	21	3	213	327	356	683	14%	63%	0.46	119	103	3.29	10
Acuna,Jose	R	22	20	SS	aa	TEX	152	14	28	5	1	2	12	12	38	8	3	187	244	274	519	7%	75%	0.30	59	124	1.75	-1
Adams,Jordyn	R	22	23	CF	aa	LAA	209	21	42	6	1	3	13	14	81	9	0	199	248	275	523	6%	61%	0.17	62	127	2.07	-52
Alexander,Blaze	R	22	23	SS	a/a	ARI	344	32	81	15	2	10	33	21	116	6	7	236	280	380	660	6%	66%	0.18	105	78	2.83	-14
Alvarez,Francisco	R	22	21	C	a/a	NYM	408	50	86	18	0	19	53	47	143	0	0	211	293	392	685	10%	65%	0.33	132	25	3.30	-5
Amaya,Jacob	R	21	23	SS	aa	LA	417	42	74	12	1	9	33	34	117	3	0	177	239	272	511	8%	72%	0.29	59	68	1.81	-27
		22	24	SS	a/a	LA	476	51	97	15	2	12	43	47	132	4	2	203	274	316	590	9%	72%	0.35	75	69	2.40	-11
Amaya,Miguel	R	21	22	C	aa	CHC	79	8	15	4	0	1	10	16	24	1	0	189	327	262	589	17%	70%	0.68	56	47	2.34	-25
		22	23	DH	aa	CHC	97	9	21	5	1	2	12	9	33	0	0	220	284	360	644	8%	66%	0.27	105	53	2.75	-16
Antuna,Yasel	B	22	23	LF	aa	WAS	91	7	11	4	0	1	3	13	36	1	2	125	231	190	421	12%	61%	0.35	62	47	0.92	-67
Arias,Gabriel	R	21	21	SS	aaa	CLE	436	48	109	26	2	10	41	29	123	4	1	250	297	387	684	6%	72%	0.24	92	75	3.22	-2
		22	22	SS	aaa	CLE	288	27	54	7	0	8	21	15	89	3	1	189	228	296	524	5%	69%	0.16	74	62	1.94	-35
Bae,Ji-hwan	L	21	22	2B	aa	PIT	320	47	78	11	3	5	23	29	89	15	9	244	307	346	653	8%	72%	0.33	64	126	2.89	-3
		22	23	2B	aaa	PIT	419	54	101	21	4	5	35	33	89	20	9	240	296	345	641	7%	79%	0.37	71	130	2.71	27
Ball,Bryce	L	22	24	1B	aa	CHC	485	47	99	24	1	7	47	42	143	1	5	204	267	300	567	8%	71%	0.29	74	46	2.01	-27
Barger,Addison	L	22	23	SS	a/a	TOR	207	24	56	10	0	9	27	16	62	1	3	271	322	456	777	7%	70%	0.25	127	37	4.29	9
Barrosa,Jorge	B	22	21	CF	aa	ARI	434	52	98	25	1	7	31	39	89	14	12	226	290	339	629	8%	80%	0.44	78	94	2.44	28
Basabe,Osleivis	R	22	22	3B	aa	TAM	228	28	64	20	2	0	18	17	30	10	0	281	332	388	720	7%	87%	0.59	77	129	3.60	64
Baty,Brett	L	21	22	3B	aa	NYM	153	12	34	6	0	4	16	16	54	1	0	219	293	331	625	9%	65%	0.30	81	35	2.82	-45
		22	23	3B	a/a	NYM	362	51	92	18	0	13	40	34	127	1	5	254	317	410	727	8%	65%	0.26	119	42	3.73	-13
Binelas,Alex	L	22	22	3B	aa	BOS	211	20	30	10	1	7	24	17	83	0	0	144	207	299	506	7%	61%	0.20	124	48	1.52	-26
Bradley,Tucker	L	22	24	LF	aa	KC	396	44	95	20	2	6	32	32	92	12	7	240	297	351	647	7%	77%	0.35	77	97	2.81	15
Breaux,Josh	R	21	24	C	aa	NYY	100	11	20	7	0	5	13	3	30	1	0	205	229	419	648	3%	70%	0.11	138	53	2.63	14
		22	25	C	a/a	NYY	370	31	64	10	1	14	35	22	136	1	0	173	219	318	537	6%	63%	0.16	105	56	1.93	-33
Brennan,Will	L	21	23	CF	aa	CLE	150	22	37	6	0	2	16	14	33	2	2	249	314	317	632	9%	78%	0.44	45	61	2.87	-14
		22	24	CF	a/a	CLE	528	44	134	33	2	9	69	32	83	13	4	253	296	373	669	6%	84%	0.38	78	87	3.09	39
Bunnell,Cade	L	22	25	SS	aa	ATL	146	17	37	10	1	6	23	23	68	0	1	255	356	462	818	14%	53%	0.33	191	69	4.45	15
Burleson,Alec	L	21	23	RF	a/a	STL	414	35	89	14	0	11	44	23	97	1	1	214	255	328	584	5%	77%	0.24	66	34	2.43	-18
		22	24	LF	aaa	STL	432	44	112	20	1	12	56	18	77	3	0	259	289	388	677	4%	82%	0.24	79	58	3.41	19
Busch,Michael	L	21	24	2B	aa	LA	409	57	89	22	1	14	46	45	151	1	3	217	295	379	673	10%	63%	0.30	117	49	2.99	-17
		22	25	2B	a/a	LA	552	70	116	29	0	21	64	42	202	2	1	211	266	379	645	7%	63%	0.21	131	57	2.80	-8
Canario,Alexander	R	22	22	CF	a/a	CHC	375	44	74	16	2	19	49	32	126	13	3	198	261	405	666	8%	66%	0.25	144	109	2.96	31
Canzone,Dominic	L	21	24	LF	aa	ARI	130	17	39	7	1	5	19	10	33	1	1	296	349	470	819	7%	75%	0.32	103	69	4.95	19
		22	25	RF	a/a	ARI	386	44	86	20	1	11	49	20	97	8	2	224	261	367	628	5%	75%	0.20	96	93	2.70	16
Carreras,Julio	R	22	22	SS	aa	COL	60	7	12	4	1	0	8	3	21	1	0	207	245	312	557	5%	65%	0.14	96	133	1.72	-14
Carroll,Corbin	L	22	22	CF	a/a	ARI	356	51	87	18	6	13	36	37	118	18	6	244	315	433	748	10%	67%	0.32	134	150	3.75	41
Carter,Evan	L	22	20	RF	aa	TEX	21	6	8	2	0	1	5	4	7	1	1	376	467	558	1	15%	68%	0.53	144	92	8.08	45
Casas,Triston	L	21	21	1B	a/a	BOS	310	50	80	16	2	10	47	45	77	6	3	257	351	424	775	13%	75%	0.58	99	94	4.25	35
		22	22	1B	aaa	BOS	264	31	63	20	1	7	26	31	73	0	0	240	320	402	721	10%	72%	0.42	120	35	3.45	18
Cerda,Allan	R	22	23	RF	aa	CIN	207	24	35	8	0	8	17	29	88	3	1	168	269	328	597	12%	57%	0.33	130	56	2.41	-23
Cespedes,Yoelqui	R	21	24	CF	aa	CHW	94	12	25	3	1	1	6	3	31	7	5	266	287	353	640	3%	67%	0.09	57	152	2.63	-35
		22	25	CF	aa	CHW	458	42	91	21	0	13	38	19	185	21	14	199	232	333	565	4%	60%	0.11	113	98	1.92	-31
Chourio,Jackson	R	22	18	CF	aa	MIL	23	0	2	1	0	0	3	2	11	1	1	75	133	112	245	6%	51%	0.14	50	69	0.27	-119
Colas,Oscar	L	22	24	RF	a/a	CHW	237	28	60	8	0	12	24	11	79	1	4	253	285	445	730	4%	67%	0.14	131	52	3.70	-2
Conine,Griffin	L	21	24	RF	aa	MIA	159	15	24	3	0	10	21	10	93	0	1	148	198	359	557	6%	41%	0.11	201	26	1.92	-52
		22	25	RF	aa	MIA	414	40	71	12	2	16	53	53	215	1	1	173	266	325	591	11%	48%	0.24	145	53	2.33	-51
Cowser,Colton	L	22	22	CF	a/a	BAL	281	48	71	14	0	12	29	32	104	1	2	251	328	425	753	10%	63%	0.31	135	54	4.08	-2
Crouch,Josh	R	22	24	DH	aa	DET	24	1	3	0	0	1	3	0	7	0	0	131	131	208	339	0%	72%	0.00	43	-7	0.80	-76
Cruz,Trei	B	22	24	3B	aa	DET	25	2	4	0	0	0	0	3	8	1	0	161	261	161	422	12%	69%	0.44	0	52	1.39	-83
Davidson,Logan	B	21	24	SS	aa	OAK	448	37	78	19	1	5	34	44	177	3	3	174	248	253	501	9%	61%	0.25	67	53	1.55	-68
		22	25	SS	aa	OAK	424	45	81	17	1	8	35	33	160	3	1	192	250	291	541	7%	62%	0.21	82	64	1.96	-49
Davis,Brennen	R	21	22	CF	a/a	CHC	323	44	71	21	0	12	35	35	122	4	4	221	298	398	696	10%	62%	0.29	132	59	3.14	-6
		22	23	CF	aaa	CHC	141	11	21	5	0	3	9	15	59	0	1	151	233	240	473	10%	58%	0.25	78	29	1.39	-75
Davis,Henry	R	22	23	C	aa	PIT	116	12	20	7	0	2	12	8	33	2	1	169	224	293	517	7%	72%	0.25	95	77	1.56	1
De La Cruz,Carlos	R	22	23	LF	aa	PHI	151	15	35	10	1	5	16	6	51	1	0	232	259	409	668	4%	66%	0.11	135	62	2.90	0
De La Cruz,Elly	B	22	20	SS	aa	CIN	190	24	52	15	2	7	24	12	71	14	2	274	316	476	791	6%	63%	0.16	167	142	4.40	40
De Los Santos,Deyvis	R	22	19	3B	aa	ARI	39	3	8	2	0	1	4	3	9	0	0	193	252	283	535	7%	76%	0.33	65	23	1.90	-22
DeLoach,Zach	L	21	23	RF	aa	SEA	185	22	36	8	1	4	17	22	69	1	2	193	280	316	596	11%	63%	0.33	90	74	2.16	-31
		22	24	RF	aa	SEA	418	52	83	11	1	9	48	46	145	3	1	199	279	298	577	10%	65%	0.32	73	74	2.34	-36
DeLuca,Jonny	R	22	24	CF	aa	LA	104	14	25	4	1	5	13	5	20	3	0	243	277	458	736	5%	81%	0.25	120	127	3.82	68
Diaz,Jordan	R	22	22	DH	a/a	OAK	491	42	127	28	1	11	52	17	88	0	0	259	284	385	669	3%	82%	0.20	82	25	3.17	10
Diaz,Yainer	R	22	24	C	a/a	HOU	445	48	108	17	3	16	61	22	96	1	0	242	277	402	680	5%	78%	0.23	96	69	3.29	22
Dingler,Dillon	R	21	23	C	aa	DET	188	18	34	3	3	3	15	7	65	1	0	181	209	274	483	3%	66%	0.10	56	105	1.51	-52
		22	24	C	aa	DET	387	38	75	18	3	9	39	31	159	1	0	194	253	326	579	7%	59%	0.19	112	77	2.11	-35
Dirden,Justin	L	22	25	CF	a/a	HOU	477	51	111	30	3	15	63	32	166	7	4	233	281	407	689	6%	65%	0.19	135	97	3.05	12
Downs,Jeter	R	19	21	SS	aa	LA	48	13	15	2	0	5	10	5	11	1	0	319	386	655	1	10%	77%	0.48	206	114	9.61	122
		21	23	SS	aaa	BOS	357	31	61	9	0	10	31	30	144	14	3	170	233	282	516	8%	60%	0.21	81	83	1.90	-54
		22	24	SS	aaa	BOS	284	36	46	10	1	10	21	24	110	12	5	162	228	307	535	8%	61%	0.22	113	124	1.84	-10
Doyle,Brenton	R	22	24	CF	a/a	COL	507	47	107	18	4	16	44	15	183	13	3	211	234	360	594	3%	64%	0.08	109	121	2.33	-13
Dunham,Elijah	L	22	24	LF	aa	NYY	415	48	83	20	2	13	45	43	122	27	8	200	276	348	624	9%	70%	0.35	104	124	2.62	23
Edwards,Xavier	R	21	22	2B	aa	TAM	291	31	77	11	3	0	21	28	48	15	12	264	329	320	649	9%	83%	0.58	36	103	2.79	13
		22	23	2B	aaa	TAM	349	34	70	16	1	3	23	31	89	5	5	201	267	279	546	8%	74%	0.35	60	71	1.89	-15
Encarnacion-Strand,C	R	22	23	3B	aa	CIN	190	16	52	7	1	9	31	7	61	1	1	272	297	468	765	4%	68%	0.11	131	48	4.28	0
Feliciano,Mario	R	21	23	C	aaa	MIL	105	8	18	2	0	2	13	3	30	1	0	170	191	246	437	3%	71%	0.09	45	49	1.37	-58
		22	24	C	aaa	MIL	285	21	62	11	0	4	25	12	63	1	2	217	250	299	548	4%	78%	0.20	56	36	2.05	-23
Fletcher,Dominic	L	21	24	RF	aa	ARI	402	41	88	15	5	10	38	17	125	2	3	219	251	353	604	4%	69%	0.14	84	85	2.31	-22
		22	25	CF	a/a	ARI	523	54	124	27	7	6	40	30	136	5	10	237	278	350	628	5%	74%	0.22	80	93	2.35	1

BATTER	B	Yr	Age	Pos	Lvl	Tm	AB	R	H	D	T	HR	RBI	BB	K	SB	CS	BA	OB	Slg	OPS	bb%	ct%	Eye	PX	SX	RC/G	BPV
Florial,Estevan	L	21	24	CF	a/a	NYY	347	55	65	15	1	14	37	37	140	10	9	186	264	355	619	10%	60%	0.26	123	100	2.36	-11
		22	25	CF	aaa	NYY	403	47	90	23	1	11	32	39	172	27	12	224	292	369	661	9%	57%	0.23	131	115	2.87	-11
Foscue,Justin	R	21	22	2B	aa	TEX	93	12	21	7	0	2	11	7	31	0	1	226	279	351	630	7%	66%	0.22	98	49	2.45	-26
		22	23	2B	aa	TEX	400	39	92	25	1	9	53	30	75	2	5	231	284	368	652	7%	81%	0.39	90	43	2.72	25
Fraizer,Matt	L	21	23	CF	aa	PIT	132	15	33	11	2	2	13	10	37	1	2	250	302	410	712	7%	72%	0.26	111	89	2.85	19
		22	24	CF	aa	PIT	439	36	77	16	5	4	28	23	128	12	1	176	218	257	475	5%	71%	0.18	60	130	1.42	-18
Frelick,Sal	L	22	22	CF	a/a	MIL	413	55	118	19	3	7	35	29	58	13	6	286	332	396	729	6%	86%	0.49	66	108	3.93	44
Garcia,Maikel	R	22	22	SS	a/a	KC	487	65	118	33	1	6	38	34	107	24	9	243	293	350	643	7%	78%	0.32	80	112	2.79	25
Gelof,Zack	R	22	23	2B	a/a	OAK	389	37	80	14	1	10	40	30	141	6	2	206	262	322	585	7%	64%	0.21	89	79	2.38	-33
Gentry,Tyler	R	22	23	RF	aa	KC	274	36	73	15	0	9	40	24	71	5	5	268	326	421	747	8%	74%	0.33	106	61	3.97	17
Gomez,Moises	R	21	23	RF	aa	TAM	269	25	38	11	0	6	17	20	133	4	3	142	201	247	448	7%	51%	0.15	97	69	1.19	-83
Gonzales,Nick	R	22	23	2B	aa	PIT	259	31	56	18	1	4	22	30	100	3	3	218	298	342	640	10%	61%	0.30	114	75	2.51	-18
Goodman,Hunter	R	22	23	DH	aa	COL	44	3	8	0	0	1	2	2	12	1	0	192	223	283	506	4%	72%	0.14	51	40	2.04	-51
Gorski,Matt	R	22	25	CF	a/a	PIT	143	17	32	7	1	3	18	10	56	7	2	222	272	363	635	7%	61%	0.18	115	137	2.65	-8
Groshans,Jordan	R	21	22	SS	aa	TOR	278	35	71	21	0	6	30	25	67	0	0	255	317	390	707	8%	76%	0.37	92	30	3.42	4
		22	23	SS	aaa	MIA	353	31	78	13	0	2	24	38	74	2	0	221	297	274	570	10%	79%	0.51	40	47	2.34	-17
Hamilton,David	L	21	24	SS	aa	MIL	133	12	28	4	3	2	9	12	38	8	3	213	277	343	620	8%	72%	0.31	76	132	2.41	5
		22	25	2B	aa	BOS	463	53	96	15	6	7	27	36	136	45	9	207	264	313	577	7%	71%	0.26	72	167	2.38	7
Harris,Brett	R	22	24	3B	aa	OAK	315	33	71	12	1	6	29	20	73	7	5	224	270	327	597	6%	77%	0.27	68	88	2.41	2
Harris,Dustin	L	22	23	LF	aa	TEX	331	38	68	13	1	11	43	27	84	12	7	205	266	347	613	8%	75%	0.33	91	100	2.48	19
Haskin,Hudson	R	22	23	CF	aa	BAL	387	38	85	19	2	12	37	28	112	3	3	220	273	368	641	7%	71%	0.25	103	68	2.69	3
Helman,Michael	R	22	26	CF	a/a	MIN	512	61	99	18	2	11	36	38	136	24	6	194	249	304	553	7%	73%	0.28	74	126	2.13	6
Henderson,Gunnar	L	22	21	SS	a/a	BAL	407	67	104	20	4	15	51	52	126	15	3	256	340	436	776	11%	69%	0.41	124	136	4.34	41
Hernaiz,Darell	R	22	21	SS	aa	BAL	53	4	5	1	0	1	5	3	17	1	1	95	147	154	301	6%	68%	0.20	41	81	0.51	-55
Hernandez,Diego	L	22	22	CF	aa	KC	124	15	31	4	0	1	7	7	29	8	4	253	295	312	607	6%	76%	0.25	43	96	2.70	-19
Herrera,Ivan	R	21	21	C	a/a	STL	367	34	68	11	0	11	42	39	104	1	3	186	265	303	568	10%	72%	0.38	71	30	2.20	-26
		22	22	C	aaa	STL	235	27	51	8	1	4	22	24	56	3	1	219	292	304	597	9%	76%	0.43	58	74	2.55	-7
Hicklen,Brewer	R	21	25	LF	aa	KC	362	53	75	14	3	11	44	40	144	31	5	209	287	353	640	10%	60%	0.27	104	149	3.03	-10
		22	26	RF	aaa	KC	480	48	91	26	2	14	48	31	229	20	2	189	238	341	579	6%	52%	0.13	146	130	2.18	-21
Hill,Darius	L	21	24	LF	aa	CHC	249	29	60	4	0	4	23	16	53	1	2	239	286	300	586	6%	79%	0.31	34	48	2.63	-30
		22	25	LF	a/a	CHC	528	51	129	28	4	6	33	21	94	4	5	244	273	342	615	4%	82%	0.22	66	80	2.46	15
Hinds,Rece	R	22	22	RF	aa	CIN	29	2	8	2	0	2	3	0	14	0	1	271	271	532	803	0%	53%	0.00	231	83	3.37	22
Holland,Will	R	22	24	RF	aa	MIN	98	13	18	1	1	2	9	11	45	7	2	184	266	273	539	10%	54%	0.24	68	158	2.07	-60
Hopkins,TJ	R	21	24	LF	aa	CIN	257	33	60	12	5	4	26	21	85	2	0	235	293	373	665	8%	67%	0.25	92	112	2.82	-8
		22	25	LF	a/a	CIN	467	46	101	22	1	17	54	33	175	5	6	216	268	373	641	7%	63%	0.19	122	61	2.70	-19
Horwitz,Spencer	L	22	25	1B	a/a	TOR	403	52	89	27	1	9	34	47	111	5	2	222	303	358	661	10%	72%	0.42	102	75	2.85	17
Howell,Korry	R	21	23	CF	aa	MIL	98	14	20	4	1	3	12	10	51	3	3	206	276	366	641	9%	48%	0.19	146	120	2.43	-35
		22	24	CF	aa	SD	146	24	29	6	2	4	13	17	63	8	1	196	281	347	628	10%	57%	0.27	126	168	2.62	3
Isola,Alex	R	22	24	DH	aa	MIN	210	21	47	8	0	6	26	21	53	0	1	226	296	349	645	9%	75%	0.39	80	25	2.97	-9
Jackson,Jeremiah	R	22	22	2B	aa	LAA	307	28	53	13	0	10	28	25	86	4	4	174	236	309	546	7%	72%	0.29	93	58	1.86	-3
Johnson,Ivan	B	22	24	2B	aa	CIN	180	21	39	10	1	3	16	9	78	3	1	215	252	338	590	5%	57%	0.11	115	112	2.17	-37
Johnston,Troy	L	22	25	1B	a/a	MIA	426	36	89	21	1	9	40	35	113	3	0	209	269	325	594	8%	73%	0.31	82	60	2.39	-5
Jones,Greg	L	21	27	C	aa	COL	20	1	2	0	0	1	1	1	12	0	0	123	150	228	378	3%	38%	0.05	102	-13	0.99	-162
		21	23	SS	aa	TAM	54	6	9	1	1	1	1	3	24	5	0	158	202	244	446	5%	55%	0.12	62	175	1.53	-64
		22	24	SS	aa	TAM	319	36	60	16	2	5	27	18	156	25	6	188	232	295	527	5%	51%	0.12	111	161	1.83	-45
Julien,Edouard	L	22	23	2B	aa	MIN	400	50	97	16	2	11	44	65	144	12	8	244	350	373	723	14%	64%	0.45	100	86	3.71	-8
Jung,Josh	R	21	23	3B	a/a	TEX	304	43	88	20	1	15	48	25	85	2	2	288	341	506	848	7%	72%	0.29	136	50	5.21	28
		22	24	3B	aaa	TEX	99	9	21	5	0	3	14	2	35	1	0	208	227	368	595	2%	65%	0.07	125	46	2.32	-21
Kavadas,Niko	L	22	24	1B	aa	BOS	81	6	15	3	0	1	7	10	45	0	0	186	279	268	547	11%	45%	0.23	97	15	2.03	-113
Keirsey,DaShawn	L	22	25	CF	aa	MIN	425	38	89	21	2	4	30	20	129	26	8	210	246	298	545	5%	70%	0.16	71	127	1.96	-15
Kessinger,Grae	R	21	24	SS	aa	HOU	297	35	52	7	0	7	20	20	94	10	6	176	229	274	503	6%	69%	0.22	62	92	1.71	-34
		22	25	SS	aa	HOU	421	44	67	10	1	10	36	43	137	14	12	160	238	261	499	9%	67%	0.31	70	98	1.56	-24
Koss,Christian	R	22	24	SS	aa	BOS	488	46	107	21	3	11	56	16	153	11	6	220	245	343	588	3%	69%	0.11	90	103	2.24	-14
Kreidler,Ryan	R	21	24	SS	a/a	DET	482	75	114	20	0	17	46	43	170	12	7	237	300	388	688	8%	65%	0.25	103	83	3.38	-15
		22	25	SS	aaa	DET	202	19	34	10	2	5	14	24	81	10	1	170	256	309	566	10%	60%	0.29	115	132	2.05	-7
LaVastida,Bryan	R	21	23	C	a/a	CLE	122	14	29	6	1	3	15	11	43	2	3	235	296	372	668	8%	64%	0.24	99	74	2.76	-23
		22	24	C	a/a	CLE	321	29	53	8	2	6	19	17	94	4	2	164	207	257	464	5%	71%	0.19	62	99	1.37	-25
Lavigne,Grant	L	22	23	1B	aa	COL	208	18	44	6	2	3	15	19	69	0	0	211	276	306	582	8%	67%	0.27	69	57	2.31	-41
Lawlar,Jordan	R	22	20	SS	aa	ARI	85	11	15	0	0	2	7	6	30	1	1	171	226	252	478	7%	65%	0.20	51	81	1.69	-61
Lee,Khalil	L	19	21	RF	aa	KC	470	69	122	22	3	7	48	61	157	49	13	259	344	363	707	12%	67%	0.39	89	189	4.47	8.98
		21	23	RF	aaa	NYM	292	46	63	16	1	9	26	48	139	6	12	216	327	372	700	14%	52%	0.35	137	83	2.92	-26
		22	24	CF	aaa	NYM	353	30	57	19	0	6	23	30	169	8	3	162	226	270	496	8%	52%	0.17	114	77	1.49	-60
Lee,Korey	R	21	23	C	a/a	HOU	220	20	46	10	1	6	23	14	51	2	1	209	256	347	603	6%	77%	0.27	82	63	2.41	6
		22	24	C	aaa	HOU	404	46	74	15	1	16	47	23	152	7	1	184	227	347	574	5%	62%	0.15	122	104	2.19	-9
Leon,Pedro	R	21	23	SS	a/a	HOU	246	29	45	7	1	7	25	28	103	12	11	183	267	302	569	10%	58%	0.27	88	97	1.98	-45
		22	24	CF	aaa	HOU	413	44	73	21	2	11	39	44	173	24	21	176	256	314	569	10%	58%	0.26	120	118	1.75	-15
Lewis,Royce	R	19	20	SS	aa	MIN	134	17	31	9	1	2	13	11	33	6	2	233	289	360	649	7%	75%	0.32	102	154	3.43	41.2
		22	23	SS	aaa	MIN	131	19	33	10	1	3	9	12	37	8	2	255	317	413	730	8%	72%	0.32	120	122	3.59	38
Lipcius,Andre	R	21	23	3B	aa	DET	341	39	71	16	2	7	36	29	86	3	1	207	270	326	596	8%	75%	0.34	74	80	2.34	0
		22	24	3B	a/a	DET	462	48	105	27	2	7	43	59	100	9	5	227	314	344	658	11%	78%	0.59	82	83	2.83	28
Lockridge,Brandon	R	21	24	CF	aa	NYY	174	26	50	8	0	8	19	11	68	10	1	285	325	476	802	6%	61%	0.16	136	97	5.20	-5
		22	25	CF	aa	NYY	418	47	76	13	1	10	34	26	151	13	5	181	229	289	518	6%	64%	0.17	83	103	1.81	-34
Loftin,Nick	R	22	24	CF	a/a	KC	516	62	105	22	1	9	39	31	107	17	7	204	249	301	550	6%	79%	0.29	65	106	2.04	15
Lopez,Otto	R	21	23	2B	a/a	TOR	451	72	128	31	3	4	52	33	98	18	4	283	331	393	725	7%	78%	0.33	74	125	3.76	25
		22	24	2B	aaa	TOR	340	40	86	17	4	2	26	29	69	11	6	254	313	350	663	8%	80%	0.42	65	120	2.91	24
Malloy,Justyn-Henry	R	22	22	LF	a/a	ATL	215	32	52	11	0	6	29	40	72	2	0	243	362	375	737	16%	67%	0.56	102	50	3.99	-3
Mangum,Jake	B	21	25	CF	aa	NYM	305	39	71	16	2	5	29	11	73	10	7	231	258	346	604	3%	76%	0.15	73	117	2.24	6
		22	26	CF	a/a	NYM	276	26	63	11	2	3	21	12	73	9	4	229	261	315	576	4%	74%	0.17	62	115	2.21	-11

BATTER	B	Yr	Age	Pos	Lvl	Tm	AB	R	H	D	T	HR	RBI	BB	K	SB	CS	BA	OB	Slg	OPS	bb%	ct%	Eye	PX	SX	RC/G	BPV
Manzardo,Kyle	L	22	22	1B	aa	TAM	99	13	27	9	0	3	19	10	23	1	1	269	338	456	794	9%	77%	0.45	131	46	4.19	48
Marlowe,Cade	L	22	25	CF	a/a	SEA	499	52	107	15	2	14	64	39	197	26	12	214	271	340	610	7%	61%	0.20	98	117	2.57	-28
Martin,Austin	R	21	22	CF	aa	MIN	330	50	79	17	2	4	26	46	91	10	4	240	333	333	666	12%	72%	0.51	66	100	3.07	-1
		22	23	SS	aa	MIN	336	38	65	11	2	1	21	31	61	22	6	194	262	249	511	8%	82%	0.50	38	132	1.84	16
Martin,Mason	L	21	22	1B	a/a	PIT	439	49	92	27	1	17	60	30	182	0	3	210	260	397	657	6%	59%	0.16	145	43	2.66	-22
		22	23	1B	aaa	PIT	481	41	83	26	3	11	48	35	213	8	3	172	229	311	540	7%	56%	0.17	128	106	1.71	-27
Martinez,Angel	B	22	20	2B	aa	CLE	82	8	18	6	1	2	13	9	20	2	1	219	296	388	685	10%	76%	0.46	114	80	2.88	42
Martinez,Orelvis	R	22	21	SS	aa	TOR	433	38	73	13	0	22	50	25	151	3	3	169	215	348	563	5%	65%	0.17	124	44	2.04	-14
Martinez,Orlando	L	21	23	LF	aa	LAA	400	44	87	20	1	12	41	24	136	4	3	219	263	365	627	6%	66%	0.18	101	71	2.58	-21
		22	24	RF	a/a	LAA	385	30	80	14	3	6	39	22	109	5	8	207	251	303	554	5%	72%	0.20	68	76	1.87	-24
Mastrobuoni,Miles	L	19	24	LF	a/a	TAM	392	49	102	9	6	3	29	38	102	13	15	261	327	337	664	9%	74%	0.37	51	155	3.41	-2.71
		21	26	SS	a/a	TAM	382	45	93	20	4	4	34	39	113	6	8	244	314	346	660	9%	70%	0.34	71	94	2.72	-13
		22	27	2B	aaa	TAM	507	61	115	25	2	10	42	42	125	15	4	227	287	342	629	8%	75%	0.34	80	106	2.75	15
Mauricio,Ronny	R	21	20	SS	aa	NYM	31	2	9	1	0	1	1	2	13	2	0	277	310	375	686	5%	59%	0.12	74	50	4.11	-79
		22	21	SS	aa	NYM	509	49	109	21	1	18	62	17	146	14	12	214	240	368	608	3%	71%	0.12	104	86	2.30	3
Mayo,Coby	R	22	21	3B	aa	BAL	128	14	28	3	0	4	14	8	54	0	0	215	261	334	596	6%	58%	0.15	96	32	2.62	-67
McCann,Kyle	L	21	24	C	aa	OAK	320	27	43	10	0	5	27	33	157	1	0	135	215	216	431	9%	51%	0.21	75	41	1.19	-103
		22	25	C	a/a	OAK	394	37	66	15	0	11	38	32	183	1	0	169	230	290	521	7%	53%	0.17	113	46	1.79	-65
McIntosh,Paul	R	22	25	C	aa	MIA	318	48	67	21	1	9	37	39	89	7	6	210	297	361	658	11%	72%	0.44	111	96	2.67	30
McLain,Matt	R	22	23	SS	aa	CIN	371	45	73	18	2	13	39	48	146	18	3	196	288	364	652	11%	61%	0.33	134	126	2.89	12
Mead,Curtis	R	22	22	3B	a/a	TAM	282	31	70	23	0	9	36	26	73	5	2	249	313	423	736	9%	74%	0.36	128	61	3.59	36
Meadows,Parker	L	22	23	CF	aa	DET	425	45	99	18	7	10	35	36	99	12	2	234	294	380	674	8%	77%	0.37	90	127	3.07	35
Mears,Joshua	R	22	21	CF	aa	SD	83	6	11	2	0	3	10	7	50	1	0	135	203	273	475	8%	39%	0.14	156	36	1.54	-89
Mervis,Matt	L	22	24	1B	a/a	CHC	412	48	97	24	2	18	57	28	97	1	0	234	284	434	718	6%	77%	0.29	127	59	3.49	40
Mieses,Luis	L	22	22	LF	aa	CHW	97	8	24	4	0	2	11	3	23	1	0	248	270	365	635	3%	76%	0.13	77	40	3.00	-13
Millas,Drew	B	22	24	C	aa	WAS	152	9	28	4	0	2	12	11	59	1	1	181	236	250	487	7%	61%	0.19	57	31	1.63	-85
Misner,Kameron	L	21	23	CF	aa	MIA	55	10	15	6	0	1	3	6	19	2	2	269	342	421	762	10%	65%	0.31	130	85	3.32	10
		22	24	CF	aa	TAM	416	54	82	20	1	10	42	59	189	22	9	197	296	320	616	12%	55%	0.31	117	105	2.53	-30
Mitchell,Garrett	L	21	23	CF	aa	MIL	129	12	21	1	0	2	8	14	47	4	1	161	244	224	468	10%	64%	0.30	40	70	1.66	-71
		22	24	CF	a/a	MIL	239	29	57	12	1	3	23	18	85	11	1	238	292	342	633	7%	64%	0.21	86	126	2.92	-20
Montgomery,Colson	L	22	20	SS	aa	CHW	48	3	6	1	0	2	5	1	16	0	0	124	149	241	390	3%	67%	0.09	78	31	0.97	-53
Morris,Tanner	L	22	24	3B	a/a	TOR	252	30	53	6	1	4	12	36	63	1	6	211	309	284	593	12%	75%	0.57	48	44	2.33	-21
Muzziotti,Simon	L	21	23	CF	a/a	PHI	41	2	9	2	0	0	6	4	7	1	0	217	290	256	546	9%	83%	0.61	30	43	2.23	-10
		22	24	CF	a/a	PHI	159	17	34	4	3	4	13	14	39	5	3	217	280	344	625	8%	75%	0.36	75	124	2.49	17
Naylor,Bo	L	21	21	C	aa	CLE	313	33	53	12	1	8	36	30	122	8	0	171	243	292	535	9%	61%	0.25	90	96	1.97	-36
		22	22	C	a/a	CLE	415	48	91	22	2	14	45	54	138	13	4	218	308	386	693	11%	67%	0.39	123	103	3.25	21
Neto,Zach	R	22	21	SS	aa	LAA	122	15	33	7	0	3	15	5	33	3	2	267	298	398	697	4%	73%	0.16	97	68	3.33	0
Noel,Jhonkensy	R	22	21	RF	a/a	CLE	257	30	51	15	1	9	28	20	78	1	0	198	257	367	624	7%	69%	0.26	121	75	2.48	14
Norby,Connor	R	22	22	2B	a/a	BAL	291	43	76	13	1	16	35	24	70	7	3	262	319	484	803	8%	76%	0.35	135	93	4.64	57
Nunez,Malcom	R	21	20	3B	aa	STL	202	19	43	4	0	4	13	13	47	1	1	212	261	288	549	6%	77%	0.29	44	43	2.23	-31
		22	21	1B	a/a	PIT	416	49	91	15	0	14	60	49	112	3	2	219	302	359	661	11%	73%	0.44	92	50	3.16	4
Nunez,Nasim	B	22	22	SS	aa	MIA	142	17	32	5	0	0	11	18	40	16	6	227	315	264	579	11%	72%	0.46	36	108	2.55	-27
O Hoppe,Logan	R	21	21	C	a/a	PHI	75	6	19	2	0	3	7	2	14	0	0	248	269	398	667	3%	81%	0.15	76	8	3.44	-6
		22	22	C	aa	LAA	360	46	84	11	1	18	50	47	84	5	4	234	322	420	742	11%	77%	0.55	109	59	3.99	36
Ornelas,Jonathan	R	22	22	SS	aa	TEX	525	56	130	17	1	9	43	30	135	9	7	247	288	334	622	5%	74%	0.22	60	76	2.83	-20
Ornelas,Tirso	L	22	22	LF	a/a	SD	455	40	101	23	1	4	33	28	103	4	2	223	268	305	574	6%	77%	0.28	62	67	2.20	-7
Ortiz,Jhailyn	R	21	23	CF	aa	PHI	77	5	14	1	0	3	4	6	31	0	0	185	244	311	555	7%	60%	0.20	82	2	2.30	-78
		22	24	RF	aa	PHI	448	45	86	20	1	12	41	29	190	6	2	192	241	324	565	6%	58%	0.15	114	91	2.08	-37
Ortiz,Joey	R	22	24	SS	a/a	BAL	539	58	124	28	4	14	54	31	112	5	2	230	273	373	646	5%	79%	0.28	91	88	2.78	29
		21	23	SS	aa	BAL	60	8	12	2	0	3	6	4	15	1	0	201	254	386	639	7%	75%	0.28	101	57	2.95	13
Outman,James	L	21	24	CF	aa	LA	166	28	39	7	1	6	17	12	60	1	2	236	286	404	691	7%	64%	0.19	115	83	3.21	-12
		22	25	RF	a/a	LA	473	60	107	24	3	21	63	40	185	8	5	227	287	422	709	8%	61%	0.22	151	99	3.33	12
Ovalles,Alexander	L	22	22	1B	a/a	TAM	42	3	5	1	0	0	2	4	15	1	0	115	197	135	332	9%	65%	0.29	21	56	0.71	-87
Pages,Andy	R	22	22	RF	aa	LA	487	46	96	24	1	20	54	40	156	4	3	198	259	375	634	8%	68%	0.26	125	62	2.58	7
Paris,Kyren	R	22	21	2B	aa	LAA	39	7	12	2	0	2	5	7	16	3	0	305	409	513	921	15%	59%	0.43	164	83	7.75	23
Peguero,Liover	R	22	21	SS	aa	PIT	483	44	106	21	4	6	40	21	120	19	7	220	252	316	567	4%	75%	0.17	67	119	2.14	0
Pereira,Everson	R	22	21	CF	aa	NYY	113	16	28	3	2	4	10	7	42	2	2	244	288	410	698	6%	63%	0.17	117	119	3.15	-6
Perez, Jr.,Robert	R	19	19	DH	aaa	SEA	64	7	14	3	1	2	6	3	26	0	0	225	262	402	664	5%	59%	0.12	151	128	3.46	5.68
Pereza,Oswald	R	21	21	SS	a/a	NYY	354	46	94	14	1	11	35	21	96	18	10	266	308	409	717	6%	73%	0.22	86	102	3.69	4
		22	22	SS	aaa	NYY	386	42	84	13	0	15	37	26	114	25	6	219	268	366	633	6%	70%	0.23	98	104	2.99	6
Pineda,Israel	R	22	22	C	a/a	WAS	114	13	25	4	0	6	19	10	27	1	0	216	280	409	688	8%	76%	0.37	114	40	3.46	27
Plummer,Nick	L	21	25	LF	a/a	STL	386	45	83	15	4	9	34	45	148	8	11	216	298	344	642	10%	62%	0.30	92	97	2.54	-28
		22	26	LF	aaa	NYM	235	18	41	8	0	4	25	15	102	5	5	175	226	265	491	6%	57%	0.15	81	61	1.51	-76
Polcovich,Kaden	B	21	22	2B	aa	SEA	128	10	14	3	0	2	11	13	47	3	1	113	194	176	370	9%	63%	0.27	47	74	0.87	-66
		22	23	2B	aa	SEA	451	47	85	16	2	8	40	39	140	12	2	188	253	286	539	8%	69%	0.28	71	110	1.98	-17
Prieto,Cesar	L	22	23	3B	aa	BAL	368	29	78	18	0	3	24	10	64	1	6	211	231	285	516	3%	83%	0.15	53	41	1.63	-8
Rafaela,Ceddanne	R	22	22	CF	aa	BOS	284	31	70	15	4	8	35	11	67	10	5	246	274	412	686	4%	76%	0.16	106	131	2.94	39
Ramos,Bryan	R	22	20	3B	aa	CHW	80	6	15	2	0	2	8	4	16	0	1	191	226	313	539	4%	80%	0.22	73	29	1.87	-4
Ramos,Heliot	R	19	20	CF	aa	SF	95	13	23	6	1	3	15	10	33	2	3	244	318	416	734	10%	65%	0.31	145	148	3.99	34.5
		21	22	CF	a/a	SF	449	50	98	22	3	9	43	32	152	11	3	218	270	341	611	7%	66%	0.21	88	106	2.50	-18
		22	23	CF	aaa	SF	427	37	77	15	1	6	27	26	128	4	7	179	226	260	487	6%	70%	0.20	61	62	1.46	-40
Redmond,Chanlder	L	21	24	1B	aa	STL	122	8	29	7	0	3	16	7	58	0	1	235	275	365	639	5%	52%	0.11	121	19	2.68	-76
		22	25	1B	aa	STL	327	27	53	8	1	10	41	20	129	0	1	162	210	286	496	6%	61%	0.15	93	50	1.59	-55
Rhodes,John	R	22	22	RF	aa	BAL	90	8	14	2	1	0	6	8	24	0	0	157	225	212	437	8%	74%	0.33	39	77	1.07	-32
Rizzo,Joe	L	21	23	3B	aa	SEA	380	39	82	15	1	9	48	34	124	3	4	216	280	333	612	8%	67%	0.27	79	54	2.53	-32
		22	24	3B	aa	SEA	488	56	104	23	0	14	46	31	126	1	1	214	261	345	606	6%	74%	0.25	89	48	2.51	-4
Rocchio,Brayan	B	21	20	SS	aa	CLE	184	28	51	13	3	5	25	11	44	6	4	275	315	457	773	6%	76%	0.25	110	128	3.75	43
		22	21	SS	a/a	CLE	510	55	110	23	1	12	43	36	115	9	10	215	266	335	601	7%	77%	0.31	80	72	2.33	11

BATTER	B	Yr	Age	Pos	Lvl	Tm	AB	R	H	D	T	HR	RBI	BB	K	SB	CS	BA	OB	Slg	OPS	bb%	ct%	Eye	PX	SX	RC/G	BPV
Rodriguez,Endy	B	22	22	C	a/a	PIT	140	20	45	15	1	6	28	13	27	1	0	321	378	561	940	8%	81%	0.48	158	61	6.32	87
Rodriguez,Johnathan	R	22	23	RF	aa	CLE	107	7	19	6	1	4	11	4	49	0	1	175	201	359	560	3%	54%	0.07	164	82	1.62	-18
Rodriguez,Jose	R	22	21	SS	aa	CHW	440	52	102	17	3	9	47	28	74	28	11	232	278	347	624	6%	83%	0.37	68	132	2.68	40
Rojas,Johan	R	22	22	CF	aa	PHI	235	30	52	7	4	3	11	15	49	20	4	222	269	321	590	6%	79%	0.31	58	170	2.48	29
Rosario,Eguy	R	21	22	SS	aa	SD	420	50	102	27	2	9	47	40	121	23	16	243	308	380	688	9%	71%	0.33	94	104	2.95	11
		22	23	2B	aaa	SD	490	54	103	26	2	12	45	34	133	12	9	211	262	342	604	7%	73%	0.26	93	92	2.28	9
Rucker,Jake	R	22	23	2B	aaa	MIN	26	2	2	0	0	1	2	1	11	1	0	88	130	155	285	5%	57%	0.11	47	83	0.61	-96
Ruiz,Esteury	R	21	22	LF	aa	SD	309	40	66	14	1	7	32	23	80	28	8	214	267	338	605	7%	74%	0.28	78	138	2.55	15
		22	23	CF	a/a	MIL	437	79	119	26	1	11	45	47	113	59	16	273	344	419	763	10%	74%	0.42	102	150	4.42	44
Sabato,Aaron	R	22	23	1B	aa	MIN	84	8	12	3	0	3	11	6	35	1	0	140	202	288	490	7%	59%	0.19	121	67	1.54	-32
Sabol,Blake	L	22	24	C	a/a	PIT	447	48	103	23	4	11	49	37	147	7	2	230	290	376	666	8%	67%	0.25	109	102	2.94	4
Saggese,Thomas	R	22	20	2B	aa	TEX	21	3	7	3	1	1	6	1	3	1	0	331	353	672	1	3%	84%	0.21	198	133	6.01	143
Sanchez,Yolbert	R	21	24	2B	aa	CHW	143	13	44	5	0	3	12	4	19	3	0	307	329	417	746	3%	87%	0.24	58	51	4.73	18
		22	25	2B	a/a	CHW	494	32	108	12	0	2	29	26	95	7	11	218	258	259	517	5%	81%	0.28	29	50	1.80	-27
Schmitt,Casey	R	22	23	3B	a/a	SF	135	9	39	10	1	2	13	4	40	1	0	287	309	428	737	3%	71%	0.10	110	62	3.84	-3
Schuemann,Max	R	21	24	2B	a/a	OAK	245	27	63	12	1	1	15	19	62	12	4	255	309	334	643	7%	75%	0.31	56	112	2.98	-6
		22	25	2B	a/a	OAK	325	39	66	12	2	5	24	32	121	14	7	202	273	290	563	9%	63%	0.26	73	112	2.11	-37
Schunk,Aaron	R	22	25	3B	aa	COL	450	37	95	27	1	9	46	20	125	4	2	211	245	335	580	4%	72%	0.16	93	62	2.13	-8
Shenton,Austin	L	21	23	3B	aa	TAM	91	8	23	7	0	2	13	5	30	0	0	251	287	400	687	5%	68%	0.16	110	20	3.19	-24
		22	24	3B	aa	TAM	195	19	36	7	1	5	19	19	85	0	0	185	258	305	563	9%	56%	0.22	105	46	2.10	-57
Shewmake,Braden	L	19	22	SS	aa	ATL	46	8	10	0	0	0	1	4	11	2	0	224	291	224	515	9%	76%	0.38	0	133	2.39	-44.2
		21	24	SS	aa	ATL	324	34	67	13	2	10	34	14	83	3	2	206	239	352	592	4%	74%	0.17	86	86	2.25	3
		22	25	SS	aaa	ATL	278	28	62	12	1	5	19	18	66	7	0	222	269	337	606	6%	76%	0.27	77	104	2.60	11
Siani,Mike	L	22	23	CF	a/a	CIN	492	58	107	17	4	11	39	47	109	37	13	217	285	335	620	9%	78%	0.43	73	131	2.69	28
Simon,Ronny	B	22	22	2B	aa	TAM	144	18	32	7	1	5	18	8	29	8	2	224	264	385	649	5%	80%	0.27	98	136	2.81	50
Smith-Njigba,Canaan	L	21	22	LF	a/a	PIT	240	27	54	10	0	4	31	36	80	10	1	225	326	321	647	13%	67%	0.45	70	76	3.16	-26
		22	23	LF	aaa	PIT	184	21	43	14	2	1	13	23	58	5	3	233	317	339	656	11%	69%	0.39	92	111	2.52	5
Soderstrom,Tyler	L	22	21	C	a/a	OAK	170	12	38	2	1	5	21	7	52	0	1	222	252	335	587	4%	69%	0.13	69	44	2.49	-45
Sosa,Lenyn	R	21	21	SS	aa	CHW	117	9	23	5	0	1	7	2	31	0	1	198	211	261	472	2%	74%	0.06	45	43	1.41	-51
		22	22	SS	a/a	CHW	483	52	126	17	1	18	53	27	95	2	5	260	299	412	712	5%	80%	0.29	89	44	3.70	18
Soto,Livan	L	21	21	SS	aa	LAA	40	2	8	1	0	0	3	2	12	0	0	195	241	218	458	6%	70%	0.20	20	19	1.49	-87
		22	22	SS	aa	LAA	456	45	105	14	1	4	37	47	116	12	9	230	302	290	593	9%	75%	0.41	44	69	2.49	-25
Steer,Spencer	R	21	24	3B	aa	MIN	249	32	51	10	2	10	30	15	83	3	0	204	249	374	622	6%	67%	0.18	109	97	2.61	-4
		22	25	3B	a/a	CIN	427	54	98	25	1	18	51	36	107	3	3	229	289	420	709	8%	75%	0.33	125	60	3.31	35
Strumpf,Chase	R	21	23	3B	aa	CHC	214	18	39	13	0	5	21	29	71	1	0	180	277	313	590	12%	67%	0.40	98	30	2.18	-20
		22	24	2B	aa	CHC	393	44	70	17	1	13	35	44	191	1	2	178	261	324	585	10%	51%	0.23	137	63	2.17	-44
Swaggerty,Travis	L	21	24	CF	aaa	PIT	41	4	7	0	0	2	5	4	9	2	0	179	258	325	584	10%	78%	0.49	69	64	2.84	9
		22	25	CF	aaa	PIT	398	35	80	13	5	5	35	38	135	13	6	201	270	299	569	9%	66%	0.28	72	121	2.06	-23
Sweeney,Trey	L	22	22	SS	aa	NYY	43	4	8	1	0	2	4	5	11	1	1	197	285	323	608	11%	74%	0.47	76	60	2.61	-3
Taylor,Samad	R	21	23	2B	aa	TOR	319	51	81	15	1	12	38	30	124	22	9	254	318	423	741	9%	61%	0.24	122	112	3.94	-5
		22	24	2B	aaa	TOR	244	31	54	9	1	7	34	20	70	17	6	220	279	358	637	8%	71%	0.28	91	133	2.86	15
Tena,Jose	L	22	21	SS	a/a	CLE	535	54	120	23	4	10	45	19	160	5	6	224	251	335	586	3%	70%	0.12	81	87	2.21	-20
Toglia,Michael	B	21	23	1B	aa	COL	143	11	28	9	1	4	12	16	53	2	0	199	280	360	639	10%	63%	0.30	121	72	2.55	-8
		22	24	1B	a/a	COL	429	43	87	17	1	19	48	33	160	5	2	203	260	376	636	7%	63%	0.21	129	64	2.74	-10
Tovar,Ezequiel	R	22	21	SS	a/a	COL	285	26	80	13	3	9	30	16	68	10	3	279	317	443	760	5%	76%	0.23	103	105	4.23	31
Tresh,Luca	R	22	22	C	aa	KC	91	10	19	4	0	3	9	8	26	1	0	211	273	345	618	8%	71%	0.30	93	47	2.71	-9
Triolo,Jared	R	22	24	3B	aa	PIT	425	43	97	19	3	5	25	43	99	16	6	229	299	327	626	9%	77%	0.43	67	112	2.68	14
Turang,Brice	L	21	22	SS	a/a	MIL	431	44	96	19	2	5	40	45	95	15	10	222	296	307	603	9%	78%	0.47	54	90	2.40	3
		22	23	SS	aaa	MIL	532	60	124	19	1	9	53	46	141	23	2	233	294	325	618	8%	74%	0.33	64	111	2.95	-3
Valdez,Enmanuel	L	21	23	2B	aa	HOU	82	9	18	5	0	4	14	10	25	0	1	221	307	434	741	11%	69%	0.40	136	24	3.54	18
		22	24	2B	a/a	BOS	500	62	125	34	1	18	71	42	140	5	3	251	309	430	738	8%	72%	0.30	127	68	3.70	28
Valera,George	L	21	21	RF	aa	CLE	86	5	21	3	0	2	18	9	33	1	0	244	316	363	679	9%	62%	0.27	85	20	3.58	-59
		22	22	RF	a/a	CLE	484	59	100	21	2	16	54	48	165	2	4	207	279	359	637	9%	66%	0.29	111	63	2.66	-8
Valera,Leonel	R	22	23	SS	aa	LA	321	41	77	10	2	10	41	21	137	15	1	239	286	377	664	6%	57%	0.15	111	140	3.37	-26
Valerio,Felix	R	22	22	2B	aa	MIL	417	41	78	11	1	9	36	34	92	21	10	188	250	283	534	8%	78%	0.37	59	109	1.93	9
Vargas,Miguel	R	21	22	3B	aa	LA	327	48	90	14	1	12	43	24	65	5	1	275	325	432	757	7%	80%	0.38	86	75	4.45	28
		22	23	3B	aaa	LA	438	58	104	25	2	11	48	40	90	9	6	236	300	377	677	8%	79%	0.44	91	92	3.06	37
Veen,Zac	L	22	21	RF	aa	COL	124	8	19	4	0	1	4	8	42	3	5	153	207	199	406	6%	66%	0.20	40	64	0.88	-69
Vellojin,Daniel	L	22	22	C	aa	CIN	94	8	15	2	0	3	9	11	38	0	1	164	253	293	546	11%	59%	0.29	96	53	1.93	-46
Veras,Wilfred	R	22	20	DH	aa	CHW	45	4	10	2	0	2	4	2	15	0	0	230	266	449	715	5%	66%	0.14	158	3	3.48	3
Vientos,Mark	R	21	22	3B	a/a	NYM	312	37	71	14	0	17	45	24	120	0	2	227	281	440	721	7%	62%	0.20	147	25	3.53	-12
		22	23	3B	aaa	NYM	378	43	84	13	1	16	47	29	148	0	2	223	279	385	664	7%	61%	0.20	123	37	3.11	-30
Vilade,Ryan	R	21	22	LF	aaa	COL	468	52	119	26	5	5	28	25	96	8	5	255	293	363	657	5%	80%	0.27	67	100	2.81	14
		22	23	RF	aaa	COL	368	36	76	13	3	3	21	27	72	6	7	205	261	282	543	7%	81%	0.38	49	92	1.82	5
Volpe,Anthony	R	22	21	SS	a/a	NYY	511	65	107	28	3	16	49	50	134	38	7	210	281	374	654	9%	74%	0.37	110	144	2.96	47
Waddell,Luke	L	21	23	2B	aa	ATL	31	3	5	0	0	0	2	2	4	1	1	148	192	148	340	5%	86%	0.40	0	80	0.74	-19
		22	24	SS	aa	ATL	162	15	38	9	0	2	22	17	25	2	2	233	306	315	622	10%	84%	0.68	58	48	2.57	19
Wagner,Will	L	22	24	2B	aa	HOU	251	25	49	9	1	4	18	22	68	3	1	196	262	290	551	8%	73%	0.33	66	83	2.02	-13
Walker,Jordan	R	22	20	3B	aa	STL	461	58	110	24	2	10	40	33	126	13	6	238	288	363	651	7%	73%	0.26	90	102	2.91	8
Wallner,Matt	L	22	25	RF	a/a	MIN	458	56	98	26	2	16	59	61	203	6	6	215	307	386	694	12%	56%	0.30	153	78	3.07	-6
Ward,Ryan	L	22	24	LF	aa	LA	459	40	95	14	1	20	50	24	135	3	1	207	247	376	623	5%	71%	0.18	109	55	2.70	-2
Warren,Zavier	B	22	23	3B	aa	MIL	92	6	19	2	0	1	7	8	32	2	0	203	270	275	545	8%	65%	0.27	56	48	2.26	-61
Wells,Austin	L	22	23	C	aa	NYY	211	25	46	6	1	9	32	22	68	5	0	217	290	382	672	9%	68%	0.32	110	88	3.40	7
Westburg,Jordan	R	21	22	SS	aa	BAL	112	11	23	5	1	3	10	10	34	2	0	202	268	357	625	8%	70%	0.30	97	96	2.56	5
		22	23	SS	a/a	BAL	544	62	119	32	2	20	68	45	163	8	3	219	278	396	674	8%	70%	0.27	125	82	2.99	22
Wiemer,Joey	R	22	23	RF	a/a	MIL	484	55	100	27	1	15	52	39	174	21	3	207	266	360	626	7%	64%	0.22	120	118	2.67	4
Williams,Alika	R	22	23	SS	a/a	TAM	38	1	6	2	0	0	3	5	18	1	1	169	265	213	478	11%	53%	0.28	57	36	1.27	-105

PITCHER	Th	Yr	Age	LvL	Org	W	L	G	Sv	IP	H	ER	HR	BB	K	ERA	WHIP	BF/G	OBA	K%	BB%	K-BB	hr/9	H%	S%	BPV
Abbott, Andrew	L	22	23	aa	CIN	7	7	20	0	91	91	51	8	40	104	5.05	1.44	19.4	261	27%	10%	17%	0.8	35%	65%	95
Abel, Mick	R	22	21	aa	PHI	1	3	5	0	23	20	9	5	11	24	3.48	1.32	19.1	231	24%	11%	13%	1.9	26%	84%	53
Acton, Garrett	R	22	24	a/a	OAK	3	9	51	9	72	72	32	10	24	76	3.93	1.32	5.9	260	25%	8%	17%	1.2	33%	75%	90
Allen, Logan	L	21	23	aa	CLE	4	0	12	0	60	46	23	10	13	66	3.40	0.98	19.0	213	29%	6%	23%	1.5	26%	74%	133
Alvarado, Elvis	R	22	23	aa	DET	5	1	20	2	24	17	10	2	6	19	3.74	0.96	4.6	198	20%	7%	13%	0.6	23%	61%	100
Armbruester, Justin	R	22	24	aa	BAL	4	1	14	2	64	53	27	14	15	51	3.77	1.06	17.7	226	20%	6%	14%	2.0	23%	76%	65
Arrighetti, Spencer	R	22	22	aa	HOU	1	1	5	0	21	13	7	3	8	25	3.13	0.99	16.0	179	31%	10%	21%	1.1	23%	74%	117
Bachman, Sam	R	22	23	aa	LAA	1	1	12	0	45	42	18	4	23	26	3.54	1.43	16.0	246	13%	12%	1%	0.7	27%	77%	38
Balazovic, Jordan	R	21	23	aa	MIN	5	4	20	0	97	108	43	9	38	86	3.96	1.50	21.0	282	21%	9%	12%	0.8	35%	75%	70
		22	24	aaa	MIN	0	7	22	0	72	104	53	16	32	63	6.65	1.88	15.4	337	18%	9%	9%	2.0	38%	69%	17
Battenfield, Peyton	R	21	24	aa	CLE	5	1	14	0	72	56	29	10	14	69	3.65	0.98	19.5	217	25%	5%	20%	1.3	26%	68%	128
Beeter, Clayton	R	21	23	aa	LA	0	2	5	0	15	10	7	2	6	20	4.10	1.09	11.7	197	33%	10%	23%	1.1	27%	66%	122
		22	24	aa	NYY	0	3	25	0	77	70	41	11	45	110	4.78	1.48	13.2	242	32%	13%	19%	1.3	35%	71%	98
Bergner, Austin	R	22	25	a/a	DET	5	5	27	0	122	100	48	15	45	95	3.53	1.18	18.1	224	19%	9%	10%	1.1	25%	74%	64
Berroa, Prelander	R	22	22	aa	SEA	2	1	9	0	35	20	15	2	21	48	3.93	1.17	15.5	166	32%	14%	18%	0.6	25%	67%	123
Bibee, Tanner	R	22	23	aa	CLE	6	1	13	0	75	55	16	4	13	70	1.90	0.91	21.6	206	25%	5%	20%	0.5	26%	81%	162
Bolton, Cody	R	19	21	aa	PIT	2	3	9	0	40	46	37	7	17	28	8.29	1.57	19.5	000	16%	10%	6%	1.6	31%	34%	25
		22	24	aaa	PIT	4	2	30	0	77	60	26	3	38	67	3.01	1.28	10.5	217	21%	12%	9%	0.4	27%	76%	83
Bowlan, Jonathan	R	21	25	aa	KC	2	0	4	0	17	16	4	0	3	19	1.99	1.10	16.7	245	29%	5%	24%	0.0	35%	80%	196
		22	26	aa	KC	1	3	9	0	39	56	31	6	15	22	7.04	1.82	20.1	336	12%	8%	4%	1.3	36%	62%	10
Boyle, Joe	R	22	23	aa	CIN	0	2	6	0	26	23	15	3	24	27	5.15	1.81	20.1	237	23%	20%	2%	1.2	29%	74%	52
Bradley, Taj	R	22	21	a/a	TAM	7	4	28	0	134	103	34	11	29	129	2.31	0.99	18.2	214	24%	5%	19%	0.7	27%	80%	137
Brito, Jhony	R	21	23	aa	NYY	3	3	8	0	48	57	31	9	9	39	5.74	1.37	25.3	295	19%	5%	15%	1.7	33%	62%	78
Brown, Aaron	L	19	27	aa	PHI	5	4	45	2	66	76	40	9	40	67	5.51	1.77	6.7	000	22%	13%	9%	1.2	36%	62%	33
		21	29	a/a	OAK	3	4	51	12	65	62	25	3	34	42	3.39	1.47	5.5	251	15%	12%	3%	0.4	29%	77%	52
		22	30	aaa	OAK	7	4	46	3	66	59	29	9	35	52	3.98	1.41	6.1	239	18%	12%	6%	1.2	27%	76%	45
Brown, Ben	R	22	23	aa	CHC	3	0	7	0	31	32	12	2	11	38	3.56	1.40	18.7	270	27%	8%	19%	0.7	38%	76%	117
Brown, Hunter	R	21	23	a/a	HOU	6	5	24	1	101	99	47	12	47	113	4.20	1.44	17.9	257	26%	11%	15%	1.1	34%	74%	82
		22	24	aaa	HOU	9	4	23	1	106	72	28	4	41	114	2.39	1.06	17.9	194	27%	10%	17%	0.4	27%	78%	122
Burke, Sean	R	22	23	a/a	CHW	2	9	21	0	80	85	44	12	33	91	4.99	1.47	16.4	273	26%	9%	16%	1.3	35%	69%	79
Burns, Tanner	R	22	24	aa	CLE	3	7	21	0	90	83	38	14	43	78	3.77	1.39	18.1	245	20%	11%	9%	1.4	28%	79%	49
Bush, Ky	L	22	23	aa	LAA	7	4	21	0	103	94	39	13	27	86	3.44	1.17	19.6	245	20%	6%	14%	1.1	29%	75%	86
Butto, Jose	R	21	23	aa	NYM	3	2	8	0	41	34	13	5	8	44	2.90	1.01	19.7	225	28%	5%	23%	1.1	29%	77%	153
Canterino, Matt	R	22	25	aa	MIN	0	1	11	0	35	18	7	1	21	41	1.71	1.09	12.5	152	28%	14%	14%	0.2	23%	84%	122
Cantillo, Joey	L	22	23	aa	CLE	4	3	14	0	62	41	14	2	26	75	1.99	1.08	17.3	189	31%	11%	20%	0.3	28%	82%	134
Carrillo, Gerardo	R	21	23	aa	WAS	3	7	23	0	97	102	61	16	50	90	5.63	1.56	18.5	271	21%	12%	9%	1.5	32%	67%	44
Castaneda, Victor	R	22	24	a/a	MIL	6	6	26	0	122	118	56	16	50	102	4.10	1.38	19.8	256	19%	10%	10%	1.2	30%	74%	55
Cavalli, Cade	R	21	23	a/a	WAS	4	8	17	0	84	83	45	5	48	87	4.86	1.55	21.7	258	24%	13%	11%	0.5	34%	68%	82
		22	24	aaa	WAS	6	4	20	0	97	80	41	3	36	85	3.77	1.19	19.5	227	21%	9%	12%	0.3	29%	67%	99
Cecconi, Slade	R	22	23	aa	ARI	7	6	26	0	131	136	55	16	27	106	3.77	1.24	20.5	269	19%	5%	14%	1.1	31%	74%	95
Church, Marc	R	22	21	aa	TEX	1	3	14	1	15	18	11	3	6	18	6.45	1.58	4.7	294	26%	9%	17%	1.9	37%	63%	68
Coleman, Carson	R	22	24	aa	NYY	2	3	35	15	44	33	15	2	10	59	3.01	0.96	4.8	208	33%	5%	27%	0.4	32%	68%	201
Criswell, Jeff	R	22	23	a/a	OAK	2	7	14	0	71	66	25	4	21	52	3.20	1.22	20.6	248	18%	7%	10%	0.5	29%	74%	81
Crouse, Hans	R	21	23	a/a	PHI	5	4	20	0	87	61	33	10	33	86	3.40	1.07	17.0	198	25%	10%	16%	1.0	24%	72%	94
Crow, Coleman	R	22	22	aa	LAA	9	3	24	0	128	132	63	18	31	112	4.46	1.28	21.9	268	20%	6%	14%	1.3	31%	69%	85
Curry, Xzavion	R	22	24	a/a	CLE	9	4	25	0	122	109	52	16	38	113	3.84	1.20	19.6	241	22%	7%	15%	1.2	29%	72%	85
Cushing, Jack	R	21	25	aa	OAK	0	5	5	0	25	39	14	1	7	16	5.02	1.83	23.2	355	14%	6%	8%	0.3	41%	71%	59
		22	26	a/a	OAK	12	6	25	0	132	154	66	13	34	91	4.49	1.42	22.4	293	16%	6%	10%	0.9	33%	70%	64
Cusick, Ryan	R	22	23	aa	OAK	1	6	12	0	41	52	28	3	26	36	6.17	1.89	16.1	311	18%	13%	5%	0.6	38%	66%	52
Dabovich, R.J.	R	21	22	aa	SF	1	1	20	6	21	14	9	1	7	29	3.81	0.99	4.0	193	36%	8%	28%	0.4	31%	60%	171
		22	23	a/a	SF	6	1	45	6	54	35	19	2	24	59	3.18	1.09	4.7	186	28%	11%	16%	0.3	26%	69%	119
Dodd, Dylan	L	22	24	a/a	ATL	3	4	10	0	55	60	23	4	14	52	3.75	1.34	23.0	276	24%	7%	17%	0.7	35%	73%	104
Dollard, Taylor	R	22	23	aa	SEA	16	2	27	0	144	106	33	7	27	115	2.06	0.93	20.0	208	20%	5%	15%	0.5	25%	80%	133
Drohan, Shane	L	22	23	aa	BOS	1	1	5	0	24	23	10	5	10	17	3.57	1.37	20.1	251	17%	10%	7%	1.7	26%	83%	28
Englert, Mason	R	22	23	aa	TEX	1	1	3	0	16	14	6	1	4	17	3.61	1.15	21.3	237	26%	7%	19%	0.5	32%	68%	129
Enlow, Blayne	R	22	23	aa	MIN	1	3	24	3	58	60	26	3	27	54	3.98	1.50	10.5	269	21%	10%	11%	0.5	34%	73%	79
Enright, Nic	R	21	24	aa	CLE	3	4	23	2	41	33	23	6	10	47	5.05	1.04	6.9	220	30%	6%	23%	1.2	28%	53%	134
		22	25	a/a	CLE	5	1	48	11	67	52	20	6	13	72	2.72	0.96	5.3	214	28%	5%	23%	0.8	28%	76%	163
Erla, Mason	R	22	25	aa	LAA	5	6	16	0	82	93	38	9	18	52	4.18	1.36	21.4	287	15%	5%	10%	0.9	32%	71%	65
Espino, Daniel	R	22	21	aa	CLE	1	0	4	0	19	9	5	4	4	31	2.41	0.68	16.7	149	46%	5%	40%	1.8	20%	86%	240
Estrada, Jeremiah	R	22	24	a/a	CHC	1	0	19	4	26	17	4	0	9	33	1.28	1.00	5.3	191	32%	9%	23%	0.0	30%	86%	162
Flores, Wilmer	R	22	21	aa	DET	6	4	19	0	85	68	27	7	19	80	2.89	1.02	17.2	222	23%	5%	18%	0.7	28%	74%	131
Fulton, Dax	L	22	21	aa	MIA	1	1	4	0	21	10	6	2	6	26	2.73	0.76	18.8	139	33%	8%	25%	0.8	19%	68%	158
Gaddis, Hunter	R	22	24	a/a	CLE	8	6	24	0	122	93	51	15	37	134	3.77	1.06	19.7	212	27%	7%	20%	1.1	27%	68%	115
Garcia, Deivi	R	19	20	a/a	NYY	5	7	22	0	95	92	57	13	47	119	5.37	1.46	18.5	000	29%	11%	18%	1.2	35%	55%	101
		21	22	aaa	NYY	3	7	24	0	92	113	79	23	67	85	7.70	1.96	18.4	303	19%	15%	4%	2.2	34%	65%	4
		22	23	a/a	NYY	4	5	20	0	66	64	50	13	30	66	6.81	1.42	14.1	254	23%	10%	12%	1.7	30%	54%	53

PITCHER	Th	Yr	Age	LvL	Org	W	L	G	Sv	IP	H	ER	HR	BB	K	ERA	WHIP	BF/G	OBA	K%	BB%	K-BB	hr/9	H%	S%	BPV
Gasser, Robert	L	22	23	a/a	MIL	3	3	9	0	48	42	18	3	23	50	3.33	1.34	22.3	235	25%	11%	14%	0.5	31%	76%	95
German, Franklin	R	22	25	a/a	BOS	5	2	43	7	51	29	16	2	18	51	2.88	0.93	4.5	168	26%	9%	16%	0.3	23%	68%	123
Gil, Luis	R	21	23	a/a	NYY	5	1	20	1	82	67	41	10	46	101	4.49	1.37	17.3	224	29%	13%	16%	1.1	30%	70%	90
		22	24	aaa	NYY	0	3	6	0	23	23	20	6	14	26	7.67	1.60	17.1	258	26%	14%	12%	2.3	30%	56%	35
Ginn, J.T.	R	22	23	aa	OAK	1	4	10	0	36	37	21	2	12	35	5.26	1.37	15.1	268	21%	7%	14%	0.5	34%	60%	98
Gomez, Yoendrys	R	22	23	aa	NYY	1	0	4	0	17	15	7	1	6	17	3.79	1.20	17.2	236	24%	8%	16%	0.5	31%	68%	106
Gordon, Tanner	R	22	25	aa	ATL	9	6	21	0	99	124	70	18	38	80	6.33	1.64	21.1	308	19%	9%	10%	1.6	35%	64%	32
Graceffo, Gordon	R	22	22	aa	STL	7	4	18	0	95	67	29	9	18	69	2.78	0.89	19.6	199	18%	5%	13%	0.9	22%	74%	108
Greene, Zach	R	21	25	aa	NYY	2	5	25	2	40	39	20	5	14	48	4.43	1.32	6.6	258	29%	8%	21%	1.1	35%	69%	110
		22	26	aaa	NYY	9	0	48	0	69	58	28	11	32	79	3.68	1.30	5.9	228	27%	11%	16%	1.5	28%	78%	78
Groome, Jay	L	21	23	aa	BOS	2	0	3	0	17	13	5	0	4	22	2.38	1.01	22.0	217	33%	6%	27%	0.0	34%	74%	200
Grove, Michael	R	21	25	aa	LA	1	4	21	0	71	92	63	18	37	72	8.00	1.82	15.7	314	22%	11%	11%	2.3	36%	60%	18
Hall, DL	L	21	23	aa	BAL	2	0	7	0	33	17	12	4	15	46	3.23	0.98	18.0	157	36%	12%	24%	1.2	21%	73%	126
		22	24	a/a	BAL	3	8	23	0	83	69	42	11	46	106	4.54	1.38	15.2	227	29%	13%	17%	1.2	31%	70%	93
Hancock, Emerson	R	21	22	aa	SEA	1	1	3	0	15	11	6	0	4	12	3.25	0.97	19.2	202	21%	7%	14%	0.0	26%	63%	122
		22	23	aa	SEA	7	4	21	0	99	80	38	13	33	81	3.41	1.14	18.7	223	20%	8%	12%	1.2	25%	76%	70
Harris, Hogan	L	22	26	a/a	OAK	2	3	16	0	62	46	22	4	31	69	3.18	1.23	15.8	207	26%	12%	14%	0.6	28%	76%	102
Harrison, Kyle	L	22	21	aa	SF	4	2	18	0	84	63	30	9	37	112	3.17	1.19	18.7	209	32%	11%	21%	1.0	30%	78%	118
Hartwig, Grant	R	22	25	a/a	NYM	2	2	18	3	28	14	3	0	12	32	0.89	0.94	5.9	154	29%	11%	18%	0.0	23%	89%	143
Headrick, Brent	L	22	25	aa	MIN	2	3	10	0	43	49	22	9	11	48	4.60	1.41	18.2	289	26%	6%	20%	1.9	35%	75%	90
Henderson, Layne	R	21	25	aa	HOU	5	2	26	0	51	47	25	6	29	51	4.36	1.48	8.5	244	23%	13%	10%	1.0	30%	73%	66
		22	26	a/a	HOU	5	4	34	0	54	41	21	5	23	56	3.44	1.18	6.4	211	26%	11%	15%	0.8	27%	73%	97
Henriquez, Ronny	R	21	21	aa	TEX	4	4	16	0	71	74	47	16	17	68	5.94	1.27	18.2	269	23%	6%	18%	2.1	30%	59%	75
Henry, Cole	R	22	23	a/a	WAS	1	0	9	0	33	15	6	2	10	28	1.72	0.76	13.2	139	24%	9%	15%	0.5	17%	81%	116
Hernandez, Adrian	R	21	21	aa	TOR	0	0	10	4	17	5	4	2	5	24	2.16	0.62	5.9	098	40%	9%	31%	1.0	12%	75%	170
		22	22	a/a	TOR	4	0	34	8	38	28	19	6	16	43	4.50	1.17	4.5	207	28%	11%	17%	1.4	25%	66%	86
Herz, D.J.	L	22	21	aa	CHC	1	4	9	0	33	23	25	4	27	37	6.68	1.51	16.0	196	23%	17%	6%	1.0	25%	55%	73
Hoeing, Bryan	R	22	26	a/a	MIA	9	6	22	0	121	138	61	13	39	60	4.52	1.46	23.6	288	12%	8%	4%	1.0	31%	71%	28
Hoffmann, Andrew	R	22	22	aa	KC	2	4	9	0	40	50	27	4	17	24	6.09	1.67	20.0	308	13%	9%	4%	0.8	34%	63%	32
Hurt, Kyle	R	22	24	aa	LA	1	5	12	0	31	36	31	3	32	38	8.87	2.21	13.0	293	22%	19%	3%	0.9	40%	58%	61
Hurter, Brant	L	22	24	aa	DET	0	2	4	0	15	23	12	1	4	14	7.29	1.73	17.3	345	21%	6%	15%	0.5	43%	55%	96
Jacob, Alek	R	22	24	a/a	SD	3	2	39	4	50	45	15	4	14	52	2.65	1.15	5.1	239	25%	7%	19%	0.7	31%	80%	123
Jameson, Drey	R	21	24	aa	ARI	8	6	20	0	47	41	22	5	17	56	4.22	1.24	23.9	237	30%	9%	21%	1.0	32%	69%	110
Jarvis, Bryce	R	21	24	aa	ARI	1	2	8	0	35	35	23	7	16	33	5.95	1.46	18.7	261	22%	11%	11%	1.9	30%	64%	41
		22	25	aa	ARI	3	6	25	0	108	144	89	21	53	88	7.41	1.82	20.1	321	18%	10%	7%	1.7	36%	61%	18
Jensen, Ryan	R	21	24	aa	CHC	1	0	4	0	18	16	7	2	7	12	3.41	1.27	18.4	237	17%	10%	7%	1.0	26%	77%	50
		22	25	aa	CHC	2	4	17	0	60	45	26	4	35	49	3.83	1.33	14.7	210	19%	13%	6%	0.6	25%	72%	69
Juenger, Hayden	R	22	22	a/a	TOR	3	7	38	2	90	66	37	18	32	86	3.71	1.08	9.3	205	24%	9%	15%	1.8	22%	76%	67
Junk, Janson	R	21	25	aa	LAA	6	3	19	1	93	87	34	11	28	80	3.26	1.23	19.8	248	21%	7%	14%	1.1	29%	78%	80
		22	26	aaa	LAA	1	7	16	0	75	78	34	8	17	55	4.02	1.26	19.2	270	18%	5%	12%	0.9	31%	70%	83
Kelly, Antoine	L	22	23	aa	TEX	0	0	7	0	20	12	14	0	16	20	6.17	1.39	12.2	175	23%	19%	5%	0.0	25%	51%	100
Kent, Zak	R	21	23	aa	TEX	0	4	6	0	30	40	21	10	9	33	6.29	1.62	22.4	318	25%	7%	18%	3.0	36%	72%	35
		22	24	a/a	TEX	3	4	24	0	111	101	44	10	38	90	3.55	1.26	18.9	244	20%	8%	11%	0.8	29%	74%	74
Kerr, Ray	L	21	27	a/a	SEA	2	1	36	5	41	31	16	2	17	49	3.59	1.16	4.6	210	30%	10%	20%	0.5	30%	68%	126
Kilian, Caleb	R	21	24	aa	CHC	4	4	15	0	80	75	27	5	12	66	3.06	1.08	20.9	248	21%	4%	17%	0.6	30%	73%	145
Kloffenstein, Adam	R	22	22	aa	TOR	2	5	19	0	86	98	53	11	37	75	5.59	1.57	19.9	287	19%	9%	10%	1.2	34%	66%	53
Knack, Landon	R	21	24	aa	LA	2	1	6	0	24	20	11	6	3	23	4.07	0.94	15.2	227	25%	3%	22%	2.1	24%	69%	178
		22	25	aa	LA	2	10	17	0	66	68	35	8	24	66	4.77	1.38	16.4	266	23%	9%	15%	1.1	33%	66%	80
Kopps, Kevin	R	22	25	aa	SD	1	2	42	4	55	47	25	4	33	50	4.10	1.46	5.6	233	21%	14%	7%	0.6	29%	72%	72
Lacy, Asa	L	22	23	aa	KC	1	2	11	0	20	9	24	2	24	20	10.74	1.65	8.1	141	19%	23%	-4%	0.7	17%	29%	77
Legumina, Casey	R	22	25	aa	MIN	2	5	30	3	73	82	38	9	30	62	4.71	1.53	10.6	284	19%	9%	10%	1.1	33%	72%	54
Leiter, Jack	R	22	22	aa	TEX	3	10	23	0	94	87	52	9	49	93	4.93	1.44	17.5	247	22%	12%	10%	0.8	31%	66%	74
Liberatore, Matt	L	21	22	aaa	STL	9	9	22	0	126	124	53	15	28	104	3.75	1.20	23.1	258	20%	6%	15%	1.1	30%	73%	93
		22	23	aaa	STL	7	9	22	0	115	116	58	12	34	94	4.54	1.31	21.6	264	19%	7%	12%	0.9	31%	67%	77
Loutos, Ryan	R	22	23	a/a	STL	1	4	37	5	50	54	18	3	18	45	3.30	1.43	5.8	278	20%	8%	12%	0.5	35%	77%	87
Lugo, Moises	R	21	22	aa	SD	0	1	6	0	15	12	3	1	8	19	1.86	1.29	10.3	216	31%	13%	18%	0.5	32%	88%	116
		22	23	a/a	SD	8	0	39	2	74	50	22	5	34	85	2.70	1.14	7.5	194	28%	11%	16%	0.5	27%	78%	113
Madden, Ty	R	22	22	aa	DET	2	2	7	0	37	29	11	5	11	41	2.62	1.07	20.7	216	29%	8%	21%	1.2	27%	83%	115
Marsh, Alec	R	21	23	aa	KC	1	3	6	0	26	23	17	4	13	34	5.79	1.38	18.3	238	31%	12%	19%	1.4	32%	60%	90
		22	24	a/a	KC	2	16	27	0	125	147	91	22	51	122	6.54	1.58	20.4	294	21%	9%	12%	1.6	35%	61%	52
Mata, Bryan	R	19	20	aa	BOS	4	6	11	0	55	65	41	7	24	51	6.73	1.62	22.3	000	21%	10%	11%	1.2	35%	50%	60
McCambley, Zach	R	21	22	aa	MIA	1	6	9	0	40	47	28	11	20	41	6.24	1.67	20.0	293	23%	11%	12%	2.6	33%	71%	18
		22	23	aa	MIA	6	8	19	0	94	91	65	11	49	86	6.19	1.50	21.4	256	21%	12%	9%	1.0	31%	59%	59
McDermott, Chayce	R	22	24	aa	BAL	1	1	6	0	28	18	19	8	19	29	5.92	1.31	19.4	187	25%	16%	9%	2.4	17%	63%	33
McGarry, Griff	R	22	23	a/a	PHI	1	5	15	0	42	21	16	3	27	41	3.41	1.13	11.1	150	24%	16%	8%	0.6	19%	71%	90
McGreevy, Michael	R	22	22	aa	STL	6	4	20	0	99	96	37	8	19	63	3.32	1.16	19.7	256	15%	5%	11%	0.8	29%	74%	84

PITCHER	Th	Yr	Age	LvL	Org	W	L	G	Sv	IP	H	ER	HR	BB	K	ERA	WHIP	BF/G	OBA	K%	BB%	K-BB	hr/9	H%	S%	BPV
Medina, Luis	R	21	22	aa	NYY	4	3	15	0	75	73	35	8	41	73	4.16	1.51	21.7	255	22%	13%	10%	0.9	32%	74%	66
		22	23	aa	OAK	5	7	24	0	94	80	47	5	53	91	4.53	1.41	16.6	231	22%	13%	9%	0.5	30%	67%	82
Melean, Alejandro	R	22	22	aa	TOR	0	4	8	0	30	26	16	5	14	21	4.70	1.33	15.6	234	16%	11%	5%	1.4	25%	69%	34
Meyer, Max	R	21	22	a/a	MIA	6	4	22	0	111	102	33	8	42	113	2.70	1.30	20.8	246	25%	9%	16%	0.7	32%	82%	98
		22	23	aaa	MIA	3	4	12	0	58	41	25	4	17	56	3.81	1.02	18.5	202	24%	8%	17%	0.7	26%	63%	113
Miller, Bobby	R	22	23	a/a	LA	7	7	24	0	113	92	46	11	30	124	3.62	1.08	18.4	225	26%	6%	20%	0.8	30%	69%	130
Miller, Bryce	R	22	24	aa	SEA	4	1	10	0	52	35	17	3	17	53	2.90	0.99	19.9	191	26%	8%	18%	0.4	25%	71%	124
Miller, Erik	L	22	24	a/a	PHI	1	1	32	0	49	42	19	4	29	51	3.55	1.45	6.5	232	24%	14%	10%	0.7	30%	77%	80
Mlodzinski, Carmen	R	22	23	aa	PIT	6	8	27	0	106	113	55	8	38	92	4.63	1.42	16.7	274	20%	8%	12%	0.7	34%	67%	78
Montes de Oca, Bryce	R	22	26	a/a	NYM	3	3	43	11	52	37	18	0	35	64	3.12	1.38	5.1	201	28%	15%	13%	0.0	31%	75%	120
Montgomery, Mason	L	22	22	aa	TAM	3	1	11	0	55	39	13	4	14	48	2.20	0.97	19.0	202	22%	6%	16%	0.6	25%	80%	115
Moore, McKinley	R	22	24	aa	PHI	4	5	39	0	51	54	25	3	25	59	4.38	1.54	5.7	272	26%	11%	15%	0.5	37%	71%	96
Morales, Francisco	R	21	22	a/a	PHI	4	14	24	0	93	87	67	12	63	105	6.45	1.61	17.2	249	25%	15%	10%	1.1	32%	60%	67
		22	23	a/a	PHI	5	3	45	3	53	35	27	1	42	59	4.55	1.43	5.0	187	26%	18%	8%	0.2	27%	65%	103
Morris, Cody	R	21	25	a/a	CLE	2	2	14	0	58	45	12	2	19	67	1.82	1.11	16.3	216	29%	8%	21%	0.3	31%	85%	137
Muller, Kyle	L	19	22	aa	ATL	7	6	22	0	113	108	64	7	78	102	5.11	1.64	23.0	000	20%	15%	5%	0.6	32%	64%	-4
		21	24	aaa	ATL	5	4	17	0	81	79	38	10	43	76	4.22	1.51	20.7	256	22%	12%	9%	1.1	31%	75%	58
Murphy, Chris	L	21	23	aa	BOS	1	3	7	0	33	34	23	4	13	40	6.22	1.40	19.9	265	29%	9%	20%	1.1	36%	55%	102
		22	24	a/a	BOS	7	11	30	0	154	135	73	13	68	121	4.24	1.32	21.3	236	19%	11%	8%	0.8	28%	69%	65
Murphy, Luke	R	22	23	aa	LAA	7	2	37	1	46	25	12	0	24	44	2.37	1.06	4.9	163	25%	13%	11%	0.0	23%	75%	114
Mushinski, Parker	L	21	26	a/a	HOU	0	4	23	1	67	76	29	6	23	68	3.88	1.46	12.5	285	24%	8%	16%	0.9	36%	75%	89
Nastrini, Nick	R	22	22	aa	LA	1	1	6	0	31	14	13	5	13	37	3.71	0.88	19.2	137	31%	11%	20%	1.4	15%	64%	108
Nelson, Ryne	R	21	23	aa	ARI	3	3	14	0	77	70	31	12	24	88	3.61	1.23	22.3	245	28%	8%	20%	1.4	31%	77%	103
Nicolas, Kyle	R	21	22	aa	MIA	3	2	8	0	40	26	13	3	25	44	2.97	1.28	20.6	188	26%	15%	11%	0.7	25%	79%	92
		22	23	aa	PIT	2	4	24	0	92	74	39	7	44	84	3.80	1.28	15.7	220	21%	11%	10%	0.7	27%	71%	78
Olson, Reese	R	21	22	aa	DET	2	1	5	0	26	20	15	1	13	17	5.24	1.28	21.5	215	16%	12%	4%	0.4	25%	56%	64
		22	23	aa	DET	8	6	26	0	121	115	55	13	35	138	4.11	1.24	18.9	251	27%	7%	20%	0.9	33%	69%	121
Ortiz, Luis	R	22	23	a/a	PIT	5	9	26	0	125	108	61	16	36	114	4.41	1.15	19.1	234	22%	7%	15%	1.2	28%	64%	90
Orze, Eric	R	21	24	a/a	NYM	3	0	21	4	31	20	8	2	7	36	2.17	0.85	5.5	181	31%	6%	25%	0.7	25%	79%	164
		22	25	aaa	NYM	4	3	32	1	48	43	25	9	13	55	4.63	1.16	6.0	241	28%	7%	21%	1.7	29%	67%	105
Pacheco, Freddy	R	21	23	a/a	STL	1	0	17	3	24	8	4	1	8	32	1.35	0.65	4.9	105	38%	9%	28%	0.3	16%	81%	182
Palmer, Trent	R	22	23	aa	TOR	1	1	7	0	33	22	12	3	13	28	3.31	1.06	18.4	193	20%	9%	11%	0.8	23%	71%	84
Parrish, Drew	L	21	24	aa	KC	5	4	18	0	83	76	38	6	26	74	4.12	1.23	18.7	246	22%	8%	14%	0.9	30%	68%	88
Peluse, Colin	R	21	23	aa	OAK	2	0	3	0	15	10	3	1	4	14	1.85	0.89	18.5	185	26%	7%	19%	0.6	24%	83%	134
		22	24	a/a	OAK	10	7	24	1	123	134	63	13	24	77	4.60	1.28	21.1	277	15%	5%	10%	0.9	31%	65%	73
Pepiot, Ryan	R	21	24	a/a	LA	5	9	26	0	104	89	52	18	41	106	4.44	1.24	16.3	231	25%	10%	15%	1.5	27%	70%	72
		22	25	aaa	LA	9	1	19	0	92	60	22	9	30	93	2.11	0.98	18.4	189	25%	8%	17%	0.8	24%	84%	114
Perez, Eury	R	22	19	aa	MIA	3	3	17	0	75	64	35	8	22	97	4.17	1.14	17.5	231	31%	7%	24%	0.9	33%	65%	143
Pfaadt, Brandon	R	21	23	aa	ARI	1	1	6	0	34	39	18	11	7	30	4.62	1.35	23.7	291	21%	5%	17%	2.8	30%	81%	58
		22	24	a/a	ARI	11	7	29	0	169	156	60	20	28	179	3.20	1.08	22.8	246	26%	4%	22%	1.1	31%	76%	167
Phillips, Connor	R	22	21	aa	CIN	1	5	12	0	47	50	26	3	32	54	4.91	1.75	18.0	274	25%	15%	10%	0.6	37%	72%	78
Povich, Cade	L	22	22	aa	BAL	2	2	6	0	24	22	18	5	10	22	6.66	1.31	16.6	242	21%	10%	12%	2.0	26%	52%	44
Priester, Quinn	R	22	22	a/a	PIT	5	5	17	0	86	74	27	4	27	72	2.79	1.17	20.2	233	20%	8%	13%	0.4	29%	76%	97
Ridings, Stephen	R	21	26	a/a	NYY	5	0	22	3	29	19	5	2	4	34	1.55	0.82	4.8	192	32%	4%	28%	0.7	26%	88%	223
Roa, Christian	R	22	23	aa	CIN	2	0	3	0	17	5	2	1	7	17	1.13	0.72	20.1	101	27%	11%	16%	0.6	12%	91%	120
Robberse, Sem	R	22	21	aa	TOR	0	3	5	0	26	19	9	4	8	16	3.13	1.03	20.2	202	16%	8%	8%	1.2	21%	76%	53
Robinson, Cam	R	22	23	a/a	MIL	0	0	24	6	29	25	12	1	12	28	3.66	1.28	5.0	233	24%	11%	14%	0.3	31%	70%	100
Rodriguez, Grayson	R	21	22	aa	BAL	6	1	18	0	81	50	24	8	20	100	2.71	0.87	16.7	180	33%	7%	27%	0.9	25%	74%	161
		22	23	a/a	BAL	2	2	16	0	77	48	22	2	23	90	2.51	0.92	18.1	180	31%	8%	23%	0.2	26%	72%	155
Rodriguez, Randy	R	22	23	a/a	SF	0	2	11	0	16	10	13	2	18	22	7.57	1.75	6.7	186	27%	22%	5%	0.9	27%	55%	92
Rodriguez, Yerry	R	21	24	a/a	TEX	4	4	27	0	83	87	50	9	33	83	5.39	1.44	13.1	270	23%	9%	14%	0.9	34%	63%	79
Rolison, Ryan	L	21	24	a/a	COL	4	3	13	0	63	71	41	9	18	51	5.79	1.41	20.6	284	19%	7%	12%	1.3	33%	61%	60
Rom, Drew	L	21	22	aa	BAL	3	1	9	0	40	37	18	6	8	39	4.06	1.15	17.6	249	25%	5%	19%	1.4	30%	70%	113
Roupp, Landen	R	22	24	aa	SF	2	1	5	0	27	21	12	3	11	26	3.92	1.18	21.7	214	24%	10%	14%	0.9	26%	69%	86
Sanchez, Sixto	R	19	21	aa	MIA	8	4	18	0	103	111	45	6	22	85	3.90	1.29	23.5	000	20%	5%	15%	0.5	34%	65%	102
Sanders, Cam	R	21	25	aa	CHC	4	7	18	0	91	85	61	17	46	86	6.06	1.44	21.6	249	22%	12%	10%	1.6	29%	61%	46
		22	26	a/a	CHC	2	9	35	0	99	74	52	10	55	89	4.76	1.30	11.7	208	21%	13%	8%	0.9	25%	65%	67
Sands, Cole	R	21	24	aa	MIN	4	2	19	0	81	66	25	6	36	80	2.73	1.26	17.4	224	24%	11%	13%	0.7	29%	81%	90
Santos, Gregory	R	21	22	aaa	SF	1	1	14	0	17	16	9	1	8	13	4.48	1.41	5.2	250	18%	11%	7%	0.4	30%	67%	68
		22	23	aaa	SF	1	2	33	1	33	29	16	3	18	29	4.35	1.41	4.2	235	20%	12%	7%	0.8	29%	70%	65
Sauer, Matt	R	22	23	aa	NYY	0	2	4	0	22	23	19	5	7	30	7.50	1.35	23.2	272	32%	7%	25%	2.0	36%	46%	107
Seabold, Connor	R	19	23	aa	PHI	3	1	7	0	40	42	13	4	11	32	2.98	1.32	23.7	000	19%	6%	13%	0.6	33%	74%	85
		21	25	aaa	BOS	3	3	11	0	54	52	27	6	20	42	4.43	1.33	20.4	254	19%	9%	10%	1.1	29%	69%	59
Seymour, Ian	L	22	24	aa	TAM	0	2	5	0	18	23	14	2	11	20	6.92	1.84	17.0	305	25%	14%	11%	0.8	40%	61%	69
Shuster, Jared	L	21	23	aa	ATL	0	0	3	0	16	23	16	6	5	14	8.87	1.74	24.7	335	19%	7%	12%	3.3	35%	55%	-6
		22	24	a/a	ATL	7	10	27	0	142	126	62	20	39	121	3.91	1.16	21.0	239	22%	7%	15%	1.3	27%	71%	80
Silseth, Chase	R	22	22	aa	LAA	7	0	15	0	83	52	19	10	24	96	2.09	0.92	20.7	181	30%	8%	22%	1.1	23%	86%	132

PITCHER	Th	Yr	Age	LvL	Org	W	L	G	Sv	IP	H	ER	HR	BB	K	ERA	WHIP	BF/G	OBA	K%	BB%	K-BB	hr/9	H%	S%	BPV
Simpson, Josh	L	22	25	a/a	MIA	7	2	50	2	70	46	33	5	33	92	4.24	1.13	5.6	189	33%	12%	21%	0.6	28%	62%	128
Small, Ethan	L	21	24	a/a	MIL	4	2	17	0	77	59	19	4	41	78	2.19	1.30	18.7	214	25%	13%	12%	0.5	28%	85%	92
		22	25	aaa	MIL	7	6	27	0	103	89	52	8	57	96	4.58	1.42	16.2	235	22%	13%	9%	0.7	30%	68%	74
Soriano, George	R	22	23	a/a	MIA	4	4	40	8	76	60	24	4	37	73	2.88	1.29	7.8	220	22%	12%	11%	0.4	29%	78%	91
Spiers, Carson	R	22	25	a/a	CIN	4	6	27	0	123	162	84	33	47	88	6.15	1.70	20.6	318	16%	9%	8%	2.4	33%	71%	-4
Stone, Gavin	R	22	24	a/a	LA	8	5	20	0	98	72	14	2	32	117	1.29	1.06	19.1	207	30%	8%	22%	0.2	31%	88%	151
Stoudt, Levi	R	21	24	aa	SEA	1	2	3	0	19	16	6	2	8	17	2.68	1.24	26.0	227	21%	10%	11%	1.0	27%	83%	72
Tamarez, Misael	R	22	22	a/a	HOU	4	7	28	1	122	81	53	17	61	126	3.88	1.17	17.4	191	25%	12%	13%	1.2	23%	72%	79
Tarnok, Freddy	R	21	23	aa	ATL	3	2	9	0	45	42	17	2	16	51	3.46	1.29	20.6	250	28%	9%	19%	0.5	35%	73%	120
Thomas, Connor	L	21	23	a/a	STL	6	6	26	1	124	134	42	12	28	96	3.03	1.30	19.7	277	19%	5%	13%	0.9	32%	80%	86
		22	24	aaa	STL	6	12	28	0	135	173	74	12	34	88	4.91	1.53	21.0	312	14%	6%	9%	0.8	35%	68%	58
Thompson, Matthew	R	22	22	aa	CHW	0	2	7	0	26	26	14	3	10	27	4.88	1.39	15.7	263	24%	9%	15%	1.0	33%	67%	83
Thompson, Riley	R	22	26	aa	CHC	2	5	19	0	57	49	26	7	29	51	4.13	1.37	12.6	234	21%	12%	9%	1.1	28%	73%	62
Torres, Eric	L	22	23	aa	LAA	2	2	42	22	51	25	8	3	21	69	1.49	0.91	4.5	150	34%	10%	23%	0.5	23%	87%	153
Varland, Louie	R	22	25	a/a	MIN	8	5	24	0	127	122	41	12	39	119	2.88	1.27	21.6	254	22%	7%	15%	0.9	31%	81%	92
Vasquez, Randy	R	21	23	aa	NYY	2	1	4	0	22	26	12	2	7	16	4.81	1.51	23.9	296	17%	7%	10%	0.9	34%	69%	57
		22	24	aa	NYY	2	7	25	0	116	115	52	11	40	102	4.07	1.33	19.3	260	21%	8%	13%	0.8	32%	71%	80
Vela, Noel	L	22	24	aa	SD	3	3	9	0	24	26	16	1	19	20	5.85	1.87	12.6	278	19%	18%	1%	0.3	35%	67%	58
Vines, Darius	R	22	24	a/a	ATL	8	4	27	0	142	151	72	19	45	131	4.53	1.38	22.1	273	22%	8%	14%	1.2	33%	70%	74
Vodnik, Victor	R	21	22	aa	ATL	1	4	11	0	35	38	26	6	23	35	6.67	1.72	14.5	277	22%	14%	8%	1.5	33%	63%	42
		22	23	a/a	ATL	2	0	31	3	36	34	11	2	19	40	2.66	1.48	5.0	251	27%	13%	14%	0.5	34%	83%	92
Waites, Cole	R	22	24	a/a	SF	3	2	25	5	29	16	4	0	17	41	1.22	1.14	4.6	162	34%	14%	20%	0.0	28%	88%	149
Waldichuk, Ken	L	21	23	aa	NYY	4	3	16	0	80	73	44	15	39	93	4.91	1.39	21.1	244	28%	11%	16%	1.6	31%	70%	70
Waldron, Matt	R	21	25	aa	SD	0	4	7	0	32	39	25	2	17	25	7.10	1.74	20.9	303	17%	11%	6%	0.5	36%	57%	53
		22	26	a/a	SD	5	10	25	0	115	138	72	11	37	79	5.62	1.52	20.0	299	15%	7%	8%	0.9	34%	63%	51
Walsh, Jake	R	21	26	a/a	STL	2	2	17	1	22	14	7	2	7	26	2.78	0.96	4.9	183	32%	9%	23%	0.7	26%	74%	140
Walston, Blake	L	22	21	aa	ARI	7	3	21	0	107	109	52	12	32	95	4.33	1.32	21.1	266	21%	7%	14%	1.0	32%	69%	84
Walter, Brandon	L	22	26	a/a	BOS	3	3	11	0	59	51	26	6	7	58	3.90	0.99	20.5	236	25%	3%	22%	0.9	30%	62%	211
Warren, Will	R	22	23	aa	NYY	7	6	18	0	94	95	43	8	31	72	4.13	1.34	21.7	263	18%	8%	10%	0.7	31%	70%	70
Weems, Avery	L	22	25	aa	TEX	2	6	26	0	91	101	50	12	30	86	4.95	1.44	14.9	282	21%	7%	14%	1.2	34%	68%	75
Weissert, Greg	R	19	24	aa	NYY	1	2	14	1	24	12	7	0	15	23	2.59	1.13	6.8	000	25%	15%	9%	0.0	22%	74%	28
		21	26	a/a	NYY	4	3	40	6	52	35	11	2	29	49	1.93	1.23	5.3	192	33%	14%	9%	0.4	25%	86%	89
Wentz, Joey	L	19	22	aa	DET	7	8	25	0	130	138	87	22	52	114	6.02	1.46	22.3	000	20%	9%	11%	1.5	31%	48%	62
		21	24	aa	DET	0	4	13	0	54	48	27	8	33	46	4.48	1.50	18.0	240	20%	14%	5%	1.3	27%	74%	43
		22	25	aaa	DET	2	2	12	0	49	40	18	5	19	42	3.23	1.21	16.5	226	21%	10%	12%	0.9	27%	77%	73
Wesneski, Hayden	R	21	24	a/a	NYY	10	5	18	0	94	100	49	13	28	88	4.71	1.36	21.8	274	22%	7%	15%	1.2	33%	68%	81
White, Brendan	R	22	24	aa	DET	6	5	48	9	68	47	21	3	16	59	2.72	0.93	5.3	198	22%	6%	16%	0.3	25%	70%	129
White, Colby	R	21	23	a/a	TAM	1	0	17	4	24	11	5	0	7	29	1.71	0.75	5.1	141	34%	8%	26%	0.0	22%	75%	180
White, Owen	R	22	23	aa	TEX	3	0	4	0	23	19	6	1	4	19	2.15	1.02	22.3	226	23%	5%	17%	0.3	28%	79%	136
Whitley, Forrest	R	18	21	aa	HOU	0	2	8	0	27	17	14	2	11	30	4.48	1.03	13.1	183	29%	10%	18%	0.8	24%	56%	113
		19	22	a/a	HOU	2	5	14	0	49	61	58	13	34	57	10.53	1.93	16.7	000	24%	15%	10%	2.3	37%	30%	37
		22	25	aaa	HOU	0	2	10	0	33	34	25	2	23	30	6.80	1.72	15.0	265	19%	15%	4%	0.5	34%	58%	64
Wicks, Jordan	L	22	23	aa	CHC	0	3	8	0	28	24	11	4	9	30	3.66	1.18	14.0	230	25%	8%	17%	1.3	29%	74%	96
Williams , Gavin	R	22	23	aa	CLE	3	3	16	0	70	47	19	9	24	71	2.45	1.02	16.8	194	25%	9%	16%	1.1	23%	84%	98
Williamson, Brandon	L	21	23	aa	SEA	2	5	13	0	68	69	29	7	23	84	3.86	1.34	21.8	264	30%	8%	22%	0.9	37%	74%	120
Winn, Cole	R	21	22	a/a	TEX	4	3	21	0	86	48	26	7	30	92	2.74	0.90	15.3	164	29%	9%	19%	0.8	21%	73%	122
		22	23	aaa	TEX	9	8	28	0	123	122	76	10	75	103	5.57	1.60	19.5	260	18%	13%	5%	0.7	31%	65%	55
Woods-Richardson, Simeon	R	21	21	aa	MIN	3	5	15	0	54	51	37	5	33	67	6.19	1.55	15.8	251	28%	14%	14%	0.8	35%	59%	91
		22	22	a/a	MIN	5	3	23	0	110	75	29	5	32	99	2.40	0.97	18.2	195	23%	7%	16%	0.4	25%	76%	119
Zerpa, Angel	L	21	22	a/a	KC	0	4	14	0	48	58	37	7	19	45	6.85	1.60	15.2	299	21%	9%	12%	1.4	36%	58%	54
		22	23	a/a	KC	2	5	19	0	73	73	30	5	21	55	3.69	1.29	15.8	262	18%	7%	11%	0.6	31%	72%	78
Zulueta, Yosver	R	22	24	a/a	TOR	1	2	12	0	22	14	9	1	16	25	3.80	1.36	7.8	183	26%	17%	9%	0.4	25%	71%	97

ORGANIZATION RATINGS/RANKINGS

Each organization is graded on a standard A-F scale in four separate categories, and then after weighing the categories and adding some subjectivity, a final grade and ranking are determined. The four categories are the following:

Hitting: The quality and quantity of hitting prospects, the balance between athleticism, power, speed, and defense, and the quality of player development.

Pitching: The quality and quantity of pitching prospects and the quality of player development.

Top-End Talent: The quality of the top players within the organization. Successful teams are ones that have the most star-quality

players. These are the players who are a teams' above average regulars, front-end starters, and closers.

Depth: The depth of both hitting and pitching prospects within the organization.

Overall Grade: The four categories are weighted, with top-end talent being the most important and depth being the least.

TEAM	Hitting	Pitching	Top-End Talent	Depth	Overall
Los Angeles Dodgers	A-	A-	A	A	A
Arizona Diamondbacks	A-	B	A-	B	B+
Cleveland Guardians	B+	A-	A-	B	B+
Baltimore Orioles	A	C	B+	C	B+
Cincinnati Reds	A	B-	B+	B	B+
Texas Rangers	A-	B	B+	A-	B+
New York Mets	A	C+	A-	C	B
New York Yankees	A	B-	B+	B	B
Pittsburgh Pirates	B+	B	B+	B	B
St. Louis Cardinals	B	B	B+	B	B
Tampa Bay Rays	B+	C	B+	A	B
Colorado Rockies	A	C-	B	B+	B
Oakland Athletics	B	B+	B	B+	B
San Francisco Giants	B	B	B	B+	B
Toronto Blue Jays	B-	B+	B	B	B
Chicago Cubs	B+	B-	B-	A-	B
Miami Marlins	C	A-	B-	C	B-
Washington Nationals	B	C	B	C-	C+
Minnesota Twins	C+	C+	C+	C-	C+
Boston Red Sox	B	D	B-	C	C
Milwaukee Brewers	B	D	B-	C	C
Houston Astros	B-	C	C	C-	C
Kansas City Royals	C	C	C	C+	C
Philadelphia Phillies	D	B-	B	D	C-
Seattle Mariners	C	D	C	C-	C-
Chicago White Sox	C	D	C-	F	C-
Detroit Tigers	C-	B	C-	D	C-
Los Angeles Angels	D	C	D	C	D+
San Diego Padres	D-	C-	D	D	D
Atlanta Braves	F	C+	F	D	D

This section of the book may be the smallest as far as word count is concerned, but may be the most important, as this is where players' skills and potential are tied together and ranked against their peers. The rankings that follow are divided into long-term potential in the major leagues and shorter-term fantasy value.

ORGANIZATIONAL: Lists the top 15 minor league prospects within each organization in terms of long-range potential in the major leagues.

POSITIONAL: Lists the top 15 prospects, by position, in terms of long-range potential in the major leagues.

TOP POWER: Lists the top 25 prospects that have the potential to hit for power in the major leagues, combining raw power, plate discipline, and at the ability to make their power game-usable.

TOP BA: Lists the top 25 prospects that have the potential to hit for high batting average in the major leagues, combining contact ability, plate discipline, hitting mechanics and strength.

TOP SPEED: Lists the top 25 prospects that have the potential to steal bases in the major leagues, combining raw speed and base-running instincts.

TOP FASTBALL: Lists the top 25 pitchers that have the best fastball, combining velocity and pitch movement.

TOP BREAKING BALL: Lists the top 25 pitchers that have the best breaking ball, combining pitch movement, strikeout potential, and consistency.

2023 TOP FANTASY PROSPECTS: Lists the top 40 minor league prospects likely to have the most value to their respective fantasy teams in 2023, then 35 more players to consider who could get the call and have the skills to produce. Remember that this section addresses 2023 value, not long-term value.

TOP 100 ARCHIVE: Takes a look back at the top 100 lists from the past eight years.

The rankings in this book are the creation of the minor league department at BaseballHQ.com. While several baseball personnel contributed player information to the book, no opinions were solicited or received in comparing players.

TOP PROSPECTS BY ORGANIZATION

AL EAST

BALTIMORE ORIOLES
1 Gunnar Henderson, 3B
2 Grayson Rodriguez, RHP
3 Jackson Holliday, SS
4 Coby Mayo, 3B
5 Colton Cowser, OF
6 Jordan Westburg, IF
7 DL Hall, LHP
8 Connor Norby, 2B
9 Heston Kjerstad, OF
10 Joey Ortiz, MIF
11 Dylan Beavers, OF
12 Hudson Haskin, OF
13 Jud Fabian, OF
14 Max Wagner, 3B
15 John Rhodes, OF

BOSTON RED SOX
1 Marcelo Mayer, SS
2 Triston Casas, 1B
3 Ceddanne Rafaela, SS/OF
4 Blaze Jordan, 1B
5 Bryan Mata, RHP
6 Nick Yorke, 2B
7 Miguel Bleis, OF
8 Wikelman Gonzalez, RHP
9 Matthew Lugo, IF
10 Brandon Walter, LHP
11 Eddinson Paulino, IF
12 Chris Murphy, LHP
13 Mikey Romero, MIF
14 Roman Anthony, OF
15 Wilyer Abreu, OF

NEW YORK YANKEES
1 Anthony Volpe, SS
2 Jasson Dominguez, OF
3 Everson Pereira, OF
4 Oswald Pereza, MIF
5 Spencer Jones, OF
6 Austin Wells, C
7 Will Warren, RHP
8 Trey Sweeney, SS
9 Drew Thorpe, RHP
10 Luis Serna, RHP
11 Estevan Florial, OF
12 Randy Vasquez, RHP
13 Yoendrys Gomez, RHP
14 Elijah Dunham, OF
15 Luis Gil, RHP

TAMPA BAY RAYS
1 Curtis Mead, IF
2 Kyle Manzardo, 1B
3 Taj Bradley, RHP
4 Mason Auer, OF
5 Junior Caminero, MIF
6 Carson Williams, SS
7 Osleivis Basabe, IF
8 Mason Montgomery, LHP
9 Willy Vasquez, IF
10 Brock Jones, OF
12 Xavier Issac, 1B
13 Cole Wilcox, RHP
13 Yoniel Curet, RHP
14 Chandler Simpson, OF
15 Ryan Cermak, OF

TORONTO BLUE JAYS
1 Ricky Tiedemann, LHP
2 Orelvis Martinez, 3B/SS
3 Brandon Barriera, LHP
4 Yosver Zulueta, RHP
5 Hayden Juenger, RHP
6 Sem Robberse, RHP
7 Tucker Toman, 3B
8 Cade Doughty, IF
9 Gabriel Martinez, OF
10 Josh Kasevich, IF
11 Addison Barger, IF
12 Adam Macko, LHP
13 Dahian Santos, RHP
14 Trent Palmer, RHP
15 Dasan Brown, OF

AL CENTRAL

CHICAGO WHITE SOX
1 Colson Montgomery, SS
2 Oscar Colas, OF
3 Bryan Ramos, 2B/3B
4 Jose Rodriguez, MIF
5 Norge Vera, RHP
6 Peyton Pallette, RHP
7 Lenyn Sosa, IF
8 Yoelqui Cespedes, OF
9 Wes Kath, 3B
10 Sean Burke, RHP
11 Noah Schultz, LHP
12 Jonathan Cannon, RHP
13 Luis Mieses, OF
14 Matthew Thompson, RHP
15 Wilfred Veras, 1B

CLEVELAND GUARDIANS
1 Daniel Espino, RHP
2 Gavin Williams , RHP
3 Bo Naylor, C
4 Will Brennan, OF
5 George Valera, OF
6 Tanner Bibee, RHP
7 Chase DeLauter, OF
8 Brayan Rocchio, MIF
9 Logan Allen, LHP
10 Cody Morris, RHP
11 Angel Martinez, MIF
12 Jhonkensy Noel, OF
13 Gabriel Arias, IF
14 Justin Campbell, RHP
15 Joey Cantillo, LHP

DETROIT TIGERS
1 Jackson Jobe, RHP
2 Jace Jung, 2B
3 Wilmer Flores, RHP
4 Ty Madden, RHP
5 Colt Keith, IF
6 Reese Olson, RHP
7 Justyn-Henry Malloy, 3B/OF
8 Peyton Graham, SS
9 Izaac Pacheco, IF
10 Cristian Santana, IF
11 Joey Wentz, LHP
12 Dillon Dingler, C
13 Dylan Smith, RHP
14 Ryan Kreidler, IF
15 Parker Meadows, OF

KANSAS CITY ROYALS
1 Gavin Cross, OF
2 Cayden Wallace, 3B
3 Tyler Gentry, OF
4 Nick Loftin, 2B
5 Frank Mozzicato, LHP
6 Ben Kudrna, RHP
7 Maikel Garcia, SS
8 Carter Jensen, C
9 Alec Marsh, RHP
10 Asa Lacy, LHP
11 Peyton Wilson, 2B/OF
12 Beck Way, RHP
13 T.J. Sikkema, LHP
14 Jonathan Bowlan, RHP
15 Luca Tresh, C

MINNESOTA TWINS
1 Brooks Lee, SS
2 Royce Lewis, SS/OF
3 Emmanuel Rodriguez, OF
4 Connor Prielipp, LHP
5 Simeon Woods-Richardson, RHP
6 Louie Varland, RHP
7 Marco Raya, RHP
8 Matt Canterino, RHP
9 Austin Martin, SS
10 Matt Wallner, OF
11 David Festa, RHP
12 Edouard Julien, 2B
13 Jordan Balazovic, RHP
14 Noah Miller, SS
15 Ronny Henriquez, RHP

AL WEST

HOUSTON ASTROS
1 Yainer Diaz, C/1B
2 Hunter Brown, RHP
3 Jacob Melton, OF
4 Drew Gilbert, OF
5 Spencer Arrighetti, RHP
6 Colton Gordon, LHP
7 Pedro Leon, 2B/OF
8 Korey Lee, C
9 Ryan Clifford, OF
10 Miguel Palma, 1B
11 Collin Price, C
12 Forrest Whitley, RHP
13 Tyler Whitaker, UT
14 Edinson Batista, RHP
15 Justin Dirden, OF

LOS ANGELES ANGELS
1 Logan O Hoppe, C
2 Zach Neto, SS
3 Edgar Quero, C
4 Denzer Guzman, SS
5 Ky Bush, LHP
6 Chase Silseth, RHP
7 Werner Blakely, IF
8 Sam Bachman, RHP
9 Ben Joyce, RHP
10 Nelson Rada, OF
11 Adrian Placencia, MIF
12 Orlando Martinez, OF
13 Landon Marceaux, RHP
14 Jeremiah Jackson, 2B
15 Livan Soto, IF

OAKLAND ATHLETICS
1 Tyler Soderstrom, C/1B
2 Gunnar Hoglund, RHP
3 Ken Waldichuk, LHP
4 Kyle Muller, LHP
5 Zack Gelof, IF
6 Max Muncy, SS
7 Esteury Ruiz, OF
8 Daniel Susac, C
9 Ryan Cusick, RHP
10 Mason Miller, RHP
11 Luis Medina, RHP
12 Denzel Clarke, OF
13 Jordan Diaz, 1B/3B
14 Henry Bolte, OF
15 J.T. Ginn, RHP

SEATTLE MARINERS
1 Emerson Hancock, RHP
2 Harry Ford, C
3 Gabriel Gonzalez, OF
4 Bryce Miller, RHP
5 Walter Ford, RHP
6 Cole Young, SS
7 Lazaro Montes, OF
8 Zach DeLoach, OF
9 Taylor Dollard, RHP
10 Bryan Woo, RHP
11 Michael Arroyo, IF
12 Prelander Berroa, RHP
13 Tyler Locklear, 3B
14 Martin Gonzalez, MIF
15 Michael Morales, RHP

TEXAS RANGERS
1 Evan Carter, OF
2 Josh Jung, 3B
3 Jose Acuña, MIF
4 Dustin Harris, 1B/OF
5 Jack Leiter, RHP
6 Owen White, RHP
7 Brock Porter, RHP
8 Aaron Zavala, OF
9 Kumar Rocker, RHP
10 Justin Foscue, IF
11 Cole Winn, RHP
12 Anthony Gutierrez, OF
13 Chandler Pollard, IF
14 Mitch Bratt, LHP
15 Yeison Morrobel, OF

TOP PROSPECTS BY ORGANIZATION

NL EAST

ATLANTA BRAVES
1   Owen Murphy, RHP
2   AJ Smith-Shawver, RHP
3   JR Richie, RHP
4   Braden Shewmake, MIF
5   Jared Shuster, LHP
6   Darius Vines, RHP
7   Jesse Franklin, OF
8   Cole Phillips, RHP
9   Cal Conley, MIF
10 Dylan Dodd, LHP
11 Adam Maier, RHP
12 Ambrious Tavarez, SS
13 Roddery Munoz, RHP
14 Spencer Schwellenbach, RHP
15 Luke Waddell, MIF

MIAMI MARLINS
1   Eury Perez, RHP
2   Max Meyer, RHP
3   Jose Salas, IF
4   Jacob Berry, 3B
5   Yiddi Cappe, IF
6   Sixto Sanchez, RHP
7   Joe Mack, C
8   Jordan Groshans, 3B
9   Kahlil Watson, MIF
10 Jake Eder, LHP
11 Troy Johnston, 1B
12 Dax Fulton, LHP
13 Jacob Miller, RHP
14 Paul McIntosh, C
15 Nasim Nunez, SS

NEW YORK METS
1   Francisco Alvarez, C
2   Brett Baty, 3B
3   Kevin Parada, C
4   Jett Williams, SS
5   Alex Ramirez, OF
6   Ronny Mauricio, SS
7   Blake Tidwell, RHP
8   Mark Vientos, 3B
9   Calvin Ziegler, RHP
10 Matt Allan, RHP
11 Dominic Hamel, RHP
12 Mike Vasil, RHP
13 Nick Morabito, OF
14 Khalil Lee, OF
15 Joel Diaz, RHP

PHILADELPHIA PHILLIES
1   Andrew Painter, RHP
2   Griff McGarry, RHP
3   Mick Abel, RHP
4   Johan Rojas, OF
5   Hao Yu Lee, MIF
6   Justin Crawford, OF
7   Andrew Baker, RHP
8   Alex McMarlane, RHP
9   Carlos De La Cruz, OF
10 Simon Muzziotti, OF
11 Francisco Morales, RHP
12 Ethan Wilson, OF
13 Alexeis Azuaje, 2B
14 Yhoswar Garcia, OF
15 Nikau Poauka-Grego, SS

WASHINGTON NATIONALS
1   James Wood, OF
2   Elijah Green, OF
3   Robert Hasselll III, OF
4   Cade Cavalli, RHP
5   Brady House, SS
6   Jarlin Susana, RHP
7   Cristhian Vaquero, OF
8   Jeremy de la Rosa, OF
9   Jackson Rutledge, RHP
10 Jake Bennett, LHP
11 TJ White, OF
12 Andry Lara, RHP
13 Cole Henry, RHP
14 Roismar Quintana, OF
15 Jose Ferrer, LHP

NL CENTRAL

CHICAGO CUBS
1   Pete Crow-Armstrong, OF
2   Brennen Davis, OF
3   Kevin Alcantara, OF
4   Matt Mervis, 1B
5   Alexander Canario, OF
6   Cristian Hernandez, MIF
7   Cade Horton, RHP
8   James Triantos, 3B
9   Ben Brown, RHP
10 Jordan Wicks, LHP
11 Hayden Wesneski, RHP
12 Owen Caissie, OF
13 Jackson Ferris, LHP
14 Moises Ballesteros, 1B
15 Caleb Kilian, RHP

CINCINNATI REDS
1   Elly De La Cruz, IF
2   Noelvi Marte, IF
3   Edwin Arroyo, SS
4   Cam Collier, 3B
5   Matt McLain, MIF
6   Spencer Steer, 3B
7   Chase Petty, RHP
8   Christian Encarnacion-Strand, 3B
9   Brandon Williamson, LHP
10 Andrew Abbott, LHP
11 Ariel Almonte, OF
12 Sal Stewart, 3B
13 Leonardo Balcazar, MIF
14 Carlos Jorge, 2B
15 Jay Allen, OF

MILWAUKEE BREWERS
1   Jackson Chourio, OF
2   Garrett Mitchell, OF
3   Sal Frelick, OF
4   Brice Turang, SS
5   Tyler Black, 2B/OF
6   Joey Wiemer, OF
7   Jacob Misiorowski, RHP
8   Ethan Small, LHP
9   Eric Brown, Jr., SS
10 Jeferson Quero, C
11 Robert Gasser, LHP
12 Luis Lara, OF
13 Robert Moore, 2B/OF
14 Logan Henderson, RHP
15 Russell Smith, LHP

PITTSBURGH PIRATES
1   Henry Davis, C
2   Termarr Johnson, 2B
3   Nick Gonzales, 2B
4   Quinn Priester, RHP
5   Liover Peguero, SS
6   Endy Rodriguez, C/2B
7   Thomas Harrington, RHP
8   Luis Ortiz, RHP
9   Bubba Chandler, RHP
10 Michael Burrows, RHP
11 Jared Jones, RHP
12 Ji-hwan Bae, IF/OF
13 Lonnie White, OF
14 Anthony Solometo, LHP
15 Kyle Nicolas, RHP

ST LOUIS CARDINALS
1   Jordan Walker, 3B/OF
2   Masyn Winn, SS
3   Tink Hence, RHP
4   Alec Burleson, OF
5   Gordon Graceffo, RHP
6   Ivan Herrera, C
7   Cooper Hjerpe, LHP
8   Matt Liberatore, LHP
9   Joshua Baez, OF
10 Leonardo Bernal, C
11 Jonathan Mejia, SS
12 Inohan Paniagua, RHP
13 Michael McGreevy, RHP
14 Brycen Mautz, LHP
15 Austin Love, RHP

NL WEST

ARIZONA DIAMONDBACKS
1   Corbin Carroll, OF
2   Jordan Lawlar, SS
3   Druw Jones, OF
4   Brandon Pfaadt, RHP
5   Blake Walston, LHP
6   Deyvison De Los Santos, 1B
7   Drey Jameson, RHP
8   Ryne Nelson, RHP
9   Landon Sims, RHP
10 Jorge Barrosa, OF
11 Wilderd Patino, OF
12 Blaze Alexander, IF
13 Ivan Melendez, 1B
14 Yu-Min Lin, LHP
15 Dominic Fletcher, OF\

COLORADO ROCKIES
1   Ezequiel Tovar, SS
2   Zac Veen, OF
3   Adael Amador, MIF
4   Benny Montgomery, OF
5   Warming Bernabel, 3B
6   Jordan Beck, OF
7   Drew Romo, C
9   Sterlin Thompson, IF
9   Gabriel Hughes, RHP
10 Jaden Hill, RHP
11 Yanquiel Fernandez, OF
12 Hunter Goodman, 1B
13 Dyan Jorge, SS
14 Julio Carreras, IF
15 Michael Toglia, 1B

LOS ANGELES DODGERS
1   Diego Cartaya, C
2   Bobby Miller, RHP
3   Miguel Vargas, 1B
4   Ryan Pepiot, RHP
5   Michael Busch, 2B/OF
6   Gavin Stone, RHP
7   Andy Pages, OF
8   Dalton Rushing, C
9   James Outman, OF
10 Nick Frasso, RHP
11 Michael Grove, RHP
12 Emmet Sheehan, RHP
13 Jose Ramos, OF
14 Nick Nastrini, RHP
15 Josue De Paula, OF

SAN DIEGO PADRES
1   Jackson Merrill, SS
2   Dylan Lesko, RHP
3   Robby Snelling, LHP
4   Adam Mazur, RHP
5   Eguy Rosario, IF
6   Samuel Zavala, OF
7   Joshua Mears, OF
8   Victor Lizarraga, RHP
9   Jairo Iriarte, RHP
10 Tirso Ornelas, OF
11 Jay Groome, LHP
12 Noel Vela, LHP
13 Henry Williams, RHP
14 Korry Howell, IF/OF
15 Yendry Rojas, SS

SAN FRANCISCO GIANTS
1   Marco Luciano, SS
2   Kyle Harrison, LHP
3   Aeverson Arteaga, SS
4   Carson Whisenhunt, LHP
5   Reggie Crawford, LHP
6   Casey Schmitt, 3B
7   Luis Matos, OF
8   Eric Silva, RHP
9   Mason Black, RHP
10 Vaun Brown, OF
11 Grant McCray, OF
12 Jairo Pomares, OF
13 R.J. Dabovich, RHP
14 Will Bednar, RHP
15 Patrick Bailey, C

TOP PROSPECTS BY POSITION

CATCHER
1 Francisco Alvarez, NYM
2 Tyler Soderstrom, OAK
3 Diego Cartaya, LA
4 Bo Naylor, CLE
5 Kevin Parada, NYM
6 Endy Rodriguez, PIT
7 Henry Davis, PIT
8 Harry Ford, SEA
9 Logan O'Hoppe, LAA
10 Yainer Diaz, HOU
11 Dalton Rushing, LA
12 Austin Wells, NYY
13 Drew Romo, COL
14 Daniel Susac, OAK
15 Edgar Quero, LAA

FIRST BASEMEN
1 Triston Casas, BOS
2 Kyle Manzardo, TAM
3 Matt Mervis, CHC
4 Niko Kavadas, BOS
5 Spencer Steer, CIN
6 Blaze Jordan, BOS
7 Lawrence Butler, OAK
8 Jhonkensy Noel, CLE
9 Xavier Isaac, TAM
10 Michael Toglia, COL
11 Mark Vientos, NYM
12 Ivan Melendez, ARI
13 Spencer Horwitz, TOR
14 Troy Johnston, MIA
15 Malcom Nunez, PIT

SECOND BASEMEN
1 Termarr Johnson, PIT
2 Connor Norby, BAL
3 Jace Jung, DET
4 Michael Busch, LA
5 Nick Gonzales, PIT
6 Edouard Julien, MIN
7 Nick Yorke, BOS
8 Lenyn Sosa, CHW
9 Ji-hwan Bae, PIT
10 Justin Foscue, TEX
11 Enmanuel Valdez, BOS
12 Hao Yu Lee, PHI
13 Nick Loftin, KC
14 Tyler Black, MIL
15 Cade Doughty, TOR

SHORTSTOP
1 Gunnar Henderson, BAL
2 Jordan Lawlar, ARI
3 Anthony Volpe, NYY
4 Elly De La Cruz, CIN
5 Ezequiel Tovar, COL
6 Jackson Holliday, BAL
7 Marcelo Mayer, BOS
8 Royce Lewis, MIN
9 Noelvi Marte, CIN
10 Marco Luciano, SF
11 Colson Montgomery, CHW
12 Masyn Winn, STL
13 Brooks Lee, MIN
14 Jackson Merrill, SD
15 Adael Amador, COL

THIRD BASEMEN
1 Miguel Vargas, LA
2 Josh Jung, TEX
3 Brett Baty, NYM
4 Curtis Mead, TAM
5 Cam Collier, CIN
6 Coby Mayo, BAL
7 Colt Keith, DET
8 Junior Caminero, TAM
9 Deyvison De Los Santos, ARI
10 Jacob Berry, MIA
11 Christian Encarnacion-Strand, CIN
12 Zack Gelof, OAK
13 Eguy Rosario, SD
14 Maikel Garcia, KC
15 Addison Barger, TOR

OUTFIELDERS
1 Corbin Carroll, ARI
2 Jackson Chourio, MIL
3 Jordan Walker, STL
4 James Wood, WAS
5 Druw Jones, ARI
6 Evan Carter, TEX
7 Robert Hassell III, WAS
8 Colton Cowser, BAL
9 Jasson Dominguez, NYY
10 Pete Crow-Armstrong, CHC
11 Elijah Green, WAS
12 Zac Veen, COL
13 Sal Frelick, MIL
14 Brennen Davis, CHC
15 Emmanuel Rodriguez, MIN
16 George Valera, CLE
17 Will Brennan, CLE
18 Esteury Ruiz, OAK
19 Gavin Cross, KC
20 Kevin Alcantara, CHC
21 Garrett Mitchell, MIL
22 Andy Pages, LA
23 Spencer Jones, NYY
24 Oscar Colas, CHW
25 Chase DeLauter, CLE
26 Aaron Zavala, TEX
27 Dustin Harris, TEX
28 Ceddanne Rafaela, BOS
29 Gabriel Gonzalez, SEA
30 Everson Pereira, NYY
31 Alex Ramirez, NYM
32 Benny Montgomery, COL
33 Justin Crawford, PHI
34 Joey Wiemer, MIL
35 Mason Auer, TAM
36 Miguel Bleis, BOS
37 Samuel Zavala, SD
38 Lazaro Montes, SEA
39 Alec Burleson, STL
40 Heliot Ramos, SF
41 Alexander Canario, CHC
42 Jacob Melton, HOU
43 Johan Rojas, PHI
44 Luis Matos, SF
45 Heston Kjerstad, BAL

RIGHT-HANDED PITCHERS
1 Grayson Rodriguez, BAL
2 Eury Perez, MIA
3 Andrew Painter, PHI
4 Daniel Espino, CLE
5 Gavin Williams, CLE
6 Bobby Miller, LA
7 Hunter Brown, HOU
8 Taj Bradley, TAM
9 Gavin Stone, LA
10 Brandon Pfaadt, ARI
11 Max Meyer, MIA
12 Mick Abel, PHI
13 Tink Hence, STL
14 Cade Cavalli, WAS
15 Jackson Jobe, DET
16 Tanner Bibee, CLE
17 Quinn Priester, PIT
18 Jack Leiter, TEX
19 Emerson Hancock, SEA
20 Ryan Pepiot, LA
21 Owen White, TEX
22 Wilmer Flores, DET
23 Griff McGarry, PHI
24 Dylan Lesko, SD
25 Cody Morris, CLE
26 Luis Ortiz, PIT
27 Reese Olson, DET
28 Kumar Rocker, TEX
29 Cade Horton, CHC
30 Gordon Graceffo, STL
31 Yosver Zuleta, TOR
32 Bryce Miller, SEA
33 Ty Madden, DET
34 Brock Porter, TEX
35 Owen Murphy, ATL
36 Jarlin Susana, WAS
37 Gunnar Hoglund, TOR
38 Simeon Woods-Richardson, MIN
39 Drey Jameson, ARI
40 Spencer Arrighetti, HOU
41 Gabriel Hughes, COL
42 Ryne Nelson, ARI
43 Sixto Sanchez, MIA
44 Chase Petty, CIN
45 Adam Mazur, SD
46 Sem Robberse, TOR
47 Thomas Harrington, PIT
48 Cole Winn, TEX
49 Jake Eder, MIA
50 J.R. Ritchie, ATL

LEFT-HANDED PITCHERS
1 Ricky Tiedemann, TOR
2 Kyle Harrison, SF
3 DL Hall, BAL
4 Ken Waldichuk, OAK
5 Brandon Barriera, TOR
6 Kyle Muller, OAK
7 Cooper Hjerpe, STL
8 Brandon Williamson, CIN
9 Jared Shuster, ATL
10 Blake Walston, ARI
11 Carson Whisenhunt, SF
12 Logan Allen, CLE
13 Robby Snelling, SD
14 Ky Bush, LAA
15 Connor Prielipp, MIN

TOP PROSPECTS BY SKILLS

2023 TOP FANTASY IMPACT

TOP POWER

Orelvis Martinez, TOR
Jhonkensy Noel, CLE
Triston Casas, BOS
Elijah Green, WAS
Brett Baty, NYM
Jordan Walker, STL
Blaze Jordan, BOS
Elly De La Cruz, CIN
Matt Mervis, CHC
Francisco Alvarez, NYM
Joey Wiemer, MIL
Noelvi Marte, CIN
Jasson Dominguez, NYY
Matt Wallner, MIN
Marco Luciano, SF
Corbin Carroll, ARI
Gavin Cross, KC
Curtis Mead, TAM
Anthony Volpe, NYY
James Wood, WAS
Jackson Chourio, MIL
Emmanuel Rodriguez, MIN
Andy Pages, LA
Gunnar Henderson, BAL
Tyler Soderstrom, OAK

TOP BA

Corbin Carroll, ARI
Gunnar Henderson, BAL
Robert Hassell III, WAS
Pete Crow-Armstrong, CHC
Jordan Lawlar, ARI
Zac Veen, COL
Francisco Alvarez, NYM
Termarr Johnson, PIT
Garrett Mitchell, MIL
Jordan Walker, STL
Josh Jung, TEX
Marcelo Mayer, BOS
Brett Baty, NYM
Brooks Lee, MIN
Endy Rodriguez, PIT
Will Brennan, CLE
Curtis Mead, TAM
Sal Frelick, MIL
Anthony Volpe, NYY
Evan Carter, TEX
Jackson Holliday, BAL
Nick Gonzales, PIT
Colton Cowser, BAL
Jace Jung, DET
Adael Amador, COL

TOP SPEED

Dasan Brown, TOR
Corbin Carroll, ARI
Zac Veen, COL
Jordyn Adams, LAA
Johan Rojas, PHI
Emaarion Boyd, PHI
Chandler Simpson, TAM
Chandler Pollard, TEX
Kahlil Watson, MIA
Elly De La Cruz, CIN
Jose Acuna, TEX
Denzel Clarke, OAK
Greg Jones, TAM
Garrett Mitchell, MIL
Anthony Volpe, NYY
Jordan Lawlar, ARI
Noelvi Marte, CIN
Sal Frelick, MIL
Royce Lewis, MIN
Ji-hwan Bae, PIT
Masyn Winn, STL
Elijah Green, WAS
Jackson Chourio, MIL
Justin Crawford, PHI
Evan Carter, TEX

TOP FASTBALL

Grayson Rodriguez, BAL
Ben Joyce, LAA
Luis Medina, OAK
Yosver Zulueta, TOR
Sixto Sanchez, MIA
DL Hall, BAL
Mick Abel, PHI
Cade Cavalli, WAS
Bobby Miller, LA
Gavin Williams, CLE
Ricky Tiedemann, TOR
Taj Bradley, TAM
Daniel Espino, CLE
Emerson Hancock, SEA
Jack Leiter, TEX
Drey Jameson, ARI
Connor Phillips, CIN
Hunter Brown, HOU
Eury Perez, MIA
Andrew Painter, PHI
Jarlin Susana, WAS
Ken Waldichuk, OAK
Luis Ortiz, PIT
Kyle Harrison, SF
Tink Hence, STL

TOP BREAKING BALL

Grayson Rodriguez, BAL
Ryan Pepiot, LA
Jackson Jobe, DET
DL Hall, BAL
Quinn Priester, PIT
Daniel Espino, CLE
Drey Jameson, ARI
Mick Abel, PHI
Max Meyer, MIA
Cade Cavalli, WAS
Ryne Nelson, ARI
Gavin Williams, CLE
Daniel Espino, CLE

Taj Bradley, TAM
Sam Bachman, LAA
Bobby Miller, LA
Eury Perez, MIA
Andrew Painter, PHI
Matt Allan, NYM
Jack Leiter, TEX
Kyle Harrison, SF
Ricky Tiedemann, TOR
JT Ginn, OAK
Tanner Bibee, CLE
Sam Bachman, LAA

THE TOP 40 • RANKED

1. Corbin Carroll (OF, ARI)
2. Gunnar Henderson (IF, BAL)
3. Josh Jung (3B, TEX)
4. Triston Casas (1B, BOS)
5. Grayson Rodriguez (RHP, BAL)
6. Royce Lewis (SS, MIN)
7. Brett Baty (3B, NYM)
8. Ezequiel Tovar (SS, COL)
9. Miguel Vargas (3B/OF, LA)
10. Hunter Brown (RHP, HOU)

11. Will Brennan (OF, CLE)
12. Anthony Volpe (SS, NYY)
13. Oswald Peraza (SS, NYY)
14. Jordan Walker (OF, STL)
15. Francisco Álvarez (C, NYM)
16. Bo Naylor (C, CLE)
17. Sal Frelick (OF, MIL)
18. Kyle Stowers (OF, BAL)
19. Spencer Steer (UT, CIN)
20. Kerry Carpenter (OF, DET)

21. Hayden Wesneski (RHP, CHC)
22. Ken Waldichuk (LHP, OAK)
23. Eury Perez (RHP, MIA)
24. Alec Burleson (OF, STL)
25. Michael Toglia (1B, COL)
26. Bobby Miller (RHP, LA)
27. Brennen Davis (OF, CHC)
28. Ryan Pepiot (RHP, LA)
29. Yainer Díaz (C/1B, HOU)
30. Garrett Mitchell (OF, MIL)

31. Matt Mervis (1B, CHC)
32. Cade Cavalli (RHP, WAS)
33. Colton Cowser (OF, BAL)
34. Taj Bradley (RHP, TAM)
35. DL Hall (LHP, BAL)
36. Esteury Ruiz (UT, OAK)
37. Matt Wallner (OF, MIN)
38. Cody Morris (RHP, CLE)
39. Curtis Mead (IF, TAM)
40. Ryne Nelson (RHP, ARI)

THE NEXT 35 • ALPHA ORDER

Ji-Hwan Bae (2B/OF, PIT)
Michael Busch (2B, LA)
Diego Cartaya (C, LA)
Jackson Chourio (OF, MIL)
Oscar Colás (OF, CHW)
Elly De La Cruz (SS, CIN)
Daniel Espino (RHP, CLE)
Wilmer Flores (RHP, DET)
Jordan Groshans (IF, MIA)
Kyle Harrison (LHP, SF)
Robert Hassell III (OF, WAS)
Iván Herrera (C, STL)
Drey Jameson (RHP, ARI)
Caleb Kilian (RHP, CHC)
Jack Leiter (RHP, TEX)
Matthew Liberatore (LHP, STL)
Marco Luciano (SS, SF)
Kyle Manzardo (1B, TAM)
Kyle Muller (LHP, ATL)
Logan O'Hoppe (C, LAA)
Luis Ortiz (RHP, PIT)
James Outman (OF, LAD)
Andrew Painter (RHP, PHI)
Quinn Priester (RHP, PIT)
Endy Rodriguez (C, PIT)
Sixto Sánchez (RHP, MIA)
Tyler Soderstrom (C/1B, OAK)
Gavin Stone (RHP, LA)
George Valera (OF, CLE)
Zac Veen (OF, COL)
Joey Wentz (LHP, DET)
Jordan Westburg (IF, BAL)
Owen White (RHP, TEX)
Gavin Williams (RHP, CLE)
Masyn Winn (SS, STL)

TOP 100 PROSPECTS ARCHIVE

2022

1. Bobby Witt, Jr. (SS, KC)
2. Julio Rodriguez (OF, SEA)
3. Adley Rutschman (C, BAL)
4. Spencer Torkelson (1B, DET)
5. Riley Greene (OF, DET)
6. CJ Abrams (SS, SD)
7. Grayson Rodriguez (RHP, BAL)
8. Shane Baz (RHP, TAM)
9. Noelvi Marte (SS, SEA)
10. Marco Luciano (SS, SF)

11. Corbin Carroll (OF, ARI)
12. Oneil Cruz (SS, PIT)
13. Anthony Volpe (SS, NYY)
14. Francisco Alvarez (C, NYM)
15. George Kirby (RHP, SEA)
16. Brennen Davis (OF, CHC)
17. Jack Leiter (RHP, TEX)
18. Gabriel Moreno (C, TOR)
19. Jordan Walker (3B, STL)
20. Zac Veen (OF, COL)

21. Triston Casas (1B, BOS)
22. Josh Jung (3B, TEX)
23. Marcelo Mayer (SS, BOS)
24. Nolan Gorman (2B, STL)
25. Vidal Brujan (2B, TAM)
26. Hunter Greene (RHP, CIN)
27. Cade Cavalli (RHP, WAS)
28. Henry Davis (C, PIT)
29. Jasson Dominguez (OF, NYY)
30. Austin Martin (SS, MIN)

31. Robert Hassell (OF, SD)
32. Alek Thomas (OF, ARI)
33. Tyler Soderstrom (C, OAK)
34. Max Meyer (RHP, MIA)
35. Brett Baty (3B, NYM)
36. Josh Lowe (OF, TAM)
37. Reid Detmers (LHP, LAA)
38. Orelvis Martinez (SS, TOR)
39. Sixto Sanchez (RHP, MIA)
40. Khalil Watson (SS, MIA)

41. Royce Lewis (SS, MIN)
42. Jordan Lawlar (SS, ARI)
43. Nick Gonzales (2B, PIT)
44. MJ Melendez (C, KC)
45. Nick Lodolo (LHP, CIN)
46. Luis Matos (OF, SF)
47. Nick Pratto (1B, KC)
48. Brady House (SS, WAS)
49. Brayan Rocchio (SS, CLE)
50. Jackson Jobe (RHP, DET)

51. Michael Harris (OF, ATL)
52. Emerson Hancock (RHP, SEA)
53. Edward Cabrera (RHP, MIA)
54. George Valera (OF, CLE)
55. Jordan Groshans (3B, TOR)
56. Cole Winn (RHP, TEX)
57. Diego Cartaya (C, LA)
58. Joey Bart (C, SF)
59. Nick Yorke (2B, BOS)
60. Eury Perez (RHP, MIA)

61. DL Hall (LHP, BAL)
62. Garrett Mitchell (OF, MIL)
63. Daniel Espino (RHP, CLE)
64. Quinn Priester (RHP, PIT)
65. Asa Lacy (LHP, KC)
66. Jarren Duran (OF, BOS)
67. Bobby Miller (RHP, LA)
68. Luis Campusano (C, SD)
69. Mick Abel (RHP, PHI)
70. Ronny Mauricio (SS, NYM)

71. Colton Cowser (OF, BAL)
72. Matthew Liberatore (LHP, STL)
73. Roansy Contreras (RHP, PIT)
74. Oswald Peraza (SS, NYY)
75. MacKenzie Gore (LHP, SD)
76. Tyler Freeman (SS, CLE)
77. Cristian Hernandez (SS, CHC)
78. Coby Mayo (3B, BAL)
79. Greg Jones (SS, TAM)
80. Cristian Pache (OF, ATL)

81. Miguel Vargas (3B, LA)
82. Gunnar Henderson (SS, BAL)
83. Kyle Harrison (LHP, SF)
84. Shea Langeliers (C, ATL)
85. Taj Bradley (RHP, TAM)
86. Bryson Stott (SS, PHI)
87. Elly De La Cruz (3B, CIN)
88. Matt McLain (SS, CIN)
89. Benny Montgomery (OF, COL)
90. Drew Waters (OF, ATL)

91. Heliot Ramos (OF, SF)
92. Drey Jameson (RHP, ARI)
93. Kevin Alcantara (OF, CHC)
94. Mark Vientos (3B, NYM)
95. Curtis Mead (3B, TAM)
96. Jordan Balazovic (RHP, MIN)
97. Spencer Strider (RHP, ATL)
98. Jeremy Pena (SS, HOU)
99. Matt Brash (RHP, SEA)
100. Gavin Williams (RHP, CLE)

2021

1. Wander Franco (SS, TAM)
2. Adley Rutschman (C, BAL)
3. Spencer Torkelson (3B, DET)
4. Jarred Kelenic (OF, SEA)
5. Julio Rodriguez (OF, SEA)
6. Marco Luciano (SS, SF)
7. MacKenzie Gore (LHP, SD)
8. Royce Lewis (SS, MIN)
9. Bobby Witt, Jr. (SS, KC)
10. CJ Abrams (SS, SD)

11. Andrew Vaughn (1B, CHW)
12. Sixto Sanchez (RHP, MIA)
13. Dylan Carlson (OF, STL)
14. Casey Mize (RHP, DET)
15. Austin Martin (SS, TOR)
16. Ke'Bryan Hayes (3B, PIT)
17. Alex Kirilloff (OF, MIN)
18. Forrest Whitley (RHP, HOU)
19. Nate Pearson (RHP, TOR)
20. Ian Anderson (RHP, ATL)

21. Michael Kopech (RHP, CHW)
22. Joey Bart (C, SF)
23. Matthew Manning (RHP, DET)
24. Spencer Howard (RHP, PHI)
25. Cristian Pache (OF, ATL)
26. Asa Lacy (LHP, KC)
27. Kristian Robinson (OF, ARI)
28. Jasson Dominguez (OF, NYY)
29. Max Meyer (RHP, MIA)
30. Vidal Brujan (2B, TAM)

31. JJ Bleday (OF, MIA)
32. Grayson Rodriguez (RHP, BAL)
33. Riley Greene (OF, DET)
34. Corbin Carroll (OF, ARI)
35. Randy Arozarena (OF, TAM)
36. Nick Madrigal (2B, CHW)
37. Nick Gonzales (SS, PIT)
38. Oneil Cruz (SS, PIT)
39. Jeter Downs (2B/SS, BOS)
40. Drew Waters (OF, ATL)

41. Tarik Skubal (LHP, DET)
42. Nolan Jones (3B, CLE)
43. Luis Patino (RHP, TAM)
44. Nolan Gorman (3B, STL)
45. Daniel Lynch (LHP, KC)
46. Jazz Chisholm (SS, MIA)
47. Zac Veen (OF, COL)
48. Jordan Groshans (SS, TOR)
49. Josiah Gray (RHP, LA)
50. Emerson Hancock (RHP, SEA)

51. Brennen Davis (OF, CHC)
52. A.J. Puk (LHP, OAK)
53. Trevor Larnach (OF, MIN)
54. Heliot Ramos (OF, SF)
55. Triston Casas (1B, BOS)
56. Brandon Marsh (OF, LAA)
57. Ronny Mauricio (SS, NYM)
58. Noelvi Marte (SS, SEA)
59. Logan Gilbert (RHP, SEA)
60. Alek Thomas (OF, ARI)

61. Brendan McKay (LHP, TAM)
62. Deivi Garcia (RHP, NYY)
63. Hunter Bishop (OF, SF)
64. Luis Campusano (C, SD)
65. Josh Jung (3B, TEX)
66. Triston McKenzie (RHP, CLE)
67. Heston Kjerstad (OF, BAL)
68. Matthew Liberatore (LHP, STL)
69. DL Hall (LHP, BAL)
70. Francisco Alvarez (C, NYM)

71. Leody Taveras (OF, TEX)
72. George Valera (OF, CLE)
73. Hunter Greene (RHP, CIN)
74. Brailyn Marquez (LHP, CHC)
75. Garrett Mitchell (OF, MIL)
76. Nick Lodolo (LHP, CIN)
77. Clarke Schmidt (RHP, NYY)
78. Xavier Edwards (2B/SS, TAM)
79. Geraldo Perdomo (SS, ARI)
80. Jordyn Adams (OF, LAA)

81. Tyler Freeman (SS, CLE)
82. Ryan Mountcastle (1B, BAL)
83. Edward Cabrera (RHP, MIA)
84. Robert Hassell (OF, SD)
85. Jordan Balazovic (RHP, MIN)
86. Austin Hendrick (OF, CIN)
87. Reid Detmers (LHP, LAA)
88. Taylor Trammell (OF, SEA)
89. Bo Naylor (C, CLE)
90. Shane Baz (RHP, TAM)

91. Bobby Dalbec (1B/3B, BOS)
92. Erick Pena (OF, KC)
93. Greg Jones (SS, TAM)
94. Matthew Allan (RHP, NYM)
95. Jesus Sanchez (OF, MIA)
96. Garrett Crochet (LHP, CHW)
97. Mick Abel (RHP, PHI)
98. Josh Lowe (OF, TAM)
99. Simeon Woods-Richardson (RHP, TOR)
100. Keibert Ruiz (C, LA)

TOP 100 PROSPECTS ARCHIVE

2020

1. Wander Franco (SS, TAM)
2. Jo Adell (OF, LAA)
3. Luis Robert (OF, CHW)
4. Gavin Lux (SS, LA)
5. MacKenzie Gore (LHP, SD)
6. Royce Lewis (SS, MIN)
7. Jarred Kelenic (OF, SEA)
8. Adley Rutschman (C, BAL)
9. Forrest Whitley (RHP, HOU)
10. Julio Rodriguez (OF, SEA)

11. Jesus Luzardo (LHP, OAK)
12. Andrew Vaughn (1B, CHW)
13. Casey Mize (RHP, DET)
14. Carter Kieboom (SS, WAS)
15. Dylan Carlson (OF, STL)
16. Nate Pearson (RHP, TOR)
17. Dustin May (RHP, LA)
18. Alex Kirilloff (OF, MIN)
19. Bobby Witt, Jr. (SS, KC)
20. Marco Luciano (SS, SF)

21. Joey Bart (C, SF)
22. Michael Kopech (RHP, CHW)
23. Cristian Pache (OF, ATL)
24. Matt Manning (RHP, DET)
25. C.J. Abrams (SS, SD)
26. Sixto Sanchez (RHP, MIA)
27. Drew Waters (OF, ATL)
28. Alec Bohm (3B, PHI)
29. Brendan McKay (LHP/DH, TAM)
30. Kristian Robinson (OF, ARI)

31. Vidal Brujan (2B, TAM)
32. A.J. Puk (LHP, OAK)
33. Brendan Rodgers (SS, COL)
34. Luis Patino (RHP, SD)
35. Spencer Howard (RHP, PHI)
36. J.J. Bleday (OF, MIA)
37. Nolan Gorman (3B, STL)
38. Heliot Ramos (OF, SF)
39. Jazz Chisholm (SS, MIA)
40. Mitch Keller (RHP, PIT)

41. Nolan Jones (3B, CLE)
42. Taylor Trammell (OF, SD)
43. Jasson Dominguez (OF, NYY)
44. Grayson Rodriguez (RHP, BAL)
45. Brusdar Graterol (RHP, MIN)
46. Ian Anderson (RHP, ATL)
47. Oneil Cruz (SS, PIT)
48. Jesus Sanchez (OF, MIA)
49. Hunter Bishop (OF, SF)
50. Trevor Larnach (OF, MIN)

51. Nick Madrigal (2B, CHW)
52. Riley Greene (OF, DET)
53. Ryan Mountcastle (1B, BAL)
54. Ke'Bryan Hayes (3B, PIT)
55. Jordan Groshans (SS, TOR)
56. Ronny Mauricio (SS, NYM)
57. Daniel Lynch (LHP, KC)
58. Xavier Edwards (SS, TAM)
59. Matthew Liberatore (LHP, TAM)
60. D.L. Hall (LHP, BAL)

61. Alek Thomas (OF, ARI)
62. Brennen Davis (OF, CHC)
63. Hunter Greene (RHP, CIN)
64. Deivi Garcia (RHP, NYY)
65. Logan Gilbert (RHP, SEA)
66. Nico Hoerner (SS, CHC)
67. Kyle Wright (RHP, ATL)
68. George Valera (OF, CLE)
69. Sean Murphy (C, OAK)
70. Corbin Carroll (OF, ARI)

71. Keibert Ruiz (C, LA)
72. Josiah Gray (RHP, LA)
73. Josh Jung (3B, TEX)
74. Evan White (1B, SEA)
75. Tyler Freeman (SS, CLE)
76. Luis Garcia (SS, WAS)
77. Shane Baz (RHP, TAM)
78. Daulton Varsho (C, ARI)
79. Triston Casas (1B, BOS)
80. Nick Lodolo (LHP, CIN)

81. Hans Crouse (RHP, TEX)
82. Tarik Skubal (LHP, DET)
83. Brandon Marsh (OF, LAA)
84. Jeter Downs (SS, LA)
85. Greg Jones (SS, TAM)
86. Luis Campusano (C, SD)
87. Clarke Schmidt (RHP, NYY)
88. Noelvi Marte (SS, SEA)
89. Jordan Balazovic (RHP, MIN)
90. Ethan Hankins (RHP, CLE)

91. Sherten Apostel (3B, TEX)
92. Robert Puason (SS, OAK)
93. Brent Honeywell (RHP, TAM)
94. Brady Singer (RHP, KC)
95. Leody Taveras (OF, TEX)
96. Francisco Alvarez (C, NYM)
97. Geraldo Perdomo (SS, ARI)
98. Adrian Morejon (LHP, SD)
99. Monte Harrison (OF, MIA)
100. Brailyn Marquez (LHP, CHC)

2019

1. Vladimir Guerrero Jr., (3B, TOR)
2. Eloy Jimenez, (OF, CHW)
3. Fernando Tatis Jr., (SS, SD)
4. Victor Robles, (OF, WAS)
5. Royce Lewis, (SS, MIN)
6. Kyle Tucker, (OF, HOU)
7. Forrest Whitley, (RHP, HOU)
8. Bo Bichette, (SS, TOR)
9. Nick Senzel, (2B, CIN)
10. Alex Kirilloff, (OF, MIN)

11. Jo Adell, (OF, LAA)
12. Wander Franco, (SS, TAM)
13. Jesus Luzardo, (LHP, OAK)
14. Brendan Rodgers, (SS, COL)
15. Michael Kopech, (RHP, CHW)
16. MacKenzie Gore, (LHP, SD)
17. Taylor Trammell, (OF, CIN)
18. Keston Hiura, (2B, MIL)
19. Sixto Sanchez, (RHP, PHI)
20. Casey Mize, (RHP, DET)

21. Dylan Cease, (RHP, CHW)
22. Mike Soroka, (RHP, ATL)
23. Joey Bart, (C, SF)
24. Carter Kieboom, (SS, WAS)
25. Alex Reyes, (RHP, STL)
26. Luis Urias, (2B, SD)
27. Ian Anderson, (RHP, ATL)
28. Brent Honeywell, (RHP, TAM)
29. Mitch Keller, (RHP, PIT)
30. Keibert Ruiz, (C, LA)

31. Peter Alonso, (1B, NYM)
32. Chris Paddack, (RHP, SD)
33. Hunter Greene, (RHP, CIN)
34. A.J. Puk, (LHP, OAK)
35. Austin Riley, (3B, ATL)
36. Kyle Wright, (RHP, ATL)
37. Alex Verdugo, (OF, LA)
38. Luis Robert, (OF, CHW)
39. Jesus Sanchez, (OF, TAM)
40. Nick Madrigal, (SS, CHW)

41. Triston McKenzie, (RHP, CLE)
42. Yordan Alvarez, (OF, HOU)
43. Brendan McKay, (1B/LHP, TAM)
44. Jonathan India, (3B, CIN)
45. Touki Toussaint, (RHP, ATL)
46. Matt Manning, (RHP, DET)
47. Francisco Mejia, (C, SD)
48. Ke'Bryan Hayes, (3B, PIT)
49. Nolan Gorman, (3B, STL)
50. Adrian Morejon, (LHP, SD)

51. Danny Jansen, (C, TOR)
52. Alec Bohm, (3B, PHI)
53. Justus Sheffield, (LHP, SEA)
54. Yusinel Diaz, (OF, BAL)
55. Jarred Kelenic, (OF, SEA)
56. Andres Gimenez, (SS, NYM)
57. Estevan Florial, (OF, NYY)
58. Luis Garcia, (SS/3B, WAS)
59. Jon Duplantier, (RHP, ARI)
60. Luis Patino, (RHP, SD)

61. Leody Taveras, (OF, TEX)
62. Nolan Jones, (3B, CLE)
63. Gavin Lux, (2B, LA)
64. Adonis Medina, (RHP, PHI)
65. Michel Baez, (RHP, SD)
66. Brusdar Graterol, (RHP, MIN)
67. Julio Pablo Martinez, (OF, TEX)
68. Matthew Liberatore, (LHP, TAM)
69. Cristian Pache, (OF, ATL)
70. Dustin May, (RHP, LA)

71. Josh James, (RHP, HOU)
72. Jonathan Loaisiga, (RHP, NYY)
73. Sean Murphy, (C, OAK)
74. Brady Singer, (RHP, KC)
75. Dane Dunning, (RHP, CHW)
76. Khalil Lee, (OF, KC)
77. Ryan Mountcastle, (3B, BAL)
78. Heliot Ramos, (OF, SF)
79. Nate Pearson, (RHP, TOR)
80. Drew Waters, (OF, ATL)

81. Jazz Chisholm, (SS, ARI)
82. Hans Crouse, (RHP, TEX)
83. DL Hall, (LHP, BAL)
84. MJ Melendez, (C, KC)
85. Oneil Cruz, (SS, PIT)
86. Kristian Robinson, (OF, ARI)
87. Ronaldo Hernandez, (C, TAM)
88. Vidal Brujan, (2B, TAM)
89. Colton Welker, (3B, COL)
90. Franklin Perez, (RHP, DET)

91. Travis Swaggerty, (OF, PIT)
92. Daz Cameron, (OF, DET)
93. Griffin Canning, (RHP, LAA)
94. Bryse Wilson, (RHP, ATL)
95. Brandon Marsh, (OF, LAA)
96. Bubba Thompson, (OF, TEX)
97. Logan Allen, (LHP, SD)
98. Justin Dunn , (RHP, SEA)
99. Miguel Amaya, (C, CHC)
100. Dakota Hudson, (RHP, STL)

TOP 100 PROSPECTS ARCHIVE

2018

1. Ronald Acuna (OF, ATL)
2. Victor Robles (OF, WAS)
3. Vladimir Guerrero Jr. (3B, TOR)
4. Eloy Jimenez (OF, CHW)
5. Gleyber Torres (SS, NYY)
6. Brendan Rodgers (SS, COL)
7. Nick Senzel (3B, CIN)
8. Alex Reyes (RHP, STL)
9. Walker Buehler (RHP, LA)
10. Michael Kopech (RHP, CHW)

11. Fernando Tatis Jr. (SS, SD)
12. Kyle Tucker (OF, HOU)
13. Bo Bichette (SS, TOR)
14. Lewis Brinson (OF, MIL)
15. Brent Honeywell (RHP, TAM)
16. MacKenzie Gore (LHP, SD)
17. Forrest Whitley (RHP, HOU)
18. Willy Adames (SS, TAM)
19. Leody Taveras (OF, TEX)
20. Royce Lewis (SS, MIN)

21. Mitch Keller (RHP, PIT)
22. Francisco Mejia (C, CLE)
23. Kyle Wright (RHP, ATL)
24. A.J. Puk (LHP, OAK)
25. Sixto Sanchez (RHP, PHI)
26. Hunter Greene (RHP, CIN)
27. Franklin Barreto (SS, OAK)
28. Juan Soto (OF, WAS)
29. Triston McKenzie (RHP, CLE)
30. Luiz Gohara (LHP, ATL)

31. Alex Verdugo (OF, LA)
32. Franklin Perez (RHP, DET)
33. Luis Robert (OF, CHW)
34. Keston Huira (2B, MIL)
35. Ryan McMahon (1B, COL)
36. Scott Kingery (2B, PHI)
37. Mike Soroka (RHP, ATL)
38. Willie Calhoun (OF/2B, TEX)
39. Kolby Allard (LHP, ATL)
40. Austin Hays (OF, BAL)

41. Jack Flaherty (RHP, STL)
42. J.P. Crawford (SS, PHI)
43. Anthony Alford (OF, TOR)
44. Austin Meadows (OF, PIT)
45. Brendan McKay (1B/LHP, TAM)
46. Luis Urias (2B/SS, SD)
47. Kyle Lewis (OF, SEA)
48. Taylor Trammell (OF, CIN)
49. Yadier Alvarez (RHP, LA)
50. Estevan Florial (OF, NYY)

51. Jay Groome (LHP, BOS)
52. Cal Quantrill (RHP, SD)
53. Nick Gordon (SS, MIN)
54. Jesus Sanchez (OF, TAM)
55. Chance Adams (RHP, NYY)
56. Jorge Mateo (SS, OAK)
57. Ian Anderson (RHP, ATL)
58. Michel Baez (RHP, SD)
59. Alec Hansen (RHP, CHW)
60. Monte Harrison (OF, MIL)

61. Keibert Ruiz (C, LA)
62. Carson Kelly (C, STL)
63. Kevin Maitan (3B, LAA)
64. Riley Pint (RHP, COL)
65. Anderson Espinoza (RHP, SD)
66. Matt Manning (RHP, DET)
67. Austin Beck (OF, OAK)
68. Dylan Cease (RHP, CHW)
69. Jorge Alfaro (C, PHI)
70. Justus Sheffield (LHP, NYY)

71. Blake Rutherford (OF, CHW)
72. Chance Sisco (C, BAL)
73. Ryan Mountcastle (3B, BAL)
74. Corbin Burnes (RHP, MIL)
75. Jake Bauers (OF/1B, TAM)
76. Pavin Smith (1B, ARI)
77. Adonis Medina (RHP, PHI)
78. Jon Duplantier (RHP, ARI)
79. Heliot Ramos (OF, SF)
80. Adrian Morejon (LHP, SD)

81. Dustin Fowler (OF, OAK)
82. Mickey Moniak (OF, PHI)
83. Shane Baz (RHP, PIT)
84. Yusniel Diaz (OF, LA)
85. Jesse Winker (OF, CIN)
86. Stephen Gonsalves (LHP, MIN)
87. Isan Diaz (2B, MIL)
88. Joey Wentz (LHP, ATL)
89. Tyler O'Neill (OF, STL)
90. Alex Faedo (RHP, DET)

91. Jo Adell (OF, LAA)
92. Austin Riley (3B, ATL)
93. Corey Ray (OF, MIL)
94. Brandon Woodruff (RHP, MIL)
95. Mitchell White (RHP, LA)
96. Yordan Alvarez (1B, HOU)
97. Michael Chavis (3B, BOS)
98. Jose De Leon (RHP, TAM)
99. Christian Arroyo (3B, TAM)
100. Chris Shaw (1B, SF)

2017

1. Yoan Moncada (2B, CHW)
2. Andrew Benintendi (OF, BOS)
3. Dansby Swanson (SS, ATL)
4. Alex Reyes (RHP, STL)
5. Lucas Giolito (RHP, CHW)
6. Victor Robles (OF, WAS)
7. J.P. Crawford (SS, PHI)
8. Tyler Glasnow (RHP, PIT)
9. Brendan Rodgers (SS, COL)
10. Austin Meadows (OF, PIT)

11. Gleyber Torres (SS, NYY)
12. Amed Rosario (SS, NYM)
13. Rafael Devers (3B, BOS)
14. Lewis Brinson (OF, MIL)
15. Anderson Espinoza (RHP, SD)
16. Willy Adames (SS, TAM)
17. Eloy Jimenez (OF, CHC)
18. Manuel Margot (OF, SD)
19. Ozzie Albies (2B, ATL)
20. Clint Frazier (OF, NYY)

21. Bradley Zimmer (OF, CLE)
22. Franklin Barreto (SS, OAK)
23. Brent Honeywell (RHP, TAM)
24. Cody Bellinger (1B, LAD)
25. Francis Martes (RHP, HOU)
26. Reynaldo Lopez (RHP, CHW)
27. Jose De Leon (RHP, LAD)
28. Mickey Moniak (OF, PHI)
29. Ian Happ (2B, CHC)
30. Kyle Tucker (OF, HOU)

31. Nick Senzel (3B, CIN)
32. Michael Kopech (RHP, CHW)
33. Aaron Judge (OF, NYY)
34. Josh Bell (1B, PIT)
35. Kyle Lewis (OF, SEA)
36. Hunter Renfroe (OF, SD)
37. Jorge Mateo (SS, NYY)
38. Amir Garrett (LHP, CIN)
39. Corey Ray (OF, MIL)
40. Jeff Hoffman (RHP, COL)

41. Tyler O'Neill (OF, SEA)
42. Josh Hader (LHP, MIL)
43. Kolby Allard (LHP, ATL)
44. Jason Groome (LHP, BOS)
45. Jorge Alfaro (C, PHI)
46. Nick Williams (OF, PHI)
47. Nick Gordon (SS, MIN)
48. Sean Newcomb (LHP, ATL)
49. Alex Verdugo (OF, LAD)
50. Blake Rutherford (OF, NYY)

51. Carson Fulmer (RHP, CHW)
52. Vladimir Guerrero, Jr. (3B, TOR)
53. David Paulino (RHP, HOU)
54. Mitch Keller (RHP, PIT)
55. Riley Pint (RHP, COL)
56. Francisco Mejia (C, CLE)
57. Brady Aiken (LHP, CLE)
58. Yulieski Gurriel (3B, HOU)
59. Braxton Garrett (LHP, MIA)
60. Tyler Jay (LHP, MIN)

61. A.J. Puk (LHP, OAK)
62. Kevin Newman (SS, PIT)
63. Robert Stephenson (RHP, CIN)
64. Sean Reid-Foley (RHP, TOR)
65. Matt Manning (RHP, DET)
66. Anthony Alford (OF, TOR)
67. Jesse Winker (OF, CIN)
68. Dominic Smith (1B, NYM)
69. Raimel Tapia (OF, COL)
70. Zack Collins (C, CHW)

71. James Kaprielian (RHP, NYY)
72. Erick Fedde (RHP, WAS)
73. Luis Ortiz (RHP, MIL)
74. Phil Bickford (RHP, MIL)
75. Jake Bauers (OF, TAM)
76. Justus Sheffield (LHP, NYY)
77. Matt Chapman (3B, OAK)
78. Luke Weaver (RHP, STL)
79. Grant Holmes (RHP, OAK)
80. Bobby Bradley (1B, CLE)

81. Ronald Acuna (OF, ATL)
82. Derek Fisher (OF, HOU)
83. Brett Phillips (OF, MIL)
84. Yadier Alvarez (RHP, LAD)
85. Leody Taveras (OF, TEX)
86. Yohander Mendez (LHP, TEX)
87. Kevin Maitan (SS, ATL)
88. Triston McKenzie (LHP, CLE)
89. Willie Calhoun (2B, LAD)
90. Ryan McMahon (3B, COL)

91. Isan Diaz (2B, MIL)
92. Ian Anderson (RHP, ATL)
93. Trent Clark (OF, MIL)
94. Alex Kirilloff (OF, MIN)
95. Harrison Bader (OF, STL)
96. Tyler Beede (RHP, SF)
97. Richard Urena (SS, TOR)
98. Mike Soroka (RHP, ATL)
99. Dylan Cease (RHP, CHC)
100. Stephen Gonsalves (LHP, MIN)

TOP 100 PROSPECTS ARCHIVE

2016

1. Byron Buxton (OF, MIN)
2. Corey Seager (SS, LAD)
3. Lucas Giolito (RHP, WAS)
4. J.P. Crawford (SS, PHI)
5. Alex Reyes (RHP, STL)
6. Julio Urias (LHP, LAD)
7. Yoan Moncada (2B, BOS)
8. Tyler Glasnow (RHP, PIT)
9. Joey Gallo (3B, TEX)
10. Steven Matz (LHP, NYM)

11. Rafael Devers (3B, BOS)
12. Jose Berrios (RHP, MIN)
13. Orlando Arcia (SS, MIL)
14. Blake Snell (LHP, TAM)
15. Trea Turner (SS, WAS)
16. Bradley Zimmer (OF, CLE)
17. Jose De Leon (RHP, LAD)
18. Brendan Rodgers (SS, COL)
19. Dansby Swanson (SS, ATL)
20. Robert Stephenson (RHP, CIN)

21. Nomar Mazara (OF, TEX)
22. Victor Robles (OF, WAS)
23. Aaron Judge (OF, NYY)
24. Manuel Margot (OF, SD)
25. Clint Frazier (OF, CLE)
26. Lewis Brinson (OF, TEX)
27. Alex Bregman (SS, HOU)
28. Jon Gray (RHP, COL)
29. Ryan McMahon (3B, COL)
30. Austin Meadows (OF, PIT)

31. Nick Williams (OF, PHI)
32. Franklin Barreto (SS, OAK)
33. David Dahl (OF, COL)
34. Brett Phillips (OF, MIL)
35. Gleyber Torres (SS, CHC)
36. Sean Newcomb (LHP, ATL)
37. Carson Fulmer (RHP, CHW)
38. Ozhaino Albies (SS, ATL)
39. Dillon Tate (RHP, TEX)
40. Andrew Benintendi (OF, BOS)

41. Jameson Taillon (RHP, PIT)
42. Raul Mondesi (SS, KC)
43. Archie Bradley (RHP, ARI)
44. Tim Anderson (SS, CHW)
45. Kolby Allard (LHP, ATL)
46. Jake Thompson (RHP, PHI)
47. Dylan Bundy (RHP, BAL)
48. Willy Adames (SS, TAM)
49. Anderson Espinoza (RHP, BOS)
50. Aaron Blair (RHP, ATL)

51. A.J. Reed (1B, HOU)
52. Jeff Hoffman (RHP, COL)
53. Jesse Winker (OF, CIN)
54. Brent Honeywell (RHP, TAM)
55. Josh Bell (1B, PIT)
56. Anthony Alford (OF, TOR)
57. Tyler Kolek (RHP, MIA)
58. Max Kepler (OF, MIN)
59. Hunter Renfroe (OF, SD)
60. Mark Appel (RHP, PHI)

61. Kyle Zimmer (RHP, KC)
62. Jose Peraza (2B, CIN)
63. Kyle Tucker (OF, HOU)
64. Cody Reed (LHP, CIN)
65. Billy McKinney (OF, CHC)
66. Nick Gordon (SS, MIN)
67. Braden Shipley (RHP, ARI)
68. Jorge Lopez (RHP, MIL)
69. Touki Toussaint (RHP, ATL)
70. Hector Olivera (3B, ATL)

71. Derek Fisher (OF, HOU)
72. Jorge Alfaro (C, PHI)
73. Raimel Tapia (OF, COL)
74. Grant Holmes (RHP, LAD)
75. Dominic Smith (1B, NYM)
76. Daz Cameron (OF, HOU)
77. Alex Jackson (OF, SEA)
78. Sean Manaea (LHP, OAK)
79. Amed Rosario (SS, NYM)
80. Reynaldo Lopez (RHP, WAS)

81. Javier Guerra (SS, SD)
82. Hunter Harvey (RHP, BAL)
83. Luis Ortiz (RHP, TEX)
84. Brady Aiken (LHP, CLE)
85. Matt Olson (1B, OAK)
86. Jorge Mateo (SS, NYY)
87. Daniel Robertson (SS, TAM)
88. Taylor Guerrieri (RHP, TAM)
89. Amir Garrett (LHP, CIN)
90. Willson Contreras (C, CHC)

91. Renato Nunez (3B, OAK)
92. Tyler Jay (LHP, MIN)
93. Tyler Stephenson (C, CIN)
94. Christian Arroyo (SS, SF)
95. Josh Naylor (1B, MIA)
96. Brian Johnson (LHP, BOS)
97. Tyler Beede (RHP, SF)
98. Garrett Whitley (OF, TAM)
99. Cody Bellinger (1B, LAD)
100. Michael Fulmer (RHP, DET)

2015

1. Kris Bryant (3B, CHC)
2. Byron Buxton (OF, MIN)
3. Carlos Correa (SS, HOU)
4. Addison Russell (SS, CHC)
5. Corey Seager (SS, LAD)
6. Francisco Lindor (SS, CLE)
7. Joc Pederson (OF, LAD)
8. Miguel Sano (3B, MIN)
9. Lucas Giolito (P, WAS)
10. Joey Gallo (3B, TEX)

11. Dylan Bundy (P, BAL)
12. Jorge Soler (OF, CHC)
13. Archie Bradley (P, ARI)
14. Julio Urias (P, LAD)
15. Jon Gray (P, COL)
16. Daniel Norris (P, TOR)
17. Carlos Rodon (P, CHW)
18. Tyler Glasnow (P, PIT)
19. Noah Syndergaard (P, NYM)
20. Blake Swihart (C, BOS)

21. Aaron Sanchez (P, TOR)
22. Henry Owens (P, BOS)
23. Jameson Taillon (P, PIT)
24. Robert Stephenson (P, CIN)
25. Andrew Heaney (P, LAA)
26. David Dahl (OF, COL)
27. Jose Berrios (P, MIN)
28. Jorge Alfaro (C, TEX)
29. Hunter Harvey (P, BAL)
30. Alex Meyer (P, MIN)

31. Kohl Stewart (P, MIN)
32. J.P. Crawford (SS, PHI)
33. Alex Jackson (OF, SEA)
34. Jesse Winker (OF, CIN)
35. Raul Mondesi (SS, KC)
36. D.J. Peterson (3B, SEA)
37. Austin Meadows (OF, PIT)
38. Josh Bell (OF, PIT)
39. Kyle Crick (P, SF)
40. Luis Severino (P, NYY)

41. Nick Gordon (SS, MIN)
42. Kyle Schwarber (OF, CHC)
43. Aaron Nola (P, PHI)
44. Kyle Zimmer (P, KC)
45. Alex Reyes (P, STL)
46. Braden Shipley (P, ARI)
47. Albert Almora (OF, CHC)
48. Clint Frazier (OF, CLE)
49. Tyler Kolek (P, MIA)
50. Mark Appel (P, HOU)

51. Rusney Castillo (OF, BOS)
52. Sean Manaea (P, KC)
53. A.J. Cole (P, WAS)
54. Matt Wisler (P, SD)
55. Raimel Tapia (OF, COL)
56. C.J. Edwards (P, CHC)
57. Dalton Pompey (OF, TOR)
58. Hunter Renfroe (OF, SD)
59. Hunter Dozier (3B, KC)
60. Brandon Nimmo (OF, NYM)

61. Tim Anderson (SS, CHW)
62. Maikel Franco (3B, PHI)
63. Mike Foltynewicz (P, HOU)
64. Nick Kingham (P, PIT)
65. Eddie Butler (P, COL)
66. Steven Matz (P, NYM)
67. Domingo Santana (OF, HOU)
68. Aaron Judge (OF, NYY)
69. Daniel Robertson (SS, OAK)
70. Stephen Piscotty (OF, STL)

71. Kyle Freeland (P, COL)
72. Kevin Plawecki (C, NYM)
73. Lucas Sims (P, ATL)
74. Yasmany Tomas (OF, ARI)
75. Jose Peraza (2B, ATL)
76. Eduardo Rodriguez (P, BOS)
77. Max Fried (P, ATL)
78. Manuel Margot (OF, BOS)
79. Matt Olson (1B, OAK)
80. Ryan McMahon (3B, COL)

81. Alex Gonzalez (P, TEX)
82. Tyler Beede (P, SF)
83. Alen Hanson (SS, PIT)
84. Grant Holmes (P, LAD)
85. Aaron Blair (P, ARI)
86. Michael Taylor (OF, WAS)
87. Trea Turner (SS, SD/WAS)
88. Christian Bethancourt (C, ATL)
89. Marco Gonzales (P, STL)
90. Michael Conforto (OF, NYM)

91. Sean Newcomb (P, LAA)
92. Alex Colome (P, TAM)
93. Jeff Hoffman (P, TOR)
94. Luke Jackson (P, TEX)
95. Lewis Brinson (OF, TEX)
96. Willy Adames (SS, TAM)
97. Jake Thompson (P, TEX)
98. Nick Williams (OF, TEX)
99. Colin Moran (3B, HOU)
100. Bradley Zimmer (OF, CLE)

AVG: Batting Average (see also BA)

BA: Batting Average (see also AVG)

Base Performance Indicator (BPI): A statistical formula that measures an isolated aspect of a player's situation-independent raw skill or a gauge that helps capture the effects of random chance has on a skill. Although there are many such formulas, there are only a few that we are referring to when the term is used in this book. For pitchers, our BPI's are control (bb%), dominance (k/9), command (k/bb), opposition on base average (OOB), ground/line/fly ratios (G/L/F), and expected ERA (xERA). Random chance is measured witih the hit rate (H%) and strand rate (S%).

*Base Performance Value (BPV): A single value that describes a pitcher's overall raw skill level. This is more useful than any traditional statistical gauge to track performance trends and project future statistical output. The BPV formula combines and weights several BPIs:

(Dominance Rate x 6) + (Command ratio x 21) – Opposition HR Rate x 30) – ((Opp. Batting Average - .275) x 200)

The formula combines the individual raw skills of power, command, the ability to keep batters from reaching base, and the ability to prevent long hits, all characteristics that are unaffected by most external team factors. In tandem with a pitcher's strand rate, it provides a complete picture of the elements that contribute to a pitcher's ERA, and therefore serves as an accurate tool to project likely changes in ERA. **BENCHMARKS:** We generally consider a BPV of 50 to be the minimum level required for long-term success. The elite of bullpen aces will have BPV's in the excess of 100 and it is rare for these stoppers to enjoy long-term success with consistent levels under 75.

Batters Faced per Game *(Craig Wright)*

((IP x 2.82) + H + BB) / G

A measure of pitcher usage and one of the leading indicators for potential pitcher burnout.

Batting Average (BA, or AVG)

(H/AB)

Ratio of hits to at-bats, though it is a poor evaluative measure of hitting performance. It neglects the offensive value of the base on balls and assumes that all hits are created equal.

Batting Eye (Eye)

(Walks / Strikeouts)

A measure of a player's strike zone judgment, the raw ability to distinguish between balls and strikes. **BENCHMARKS:** The best hitters have eye ratios over 1.00 (indicating more walks than strikeouts) and are the most likely to be among a league's .300 hitters. At the other end of the scale are ratios

less than 0.50, which represent batters who likely also have lower BAs.

bb%: Walk rate (hitters)

bb/9: Opposition Walks per 9 IP

BF/Gm: Batters Faced Per Game

BPI: Base Performance Indicator

*BPV: Base Performance Value

Cmd: Command ratio

Command Ratio (Cmd)

(Strikeouts / Walks)

This is a measure of a pitcher's raw ability to get the ball over the plate. There is no more fundamental a skill than this, and so it is accurately used as a leading indicator to project future rises and falls in other gauges, such as ERA. Command is one of the best gauges to use to evaluate minor league performance. It is a prime component of a pitcher's base performance value. **BENCHMARKS:** Baseball's upper echelon of command pitchers will have ratios in excess of 3.0. Pitchers with ratios under 1.0 — indicating that they walk more batters than they strike out — have virtually no potential for long term success. If you make no other changes in your approach to drafting a pitching staff, limiting your focus to only pitchers with a command ratio of 2.0 or better will substantially improve your odds of success.

Contact Rate (ct%)

((AB - K) / AB)

Measures a batter's ability to get wood on the ball and hit it into the field of play. **BENCHMARK:** Those batters with the best contact skill will have levels of 90% or better. The hackers of society will have levels of 75% or less.

Control Rate (bb/9), or Opposition Walks per Game

BB Allowed x 9 / IP

Measures how many walks a pitcher allows per game equivalent. **BENCHMARK:** The best pitchers will have bb/9 levels of 3.0 or less.

ct%: Contact rate

Ctl: Control Rate

Dom: Dominance Rate

Dominance Rate (k/9), or Opposition Strikeouts per Game

(K Allowed x 9 / IP)

Measures how many strikeouts a pitcher allows per game equivalent. **BENCHMARK:** The best pitchers will have k/9 levels of 6.0 or higher.

*Expected Earned Run Average (*Gill and Reeve*)

(.575 x H [per 9 IP]) + (.94 x HR [per 9 IP]) + (.28 x BB [per 9 IP]) - (.01 x K [per 9 IP]) - Normalizing Factor

"xERA represents the expected ERA of the pitcher based on a normal distribution of his statistics. It is not influenced by situation-dependent factors." xERA erases the inequity between starters' and relievers' ERA's, eliminating the effect that a pitcher's success or failure has on another pitcher's ERA.

Similar to other gauges, the accuracy of this formula changes with the level of competition from one season to the next. The normalizing factor allows us to better approximate a pitcher's actual ERA. This value is usually somewhere around 2.77 and varies by league and year. BENCHMARKS: In general, xERA's should approximate a pitcher's ERA fairly closely. However, those pitchers who have large variances between the two gauges are candidates for further analysis.

Extra-Base Hit Rate (X/H)

(2B + 3B + HR) / Hits

X/H is a measure of power and can be used along with a player's slugging percentage and isolated power to gauge a player's ability to drive the ball. BENCHMARKS: Players with above average power will post X/H of greater than 38% and players with moderate power will post X/H of 30% or greater. Weak hitters with below average power will have a X/H level of less than 20%.

Eye: Batting Eye

h%: Hit rate (batters)

H%: Hits Allowed per Balls in Play (pitchers)

Hit Rate (h% or H%)

(H—HR) / (AB – HR - K)

The percent of balls hit into the field of play that fall for hits.

hr/9: Opposition Home Runs per 9 IP

ISO: Isolated Power

Isolated Power (ISO)

(Slugging Percentage - Batting Average)

Isolated Power is a measurement of power skill. Subtracting a player's BA from his SLG, we are essentially pulling out all the singles and single bases from the formula. What remains are the extra-base hits. ISO is not an absolute measurement as it assumes that two doubles is worth one home run, which certainly is not the case, but is another statistic that is a good measurement of raw power. BENCHMARKS: The game's top sluggers will tend to have ISO levels over .200. Weak hitters will be under .100.

k/9: Dominance rate (opposition strikeouts per 9 IP)

Major League Equivalency (*Bill James*)

A formula that converts a player's minor or foreign league statistics into a comparable performance in the major leagues. These are not projections, but conversions of current performance.

Contains adjustments for the level of play in individual leagues and teams. Works best with Triple-A stats, not quite as well with Double-A stats, and hardly at all with the lower levels. Foreign conversions are still a work in process. James' original formula only addressed batting. Our research has devised conversion formulas for pitchers, however, their best use comes when looking at BPI's, not traditional stats.

MLE: Major League Equivalency

OBP: On Base Percentage (batters)

OBA: Opposition Batting Average (pitchers)

On Base Percentage (OBP)

(H + BB) / (AB + BB)

Addressing one of the two deficiencies in BA, OBP gives value to those events that get batters on base, but are not hits. By adding walks (and often, hit batsmen) into the basic batting average formula, we have a better gauge of a batter's ability to reach base safely. An OBP of .350 can be read as "this batter gets on base 35% of the time."

Why this is a more important gauge than batting average? When a run is scored, there is no distinction made as to how that runner reached base. So, two thirds of the time—about how often a batter comes to the plate with the bases empty—a walk really is as good as a hit. BENCHMARKS: We all know what a .300 hitter is, but what represents "good" for OBP? That comparable level would likely be .400, with .275 representing the level of futility.

On Base Plus Slugging Percentage (OPS): A simple sum of the two gauges, it is considered as one of the better evaluators of overall performance. OPS combines the two basic elements of offensive production — the ability to get on base (OBP) and the ability to advance baserunners (SLG). BENCHMARKS: The game's top batters will have OPS levels over .900. The worst batters will have levels under .600.

Opposition Batting Average (OBA)

(Hits Allowed / ((IP x 2.82) + Hits Allowed))

A close approximation of the batting average achieved by opposing batters against a particular pitcher. BENCHMARKS: The converse of the benchmark for batters, the best pitchers will have levels under .250; the worst pitchers levels over .300.

Opposition Home Runs per Game (hr/9)

(HR Allowed x 9 / IP)

Measures how many home runs a pitcher allows per game equivalent. BENCHMARK: The best pitchers will have hr/9 levels of under 1.0.

Opposition On Base Average (OOB)

(Hits Allowed + BB) / ((IP x 2.82) + H + BB)

A close approximation of the on base average achieved by opposing batters against a particular pitcher. BENCHMARK: The best pitchers will have levels under .300; the worst pitchers levels over .375.

Opposition Strikeouts per Game: See Dominance Rate.

Opposition Walks per Game: See Control Rate.

OPS: On Base Plus Slugging Percentage

RC: Runs Created

RC/G: Runs Created Per Game

Runs Created *(Bill James)*

(H + BB - CS) x (Total bases + (.55 x SB)) / (AB + BB)

A formula that converts all offensive events into a total of runs scored. As calculated for individual teams, the result approximates a club's actual run total with great accuracy.

Runs Created Per Game *(Bill James)*

Runs Created / ((AB - H + CS) / 25.5)

RC expressed on a per-game basis might be considered the hypothetical ERA compiled against a particular batter. BENCHMARKS: Few players surpass the level of a 10.00 RC/G in any given season, but any level over 7.50 can still be considered very good. At the bottom are levels below 3.00.

S%: Strand Rate

Save: There are six events that need to occur in order for a pitcher to post a single save...

1. The starting pitcher and middle relievers must pitch well.
2. The offense must score enough runs.
3. It must be a reasonably close game.
4. The manager must choose to put the pitcher in for a save opportunity.
5. The pitcher must pitch well and hold the lead.
6. The manager must let him finish the game.

Of these six events, only one is within the control of the relief pitcher. As such, projecting saves for a reliever has little to do with skill and a lot to do with opportunity. However, pitchers with excellent skills sets may create opportunity for themselves.

Situation Independent: Describing a statistical gauge that measures performance apart from the context of team, ballpark, or other outside variables. Strikeouts and Walks, inasmuch as they are unaffected by the performance of a batter's surrounding team, are considered situation independent stats.

Conversely, RBIs are situation dependent because individual performance varies greatly by the performance of other batters on the team (you can't drive in runs if there is nobody on base). Similarly, pitching wins are as much a measure of the success of a pitcher as they are a measure of the success of the offense and defense performing behind that pitcher, and are therefore a poor measure of pitching performance alone.

Situation independent gauges are important for us to be able to separate a player's contribution to his team and isolate his performance so that we may judge it on its own merits.

Slg: Slugging Percentage

Slugging Percentage (Slg)

(Singles + (2 x Doubles) + (3 x Triples) + (4 x HR)) / AB

A measure of the total number of bases accumulated per at bat. It is a misnomer; it is not a true measure of a batter's slugging ability because it includes singles. SLG also assumes that each type of hit has proportionately increasing value (i.e. a double is twice as valuable as a single, etc.) which is not true. BENCHMARKS: The top batters will have levels over .500. The bottom batters will have levels under .300.

Strand Rate (S%)

(H + BB - ER) / (H + BB - HR)

Measures the percentage of allowed runners a pitcher strands, which incorporates both individual pitcher skill and bullpen effectiveness. BENCHMARKS: The most adept at stranding runners will have S% levels over 75%. Once a pitcher's S% starts dropping down below 65%, he's going to have problems with his ERA. Those pitchers with strand rates over 80% will have artificially low ERAs, which will be prone to relapse.

Strikeouts per Game: See Opposition Strikeouts per game.

Walks + Hits per Innings Pitched (WHIP): The number of baserunners a pitcher allows per inning. BENCHMARKS: Usually, a WHIP of under 1.20 is considered top level and over 1.50 is indicative of poor performance. Levels under 1.00 — allowing fewer runners than IP — represent extraordinary performance and are rarely maintained over time.

Walk rate (bb%)

(BB / (AB + BB))

A measure of a batter's eye and plate patience. BENCHMARKS: The best batters will have levels of over 10%. Those with the least plate patience will have levels of 5% or less.

Walks per Game: See Opposition Walks per Game.

WHIP: Walks + Hits per Innings Pitched

Wins: There are five events that need to occur in order for a pitcher to post a single win...

1. He must pitch well, allowing few runs.
2. The offense must score enough runs.
3. The defense must successfully field all batted balls.
4. The bullpen must hold the lead.
5. The manager must leave the pitcher in for 5 innings, and not remove him if the team is still behind.

X/H: Extra-base Hit Rate

*xERA: Expected ERA

---

* Asterisked formulas have updated versions in the Baseball Forecaster. *However, those updates include statistics like Ground Ball Rate, Fly Ball Rate or Line Drive Rate, for which we do not have reliable data for minor leaguers. So we use the previous version of those formulas, as listed here, for the players in this book.*

Back in Florida!

March 3-5, 2023

DoubleTree by Hilton Palm Beach Gardens

Interactive sessions • Player analysis

Injury updates • Current ADP feedback

Gaming strategies • Live drafts

Spring training games

Plus the LABR experts drafts in-person

.... and a whole lot more!

Details: www.baseballhq.com/first-pitch-florida

BONUS DATE: First Pitch Arizona at the Arizona Fall League • November 2-5, 2023

Get Baseball Insights Every Single Day.